,18

**DATE DUE**

A GUIDE TO THE BIRDS OF VENEZUELA

A GUIDE TO THE

# Birds of Venezuela

By Rodolphe Meyer de Schauensee

and William H. Phelps, Jr.

53 COLOR AND BLACK AND WHITE PLATES WITH

FACING-PAGE NOTES BY

## Guy Tudor

AND H. WAYNE TRIMM, JOHN GWYNNE,

AND KATHLEEN D. PHELPS

LINE DRAWINGS BY

MICHEL KLEINBAUM

PRINCETON UNIVERSITY PRESS

DEDICATED TO THE MEMORY OF

DR. WILLIAM H. PHELPS

1875–1965

who for thirty years enthusiastically ex-
plored Venezuela to further his studies of
the ornithology of the country, and through
whose efforts its avifauna has become the
best known in South America.

# CONTENTS

# FOREWORD

This book on the birds of Venezuela will be of particular interest to the amateur visiting Venezuela and to the more serious scholar interested in identifying the birds which he sees in his studies of Venezuelan birds relating to community structure, ecology, zoogeography, etc.

One could not find a better combination of scientists to write such an important book than Mr. R. Meyer de Schauensee and Mr. William H. Phelps, Jr. Mr. de Schauensee has spent considerable time in the Amazon and Rio Negro areas of Brazil. He has painstakingly studied the birds of Venezuela represented in some of our most important ornithological collections. These studies have been accompanied by a thorough study of the literature on the Venezuelan avifauna. Mr. de Schauensee has a broad and thorough knowledge of the birds of the world, particularly of tropical areas, and therefore is well qualified to discuss the Venezuelan avifauna. He is a Curator in the Ornithology Department of the Academy of Natural Sciences, a Fellow of the American Ornithological Union, a Director of the Philadelphia Zoological Society, and a member of the Board of Trustees of the Academy of Natural Sciences. He is the author of *Birds of Colombia, The Species of Birds of South America,* and *A Guide to the Birds of South America.*

Mr. Phelps and his father accumulated in Caracas the finest scientific collection of Venezuelan birds in the world and he has continued to add to it since his father's death. His vast knowledge is based on 35 years field experience and on 20 major ornithological expeditions led by him to unexplored regions of his native land. Mr. Phelps and his father are the authors of *Lista de las Aves de Venezuela y su Distribución,* the authoritative checklist of the birds of that country. He is a member of the Venezuelan Academy of Physical, Mathematical and Natural Sciences, a Research Associate of the Department of Ornithology of The Academy of Natural Sciences and of The American Museum of Natural History, an Elective Member of The American Ornithologists' Union and past-President of the Venezuelan Society of Natural Sciences.

The excellent illustrations, together with the descriptions of the species will be of immeasurable value in the identification of Venezuelan birds, particularly as no guidebook to the birds of that country exists. Furthermore, because it is such an exhaustive study of the birds of Venezuela, it will enable one to determine changes in the fauna over time, and to determine those changes probably due to the shifting of the natural environment and those due to man's activities. This book will also have value in determining trends in the bird populations of Venezuela.

*Ruth Patrick*
*Honorary Chairman of the Board of Trustees*
*The Academy of Natural Sciences*
*Philadelphia*

# INTRODUCTION

South America can well be called the Bird Continent, for its mountains, forests, and plains are inhabited by no less than 2936 different species of birds, or about 33 percent of the 9016 species found throughout the world. The richness of the Venezuelan avifauna is attested to by the fact that about 44 percent of all the species found in South America occur within the boundaries of the republic. Actually 20 orders, 81 families, 589 genera, 1296 species, and 2102 subspecies have been recorded from Venezuela. Endemic to Venezuela are 46 species. About 115 species of birds, mostly warblers, migrate from North America to South America in the boreal winter; some stop in Venezuela but most continue their migration southward. A few come from the West Indies and others migrate northward from southern South America during the austral winter. Arctic shore birds begin to arrive as early as July; several of these, and some other migrants, stay as late as May.

On the Venezuelan islands in the Caribbean a few oceanic species breed by the thousands from May to August, begin to leave in September, then disappear almost completely and return from January to March. Where they go during their absence is still not well known.

Vagrants and regular pelagic migrants from the North and South Atlantic Ocean also visit Venezuelan waters.

## THE GEOGRAPHY OF VENEZUELA

Venezuela is bounded by the Caribbean on the north, by Colombia on the west, the Atlantic and Guyana on the east, and Brazil on the south. It covers 352,141 square miles, an area which is roughly similar to that occupied by Texas and Utah.

For the purpose of this book, Venezuela may be divided into three well-defined geographical areas: the northern region, the central region, and the southern region.

### The Northern Region

The northern region is composed of the Caribbean littoral, three groups of mountain ranges, and the Lake Maracaibo basin.

The dry littoral extends along the northern coastal fringe; it includes Margarita and other Caribbean islands and penetrates inland in northern Zulia and western Lara. This semi-arid part of the country is predominantly a scrubby xerophytic area that in places becomes desert-like.

The mountain ranges may be divided into three groups, the western, north-central, and northeastern. The western group includes the Sierra de Perijá, which is an extension of the Eastern Andes of Colombia and which rises to an altitude of 3650 m. along the western border of Zulia. A very small area of the Eastern Andes proper in extreme western Táchira also borders Colombia. Another extension of the Eastern Andes, which consists of the main Venezuelan Andes, is the snow-capped Cordillera de Mérida. This range extends northeastwards from Táchira to Lara, and rises to slightly over 5000 m. Included in this western group of mountains is the much lower, outlying range to the east of Lake Maracaibo in eastern Zulia and western Lara that faunistically also pertains to the Andes.

The north-central group consists of the Cordillera de la Costa Central which rises to 2765 m., and its adjacent, parallel, southern chain, the Cadena del Interior. They extend from Carabobo to Miranda and the outlying Sierra de San Luis in Falcón and the Sierra de Aroa in Yaracuy also pertain faunally to this Central Coast Range.

The eastern group consists of the Cordillera de la Costa Oriental. It extends from Anzoátegui to Sucre and includes the narrow mountain range along the Paria Peninsula that extends eastward to within 10 miles of Trinidad.

The Maracaibo basin, mostly low-level terrain, is about one-fourth occupied by Lake Maracaibo, which opens to the Caribbean sea and is the largest lake in South America. The lake is brackish only near its opening to the sea. Most of the basin is densely forested, especially the southern part, which is periodically inundated in the rainy season. The annual rainfall decreases gradually to the north where the terrain becomes arid and characteristic of the Caribbean littoral.

*The Central Region*

The central region includes the llanos and the Orinoco delta. The llanos are extensive, flat, grassy savannas, not much more than 200 m. above sea level. They begin near the foothills of the northern cordilleras and continue south to the Orinoco and Meta rivers; similar savannas and open grassy terrain extend south of the Orinoco in many places in northern Bolívar. Large areas of the llanos are flooded every year in varying degrees depending on the intensity of the rainy season, which usually lasts from May to November. The eastern extremity of the central region is formed by the delta of the Orinoco, covered by great expanses of mangroves. Between the coastal mangrove swamps of the delta and the llanos proper, in eastern Monagas and the Territorio Delta Amacuro, there is a wide area of luxuriant, periodically flooded, rain forest.

## The Southern Region

The southern region, south of the Orinoco, comprises the state of Bolívar and the Territorio Amazonas. In northern Bolívar, besides the many savannas and the open, grassy terrain mentioned above, are found several low, densely forested mountain ranges. Most of the southern region consists of heavily forested lowlands, although there are also many savannas, some at elevations of 1000 m. or more, like the Gran Sabana, and numerous other smaller open, grassy areas at lower altitudes. The southern part of the region, in the upper reaches of the Orinoco and its tributaries, forms the northern extremity of the great Amazonian forest which extends southward, almost uninterruptedly, to Misiones, Argentina. This region is especially remarkable for the dozens of tepuis, the Indian name for the spectacular, isolated, sandstone, table-top mountains found irregularly scattered throughout the area and in the adjacent border districts of Brazil and Guyana. The flat summits of the tepuis vary greatly in size, some covering only 3 or 4 km.², the larger ones ranging up to 700 km.² in area. Standing like islands, their summits and upper talus slopes support many forms of birds peculiar to them. The tepuis rise to an altitude between 1250 m. to slightly more than 3000 m., but most range between 1600–2400 m. in height. The highest point is Pico Phelps on Cerro de la Neblina which reaches 3045 meters, the highest mountain in South America outside of the Andes and the Sierra Nevada de Santa Marta in northeastern Colombia.

## ALTITUDINAL ZONES

The various avifaunal life zones, as delimited by Chapman (1917), occur in Colombia at the following altitudes.

Tropical Zone
sea level to 4500–5500 ft. (1400–1700 m.)

Subtropical Zone
4500–5500 (1400–1700 m.) to 7500–8500 ft. (2300–2600 m.)

Temperate Zone
7500–8500 (2300–2600 m.) to 9500–11.500 ft. (2900–3500 m.)

Páramo Zone
9500–11.500 ft. (2900–3500 m.) to snow line.

There are no rigid limits to these life zones; many species vary in their altitudinal flexibility, and some actually live between two of these climatic or ecologic belts, but most of them always remain within the altitudinal limits given by Chapman.

When the same upper zonal species are encountered in the northern mountain ranges of Venezuela, they are usually at somewhat lower elevations than in Colombia.

About 90 percent of Venezuela is in the tropical zone. In this vast area the rainfall, vegetation, and terrain vary greatly and create a large diversity of habitats: desert-like areas and mangrove swamps in the Caribbean littoral; enormous expanses of mangroves and flooded forests in the Orinoco delta; grasslands with scattered trees and shrubs; deciduous and gallery forests in the llanos and innumerable savannas; flooded forests in the tributaries of the Caño Casiquiare; also many rivers, lagoons, lakes and swampy areas. Where the annual rainfall is heavy there are immense, dense rain forests, mainly of broadleaf evergreen trees, with a great variety of species of plants that include lianas and epiphytes.

The subtropical zone, when it is found in its original condition in the Andes and the other northern mountains, and as it still exists almost intact on the slopes of the tepuis, far south of the Orinoco, is a region of heavy annual rainfall and luxuriant cloud, or montane forest, characterized by a damp and relatively cool climate and where the broadleaf evergreen trees are covered with epiphytes and mosses but are not as high as in the rain forests of the tropical zone below. Large tree ferns are abundant in this humid, misty atmosphere. The cordilleras in the north with their excellent climate, have been well populated for hundreds of years and consequently their forests and other original habitats have either disappeared or are being destroyed or modified.

The temperate zone forms the transition between the cloud forests and the open páramos; it is a sparsely wooded area of dense, stunted forests, the trees with twisted trunks are covered with mosses and epiphytes.

The páramo zone in the Andes, with its magnificent landscapes, is found above the stunted forests and extends up to the perpetual snow line. Hundreds of different kinds of plants burst into bloom from October to December and blanket the zone with the most resplendent colors. This is an area of open, undulating plains with steep slopes and rocky outcrops and characteristic low, scrubby vegetation and grasses. Small lakes, ponds, and bogs are found throughout the zone.

## THE RIVER SYSTEMS

The principal river in Venezuela is the Orinoco, over 1500 miles in length. It rises on the slopes of the Sierra Parima bordering Brazil in southern Venezuela and flows from its slopes in a northwesterly direction. At its juncture with the Río Guaviare, flowing into it from the west and the much smaller Río Atabapo from the south, the river flows north forming the border with Colombia until it is joined by the Río Meta, flowing into it from the west. Here it turns eastward, receives the waters of the Ríos Arauca and Apure, which rise on the eastern slopes of the Andes, and eventually reaches the Atlantic just south of Trinidad. The main affluent flowing into it from the east is the Río Ventuari at about 4°N of the Equator. From the south two large rivers, each over 300 miles long, the Caura and the Caroní are its principal affluents.

At the upper reaches of the Orinoco the Caño Casiquiare connects that system with that of the Amazon. It links the Orinoco with the Río Negro, the latter forming the border with Colombia for a short distance and eventually flowing into the middle Amazon.

Draining the Gran Sabana are the Río Caroní and its affluents the Ríos Paragua, Aponguao, and Cuquenán and the Río Cuyuni, which, after flowing northward through the Gran Sabana, turns eastward through Guyana, and enters the Essequibo River just south of Georgetown. No rivers of any consequence flow into the Caribbean, the coastal ranges forming an effective barrier.

In the northwestern part of the country many small rivers flow into Lake Maracaibo, the principal one of which is the Río Catatumbo.

## TRAVEL

Caracas is less than 5 hours from New York by air. The modern highways that connect all major cities are supplemented by a network of excellent paved roads to all the important towns and well-maintained dirt roads lead to villages and hamlets. This road system, the best in Latin America, makes much of Venezuela accessible to the bird student. Cable cars in the Andes and in the Caracas area give access to altitudes of nearly 5000 m. and 2000 m., respectively, and the Transandean Highway goes over the Páramo of Mucuchíes at 4000 m. altitude. Many scheduled airplane flights also make it easy to reach remote places throughout the entire country.

The Brazilian border in the southeast can now be reached by a highway that traverses the great Cuyuni tropical forest before it ascends the spectacular northern escarpment of the eastern Pantepui area; the road then cuts across the Gran Sabana from north to south and offers the traveler dramatic views of some superb sandstone tepuis such as Ptaritepui, Sororopán-tepui, Auyán-tepui, Cuquenám, and Roraima, all of them isolated table-top mountains over 2500 m. high.

Of course, river boats ply the waters and offer another type of transportation.

## Book Plan

Although this is the first book containing illustrations of practically all the birds of Venezuela, it was preceded by *Aves de Venezuela, cien de las mas conocidas,* written and illustrated by Kathleen D. Phelps in 1954; three editions in Spanish and one in English were published in Caracas. That book, written "to stimulate a greater interest in the knowledge and protection of our Venezuelan birds," amply realized the wish of the author and is greatly responsible for the appearance of this guide, for which Mrs. Phelps has painted two beautiful plates.

This book contains a description of all the species of birds known at present to inhabit Venezuela and its adjacent islands, and their range within the republic is noted. Extralimital ranges are given in square brackets.

In cases where a species is represented by one or more subspecies, which differ among themselves sufficiently to affect field identification, the salient difference is noted parenthetically within the main description. This note is followed by a letter corresponding to a letter in the range that denotes the area occupied by the particular subspecies. The measurement of the bird (total length) is given in inches and centimeters. Altitudes are given in meters. When a bird's altitudinal range is given as being found, say, to 1000 m., this means from at or near sea level to 1000 m.

As almost every species found in Venezuela is illustrated, no key is provided. It is suggested that the observer look through the plates to find the bird seen, then check the identification with the description.

Short notes on habits, habitats, and vocalization are given that will be useful in field work. As the habits of many Venezuelan birds are not yet well known, the local bird students and those visiting the country can make valuable contributions to knowledge in this field.

A short account of each family precedes the description of the birds belonging to it. Alexander Wetmore's sequence of families (Smiths. Misc. Coll., *1960,* 139, no.11, pp. 1–37) is for the most part adhered to.

Latin and English names follow those used in *The Species of Birds of South America* (Meyer de Schauensee, 1964); Spanish names are those used in *Lista de las Aves de Venezuela y su Distribución* (Phelps and Phelps, 1950). A short bibliography will be found at the back of the book listing works of use to students of Venezuelan birds.

## The Illustrations

The value of a guidebook to birds depends largely on the quality of the color plates and other illustrations it contains.

Guy Tudor is much to be congratulated for the exceptionally fine paintings of Venezuelan birds reproduced in this book. In addition, Tudor has contributed the notes accompanying the plates, which give salient characters as an aid to the identification of the birds seen. These notes will be extremely useful and add immeasurably to the value of this guide.

In addition to the plates by Tudor, nine plates have been painted by H. Wayne Trimm, five by John Gwynne, and two by Kathleen D. Phelps. These will be found to be of high quality, and the artists are commended for their work. The exceptionally fine line drawings are the work of Michel Kleinbaum. The 40 color and 13 black and white plates as well as the line drawings show virtually all of the resident species of birds found in Venezuela. North American migrants, some of which are not shown, can be found figured in any of the several guides to North American birds.

The American Museum of Natural History, New York, has been generous in lending the artists specimens from their collection, which have been used in preparing the illustrations.

We are grateful to Miss Maude Meyer de Schauensee for drawing the splendid maps of Venezuela that are used as end sheets.

# ARTIST'S ACKNOWLEDGMENTS

Upon my initial involvement with this enterprise, it was decided that as much of the Venezuelan avifauna should be illustrated as possible within spatial limitations. It did not take long before I realized that some artistic collaboration would be required if the task were to be accomplished. Eventually, I had the good fortune in persuading several excellent bird artists to undertake the arduous chore of preparing many of the illustrations in this guide, with the result that we have been able to depict a very large percentage of the total species.

Foremost, I would like to express my gratitude to Wayne Trimm who consented to paint nine of the color plates—nos. 16, 32–34 and 36–40—and to John Gwynne who agreed to handle plates 15 ,17, 35, VIII and IX. Without their professional skill and continued dedication the publication would have been critically delayed. Kathleen Phelps kindly contributed plates 13 and 25. The attractive pen-and-ink drawings in the text were executed by Michel Kleinbaum, here making an impressive debut. These artists have had to labor under the often restrictive demands of the original conception and format, a largely unrecognized accommodation for which I am most appreciative. The composition of all the identification notes on the facing-page plate legends, however, remains my responsibility; I accept full liability for any misjudgments or omissions contained therein.

With few exceptions, all of the portraits and identification notes were prepared from study specimens in the American Museum of Natural History. I wish to thank Drs. Wesley Lanyon and Dean Amadon for providing me with liberal access to and special privileges with this valuable material during the long term of the project. Throughout, Allan O'Connell was always ready to furnish assistance with the collection.

The attitudes and configurations of the species were based upon as much first-hand information as was reasonably obtainable, although extrapolation became necessary with many of the lesser known birds. In furtherance of this goal, the aggregate contributions of Peter Alden, Tom Davis, Michael Gochfeld, Michel Kleinbaum and Robert Ridgely have been of the utmost importance to me. The countless hours of discussion and shared field experience, together with their expertise with the camera, were indispensable.

Four major bird painters—Al Gilbert, John Gwynne, Jorge Mata and John O'Neill—have lent advice on various aspects relating to identification or appearance of Neotropical species. Moreover, they have repeatedly and generously gone out of their way to supply me with many unique and vital color slides of netted, collected or captive examples from their personal files.

I have benefitted considerably from extensive conversations with John Farrand, David Hill and Ted Parker on taxonomy and distribution. Lee Morgan has been of great aid to me in photographing zoo specimens. Others to whom I am chiefly indebted for information, suggestions, reprints or picture material are: Kenneth Berlin, Emmet Blake, Walter Bock, Ned Boyajian, Paul Buckley, John Bull, Thomas Butler, Charles Collins, Robert Dickerman, John Dunning, David Ewert, Robert Gochfeld, Jürgen Haffer, Stuart Keith, Ben King, Wesley Lanyon, Helen Lapham, Chris Leahy, Mary LeCroy, Alain Loiseau, John Morony, Peter Post, Jaime Pujals, Richard Ryan, Paul Schwartz, Lester Short, Robert Smart, Neal Smith, Gary Stiles, John Terborgh, Joanne Trimble, the late Charles Vaurie, François Vuilleumier, Dora Weyer, Edwin Willis and John Yrizarry.

During research sojourns to various countries, I have often received assistance with travel arrangements, lodging and local field directions from resident naturalists, most notably: William Phelps, Jr., Ramón Aveledo, Paul Schwartz and Dr. Gonzalo Medina (Venezuela); the late Dr. Carlos Lehmann (Colombia); Dr. J. P. Schulz (Surinam); Will Houston (Trinidad); and Roger Morales (Costa Rica).

Eugene Eisenmann, the ultimate synthesizer of Neotropical ornithology, must be singled out for special acknowledgment and thanks. An early proponent of my work and a steadfast mentor over the years, he has functioned as an invaluable source of information, counsel and enlightened criticism not only within the scope of this guide but also throughout my career as well. Finally, I cannot overlook the contribution of my wife, Elizabeth, who more than anyone else enabled me in a very specific way to continue painting Venezuelan birds.

*Guy Tudor*
*New York City*
*May 1976*

# CHART OF A BIRD

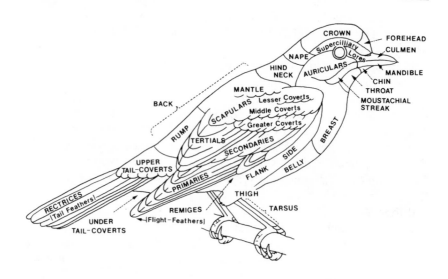

*Not shown on the above chart are:*

RICTAL BRISTLES: hair like filaments at the base of the bill, usual among flycatchers.

ORBITAL RING: a contrasting ring around the eye.

CHEEKS: the area below the eye in front of the ear coverts (auriculars in the above chart).

AXILLARS: feathers on the underside of the wing (sometimes elongated) between it and the body.

SPECULUM: a colored area on the wing, contrasting in color with the rest of it.

# LIST OF FAMILIES OF VENEZUELAN BIRDS

ANTBIRDS (Formicariidae)   201
AVOCETS, STILTS (Recurvirostridae)   81
BARBETS (Capitonidae)   167
BARN OWLS (Tytonidae)   115
BOAT-BILLED HERONS (Cochleariidae)   20
BOOBIES (Sulidae)   11
COCKS-OF-THE-ROCK (Rupicolidae)   237
CORMORANTS (Phalacrocoracidae)   12
COTINGAS (Cotingidae)   226
CUCKOOS (Cuculidae)   110
CURASSOWS (Cracidae)   53
DARTERS (Anhingidae)   13
DIPPERS (Cinclidae)   288
DUCKS & GEESE (Anatidae)   27
FALCONS, CARACARAS (Falconidae)   48
FINCHES (Fringillidae)   352
FLAMINGOS (Phoenicopteridae)   24
FRIGATEBIRDS (Fregatidae)   14
GNATCATCHERS (Sylviidae)   301
GREBES (Podicipedidae)   6
GULLS, TERNS (Laridae)   84
HAWKS, EAGLES (Accipitridae)   34
HERONS, EGRETS (Ardeidae)   14
HOATZINS (Opisthocomidae)   109
HUMMINGBIRDS (Trochilidae)   131
IBISES (Threskiornithidae)   22
JACAMARS (Galbulidae)   162
JACANAS (Jacanidae)   66
JAYS (Corvidae)   287
KINGFISHERS (Alcedinidae)   159
LIMPKINS (Aramidae)   58
MANAKINS (Pipridae)   238
MOCKINGBIRDS (Mimidae)   294
MOTMOTS (Momotidae)   161
NIGHTJARS (Caprimulgidae)   122
OILBIRDS (Steatornithidae)   121
ORIOLES, CACIQUES (Icteridae)   308
OSPREYS (Pandionidae)   47
OWLS (Strigidae)   116
OYSTERCATCHERS (Haematopodidae)   66
PARROTS, PARAKEETS (Psittacidae)   98
PARTRIDGES, QUAILS (Phasianidae)   57
PELICANS (Pelecanidae)   10

A GUIDE TO THE BIRDS OF VENEZUELA

# TINAMIFORMES

## TINAMOUS: Tinamidae

Tinamous form an exclusively American family of grouse-like birds, compact and rounded in shape without an obvious tail, and with rather short legs. Terrestrial, they are shy and retiring inhabitants of forest and scrub, and are more often heard than seen. They are clothed in shades of brown; many species are conspicously barred. They live on insects, seeds, and fruit. Their notes consist of melodious flute-like whistles. Their eggs are notable for their enamel-like surface, often green, blue or purple in color, and are incubated only by the male. Tinamous are often hunted for sport and trapped for food as they are very good to eat.

### GRAY TINAMOU
*Tinamus tao*
GALLINA AZUL

Pl. 1

18″ (46 cm.). Head and neck black, neck spotted with white, throat white (or head and neck gray, hindneck speckled with white, a). Back and wings gray, speckled or finely barred black (or above olive gray speckled and finely barred dusky brown, a). Below olive gray, vermiculated with black (or below light brownish gray vermiculated dusky, a). Under tail coverts cinnamon.
Tropical and lower subtropical zones. Nw Zulia, sw Táchira, the Andes from Mérida to Lara and Yaracuy, e along the coastal Cordillera to the Distr. Federal (*larensis*, a). The coastal Cordillera in Sucre and Monagas (*septentrionalis*). [Guyana; n and w Colombia, e Ecuador to Bolivia and Amazonian Brazil.]
Humid areas in rain and cloud forests to 1900 m. Dense second growth. Very secretive, sneaks away through the underbrush; seldom flies. Although responds to an imitation of its song, it is difficult to observe. Call: loud, high-pitched, rolling trill of 3 or 4 tones, usually at dusk.

### GREAT TINAMOU
*Tinamus major*
GALLINA DE MONTE

Pl. 1

18″ (46 cm.). Forehead, auriculars, eyebrow and well-developed occipital crest sooty, crown and neck rufous. Back and wings olive brown, spotted and barred with black, variable in intensity; underparts lighter and grayer than back. Throat whitish. Under tail coverts cinnamon. (Or generally similar but paler and more olivaceous with forehead and sides of head rufous, and a less developed occipital crest, a).
Tropical zone. The L. Maracaibo region, Zulia; n Mérida; ne Monagas; nw Bolívar; Amazonas from Caño Cataniapo s (*zuliensis*, a). Delta Amacuro; e Bolívar from the Altiplanicie de Nuria to the upper Río Caroní and w to the Río Paragua; Delta Amacuro (*major*). [S Mexico to w Ecuador, the Guianas, Amazonian Brazil and n Bolivia.]
Rain and cloud forests, second growth, to about 200 m. n of the Orinoco, to 1500 m. s of it. Near water. Secretive, not excessively shy, usually alone. Call: frequently whistles 2 long, plaintive, vibrating notes. The nest is invariably at the base of a tree trunk.

### WHITE-THROATED TINAMOU
*Tinamus guttatus*
GALLINETA CHICA

13″ (33 cm.). Crown slaty, throat white, neck dusky with pale spots. Back dark brown vermiculated dusky; paler below with wider dusky vermiculation. Inner remiges, lower back, upper tail coverts and belly with *yellowish buff spots;* flanks with a few dark bars.
Tropical zone. W Amazonas from Caño Cuao s to the Brazil border. [Se Colombia to n Bolivia and Amazonian Brazil.]
Rain forest, 100–200 m. Frequently in pairs. Song: Melancholy and arresting. A long mellow note followed by a short

one, one half tone lower, then a pause, then a series of notes on the same tone as the last one, increasing in rapidity, then a pause, then the first 2 notes repeated. [M.deS]

## HIGHLAND TINAMOU
*Nothocercus bonapartei*
GALLINA CUERO

Pl. 1
15" (38 cm.) Crown blackish, throat tawny. Back dark brown, flecked with black; below rufescent with thin, wavy black bars. Wings and belly palespotted.
Subtropical zone. Nw Zulia; the Andes of Táchira, Mérida and Lara, and the coastal Cordillera in Carabobo and Aragua (*bonapartei*). [Costa Rica to e Ecuador and ne Peru.]
Cloud forests, 1300–2500 m. Low thickets in humid areas. Shy, solitary or in groups up to 5. Several females lay 4–10 turquoise blue eggs on the ground; no proper nest is built. Song: high, penetrating, audible one km. away.

## TAWNY-BREASTED TINAMOU
*Nothocerus julius*
CHÓCORA DE TAMÁ

15" (38 cm.). Forecrown and sides of head *bright chestnut*. Back olivaceous brown waved and barred with black, inner remiges spotted pale buff. Upper throat gray; breast and flanks olivaceous brown, rest of underparts bright cinnamon rufous.
Páramo de Tamá, sw Táchira. [The Andes of Colombia and Ecuador.]
Low, fairly open woodland, 2500 m.

## CINEREOUS TINAMOU
*Crypturellus cinereus*
PONCHA

11" (28 cm.). Uniform smoky, grayish brown except for dull reddish brown crown and neck. Dark phase: mostly sooty brown.
Tropical zone. W Amazonas s to the lower Río Ventuari. [E Colombia and the Guianas to n Bolivia and Amazonian Brazil.]

Rain forests, 100–150 m. Terrain between woodland and savanna covered by bushes, thickets and scattered trees, plantations. Shy, secretive. Call: loud, penetrating notes, like those of a police whistle, at dawn and dusk.

## LITTLE TINAMOU
*Crypturellus soui*
PONCHITA

Pl. 1
9" (23 cm.). Top and sides of head and back of neck sooty; back and wings cinnamon brown to auburn (or less rufescent above, a). Throat white, foreneck brownish, becoming clay color on breast and cinnamon buff on rest of underparts (or duller below, a). ♀: top and sides of head blacker than in ♂, underparts darker (or with crown and sides of head sooty gray, a).
Tropical and lower subtropical zones. Nw Zulia; w Mérida; n Táchira (*mustelinus*, a). Elsewhere n of the Orinoco (*andrei*, a), s of the Orinoco (*soui*). [Mexico to w Ecuador, the Guianas, n Bolivia, Amazonian, e and se Brazil, Trinidad, a.]
Rain and cloud forests, second growth, forest edge, humid areas, to 1700 m. n of the Orinoco, to 1600 m. on the slopes of the tepuis. Thick tangled undergrowth, clearings, plantations, damp thickets. Not active; shy, solitary, secretive. Will flush when less than 5 m. away. Call: long, clear, tremulous, wailing, whistle. Vespertine singer. Rarely responds to imitated whistle. Nests on ground; eggs pinkish clay. Feeds on vegetable matter.

## TEPUI TINAMOU
*Crypturellus ptaritepui*
PONCHA DEL PTARI-TEPUI

11" (28 cm.). Top of head and hindneck rufous brown, sides of head, chin and throat light gray; back rufous brown darker than crown and neck. Underparts dusky with a rufous sheen on upper breast. Maxilla black, mandible yellow, tipped black; legs olive.
Subtropical zone. Known only from Cerros Ptari-tepui and Sororopán-tepui, se Bolívar.
Endemic species to Pantepui. Cloud forests, 1350–1800 m. The only tinamou at those altitudes on the two tepuis.

## BROWN TINAMOU
*Crypturellus obsoletus*
PONCHA MONTAÑERA

Pl. 1
11″ (28 cm.). Crown and nape grayish black, sides of head and neck gray, paler on throat. Back brown; foreneck and breast cinnamon rufous, becoming darker on belly (or darker above and below, a); flanks and under tail coverts barred blackish brown. Bill black; legs olive.
Cloud forest in the subtropical zone on the n slope of the Andes of Mérida (La Azulita, 1200 m.) and the forests of Terepaima, s of Barquisimeto in Lara (*knoxi*). Subtropical zone on the isolated mountain ranges in w Lara (Cerro El Cerrón, 1700 m.) on the common border with Zulia and Falcón; on the Sierra San Luis, Falcón (Curimagua, 1300 m.); on the Cordillera de la Costa Central and Colonia Tovar in Aragua (*cerviniventris*). [E Colombia to s Brazil, Bolivia, Paraguay and the Argentina chaco.]
Cloud forests and low vegetation near mountain ridges, 1300–2200 m. Secretive. Call: a dull whistle. Nests at the base of trees: eggs deep pink.

## UNDULATED TINAMOU
*Crypturellus undulatus*
GALLINETA ONDULADA

Pl. 1
11″ (28 cm.). Forecrown dusky brownish merging into brownish hindneck, back light cinnamon brown, grayish on rump; entire upperparts finely vermiculated black; tail gray. Chin white, merging into pale gray throat which is heavily spotted with white; breast and sides grayish olive with fine dusky vermiculations; crissum whitish, conspicuously barred brownish black. Bill black; legs yellowish green.
Tropical Zone. W Amazonas on the Río Manapiare, upper Río Ventuari (*manapiare*). [E Colombia, Guyana, e Ecuador to Bolivia, Amazonian Brazil and w Argentina.]
Rain forest and forest edge, 150–200 m. Secretive. Song: most frequently a melodious, melancholy whistle which sounds like the first 3 notes of the Bar-

carolle in Offenbach's opera, *The Tales of Hoffmann.*

## VARIEGATED TINAMOU
*Crypturellus variegatus*
GALLINETA CUERO

Pl. 1
13″ (33 cm.). Top and sides of head black, throat white, neck and upper breast and upper back rufous, wing coverts and rest of back conspicuously banded with light ochraceous. Lower breast and belly white, sides tinged cinnamon, lightly barred dusky. Bill yellowish, comparatively long; legs olive yellow.
Tropical, lower subtropical zones. Nw Bolívar e across the upper Río Paragua to the Gran Sabana from Cerro Guaiquinima to Cerro Roraima; Amazonas from Caño Cuao to the Brazilian border. [E Colombia, the Guianas to central Peru and Amazonian and se Brazil.]
Rain forests, clearings and open, relatively dry areas, 100–1300 m. Secretive. Call: a wailing whistle. Eggs brown washed with pinkish violet, or of a purple shade.

## RED-LEGGED TINAMOU
*Crypturellus erythropus*
SOISOLA PATA ROJA

Pl. 1
12″ (30 cm.). Crown sooty black (or dull brown, a; or mouse gray, b); throat variable, white to tawny; hindneck and mantle dull brown (strongly tinged grayish, c) vermiculated black, lower back and upper tail coverts obscurely barred black; wing coverts and inner webs of secondaries with scattered black and buff spots. Foreneck and upper breast mouse gray washed brownish, rest of underparts tawny cinnamon barred blackish on sides, (or buffy, barred black and white at sides, a). Lower mandible flesh color; legs salmon to scarlet pink. ♀: differs from respective ♂ by lower back and rump evenly barred black and ochraceous.
Tropical zone. Nw Zulia in the Perijá region (*idoneus*, a). S Táchira (*cursitans*, b). Falcón, Mérida, the Distr. Federal, Aragua, e Guárico and central Anzoátegui (*spencei*, c). The Paria Pen., Sucre, nw Monagas, ne Bolívar from the Río Paragua e to the Sierra de Imataca

and the Río Cuyuni (*erythropus*). Margarita I. (*margaritae*, c). [Ne Colombia, the Guianas, Brazil n of the Amazon.] Open forest, second growth, dry, low, deciduous forest, thorny thickets to 1300 m. n of the Orinoco, to 700 m. s of it. Solitary or very scattered individuals; active, not very shy, curious, sometimes heard running over dry leaves. Song: vespertine singer; fairly clear, slightly scolding 3-note whistle, "soy-so-la." Responds to an imitation of its whistle. Eggs light brownish pink.

Note: *C. erythropus* and its races were treated as subspecies of *C. noctivagus* in Lista Av. Venez. In Sp. Bds. S Amer. they were regarded as races of *atrocapillus* except for *idoneus*, which was included in *C. cinnamomeus*. The present arrangement of the genus *Crypturellus* is based on recent studies by P. Schwartz and E. Eisenmann based on voice and egg color.

## GRAY-LEGGED TINAMOU

*Crypturellus duidae*
SOISOLA PATA GRIS

12" (30 cm.). Head and neck rufous, throat white; back dark brown indistinctly barred on lower back; breast clear rufous with a slight grayish tinge on upper breast, belly buffy banded at sides with blackish. Legs grayish olive. ♀: like ♂ but lower back and inner remiges darker, narrowly barred light buffy.

Tropical zone. Amazonas from Caño Cuao and Sanariapo s to the foot of Cerro Duida. [Colombia in s Meta.]

Rain forest, open woodland, 100–200 m. Behavior similar to that of its congeners.

Note: *C. duidae* was treated as a race of *noctivagus* in Lista Av. Venez. In Sp. Bds. S Amer. *C. e. cursitans* was treated as a race of *duidae*.

## BARRED TINAMOU

*Crypturellus casiquiare*
SOISOLA BARRETEADA

10" (25 cm.). Head and neck bright chestnut, throat white. Entire upperparts boldly barred black and dark ochraceous. Breast, front and sides of neck light gray, belly white, flanks barred cream color and black. Legs olive green. ♀: like ♂ but back paler.

Tropical zone. S Amazonas at the mouth of Caño Casiquiare and along the Yavita-Pimichín Trail. [Adjacent Colombia.]

Rain forests, 100–200 m. Behavior similar to that of its congeners.

# PODICIPEDIFORMES

# GREBES: Podicipedidae

ZAMBULLIDORES

Grebes form a small family of water birds of virtually world-wide distribution. They are expert divers and differ from ducks by their slender, narrow bills and individually webbed toes. They frequent ponds, reservoirs, marshes, lagoons and rivers, usually where there is abundant vegetation. They live chiefly on fish, insects and other aquatic life. Their nests, which float upon the water, are made of aquatic vegetation.

## LEAST GREBE

*Podiceps dominicus*
PATICO ZAMBULLIDOR

Fig. 1
8" (20 cm.). Ashy gray; throat black (white in winter); belly dirty white. Flight feathers mainly white. Bill thin, black with light tip. Iris yellow.

Tropical, casually subtropical zone. Locally n of the Orinoco e to Miranda, Guárico and Monagas; s of the Orinoco in e Bolívar; Margarita I. (*speciosus*).

[Texas to w Peru and Tierra del Fuego. Caribbean islands. Trinidad, Tobago.] Sea level to 1950 m. Solitary and in small groups and flocks up to 50. Distinguished from the Pied-billed Grebe by its white wing patch.

## PIED-BILLED GREBE

*Podilymbus podiceps*
Buzo

Fig. 1
13″ (33 cm.). Dusky brownish gray, throat black. Under tail coverts white. In winter throat, foreneck and under-parts dirty white. Bill thicker than in other grebes, yellowish white with a black band in breeding season. Iris brown.

Tropical zone. Locally distributed n of the Orinoco, where recorded in Zulia (L. Maracaibo), Carabobo (L. Valencia), Aragua (Suata reservoir), and w Monagas (Caicara) (*antarcticus*). [Canada to Tierra del Fuego. Caribbean islands. Trinidad, Tobago.]

Sea level to 500 m. More solitary than previous species, usually in pairs or small groups. Call: a loud chatter, "cao-cao-cao."

# PROCELLARIIFORMES

## PETRELS, SHEARWATERS: Procellariidae

### PETRELES

Shearwaters are truly pelagic birds coming to land only for nesting. One species nests in Venezuelan territory, but others, like the Greater Shearwater taken off Los Roques, can possibly be seen off the coasts for they have been recorded as accidental from nearby countries: Caribbean Colombia, the Dutch West Indies, Trinidad and Guyana. These are: Black-capped Petrel (*Pterodroma hasitata*), Cory's Shearwater (*Puffinus diomedea*), Mediterranean Shearwater (*Puffinus kuhli*), Manx Shearwater (*Puffinus puffinus*) and Bulwer's Petrel (*Bulweria bulwerii*).

### GREATER SHEARWATER

*Puffinus gravis*
Petrel Cauicho

18″ (46 cm.). Cap and sides of head dusky, back grayish brown with a pale nuchal collar. Below white, grayish brown on flanks and under tail coverts. Wing lining white. Tips of longer tail coverts white. Tail blackish. Bill black, legs pinkish.

One specimen only, taken 5 m. (8 km.) off the Los Roques Archipelago, June 19. [Breeds in the Tristan da Cunha group of islands, s Atlantic. Ranges in the n Atlantic to the Arctic Circle in the non-breeding season. Recently reported as breeding in the Falkland Is., a record needing confirmation.]

The specimen taken near Los Roques is reliably reported to have laid an elon-gated, very soft-shelled egg a few hours after it was captured. The egg was trampled on by the bird and lost.

Note: New record since publication of Lista Av. Venez.

### DUSKY-BACKED (OR AUDUBON'S) SHEARWATER

*Puffinus lherminieri*
Petrel Garrapatero

Fig. 2
11″ (28 cm.). Above slaty blackish; sides of head; underparts and wing lining white. Feet flesh colored. A black phase exists.

Nests on El Morro (adjacent to Gran Roque), Selesquí, Bequevé, and Espenquí, all islands of the Los Roques archipelago; La Orchila and Los Hermanos, islands off the Caribbean coast (*loye-*

Fig. 1. PIED-BILLED GREBE (left), LEAST GREBE (right)

Fig. 2. LEACH'S STORM-PETREL (left), DUSKY-BACKED SHEARWATER (right)

*milleri*). [Breeds in Bermuda, Tobago, Caribbean islands, Caribbean w Panama, Ascension I., Galápagos Is. Recorded off Ecuador.]
Nests, Feb.-May, in crevices formed by coral rock debris near the shore. In and near the nesting area may be located at night, usually between 8 P.M. and midnight, by its high melodious series of soft, musical whistled notes, uttered while flying or from the nest crevices. Banking and gliding flight with stiff wing beats. Offshore, also pelagic. Usually in small flocks; feeds on fish and squid.

## STORM-PETRELS: Hydrobatidae

### GOLONDRINAS DE MAR

Storm-Petrels are only casual visitors, during the non-breeding season, to the Venezuelan coast and islands. They are small, dark, pelagic birds, sometimes variegated with white, that flit close over the water.

**WILSON'S STORM-PETREL**

*Oceanites oceanicus*
PETREL DE LAS TORMENTAS

6.5″ (16.5 cm.). *Tail rounded.* Brownish black; rump white; a pale ashy brown band across wing; wing lining black. Legs long, feet extending beyond tail when flying; webs of toes yellow.
Recorded 15 m. (24 km.) off Placer de la Guaira, Distr. Federal, in July. [Recorded off Guyana, Surinam. Breeds in the Antarctic. Migrates north to Labrador, British Is., Japan.]
Pelagic. Usually solitary but sometimes in small flocks up to 20. Glides along the waves pattering near the surface of the water. Off the n coast, often near whales. Food: crustaceans, squids.

**LEACH'S STORM-PETREL**

*Oceanodroma leucorhoa*
GOLONDRINA DE MAR

Fig. 2
7.5″ (19 cm.) *Tail forked.* In general color much like Wilson's Petrel. Feet black.
Recorded from the Gulf of Paria and the mouth of the Río San Juan, Monagas, and the delta of the Orinoco (*leucorhoa*). [Recorded off Guyana, Surinam, Brazil. Trinidad. Breeds in the n Atlantic and n Pacific. Migrates to New Zealand and Cape of Good Hope.]
Pelagic. Often glides, but usually has an erratic, broken, fluttering flight, close to the surface. Food: crustaceans; feeds at night.

# PELECANIFORMES

## TROPICBIRDS: Phaethontidae

### CHÍPAROS

Tropicbirds, except in the nesting season, are found far out to sea. They are distinguishable from other gull-like birds by the very long, quill-like central tail feathers. Their flight is rapid and direct. They feed on squid and other fish, which they catch by diving. When on the water they float high, the tail held elevated.

**RED-BILLED TROPICBIRD**
*Phaethon aethereus*
CHÍPARO

Fig. 3
24" (60 cm.), with quills 40" (1 m.).
Mainly white, line through eye, extensive
wing band and tip of wing black. Bill
red. Imm.: back narrowly banded with
black, no streamers in tail. Bill yellow.

Breeds on Los Hermanos and Los Roques
(*mesonauta*). [Nests on St. Giles Is. and
Little Tobago. Curaçao. Also on islands
off Pacific S Amer. Accidental off
Brazil.]
Near the sea cliffs and steep promontories
of Gran Roque, Los Roques and Los
Hermanos; also other precipitous head-
lands. Alone or in pairs. Reported nesting Feb.-Apr.

## PELICANS: Pelecanidae

ALCATRACES

Pelicans are recognizable in flight by their majestic aspect and the somewhat hunch-
backed appearance caused by flying with the head retracted. They catch fish in their

Fig. 3. BROWN PELICAN (left), MAGNIFICENT FRIGATEBIRD (male,
upper right), RED-BILLED TROPICBIRD (lower right)

large, pouched bills by diving after them head first, hitting the water with a splash. Pelicans do not often venture far from land and nest in low trees and bushes along the shore line.

## BROWN PELICAN
*Pelecanus occidentalis*
ALCATRAZ

Fig. 3
38–54″ (1 m.–1 m. 35 cm.). Head and stripe down neck white, rest of neck chestnut (or head and neck white in non-breeding plumage). Body plumage silvery gray, browner below. Imm.: head, neck and back pale brown, below whitish.

Generally distributed along the coast and islands and nesting locally (*occidentalis*). Erratic migrant recorded from Aragua, Sucre and Margarita I. (*carolinensis*). [S US to Chile and n Brazil.]
Nesting colonies on several islands in Los Roques, in La Tortuga and in the Gulf of Cariaco. Seen nesting Feb.–July but may also nest sporadically the rest of the year. Plunges for fish at the surface, filtering the contents of the bill.

# BOOBIES: Sulidae

## BOBAS

Boobies are narrow-winged, wedge-tailed, web-footed marine birds related to pelicans. They are much smaller, however, with much smaller bills, which have a small pouch at the base. They nest in colonies and, like pelicans, feed on fish which they catch by diving.
The immature birds of the various species look much alike in their brownish or grayish plumage. The adults, however, are very distinctive.

## MASKED (WHITE OR BLUE-FACED) BOOBY
*Sula dactylatra*
BOBA BORREGA

Fig. 4
34″ (86 cm.). White; tail, primaries, and tips of inner remiges brownish black. Facial skin black, slaty blue near bill. Bill and feet yellow; ♀: bill and feet pink or light red.
Nests on Los Roques, Los Monjes and Los Hermanos (*dactylatra*). [Coasts of S Amer. to Brazil and Peru. Caribbean islands. Tropical Pacific and Indian Oceans.]
Rare. In Los Roques, on Selesquí I.; the number of nests fluctuates from 1–15 in different years. Conspicuous in the open sea between the islands and the mainland, especially near Los Hermanos. Nests on the ground; recorded nesting Feb.–Nov. Plunges for fish. Usually coastal and offshore, occasionally pelagic.

## RED-FOOTED BOOBY
*Sula sula*
BOBA RABO BLANCO

Fig. 4
28″ (71 cm.). White; wing tips black. Bill bluish, red at base; legs red. Brown and gray phases exist but the white tail is always the distinguishing character.
Locally on Caribbean coast from Los Monjes Is. to Cape Codera and on Margarita I. Breeds on Las Aves, Los Roques, Los Testigos and Los Hermanos (*sula*). [Breeds on islands in the Caribbean, s Atlantic and w and central Pacific.]
Nests on mangroves and low bushes. Open sea between the islands and the mainland, especially near Los Roques. The largest colony, estimated at some 5000 birds, is in Las Bubias, Los Roques; it is occupied all year round; nesting begins in Oct. Plunges for fish. Usually coastal and offshore, occasionally pelagic.

Fig. 4. MASKED BOOBY (left), BROWN BOOBY (center),
RED-FOOTED BOOBY (right), brown phase flying

## BROWN BOOBY

*Sula leucogaster*
BOBA MARRÓN

Fig. 4
40″ (·1 m.). Chocolate brown; lower breast, and belly and wing lining white. Bill and feet yellow.
The Caribbean coast from Falcón to Sucre and all coastal islands. Breeds on Los Monjes, Las Aves, Los Roques, La Orchila, Los Hermanos (*leucogaster*). [Breeds on islands in the Caribbean and tropical Atlantic, Pacific and Indian Oceans. Aruba to Trinidad and Tobago.] The most common booby. Solitary or in small groups in the open sea between the islands and the mainland. Plunges powerfully after fish and disappears below the surface for several seconds. Breeds on several islets of the Los Roques group. Nests Feb.–Oct. Usually coastal and offshore, occasionally pelagic.

## CORMORANTS: Phalacrocoracidae

### COTÚAS

Only one species of cormorant is found in Venezuela. These aquatic birds are recognizable by their rather long necks and dark coloration. They are expert divers and catch fish under water. In flight they fly with neck extended, the wings and tail are

Fig. 5. NEOTROPIC CORMORANT (left), ANHINGA (male, right)

narrow. Their bills are slender and hooked. rocks or branches overhanging the water. waters.

They often perch, with wings dangling, on Cormorants frequent coastal and inland

## NEOTROPIC (OR OLIVACEOUS) CORMORANT

*Phalacrocorax olivaceus*
COTÚA OLIVÁCEA

Fig. 5
26" (66 cm.). Purplish black, somewhat bronzy on wings. Face and gular sack yellow, outlined from eye to eye with white; a tuft of white, hairlike plumes behind ear coverts in breeding season. Imm.: dull brown above, pale brown below.

Locally distributed on coasts, lakes and rivers from the tropical to the temperate zone. Los Roques, Margarita and Coche Is. (*olivaceus*). [S US to Panama, Colombia and Cape Horn. Aruba to Trinidad.]
On inland lakes and rivers, and in coastal waters, occasionally offshore, often in flocks of 50 or more. Because of their fast wing beat and V-flock formation may be confused with ducks. They dive in pursuit of fish. In flight the tail appears short and pointed, the neck extended.

# DARTERS: Anhingidae

## COTÚAS AGUJITAS

Darters are easily distinguishable from cormorants by their very thin necks, small heads and thin, very pointed yellow bills and long fanshaped tails. Like cormorants they feed on fish, but unlike them, spear them with their sharply pointed bills, rather than seizing them between the mandibles.

Anhingas often swim submerged with only the head and neck showing above the water. They frequent fresh-water swamps, lakes and rivers. When perching they often hold their wings dangling to dry the feathers. Their flight consists of alternate flapping and sailing.

## ANHINGA

*Anhinga anhinga*
Cotúa Agujita

Fig. 5

32" (81 cm.). Bill long, thin, pointed. Neck very long and thin, head very small. Tail long, fanshaped. Mainly glossy greenish black; wing coverts and edges of inner remiges silvery white. ♀: head, neck and breast buffy brown, rest of plumage like ♂ but brownish black rather than greenish black.

Tropical zone. Nw Zulia (*leucogaster*). Aragua on Lake Valencia and at Turiamo; generally in the Orinoco basin (*anhinga*). [Southern US to Argentina. Trinidad; W Indies.]

During the breeding season nests in colonies; sometimes joins herons and ibises in the extensive *garceros* or nesting colonies in the llanos.

## FRIGATEBIRDS: Fregatidae

### Tijeretas de Mar

Frigatebirds are recognizable from other large seabirds in flight by their long, forked tails, which they often open and shut, and long narrow wings. They are graceful, effortless, soaring fliers who feed from the surface of the water, take fish or squids by dipping, or rob other birds of their catch. Coastal waters, also offshore and pelagic; occasionally a few km. inland.

Frigatebirds are gregarious and nest in colonies, placing their nests in low trees and bushes along the ocean front.

## MAGNIFICENT FRIGATEBIRD

*Fregata magnificens*
Tijereta de Mar

Fig. 3

40" (1 m.). Entirely glossy black; tail long, deeply forked. Gular sack red, inflated and balloonlike in courtship. ♀: like ♂ but breast and upper abdomen white. Imm.: head, neck and underparts white.

Breeds on Los Hermanos and Los Testigos. Generally distributed off the Caribbean and Atlantic coasts (*rothschildi*). [Tropical Atlantic and Pacific Oceans.]

In the islands their principal targets seem to be the Red-footed Boobies, which they harass as the boobies approach their breeding colonies. In an attempt to force a booby to expel its catch they may seize it in their bills by a wing tip or by the tail, and dangle it for several seconds before releasing it unharmed.

# CICONIIFORMES

# HERONS, EGRETS, BITTERNS: Ardeidae

## Garzas

Herons, egrets and bitterns inhabit swamps, river banks and reed beds. They feed in shallow water where they catch fish, frogs and other animal life.

Herons fly with head retracted, thus differing from storks and ibises, which fly with neck extended. They further differ from ibises by their straight, daggerlike, instead of curved, bills.

## GREAT BLUE HERON
*Ardea herodias*
GARZÓN CENIZO

Fig. 6
46″ (1 m. 16 cm.). Center of crown and sides of head white, sides of crown and long occipital crest black. Back blue gray, sides and back of neck violaceous gray, front of neck white with a ragged black line down center. Sides of belly blackish, center of belly mixed gray and white with a little rufous, *thighs rufous.* (Or all white, or mottled gray and white, or similar but smaller, a.) Bill yellow, ridge dusky. Legs dusky, yellow in white form. Imm.: crown all black, no occipital crest.

Accidental visitor, Sept.–Dec., to Miranda, Guárico and Apure (*herodias*). Islands off the Caribbean coast, known to breed on Esparquí, in Los Roques (in Los Roques where the birds are approximately 20% white, 20% gray and white, 60% gray); occurs on Las Aves, La Orchila, and Margarita Is.; accidental on coast of Falcón and Aragua (*repens,* a). [Migrants breed in N. Amer., and the Greater Antilles and winter to northern S Amer., Trinidad, Tobago. Galápagos Is.]

Wades along fresh- and salt-water shores;

Fig. 6. GREAT BLUE HERON (left), WHITE-NECKED HERON (right)

beaches and mangrove areas; llanos. Solitary or dispersed individuals, shy, alert. The white phase in found only in salt water.

## WHITE-NECKED HERON

*Ardea cocoi*
GARZA MORENA

Fig. 6
48" (1 m. 21 cm.). Differs principally from the Great Blue Heron by all black crown, white neck, all black belly and *white thighs*. Bill orange. Imm.: looks much like the Great Blue Heron but thighs white instead of rufous.
Tropical zone. [Panama to Chile and s Argentina. Trinidad.]
Wades along salt- and fresh-water beaches, lagoons, forest rivers, swamps, llanos to 1200 m. Solitary, shy.

## GREAT (OR COMMON) EGRET

*Casmerodius albus*
GARZA BLANCA REAL

Fig. 7
38" (96 cm.). All white. Bill yellow, *legs black*. Distinguishable from white form of Great Blue Heron by black instead of yellow legs.
Tropical zone, including Margarita I. (*egretta*). [N, Central and S Amer. to the Strait of Magellan. The Antilles. Trinidad. Se Europe; Africa; Asia; Australia.]
The largest white heron on the mainland; near fresh- and salt-water areas, open savannas, sea level to 300 m. Swamps, flooded pastures, llanos. Forages in scattered groups but roosts in low trees in flocks up to several hundred. Feeds on fish, lizards, frogs. Nests in mixed colonies with other herons.

Fig. 7. White Herons (non-breeding plumage): GREAT EGRET (left), SNOWY EGRET (center), LITTLE BLUE HERON (juvenal, upper right), CATTLE EGRET (lower right)

## SNOWY EGRET
*Egretta thula*
GARCITA BLANCA

Fig. 7
23" (58 cm.). All white. *Bill and legs black, feet yellow.*
Tropical zone (*thula*). [Southern US to Argentina and Chile. Antilles. Trinidad.]
Various habitats, on level areas, near water, in the *garceros* of the llanos, to 500 m. Solitary or in small groups. Roosts in large flocks. A migrant from the e coast of the US has been recorded in Venezuela.

## LITTLE BLUE HERON
*Florida caerulea*
GARCITA AZUL

Pl. 2, Fig. 7
24" (60 cm.). Head and neck dark purplish brown, rest of plumage slate blue. Bill bluish gray, distal third black. Imm.: white, bill bluish, distal third black, legs pale greenish.
Resident. Tropical zone (*caerulescens*). A few birds banded in N Amer. casually reach Venezuela and Colombia in winter (*caerulea*). [Alaska and Canada to w Peru, Brazil and Uruguay. Trinidad, Tobago.]
Stream borders, wet terrain, mud flats along rivers, estuaries, to 1600 m. Sometimes on sea beaches. Solitary or in pairs, but congregates for nesting. Small flocks of adults and young are seen occasionally flying a few hundred m. off the central n coast, always in an easterly direction. Feeds on frogs, insects, fish.

## REDDISH EGRET
*Dichromanassa rufescens*
GARZA ROJIZA

Pl. 2
30" (76 cm.). Head and neck rufous brown, the feathers somewhat shaggy, rest of plumage gray; bill pink, distal third black, legs dusky. White phase: white; *bill pink, distal third black,* the bill color separates it from other white egrets. However imm. birds in white phase have blackish bills.
Winter resident, Aug.–May. Recorded from Falcón and Sucre, Los Roques, La

Orchida, La Tortuga, Las Aves and Margarita Is. (*colorata*). [Breeds from s US to Mexico, the Bahamas and Greater Antilles. Winters to El Salvador. Recently recorded from ne Colombia where it may breed. Specimens seen in late June. Aruba, Curaçao; Bonaire where it breeds.]
A bird from Los Roques in the collection of the Field Mus. (Chicago, Ill.) was identified by Conover as belonging to the n race, *D. r. rufescens,* and listed as an accidental visitor to Venezuela.
Salt marshes, coastal lagoons, ocean beaches, reefs, mangroves; recorded only at sea level. Feeds erratically, actively running to and fro with sudden changes of direction.

## TRICOLORED (OR LOUISIANA) HERON
*Hydranassa tricolor*
GARZA PECHIBLANCA

Pl. 2
24" (60 cm.). Blue gray, front of neck white with a ragged black and rufous line down front; *belly white.* Breeding season: plumes of lower back pinkish gray; occipital crest white.
Caribbean coast; Margarita, Los Roques, La Orchila Is. (*ruficollis*). [S US, Mid. Amer. to w Peru and e Brazil. Aruba to Trinidad.]
Near salt and fresh water to about 1500 m. Streams and ponds, mangroves, lagoons, coral and sand beaches. Perches in bushes and low trees. Solitary; not shy.

## GREEN HERON
*Butorides virescens*
CHICUACO CUELLO ROJO

18" (46 cm.). Crown glossy greenish black, sides of head and sides and back of neck and sides of breast *purplish chestnut,* front of neck white with a ragged black line down center; center of breast white streaked blackish; belly pale brown. Back light grayish green. Imm.: dark brown above; below white, streaked dusky.
Tropical, casually subtropical zone. Winter visitor recorded from Mérida, Falcón and Aragua (*virescens*). The smaller resident race on Caribbean coast and islands (*maculatus*). [Breeds from N

Amer. to n S Amer. Antilles, Trinidad, Tobago.]

Mangroves, salt- and fresh-water marshes and mud-flats, coral beaches. In contrast to the Reddish Egret crouches motionless for prolonged periods before spearing its prey with a lightning jab. Wades in deep water. Sea level, accidentally subtropical zone (*maculatus*).

## STRIATED HERON

*Butorides striatus*
CHICUACO CUELLO GRIS

Pl. 2

16″ (41 cm.). Much like the Green Heron but instantly separable by *gray instead of chestnut* sides of head and sides and back of neck. Imm.: resembles Green Heron but neck more grayish, less brownish.

Tropical zone on the mainland (*striatus*). Margarita I. (*robinsoni*). [Panama, the Guianas to Bolivia, Uruguay and Argentina. Trinidad, Tobago.]

Fresh- and salt-water environments; habits similar to the Green Heron. To 1000 m. n of the Orinoco, to 250 m. s of it. Llanos, gallery forest.

## CHESTNUT-BELLIED HERON

*Agamia agami*
GARZA PECHICASTAÑA

Pl. 2

28″ (70 cm.). Top of head black, long occipital crest lavender gray. Throat and foreneck white, sides and back of neck chestnut. Back, wings and tail shining bottle green, breast with long lavender gray plumes in breeding season; belly chestnut. Bill long, greenish yellow. Imm.: above brown, below buffy white, streaked dusky. Wings glossed with bottle green. Has somewhat shorter legs than other herons of similar size.

Spottily recorded n and s of the Orinoco to 1000 m. in Mérida, Sucre, Bolívar and Amazonas. [Mexico to Bolivia and s Brazil. Trinidad.]

The most colorful of all herons. Small streams, marshes, swamps and other wet places in forests. Shy, solitary.

## CATTLE EGRET

*Bubulcus ibis*
GARCITA REZNERA

Fig. 7

17″ (43 cm.). White; crown, dorsal plumes, neck and breast intense pinkish buff in breeding season. Bill yellow, legs greenish yellow to dusky.

Tropical zone. Emigrant from Africa, now widely distributed n of the Orinoco, but probably occurs throughout in pasturelands accompanying cattle (*ibis*). [From Newfoundland to Peru and Bolivia; w Indies, Trinidad, Tobago. S Europe, Africa, Asia, Australia.]

Grassy and newly plowed fields generally. Not shy. Feeds on insects disturbed by cattle as they graze; also vertebrates.

## WHISTLING HERON

*Syrigma sibilatrix*
GARZA SILBADORA

Pl. 2

21″ (53 cm.). Crown and occipital crest black or slaty gray, neck buffy. Lower back, tail and underparts creamy white, wing coverts reddish buff *streaked black*. Upper mantle and secondaries gray, primaries slaty black. Bare orbital skin bright blue; bill reddish pink, tipped black.

Tropical zone n of the Orinoco from Barinas and Apure e to Monagas and at Caicara, Bolívar (*fostersmithi*). [The llanos of e Colombia. S Brazil, Paraguay, e Bolivia, Uruguay to central Argentina.]

Open, shallow lagoons, damp and marshy places in the llanos to 500 m. Solitary or with a few other scattered individuals.

## CAPPED HERON

*Pilherodius pileatus*
GARCIOLA REAL

Pl. 2

22″ (56 cm.). Forehead white, crown black, 2 long, narrow, white occipital plumes. Body plumage white, strongly tinged buff in breeding season; wings and tail white, shafts of wing feathers black. Bare facial skin and base of bill cobalt blue; bill dark gray, tip black, intervening part of bill livid blue. Imm.: like ad., but crown streaked white.

Tropical zone n of the Orinoco; w Zulia; n Bolívar from Caicara to Ciudad Bolívar; Gran Roque, Los Roques Is. [Panama, Colombia, the Guianas to Bolivia, n Paraguay, s Brazil.] Swampy woodland, gallery forest edge, forested rivers, muddy areas, llanos to 500 m. Very wary; solitary or in pairs.

## BLACK-CROWNED NIGHT-HERON
*Nycticorax nycticorax*
GUACO

Pl. 2
22″ (56 cm.). Crown, mantle and scapulars black. Forehead, sides of head, occipital plumes, neck all around and underparts white; wings, lower back and tail gray. Bill black; legs yellow. Imm.: brown, spotted buffy above and below. Tropical zone. Generally n of the Orinoco; n Bolívar from Caicara to Ciudad Bolívar; Delta Amacuro. Las Aves, La Orchila, Los Roques, Margarita I. (*hoactli*). [S Canada to Chile and Argentina. Antilles. Trinidad, Tobago. Eurasia, Africa, Philippines, Japan, Hawaii.] Thick vegetation, near water to 500 m.; mangroves, salt- and fresh-water marshes, wooded swamps. Not shy, usually in pairs or groups up to 10. Forages at night. Call: a loud "quock."

## YELLOW-CROWNED NIGHT-HERON
*Nyctanassa violacea*
CHICUACO ENMASCARADO

Pl. 2
23″ (58 cm.). Forecrown yellow; hindcrown, occipital plumes and conspicuous patch at sides of head white; throat and sides of head black (except for white patch). Neck and body blue gray, dorsal plumes with black centers. Bill black, legs yellow. Imm.: much like the Black-crowned Night-Heron but bill shorter and thicker, pale spots on back and underparts smaller. The islands of Las Aves (Aves de Barlovento), Los Roques, La Orchila, La Blanquilla, Margarita and Los Testigos; accidental on coast of the Distr. Federal and Sucre (*bancrofti*). Generally n of the Orinoco and in Delta Amacuro and n Bolívar (*cayennensis*). [Central and e US to nw Peru and s Brazil. Aruba to Trinidad. W Indies. Galápagos Is.]

Near water in varied habitats to 500 m. Mangroves, fresh water streams, swampy woodland, lagoons, beaches. Not shy. Usually alone or in pairs. At night utters frequent, loud "quock." Feeds on insects, crabs.

## RUFESCENT TIGER-HERON
*Tigrisoma lineatum*
PÁJARO VACO

Pl. 2
28″ (71 cm.). Head and neck chestnut, sometimes barred lightly with black; line down front of neck white. Back chestnut finely vermiculated black and streaked brown and black; belly tawny, sides of body barred black and white. Imm.: broadly banded black and rufous above and below, including wings. Locally distributed throughout in tropical zone; Margarita I. (*lineatum*). [Honduras to w Ecuador, Colombia and the Guianas to central Argentina. Trinidad.] Forest rivers and small streams, lagoons, llanos, gallery forest, mangroves, to 300 m. Open and wooded marshy areas. Usually solitary, not shy. Active at night. Remains motionless when alarmed. Feeds on fishes, insects.

## FASCIATED TIGER-HERON
*Tigrisoma fasciatum*
PÁJARO VACO OBSCURO

Pl. 2
26″ (66 cm.). Crown black; neck and back slaty black finely vermiculated buff; breast brown streaked white, belly grayish brown. Imm.: resembles Rufescent Tiger-Heron but bill shorter and stouter. Tropical and upper tropical zones. Spottily recorded in nw Zulia, Lara, Distr. Federal, Guárico and Sucre (*salmoni*). [Costa Rica through Colombia and e Ecuador to nw Argentina. S Brazil.] Streams and humid mountain forests, 300–700 m. Usually solitary. Feeds on fishes and large insects. Note: Called *T. s. salmoni* in Lista Av. Venez.

## ZIGZAG HERON
*Zebrilus undulatus*
GARZA ZEBRA

Pl. 2
13″ (32 cm.). At once separable from Rufescent and Fasciated Tiger-Herons by

its small size. Crown and ample crest black, sides of head and neck chestnut. Above black, back and wing coverts crossed by narrow, wavy buff lines; underparts buff. Rufous phase: fore-crown maroon, the crown tinged chestnut, upper parts more coarsely banded.
Tropical zone. The delta region in Monagas and Delta Amacuro; n Bolívar w to Caicara and s to Salto Guaquinima; s Amazonas. [The Guianas, e Colombia to e Peru and s Brazil.]
Undergrowth near forest ponds, streams, swamps; sea level to 800 m. Terrestrial but occasionally perches at mid-level of trees. Not particularly shy.

## STRIPE-BACKED BITTERN

*Ixobrychus involucris*
GARZA ENANA AMARILLA

Pl. 2
13" (33 cm.). Sandy buff above, line down center of crown and bold stripes down back black. Below buffy white, streaked fawn. Wing tips tawny.
Tropical zone. Local; recorded from Lake Valencia, Carabobo; Aragua (Suata reservoir; Ocumare de la Costa); El Valle, Distr. Federal and Aparición, Portuguesa. [The Guianas, ne Colombia. Se Brazil to s Argentina, s Bolivia and central Chile. Trinidad.]
Fresh-water lakes, marshes, etc., to 500 m., always in reedbeds, rushes and similar dense aquatic vegetation. Small, secretive. Like all bitterns, freezes when alarmed. Partly nocturnal. Feeds on fishes, insects and small aquatic animals. Like the Least and Pinnated Bitterns seen only when flushed, always close at hand.

## LEAST BITTERN

*Ixobrychus exilis*
GARZA ENANA

10" (25 cm.). Crown, nape, back and tail glossy greenish black, a white stripe at each side of back. Sides of head, back and sides of neck and breast, and upper mantle chestnut; breast and belly buffy. Shoulders extensively pale buff, flight feathers dusky, the pale shoulders conspicuous in flight.
Tropical zone. Local; recorded from Guárico (Sta. María de Ipire) and Miranda (Río Chico) (*erythromelas*). [S Canada, US, Mid. Amer., The Guianas, to w Peru, Bolivia, Paraguay and s Brazil. Trinidad.]
The smallest heron. Frequents fresh-water marshes and swamps with high grasses and reedbeds near sea level. Solitary, inconspicuous.

## PINNATED BITTERN

*Botaurus pinnatus*
MIRASOL

Pl. 2
25" (64 cm.). The only heron with a prominent *black moustacial streak*. Crown black; above brown variegated and vermiculated buff. Throat white, rest of underparts buffy white, streaked buffy brown. *Flight feathers black*.
Tropical and subtropical zones. Recorded from Mérida, Aragua, Guárico, Delta Amacuro, and the Gran Sabana, Bolívar, but probably occurs throughout. [E Mexico to Colombia, w Ecuador, the Guianas, se and central Brazil and central Argentina. Trinidad.]
Fresh-water ponds, marshes with high grasses, rivers, reedbeds, near sea level. Solitary, secretive. Feeds on fishes, frogs, snakes.

# BOAT-BILLED HERONS: Cochleariidae

PATOS CUCHARA

Probably related to night-herons but differs from any heron by its very broad, flat bill. Boat-bills inhabit wooded swamps, nest in colonies and are somewhat nocturnal.

## BOAT-BILLED HERON

*Cochlearius cochlearius*
PATO CUCHARA

Pl. 2
23″ (58 cm.). Forehead white, crown and very ample crest black. Upperparts mostly pale, pearl gray. Breast pinkish buff, center of abdomen chestnut, sides of body black. Imm.: mostly dull brown above, paler below. Always distinguish-able by shape of bill from any other heron.
Tropical zone (*cochlearius*). [Mexico to n Colombia, the Guianas, e and w Ecuador to Bolivia and central Argentina. Trinidad.]
Edge of salt- and fresh-water swamps, mangroves, gallery forest, river banks, sea level to 300 m. Shy, wary. Crepuscular and noctural, gregarious. Sometimes perches with other herons on small trees. Call: a heavy "quock."

# STORKS: Ciconiidae

GABANES Y CIGÜEÑAS

Storks resemble herons but have very much heavier bills. Much less dependent on water, they frequent savannas, pastures, and marshy fields.
Unlike herons they fly with necks extended, and often soar in flight. They feed on frogs, small reptiles, fish and other animal life.

## AMERICAN WOOD-IBIS (OR WOOD-STORK)

*Mycteria americana*
GABÁN

Fig. 8
40″ (1 m.). Bill and bare head and neck grayish black (imm.: bill dirty yellow). Plumage white, flight feathers and tail black. Legs blackish, feet pinkish.
Tropical zone. Generally distributed n of the Orinoco from Zulia and Apure to Anzoátegui. S. of the Orinoco in n Bolívar and central Amazonas. [S US to nw Peru, Brazil, Uruguay and central Argentina. Greater Antilles. Trinidad.]
Llanos, open bushy areas, gallery forest, to 200 m. Gregarious, they soar high in flocks of 50 or more. Perches high on dead trees. Nests in trees.

## MAGUARI STORK

*Euxenura maguari*
CIGÜEÑA

Fig. 8
40″ (1 m.). White; wings and tail black. Bill, facial region and legs orange red. Imm.: has considerable amount of black on wing coverts; bill dirty yellow tipped black.
Tropical zone. Locally distributed n of the Orinoco from Zulia and Apure to Sucre and Monagas; s of the Orinoco from nw Bolívar to the Gran Sabana. [E Colombia, the Guianas to s Chile and Argentina.]
Llanos, savanna ponds, swampy areas, near sea level. Solitary or in pairs. Builds large nests of sticks on palms, low trees and bushes, often near heron colonies. Feed on reptiles, small mammals, frogs, insects.

## JABIRÚ

*Jabiru mycteria*
GARZÓN SOLDADO

Fig. 8
52″ (1 m. 30 cm.). Bill very heavy, black. Head and neck bare, black, bare patch at base of neck red. Plumage white, including wings and tail.
Tropical zone. Locally and widely distributed, commonest along the Ríos Apure, Orinoco and Ventuari. [Mid. Amer., Colombia, the Guianas, Brazil, e and w Peru, Paraguay, Uruguay and n Argentina.]
Open marshy terrain, llanos, near sea level. Very large; conspicuous as it forages in the open, usually alone. Wary. Builds nests near tops of trees but usually on top of palm trees. Soars in flocks. Feeds on fish, frogs, snakes, insects.

Fig. 8. MAGUARI STORK (left), JABIRÚ (center), AMERICAN WOOD-IBIS (right)

## IBISES: Threskiornithidae

### COROCOROS, GARZAS PALETA

Ibises are distinguishable from herons by their long, thin, curved bills. Unlike herons, but like storks, they fly with neck extended. Ibises are gregarious, nest in colonies and live in marshes, wooded swamps and savannas where they feed on fish and crustaceans.

Young ibises of the various species resemble each other in their brown upperparts and necks, and whitish underparts.

### BUFF-NECKED IBIS

*Theristicus caudatus*
TAUTACO

Pl. 3
29″ (74 cm.). Head, neck and breast buffy white, shaded cinnamon on head and breast. Back gray; greater wing coverts white; lower breast and belly black.

Tropical zone. Widely distributed n of the Orinoco especially in the llanos; s of the Orinoco in n Bolívar (*caudatus*). [Casual in e Panama through the more open parts of S Amer. to Tierra del Fuego. The Andes of Ecuador and Peru.] Savannas along river and lake borders, open swampy places, open forests, to 300 m. Colonial breeders. Build bulky nests, usually in trees. Call: metallic clanking, uttered when flying and also on the ground. Loose flocks.

## SHARP-TAILED IBIS
*Cercibis oxycerca*
TAROTARO

Pl. 3
30″ (76 cm.). A bushy occipital crest. Plumage glossy greenish black, glossed purple on back. Bill, legs and bare ocular region orange red.
Tropical zone. Locally distributed on the llanos and along the Ríos Apure and Orinoco in Apure, Barinas and nw Bolívar. [Ne Colombia, Guyana, Surinam, w Amazonian Brazil.]
Savannas along rivers and lake borders, open swampy places, to 300 m. Nests in trees.

## GREEN IBIS
*Mesembrinibis cayennensis*
COROCORO NEGRO

Pl. 3
23″ (58 cm.). A bushy nuchal crest. Head gray, nape and back of neck shining green; wings and upperparts bronzy green; below dusky purplish. *Bill and legs dark green,* facial area gray.
Tropical zone. Locally distributed in the basins of the Ríos Apure and Orinoco. [Costa Rica to Colombia and the Guianas to Bolivia and Argentina.]
Forest, second growth, to 500 m. Wooded, wet, muddy places; gallery forest edge. Solitary or in small loose flocks. Shy. Nest is a frail-looking structure, high in trees. Mellow rattling calls at twilight. Not a colonial breeder.

## BARE-FACED (OR WHISPERING) IBIS
*Phimosus infuscatus*
TARA

Pl. 3
19″ (48 cm.). Greenish black, wings bluish green. Face, *bill* and *legs red.*
Tropical, casually subtropical zone. Locally distributed s to the s bank of the Orinoco in Bolívar and nw Amazonas (*berlepschi*). [Colombia, Guyana, Surinam to n Bolivia, Paraguay, Brazil and central Argentina.]

Wooded swamps and streams, pastures and open fields near sea level; once at 1950 m. Nests in colonies in low trees. Nest is a rude, flat platform of sticks, very small for the size of the bird, 30–35 cm. in diameter.

## WHITE IBIS
*Eudocimus albus*
COROCORO BLANCO

Fig. 9
23″ (58 cm.). White; wing tips black. Face, bill and legs red. Imm.: head and neck pale brown, wings and tail dark brown, rump and belly white.
Tropical zone. Locally distributed along the coast from Falcón (Adícora) to Anzoátegui, Aragua and Carabobo (L. Valencia); nests in Apure. [S US to n Colombia, French Guiana. Greater Antilles. Curaçao. Trinidad.]
Near large bodies of water; coastal mangrove swamps, tidal mud flats, llanos, flooded areas. Gregarious. Joins flocks of Scarlet Ibises, but much less common. Nests in trees, often in colonies with other ibises and herons.

## SCARLET IBIS
*Eudocimus ruber*
COROCORO COLORADO

Pl. 3, Fig. 9
23″ (58 cm.). Scarlet; wing tips black. Imm.: like imm. White Ibis, but tinged pink on rump.
Locally throughout except in Amazonas & s Bolivar; Margarita I.; nests in Falcón Apure and Delta Amacuro. [N and e Colombia, the Guianas, coastal Brazil. Trinidad.]
Habitat similar to the White Ibis but much more common. Usually in flocks up to 30. Very common in the mudflats and mangroves of the Orinoco delta region. Often nests with other ibises and herons.

## GLOSSY IBIS
*Plegadis falcinellus*
COROCORO CASTAÑO

Pl. 3
19″ (48 cm.). Maroon chestnut (appears black at a distance); greater wing coverts iridescent purple green. Face *blackish,* outlined in white in breeding sea-

Fig. 9. WHITE IBIS (left), SCARLET IBIS (right)

son. Imm.: resembles imm. White Ibis but front and sides of neck white, bill dusky.

Tropical zone. Reported breeding in Aragua (*falcinellus*). [S US to Colombia, Greater Antilles. Europe. Asia. Africa. Australia.]

Sight records of *P. chihi* in Apure and Aragua probably belong here. *P. chihi* differs from *P. falcinellus* by broader white line outlining face and *red facial area*. In non-breeding season very similar to *falcinellus;* imm. not distinguishable from *falcinellus*.

Water's edge, mud flats, near sea level.

**ROSEATE SPOONBILL**
*Ajaia ajaja*
GARZA PALETA

Fig. 10

28″ (71 cm.). *Bill* long, *flat, expanded* and *rounded at the end*. Bill and bare skin of head yellowish green. Plumage mostly pink, shoulder bar and rump rosy crimson. Imm.: white with a pink tinge.

Locally n of the Orinoco s to the s bank at Caicara, nw Bolívar; Delta Amacuro; Margarita I. [S US to s Bolivia, Uruguay and central Argentina. Antilles, Aruba, Bonaire. Trinidad, Tobago.]

Llanos, swampy woods, marshes, mud flats, ponds in savannas and other open areas, near sea level. Mangroves. Alone or in small groups. Feeds by moving the bill from side to side in the mud and shallow water. Nests in trees in the llanos, often with other ibises and herons.

# FLAMINGOS: Phoenicopteridae

## FLAMENCOS O TOCOCOS

Flamingos are recognizable at a distance by their very long, slender necks and legs; this is true also in flight for their legs and necks are carried extended. Flamingos are

Fig. 10. ROSEATE SPOONBILL (juvenal at left; adult at right)

Fig. 11. AMERICAN FLAMINGO

found in shallow coastal lagoons where they feed on minute crustaceans, algae and diatoms which they sift with their bills. The bill is curiously shaped, being sharply bent downward in the middle. It is short, basally pink with a wide black tip. Flamingos nest in colonies and build columnar mud nests.

**AMERICAN FLAMINGO**

*Phoenicopterus ruber*
FLAMENCO O TOCOCO

Fig. 11
46" (1 m. 20 cm.). General plumage orangy pink, primaries black. Legs pink. Bill strongly curved, thick, distal half black.

Locally distributed along the Caribbean coast and islands. Falcón (Adícora; Chichiriviche); Miranda (Laguna de Tacarigua); Margarita, La Orchila, Los Roques, Las Aves Is. [Bahamas; Hispaniola; Cuba. Yucatan; ne Colombia. The Guianas, ne Brazil. Aruba, Curaçao, Bonaire. Galápagos Is.]

Most numerous in Falcón; single birds and flocks up to 100 often on Los Roques. Formerly bred on La Orchila and still visits there.

# ANSERIFORMES

## SCREAMERS: Anhimidae

ARUCOS, CHICAGÜIRES

These large, ungainly birds frequent swamps and marshy open country, where they may be seen walking with slow, dignified steps. They have very large feet, the toes unwebbed. The bill is short and chickenlike. Screamers are remarkable in having an airspace between the body and skin. They often fly to great heights and sail in wide circles, and are well known for their very loud, sonorous trumpeting calls uttered both on the ground and on the wing. They feed on vegetable matter.

**HORNED SCREAMER**

*Anhima cornuta*
ARUCO

Fig. 12
32" (81 cm.). Mainly glossy greenish black; belly, shoulders and mottling on head and neck white. Head adorned with a thin, long quill (3", 7.6 cm.). A pair of large spurs at shoulders. Legs rather short, thick, feet very large.

Locally distributed, probably throughout but recorded presently from Zulia, Mérida, Guárico, Anzoátegui, Sucre, Monagas, and Delta Amacuro. [The Guianas, Colombia, e and w Ecuador to Brazil and Bolivia. Formerly Trinidad.]

Llanos, forest edge, bushes, to about 300 m. Not shy. Usually in pairs, they stand on exposed river bars and banks. Perch on trees. Heavy, fast wing beats as it takes flight, alternating with short glides. Nests near aquatic vegetation. Honks and squeaks in the morning.

**NORTHERN SCREAMER**

*Chauna chavaria*
CHICAGÜIRE

Fig. 12
34" (86 cm.). Head and crest gray, throat and sides of head white, forming a band; neck black; rest of plumage dark gray, glossed green above.

Locally distributed in the basin of L. Maracaibo in Zulia, Mérida and Trujillo. [N Colombia.]

From near sea level to 1200 m. They stand on exposed river banks and marshes. Usually in pairs or scattered flocks of 10 or more. Breeds in May. Nest is a mass of rushes accumulated above the water in the aquatic vegetation. Lays 2 to 7 eggs. Call: strident.

Fig. 12. HORNED SCREAMER (left), NORTHERN SCREAMER (right)

# DUCKS, GEESE: Anatidae

## PATOS

Many species of ducks are found in Venezuela, some of them migrants from the north. They are found on rivers, lakes and marshes, mostly in the tropical zone.

In habits they do not differ, except for the torrent ducks, from ducks in other parts of the world. In the non-breeding season the males of many species assume an eclipse plumage which closely resembles that of the female.

Whistling-Ducks have longer necks and legs than is usual in ducks and are rather gooselike in appearance. Partially nocturnal. Their high whistling notes are often heard at night.

### FULVOUS WHISTLING- (OR TREE-) DUCK

*Dendrocygna bicolor*
YAGUASO COLORADO

Pl. 3
19″ (48 cm.). Head, neck, and underparts tawny brown, a black line down back of neck; back dark brown, barred with buffy rufous; upper and under tail coverts white. Lengthened feathers at sides of body cream color, forming a stripe. Slight crest on back of head. Bill slaty gray, legs bluish gray.

Tropical zone. Recorded from Zulia, Táchira, and the llanos of Cojedes and Aragua, Portuguesa, Apure and Guárico but undoubtedly more widely distributed. [E Panama, Colombia to the temperate zone, to s Brazil, central Argentina and Chile. Trinidad. E Africa, Madagascar, se Asia.]

Sea level to 500 m. Numerous n of the llanos but flocks of thousands in the llanos, especially in the dry season, inundated savannas. Associated with White-faced and Black-bellied Whistling-Ducks. Occasionally in muddy coastal lagoons or rice fields. Seldom perches on trees. Nests in the llanos at the end of the rainy season. Call: long, squealing whistle.

## WHITE-FACED WHISTLING- (OR TREE-) DUCK

*Dendrocygna viduata*
YAGUASO CARIBLANCO

Pl. 3

17″ (43 cm.). Face and foreneck white; back of head and neck—and sometimes a band across throat—black. Back reddish brown, feathers pale-edged; rump, tail and center of underparts black; breast rufous chestnut, side of body barred black and white.

Tropical zone. N of the Orinoco from Zulia, Mérida, Táchira and Apure to Sucre and Monagas. [Costa Rica to central Argentina. Greater Antilles, Curaçao, Trinidad. Africa s of the Sahara.]

Sea level to 1500 m. Flocks of thousands in the llanos. Associates with Fulvous and Black-bellied and Whistling-Ducks. Rice fields, mud flats on the n coast, Nov.–March. Nests in the llanos at the end of the rainy season. Call: thin, high whistle, "vee-see-seee."

## BLACK-BELLIED WHISTLING- (OR TREE-) DUCK

*Dendrocygna autumnalis*
GUIRIRÍ

Pl. 3

19″ (48 cm.). Crown and back of neck dark reddish brown, front and sides of neck and sides of head gray. Back and upper breast chestnut brown, lower breast gray, belly black, under tail coverts barred black and white. Large area on upper side of wings white, wing lining black. Bill bright pink, pale-tipped.

Tropical zone, n and s of the Orinoco; Margarita I. (*discolor*). [Texas to Panama. Colombia to w Peru, Bolivia, Paraguay, s Brazil and n Argentina. Trinidad. W. Indies.]

Sea level to 600 m. Flocks of thousands in the llanos. Associates with Fulvous and White-faced Whistling-Ducks. Rice fields. Often wades. Perches on high branches of trees near marshes. Call: high thin whistles, sounding like its local name, "wee-ree-reee."

## ORINOCO GOOSE

*Neochen jubata*
PATO CARRETERO

Pl. 3

23″ (58 cm.). Head and neck, breast and extreme upper back grayish buffy white, darkest on hindneck. Back, tail, lesser wing coverts and primaries black with a purplish gloss. Secondaries metallic green, wing speculum rusty cinnamon; belly chestnut; under tail coverts white. Feet and legs salmon pink.

Wooded banks of the Orinoco and its affluents. [Colombia and the Guianas to s Bolivia, nw Argentina, Paraguay and s Brazil.]

Sea level to 200 m. Alone or in pairs, seldom in groups. Not shy.

## SPECKLED TEAL

*Anas flavirostris*
PATO SERRANO

Pl. 3

15″ (38 cm.). Somewhat crested. Head and neck freckled buffy and blackish. Back blackish brown, feathers pale-edged. Below buffy white, the feathers dark-centered, giving a somewhat mottled appearance. Wing speculum black with a slight purplish green reflection, bordered above with rufous, below by buffy. Bill blue gray.

Páramo zone of the Andes, from Trujillo to sw Táchira (*altipetens*). [Andes from Colombia to Tierra del Fuego. Paraguay. Se Brazil. Uruguay. Falkland Is.]

Small lakes 3200–3800 m. Not shy; in pairs or small groups. Nests in the grass, near the lagoons, reportedly in Aug.

## AMERICAN WIGEON

*Anas americana*
PATO CALVO

20″ (51 cm.). Crown white, green stripe through eye, meeting at back of neck;

cheeks and neck white freckled with black. Upper back pinkish gray, vermiculated black, lower back black vermiculated white, Upper breast and sides of body pinkish. Flanks and broad patch on forewing white. Wing speculum black with bronzy reflections. ♀: head and neck freckled black and white, dusky band through eye, otherwise much like ♂ but back browner, the feathers pale-edged.

Known to occur only from a leg band recovered in L. Maracaibo, Zulia. [Breeds in N Amer. Winters to Colombia.]

Shallow fresh- and salt-water lagoons and marshes on and near the coast.

Note: Called *Mareca americana* in Lista Av. Venez.

[GREEN-WINGED TEAL (*A. crecca carolinensis*)] is probably an accidental winter visitor, for it has been taken in the e Andes of Colombia and on Tobago.

## WHITE-CHEEKED (OR BAHAMA) PINTAIL
*Anas bahamensis*
PATO MALIBÚ

Pl. 3
16″ (41 cm.). Top half of head dark brown, lower half white, very sharply defined. Throat and foreneck white, hindneck brown freckled with black. Upper back and underparts light brown, spotted dusky, lower back dark brown; tail long, pointed, light cinnamon. Bill orange red at base, rest blue gray. Sexes similar.

Known from Falcón, Aragua, Sucre, Margarita I. (*bahamensis*). [N Colombia, sw Ecuador, the Guianas, n Brazil to Uruguay, Argentina and Chile. Antilles. Curaçao, Bonaire. Trinidad. Galápagos Is.]

Fresh- and salt-water ponds, sloughs, in open areas, swamps. Sea level. Usually in small groups but also in flocks of more than 500. Shy, alert. Nests on the ground in grassy areas or near bushes, July–Dec.

## COMMON (OR NORTHERN) PINTAIL
*Anas acuta*
PATO RABUDO

26″ (66 cm.). Head and neck chocolate brown with white stripe from behind ear coverts down sides of neck. Lower neck and underparts white, upper back and sides of body grayish, vermiculated dusky. Lower back mostly gray. Scapulars and tertials long, narrow, pointed, black, edged white. Middle tail feathers black, very long, narrow and pointed. Wing speculum bronzy brown. ♀: brown, mottled dusky. Distinguishable from other similar ducks by long neck, and narrow, long, pointed middle tail feathers, good field characters in both sexes.

Casual winter visitor, November. Carabobo; Anzoátegui. [Breeds in N Amer., Europe and Asia. Winters to Panama, Colombia, Guyana, Africa, India and the Philippines.]

Lagoons in open foothills and in the llanos, to 500 m. Usually in small flocks up to 12.

## BLUE-WINGED TEAL
*Anas discors*
BARRAQUETE ALIAZUL

Pl. 3
15″ (38 cm.). Head and neck blue, a *conspicuous white crescent in front of eye*. Back dark brown, the feathers pale-edged; lower parts pinkish cinnamon spotted with dusky. A broad patch on forepart of wing pale blue; wing speculum green, outlined with white posteriorly, wing lining and flanks white. ♀: brown, mottled dusky, wing patch and speculum as in ♂.

Tropical to temperate zones. Winter resident, Sept.–May, n of the Orinoco, including La Tortuga, Los Roques and Margarita I. (*discors*, more rarely *orphna*). [Breeds in N Amer. Winters to n Chile and central Argentina. Aruba, Curaçao, Bonaire. Trinidad, Tobago.]

Fresh- and salt-water lagoons in open areas to 3500 m., as well as in mangrove swamps. Usually in small groups but also in flocks up to 400.

## CINNAMON TEAL
*Anas cyanoptera*
BARRAQUETE COLORADO

15″ (38 cm.). Head, neck and underparts cinnamon red, otherwise like Blue-winged Teal. ♀: much like ♂ Blue-wing but wing speculum brown only slightly glossed bronzy green.

Casual winter visitor. Taken once: Páramo de Conejos, Mérida, in Oct. (*septentrionalium*). [Breeds in N Amer., winters occasionally to Colombia. Resident in Colombia and in S Amer.]

Inconspicuous, small, chestnut red duck. Note: Resident S Amer. races (♂) have the breast slightly speckled with black.

## TORRENT DUCK
*Merganetta armata*
PATO DE TORRENTES

Pl. 3

15" (38 cm.). Crown, back of neck and *stripe through eye continued down sides of neck black,* sides of head and rest of neck white. Upperparts striped sandy and black, rump vermiculated gray and black. Underparts white streaked with gray. Wing speculum green bordered above and below with white. Tail long, shafts of feathers very stiff. Bill very narrow, orange red, tipped yellow. ♀: above like ♂ but throat, sides and front of neck and entire underparts orange rufous. No stripes on sides of neck. Bill as in ♂. Both sexes have a spur on shoulder.

Subtropical and temperate zones. The Andes from n Mérida to sw Táchira (*colombiana*). [Colombia through the Andes to Tierra del Fuego.]

Fast-flowing rivers and streams in heavily wooded mountain areas, 2000–2800 m. Excellent swimmers and divers, the adults as well as the ducklings can remain stationary in the fastest rushing waters. Seldom flies. Feeds on aquatic insects. Nests in burrows near the torrents it frequents.

Note: Called *M. colombiana* in Lista Av. Venez.

## SOUTHERN POCHARD
*Netta erythrophthalma*
PATO NEGRO

Fig. 13

20" (51 cm.). A blackish duck (actually dark brown) with white wing speculum and white inner webs to secondaries. Bill gray blue, tip black. ♀: uniform dull brown; throat, foreneck and area around bill whitish. Bill as in ♂. Not unlike Lesser Scaup but much larger, with dark underparts and basally white secondaries. Zulia and Aragua (*erythrophthalma*).

Fig. 13. SOUTHERN POCHARD (top) (male left; female right), LESSER SCAUP (bottom) (male left; female right)

[Colombia to temperate zone, s to Chile. Casual in e Brazil. E and s Africa.] Recorded alone or in pairs, does not associate with other species. Sea level to 500 m.
Note: Called *Aythya erythrophthalma* in Lista Av. Venez.

## LESSER SCAUP
*Aythya affinis*
PATO ZAMBULLIDOR DEL NORTE

Fig. 13
15" (38 cm.). Head and neck black shot with purple; breast brownish black. Belly white, sides of body heavily vermiculated with brown. Back white narrowly barred with wavy blackish lines. Secondaries mostly white showing as a wing stripe in flight. Bill gray blue. ♀: mostly brown, darkest on head and neck. Area surrounding bill including forehead white. Secondaries mostly white showing as a wing stripe in flight. Bill as in ♂.
Winter resident. Recorded in Falcón, Aragua, Miranda and Monagas; Margarita I. [Breeds in N Amer. Winters to Surinam, w Ecuador, and Trinidad.]
Sea level to 500 m. A diving duck of placid waters. Feeds on aquatic vegetation and insects, snails.

## RING-NECKED DUCK
*Aythya collaris*
PATO ZAMBULLIDOR DE COLLAR

15" (38 cm.). Very similar to Lesser Scaup. Best distinguished by blackish back, pale brownish gray, dark-tipped primaries, blue gray secondaries with no white and *differently colored* bill which is white basally, gray in the middle, followed by a white band and black tip. Head has green gloss, chin white; dark chestnut collar around base of neck is not very evident. ♀: much like ♀ Lesser Scaup but with less white on head, no white on forehead. Secondaries mostly grayish instead of white showing as a wing stripe in flight. The bill in both sexes differs from that of Southern Pochard and Lesser Scaup by having a distinct pale ring behind black tip.
Casual in winter. Recorded once in Dec. in Carabobo and on Margarita I. [Breeds in N Amer. Winters to Panama and Trinidad.]

Sea level to 500 m. A diving duck. Feeds on aquatic vegetation and insects.

## BRAZILIAN DUCK
*Amazonetta brasiliensis*
PATO BRASILEÑO

Pl. 3
16" (41 cm.). Top of head, back of neck, lower back and rump black, sides of head and neck grayish. Wing coverts and outer secondaries brilliant metallic green, turning purplish on inner secondaries, wing speculum white bordered above by black. Underparts brownish, spotted dusky on breast. *Bill and feet bright orange red.* ♀: like ♂ but duller, with face blotched with whitish. Bill and feet olive.
Río Apure and its tributaries in Táchira, Apure, Barinas and Guárico; the middle Orinoco from Caicara to Ciudad Bolívar (*brasiliensis*). [Colombia and the Guianas to Bolivia, Argentina and Uruguay.]
Sea level to 300 m. Called *Roppong* by the Indians in Guyana in imitation of its call. Nests in the grass. A small duck appearing brownish gray at a distance.

## COMB DUCK
*Sarkidiornis melanotos*
PATO DE MONTE

Fig. 14
♂ 30" (76 cm.), ♀ 22" (56 cm.). Head, neck, breast and central underparts white, head and neck speckled with black. *Bill black with a tall, fleshy comb.* Back and sides of body and wing black glossed with oily green and purple. ♀: like ♂ but much smaller, sides of body grayish. No comb.
Recorded only from the llanos of Guárico and n and central Anzoátegui (*sylvicola*). [Colombia and the Guianas to Ecuador, e Peru, Paraguay, Uruguay and central Argentina. India, Burma, Thailand.]
Sea level to 300 m. Ponds in the llanos and adjacent woodland. Goose-like. Shy. In pairs and small groups but in the dry season gathers in flocks of over 100. Call: Usually silent.

## MUSCOVY DUCK

*Cairina moschata*
PATO REAL

Fig. 14
♂ 33" (84 cm.); ♀ 26" (66 cm.). A big, black forest duck with a large white wing patch. Head somewhat crested, general plumage black glossed with green. Base of bill and ocular region adorned with red caruncles, bill black with a livid bluish white band. ♀: similar but much smaller, crest much reduced. No caruncles.

N and s of the Orinoco along wooded streams, and in the delta. [Mexico to sw Ecuador, s Bolivia, Uruguay and central Argentina.]

Sea level to 300 m. In pairs or in small flocks. Roosts in trees. Call: usually silent but emits a choked call, "cua-cua," and squealing whistles. Nests in holes in trees and dry logs.

## MASKED DUCK

*Oxyura dominica*
PATICO ENMASCARADO

Pl. 3
15" (38 cm.). Face black; neck, back of head and back bright chestnut, the back heavily spotted with black, forming stripes. Underparts buffy brown, wings and tail black, the wings with a large white patch. Tail fanshaped, carried erect at times when swimming. ♀: top of head brownish black, sides of head white with a *black stripe through eye,* and *another below it.* Back brown, mottled black; breast and sides pale brown, belly white; wings dark brown with a large white patch.

Tropical zone generally, but locally n of the Orinoco; s of the Orinoco in extreme ne and se Bolívar. [Texas to Chile and Argentina. Trinidad, Tobago.]

Fig. 14. Large, perching ducks:
COMB DUCK (upper left) (female left; male right),
MUSCOVY DUCK (lower right) (male left; female right)

Sea level to 500 m. Forested rivers and marshes; ponds heavily overgrown with vegetation; rice fields; occasionally seen flying or on sandy open beaches. Shy, secretive, dives when alarmed. In pairs and flocks up to 30. Call: described as a cackling *kirri-birroo, kirri-birroo, kirroo, kirroo.*

# FALCONIFORMES

## VULTURES: Cathartidae

ZAMUROS

Except for the beautiful King Vulture, American vultures are mainly black with bare heads and necks and of rather unprepossessing appearance. The Black Vulture serves a very useful purpose in cleaning up garbage and refuse in many towns and villages. All are scavengers. Except for the Black Vulture and occasionally the Turkey Vulture they inhabit llanos, swamps and forested areas.

**ANDEAN CONDOR**
*Vultur gryphus*
CÓNDOR

42″ (1 m. 10 cm.). Wingspread about 10′ (3 m.). Head bare, dusky flesh, surmounted by a fleshy comb. Plumage mainly black; ruff of white down around neck, not quite meeting in front. Median and greater wing coverts and inner remiges silvery gray. ♀: similar but without comb. Imm.: brownish black, ruff brownish.
Formerly the Andes of Mérida, now probably extinct there; last reported in 1912. [The Santa Marta Mts., ne Colombia s through the Andes and s Pacific coast to Tierra del Fuego.]
The largest flying bird in the world; weighs about 11 kilos. Gregarious. Nests in caves in precipitous cliffs on the páramos.

**KING VULTURE**
*Sarcoramphus papa*
REY ZAMURO

Pl. I
30″ (76 cm.). Easily recognizable by its white body and black wings. Bill, cere, wattles, eye ring and neck bright orange, head purplish black, crown orange, head covered with sparse bristles. *General body color creamy white,* ruff around base of neck slaty gray almost black on hindneck. *Wings,* tail and rump *black.* Imm.: black, neck orange, head blacker than in ad., base of bill orange, no wattles.
Tropical zone, virtually throughout. [Mexico to sw Peru, Bolivia, Paraguay, Uruguay and central Argentina. Trinidad.]
Soars in forested areas in the lowlands but also high over cities. Usually flies alone or in widely scattered groups. Called King Vulture, or Rey Zamuro because all the other vultures that are feeding on carrion immediately retreat to a safe distance as this much larger bird approaches. Nests in caves and hollow trees.

**BLACK VULTURE**
*Coragyps atratus*
ZAMURO

Pl. I
22″ (56 cm.). Wingspread 54″ (1 m. 40 cm.). Black; front and sides of head and throat bare, slaty black. *A large white patch on underside of wings* near tip. *Tail short, rounded. Flight heavy, short glides interrupted by flapping;* in flight wings held horizontal to body, wing tips pointed forward, feet extending beyond tail. Legs gray.
Tropical to temperate zones throughout including Margarita, Coche and Cu-

bagua Is. (*brasiliensis*). [S US to Chile and Argentina. Trinidad.]
All habitats to 3500 m. Forests, fields, cities, garbage dumps. Gregarious. Nests in crevices in rocks. Alone and in flocks up to 200.

## TURKEY VULTURE

*Cathartes aura*
ORIPOPO

Pls. 4, I
25″ (63 cm.). Wing spread 72″ (1 m. 80 cm.). Brownish black, head bare, dusky red (blackish in imm.). *Tail rather long, square.* Soaring flight in wide circles; pointed wings are held slanted up from body in flight, but do not extend beyond long, narrow tail when bird is perched. Legs pinkish.
Tropical to páramo zone throughout; Margarita I. (*ruficollis*). [S Canada and US to Cape Horn and the Falkland Is. W Indies. Trinidad.]
Various habitats, sea level to near páramos. Usually the most common vulture after the Black Vulture. Lagoons, open country with scattered trees. Inhabited and uninhabited areas but seldom in towns.

## LESSER YELLOW-HEADED VULTURE

*Cathartes burrovianus*
ORIPOPO CABEZA AMARILLA MENOR

Pls. 4, I
30″ (76 cm.); [or 23″ (59 cm.), a]. In flight outline like the Black Vulture. Above dull black, feathers edged brownish black, back slightly glossed green. White shafts of base of primaries show in flight as a distinct white patch on underside of wing. Head bare; cere, forecrown, nape, sides of neck and throat dull orange red, center of crown dull bluish gray, sides of *head bright orange,* lores greenish yellow, spot in front of eye bluish gray.
Range of the two forms found in Venezuela still remains to be worked out. Locally from Zulia, Falcón and Aragua e to Anzoátegui, Delta Amacuro and the middle and lower Orinoco in Bolívar (*burrovianus,* a). Birds from s Venezuela probably belong to the larger, southern race (*urubutinga*). [Mexico to Colombia, the Guianas and Argentina. Trinidad.]
Forests, near rivers and forest edge; usually near sea level but observed up to 1800 m. Marshy grasslands, llanos and woodland, away from habitations. Nests in holes in trees.

## GREATER YELLOW-HEADED VULTURE

*Cathartes melambrotus*
ORIPOPO CABEZA AMARILLA MAYOR

Pls. 4, I
33″ (84 cm.). Differs from Lesser Yellow-headed Vulture by duller, yellower head without red on forecrown, larger size and longer tail. Plumage blacker, glossy black with a greenish gloss, rather than brownish black. No white patch on underside of wing.
Tropical zone. Recorded in Delta Amacuro and s Amazonas, but probably widespread in forested country of the s. [The Guianas to e Peru, Bolivia and e Brazil.]
Forested lowland areas. Difficult to differentiate with certainty in the field from Lesser Yellow-head.
Note: The original spelling of this name is as above, not *melambrotos.*

# KITES, HAWKS, EAGLES: ACCIPITRIDAE

## GAVILANES, AGUILAS

The Accipitridae divide themselves conveniently into 4 distinct groups: the kites, the accipiters, the harriers and the buteos, which include the eagles.

Kites are birds of rapid and graceful flight, hovering over their prey when they spot it, then gliding down, seizing it with their feet and swooping up with it again. Their food consists of small reptiles, mammals and large insects. Some, however, subsist exclusively on marsh-inhabiting snails which are seized in the water while the bird is in flight. Kites have long, narrow tails (in one species deeply forked) and the wings are rather narrow and pointed. They inhabit open country and swamps.

Accipiters fly rapidly with quick wing beats interrupted by short glides. They feed chiefly on small birds and mammals and in the smaller species on large insects. They have broad, short, rounded wings and long tails. They inhabit open country and forest.

Harriers live in open, often grassy country where they sail gracefully, close over the ground, the wings held above the level of the back. The wings are rather broad, the body slim, the legs and tail rather long. Males and females are very different in plumage. Harriers feed on rodents, frogs and small reptiles.

Buteos, known as buzzards in Europe, form the largest group in the family and include eagles. They have short, spreading tails and broad wings, suited to the soaring flight which helps to distinguish them from other hawks. Their toes are rather short and thick. They secure their prey—small mammals, reptiles and birds, and even monkeys, sloths and fairly large mammals for certain eagles—by suddenly diving on it and seizing it with their talons. In this group certain species have the tarsi feathers to the toes. Buteos are found in open country, forest, and open mountain slopes.

Although hawks are much persecuted by man on the supposition that they kill domestic birds and mammals, this happens only infrequently and their propensity for keeping down the rodent and insect population far outweighs any harm they might do. They should be protected.

## WHITE-TAILED KITE

*Elanus leucurus*
GAVILÁN MAROMERO

Pl. VII
15″ (38 cm.). Upperparts, wings and central tail feathers pale gray; rest of tail feathers, forehead, sides of head and underparts white. *Shoulders extensively black.* In flight both ad. and imm. have a *black patch at bend on underside of wing.* Imm.: mottled brown and white above; below pale cinnamon, streaked dusky.

Tropical zone. Generally n of the Orinoco; s of it recorded only from Cerro Roraima, Bolívar. [S US to Panama, n Colombia, the Guianas to se Brazil, Paraguay, Uruguay, Argentina and Chile. Trinidad.]

Open terrain, with isolated trees, often near water, to 1200 m. Marshy llanos, pastures, second growth. Not shy. Alone or in pairs, courses low over fields; soars and hovers, often near streams. Perches on small trees and wires. Nests in isolated trees (Feb.).

## PEARL KITE

*Gampsonyx swainsonii*
CERNÍCALO

Pls. 5, VII
8″ (20 cm.). Forehead and sides of head buff, crown, ocular region, and nape

black, narrow white nuchal collar edged below with dull rufous. Upperparts, wings and tail slaty gray, inner remiges conspicuously edged white. Underparts white including wing lining; a patch of black or rufous at sides of breast, thighs pale rufous. Imm.: differs from ad. by feathers of back edged rufous brown, below suffused with yellowish buff.

Tropical zone, probably throughout including Margarita I. (*leonae*). [Nicaragua. N Colombia, Guyana, Surinam to Chile and Argentina. Trinidad.]

One of the smallest hawks in Venezuela. Various habitats to 1000 m. Rain forest, deciduous woodland, xerophytic areas, llanos, pastures, second growth. Usually alone; perches on telephone poles. Feeds on insects, lizards.

Note: Placed in Falconidae in Lista Av. Venez.

## SWALLOW-TAILED KITE

*Elanoides forficatus*
GAVILÁN TIJERETA

Pl. VII
24″ (60 cm.). *Tail long, deeply forked.* Head, neck, underparts and wing lining white. Back, wings and tail black, inner remiges white, interscapular region glossed oily green. Imm.: like ad. but head and underparts finely streaked.

Tropical to subtropical zones. From Zulia, Lara, Mérida and Barinas to Aragua,

Miranda and n Monagas, and from Delta Amacuro to n and se Bolívar (*yetapa*). [Breeds from US to Argentina. Trinidad. Migration routes of northern birds (*forficatus*) little known; recorded from w Ecuador and s Brazil. They differ from *yetapa* by purple-glossed instead of green-glossed interscapular region.]

Open woodland areas, plantations, second growth forest edge, along rivers, clearings, to 1800 m. Unmistakable for its long, forked tail. Glides and soars gracefully in circles, usually in small groups but sometimes 30 or more. While flying seizes insects with its talons and eats them. Also eats frogs and snakes. Seldom observed perched.

## GRAY-HEADED KITE
*Leptodon cayanensis*
GAVILÁN PALOMERO

Pls. III, V
18–20" (46–51 cm.). Head and nape dark gray, throat and upper breast grayish white, rest of underparts white. Back and wings blackish, remiges with dark gray bars; upper tail coverts gray; tail long, black with 3 light gray bands and white tip. From below: lesser *under wing coverts jet black,* remiges barred dusky and white; tail wedge-shaped with 3 white bars. Facial skin, cere, legs and feet *light blue* in either plumage. Imm., dark phase: head, neck, back and wings brown; underparts buffy white, very heavily (or very lightly) streaked dusky. Tail dusky brown with 3 gray bars. Light phase: center of crown blackish, or streaked dusky; forehead, sides of head, neck, upper back and entire underparts white. Back, wings and tail as in dark phase, but under wing coverts white. In color much like Black-and-white Hawk Eagle but smaller, and with fewer bars in tail; tail longer. In addition the Black-and-white Hawk Eagle has feathered tarsi, *L. cayanensis* does not.

Tropical and subtropical zones. Recorded from Zulia, Mérida, Apure, Guárico, Carabobo, Distr. Federal, Monagas, Bolívar and Amazonas. [Mexico to Argentina. Trinidad.]

Humid forests, savannas, forest edge, often near water, to 2000 m. Forages and perches in the treetops, difficult to see in the foliage. Alternates glides with a few wing beats; soars. Consumes a wide variety of food, from insects and birds to snakes and honey.

## HOOK-BILLED KITE
*Chondrohierax uncinatus*
GAVILÁN PICO GANCHUDO

Pls. 4, II, III, V
15–18" (38–46 cm.). Bill large, strongly hooked. Above dark blue gray, pale gray below, or breast and belly, sometimes throat as well, with very narrow or rather broad white bars. Wings like back, outer remiges barred black. Tail black with 2 visible gray to whitish bars and tip. From below: remiges broadly barred black and white; tail silvery gray with 2 broad pinkish white bars and tip. ♀: crown and nape dark brown, sides of head gray; nuchal collar cinnamon, back dark brown. Entire underparts regularly and evenly barred chestnut and white. Wings and tail marked as in ♂. Dark phase: brownish black, wings browner, remiges barred very dark grayish brown. Tail blackish with 1 very broad or 2 rather narrow white bars. In this phase can be confused with the Common Black Hawk. Imm.: brownish above, feathers edged rusty rufous, collar on hindneck and underparts white, latter with a few dark bars or streaks. Tail black with 3 brownish gray bars. From below: remiges white with 7 narrow black bars; tail pinkish with 4 dusky bars.

Generally n of the Ríos Meta and Orinoco; s of them in n Amazonas and n and central Bolívar (*uncinatus*). [S Texas to w Peru, Bolivia and n Argentina. Trinidad. Grenada. Cuba.]

Rain and cloud forest, gallery forest, deciduous forest, savannas, to 2500 m. Secretive but not shy. Forages in the treetops and in dense undergrowth. Feeds principally on large land snails, reptiles, insects, birds. Emits a shrill, musical whistle.

## DOUBLE-TOOTHED KITE
*Harpagus bidentatus*
GAVILÁN BIDENTE

Pl. 5, II
12–14" (31–35 cm.). Above, including sides of head, wings and tail slaty gray.

*Throat white with a black line down center;* below rufous chestnut virtually solid or more or less barred with white. Primaries inconspicuously barred dusky, barred whitish below. Tail with 3 gray bars and narrow gray tip. ♀: like ♂ but dark brown, above, more conspicuously barred below. Imm.: above grayish; below white streaked on breast, barred on sides with blackish. Tail dusky with 4 gray bars and gray tip.

Tropical and lower subtropical zones virtually throughout (*bidentatus*). [Mexico through Mid. Amer. to w Ecuador, central Peru, e Bolivia, Amazonian and e Brazil. Trinidad.]

Rain and cloud forests to 1800 m. n of the Orinoco, to 900 m. s of it. Second growth, forest edge, clearings, pastures, near streams. Not shy; alone or in pairs. Hunts from high and low perches. Forages in the trees for lizards and insects; also eats birds. Nests high in trees. Call: high, shrill.

## PLUMBEOUS KITE

*Ictinea plumbea*
GAVILÁN PLOMIZO

Pls. 4, VII
13–15″ (33–38 cm.). Head and underparts gray, throat paler. Back dark gray. Wings dark gray, *the inner web of primaries bright rufous chestnut.* Tail square, blackish with 2 dark grayish bands. From below tail has 2 distinct white spots on inner web, forming a band. Imm.: head and underparts white, *streaked gray.* Back, wings and tail brownish black, feathers pale-edged. Tail as in ad.

Tropical and subtropical zones. [Mid. Amer. to w Ecuador and n Argentina. Trinidad.]

Rain and cloud forests, mangroves, to 1700 m. n of the Orinoco, to 1400 m. s of it. Deciduous forest, forest and llano rivers, forest edge, coffee plantations. Soars in circles, often in small groups. Joins other kites. Perches and nests high in trees. Feeds on reptiles, frogs.

[MISSISSIPPI KITE (*I. misisippiensis*)] has not been recorded from Venezuela but it probably passes through the nw on migration. The ad. differs from *I. plumbea* chiefly by having the remiges blackish without rufous. The imm. has the underparts heavily *streaked with rufous* instead of streaked with gray. The tail is slightly forked instead of square. Recently a flock of 200 was observed in November in the outskirts of Barranquilla, Colombia. (Dugand, in litt.) The species breeds in US, presumably migrates through Mid. Amer. and winters in Paraguay and Argentina. Information regarding its movements in winter is desirable.

## SNAIL (OR EVERGLADE) KITE

*Rostrhamus sociabilis*
GAVILÁN CARACOLERO

Pls. 4, III
16″ (41 cm.). Bill black, curved, very slender; facial skin and legs bright orange red. General color slaty black, upper and under tail coverts and *basal part of tail white,* latter tipped ashy. ♀: above brownish black, below dark brown with whitish or rufous clouding. Forehead, throat and line behind eye whitish. Tail as in ♂. Imm.: dark brown above, feathers edged light brown. Forehead and line behind eye and underparts buff, streaked dusky on breast and belly. *Tail basally white, distal part dusky brown tipped whitish.*

Tropical zone. From Zulia and Apure to Delta Amacuro and the s bank of the Orinoco in Bolívar; probably occurs throughout in suitable localities (*sociabilis*). [S US through Mid. Amer. to w Ecuador, n Argentina and Uruguay. Trinidad.]

Lagoons, fresh-water marshes, swamps, rivers, mangroves, to 500 m. Alone or in groups. Feeds on snails and crustaceans. The snails are seized with one foot and eaten on a favorite perch under which hundreds of shells may accumulate.

## SLENDER-BILLED KITE

*Helicolestes hamatus*
GAVILÁN PICO DE HOZ

Pls. 4, III
14–15″ (35–38 cm.). Bill and legs as in Snail Kite but immediately distinguishable from it by its uniform gray plumage

without any white, and much shorter tail. ♀: like ♂. Imm.: like ad. but wing and tail coverts edged white or rusty, primaries with narrow white bars on under surface, tail with 2–4 white bars. Can be confused with dark phase of Hook-billed Kite.

Known from El Amparo, w Apure, Caicara, nw Monagas and Carabobo on the Río Cuyuni, e Bolívar. [E Panama. N and se Colombia. Amazonian Brazil, e Peru. Surinam.]

Rain forest, near water, to 400 m. Solitary or in pairs; sometimes small groups soar in circles. Feeds on snails which it captures by leaping down when perched in shady low branches or dense undergrowth in marshes and swamps. Nests high in trees. Call: noisy, repeated mewing. Little is known of its habits. Very local.

## BICOLORED HAWK

*Accipiter bicolor*
GAVILÁN PANTALÓN

Pl. 5

14–17″ (35–43 cm.). Crown black, sides of head dusky gray, back slaty gray, tail black with 2 or 3 gray bands. Below either pale gray with white throat and under tail coverts, or dark leaden gray with indistinct dusky shaft streaks. *Thighs bright rufous chestnut.* From below: under wing coverts mixed rufous and white, wings blackish heavily barred white. Tail with 2 or 3 white bars. Imm.: crown black, cheeks brownish. Upperparts blackish, tail with 3 or 4 pale bars and white tip. Below from almost white to dark ochraceous, in pale-colored birds an indistinct light nuchal collar.

Tropical and subtropical zones. From Zulia, Mérida, Barinas and Carabobo e to n Monagas; n and e Bolívar; central Amazonas (*bicolor*). [Mexico to nw Peru and Tierra del Fuego.]

Mostly forested areas, to 2000 m. n of the Orinoco, to 1000 m. s of it. Second growth, open and deciduous forest, clearings, forest edge. Usually alone; shy, secretive. Perches quietly in trees, fairly high or in exposed dry branches. Flies speedily, weaving through the forest. Feeds on birds. Calls: include a clear whistle.

## TINY HAWK

*Accipiter superciliosus*
GAVILÁN ENANO

Pl. 5

8–11″ (20–28 cm.). *The smallest hawk* in Venezuela. Crown and nape blackish, back slaty gray, tail dusky brown with 4 paler brownish bars. Below white, narrowly barred, except on throat, with grayish brown. Rufous phase: above rufous brown barred dusky; below buffy rufous, barred rufous brown. Tail with 4 broken black bars. Imm.: grayish brown above, tail with 5 dark bars; below whitish to buff, barred rufous brown. Iris yellow.

Tropical and subtropical zones. Sw Táchira, Mérida, Carabobo, Barinas, Apure, Amazonas and n Bolívar (*superciliosus*). [Nicaragua to w Ecuador, Brazil and Argentina.]

Open rain and cloud forest, to 1800 m. Forest edge, humid clearings, second growth, gallery forest in the llanos, thickets. Alone or in pairs. Attacks by swooping from a perch, usually low or in exposed branches. Feeds on birds.

## SEMICOLLARED HAWK

*Accipiter collaris*
GAVILÁN ACOLLARADO

12–14″ (31–36 cm.). Above blackish brown; interrupted collar on hindneck white, the feathers edged black. Tail dark gray with 5 brownish black bands. Sides of head narrowly barred black and white; *underparts* white, *conspicuously barred with brown*, except on throat. Rufous phase: much "redder" throughout. Tail rufous with 5 black bars. Imm.: like ad. but somewhat browner, nuchal collar rufous but indistinct, tail with 6 black bars. Below white or buffy broadly barred with rufous brown.

The Andes of Táchira and Mérida. [Colombia w of the e Andes, w Ecuador.]

Cloud forests, 1300–1800 m. Habits unknown.

## GRAY-BELLIED HAWK

*Accipiter poliogaster*
GAVILÁN VIENTRIGRIS

Pl. 5

17–20″ (43–51 cm.). Superficially like Slaty-backed Forest-Falcon, but legs shorter and less orange. Crown blackish, sides of head blackish or gray. Back dull blackish, the feathers obscurely edged with gray. Tail black with 3 rather narrow gray bars and white tip. Throat white, rest of underparts pale gray with dark hair streaks. Underside of wings grayish white, feathers marbled and mottled dusky near base. Imm.: quite different from ad., remarkably like the Ornate Hawk Eagle but considerably smaller. Crown and nape black; back dark brown, the feathers edged whitish; tail blackish, evenly banded with gray. Nuchal collar, sides of head, throat and breast rufous, moustacial streak black, continued down sides of breast; throat and upper breast white, rest of underparts, including thighs white, barred and spotted with black.

Tropical zone. Known from Burgua, Táchira; Caño Cataniapo and Cerro Yapacana, Amazonas, and s Bolívar on the Río Paragua and the Gran Sabana. [Guyana, Surinam, ne Colombia, e Ecuador through Brazil to Bolivia, Paraguay and ne Argentina.]
Rain forests to 400 m. Little is known of its habits. Reported to feed on birds and mammals.
Note: *A. pectoralis* in Lista Av. Venez. is based on the immature plumage of this species.

## SHARP-SHINNED HAWK

*Accipiter striatus*
GAVILÁN ARRASTRADOR

Pls. 5, II
11–13″ (28–33 cm.). Above gray; below variable, usually white or buffy white with a few dusky streaks on breast, or cinnamon rufous below, palest on throat and center of belly, barred on sides, sometimes on breast, with white and grayish bars (or anything between the two extremes); thighs rufescent. Tail dusky with 3 gray bars and white tip. Imm.: crown streaked brown and white, back and wings brown, the feathers edged rufescent. Below white, coarsely streaked dark brown.

Tropical to temperate zones. Generally distributed in hilly and mountainous country n of the Orinoco; s of it in n Amazonas and in the Gran Sabana,

Bolívar (*ventralis*). [N Amer. to Bolivia, n Argentina and Uruguay.]
Forested areas mostly in the subtropical zone, 300–3000 m. n of the Orinoco, 1400–1800 m. on the tepuis. Forest edge, second growth, open woodland, pastures, clearings. Solitary, secretive. Perches at any height in the forest; feeds on birds, lizards, rodents, insects. Graceful, speedy flight. Call: shrill cackles near nest; squealing cries.

## BLACK-CHESTED BUZZARD-EAGLE

*Geranoaetus melanoleucus*
AGUILA REAL

Pls. IV, VII
24–27″ (60–68 cm.). *Wings very broad; tail short, wedge-shaped.* Slaty black above, shoulders extensively pale gray, finely barred dusky. Breast and sides of head slaty black, throat grayish white, rest of underparts white with fine gray bars. Feathers of head, nape and breast lengthened. Tail black narrowly tipped with white. Imm.: tail longer than in ad., gray with numerous blackish bars. Above not unlike ad. but no pale area on shoulders. Below buff, breast coarsely streaked, belly barred blackish.

Páramo zone of the Andes of Mérida (*australis*). [Colombia through the Andes to Tierra del Fuego.]
3500–4500 m. Beautiful, effortless, soaring flight. Wary. Feeds on mammals and snakes, usually consumed on the ground, rarely in trees. Nests on ledges, seldom in trees. Call: harsh, cackling.
Note: Called *Buteo fuscescens* in Lista Av. Venez.

## WHITE-TAILED HAWK

*Buteo albicaudatus*
GAVILÁN TEJÉ

Pl. IV
21–24″ (53–60 cm.). *Tail white with a conspicuous black subterminal band,* rectrices with many inconspicuous narrow gray cross lines. Above light gray (or dark gray, a), shoulders and scapulars rufous; underparts white, occasionally breast or entire underparts gray. Dark phase: dark brown, some rufous on shoulders, tail as in normal phase. From below: under wing coverts white,

remiges barred. Tail white with a conspicuous black subterminal band. Imm.: dark brown above with some rufous on shoulders, below buffy, streaked dusky on underparts. Tail plain pale grayish, sometimes with the black subterminal band suggested.

Tropical and subtropical zone. Sierra de Perijá, Zulia; Andes of Mérida and Lara. (*hypospodius, a*). Elsewhere, including Margarita I. (*colonus*). [Texas to Argentina. Curaçao, Aruba, Bonaire. Trinidad.]

Open dry country, thorny scrub, xerophytic areas, llanos, plantations, pastures, to 1900 m. Soars high. Attracted by savanna fires where it feeds on fleeing animals. Perches on telephone poles. Feeds on lizards, snakes, small mammals, and birds. Call: high whistle.

## ZONE-TAILED HAWK
*Buteo albonotatus*
GAVILÁN NEGRO

Pls. II, III
19–21″ (48–53 cm.). Slaty black, tail black with 3 gray bands, the bands becoming narrower toward base of tail. From below: tail bands white, wing lining black, remiges narrowly barred black and white. Imm.: much like ad. but spotted with white. Tail pale with several gray bands and broad black terminal band.

Tropical zone. Hilly country of the n from Zulia to Anzoátegui; ne Bolívar. [Southern US to w Peru, Bolivia, Paraguay and se Brazil. Trinidad.]

Savannas, deciduous forest 300–500 m. Soars like a turkey vulture, which it probably mimics. Feeds on reptiles, mammals, birds. Screaming call.

## SWAINSON'S HAWK
*Buteo swainsoni*
GAVILÁN LANGOSTERO

18–20″ (46–51 cm.). Above brown, the feathers pale-edged. Forehead and short eyebrow white. Breast, or sides of breast, rufous brown, rest of underparts white, somewhat barred rufescent at sides. Tail gray, whitish near base, finely barred dusky with a broad black subterminal bar. From below: white with rufous brown breast. Wing lining white; remiges barred, with a conspicuously broader subterminal bar outlining trailing edge of wing. Tail pale with numerous fine bars and broader black subterminal bar. Dark phase: rare. Dusky brown, forehead and throat whitish; wing lining dusky brown, remiges as in normal phase but bars not as contrasting. Imm.: head and nape streaked brown and white, back brown mixed with white, the feathers pale-edged. Throat white, rest of underparts white streaked and spotted with dark brown. Tail as in ad. but not as clearly barked.

Probably transient. Recorded in Sept. from Mérida. [Breeds in w N Amer. Winters chiefly in Argentina, migration route little known.]

Recorded in open country near rivers, 2500 m. Feeds on insects and small mammals.

## BROAD-WINGED HAWK
*Buteo platypterus*
GAVILÁN BEBEHUMO

Pls. 5, II
14–17″ (35–43 cm.). Above grayish brown, tail coverts tipped white; tail black, tip white with a sharply defined white bar near middle and a narrower one near base. Throat white, rest of underparts evenly and narrowly barred rufous and white. From below: wings whitish, remiges narrowly barred grayish brown, primaries tipped black. Imm.: crown and nape streaked and mottled white and reddish brown, back brown, the feathers pale-edged. Below white, streaked reddish brown. Tail with several light gray bars. Primaries tipped black and lightly barred grayish brown.

Tropical to temperate zones. Winter resident Aug.–May; widespread n of the Orinoco; s of it along the upper Ríos Ventuari and Caura in Amazonas and Bolívar (*platypterus*). [Breeds in N Amer., winters in Mid. Amer., and w S Amer. Resident races in Antilles. Trinidad (migrant). Tobago (resident).]

Partly open terrain, llanos to páramos, to 3000 m. n of the Orinoco, to 500 m. s of it. Second growth, coffee plantations, clearings, forest edge. Solitary, sluggish, not shy, not inside forest. Soars. Perches on telegraph poles and in mid-level of trees. Feeds on frogs, reptiles, mammals, crabs.

# ROADSIDE HAWK
*Buteo magnirostris*
GAVILÁN HABADO

Pls. 5, II
13–15″ (33–38 cm.). Head, breast, back and wings pale gray (or brownish gray, a) inner webs of primaries barred with rufous. Lower breast and belly regularly and narrowly barred cinnamon and white (or cinnamon brown and white, a). Tail brown with 4 or 5 gray bars. From below: the rufous in wing is noticeable. Imm.: above brown, below tawny streaked brown on throat and breast, barred reddish brown on belly.
Tropical and subtropical zones. Generally distributed n of the Orinoco including Patos I. (*insidiatrix*). Amazonas, Bolívar and Delta Amacuro (*magnirostris, a*). [Mexico to w Peru and central Argentina.]
Fairly open terrain, to 2500 m. n of the Orinoco, to 1400 m. s of it. Llanos, gallery forest, second growth, forest edge, clearings, coffee plantations. Not shy. Solitary or in pairs. Perches low. Attracted by savanna fires. Feeds mostly on insects. Call: high-pitched whistle.

# WHITE-RUMPED HAWK
*Buteo leucorrhous*
GAVILÁN RABADILLA BLANCA

Pl. II
14–15″ (35–38 cm.). Deep black, rump and upper tail coverts white; under tail coverts buffy white, thighs dull rufous with a few black bars. Tail with 1 white bar near end. From below: tail with 2 white bars, under wing coverts buff. Pale phase: above ashy brown, forehead and underparts white; thighs dull rufous. Tail ashy brown with 1 white bar above, 2 below. Imm.: blackish above mottled and streaked rufous. Below rufous mottled with black. Upper tail coverts white, tail blackish with 1 ashy bar above, 2 bars below.
Subtropical and temperate zones. Sierra de Perijá, Zulia; Andes of Mérida and Trujillo; the coastal Cordillera in the Dist. Federal. [Colombia to nw Peru, n Argentina and se Brazil.]
Cloud forest, forest edge, clearings, 1800–3000 m. Feeds on reptiles, frogs, insects.

# WHITE-THROATED HAWK
*Buteo albigula*
GAVILÁN GARGANTIBLANCO

Pl. II
16–19″ (41–48 cm.). Above dark brown, sides of neck and breast chestnut brown. Below white, sides of body streaked and splotched brown, a solid dark brown patch at sides of belly; thighs buffy, barred ferruginous. Tail dark brown with numerous inconspicuous dark bars. Not unlike imm. of Broad-winged Hawk but chestnut brown sides of neck and breast distinguish it. A black phase exists but is very rare. Imm.: much like ad. but duller; thighs buff, barred black. Always distinguishable from imm. Broadwinged Hawk by unstreaked throat. Not unlike ad. Short-tailed Hawk but always separable by longer tail.
Subtropical zone. Mountains of n and w Venezuela; ne Bolívar. [Colombia through the Andes to nw Argentina.]
Dwarf forest, 3000 m. Feeds on rodents and birds. A little-known species.

# SHORT-TAILED HAWK
*Buteo brachyurus*
GAVILÁN COLA CORTA

Pl. II
14–16″ (35–41 cm.). Above slaty black, forehead and underparts white. From below: wing lining white, remiges white barred dusky, tipped black. Tail with 3 white bars and white tip, subterminal black band widest. Dark phase: entirely dark slaty gray, including wing lining, otherwise like normal phase from below. Tail considerably shorter than in the White-throated Hawk. Imm.: brown above, the feathers edged reddish brown and mixed with white, below buffy white streaked brown. Tail from below buffy with 3 narrow dark bars and a broad terminal black portion.
Tropical and subtropical zones. Sierra de Perijá, Zulia; the Andes of Lara, Trujillo and Mérida; Turiamo, Carabobo; Patos I. Sucre; nw Amazonas; Bolívar in the Gran Sabana (*brachyurus*). [Chacachacare I. S US to Argentina.]
Forested areas, open and semi-open country, sea level to 2200 m. Xerophytic areas as well as soggy, cool, meadows and low, open forest. Not shy. Soars. Drops swiftly on prey spotted from high

in the air. Feeds on rodents, birds, reptiles, insects. Call: a shrill whistle.

## GRAY HAWK
*Buteo nitidus*
GAVILÁN GRIS

Pls. 4, 5, II

15–17" (38–43 cm.). Pale gray above, rump whitish; entire underparts including wing lining finely and regularly barred gray and white. Under tail coverts white. Tail black with 2 narrow white bands and tip. Imm.: blackish brown above mottled with white and buff. Tail with several inconspicuous dark bands and a broader subterminal one. Dull white below, throat with a central dark stripe, bordered by dark moustacial streak, breast streaked dark brown, belly with heartshaped dark spots.

Tropical zone. Generally n of the Orinoco, s of it in nw Amazonas; n Bolívar from the mouth of the Río Apure e to the Río Cuyuni; Patos I. (*nitidus*). [Sw US to n Colombia, the Guianas, ne and s Brazil; Bolivia, Paraguay, n Argentina. Trinidad.]

Rain forest edge, deciduous forest, pastures, open country with scattered trees, to 1000 m. n of the Orinoco, to 250 m. s of it. Solitary, often on isolated trees. Soars. Perches quietly, high on leafy trees; wiggles tail on alighting. Feeds on rodents, birds, snakes, insects. Call: kree-ee-ee; also whistled notes. Nests high in trees.

## BAY-WINGED (OR HARRIS') HAWK
*Parabuteo unicinctus*
GAVILÁN ANDAPIÉ

Pls. 4, III

19" (48 cm.). Dark ashy brown, shoulders and thighs chestnut, upper and under tail coverts white. Tail black, extensively white at base with a white terminal band. From below: wing lining chestnut, remiges blackish, tail as above. Imm.: head and underparts buffy white streaked dusky; thighs barred chestnut. Back dark brown, shoulders mottled with chestnut, tail as in ad. but dark portion with numerous black bars, white portion tinged buffy. From below: forepart of wing chestnut, rest whitish with narrow dusky bars; tail evenly barred black and white, tip white.

Tropical zone. Locally distributed in Falcón including the Paraguaná Pen., Aragua, Guárico, Anzoátegui, Monagas, Sucre; n Bolívar along the middle Orinoco, Margarita I. (*unicinctus*). [S Texas s to w Ecuador, Bolivia and s Argentina.]

Open woodland, savannas, deciduous forest, to 800 m. Solitary. Feeds on mammals, birds, reptiles, and other animals. Walks on the ground after animals. Call: harsh screams.

## WHITE HAWK
*Leucopternis albicollis*
GAVILÁN BLANCO

Pl. V

18–22" (46–56 cm.). A black and white hawk. White; lores black, crown spangled with black, the spots almost forming a nuchal collar on hindneck (or crown and nape white, unspotted, a). Interscapulars black broadly margined with white, remiges black, secondaries margined white, tertials evenly barred black and white, lesser wing coverts black and white (or with all these parts much blacker, the white margins to feathers very narrow, a). Tail white, with a black subterminal band (or black, white near base, with a white terminal band, a). Imm.: much like ad.

Tropical and subtropical zones. Sierra de Perijá, Zulia (*williaminae*). The n Cordilleras from Carabobo to Sucre; the w llanos in Táchira; n Amazonas and Bolívar at Ciudad Bolívar (*albicollis, a*). [Mid. Amer., n and e Colombia, the Guianas to n Bolivia and Amazonian Brazil. Trinidad.]

Open, partially forested areas, to 1500 m. Conspicuous, extremely handsome. Usually alone, soars above open woodland and near forest edge. Not shy. Feeds on reptiles, insects. Call: harsh screams.

## BLACK-FACED HAWK
*Leucopternis melanops*
GAVILÁN CARINEGRO

Pl. V

16" (41 cm.). Black and white. Head, neck and underparts white, lores black,

streaks on crown and nape black. Upper-parts slaty black, scapulars spotted with white. Wings and tail black, latter with a white band toward end. Imm.: like ad. but streaks on head only faintly indicated.
Amazonas; Bolívar along the Río Caura e to the Gran Sabana. [Se Colombia, ne Ecuador, n Amazonian Brazil, the Guianas.]
Rain forest, clearings, forest edge, mangroves, to 1000 m. Usually inside the forest, but also in savannas. Not shy. Feeds on reptiles and sometimes on birds following army ants.

## SLATE-COLORED HAWK
*Leucopternis schistacea*
GAVILÁN AZUL

Pls. 4, III
15–17″ (38–43 cm.). Uniform bluish slate, darker on head. Tail black with a median white band. Imm.: like ad. but belly lightly barred white, upper tail coverts tipped white.
Tropical zone. W Amazonas on the Orinoco. [E Colombia to n Bolivia and Amazonian Brazil s of the Amazon.]
Rain forests, 100–200 m., near rivers. Feeds on snakes, frogs.

## BLACK-COLLARED HAWK
*Busarellus nigricollis*
GAVILÁN COLORADO

Pls. 4, IV
18–20″ (46–51 cm.). *Bright cinnamon rufous, head buffy white. Black patch on the breast.* Tail black with rufous bars near base and at tip. From below: wing lining cinnamon rufous, remiges black, wings very broad. Imm.: head whitish, streaked dusky; patch at base of throat black; breast buff, streaked dusky; belly brown, barred black. Thighs and under tail coverts barred buffy and black. Back and wings reddish brown, barred and spotted dusky. Tail barred rufous and black.
Tropical zone. Widely distributed along rivers and in marshes n of the Orinoco, s of it in n Bolívar and Delta Amacuro (*nigricollis*). [Mexico to n Argentina. Trinidad.]
Near water in forested areas as well as llanos in Moriche palm swamps; flooded

rice fields, mangroves, to 300 m. Soars. Not shy, perches in middle branches, telegraph poles. Feeds mainly on fish and crabs. Various screeching cries. Also called Fishing Hawk.

## SAVANNA HAWK
*Heterospizias meridionalis*
GAVILÁN PITA VENADO

Pls. 4, IV
20–25″ (51–64 cm.). Mostly rufous, tail black with one white bar. Whole head, neck, shoulders and basal part of remiges bright rufous; below rufous, lightly barred with black. Back slaty; rump, upper tail coverts and tail black, tail with a conspicuous central white bar and tip. From below: wing lining rufous, remiges black, tail black with a central white bar. Legs pale yellow to orange. Imm.: blackish above mottled with rufous on shoulders. Below buffy white with a dusky patch at sides of breast and streaks at sides of body. Thighs rufescent, narrowly barred dusky, belly and under tail coverts buffy, more widely barred dusky. Bases of remiges with considerable rufous.
Tropical zone. Widely distributed in marshes and savanna n of the Orinoco; extreme n Amazonas; n Bolívar from Caicara to the Altiplanicie de Nuria. [Panama to w Ecuador and Argentina. Trinidad.]
Llanos, deciduous forest edge, swampy savannas and similar open country, to 500 m. Perches on palms and low trees. Attracted by savanna fires to feed on fleeing mammals, insects, reptiles. Walks on the ground, seldom soars. Call: loud, whistled screams.

## RUFOUS CRAB-HAWK
*Buteogallus aequinoctialis*
GAVILÁN DE MANGLARES

Pl. 4
18″ (46 cm.). Not unlike White-tailed Hawk but *much darker* and smaller. Head, neck and upperparts blackish brown, scapulars, feathers of back and wing coverts edged rufous. Inner primaries and secondaries rufous, tipped black. Underparts rufous with narrow, rather inconspicuous fine bars. Tail black with a narrow, sometimes incom-

plete white bar across middle, and white tip. Imm: cere and legs orange, head black, mixed with white on cheeks. Back blackish brown. Below whitish streaked dusky, rather heavily so on breast, thighs narrowly barred. Wings with a tawny patch. Tail gray with numerous narrow dark bars. Legs ochre.

A coastal and mangrove species recorded from Pedernales and Corocoro I., Delta Amacuro. [Coast of the Guianas and Brazil to Panama.]

Mangroves; flooded forest at sea level. Alone or in pairs. Forages in mud flats where it feeds on crabs, which it pounces upon from a low perch or captures on the wing. Call: laughter-like cry, melodious whistle.

## COMMON BLACK HAWK
*Buteogallus anthracinus*
GAVILÁN CANGREJERO

Pl. IV

18–21" (46–51 cm.). Sooty black; a broad white median band on tail, and white tip. Facial skin bright yellow, legs straw yellow. Could be confused with black phases of the Hook-billed Kite. From below: wing lining black, *base of outer primaries white,* tail with a broad white median band and white tip. *Wings exceptionally broad.* Imm.: blackish brown above, tail black with 4 prominent, irregular white bars and white tip. Below buff streaked dusky, thighs barred. From below: wing lining clear buff, remiges with dark bars and black tip.

Tropical zone. Generally but locally distributed n of the Orinoco from Zulia and Táchira through Barinas, Mérida and Yaracuy to Carabobo thence to Sucre, Monagas, and Delta Amacuro (*anthracinus*). [Sw US to nw Peru and Argentina. Antilles. Trinidad.]

Sea and lake shores, mud flats, mangroves, streams, to 1100 m. Feeds on crustaceans, fish, reptiles and insects. Usually alone, not shy. Soars. Perches low near water, walks on sand bars. Call: a series of high whistles.

## GREAT BLACK HAWK
*Buteogallus urubitinga*
AGUILA NEGRA

Pl. IV

25" (64 cm.). Black; rump and upper tail coverts white; tail black, basally white,

with a broad white median band and white tip. Very like Common Black Hawk but larger, with white rump and dark, instead of yellow, lores. From below: wing lining black with a white patch at base of primaries. Tail band much wider than in the Common Black Hawk. Imm.: much like imm. Common Black Hawk but larger with more bars in tail.

Tropical zone. Generally n of the Orinoco and in Bolívar, n and central Amazonas. Apparently not recorded from Delta Amacuro where it undoubtedly occurs (*urubitinga*). [Mexico to Chile, the Guianas, Brazil and Argentina. Trinidad, Tobago.]

Forest edge, along forest rivers, deciduous forest edge, mangroves, sea coasts, to 500 m. Llanos, gallery forest. Not shy; soars. Usually alone, perches on highest treetops. Attracted to savanna fires. Feeds on frogs, lizards, snakes, turtles, crabs, carrion. Call: prolonged shrill whistle.

## SOLITARY EAGLE
*Harpyhaliaetus solitarius*
AGUILA SOLITARIA

Pl. IV

26–28" (66–71 cm.). Head with a short bushy crest, *tail very short.* Dark bluish gray, upper tail coverts edged white. Tail black with a median white band and white tip. Tarsus bare, yellow. From below: wing lining pale gray, tips of remiges black. Imm.: head slightly crested. Dark brownish gray above, feathers of back edged cinnamon. Sides of head and underparts ochraceous tawny, streaked black. Tail black marbled with gray, terminal band black.

Tropical and subtropical zones. Recorded from Carabobo and Aragua (*solitarius*). [Mexico to Colombia and e Peru and Salta, Argentina.]

Forested hilly areas to 1700 m. Feeds on mammals, snakes, large birds. Nests high on tall trees.

## CRESTED EAGLE
*Morphnus guianensis*
AGUILA MONERA

Pl. VI

32–34" (81–86 cm.). Long, narrow, occipital crest black, tipped white. Head, neck and upper breast pale gray, throat and lower breast and belly white. Back black. Tail blackish with 3 broad grayish bands. Primaries from below conspicuously barred black, wing lining white. Tarsus bare. Dark phase: sides of head and upper breast blackish, throat paler, rest of underparts boldly or lightly barred black and white. Imm.: head, neck and underparts white, occipital crest white, tipped black. Primaries conspicuously barred; tail gray with numerous dusky bars.

Tropical zone. Nw Zulia; Aragua (sight). [Colombia, the Guianas to w Ecuador and Bolivia, Paraguay, se Brazil and ne Argentina.]

Forested areas, 500–1600 m. Soars high. Alone or in pairs. Perches on highest treetops. Feeds on monkeys, other arboreal mammals, iguanas, and large birds. Longer-tailed than Harpy Eagle.

## HARPY EAGLE
*Harpia harpyja*
AGUILA HARPÍA

Pl. VI
34–37" (86–93 cm.). Head with a ruff and bushy, divided crest, hornlike when erected. Head ashy gray, crest blackish, the feathers pale-edged. Back, neck, large patch on each side of breast and the wings black, the latter indistinctly barred dusky gray above. Bend of wing and underparts white, thighs barred black; tarsus very thick, bare. Tail black with 3 broad gray bars. From below: wings whitish, barred and spotted with black, a clear white patch in center. Tail with 3 gray bars. Black chest patch clearly visible. Imm.: head, crest and underparts white. Back and wings brownish gray. Tail marbled and barred with black.

Tropical and lower subtropical zones. Carabobo; Aragua; Distr. Federal; Miranda; Bolívar on the upper Río Caura and the Gran Sabana. [Mexico to n Argentina.]

One of the greatest and mightiest eagles in the world. Forests, occasionally open terrain near forest edge, and river banks, 100–1800 m. Soars. Perches on highest protruding branches in the treetops; on low trees in open areas. Feeds on monkeys, sloths, other arboreal animals, and

large birds which it pursues through the branches with great agility. Constructs very bulky nests in the high branches of the tallest trees.

## BLACK-AND-CHESTNUT EAGLE
*Oroaetus isidori*
AGUILA DE COPETE

Pls. VI, VII
25–29" (63–74 cm.). Head with a long, black crest, usually elevated. Head, throat and upper back black; underparts chestnut, streaked black. Thighs black; tarsus feathered, chestnut. Tail pale grayish with broad black subterminal band. From below: wing coverts chestnut with black streaks, remiges grayish, whitish near base with a few dark bars and black tips. Tail with a broad black subterminal band. Imm.: above brown, feathers pale-edged, crest tipped black; below white. Tail gray with 3 black bands. Not unlike Black-and-white Hawk-Eagle but rarely found in tropical zone.

Upper tropical and subtropical zones. The Sierra de Perijá, Zulia; the Andes of Mérida and the coastal Cordillera in Carabobo and Aragua. [Colombia through the Andes to nw Argentina.]

Forested mountain slopes, 600–2500 m. Alone or in pairs. Not conspicuous; soars above forest; perches in high trees. Feeds on arboreal mammals and large birds. Constructs large nests near treetops.

## BLACK-AND-WHITE HAWK-EAGLE
*Spizastur melanoleucus*
AGUILA BLANQUINEGRA

Pl. V
22–24" (56–60 cm.). Head, neck and underparts and *feathered tarsi* white. Orbital region, crown patch and short crest black. Back and wings brownish black. Tail evenly barred black and grayish brown (cf. light phase, Grayheaded Kite). From below: wing lining pure white, remiges pale, lightly barred. Tail with 4 narrow black bars and a wider subterminal one. Imm.: like ad. but browner above with white-tipped wing coverts.

Tropical and subtropical zones. The coastal

Cordillera in Aragua, Distr. Federal and Miranda; w Amazonas; se Bolívar. [Mexico to n Argentina.] Mostly forested areas to 1500 m. Forest edge, semi-open woodland near rivers. Perches low and in the treetops. Soars. Usually alone. Feeds on mammals, large birds, and reptiles.

## ORNATE HAWK-EAGLE
*Spizaetus ornatus*
AGUILA DE PENACHO

Pls. V, VI
23–25" (58–63 cm.). Much like imm. Gray-bellied Hawk but tarsus feathered instead of bare. Crown and *long crest* black. Throat white bordered on each side by a broad black band; hindneck, *sides of head and sides of breast tawny rufous;* upper breast white, rest of underparts, including tarsi, white broadly barred black. Back slaty black, upper tail coverts margined white. Tail long, conspicuously and evenly barred black and grayish brown. From below: underside of wing whitish narrowly barred with blackish. Tail grayish brown with 5 black bars. Sides of breast rufous. Imm.: head, neck and underparts white, thighs finely barred black. Crest white, back blackish brown. Tail grayish brown with 6 blackish bars.
Tropical zone. Locally in Táchira, Carabobo, Aragua, Guárico and Sucre; n and central Amazonas; central Bolívar on the lower Río Paragua (*ornatus*). [Mexico to w Ecuador and Argentina. Trinidad, formerly Tobago.] Mostly forested areas and open terrain; llanos, 300–1100 m. Perches near treetops, sometimes low. Soars. Usually alone. Feeds on mammals, large birds. Call: ringing, high-pitched. Nests near the top of tall trees.

## BLACK HAWK-EAGLE
*Spizaetus tyrannus*
AGUILA TIRANA

Pl. VI
25–28" (63–71 cm.). Black; bases of long bushy crest feathers white. Belly, thighs and tibial feathers barred with white, sometimes belly spotted white. Tail long, black with 3 grayish brown bars. From below: body black, wings boldly banded all over black and white. Tail with 4 pale bars and white tip. Imm.: brownish black above, lower back and upper tail coverts barred with white. Throat white, breast buffy streaked with black, rest of underparts blackish, barred and spotted with white. Tail with 5 or 6 blackish bars.
Tropical zone. Spottily recorded in Mérida, Sucre, Monagas and Delta Amacuro (*serus*). [Mexico to n Argentina. Trinidad.] Mostly forested areas, semi-open, second growth, forest edge, to 1500 m. Seldom perches near treetops. Solitary. Feeds on large birds and mammals. Call: noisy, loud screams. Responds to an imitation of its call.

## NORTHERN HARRIER
*Circus cyaneus*
AGUILUCHO PÁLIDO

18–21" (45–53 cm.). Head, neck, breast and back light gray; rump white. Central rectrices like back, with 4 dark bars and white tip, rest light gray, barred rufescent. Lower breast and belly white lightly barred rufescent. ♀: above dark brown, crown and wing coverts mixed with rufous; rump white. Underparts tawny buff streaked dark brown. Tail grayish, becoming buff toward outer feathers, with 4 or 5 dark bars. Imm.: like ♀ but paler below and more heavily streaked.
Casual winter visitor, taken once in Dec. in Mérida, at about 2500 m. in cloud forest (*hudsonicus*). [Breeds in the N Hemisphere. Winters to Mid. Amer., casually to nw S Amer. W Indies. Europe. Africa. N Asia.] Usually swampy areas with thick tall growths of reeds and grassy aquatic vegetation. Feeds on rodents, reptiles, frogs. Sails low over ground, wings held above body. Flight erratic.
Note: New record since the publication of Lista Av. Venez.

## LONG-WINGED HARRIER
*Circus buffoni*
AGUILUCHO DE CIÉNAGA

Pl. III
18–24" (45–60 cm.). Upperparts and shoulders, throat, neck and upper breast

slaty black; forehead and eyebrow white, ruff speckled with white; rump white; tail silvery gray with 5 black bands and white tip, the outer feathers with rufous next to the black bars. Remiges silvery gray, banded with black. Breast and rest of underparts white lightly spotted with black. Dark phase: sooty black, browner below, rump white. Ruff, eyebrow, wings and tail as in normal phase. ♀: brown above, the feathers edged rufous; rump white. Forehead, eyebrow and throat buff, narrow band across lower throat brown, upper throat and rest of underparts buffy, streaked dark brown; thighs tawny. Remiges and tail as in ♂. Imm.: similar to ♀ but more heavily streaked below. Dark phase: similar to ad. in dark phase, but thighs and under tail coverts rufous.

Tropical zone n of the Orinoco from Zulia to Carabobo, Aragua, and Monagas, and s to the Orinoco in Anzoátegui and Delta Amacuro. [E Colombia and the Guianas to Uruguay and Argentina. Trinidad.]

Edges of mangroves and lakes, open terrain; rice fields, to 600 m. Usually alone; low buoyant flight. Feeds on small mammals, reptiles, birds and birds' eggs. Call: plaintive cry. Nests on the ground in tall grassy vegetation, often near fresh water.

Note: Called *C. brasiliensis* in Lista Av. Venez.

## CRANE HAWK
*Geranospiza caerulescens*
GAVILÁN ZANCÓN

Pls. 4, III

17–21″ (43–53 cm.). *Legs long, orange red.* Light blue gray; belly and thighs sometimes with narrow white bars. Tail long, black with a white basal and median bar and narrow white tip. Primaries black with a white spot on inner web forming a bar. *From below* recognizable from any other hawk by a *white crescent near tip* of *wing* formed by the spots on the primaries. Imm.: much like ad. but browner with a buffy eyebrow; a narrow brown band across lower throat; upper throat and rest of underparts buffy, streaked dark brown. Remiges and tail as in ad.

Tropical zone, n of the Orinoco from Zulia to Carabobo, Aragua and Monagas; s to Ríos Meta in Apure and Orinoco in Anzoátegui and Delta Amacuro (*caerulescens*). [E Colombia and the Guianas s to Uruguay and Argentina.]

Wet forests, mangroves, river banks, deciduous open woodland, second growth, to 300 m. Gallery forest, llanos, pastures. Solitary, forages from mid-level to tree tops, clambering along tree branches, in search of tree frogs, snakes, lizards, insects hidden in the epiphytic vegetation. Often on the ground. Flies with alternate glides and wing beats. Call: a hollow "how." Nests high in trees.

# OSPREYS: Pandionidae

## AGUILAS PESCADORAS

Ospreys are found along sea coasts and large inland lakes and live on fish, which they catch by plunging into the water and seizing with their claws. Ospreys can be told from other hawks by their habit of often flying with feet dangling. When they fly overhead in sunlight the tail appears translucent.

## OSPREY
*Pandion haliaetus*
AGUILA PESCADORA

Pl. I

22″ (56 cm.). Head and underparts white, a dark stripe through the eye and down side of neck, a few dark streaks on breast. Head slightly crested. Upperparts dark brown, tail with 4 grayish brown bars. From below: wings angled backwards more than in other hawks. Wing lining pale, a dark patch at angle of wing; remiges rather narrowly barred. Tail barred, black subterminal bar wider than others. Imm.: much like ad. but breast heavily streaked. Winter resident; a few may remain the year round but do not breed. Occurs along coasts, Caribbean islands, and large inland bodies of water (*carolinen-*

*sis*). [Breeds in N Amer.; Greater Antilles, Eurasia, Australasia. Winters to southern S Amer., s Africa, India.] Solitary, sometimes in pairs; active. Perches quietly on trees or rocks near water. During migration passes over mountains. Call: sharp whistles.

# FALCONS, CARACARAS: Falconidae

## HALCONES, CARICARES

Falcons are distinguishable from other hawks by their narrow, pointed and angled wings. They seldom soar, but fly swiftly on rapidly beating wings, sometimes stopping to hover over one spot in search of prey. They are fierce hunters of birds and small mammals, catching birds in flight by diving after them. They inhabit forest and open country.

A very distinct member of this group, so distinct as to be regarded by some as forming a subfamily, is the Laughing Hawk, a sluggish bird which feeds almost exclusively on snakes. It sometimes remains for long periods of time perched on a branch and has the ability to turn its head 180° like an owl.

The Caracaras, although very different-looking from ordinary falcons, are closely related to them. Some are distinguishable from them by their bare and brightly colored faces, and sometimes throats, and mostly black plumage.

Rather than pursuing their prey with swift flight, caracaras are for the most part terrestrial. They feed on carrion and insects, one species subsisting mainly on wasp larvae, while another eats ticks which it picks from the backs of domestic animals.

**LAUGHING HAWK**

*Herpetotheres cachinnans*
HALCÓN MACAGUA

18–22" (46–56 cm.). Bushy crest and crown buffy white with black shaft streaks, *mask* extending around back of head *black*. Nuchal collar and entire underparts buffy white. Back and wings dark brown, upper tail coverts buff. Tail evenly barred black and buff, the 4 buff bars slightly narrower than black ones, tip of tail buff. From below: wings pale with narrow dusky bars, wing coverts buff, spotted with blackish. Tail with 6 narrow blackish bars, black mask visible. Imm.: much like ad.
Tropical zone. Zulia and Táchira to Sucre; central Anzoátegui, central Monagas; Delta Amacuro; Bolívar on lower Río Caura and Río Paragua (*cachinnans*). [Mexico to w Peru and Argentina.]
Open forest, forest edge, llanos, deciduous woodland, open terrain, to 500 m. Not shy, usually alone. Perches high on bare branches. Apparently feeds exclusively

on snakes pouncing on them on the ground. Call: noisy, repeated, like loud laughter.

**COLLARED FOREST-FALCON**

*Micrastur semitorquatus*
HALCÓN SEMIACOLLARADO

Pls. 4, 5, VI
18–24" (46–60 cm.). *Tail long, wedge-shaped;* a ruff around the face. Sooty brown above with a white or buff collar on hindneck. Cheeks and underparts white (or tawny buff, tawny phase; or brown, dark phase). Tail blackish with 3 or 4 narrow white bars and white tip, outer feathers with 6 bars. From below: primaries barred black and white, wing lining white, finely barred. Imm.: very variable; above dark brown, blackish on crown and tail, the feathers of back and wings barred and tipped amber brown. Below white, with crescent-shaped black marks, sometimes coalescing into heavy bars. An indistinct pale collar across hindneck and a chestnut wash across breast. In tawny phase underparts tawny

buff with brown crescentic marks, sometimes unmarked. Tail barred with brown.
Tropical zone. Locally recorded from Zulia and Mérida to Guárico, Aragua and the Distr. Federal; central Amazonas; nw and se Bolívar; Delta Amacuro (*semitorquatus*). [Mexico to Argentina.]
Rain and cloud forests, gallery forest, mangroves, to 1500 m. Alone or in pairs, not often seen. Perches quietly in the foliage, drops swiftly on its prey or chases it on the ground. Feeds on reptiles, birds, insects, mammals. Responds to an imitation of its call, which resembles that of the Laughing Hawk.

## SLATY-BACKED FOREST-FALCON
*Micrastur mirandollei*
HALCÓN DE LOMO PIZARREÑO

Pl. 5
14–16″ (35–41 cm.). Superficially like Gray-bellied Hawk. Above slaty gray, darker on head, below creamy white, sometimes with black shaft streaks. Tail black with 3 white or grayish white bars and tip. Imm.: like ad. but feathers of underparts edged pale gray giving a scaled appearance.
Tropical zone. Amazonas s of the Río Ventuari; Bolívar along the upper Río Caura. [Costa Rica to Bolivia and s and e Brazil.]
Rain forest near rivers, 100–200 m. Solitary. Usually perches low in trees. Sometimes forages on the ground. Calls reported: a repeated "weet"; nasal calls; a long series of loud repeated "haw." Rare. Responds to a squeak. Feeds on snakes, birds, lizards.

## BARRED FOREST-FALCON
*Micrastur ruficollis*
HALCÓN PALOMERO

Pl. 5
11–14″ (28–35 cm.). Uniform slaty gray above, throat and sides of neck light gray or tinged rufous brown, rest of underparts including thighs and under tail coverts evenly and narrowly barred blackish gray and white. Remiges barred black and white on basal portion. Tail black with 2 or 3 narrow white bars and white tip. Imm.: a miniature replica of

imm. Collared Forest-Falcon, showing the same phases.
Upper tropical and subtropical zones. The Andes and n Cordilleras e to Miranda; s of the Orinoco recorded from Cerro Tabaro, Río Nichare, nw Bolívar (*zonothorax*). [Mexico to nw Ecuador, se Brazil and Argentina.]
Forested, mountainous terrain from 1200 to about 2500 m. n of the Orinoco, found at 1000 m. s of it. Dense second growth and forest undergrowth. Difficult to observe. Solitary. Perches hidden in the lower and middle branches. Feeds on birds and lizards which it captures by chasing through the dense vegetation. Attracted to birds following army ants. Call: a series of barking sounds like that of a small dog.

## LINED FOREST-FALCON
*Micrastur gilvicollis*
HALCÓN PALOMERO DEL SUR

Pl. 5
10–13″ (25–33 cm.). Differs from Barred Forest-Falcon by lighter gray upperparts; white belly, thighs and under tail coverts only very lightly, if at all, barred; tail shorter, black with 1 or 2 white bars. Iris white.
Tropical zone. Nw Amazonas. Nw Bolívar (Cerro El Negro, Río Cuchivero), the Río Paragua and the Gran Sabana (*gilvicollis*). [Colombia, the Guianas to w Ecuador, Bolivia, s Brazil.]
Rain forests, 100–1100 m. Habits similar to those of Barred Forest-Falcon.

## BLACK CARACARA
*Daptrius ater*
CHUPACACAO NEGRO

Pl. I
17–19″ (43–48 cm.). Glossy greenish black, base of tail white. Throat bare, lemon yellow shading to reddish flesh color on sides of head; legs light orange yellow. From below: all black except for white base of tail. Imm.: duller black than ad., basal third of tail white with 3 or 4 black bars which also show from below. Soft parts as in ad.
Tropical zone. Zulia, Táchira and Barinas; Sucre and Monagas; nw Bolívar e to the Río Paragua; Amazonas. [E Colombia, the Guianas to e Peru, n Bolivia and Amazonian Brazil.]

Forest edge, savannas with scattered trees, second growth, mangroves, to 300 m. Clearings, pastures, along rivers. In pairs or small groups. Not shy. Feeds on carrion, insects, fruit, fish. Call: a long, shrill, wailing cry, "eeeeeeeeah," similar to that of the Yellow-headed Caracara.

## RED-THROATED CARACARA

*Daptrius americanus*
CHUPACACAO VENTRIBLANCO

Pl. I

19–22" (48–56 cm.). Black glossed with green or blue, sides of head streaked white; belly, thighs and under tail coverts white. Tail all black. Bare throat and cheeks red; legs bright orange red. Imm.: like ad. but with fewer streaks at sides of head, facial skin not as bright, yellower.

Tropical zone. Zulia, Táchira, Mérida, Barinas and Portuguesa; Monagas; Delta Amacuro; Bolívar from the Altiplanicie de Nuria to the n Gran Sabana and the Río Paragua; n Amazonas southward (*americanus*). [Mexico to w Ecuador, the Guianas, e Peru and Amazonian and e Brazil.]

Rain forest, deciduous woodland, forest edge, second growth, plantations, to 500 m. Near rivers. Not shy, social, curious. Forages in pairs or small noisy bands in the upper branches. Feeds on wasp larvae, fruit, seeds, bees. Call: a series of hoarse loud caws, "ca-ca-ca-ca-cá-o."

## YELLOW-HEADED CARACARA

*Milvago chimachima*
CARICARE SABANERO

Pls. 4, I

16–18" (41–46 cm.). Head, neck and underparts buffy white, a black postocular streak. Back brown, the feathers pale-edged. Tail buff with many wavy, narrow, black lines and a broad, blackish terminal band, tipped white. From below: wing lining plain buff, remiges blackish with a broad pale area toward tip of wing; tail with a broad dusky terminal band. Imm.: head, neck and underparts buffy, profusely streaked dusky. Under wing coverts and remiges barred dusky; tail with terminal black band, narrowly barred white.

Tropical zone. N of the Orinoco from Táchira, Barinas and Carabobo e to Monagas and s to Apure, n Amazonas, and n Bolívar e to Ciudad Bolívar and the n Gran Sabana; Delta Amacuro (*cordatus*). [Costa Rica to n Bolivia, n Argentina and Uruguay. Chacachacare I.; Curaçao (sight).]

Open terrain with bushes and scattered trees, forest edge, llanos, often with cattle; sea level to 900 m. Gallery forest, near roads; feeds on animals killed by automobiles. Perches high on trees, often in palms. Also forages on the ground. Feeds on ticks, small mammals, insects, carrion, fruit. Call: a repeated, shrill, wailing cry, descending in pitch, "heeeeeeeeee."

## CRESTED CARACARA

*Polyborus plancus*
CARICARE ENCRESTADO

Pl. I

19–21" (48–53 cm.). Head slightly crested, face bare, red. Crown black, throat and sides of neck dull white; upper back and breast narrowly banded black and buffy white; rest of back, belly and thighs black, upper and under tail coverts white. Tail buffy white with many narrow, wavy black bars and broad black terminal bar. Legs long, yellowish. From below: wing lining black, remiges gray, conspicuous white patch at wing tip. Imm.: much like ad. but browner, belly with pale shaft streaks.

Tropical zone. Locally n of the Orinoco including Margarita and La Blanquilla Is., s of it in e Bolívar; Delta Amacuro (*cheriwayi*). [Southern US to Tierra del Fuego. Cuba. Aruba, Curaçao and Bonaire. Trinidad.]

Partially open terrain, deciduous forest edge, mangroves, savannas with scattered trees, to 850 m. Freshly plowed fields; near highways. Partially terrestrial, walks and runs on the ground. Social; often in pairs or groups to 20 or more. Attracted by grass fires. A scavenger. Feeds on carrion, small mammals, reptiles. Call: low, rattling. Nests in trees.

Note: Called *Caracara plancus* in Lista Av. Venez.

## PEREGRINE FALCON
*Falco peregrinus*
HALCÓN PEREGRINO

Pl. VII
15–20″ (38–51 cm.). Crown, hindneck and *patch extending down over eye to cheeks* black, a small white patch between moustacial streak and ear coverts (or without white patch, a). Back blue gray with indistinct dusky bars; tail like back with 5 or 6 indistinct dusky bars and with a blackish subterminal area and white tip. Throat and breast white to buffy white, rest of underparts buffy white narrowly barred gray on sides. From below: wing lining narrowly barred blackish and white, remiges more broadly barred. Tail whitish with 4 or 5 dark bars, and broad black subterminal band and narrow white tip. ♀: differs from ♂ by often darker lower back and rump, and by having large drop-shaped marks on upper breast. Imm.: brown above, the feathers margined buff, below buffy broadly streaked dusky. Facial pattern as in ad.
Winter resident probably Oct.–March. Known in Venezuela from Margarita I. and sight records in Aragua, Miranda and Los Roques, La Orchila and Los Hermanos Is. (*anatum*). [Breeds in the N and S Hemispheres, northern breeders migrating south, southern breeders migrating north. N Amer. birds winter to Chile and Argentina. S Amer. breeders, *F. p. cassini*(a), migrate n through the Andes to Colombia, and may be found in nw Venezuela.]
Sea coasts and open country, usually at sea level. Solitary. Flies very swiftly, with great agility catches flying birds. Hunts along forest edge, savannas and often close to the waves in the open seas near oceanic islands where birds are nesting. Perches high on trees, posts, lighthouses, towers.

## ORANGE-BREASTED FALCON
*Falco deiroleucus*
HALCÓN PECHIANARANJADO

Pl. 5
13–15″ (33–38 cm.). Very like Bat Falcon but larger. Above black, the feathers of back and wing coverts edged gray. Sides of head black, broken collar around

hindneck orange rufous; throat white, breast and belly orange rufous, lower breast and upper belly conspicuously barred black and buffy rufous, under tail coverts spotted with black. Tail black with 3 narrow white bars and white tip. From below: under wing coverts black, spotted with buff and white, remiges dark gray with white bars. Imm.: much barred on lower breast with black.
Tropical and subtropical zones. Known from Mérida, Carabobo and the Gran Sabana, Bolívar. [Mid. Amer. to w Colombia and n Argentina. Trinidad.]
Forested mountainous regions, forest edge, sea level to 1700 m. n of the Orinoco, to 1200 m. s of it. Solitary. Perches in treetops, tall dead trees. Swoops down to capture flying birds. Call: aczeek, aczeek. Nests in trees, including palm trees.

## BAT FALCON
*Falco rufigularis*
HALCÓN GOLONDRINA

Pls. 5, VII
9–12″ (23–30 cm.). Very like the Orange-breasted Falcon but much smaller. Differs in color chiefly by having the central portion of the underparts black, barred with white.
Tropical zone. Apure and Táchira n to Zulia, and Carabobo to Sucre and Monagas; s of the Orinoco in Amazonas and Bolívar (*rufigularis*). [Mid. Amer. to w Ecuador and Argentina. Trinidad.]
Much more common than Orange-breasted Falcon. Forest edge, clearings, second growth, open woodland, near water, plantations, to 1450 m. Alone or in pairs. Perches in treetops. Flight very swift. On the wing, catches birds including small parrots, insects. Hunts bats at dusk. Call: a series of shrill "kin, kin, kin." Nests in holes in trees.

## APLOMADO FALCON
*Falco femoralis*
HALCÓN APLOMADO

Pls. 5, VII
15–18″ (38–46 cm.). Above slaty gray; forehead, lores *and band from behind eye and below it slaty gray*. Broad band across central underparts blackish, lightly

barred white, throat and upper breast
buffy, belly, flanks and under tail coverts
tawny buff. Tail blackish with 5 white
bars and tip. From below: wing coverts
and remiges checkered black and white.
Imm.: like ad. but browner, breast
streaked dusky, band on central under-
part brownish without white bars.
Tropical, occasional subtropical zone.
Locally n of the Orinoco from Zulia
and Apure e to Anzoátegui and Delta
Amacuro; nw Bolívar e to the Gran
Sabana; Margarita I. (*femoralis*). [Sw
US to Tierra del Fuego. Trinidad.]
Llanos, gallery forest, deciduous forest
clearings, dry open country, along rivers,
plantations, to 600 m. n of the Orinoco,
to 1800 m. on the tepuis. Usually in
pairs, not shy, perches on posts and near
the ground. With graceful flight captures
its prey on the wing. Attracted to grass
fires. Feeds on various animals, including fish, but preys principally on birds
caught in the air or on the ground. Call:
high-pitched cackling; shrieks. Lays eggs
in abandoned nests of other birds.

## MERLIN (OR PIGEON HAWK)
*Falco columbarius*
HALCÓN MIGRATORIO

Pl. VII
10–13″ (25–33 cm.). *No facial pattern.*
Above dark slaty blue, narrowly streaked
black, rump lighter, tail with 3 even gray
and black bars, wide black subterminal
bar and white tip. Forehead, eyebrow,
nuchal collar buff, narrowly streaked
blackish; throat white, rest of underparts
buff, streaked brown or rufous brown,
thighs brighter, with a few narrow dusky
streaks. ♀: back brown, gray on rump
and upper tail coverts; below streaked
like ♂. Imm.: differs from ♀ by brown
rump and upper tail coverts.
Tropical and subtropical zones. Winter
resident, Oct.–May. Locally n of the
Orinoco including La Tortuga and Margarita Is.; nw Bolívar (*columbarius*).
[Breeds in N Amer. and Eurasia. Winters
to Colombia and Peru, accidentally to
Bahia, Brazil. Aruba to Trinidad. Tobago.]

Small, bold falcon. Generally open country but found in a variety of habitats,
sea shores, xerophytic areas; cloud forest
edge, to 1800 m. n of the Orinoco, recorded only at sea level s of it. Not shy.
Perches in treetops. Flight very swift.
Preys chiefly on small birds, mammals.

## AMERICAN KESTREL (OR SPARROW HAWK)
*Falco sparverius*
HALCÓN PRIMITO

Pls. 5, VII
9–11″ (23–26 cm.). Center of crown chestnut surrounded by gray. Throat and
sides of head white, 2 vertical black
stripes on sides of head and black spot
on ear coverts. Back chestnut barred
black. Shoulders and inner remiges
gray. Tail rufous with a black subterminal band and white tip, outer
rectrix with black-barred white outer
web. Below buffy white to buffy cinnamon becoming paler on belly and under
tail coverts, more to less spotted on
breast and sides. ♀: head much as in ♂.
Back, shoulders, inner remiges and tail
rufous brown barred black; below like
♂ but streaked reddish brown on breast
and sides. From below: wings barred
black and white. Imm.: ♂ much like
ad. but more heavily spotted and
streaked below, tail feathers with brown
tips. ♀: imm. like ♀ ad.
Tropical to temperate zone. The Andes of
Táchira, Mérida, Barinas and Trujillo
(*ochraceus*). Elsewhere n of the Orinoco
including Margarita I. and in n Amazonas and Bolívar (*isabellinus*). [Open
or lightly wooded country in N, Central
and S Amer. to Tierra del Fuego. Antilles. Aruba to Trinidad.]
Rain forest edge and xerophytic areas in
the lowlands to humid cloud forest edge
and wet páramos in the Andes to 3000
m. n of the Orinoco, to 950 m. s of it.
Gallery forest, llanos, open fields. Shy,
active. Usually alone. Perches in treetops and on wires and poles. Feeds
mainly on large insects which it captures
on the wing in graceful rapid flight.
Nests in holes in trees and poles.

# GALLIFORMES

## CHACHALACAS, GUANS, CURASSOWS: Cracidae

### GUACHARACAS, PAVAS, PAUJIES

These large, gregarious game birds inhabit thickets and high forest. They are more arboreal than most game birds and can be distinguished from other members of the order by having a well-developed hind toe.

They feed on fruit and vegetable matter that they find on the ground or in the treetops. Guans are particularly partial to an arboreal life, but curassows often feed on the ground on fallen fruit, quickly flying up into the trees if disturbed. Chachalacas live, well concealed, in thickets, often revealing their presence by their loud, chattering note. All these species nest in trees.

All are excellent table birds and are assiduously hunted for food.

**RUFOUS-VENTED CHACHALACA**
*Ortalis ruficauda*
GUACHARACA DEL NORTE

Pl. 1
21″ (53 cm.). Top and sides of head grayish; back bronzy olive, throat blackish gradually turning along neck to grayish olive on breast and to pale gray on abdomen; under tail coverts rufous chestnut. Wings brownish gray; tail feathers bronzy olive green, broadly tipped rufous (or white, a). Bare eye ring gray; sides of throat pale red; legs gray.
Tropical zone. Extreme nw Zulia at the base of the Goajira Pen. (*ruficrissa*, a). W Zulia, s of the range of *ruficrissa*, south to w Apure and through Mérida to Lara, Trujillo and Falcón and to Sucre and Delta Amacuro; Margarita I. (*ruficauda*). [E Colombia. Tobago.] In the Maracaibo region birds with buffy tail tips intermediate between the two races are found. The subspecies *lamprophonia* of the Goajira Pen. and *baliolus* from the Maracaibo region are considered synonyms of *ruficrissa* by Vaurie.
Forest edge, scrub, gallery forest, llanos, xerophytic areas, to 1600 m. Second growth, cleared areas, deciduous forest; along rivers and near lagoons. Shy, secretive, descends to the ground, hides in thickets. Flocks of 4 to 20. Feeds on fruits, seeds and leaves. Often on the ground. Call: raucous early-morning song "guacharáca," usually in duets and repeated with variations. Nests low or quite high on bushes and trees.

**LITTLE CHACHALACA**
*Ortalis motmot*
GUACHARACA GUAYANESA

21″ (53 cm.). Top and sides of head and neck and band across lower throat rufous chestnut. Back, wings and 4 central tail feathers bronzy olive brown, rest chestnut. Below grayish, under tail coverts rufous brown. Facial skin bare, black; sides of throat and legs red.
Tropical zone, s of the Orinoco in Amazonas and Bolívar (*motmot*). [The Guianas, Colombia to Bolivia, s Brazil.] Includes *superciliaris* of e Brazil and *guttata* of Colombia to Brazil and Bolivia as races, following Delacour and Amadon; considered distinct species in Sp. Bds. S. Amer.
Rain and cloud forest edge, second growth, clearings, to 1700 m. Thick shrubbery; low trees; descends to the ground. In pairs or small flocks. Call: from dawn into the morning monotonous, harsh-sounding duets, "guachaco guachaco" during nesting season. Nest of sticks in low trees.

**BAND-TAILED GUAN**
*Penelope argyrotis*
CAMATA

Pl. 1
24″ (60 cm.). Head crested, the feathers at forecrown edged basally with white; eyebrow and malar streak conspicuously silvery. Above bronzy olive brown, lower back rufescent brown, feathers of

mantle edged silvery white laterally giving a streaked appearance. Throat bare, red; lower neck, breast and upper belly bronzy olive brown, somewhat browner than mantle, streaked white: belly and under tail coverts reddish brown, slightly vermiculated black. Four central tail feathers like back, rest blackish, tipped with a diffused dark rufous (or whitish, a) band. Legs salmon pink.

Tropical and subtropical zones. Upper Río Negro, Sierra de Perijá, Zulia (*albicauda*, a). Sw Táchira; the Sierra de San Luis, Falcón, s through Lara to Trujillo, Mérida and Barinas to e Táchira, and along the coastal and interior Cordilleras from Carabobo to Miranda and in Anzoátegui and Sucre (*argyrotis*). [E Colombia.]

The 3 races described from Venezuela, *albicauda* (Sierra de Perijá), *mesaeus* (sw Táchira), and *olivaceiceps* (Anzoátegui and Sucre), are not recognized by Vaurie; *barbata,* from Ecuador and Peru, is regarded as a distinct species by Delacour and Amadon but included in *argyrotis* by Vaurie. In our opinion *albicauda*, because of its white tail tip, deserves recognition.

Rain and cloud forest in the Cordilleras, 300–2400 m. Plantations. In pairs or groups up to 8. Especially active before dawn during the nesting season, Mar.–June. Noisy, not shy. Perches from the lower to the middle branches of trees, seldom seen on the ground. Melancholy notes in the early evening; alarm call, "gi-gi-gigigik."

## ANDEAN GUAN
*Penelope montagnii*
PAVA ANDINA

Pl. 1

24″ (60 cm.). Head, crest, sides and back of neck, breast, mantle, wings and tail bronzy olive, feathers of sides of head, neck, upper mantle and breast edged all around by white giving a scaled appearance. Chin and upper throat feathered, the feathers sometimes edged silvery, sometimes entirely dusky. Lower back, rump and upper tail coverts reddish brown, coarsely but not conspicuously vermiculated black, belly similar but grayer and paler. Legs salmon red.

Subtropical and temperate zones. The Sierra de Perijá, Zulia; the Andes of Táchira through Mérida to Trujillo (*montagnii*). [Colombia to nw Argentina.]

Cloud and dwarf forest, 1800–3200 m. Gathers at favorite feeding places. Responds to an imitation of its whistling call.

## MARAIL GUAN
*Penelope marail*
PAVA BRONCEADA

25″ (63 cm.). Upperparts dark olive green with a distinct gloss; lower throat and upper breast olive green, duller than back. Feathers at front and sides of crest narrowly edged grayish, feathers of mantle narrowly, those of breast more broadly, edged white. Lower breast and belly dark dull brown, slightly mottled with dusky. Primaries and tail brown. Throat bare; legs red.

Tropical zone. Bolívar e of the lower Río Caura and the middle Río Paragua to the Río Cuyuni and the Gran Sabana (*marail*). [The Guianas, n Brazil.] Vaurie finds that birds from Brazil are recognizable as distinct, *P. m. jacupeba*.

Rain forest, 100–600 m. Second growth. Shy. Arboreal. Alone or in small groups, forages in trees, but descends to the ground. Call: a series of grunts.

## SPIX'S GUAN
*Penelope jacquacu*
ÚQUIRA

Pl. 1

28″ (71 cm.), (or 32″ [81 cm.], a). Crest well developed, the feathers edged pale gray. Bronzy olive green above (or bronzy bluish green, a); feathers of mantle and breast edged white; rump and upper tail coverts tobacco brown. Lower breast and belly rufous brown. Four central tail feathers like back, rest much darker and bluer. Throat bare, pinkish crimson; legs salmon red.

Tropical zone. Extreme nw Amazonas (Caño Cataniapo); generally through Bolívar (*granti*, a). From ne Amazonas (Cerro Yaví, Caño Parucito) s through the Río Ventuari basin to Caño Casiquiare and the Brazilian border (*orienticola*). [E Colombia to n Bolivia and w and central Brazil.]

Rain and cloud forest, 100–1600 m. Habits similar to those of its congeners.

Note: Considered a distinct species (a), with *orienticola* as a race, in Lista Av. Venez.

## CRESTED GUAN
*Penelope purpurascens*
PAVA CULIRROJA

36″ (91 cm.). Crest bushy. General color glossy dark olive to dark bronzy olive (or bronzy olive brown, a), the feathers of breast broadly edged white, sometimes a few white edges to feathers of mantle. Lower back and belly chestnut. Central tail feathers like back, rest blackish (or central tail feathers browner and more coppery than back, a). Face bare, blue black; throat red; legs dark red.
Tropical zone. The L. Maracaibo basin in Zulia and se Mérida (*brunnescens*, a). Generally n of the Orinoco (except the Maracaibo region) and in Delta Amacuro (*aequatorialis*). [Mexico to sw Ecuador.]
Rain forest to 1100 m. Shy. Alone or in small groups in high branches or the canopy of the forest; seldom on the ground. Call: a repeated honk, also strident calls, "ki-ki-kui."

## BLUE-THROATED PIPING GUAN
*Pipile pipile*
PAVA RAJADORA

Pl. VIII
24″ (60 cm.). Crest and nape white; general plumage glossy black with a strong bluish green sheen. Breast and wing coverts streaked white. Large wing patch white. Bare skin of face and throat bright cobalt blue. Legs red.
Tropical zone, generally s of the Orinoco, but local in Amazonas, (*cumanensis*). [The Guianas, e Colombia through w Brazil to n Bolivia. Trinidad.]
Rain forest, often near rivers, to 1000 m. Not shy but secretive. Runs along the upper branches. Roosts in flocks of 20 or more. Noisy at daybreak as it flies, when, with its wings, it makes an unusual, loud, rattling noise which sounds like the tearing of a piece of canvas. Its name, *Rajadora*, refers to this rending sound. Call: uíi- uíi-uíi.
Note: Called *Pipile cumanensis* in Lista Av. Venez. and Sp. Bds. S Amer.

## WATTLED GUAN
*Aburria aburri*
PAVA NEGRA

Pl. VIII
28″ (71 cm.). Uniform glossy greenish black. Base of lower throat bare; from it springs a thin, pendulous yellowish white wattle about 1.5″ (4 cm.) long. Bill cobalt blue; legs pale yellowish flesh.
Tropical and subtropical zones. Locally in the Sierra de Perijá, Zulia, s Táchira and w Mérida. [Colombia to Peru.]
Rain and cloud forests to 1400 m. Congregates in fruiting trees. Sometimes calls several hours before daybreak.

## NOCTURNAL CURASSOW
*Nothocrax urumutum*
PAUJÍ NOCTURNO

Pl. VIII
24″ (60 cm.). Crown and long crest black. Back, closed wing and tail reddish brown heavily vermiculated blackish. Hindcrown, uppermost mantle, sides of neck and underparts rufous chestnut slightly vermiculated dusky on sides of body; center of abdomen and under tail coverts cinnamon buff. Outer tail feathers blackish, tail feathers tipped buff, buff tip increasing in size toward outermost. Sides of head bare, dark blue, a vivid yellow streak above eye; bill high, arched, coral red; legs rose red: ♀: like ♂ but sides more heavily vermiculated.
Tropical zone. S Amazonas from Cerro Duida s to Caño Casiquiare and the Río Guainía. [Se Colombia to nw Brazil and e Peru.]
Rain forests, 100–200 m. Near rivers. Alone or in pairs. Perches on trees at medium heights. Call: nocturnal; clear, melodious, hollow boom, with a pitch like that of a large pigeon, is similar to that of other curassows.

## LESSER RAZOR-BILLED CURASSOW
*Mitu tomentosa*
PAUJÍ CULO COLORADO

Pl. VIII
33″ (84 cm.). Blue black; belly, flanks and under tail coverts chestnut. Tail tipped with a chestnut band. Bill red, compressed, arched; legs red.
Tropical zone. W Apure; w Amazonas; nw

and central Bolívar. [Guyana; e Colombia; n Brazil.]
Rain forests, along rivers, to 600 m. Gallery forest. Alone or in pairs. Walks and runs on the ground in thick undergrowth. Flies up into trees if disturbed. Perches in trees at night. Call: a deep boom with a pitch like that of a large pigeon. Sings on moonlit nights and intermittently during the day. Nests low in trees.
Note: Included in *Crax* by Delacour and Amadon, but not by Vaurie.

## HELMETED CURASSOW
*Pauxi pauxi*
PAUJÍ COPETE DE PIEDRA
Pl. VIII
38″ (96 cm.). A large bony, fig-shaped, bluish casque springing from forehead (or casque smaller and less swollen, a). General plumage glossy blue black, the feathers edged dull black. Belly, under tail coverts and band at tip of tail white. ♀: two color phases; either like ♂ or more rarely mostly brown, but always recognizable by the bony fig-shaped casque. Bill dark red; feet dull carmine red.
Upper tropical and subtropical zones. The Sierra de Perijá s to the Río Tucuco, 10°10′ N, Zulia (*gilliardi*, a). S Táchira n through the Andes of Mérida, Lara and Yaracuy to e Falcón, the coastal Cordillera in Carabobo, the Distr. Federal and the central Cordillera in Miranda on Cerro Negro (*pauxi*). [Ne Colombia in Norte de Santander and possibly w Arauca.]
Dense cloud forests on the steep slopes of mountainous terrain, 500–2200 m., but usually between 1000–1500 m. Alone or in pairs, forages on the ground, in the undergrowth; perches in trees. Call: a deep, moaning, boom, "oom, oom"; also a cackle. Nests low in trees.
Note: Included in *Crax* by Delacour and Amadon, but not by Vaurie. We agree with Vaurie in keeping *P. pauxi* and *P. unicornis* of Bolivia and se Peru as distinct species rather than uniting them as do Delacour and Amadon.

## BLACK CURASSOW
*Crax alector*
PAUJÍ CULO BLANCO
Pl. VIII
38″ (96 cm.). Head crested, crest low,

feathers curled forward. Entirely glossy black with a purplish blue sheen, except for white belly and under tail coverts. Thighs black. Bill blackish, light red on cere and at base; legs blue gray. ♀: like ♂, except crest feathers barred with white.
Tropical zone, s of the Orinoco in Amazonas, Bolívar and Delta Amacuro (*erythrognatha*). [The Guianas; e Colombia; n Brazil.]
Rain and cloud forest to 1500 m. Often near rivers. Alone or in pairs. Sings on moonlit nights and intermittently during the day. Joins *Psophia crepitans* (p. 60) on the ground. Call: like that of the Lesser Razor-billed Curassow. Builds a loose nest of sticks.
Note: Delacour and Amadon find that Venezuelan birds differ from Guiana specimens by having the base of the bill light red, instead of yellow, and that birds from extreme e Venezuela are intermediate with typical *alector*.

## YELLOW-KNOBBED CURASSOW
*Crax daubentoni*
PAUJÍ DE COPETE

Pl. VIII
33″ (84 cm.). Like Black Curassow in pattern but with a green sheen and the outer tail feathers tipped white. Crest highly developed, curled forward. Bill black, large knob at base of culmen and wattles at base of mandible bright yellow. ♀: differs from ♂ by having the crest indistinctly marked with white; wing coverts, breast and sides of body with narrow white bars.
Tropical zone. Locally distributed n of the Ríos Meta and Orinoco from Zulia, Mérida and Apure, and through Falcón and Guárico to Carabobo, Aragua to Sucre and Monagas. [Ne Colombia.]
Rain, deciduous and gallery forests, llanos, savannas with scattered trees, semi-arid vegetation, 100–500 m. Often near rivers. Forages from the ground to tree-tops. Shy. Flocks of 3 to 15 or more in the dry season, small family groups at other times. Perches in the highest branches of tall trees. Call: a slow, deep whistle, "yiiiiiiii," lasting 4–6 sec.

# WOOD-QUAILS, BOBWHITES: Phasianidae

## PERDICES

No true pheasants occur in South America, where the family is represented by quails and wood-quails.

The former is represented by a bobwhite found in small coveys along woodland borders and scrub. The larger wood-quails live in the forests and thick scrub and are found in family groups and small coveys.

Members of this family are ground dwellers living on seeds, fallen fruit and insects; they nest on the ground and are non-migratory.

### CRESTED BOBWHITE

*Colinus cristatus*
PERDIZ ENCRESTADA

Pl. 1

8″ (20 cm.). Long, thin crest smoky white (or sooty brown, a), forehead and lores white; eyebrow, commencing above eye and continuing to sides of nape, cinnamon surmounted by a mixed black and white stripe, which expands broadly on sides of neck and narrowly borders base of cinnamon to whitish throat. Ear coverts smoky gray to white. Upper parts pinkish brown to grayish vermiculated black on mantle, spotted with black on lower back, and black and white on wing coverts and scapulars. Tail vermiculated grayish black with narrow black cross bars. Breast plain pinkish chestnut, rest of underparts with conspicuous white, black-bordered spots (or underparts, except throat, thus spotted, belly plain light chestnut, a; or underparts, except throat, white, tinged buff, feathers of breast with a median black horizontal bar, of belly and sides with a median black vertical line, center of belly plain buff, b). ♀: much like ♂ but throat white to pale buff, lightly to heavily streaked black.

Tropical and subtropical zones. Zulia from the Goajira Pen. e to Falcón and s to Lara and Trujillo (*continentis,* b). The Andes of Mérida (*horvathi*). W. Barinas to n Portuguesa (*barnesi,* a). Anzoátegui, Sucre, Monagas and Margarita I. (*mocquerysi*). Most of Venezuela n of the Orinoco, except areas occupied by other races (*sonnini*). Apure, n of the Orinoco in s Anzoátegui; s of the Orinoco in n Amazonas; n Bolívar from the Río Cuchivero to the Río Paragua, thence south to the Cerro Guaiquinima region (*parvicristatus*). [Pacific slope of central and w Panama. Aruba, Curaçao. N Colombia, the Guianas, n Brazil.]

Open habitats, grassland, second growth, to about 1500 m. n of the Orinoco, to 1000 m. s of it. Llanos, xerophytic areas, plantations. Habits and notes similar to the N Amer. Bobwhite. Shy, secretive, in coveys of about 12. When flushed flies a short distance and drops into the grass. Call: 3-noted whistle. Lays 8–16 eggs.

### MARBLED WOOD-QUAIL

*Odontophorus gujanensis*
PERDIZ COLORADA

Pl. 1

11″ (28 cm.). A dark bird with no definite pattern, looking dusky brown from a distance. Face rufescent, head crested. General color dark brown to grayish brown marbled with black; below somewhat lighter (or ochraceous tawny, a) with broken bars and spots of black, buff and white, very variable in the amount of barring or spotting. Wings and wing coverts barred and spotted with dark chestnut and buffy white and blotched with black.

Tropical and lower subtropical zones. Zulia and Lara s to Barinas, w Apure and Táchira (*marmoratus*). Amazonas throughout; w and central Bolívar to the upper Río Paragua and Cerro Guaiquinima (*medius,* a). From the lower Río Paragua e to the Altiplanicie de Nuria and s through the Gran Sabana (*gujanensis*). [Costa Rica to n and e Colombia and the Guianas, and to Bolivia and Amazonian Brazil.]

Rain and cloud forests, to 1500 m. n of the Orinoco, to 1800 m. on the tepuis. Very wary and secretive, usually seen only when flushed close at hand. Forages in dense undergrowth. Alone, in pairs or family groups. Call: loud, ventriloquial, roosterlike. Nests at the base of trees.

**BLACK-FRONTED WOOD-QUAIL**
*Odontophorus atrifrons*
PERDIZ FRENTINEGRA

12″ (30 cm.). *Forecrown, cheeks and throat black*, hindcrown and nape chestnut, mantle olivaceous brown finely vermiculated sandy, lower back pale sandy brown; wing coverts edged rufous blotched with black. Breast olivaceous brown, somewhat spotted with white; center of belly buff, streaked black; sides grayish brown.
Subtropical zone. Sierra de Perijá, Zulia (*navai*). [Ne Colombia.]
Cloud forests, 1650–2600 m. Habits similar to those of Marbled Wood-Quail.

**VENEZUELAN WOOD-QUAIL**
*Odontophorus columbianus*
PERDIZ MONTAÑERA
Pl. 1
11″ (28 cm.). Crown brown, freckled black; hindneck rufescent; inconspicuous superciliary mottled buff and black. Back grayish brown, feathers with a central buff streak, margined black, giving a spotted appearance. Scapulars and inner remiges splotched dark brown and spotted buff. Throat white, barred black mostly at sides, and surrounded by a broad black line. Underparts reddish brown, the feathers with white, black-bordered spots giving the under surface a spotted appearance; belly and under tail coverts brown freckled sandy buff and black. Central tail feathers like back, outer ones more rufescent.
Subtropical zone. Sw Táchira along the Río Chiquito; the coastal Cordillera from Carabobo to w Miranda.
Cloud forests; edge of open terrain at the highest altitudes, 1300–2400 m. Habits similar to those of the Marbled Wood-Quail.

# GRUIFORMES

# LIMPKINS: Aramidae

## CARRAOS

The long, curved bill of the limpkin resembles that of an ibis. Like ibises, limpkins fly with neck and legs extended, but are not related to them, being actually close to rails.

Limpkins are partly nocturnal, and live in wooded swamps and marshes; they feed almost exclusively on snails and fresh-water mussels, but will also eat crayfish, small reptiles and worms.

The limpkin's 3-note wailing cry has given it its South American name, *Carrao*.

**LIMPKIN**

*Aramus guarauna*
CARRAO

Pl. 3
26″ (66 cm.). Tobacco brown heavily streaked on neck and back with white, and with concealed white streaks on underparts. Bill long, curved, black, base of mandible yellow; legs dusky.

Tropical zone (*guarauna*). [Se US to central Argentina. Greater Antilles. Trinidad.]
Swamps, marshes, flooded pastures, llanos, near large trees, to 300 m. Not shy, conspicuous. Alone or in small groups, or with other aquatic birds. Walks with a halting, limping gate. Heavy, awkward, flapping flight. The call carries very far and is especially notable at night. Builds nests in high marsh grass.

# TRUMPETERS: Psophiidae

### GRULLAS

Trumpeters form a small family of birds, found chiefly in Amazonia, intermediate between cranes and rails. Shaped rather like a small rhea, they have short, fowl-like bills and long legs. Their necks and heads are clothed in short, plushlike, black feathers, and the inner remiges end in long, hairlike filaments.

Trumpeters are gregarious, sometimes forming flocks up to 100. They are terrestrial but perch in trees at night. They nest in natural cavities in trees and line their nest with leaves, laying up to 6 eggs. Shortly after the young hatch the parent is said to grasp them with its bill and transport them to the ground.

Trumpeters feed mainly on insects and vegetable matter. They produce a variety of notes, the most characteristic being a loud, booming sound. Trumpeters become very tame in captivity, make intriguing pets, and in Venezuela are often kept around houses as "watch dogs" and for their alleged prowess in killing snakes.

Fig. 15. GRAY-WINGED TRUMPETER

**GRAY-WINGED TRUMPETER**
*Psophia crepitans*
GRULLA

Fig. 15
24″ (60 cm.). Head and neck covered with short plushlike black feathers; base of neck metallic purple, rest of plumage black, except for ochraceous tip to feathers of lower mantle and gray inner remiges.

Tropical zone. N of the Orinoco in se Sucre and ne Monagas; generally s of the Orinoco in Bolívar and Amazonas. [Se Colombia, the Guianas to ne Peru and n Amazonian Brazil.]
Rain forests to 700 m. Forages slowly in small flocks, sometimes with *Crax alector* (p. 56). When flushed, perches in trees. Responds to an imitation of its call.

# RAILS, COOTS: Rallidae

## COTARAS, POLLAS DE AGUA, GALLINETAS

Typical rails inhabit mangroves, dense vegetation in salt- and fresh-water marshes and moist meadows. A few prefer forest and dry woodlands, sometimes far removed from water. Rails are terrestrial birds with either long and slender or short, quail-like bills. They rarely fly, preferring to run from danger, and are difficult to observe. They feed on insects and other animal life, seeds and vegetable matter even including fruits.

Gallinules and coots differ from typical rails in possessing a frontal shield, and coots differ additionally by having webbed toes. Both groups are excellent swimmers and are sometimes mistaken for ducks.

Wood-Rails are not as dependent on water as are other rails, sometimes being found in dry woodland, far from water.

**CLAPPER RAIL**

*Rallus longirostris*
POLLA DE MANGLE

13″ (33 cm.). Bill long (2″ [5 cm.]). Crown and hindneck brown, sides of head gray. Short eyebrow and throat white. Back brownish black, the feathers edged gray giving a streaked appearance. Foreneck and breast buff, belly and under tail coverts white, *sides of body brownish black barred white*. Upper mandible black, *lower coral with black tip*.
Tropical zone. Falcón and Carabobo (*phelpsi*). Laguna Arestinga, Margarita I. (*margaritae*). [Coastal marshes of the US to Honduras; W Indies. Coasts of S Amer. to nw Peru and se Brazil. Trinidad.]
Usually alone, secretive, shy; forages in the mud and on the grassy edge of coastal mangroves. Call: loud, rattling. Nests are placed near the mangrove roots.

**PLAIN-FLANKED RAIL**

*Rallus wetmorei*
POLLA DE WETMORE

Pl. 6
13″ (33 cm.). Above olive brown, the feathers centered blackish giving a streaked appearance. Chin whitish, rest of underparts uniform light pinkish brown, flanks grayer, *unbarred*. Under tail coverts brown, barred white.
Tropical zone. Falcón (Tucacas); Carabobo (Puerto Cabello); Aragua (La Ciénaga).
Coastal mangroves; shallow saltwater lagoons.

**SPOTTED RAIL**

*Rallus maculatus*
POLLA PINTADA

Pl. 6
10″ (25 cm.). Conspicuously spotted and barred with white. Head, neck, upper mantle and breast blackish, handsomely spotted with white. Throat white, belly banded black and white. Back olive

brown, streaked with black and white. Bill olive yellow, base orange red; legs red.

Tropical, occasionally subtropical zone. Fresh-water marshes in Mérida, Portuguesa, Carabobo and Aragua (*maculatus*). [E Mexico, Brit. Honduras; Costa Rica. Trinidad. Cuba.] Marshes with rushes, wooded swamps, 500–1700 m. Wades, forages at water's edge. Feeds on insects, small fishes. Nests in the low aquatic vegetation. Call: a series of whistles, grunts.

## UNIFORM CRAKE
*Amaurolimnas concolor*
COTARA UNICOLOR

9″ (23 cm.). Upperparts, wings and tail dark chestnut brown. Throat buffy white, rest of underparts rufous brown, darkest on flanks. Iris red; bill short, olive green, ridge black; legs dusky pink.
Tropical zone. Boquerón, Carabobo (*castaneus*). [Mexico to w Ecuador, e Peru, Guyana, Amazonian and e Brazil, e Bolivia.]
Swampy woodland; recorded at about 700 m. Thickets, second growth, marshy areas.
Note: New record since the publication of Lista Av. Venez.

## RUFOUS-NECKED WOOD-RAIL
*Aramides axillaris*
COTARA MONTAÑERA

Pl. 6
12″ (30 cm.). Head, neck, breast, sides of body and flight feathers rufous chestnut; center of throat whitish. Mantle blue gray, lower back, upper and under tail coverts and tail, belly and thighs black. Under wing coverts and axillaries barred black and white.
Tropical, occasionally subtropical zone. Zulia, Falcón, Lara and Carabobo to Monagas; Patos and Los Roques Is. [Mexico to Panama. N and w Colombia, w Ecuador, Guayan, Surinam. Trinidad.]
Rain forest and edge, xerophytic areas, open cloud forest, to 1800 m. Coastal marshes, mangroves, dense underbrush, deciduous woodland, forested swamps, mud flats at edge of swamps. Terrestrial, secretive, shy. Often calls at night, a

high, prolonged yelping, answered by other birds. May respond to an imitation of the calls of the chicks, like the peeping of young chickens.

## GRAY-NECKED WOOD-RAIL
*Aramides cajanea*
COTARA CARACOLERA

Pl. 6
15″ (38 cm.). Head and neck gray, darkest on crown, palest on throat. Back olive; flight feathers rufous chestnut. Breast and sides of body buff, center of belly, thighs, upper and under tail coverts black. Bill proportionately rather short, yellow; legs coral red.
Tropical and subtropical zones (*cajanea*). [S Mexico to Colombia, the Guianas and central Argentina. Trinidad.]
Rain forests, second growth, deciduous woodland, mangroves, swamps, wooded marshes, humid forest, also drier ground with grass, shrubbery, bushes, to 1900 m. n of the Orinoco, to 650 m. s of it. Shy, active, secretive, usually alone. Call: loud rolling guttural sound, then a rising, rolling trill; in the evening often calls in pairs or groups. May respond if imitated.

## SORA
*Porzana carolina*
TURURA MIGRATORIA

Pl. 6
7.5″ (19 cm.). Forehead, center of crown, lores, ocular region and center of throat and foreneck black. Sides of crown and hindneck olive brown, back olive brown mottled with black and streaked white. Sides of head and neck gray, breast gray fading to white in center of abdomen, under tail coverts white, sides of body dusky brown barred white. Bill short, pale yellow, tipped black. Legs pale yellow. Imm.: like ad. but lacks black on neck; upper throat white.
Tropical and subtropical zones. Winter resident, probably Sept.–May. Fresh- and salt-water marshes n of the Orinoco from Zulia, Falcón, Mérida and Portuguesa to Anzoátegui; s Amazonas. Margarita I. Transient in the fall in Los Roques. La Orchila. [Breeds in N America. Winters from the s US to

Guyana and Peru. Curaçao, Bonaire. Trinidad.]

Mangroves, muddy margins of swamps, streams and lagoons, savanna edge, rice fields, flooded pastures, sea level to about 2500 m. Shy, secretive, mostly silent; broken, shifting flight. Alone or in groups up to 20. Call: rarely, a shrill whistle.

## ASH-THROATED CRAKE
*Porzana albicollis*
TURURA GARGANTIBLANCA

Pl. 6

8″ (20 cm.). Bill longer and more slender than Sora, yellowish green. Upperparts reddish olive brown, feathers with black centers, narrowest on head giving a streaked appearance; center of throat white, sides of head and neck, breast and center of abdomen gray, sides of belly and under tail coverts black barred with narrow white bars. Legs yellowish green.

Tropical zone. Zulia, Portuguesa, Carabobo and Aragua; nw and se Bolívar (*typhoeca*). [N Colombia and the Guianas to central Argentina. Trinidad.]

Clearings, second growth, marshes, pastures, Moriche swamps, to 1200 m. Usually alone; shy, flushes suddenly from almost under one's feet. Feeds on insects, seeds. Nests in reeds on or near the ground.

## YELLOW-BREASTED CRAKE
*Porzana flaviventer*
POLLA ENANA

Pl. 6

5.5″ (14 cm.). Eyebrow yellowish white, crown and *stripe through eye black.* Foreneck and breast buffy yellow, flanks heavily barred black and white. Hindneck brown, back black streaked white. Closed wing brownish mottled and barred black and white. Legs dull yellow.

Tropical and subtropical zones. Locally in Mérida, Portuguesa, Carabobo, Distr. Federal and Miranda; ne Bolívar near the border of Delta Amacuro (*flaviventer*). [Spottily in Mid. Amer. N Colombia, the Guianas, n and e Brazil to central Argentina.]

Mangroves, lake vegetation, grassy lagoon margins and marshes, flooded pastures, to about 2500 m. Not shy; flushes only when closely approached. Call: a thin "peep."

## GRAY-BREASTED CRAKE
*Laterallus exilis*
COTARITA CUELLIRRUFA

Pl. 6

6″ (15 cm.). Head, neck and breast gray, throat white; nape, hindneck and upper mantle chestnut; back and wings light olive brown, wing coverts barred white. Flanks, rump, upper and under tail coverts black, barred white. Bill short, greenish black, legs yellowish brown.

Tropical and subtropical zones. Mérida, Portuguesa (Aparición), Miranda and Monagas. [Brit. Honduras to Nicaragua. Panama, Colombia, the Guianas to w Ecuador, e Peru, n Amazonian Brazil. Trinidad.]

Marshes, dense low vegetation, wet grassy places, to about 1700 m. Solitary, shy, secretive; seen only when flushed.

## RUFOUS-SIDED CRAKE
*Laterallus melanophaius*
COTARITA PECHIBLANCA

7″ (18 cm.). Above olive brown, tail black. Supraloral streak white, sides of head, neck and breast orange rufous, under tail coverts chestnut, rest of underparts white heavily barred with black on flanks. Bill and legs pale yellowish.

Tropical zone. Known from Caracas, and Cumaná, Sucre (*melanophaius*). [Nicaragua to w Ecuador and central Argentina.]

Forest, swamps, wet marshy meadows, mud flats, lagoons, dry grassland, to 900 m. Shy, secretive, hides in rushes. Call: frey-eeé, frey-ee, frey-o-o-o.

## RUSTY-FLANKED CRAKE
*Laterallus levraudi*
COTARITA DE COSTADOS CASTAÑOS

Pl. 6

6.5″ (16.5 cm.). Much like the Rufous-sided Crake, but without black and white bars on flanks. Dark olive brown above; supraloral streak buffy white; forecrown, sides of head, neck, breast, flanks and under tail coverts reddish chestnut, rest of underparts white.

Tropical zone. Yaracuy and Carabobo to ne Miranda.
Lakes, lagoons, swamps, flooded pastures, sometimes dry grassland to 600 m. Shy, secretive.

## RUSSET-CROWNED CRAKE
*Laterallus viridis*
COTARITA CORONA RUFA

Pl. 6
6.5" (16.5 cm.). Crown rufous chestnut, sides of head gray. Above uniform olive brown, below orange ochraceous, palest on throat and belly. *Bill blackish;* legs salmon; iris orange; eye ring red.
Tropical zone. Delta Amacuro; central Amazonas; Bolívar from the lower Río Paragua to the Gran Sabana (*viridis*). [N Colombia, the Guianas to e Peru and s Brazil.]
Swamps, wet marshy meadows, sometimes dry grassland, second growth, to 1200 m. Shy, secretive. Feeds on seeds, insects. Noisy in the evenings and at dawn.

## OCELLATED CRAKE
*Micropygia schomburgkii*
COTARITA DE OCELOS

Pl. 6
5.5" (14 cm.). Mostly ochraceous; crown black, dotted white. Back, wing coverts and sides of breast with white, *black-encircled* dots; center of abdomen white.
Tropical zone. Very local, probably throughout. [Costa Rica. The Guianas; e Colombia. Se and central Brazil. Accidental Galápagos Is.]
Savannas, open fields, marshy grassland, 450–1400 m.

## SPECKLED CRAKE
*Coturnicops notata*
COTARITA MOTEADA

5.5" (14 cm.). Above dark olive brown dotted with black and white. Throat whitish, neck and breast olive, finely and closely streaked white; belly dusky olive finely barred white. Iris red; bill and legs black.
Tropical zone. Known from Mérida (June) and Aparición, Portuguesa (Aug.). Possibly migrant. [E Colombia (Mar.), Guyana (Sept.), Paraguay (Dec.), s

Brazil (Sept.), Uruguay (Apr. and probably Nov. or Dec.), s Argentina, Falkland Is.?]
Rice and alfalfa fields, swamps, humid woodland edge, 200–1500 m.
Note: New record since publication of Lista Av. Venez.

## PAINT-BILLED CRAKE
*Neocrex erythrops*
POLLA PICO ROJO

Pl. 6
8" (20 cm.). Upperparts dark olive brown; forecrown, sides of head, and throat white, rest of underparts blue gray; flanks, under tail coverts, axillaries and under wing coverts blackish, barred with white. Bill yellow, bright orange red basally, legs salmon.
Tropical zone. Mérida, Portuguesa and Carabobo to Miranda and Monagas; e Amazonas; Bolívar in the Gran Sabana (*olivascens*). [E Panama, to w Peru; e and s Brazil; Paraguay; nw Argentina.]
Rice fields, humid woodland and pastures, reedbeds, llanos, swampy areas with low thick vegetation, lagoons, 200–900 m. Feeds on seeds, insects. Sometimes called locally Turututú because of its call.

## COMMON GALLINULE
*Gallinula chloropus*
GALLINETA DE AGUA

Fig. 16
11" (28 cm.). Head, neck and underparts slaty gray, back darker gray, tinged olive brown, *a white line* along flanks dividing the two colors; central under tail coverts black, lateral ones white forming two white lines. Bill chickenlike, frontal shield and bill red, latter tipped yellow; upper part of tibia red, rest of legs and the feet yellow.
Tropical zone. Locally in Zulia, Carabobo, Aragua and Monagas (*galeata*). [S Canada to Chile and Argentina. W Indies. Trinidad. Eurasia, Africa.]
Lakes, rivers, streams, ponds, marshes, always near aquatic vegetation, to 500 m. Swims near shore. Alone or in flocks up to 35. Clucking, chattering calls. Nests in marsh vegetation.

## PURPLE GALLINULE

*Porphyrula martinica*
GALLITO AZUL

Pl. 6
12″ (30 cm.). Head, neck and underparts bluish purple, back bronzy green, under tail coverts white. Frontal shield bluish white, bill chickenlike, red, tipped yellow, legs greenish yellow. Imm.: light brown above, neck and underparts paler, breast whitish, lower back and quills greenish. Legs dull greenish yellow.
Tropical zone throughout. [S US to Bolivia, Argentina and Uruguay. Curaçao, Aruba. Trinidad, Tobago.]
Lagoon and river margins with floating, dense vegetation; muddy and reedy shores, rice fields, to 500 m. Usually in pairs; flocks of over 50. Feeds on grass seeds, insects, spiders. Call: noisy, reedy clucking, guttural deep cackling.

## AZURE (OR LITTLE) GALLINULE

*Porphyrula flavirostris*
GALLITO CLARO

Pl. 6
10″ (25 cm.). Sides of head, neck, breast and wing coverts light blue, center of underparts dull white. Crown, hindneck and mantle olive brown, rest of upperparts blackish, feathers pale-edged. Frontal shield and bill greenish; legs dull yellow.
Tropical zone. Spottily distributed. Apure (Guasdualito). Delta Amacuro (Jobure). Bolívar (upper Río Caura), Amazonas (Río Ventuari). [Spottily distributed n of the Amazon. Widespread s of it to Paraguay, se Brazil and n Bolivia.]
Swampy river margins, rice fields, marshes, to 300 m. Feeds on seeds, insects.

## CARIBBEAN COOT

*Fulica caribaea*
GALLINETA PICO PLATA

Fig. 16
15″ (38 cm.). General plumage dark slate gray, inner remiges edged white. *Frontal shield white* to pale sulphur, *bill white,* chickenlike; feet dull olive, toes webbed.
Tropical zone. Zulia (Lagunillas); Aragua (Suata reservoir). [The Antilles; Curaçao. Trinidad, Tobago.]
Lakes, ponds, marshlands, to 500 m. Swamps with floating vegetation. Not shy, usually in groups.

Fig. 16. COMMON GALLINULE (left), CARIBBEAN COOT (right)

# SUNBITTERN: Eurypygidae

## Tigana

Except for its long tail the sunbittern looks rather like a small heron. It lives along streams in the forest, capturing its prey with a lightning-fast thrust of its long bill. Nests are built in low trees near the banks of streams. The one species comprising the family is exclusively neotropical.

### SUNBITTERN

*Eurypyga helias*
Tigana

Pl. 6
18″ (46 cm.). Wings and tail strikingly patterned. Primaries broadly banded gray, black, white and chestnut; scapulars with round white spots; much mustard yellow on inner remiges. Tail narrowly barred black and white and crossed by two broad black bars, edged above with chestnut. Back narrowly barred rufescent and black (or olivaceous gray and black, a), rump and upper tail coverts black with narrow white bars. Top and sides of head black with a white bar above and another below the eye. Throat, lower breast and abdomen white, center of foreneck buff, rest of neck finely barred buff and black, breast coarsely marked with dusky bars and streaks. Lower mandible and legs orange.

Tropical and subtropical zones. Sierra de Perijá, Zulia; Aragua at Rancho Grande (*major,* a). N of the Orinoco, s of the n Cordilleras from Táchira, Apure, Barinas and Portuguesa to central Monagas and se Sucre; Delta Amacuro; n Bolívar; Amazonas s to the Río Ventuari (*helias*). [Mexico to n Bolivia and s Brazil.]

Shores of large forested rivers and of smaller forest streams and swamps; gallery forests; 500–1800 m. in the Sierra de Perijá and the central n Cordilleras, s of them from sea level to 500 m. Shy, usually solitary, perches low on branches, also swims. Undergrowth of rain forest. Feeds on a variety of animals, fish, flies, frogs, beetles. Call: soft penetrating high double whistle, also a low trill. Large orange spot visible as it opens wings.

# SUNGREBES: Heliornithidae

## Zambullidor de Sol

These small aquatic birds superficially resemble grebes but are related to rails. They have rather long, slender bills, and webbed toes which are banded dull yellow and black.

Sungrebes live on quiet streams among thick vegetation. They dive easily, take wing readily and live on aquatic life and seeds. The family is also represented by one species in Africa and another in Asia.

### SUNGREBE

*Heliornis fulica*
Zambullidor de Sol

Pl. 6
11″ (28 cm.). Crown and hindneck black, white stripe extending backward from above eye, almost joining another white band down side of neck, black stripe behind eye joining another black stripe down sides of neck, giving the sides of neck a broadly black and white striped appearance. Cheeks ochraceous. Throat, foreneck and underparts white, breast and sides tinged buffy. Back olive brown, tail rather long wide, black, tipped white.

Tropical zone. Very local. N of the Orinoco recorded only from the Río Meta, Apure and Monagas (Caicara); s of it in se Bolívar and in Amazonas s of the Río Ventuari. [Mexico to Argentina. Trinidad.]

Margins of large forest rivers and deep streams, 100–400 m. Usually in quiet waters. Swims half-submerged; solitary.

Feeds on insects, molluscs. Call: "kow," usually repeated; also reported, "wak-wak-wak." Builds nest of sticks in bushes above the water; transports its chicks in cavities on its side; swims and flies perfectly carrying its young until they fledge.

# CHARADRIIFORMES

## JACANAS: Jacanidae

### GALLITOS DE LAGUNA O DE AGUA

Jacanas are unique among waders for their long toes and very long nails, which allow them to run over the water on floating vegetation. They swim and dive easily and feed on vegetable matter, snails, insects and other animal life.

In this order, especially among the plovers, sandpipers and gulls, immature migrants of many North American species that require two or more years before breeding are found in South America the year round.

**WATTLED JACANA**

*Jacana jacana*
GALLITO DE LAGUNA

Pl. 6
9" (23 cm.). Black; back chestnut maroon (or purple maroon, a). Primaries and secondaries pale yellow, with blackish tip. Frontal shield and wattles at gape red, bill yellow. Imm.: bronzy brown above, broad eyebrow buffy; underparts dull white.

Tropical zone. The L. Maracaibo region, Zuia (*melanopygia,* a). Elsewhere n of the Orinoco and in n Amazonas, n Bolívar and Delta Amacuro (*intermedia*). [Panama to nw Peru and Argentina.]
Shores of marshes, lakes, ponds, with floating vegetation, flooded pastures, llanos. to 720 m. n of the Orinoco, to 300 m. s of it. In pairs or flocks up to 50. Noisy, conspicuous. As the birds alight their lemon-colored wings are held for a moment straight up. Call: shrill cackles. Nests on aquatic vegetation.

## OYSTERCATCHERS: Haematopodidae

### CARACOLEROS

These inhabitants of rocky shores and beaches are recognizable by their strikingly contrasted white and dusky coloration; they are thickset birds with rather short flesh-colored legs. The highly specialized, long, red bill is laterally compressed and bladelike at the tip. It is used to pry open molluscs, their main food.

**AMERICAN OYSTERCATCHER**
*Haematopus palliatus*
CARACOLERO

Fig. 17
16" (41 cm.). Head, neck, and upper breast black. Back grayish brown, darker on rump, upper tail coverts white, tail black. Below white; secondaries mostly white, showing as a conspicuous white wing stripe in flight.

Tropical zone. Coastal Zulia to Aragua (*palliatus*). Islands off the Caribbean coast (*prattii*). [Atlantic, Pacific and Caribbean coasts of the Americas from Lower California and New Jersey to Chile and Argentina.]
Sea beaches. In pairs. Shy. Feeds on crabs, molluscs, fish. Call: high-pitched, varied, penetrating clear whistles, or repeated loud, single notes when alarmed. Called Pito (whistle) by fishermen.

Fig. 17. AMERICAN OYSTERCATCHER

# LAPWINGS, PLOVERS: Charadriidae

## ALCARAVANES, PLAYEROS

Plovers differ from sandpipers by their proportionately shorter bills, which are noticeably swollen near the tip. They frequent sandy beaches, and not uncommonly, meadows and mountain grasslands. The winter, or non-breeding plumage of most plovers is different from that of the breeding plumage. Many plovers are migratory.

### SOUTHERN LAPWING
*Vanellus chilensis*
ALCARAVÁN

Pl. 6
13" (33 cm.). *A long, thin, black occipital crest.* Forecrown black, bordered white behind, hindcrown, neck and upperparts light bronzy grayish green; rump white; tail black, base and tip white. Greater wing coverts white, median wing coverts shiny, metallic purplish green, scapulars rosy bronze, basally white, distally black; outer remiges black. Breast and center of throat black; belly white. A long, sharp, red spur at bend of wing. Bill basally red, distally black, legs reddish flesh.
Tropical zone, but not recorded in central and s Amazonas (*cayennensis*). [E Panama to Tierra del Fuego. Trinidad.]
Llanos, savannas, open lands wet or dry to 300 m. n of the Orinoco, to 1200 m. s

of it. Usually in groups up to 10 or more, also flocks up to 100. Very easily alarmed; communicates its alarm by a continued, insistent, strident series of loud "keks" which warns all animals within hearing distance.
Note: Called *Belonopterus cayennensis* in Lista Av. Venez.

### PIED LAPWING
(OR PLOVER)
*Hoploxypterus cayanus*
ALCARAVANCITO

Pl. 6
9" (23 cm.). Looks like a large, long-legged plover with strongly patterned black and white wings conspicuous in flight. Forecrown, sides of head and neck black, which continues to form a broad band across breast and around upper mantle; upperparts sandy brown, crown and nape outlined with white; rump and upper tail coverts white.

Scapulars white, externally margined black, forming a conspicuous longitudinal black and white band at sides of back. Primary coverts and primaries black, outer secondaries white, tipped black, tertials sandy brown like back. Throat and underparts white. Tail white with a broad, white-tipped, black terminal band. Bill blackish, flesh colored basally; eye ring and legs brick red to orange.

Tropical zone, but not recorded from Delta Amacuro. [S Amer. generally e of the Andes in open country s to Argentina.]

Pools in savannas, llanos; sandy river banks and sand bars, to 450 m. Gallery forest edge. Solitary or in pairs. Feeds on insects, molluscs. Call: low-toned, clear, mellow whistle consisting of 2 notes, the first higher-pitched.

## BLACK-BELLIED PLOVER

*Pluvialis squatarola*
PLAYERO CABEZÓN

Fig. 18
9″ (23 cm.). Breeding plumage: forehead, face, sides and front of neck, breast and upper belly black; lower belly and under tail coverts white. Forecrown white, the white continued around ear coverts and down sides of neck and breast. Back and wing coverts black spotted with white, rump white. White wing flash prominent in flight. Axillars black. Tail white, barred black. Bill and legs black. Winter: crown dusky, forehead and eyebrow white. Upperparts light grayish, rump white; underparts dull white slightly streaked. Tail white, barred dusky. Wing flash white. Note black axillars in flight. Head looks rather large, eye prominent.

Winter resident, Aug.–Apr. Coastal Zulia and Aragua; Los Roques; La Orchila, Margarita. [Breeds in circumpolar regions. Winters in s US s, chiefly in w S Amer., rare in the e, to Chile and Argentina. Aruba to Trinidad. Africa, s Asia, Australia.]

Sea shores. Shy, usually alone, forages on mud flats and sandy beaches. Feeds on

Fig. 18. BLACK-BELLIED PLOVER (non-breeding plumage)

molluscs, crabs, insects. Call: rarely, a mellow whistle.
Note: Called *Squatarola squatarola* in Lista Av. Venez.

## LESSER GOLDEN PLOVER
*Pluvialis dominica*
PLAYERO DORADO

9″ (23 cm.). Much like Black-bellied Plover but back black spotted with straw yellow *including rump*. Lower *belly* and *under tail coverts black* instead of white. No flash in wing. Tail obscurely barred. Axillars pale grayish instead of black. Winter: darker above than Black-bellied Plover with *no flash* in wing. Rump and tail dark brownish gray, indistinctly spotted with white, instead of white rump and white, dark-barred tail.
Chiefly transient but some winter, Sept.–Dec. Recorded along the Caribbean coast from Aragua to Sucre and in interior Anzoátegui and Monagas, also in e and se Bolívar (*dominica*). [Breeds in N Amer. and Asia. Winters chiefly in s S Amer. and in s Asia and Pacific islands.]
Sandy beaches and mud flats, llanos, savanna ponds, open fields to 1200 m. Call: loud whistle.

## SEMIPALMATED PLOVER
*Charadrius semipalmatus*
PLAYERO ACOLLARADO

Fig. 19
6″ (15 cm.). Narrow black band across forehead, lores, black band across center of crown, and across chest continued across upper mantle. Forecrown, spot behind eye, throat, *collar across hindneck,* and the underparts white. Hindcrown, back and closed wing dark grayish brown. Tail like back with a broad black distal band, tip and outer feathers white. In flight a conspicuous white wing stripe, edged black behind. Bill black, *base of bill and legs dull orange, eye ring orange.* In winter the black portions of plumage become brown, forehead and eyebrow white. *Legs yellow.*
Winter resident, Aug.–May. The Caribbean coast and islands, occasionally in the n interior. [Breeds in arctic Amer. Winters from s US to Chile and Argentina.]

Sea beaches, coastal lagoons and mud flats, occasionally inland in savanna pools, to 200 m. Alone or in small flocks, forages for small crabs, insects.

## SNOWY PLOVER
*Charadrius alexandrinus*
FRAILECITO

Fig. 19
5.5″ (14 cm.). *No collar across breast.* Forecrown white, ear coverts and bar across crown black, hindcrown and nape pale sandy gray as is back and closed wing. Sides of head, collar around hindneck and the underparts white, a black bar at sides of breast. Tail mostly blackish, outer tail feathers white. In flight a conspicuous white wing stripe, edged dusky behind. *Bill and legs blackish.* In non-breeding season black markings replaced by brown.
Resident. Islands off the Caribbean coast (*tenuirostris*). [Breeds on Curaçao and Bonaire. Also in the s and w US. Europe. N Africa. Asia. Winters to Panama, accidental w Ecuador. Antilles. Africa. S Asia. Australia.]
Sandy salt flats and lagoons near marine beaches; alone or in pairs; runs surprisingly fast; usually flushes only when closely approached. Call: high, clear whistle when flushed. Nests on the sand, away from the shore.

## COLLARED PLOVER
*Charadrius collaris*
TURILLO

Fig. 19
5″ (13 cm.). Forehead white, lores and center of crown black, bordered cinnamon posteriorly. Hindcrown and upperparts sandy brown *with no white nuchal collar.* Underparts white with a black band across breast. Ear coverts and sides of neck more or less tinged cinnamon. Central tail feathers dark brown, outer ones white, remainder pale brown. Bill black, *extreme base orange, legs flesh.*
Resident. Seashore and inland ponds and rivers throughout including islands off the Caribbean coast. [S Mexico to w Ecuador and Argentina.]
Llanos, beaches, gallery forest edge, salt and mud flats, open savannas, flooded

fields with low vegetation, to 200 m. In pairs and small flocks. Call: soft, short, rolling whistle; sharp "peep-peep."

## KILLDEER
*Charadrius vociferus*
PLAYERO GRITÓN

9" (23 cm.). Below white with *two black bands*. Forehead, subocular region, broad stripe behind eye white; black line below eye, continued across ear coverts. Throat, sides of neck white, continued to form a nuchal collar; underparts white with a black collar across foreneck continued around upper mantle and a black collar across breast. Hindcrown, back and closed wings dark grayish brown, *rump and upper tail coverts cinnamon.* Outer tail feathers cinnamon with a subterminal black band and *white tip,* 3 central pairs grayish brown with a broad black band near tip. In flight a striking white band on wing, trailing edge of wing black. Bill black, legs flesh, eye ring red.

Recorded from the Páramo de Mucuchíes, 4500 m., Mérida, and the Gulf of Cariaco, Sucre (*vociferus*). [Breeds in N Amer., W Indies and the coast of Peru. N breeders winter from s US to the Antilles, Colombia and w Ecuador. Winter visitor to Aruba, Curaço, Bonaire, Tobago.]

Open habitats. Lagoons, tidal flats, wet grasslands, Nov.–Dec.

## THICK-BILLED (OR WILSON'S) PLOVER
*Charadrius wilsonia*
PLAYERO PICOGRUESO

Fig. 19
8" (20 cm.). *Bill all black,* heavier and larger than in similar species. *Legs blue gray.* Forehead, eyebrow, throat and collar on hindneck white. Lores and bar across center of crown black. Above *sandy brown including rump.* Tail like back with a black area toward tip, outer feathers and tip white. Below white with a broad black band across breast. Wing stripe prominent, white. The breeding race (a) is strongly tinged rusty on

Fig. 19. SNOWY PLOVER (upper left), THICK-BILLED PLOVER (center, male), COLLARED PLOVER (lower left), SEMIPALMATED PLOVER (right, non-breeding plumage)

crown and sides of neck. ♀: like ♂ but breast band sandy brown (or strongly tinged cinnamon, a), no black bar on crown and sides of head. ♂ in winter plumage resembles ♀.
Resident along the Caribbean coast from Carabobo to Sucre and islands off the coast (cinnamominus, a). Winter resident. Recorded from coastal Anzoátegui and Sucre and on Margarita, Las Aves and Los Roques Is. (wilsonia). [Breeds in N Amer. from New Jersey to nw Peru and ne Brazil. N Amer. birds migrate s to Bahia, Brazil, and to Ecuador. Aruba to Trinidad.]
Mangroves, sandy sea beaches. Call: short, soft "wheet" or "chirrip."

# SANDPIPERS, SNIPES: Scolopacidae

## PLAYEROS, BECASINAS

Sandpipers differ from plovers by usually having longer and more slender bills and longer necks; especially in breeding plumage, the upperparts are dusky, the feathers pale-edged, giving a patterned appearance.
All the species of sandpipers found along South America shores are migrants from their breeding grounds in the far north; some species may be found on inland waters, even high in the mountains.
Snipes differ from most sandpipers in habits: they live in swamps and Andean bogs and do not occur on ocean beaches.

## SOLITARY SANDPIPER

*Tringa solitaria*
PLAYERO SOLITARIO

7″ (18 cm.). Olive brown above streaked with white on crown and hindneck, finely spotted with white on back and closed wing; central tail feathers olive brown, outer feathers white, barred with dusky. Underparts white streaked on sides of neck and breast and lightly barred on flanks with olive brown. In flight wings dark *with no white stripe*. Bill and legs black. Winter: similar but grayer with markings less distinct. (markings distinctly buff in fall instead of white, a).
Winter resident on coastal and inland waters throughout, Aug.–May (*solitaria*). The race breeding in w N Amer. has been recorded once at Caicara, Monagas (*cinnamomea*, a). [Breeds in Alaska and Canada. Winters to Uruguay and Argentina.]
Open savannas, river banks, muddy shores of lagoons, mangroves, flooded terrain at woodland edge, páramos, to 3600 m. N of the Orinoco, to 500 m. s of it. Rarely on sandy beaches. Gallery forest. Solitary, not shy. Feeds on insects. Call sounds like Tin-güin, one of its local names.

## LESSER YELLOWLEGS

*Tringa flavipes*
TIGÜI-TIGÜE CHICO

Fig. 20
9″ (23 cm.). Above dark brown spotted and barred with white, rump white, tail white lightly barred dusky. Below white streaked on sides of neck and breast with dusky. *No wing stripe*. Bill long; *legs long, yellow*. Winter: more or less plain gray above, rump white; dull white below. Flight feathers blackish; tail light grayish, unbarred.
Winter resident, most common Aug.–Nov. Coastal and inland waters generally n of the Orinoco and in the Caribbean islands. [Breeds in Canada and Alaska. Winters from Florida and the Gulf States to Tierra del Fuego.]
Salt- and fresh-water lagoons, beaches, gallery forest edge, river banks, llanos, mangroves, to 200 m. Solitary and flocks up to 60. Keeps wings raised as it lands. Feeds on molluscs, insects. Call: a thin 2-note whistle when flushed.
Note: This and the Greater Yellowlegs were placed in the genus *Totanus* in Lista Av. Venez.

## GREATER YELLOWLEGS

*Tringa melanoleuca*
Tigüí-tigüe Grande

Fig. 20
11″ (28 cm.). Virtually identical to Lesser Yellowlegs in both breeding and winter plumage but considerably larger with a longer bill, which is slightly upturned. *Legs long, yellow.*
Winter resident, Aug.–Mar. Tropical to páramo zone throughout including Caribbean islands. [Breeds in Alaska and Canada. Winters from the US to Tierra del Fuego.]
Habits and habitat similar to Lesser Yellowlegs but with a remarkable vertical range from sea level to 4100 m. Call: when flushed gives a clear 3 to 5 note whistle.

## SPOTTED SANDPIPER

*Actitis macularia*
Playero Coleador

Fig. 21
7.5″ (19 cm.). Constantly *teeters while walking.* Grayish olive brown above finely marked with dusky lines and irregularly freckled with black. A broad white eyebrow. Underparts white marked *with round black spots.* Inner remiges tipped white forming a white band on inner part of wing, conspicuous in flight. Central tail feathers like back, outer ones white, barred black. Bill basally pinkish, distally black; legs flesh color. Winter: above plain grayish olive brown, eyebrow and underparts white with a gray wash on sides of neck and breast. No spots. Wings and tail as in breeding plumage.
Winter resident, July–Apr. Found throughout including the Caribbean islands probably to the temperate zone (*macularia* and *rava*). [Breeds in N Amer. Winters to Argentina and Chile. Aruba to Trinidad and Tobago.]
Near water, to 1600 m. n of the Orinoco, to 1800 m. s of it. Rain, cloud forest and gallery forest, lagoons, mangroves, sandy and rocky ocean beaches, river banks, mud flats. Not shy; solitary or in groups up to 5. Dips or bobs repeatedly,

Fig. 20. Greater Yellowlegs (left),
Lesser Yellowlegs (right), Solitary Sandpiper (center)

Fig. 21. SPOTTED SANDPIPER (non-breeding plumage)

lowering and lifting the tail as it walks or while standing.
Note: Cf. Wetmore, Bds. Panama, I, p. 405, for distribution.

## WILLET

*Catoptrophorus semipalmatus*
PLAYERO ALIBLANCO

Fig. 22

15″ (38 cm.). Above brownish gray (or paler ashy gray, a). Crown and hind-neck streaked, back and scapulars barred and spotted with dusky; rump white, tail white with a dusky area toward tip. Underparts white, foreneck and upper breast spotted, sides barred with dusky (or barring paler and less distinct, a). Greater upper wing coverts black, re-miges basally white, distally blackish. Under wing coverts and axillars black, the black and white of remiges showing in flight from above and below *as a bold white bar contrasting strongly with the black parts.* Bill black, legs gray. Winter: pale solid grayish above, white below. Wings as above.
Winter resident, July–May. Caribbean coast and salt marshes from Zulia to Sucre, and the islands off the coast.

Breeds on Los Roques, Apr.–June (*semipalmatus*). Rancho Grande, Aragua, Aug. 4, Coche I., Aug. 26 (*inornatus, a*). [Breeds in e N Amer.; winters from the Gulf States to Trinidad, Guianas and ne Brazil. Breeds also in w and central N Amer.; winters to Peru and the Galápagos Is. (*inornatus*).]
Sandy shores and beaches, mud flats, mangroves. Not shy. Solitary or in small flocks. Feeds on molluscs, fish. Raises wings after alighting showing the white bar.

## RUDDY TURNSTONE

*Arenaria interpres*
PLAYERO TURCO

Fig. 22

8″ (20 cm.). In flight strikingly patterned with cinnamon chestnut, black and white in breeding plumage. Bill rather short, slightly upturned, legs short, red, body plump. Head mostly white, lores black, black stripes at sides of head connected to a broad black band across breast, rest of underparts white. Back chestnut with two broad black lateral stripes, rump white, upper tail coverts black, the long-est ones tipped white; tail basally white

Fig. 22. WILLET (left and flying), RUDDY TURNSTONE (right),
(both in non-breeding plumage)

with a broad black subterminal band and white tip. Winter: no cinnamon chestnut, back mostly grayish brown, black parts of plumage replaced by dusky brown, head with almost no white. Legs red.

Mostly winter resident. Zulia; Aragua; the Caribbean islands (*morinella*). [Breeds in circumpolar regions; winters from US to Chile and Argentina; s Africa; s Asia.]

Sandy or rocky coasts, usually in small groups up to 10. Found throughout the year but much more frequently from Aug. to Apr.

Note: This species has been transferred to the Scolopacidae from the Charadriidae where it was placed in Lista Av. Venez. and Sp. Bds. S Amer.

## RED KNOT

*Calidris canutus*
PLAYERO PECHO RUFO

10″ (25 cm.). A plump, short-legged sandpiper with *cinnamon underparts* in breeding plumage. Above gray, variegated with black and rufous, rump pale gray barred with black, tail brownish gray narrowly tipped white. Eyebrow and underparts cinnamon, lower ab-domen white. Flight feathers dusky, greater coverts tipped white, forming a narrow wing stripe visible in flight. Winter: above brownish gray, the feathers narrowly edged grayish white giving a streaked appearance, rump white, lightly barred, the white *extending* upward *in a point to lower back,* tail grayish brown. Below white, barred lightly with gray at sides. Wings dusky, coverts and inner edged grayish white, in flight a narrow white wing stripe. Legs greenish.

Casual in winter. Recorded from the ne Goajira Pen., Zulia (Nov.); Cumaná, Sucre, May (*rufa*). [Breeds in circumpolar regions. Winters in southern S Amer.; Africa; s Asia.]

Sandy beaches, rocks, mud flats. Resembles a sanderling but it is quite stocky and about twice as large. Feeds on molluscs.

## LEAST SANDPIPER

*Calidris minutilla*
PLAYERITO MENUDO

Fig. 23

5.5″ (14 cm.). The *only small* sandpiper with *yellowish legs.* Above dark brown, feathers edged rufous, lower back, rump and central tail feathers black, outer tail feathers gray. Eyebrow, throat and belly white, breast grayish heavily streaked with dusky. In flight a narrow wing stripe white. In winter similar but markings, especially on breast, less pronounced.

Rather like Baird's Sandpiper but considerably smaller and not as definitely marked above. Found throughout the year, more common in spring and fall. N of the Orinoco ˙s to the Río Meta, Apure, n Amazonas and n Bolívar; Caribbean islands. [Breeds in arctic Amer. Winters to n Chile and Brazil.]

Sea beaches, salt lagoons, mangrove edge, llanos, gallery forest edge, flooded terrain, margins of forested rivers, to 400 m. Not shy. Alone or in small groups. Feeds on insects.

Note: Birds placed in the genus *Erolia* in Lista Av. Venez. are included here in *Calidris*.

## BAIRD'S SANDPIPER

*Calidris bairdii*
PLAYERO DE BAIRD

6″ (15 cm.). Much like Least Sandpiper but upperparts have a scaled appearance, *legs black* instead of yellowish; also much like White-rumped Sandpiper but differs by black instead of white middle upper tail coverts. Winter: much like breeding plumage but edges to feathers of upperparts much paler, white to buffy white instead of buff to cinnamon buff. Legs black.

Transient. Recorded from Ocumare, Aragua (Oct.). [Breeds in ne Siberia and arctic Amer. Winters on the seacoast and Andes of s S Amer.]

Recorded from a lagoon near a sandy sea beach. In winter quarters usually found inland.

Fig. 23. Small Sandpipers (all in non-breeding plumage):
STILT SANDPIPER (upper left)          PECTORAL SANDPIPER (upper right)
WHITE-RUMPED SANDPIPER (middle left)          SANDERLING (middle right)
LEAST SANDPIPER (lower left)          WESTERN SANDPIPER (lower right)

## WHITE-RUMPED SANDPIPER
*Calidris fuscicollis*
PLAYERO DE RABADILLA BLANCA

Fig. 23
6" (15 cm.). Upperparts much as in Baird's Sandpiper, but upper tail coverts usually with some white, breast not as heavily marked. Central tail feathers black, rest dusky brown. White rump visible in flight or when wings are raised. Can always be distinguished in the hand from Baird's by broadened, pitted tip of bill, (Baird's is narrow and unpitted at tip). Legs black. Winter: brownish gray with concealed black and buff markings. Eyebrow white. Below white with light grayish streaks on breast.
Transient. Recorded coastally from Zulia to Delta Amacuro and in nw and se Bolívar; La Orchila, La Tortuga I. [Breeds in N Amer. Winters in s S Amer. Aruba to Trinidad.]
Sea beaches, river banks, open fields, marshes; at sea level n of the Orinoco, to 450 m. s of it. Not shy. Solitary or in small groups. Feeds on crustaceans and insects. More abundant in the spring and fall.

## PECTORAL SANDPIPER
*Calidis melanotos*
TIN-GÜÍN

Fig. 23
7.5" (19 cm.). A medium-sized sandpiper with comparatively short bill and greenish legs, breast heavily streaked, *sharply demarcated from white underparts*. Wings dark with *no wing stripe*. Upperparts blackish, the feathers broadly edged with buff and rufous; crown strongly rufous; rump and middle tail feathers black, outer tail feathers dark grayish brown. Below white, the breast heavily streaked dusky and rufescent abruptly demarcated from white belly. Winter: rufous markings reduced or absent. Underparts white, foreneck and breast tinged grayish, markings duller.
Transient. Recorded along the coast, including offshore islands, and inland from Zulia to Sucre and in Portuguesa and Apure, n Amazonas and Bolívar. [Breeds in arctic Amer., winters in s S Amer. Aruba to Trinidad.]
Sea beaches, salt lagoons and estuaries,

llanos, savanna ponds, rice fields, marshes, sand banks of rain forest rivers; to 500 m. n of the Orinoco, to 1300 m. s of it. Usually solitary but also in flocks of 5 to 30. Feeds on insects. Most common Aug.–Oct., but also recorded in Nov. and Feb.

## SEMIPALMATED SANDPIPER
*Calidris pusilla*
PLAYERITO SEMIPALMEADO

5" (13 cm.). Bill comparatively thick, legs black, *breast streaked only at sides.* Narrow white wing stripe (cf. Western Sandpiper). Brownish gray above, feathers of crown and back narrowly edged buff, crown streaked and back heavily spotted with black; rump and central tail feathers black, outer feathers grayish brown. Below white streaked at sides with dusky. Winter: grayish brown above, narrowly streaked dusky. Eyebrow, sides of head and underparts white, sides lightly streaked dusky.
Winter resident, Jul.–May. Chiefly coastal but occasionally inland from Zulia to Sucre and Delta Amacuro, Monagas and in Apure, Caribbean islands. [Breeds in arctic Amer., winters to Chile and Argentina. Aruba to Trinidad and Tobago.]
Sea beaches, salt marshes and lagoons, mangrove swamps, lake shores, river margins; to 400 m. n of the Orinoco, to 100 m. s of it. Alone or in small groups, large flocks in mangrove and tidal mudflats. Most abundant in Feb.–Mar. and Aug.–Oct.

## WESTERN SANDPIPER
*Calidris mauri*
PLAYERITO OCCIDENTAL

Fig. 23
6.5" (16 cm.). Very similar to Semipalmated Sandpiper, but bill with a *very slightly curved tip* instead of straight. Above somewhat more rufescent than Semipalmated. Best distinguishing character is longer bill, "♂♂ 20.5–23.5 (22.5); ♀♀ 23–28 (25.9)" vs. for Semipalmated ♂♂ 17–20 (18.6), ♀♀ 18–22 (20.8 mm.)" *fide* Wetmore.
Winter resident, Aug.–Mar. Coastally from Zulia to Delta Amacuro and Caribbean islands. [Breeds in Alaska. Winters from

s US to Argentina and Chile. Aruba to Trinidad and Tobago.]
Sea beaches, mud flats, lagoons, mangrove swamps. Singly and in small or large flocks. Feeds on crustaceans and insects. Most abundant in Feb.–Mar. and Aug.–Oct.

## SANDERLING
*Calidris alba*
PLAYERO ARENERO

Fig. 23
6.5" (16.5 cm.). Cinnamon rufous above streaked and spotted with black, white around base of bill; sides of rump white, stripe down center of rump and central tail feathers black, rest of tail feathers gray. Below white, neck and breast cinnamon buff with dark streaks. Broad wing stripe white. Bill black, rather thick; legs black. Winter: very pale gray above, white below. Wings, rump and tail as in summer.
Winter resident, Sept.–Apr. Sandy beaches; recorded from Zulia to Anzoátegui; Caribbean islands. [Breeds in circumpolar regions. Winters from s US to Chile and Argentina; Africa; s Asia.]
Not shy. In small groups. Runs back and forth, following the waves as they advance and racing over the wet sand as they retreat. Feeds on marine invertebrates. Most numerous Feb.–Apr.

## STILT SANDPIPER
*Micropalama himantopus*
PLAYERO PATILARGO

Fig. 23
7.5" (19 cm.). *Legs long, yellowish green.* In breeding plumage a broad cinnamon *rufous band* across sides of head. Crown mixed rufous, black and buff; eyebrow whitish. Upperparts mixed blackish and gray the feathers edged with buffy. Rump and upper tail coverts white, barred with black; tail gray, outer feathers basally white with white tip. Below white, neck streaked, *breast and belly heavily barred dusky.* No wing stripe, trailing edge of wing blackish. Winter: above plain brownish gray, rump and upper tail coverts white. Eyebrow white, line through eye dusky; underparts white unobtrusively streaked with gray on neck and sides.

Transient. Recorded coastally from Aragua to Sucre. Las Aves Is. [Breeds in arctic Amer. Winters chiefly from Bolivia and s Brazil to central Argentina. Antilles, Trinidad, etc.]
Sea beaches, shallow coastal pools and mud flats. Wades up to its breast, pokes head under water. Feeds on insects, molluscs, seeds. Most frequently found Aug.–Oct.

## BUFF-BREASTED SANDPIPER
*Tryngites subruficollis*
PLAYERITO DORADO

7" (18 cm.). *Bill short,* legs yellowish, entire *underparts pinkish buff.* Eye ring white. Upperparts black, the feathers sharply edged buff, giving a handsomely scaled appearance. Central tail feathers blackish tipped buff, the outer feathers grayish brown, blackish toward end, tipped and edged with deep buff. No wing stripe, wing lining white in contrast to pinkish buff underparts. Winter: like breeding plumage.
Transient, probably to temperate zone in short grass meadows. Recorded in May from e Zulia and in Mar. from nw Amazonas. [Breeds in w arctic Amer. Winters chiefly in Argentina.]
Rain forest river banks, marshes; also on the sea shore and in pastures. In small flocks.

## UPLAND SANDPIPER
*Bartramia longicauda*
TIBI-TIBE

Fig. 24
10" (25 cm.). Head small, neck and tail long. Apt to hold *wings elevated after landing.* Crown dusky with an indistinct central stripe. Upperparts streaked buffy and black, rump and central tail feathers black, outer tail feathers buffy, barred with black. In flight primaries dusky in contrast to rest of upperparts, under wing coverts and axillars barred black and white. Below buffy white, lower neck, breast and sides barred dusky, throat and center of belly pure white. Legs greenish yellow. Winter: similar.
Transient, recorded in Sept.–Oct., March–May to the temperate zone from Mérida and Barinas to Anzoátegui and Monagas, and in Amazonas. [Breeds in N Amer.

Fig. 24. UPLAND SANDPIPER

s to Colorado and Virginia. Winters principally in Paraguay and Argentina. Recently found to winter in small numbers in Surinam.]

Savanna and open fields, 100–200 m. Llanos, wet grasslands, forested river margins, suburban lawns. Solitary or in small groups. Feeds on insects. Raises wings when it lands.

## WHIMBREL

*Numenius phaeopus*
CHORLO REAL

Fig. 25

17" (43 cm.). *Bill very long* (3.4" [8.5 cm.]), *curved,* black. Stripe at each side of crown and through eye blackish, central crown stripe and eyebrow buffy white. Back blackish brown variegated with buff. Below buffy white streaked on neck and breast and barred on sides with dusky. Tail barred, brown and blackish. Remiges dusky barred with buff on inner web. Axillars and under wing coverts pale cinnamon buff heavily barred dusky. Legs blue gray.

Winter resident, Aug.–Apr., chiefly on mud flats and estuaries of rivers from Falcón to Sucre and Monagas and inland on the middle Orinoco in Bolívar; Margarita, Los Roques, Las Aves Is. (*hudsonicus*). [Breeds in circumpolar regions. Winters to Tierra del Fuego, s Africa and nw India.]

Sand beaches, coral flats, mangrove borders. Solitary. Feeds on molluscs, crabs.

## HUDSONIAN GODWIT

*Limosa haemastica*
BECASA DE MAR

13" (33 cm.). Bill very long (3.3" [8.5 cm.]), slightly *upcurved,* basal half pink. Crown blackish, sides of head and throat whitish streaked black, eyebrow white. Back variegated black, cinnamon and buff. Lower back and tail black with a broad white bar across rump, tail tipped white. Shoulders plain gray. Neck and underparts chestnut, the neck streaked, the underparts barred with black. In flight a white wing stripe. Winter: crown dusky, upper back gray, lower back and tail black, bar across rump and tip of tail white. Sides of head, neck and underparts pale ashy gray, belly white. Wing stripe white.

Transient. Recorded in Oct. from L. Valencia, Carabobo, and Barcelona, Anzoátegui. [Breeds in arctic Amer. Winters in S Amer. to Tierra del Fuego.]

Lake shores, sand beaches. Swampy grassland, lagoons, to 400 m. Feeds on shellfish, insects.

## COMMON DOWITCHER
*Limnodromus griseus*
BECASINA MIGRATORIA

Fig. 25
10" (25 cm.). Bill comparatively long, (2.2" [5.5 cm.]), black. Legs rather short, yellowish green. Eyebrow white. Above cinnamon buff, streaked on crown, hindneck and breast, spotted on scapulars with black. Lower back rump and upper tail coverts extensively white, rump spotted, tail barred black and white, bars of equal width. Below pinkish cinnamon, streaked and spotted on neck and upper breast with dusky, lower breast and upper belly splotched with white, belly white. Narrow wing stripe and trailing edge of wings whitish. Winter: eyebrow white. Above gray, *white of lower* back *extending* well up in a point *almost to center of back.* Tail as in breeding plumage. Below white, foreneck, breast, sides clouded with gray, sides and under tail coverts barred dusky. Narrow wing stripe and trailing edge of inner remiges white.

Winter resident. Caribbean coast from Miranda to Sucre; Margarita, Los Roques, Las Aves de Barlovento Is. (*griseus*). [Breeds in Alaska and Canada. Winters from California and S Carolina to Colombia and the Antilles.]

Mangrove edge, sand beaches, mud flats. In small flocks. Feeds on insects, molluscs. Most abundant July–Oct.

## COMMON SNIPE
*Gallinago gallinago*
BECASINA CHILLONA

11" (28 cm.). Bill long, straight, (2.5" [6.5 cm.]), legs short. Crown blackish with a median stripe, sides of crown buff. Hindneck streaked pale cinnamon and blackish, back variegated black, buff

Fig. 25. WHIMBREL (top), COMMON DOWITCHERS (bottom)

and cinnamon, upper tail coverts barred pale cinnamon and buff; scapulars black edged buffy white. Throat white, foreneck and upper breast buff, streaked dusky, sides barred heavily to lightly with black and white, center of lower breast and belly white. Axillars and under wing coverts heavily barred black and white, the bars of about equal width. Outer tail feathers buffy, barred black, rest black basally, rufous distally with a black subterminal bar and white tip, the black basal coloring increasing in extent toward central feathers.

Winter resident, tropical to páramo zone, July-Apr. From Zulia and Táchira e to Anzoátegui and Monagas; nw Bolívar to the Río Paragua (*delicata*). [Breeds in N Amer. to California and Pennsylvania. Winters to the Guianas and e Ecuador. Curaçao, Bonaire. Tobago. Breeds also in Europe and Asia wintering to s Asia and Africa.]

Boggy, wet grassland, marshes, swamps, páramos, 500–3500 m. n of the Orinoco, 200–300 m. s of it. Secretive, alone, in pairs and scattered groups. Flushes when nearly stepped on. Zigzag flight.

### PARAGUAYAN SNIPE
*Gallinago paraguaiae*
BECASINA PARAGUAYA

Fig. 26

10″ (25 cm.). Not distinguishable in the field from the Common Snipe. Differs by narrower outer tail feathers which are much paler, whiter, less buffy and by having the black bars on the axillars narrower than the white ones. Upper tail coverts usually grayer, less buffy.

Tropical, occasionally lower subtropical zone. Locally from Mérida, to Táchira, Apure, Barinas e through Falcón and Aragua to Sucre and Monagas; nw and se Bolívar; n Amazonas (*paraguaiae*).

Fig. 26. Snipes: GIANT SNIPE (upper left), NOBLE SNIPE (upper right), PARAGUAYAN SNIPE (lower left), ANDEAN SNIPE (lower right)

[Llanos and open country e of the Andes to Tierra del Fuego.]
Mucky borders of streams, lakes, lagoons; wet savannas and marshy coastal areas. Sea level to 350 m. n of the Orinoco, to 1300 m. s of it. Behaves like the Common Snipe.
Note: Here regarded as a distinct species instead of a race of *G. gallinago* as it was in Lista Av. Venez. and Sp. Bds. S Amer.

## NOBLE SNIPE

*Gallinago nobilis*
BECASINA PARAMERA

Fig. 26
12" (30 cm.). Distinguishable from the Common Snipe by much larger size and longer bill (3.5" [9 cm.] vs. 2.5" [6.5 cm.]). In color virtually indistinguishable.
Temperate and páramo zones, occasionally upper subtropical. Táchira on the Páramo de Tamá. [The Andes of Colombia and Ecuador.]
Open grassy swamps, lagoons and streams in páramos, 2700–3300 m. Alone or in pairs, active, restless, secretive. Call: clear, melodious. Makes nest of aquatic vegetation on the ground.

## GIANT SNIPE

*Gallinago undulata*
BECASINA GIGANTE

Fig. 26
15" (38 cm.). Very large size and long bill (4.1" [10.5 cm.]), *primaries barred black and sandy buff,* at once distinguish it from other snipes, whose primaries are uniform dusky brown. Underparts with more rufous than in other species.

Throat and sides of head white with a very prominent dark line from eye to bill. Neck streaked buff and dusky, underparts white, sides barred blackish.
Tropical and lower subtropical zone. Very local. Carabobo; central Monagas; Bolívar in the vicinity of Cerros Auyan-tepui and Roraima; central Amazonas (Río Asisa) (*undulata*). [E Colombia, the Guianas, ne and s Brazil to Paraguay and Río Grande, Tierra del Fuego.]
Dry or marshy grassy savannas, swamps, 200–700 m. Llanos, pastures. Solitary.

## ANDEAN SNIPE

*Chubbia jamesoni*
BECASINA ANDINA

Fig. 26
13" (33 cm.). Bill (3.5" [9 cm.]) heavier, particularly at base, than in other snipes. Upperparts much as in other species. Below *barred on foreneck, breast and belly* dull white and dusky brown. Axillars black, barred narrowly with white. Central tail feathers mostly black, with a few sandy bars on outer web, no rufous, outer feathers dark brown with a few broad grayish brown bars on inner web. Differs from other snipe by having the tibia feathered almost to the joint.
Páramo zone. Locally in Táchira, Mérida and Trujillo. [The mountains of Colombia to Bolivia.]
Open, grassy, boggy páramos with low vegetation, 3200–3300 m. Secretive, solitary. Hides in the vegetation during the day, active and noisy at dusk and at night. Displays by flying in circles and calling repeatedly.
Note: Made a subspecies of *C. stricklandii* of Chile in Sp. Bds. S Amer. and placed in *Gallinago.*

# STILTS: Recurvirostridae

## PLAYEROS PATILARGOS

Stilts are easily identifiable among shorebirds by their exceedingly long, pink legs and striking black and white plumage.
They are found on mud flats and in shallow salt- and fresh-water lagoons, are gregarious and nest in colonies. They may often be seen wading and swishing their bills from side to side in search of the crustaceans and other animal life on which they feed.

Fig. 27. COMMON STILT

**COMMON STILT**

*Himantopus himantopus*
VIUDA PATILARGA

Fig. 27
15″ (38 cm.). Above mostly black; forehead, spot above eye and entire underparts white. In flight lower back white, tail pale gray. Bill long, black; legs very long, coral pink.

Tropical and subtropical zones. Generally n of the Orinoco, s of it in nw Bolívar and in the Río Paragua; n Amazonas; Caribbean islands (*mexicanus*). [Virtually world-wide in warmer temperate and tropical regions. N Amer. breeders are migratory, some reaching n S Amer.] Alone, in pairs and flocks over 100. Call: loud, repeated, strident bark when flying alarmed.

## THICK-KNEES: Burhinidae

### DARAS

Thick-knees look like enormous plovers. They live in open, arid, often stony country and are crepuscular in habits. They have rather short bills, thick, longs legs and very large eyes. They feed on animal matter and are not dependent on the proximity of water.

**DOUBLE-STRIPED THICK-KNEE**

*Burhinus bistriatus*
DARA

Fig. 28
18″ (46 cm.). Upperparts streaked dark brown and buff. Broad superciliary, throat and belly white, sides of body barred buff and black. Primaries black with a white bar. Tail white, barred and tipped black. Legs olive.

Tropical zone. Goajira Pen., Zulia, extending e along the arid coast of Falcón

Fig. 28. DOUBLE-STRIPED THICK-KNEE

(*pediacus*). Barinas, Lara, and Guárico e to Anzoátegui, Sucre, Monagas and Delta Amacuro; n Bolívar; Margarita I. (*vocifer*). [Ne and e Colombia; Guyana; ne Brazil. Curaçao. Se Texas to nw Costa Rica.]

Inconspicuous, in pairs and small, scattered bands. Seldom flies. Frequently seen when driving through open terrain at night. Call: a series of short, chattering, strident calls.

## SKUAS, JAEGERS: Stercorariidae

### SALTEADORES O ESTERCORARIOS

These dark-colored marine birds breed in arctic and antarctic regions and migrate south or north during their respective winters. One species is recorded as not uncommon off the Caribbean coast of Venezuela in winter, and others may occur casually.

**POMARINE JAEGER**

*Stercorarius pomarinus*
SALTEADOR

Fig. 29
22″ (56 cm.). Cap blackish. Upperparts and wings dark chocolate brown; a prominent white wing patch. Sides of neck yellowish, collar on hindneck and underparts white, band across breast chocolate brown. *Central tail feathers narrow, twisted, protruding 2–4″ (5–10 cm.) beyond rest.* Dark phase: chocolate brown below. Imm.: below barred dusky; central tail feathers barely protruding.
Common from Dec. to Mar. (once in Sept.) off Placer de la Guayra, 18 km. off the coast of the Dist. Federal; coast of Higuerote, Miranda. Margarita I.

Fig. 29. POMARINE JAEGER
(light phase)

[Breeds in arctic regions. Winters at sea from s US to Guyana, Africa and Australia.]
High seas off the coast, Dec.–Mar. Gull-like in appearance, flies with steady wing beats about 20 m. above the waves. Called by some fishermen Cauicho or Guincho. Piratical, but also feeds on fish by dipping and plunging. It maneuvers with surprising speed and agility when pursuing terns near the surface of the sea.

PARASITIC JAEGER (*S. parasiticus*) although not recorded from Venezuela, is likely to be found in the open ocean off its coasts for it is recorded as accidental from Curaçao and the interior of n Brazil in Roraima. The Great Skua (*Catharacta skua*) has been recorded once (bird banded in the Shetland Is.) off Georgetown, Guyana, June 19.

# GULLS, TERNS: Laridae

## GAVIOTAS, TIÑOSAS

Gulls and most species of terns inhabit coastal waters and not a few are found inland along rivers and on larger lakes. A few however, are often seen far from land.

Gulls have broad wings, square or rounded tails and rather thick, hooked bills. Terns differ from them by having narrow, pointed wings, forked tails, sometimes deeply so, and rather thin, pointed bills. Winter, or non-breeding plumage in both gulls and terns differs from breeding plumage.

Gulls are more or less omnivorous, while terns feed chiefly on fish which they catch by diving.

Gulls are apt to prefer temperate climates, while most terns inhabit tropical regions.

**LAUGHING GULL**
*Larus atricilla*
GUANAGUANARE

Fig. 30
16″ (41 cm.). Head slaty black with a short white bar above and another below the eye. Back and wings gray; neck, underparts, rump and tail white. In flight trailing edge of wing white, no white wing tip. Bill red, feet brown. Winter: head white, mottled with brownish gray. Bill black. Imm.: above brownish, rump and tail white, tail with a broad, black subterminal band; breast brown, throat and belly white.

Resident and migrant. Generally distributed along the Caribbean coast and Gulf of Paria. Nests on La Orchila, Los Roques, Las Aves and Coche Is. [Breeds from Nova Scotia to the Caribbean. Migrates to Peru and ne Brazil.]
Largely coastal but found in L. Maracaibo and occasionally L. Valencia. Piratical, but also feeds on fish and carrion seized on the surface by dipping. Present year-round in small numbers along the coast but very common in Los Roques and

Fig. 30. LAUGHING GULL (non-breeding in flight)

other oceanic islands during the greatest nesting activity, May–July, when their loud, laughing calls are frequently heard. Nests on the ground.

RING-BILLED GULL (*L. delawarensis*) has been recorded from Trinidad and Panama and may occur in winter as a migrant. It can be told from any other gull by the yellow bill, which has a black ring around it toward the tip.

## BLACK TERN
*Chlidonias niger*
GAVIOTA NEGRA

Fig. 31
9" (23 cm.). Head, neck and underparts blackish, under tail coverts white. Back, wings and tail dark gray. Tail forked. Bill black, feet purplish brown. Winter: forehead, nuchal collar and underparts white, a *dark patch at sides of head* and of breast; back, wings and tail dark gray.
Winter visitor. Recorded only from Coche I. off the coast of Sucre (*surinamensis*). [Breeds in inland marshes and lakes in

Canada and the northern US and in Europe. Winters s to Peru and Surinam. Nw Argentina. Trinidad. Also s Asia and Africa.]
Salt- and fresh-water marshes and lagoons, salt flats, also coastal and offshore. Dips for fish.

## LARGE-BILLED TERN
*Phaetusa simplex*
GUANAGUANARE FLUVIAL

Fig. 32
15" (38 cm.). *Bill thick,* long, *yellow.* Forehead white, crown glossy black; neck and underparts white; back and tail dark gray. Inner remiges and lesser wing coverts gray, middle and greater wing coverts and most of secondaries white, primaries black; in flight a *white triangle in wing behind black primaries.* Tail short, slightly forked. In non-breeding season crown mottled with white.
Generally around the mouths of rivers and upstream, and on larger lakes. Zulia on L. Maracaibo; the Orinoco to Puerto Ayacucho, Amazonas; along the Ríos

Apure and Meta and the larger rivers of Bolívar; Margarita I. (*simplex*). [Large rivers flowing into the Caribbean and Atlantic s to Buenos Aires, Argentina. W of the Andes in Ecuador; recorded from Peru.]

Rivers, lakes, estuaries, salt-water lagoons and coasts; ranges up to 500 m. Solitary or in small groups. Plunges for fish, hawks for insects. Rests on sand bars, lays eggs on sandy beaches.

## GULL-BILLED TERN
*Gelochelidon nilotica*
GAVIOTA PICO GORDO

Fig. 31
13″ (33 cm.). *Bill thick,* gull-like, *black;* legs black, long for a tern. Crown and nape black; upperparts, wings and tail very light gray; underparts white. A very "white" tern, with rather broad wings. Non-breeding season: crown and nape white, crescent in front of eye and patch on auriculars dark gray.

Transient? Known from Barcelona on the coast of Anzoátegui in May and Oct., and Laguna de Tacarigua in Miranda in May (*aranea*). [Breeds in N Amer. to Mexico, the Bahamas and the Virgin Is. Breeds also in w Ecuador where recorded in Feb., June, July, Sept. and in Brazil. Winters s through Mid. Amer. to w Peru and interior and coastal Argentina. Breeds also in much of the Old World, wintering to s Africa, the E Indies and s Asia.]

Found chiefly inland on fresh water. Flight gull-like. Picks food from the surface rather than "hitting" the water like most terns. Feeds on fish, hawks for insects, has been seen carrying a small lizard.

Fig. 31. COMMON TERN (upper left; flying, breeding plumage), GULL-BILLED TERN (lower left), ROSEATE TERN (upper right; flying, breeding plumage), BLACK TERN (lower right)

## COMMON TERN
*Sterna hirundo*
TIRRA MEDIO CUCHILLO

Fig. 31

14″ (35 cm.). Bill red, tip black (only in breeding season); legs red; tail deeply forked. Crown, nape and sides of head to eyes black. Back and wings gray; rump and tail white, outer web of outer tail feather dark gray. Outer primaries black on outer web in contrast to rest of wing, observable in flight. Non-breeding season: similar but only nape black and bill black with red base.

Resident and migrant. Breeds on Los Roques and Las Aves de Barlovento, May–July. Migrants and probably some residents are found generally on the Caribbean ccast, from L. Maracaibo and the islands offshore to Delta Amacuro. Banded migrants recorded Sept.–Apr. (*hirundo*). [Breeds from se Canada to the Virgin Is. Winters s to Argentina, recorded in interior s Brazil. Breeds in Eurasia, winters to E Indies, s Africa.]

Coastal and offshore, occasionally pelagic. Alone or in flocks up to 50. At rest, wing tips reach tip of tail (cf. Roseate Tern). Gray outer edge of outer tail feathers (white in Roseate Tern) often visible when the bird flies overhead. Dips and plunges for fish. Calls: harsh, shrill "kee-arr," a repeated "kik, kik, kik" and a bubbling trill. Nests on sand near beaches, salt flats and lagoons.

## ROSEATE TERN
*Sterna dougallii*
TIRRA ROSADA

Fig. 31

15″ (38 cm.). Differs from Common Tern, by much more *deeply forked* and longer tail, the outer feathers of which are all white. Bill black with red base in breeding season. Outer webs of outer primaries only slightly paler than in Common Tern, breast faintly tinged rosy. Winter: bill all black, black of crown confined to nape, breast without rosy tinge.

Resident and migrant. Nests on Los Roques and Las Aves Is. Migrant and perhaps resident, recorded from Falcón and Anzoátegui, and La Tortuga, Margarita and Coche Is. (*dougallii*). [Breeds from Nova Scotia to the W Indies. Winters chiefly in the e Caribbean and adjacent Atlantic. Breeds also in Brit. Is. and Denmark to n Africa, s Asia, Australia. etc. Winters to s Africa.]

Habits and habitat similar to Common Tern. Note that at rest tip of tail extends well beyond wing tips (cf. Common Tern). Call: a soft "chivy" uttered repeatedly during nesting season, occasionally a harsh "z-a-a-a-p."

## BRIDLED TERN
*Sterna anaethetus*
GAVIOTA LLORONA

Fig. 34

14″ (35 cm.). Forehead and eyebrow extending *well behind eye white;* conspicuous stripe through eye blackish; crown, nape and ear coverts blackish, nuchal collar whitish; back and all but outer tail feathers smoky grayish brown, outer tail feathers white, tail conspicuously forked. Underparts white. Bill and feet black. Winter: similar but forecrown white.

Nests on Los Roques and Las Aves; recorded from Falcón (Cayo Borracho); Distr. Federal (Placer de la Guayra), La Tortuga and Coche Is. (*recognita*). [Breeds in tropical and subtropical oceans and seas. Breeds on Aruba and Curaçao. N Amer. breeders migrate s to Gulf States, coastally to e US; and in the Pacific to Japan.]

Coastal, occasionally seen singly or in small groups offshore and in the open sea. In early Mar. it is heard at night in Los Roques, but is not seen by day until late Mar. Flight slow and buoyant. Dips for fish and squids; occasionally feeds at night. Called locally *Llorona* ("cry baby") because its very distinctive, repeated, single, deep, nasal "wong," uttered when flushed, sounds like a series of complaining moans. Nests near the shore where it lays 1 egg on the ground, usually hidden in crevices formed by coral debris, but also often hidden in low, thick vegetation.

## SOOTY TERN
*Sterna fuscata*
GAVIOTA DE VERAS

Fig. 34

16″ (41 cm.). *Much darker than Bridled Tern.* White of forehead and eyebrow reaching *only to eye. Back, wings and tail blackish,* tail conspicuously forked, outer feathers white. Below white, tinged gray on belly. Bill and feet black. Imm.: dark brown, (no white on head) feathers of back edged with *crescentic white marks.* Tail forked. The forked tail and white crescents on back distinguish it from the noddies (*tiñosas*).

Breeds in small colonies on Los Roques Is. and in large colonies on Los Hermanos (Morro Fondeadero, La Horquilla) and La Orchila; recorded from Isla de Aves (*fuscata*). [Breeds in the Caribbean, on the Dry Tortugas off Florida, Trinidad, Tobago. Also virtually world-wide in tropical and subtropical waters.]

Offshore, seldom on the continental coast. In immense flocks on islands during breeding period (Jan.–Mar., but may vary from year to year). Hundreds of thousands nest on Isla de Aves, and nearly as many nested recently on La Orchila, perhaps only half that number now. Feeds on fish and squid, dips for food, occasionally feeds at night. Calls frequently in flight, even at night in the open ocean. Strident, staccato calls transcribed variously as "wide awake," "de veras" or "ker-wacky-wack." More often heard before it is seen. Nests in bushes or on open sand.

### YELLOW-BILLED TERN
*Sterna superciliaris*
GAVIOTA PICO AMARILLO

Fig. 32

10″ (25 cm.). A small fresh-water tern. Forehead and eyebrow white; lores, crown and nape black. Upperparts pale gray; below white. Primaries black. Tail

Fig. 32. LEAST TERN (lower left; flying at upper left),
LARGE-BILLED TERN (center; flying at upper right),
YELLOW-BILLED TERN (right; flying at center)

gray, short and only slightly forked. Bill rather long, yellow; legs yellow. Winter: crown streaked with white.

Tropical zone. L. Valencia, Carabobo; Aragua; Laguna de Tacarigua, Miranda; Guárico; Urica, Anzoátegui; Apure; n Bolívar; Delta Amacuro; Amazonas s to Caño Casiquiare. [Colombia and the Guianas s, e of the Andes, to Argentina and Bolivia.]

Habits and habitat like those of the Large-billed Tern.

## LEAST TERN

*Sterna albifrons*
GAVIOTA FILICO

Fig. 32

9″ (23 cm.). A marine species distinguishable from the Yellow-billed Tern by somewhat more forked tail, only outer web of outer 2 primaries black, bill shorter, yellow with black tip (all black in winter) and orange yellow legs.

Resident and migrant. Breeds on Margarita and Los Roques Is., reported from Isla Aves de Sotavento, La Orchila, Coche, La Tortuga Is. and on the coast from Aragua to Anzoátegui, and on L. Maracaibo, Zulia (*antillarum*). [Breeds from the s US to the Caribbean and in Europe. N birds winter to Panama, Brazil and Argentina. Also in Eurasia and Africa.]

Coastal, occasionally offshore. Salt flats, lagoons. Nests on beaches in a depression in the sand, beginning to arrive at the nesting areas at the end of Mar., staying until end of Oct. Dips and plunges for fish. Call: clear and very high-pitched, repeated shrill whistles, incessant screeching when disturbed.

## ROYAL TERN

*Sterna maxima*
TIRRA CANALERA

Fig. 33

18″ (46 cm.). Head somewhat crested, crown to below eye black, the feathers

Fig. 33. SANDWICH TERN (flying), CAYENNE TERN (left),
ROYAL TERN (right)

of hindcrown lengthened and pointed. Back and wings pale gray, lower back and tail white, tail strongly forked. Neck, sides of head and entire underparts white. Bill yellow, feet and legs dusky. Winter: similar but forecrown white, hindcrown streaked with white.

Resident and migrant. Nests on Las Aves de Barlovento and Sotavento and Los Roques; recorded on La Tortuga, La Blanquilla, La Orchila, Los Hermanos and Margarita Is., along the Caribbean coast from Aragua to Anzoátegui, and on L. Maracaibo, Zulia (*maxima*). [Breeds in s N Amer., W Indies and W Africa. Winters from s US along Atlantic coast to s Argentina.]

The largest Venezuelan tern. Coastal and offshore, sand beaches, mangroves, estuaries, lagoons. Solitary or near nesting sites only, in flocks of 100 or more. Dips and plunges for fish.

CASPIAN TERN (*S. caspia*) occurs as a winter migrant in Panama and ne Colombia and should be looked for in nw Venezuela. It resembles the Royal Tern but is somewhat larger (20", 51 cm.), has a thick red bill and in winter plumage the forecrown is streaked black and white, not pure white as in the Royal Tern. The tail is much less forked. Its range is virtually cosmopolitan in salt and fresh water, except for most of Middle and S. Amer. Very recently 3 banded specimens have been taken in Zulia at the entrance to L. Maracaibo.

### CAYENNE TERN
*Sterna eurygnatha*
GAVIOTA TIRRA

Fig. 33
16" (41 cm.). Much like Royal Tern but slightly smaller and with a straw yellow bill.

Breeds on Las Aves de Sotavento and Barlovento and on Los Roques. Recorded from La Orchila and Margarita I. and the coast of Miranda and Monagas. [Aruba to Trinidad, Atlantic coast from Guyana to Argentina. Breeds on Macaé I. off coast of Rio de Janeiro.]

Coastal, seldom far from shore. Alone or in pairs, also in noisy, compact flocks of over 100. Dips and plunges for fish. Call: a high, shrill, rasping "keee-rack." Nests on the sand.

Note: Called *Thalasseus sandvicensis eurygnatha* in Lista Av. Venez.

### SANDWICH TERN
*Sterna sandvicensis*
GAVIOTA PATINEGRA

Fig. 33
16" (41 cm.). Very similar to Cayenne Tern but differs by black, yellow-tipped bill. Interbreeds with Cayenne when black bill shows varying amount of yellow.

Probably occurs along the Venezuelan coasts, for it breeds occasionally on Soldado Rock near the sw tip of Trinidad and has been recorded off Panama and Cartagena, Colombia in winter (*acuflavida*). [Breeds in the US Gulf and s Atlantic states and Cuba. Winters to Uruguay and n Chile. Also found in Europe, Africa and Asia.]

### BROWN NODDY
*Anous stolidus*
TIÑOSA

Fig. 34
15" (38 cm.). Dark brown, cap white; tail *wedge-shaped*. Bill black.

Breeds in large numbers on Aves de Barlovento and Sotavento, Los Roques, Los Hermanos (Morro Fondeadero, La Horquilla). Recorded also from Margarita, Los Testigos and La Orchila. Observed on Los Monjes Is. and off the coast of Falcón and Dist. Federal (*stolidus*). [Breeds on islands in the Gulf of Mexico and Caribbean, tropical Atlantic and Pacific and Indian oceans.]

Coastal, offshore. Swift, twisting flight. Alone or in small loose groups, but during breeding season congregates to feed in flocks of hundreds, with Lesser Noddy. Dips and plunges for fish and squid. Fledged young call loudly night and day from the mangroves, a plaintive "peeeeeo." Adults emit an angry-sounding, rattling, low growl, often at night, "yourrn." Nests on ground or in large, conspicuous nests of sticks and grass stems in the lower and middle branches of mangroves.

Fig. 34. Pan-tropical Terns:
BROWN NODDY (upper left), SOOTY TERN (upper right),
LESSER NODDY (lower left), BRIDLED TERN (lower right)

**LESSER NODDY**

*Anous tenuirostris*
TIÑOSA CHOCORA

Fig. 34

12″ (30 cm.). Smaller and blacker than Brown Noddy with a white cap and proportionately longer bill.

Breeds on Los Roques and probably Islas Las Aves (*americanus*). [Breeds in many small islands in the Caribbean, tropical Atlantic and Pacific Oceans.]

Coastal, offshore. Swift, twisting flight. Alone or in small loose groups, but during breeding season feeds in flocks of up to 100, with Brown Noddies. Call: a deep, throaty gargle; also "cho-cho-chocóra, cho-córa." Inconspicuous, small nest, about 6″ (15 cm.) in diameter, is made of seaweed and placed in a fork in the upper branches of mangroves.

Note: Called *A. minutus* in Lista Av. Venez.

# SKIMMERS: Rynchopidae

## PICOS DE TIJERA

Skimmers differ from gulls and terns by large, much compressed, bladelike red bills in which the mandible is considerably longer than the maxilla. The wings are long, pointed and strongly angled backward.

Skimmers assemble in large flocks on sand banks and beaches and fly very low over the water, the mandible skimming the surface. When the bill comes in contact with food it quickly snaps shut.

Skimmers are found on the seacoast and inland along the larger rivers.

Fig. 35. BLACK SKIMMER

**BLACK SKIMMER**

*Rynchops nigra*
PICO DE TIJERA

Fig. 35

17″ (43 cm.). Black above; forehead, underparts and trailing edge of wing white. Tail slightly forked, pale (or dark, a) gray, feathers edged white. Basal part of bill bright red, distal part black. In non-breeding season a whitish band across hindneck.

Resident and casual migrant. From Aragua (L. Valencia) coastally to Sucre, Monagas and Delta Amacuro; along the Orinoco for its entire length and along the Río Apure to San Fernando; La Tortuga, Margarita Is.; sight records from La Orchila (*cinerascens,* a). Migrant recorded once from the Gulf of Cariaco, Sucre, Jan. (*nigra*). [S US to w Ecuador, Amazonian Peru, s Argentina and Tierra del Fuego.]

Coastal; sandy shores, beaches, rivers, lakes, lagoons, swamps, mangrove swamps, estuaries. Small groups to flocks of several hundred on sand bars. Partially noctural. Nests in large colonies on sandy beaches, lays 1 egg.

# COLUMBIFORMES

# PIGEONS AND DOVES: Columbidae

## PALOMAS Y TORTOLITAS

Pigeons and doves are of world-wide distribution in temperate and tropical regions. They inhabit all types of country and feed on seeds and fruits. Some species are gregarious, others are solitary and both are either arboreal or terrestrial. The species found in South America are for the most part rather soberly colored, but quite a few show iridescent, metallic colors on the sides of the neck and upper mantle.

The domestic pigeon (*Columba livia*) familiar to everyone in cities of Europe and North America is also established in cities of South America and is probably feral in suburban areas.

## BAND-TAILED PIGEON
*Columba fasciata*
PALOMA GARGANTILLA

Pl. 7
14″ (35 cm.). Head and underparts dark vinaceous, *band across nape white,* throat gray. Feathers at base of hind-neck and on upper mantle metallic bronze green; lower back, rump and upper tail coverts gray (strongly glossed with olive green, a). Wings bronzy dark brown; tail gray, paler on terminal half. Bill and feet yellow, eye ring blue.
Subtropical and temperate zones. Generally distributed in the n mountains from Zulia and Táchira to Sucre and Monagas (*albilinea*). The high tepuis of Bolívar and Amazonas (*roraimae,* a). [W N Amer. through Mid. Amer. and the Andes to nw Argentina. Adj. Brazil.]
Páramos, open fields with scattered trees, savannas, second growth, wheat fields, 900–3000 m. n of the Orinoco, 1200–2000 m. s of it. Arboreal but descends to the ground for seeds. Shy and usually alone. Sometimes congregates in flocks of about 100 high on fruiting trees. Call: an owl-like "hoo." Nest, a frail flat structure.

## SCALY-NAPED PIGEON
*Columba squamosa*
PALOMA ISLEÑA

15″ (38 cm.). Dark bluish gray; head, neck and upper breast dull vinous, feathers on sides and back of neck metallic purple edged maroon red. Bill yellow with red base; conspicuous bare orbital area red. Los Frailes Is., Los Testigos. [Curaçao, Bonaire, formerly Aruba.]
Arid woodland to 100 m. Secretive, inconspicuous. Alone or in small groups. Perches in the treetops. Feeds on seeds, snails. Call: very loud frequently repeated cooing, "coo-róo-coo." Nests in holes and crevices on rock ledges.

## SCALED PIGEON
*Columba speciosa*
PALOMA GUACOA

Pl. 7
12″ (30 cm.). No gray in plumage, *scaled appearance* distinctive at close quarters. Top of head, wing coverts, inner remiges and lower back vinous chestnut. Primaries dusky brown, tail black. Feathers of neck and upper breast with a white subterminal spot and metallic purple black fringe, those of mantle coppery gold with a metallic greenish black fringe. Lower breast buffy, belly whitish with dull purplish edges to the feathers giving a scaled appearance; under tail coverts white. Orbital skin dark red, bill bright red. ♀: much duller than ♂, back brown, feathers edged black with little or no metallic reflections.
Tropical and subtropical zones. Zulia, Táchira and Lara e through Carabobo to Sucre and Monagas; n Bolívar; n Amazonas s to the Río Ventuari. [S Mexico to w Ecuador, Bolivia and n Argentina.]
Rain forest edge, open forest, savannas with scattered trees, second growth to 1400 m. n of the Orinoco, to 950 m. s of it. Perches alone on the treetops. In small groups or flocks over 100. Feeds on fruits. Call: harsh, very low, raw-voiced "cooo" heard at considerable distance, like distant cattle; one local name is Paloma tora (bull pigeon). Nest a frail, cup-shaped platform of twigs.

## BARE-EYED PIGEON
*Columba corensis*
PALOMA ALA BLANCA

Pl. 7
13″ (33 cm.). *A conspicuous white patch in wing.* Head, neck and underparts light vinous pink, becoming whitish on lower belly and under tail coverts. Feathers on back and sides of neck silvery, edged

blackish; feathers of upper mantle bronzy pink edged black. Upper back and lesser wing coverts brown; lower back and tail light gray; greater wing coverts broadly edged white, forming a broad white line along closed wing, and a broad band across wing in flight. Large, bare orbital patch smooth and blue near eye, rough and reddish brown on outer portion. Bill flesh; legs dark red.

Tropical zone. Falcón, Lara, ne Guárico, central Anzoátegui and in Monagas; Margarita I. [Ne Colombia. Aruba, Curaçao, Bonaire.]

Deciduous forest, xerophytic areas, thorny scrub, cacti, to 400 m. In treetops. Alone or in pairs; flocks of over 500. Flaps wings noisily when flushed. Feeds on fruits, seeds. Call: has been transcribed as "roo-oo-cóoo" and "coooo, chuck-chuck, chooo." Nest, a frail transparent platform of twigs.

## PALE-VENTED PIGEON
*Columba cayennensis*
PALOMA COLORADA

Pl. 7

13″ (33 cm.). Head gray, crown and nape metallic bronzy green, throat white. Hindneck, upper back and wing coverts vinous brown with a strong purple gloss; lower back gray; tail grayish brown. Foreneck and breast paler than back without purple gloss, rest of underparts gray. Orbital skin red; bill black. ♀: much duller than ♂.

Tropical zone. N of the Orinoco (*pallidicrissa*); s of the Orinoco (*cayennensis*). [S Mexico to Uruguay and n Argentina. Trinidad and Tobago.]

Found in a variety of habitats including mangroves but not in rain forest, to 800 m. n of the Orinoco, to 1300 m. s of it. Gregarious, wary, inconspicuous. Alone, in groups, or flocks of over 500. Wings clap when flushed. Call: a mournful, owl-like hooting "kuk-tu-coooo." Nest a flimsy platform of twigs in trees and palms.

## RUDDY PIGEON
*Columba subvinacea*
PALOMA MORADA

Pl. 7

12″ (30 cm.). Mainly purplish brown, upper mantle shot with metallic violet;

back wings and tail bronzy brown. Under wing coverts dull cinnamon. Bill black, legs dark red.

Tropical and subtropical zones. Zulia, Táchira, Barinas, Mérida, Lara and Carabobo e to Miranda (*zuliae*). Sucre (*peninsularis*). S of the Orinoco in Amazonas, Bolívar and Delta Amacuro (*purpureotincta*). [Costa Rica to w Ecuador and e of the Andes to n Bolivia and s Brazil.]

Rain and cloud forest, clearings, second growth, to 2200 m. n of the Orinoco, to 1100 m. s of it. Woodland edge. In pairs or bands up to 15, not shy. Inconspicuous, in leafy middle heights to treetops. Sometimes on the ground. Call: harsh, strongly accented series of "hoos" from near treetops.

## PLUMBEOUS PIGEON
*Columba plumbea*
PALOMA PLOMIZA

13″ (33 cm.). Very similar to Ruddy Pigeon but slightly larger, upper mantle pinker without any metallic violet reflections. Back duller, tinged olivaceous, underparts lighter, pinker, somewhat tinged gray. Throat buffy, under wing coverts brown. Bill black, legs dark red.

Tropical and subtropical zone. Sierra de Perijá, Zulia; w and central Mérida (*bogotensis*). Río Cuyuni, s Bolívar; s Amazonas (*wallacei*). [The Guianas, Colombia, e and w Ecuador, to Bolivia, se Brazil and possibly ne Argentina.]

Rain and cloud forests, second growth, 1200–1900 m. n of the Orinoco, 200–300 m. s of it. Usually solitary. Feeds on fruits and seeds in the forest canopy. Very difficult to see among the leaves as they remain silent and motionless when alarmed. Cooing is heard in the morning and in the afternoon.

## EARED DOVE
*Zenaida auriculata*
PALOMA SABANERA

Pl. 7

9″ (23 cm.) (or 11″ [28 cm.], a). Tail graduated, pointed. Top of head gray, forehead, sides of head and breast pinkish cinnamon. Two black marks at side of head; sides of neck metallic purple with gold and pink reflections. Upper-

parts olive brown, inner remiges spotted with black. Flanks and under wing coverts light blue gray. Central tail feathers like back, next pair gray with a dark median bar, remainder similar but broadly tipped rusty buff.
Tropical zone. Coastal Falcón (*vinaceorufa*). The rest of Venezuela (except areas occupied by other races) and not recorded from Sucre, s Bolívar or Amazonas; found on La Tortuga, Margarita and Los Testigos Is. (*stenura*). Subtropical zone in the Andes of Táchira, Mérida and Trujillo (*pentheria,* a). [Generally distributed s to Tierra del Fuego. S Lesser Antilles. Aruba to Trinidad and Tobago.]
Rain and cloud forest edge, deciduous and gallery forest edge, llanos, xerophytic areas, to 3000 m.; at the highest altitudes in artificially cleared fields and cultivated areas. Gregarious, often on the ground, in pairs or small groups. In the e llanos very large flocks form in Mar. Feeds on grains, seeds. Constructs a flimsy nest of sticks in low trees and bushes.

## COMMON GROUND-DOVE
*Columbina passerina*
TORTOLITA GRISÁCEA

Pl. 7
6″ (15 cm.). Forehead, sides of head and the underparts pinkish, feathers of breast and sides of neck with dark centers giving a scaled appearance. Belly pinkish fading to white on under tail coverts. Above grayish brown, wings with conspicuous purple black spots. Under wing coverts and primaries bright rufous, latter tipped black. Tail short, rounded, black outer feather tipped white. Bill pinkish with black tip, (or all black, a).
Tropical zone. Generally distributed (*albivitta*). Extreme sw Amazonas along the Río Negro (*griseola,* a). La Tortuga, La Orchila, Los Roques, La Blanquilla and Los Hermanos Is. (*tortugensis*). [S US to Ecuador and e Brazil, Aruba to Trinidad.]
Open terrain, second growth, clearings, scrub, scattered trees, suburban areas, savannas, gallery forest edge, llanos, to 1600 m. n of the Orinoco, to 500 m. s of it. Not shy, feeds on the ground in pairs or flocks up to 40 or more. Call: soft,

repeated, monotonous "coo-coo-coo." Nest of small sticks and grass placed in low bushes and on the ground.
Note: Birds listed under *Columbigallina* in Lista Av. Venez. are here included in *Columbina*.

## PLAIN-BREASTED GROUND-DOVE
*Columbina minuta*
TORTOLITA SABANERA

Pl. 7
6″ (15 cm.). Best distinguished from Common Ground-Dove by the plain pinkish breast and neck without the dark centers which give the latter its scaled appearance. Bill grayish or brown. ♀ has underparts grayish olive with white throat and belly, and less rufous in wing.
Tropical zone. S of the Orinoco in Bolívar and Amazonas; occasional n of the Orinoco where recorded from Zulia and Aragua, and in Barinas, Apure and Delta Amacuro (*minuta*). [Spottily distributed from s Mexico to n Colombia and the Guianas to w Peru, Bolivia and central Argentina. Trinidad.]
Rain forest edge, second growth, deciduous forest, savannas with scattered low bushes, gallery forest, to 850 m. n of the Orinoco, to 500 m. s of it. Alone or in pairs, groups up to 15. Mostly on low bushes, but feeds on the ground. Call: insistent, repeated, low cooing, "woo-ahk, woo-ahk, woo-ahk." Nests of grass placed on the ground, or in low bushes.

## RUDDY GROUND-DOVE
*Columbina talpacoti*
TORTOLITA ROJIZA

Pl. 7
6.5″ (16.5 cm.). Forehead pale gray darkening on crown. Upperparts cinnamon; underparts pinkish cinnamon, under tail coverts chestnut. Inner remiges like back with black spots and bars, primaries black, chestnut on inner web tipped black (or primaries brownish black, sometimes tinged rufous on inner web, a). Outer under wing coverts chestnut, inner ones black (or all black, a). ♀: much duller than ♂, mantle olivaceous brown, underparts much paler, brownish gray, tinged pinkish. Central tail feathers like back, outer ones black, tipped chestnut.

Tropical, occasionally subtropical zone. N of the Orinoco including Margarita and Patos Is.; Río Meta, Apure; Amazonas generally; n Bolívar; Delta Amacuro (*rufipennis*). The se corner of Bolívar (*talpacoti, a*). [S Mexico to nw Peru, Bolivia, central Argentina and Chile.]

Rain and cloud forest edge, second growth, gallery forest, grassy savannas with scattered trees, llanos, suburban areas, pastures, scrub, to 1600 m. n of the Orinoco, to 900 m. s of it. In pairs or flocks up to 50. Feeds on the ground on vegetable matter, perches in low bushes. Call: single, soft, repeated, "hoo-hoo-hoo" with a rising inflection.

## BLUE GROUND-DOVE

*Claravis pretiosa*
PALOMITA AZUL

Pl. 7

8.5" (22 cm.). Above blue gray, below pale gray, lightest on throat, darkest on under tail coverts. Upper wing coverts and scapulars spotted with black, inner remiges with 2 purple black bars. Central tail feathers like back, rest black. ♀: quite different. Mainly olive or tawny brown, abdomen pale gray. Rump and central tail feathers rufous, outer tail feathers black. Wing coverts spotted purple chestnut, inner remiges barred purple chestnut, bars narrowly edged white posteriorly.

Tropical zone throughout except in extreme S. [Mexico to nw Peru, Bolivia and n Argentina. Trinidad.]

Semi-open rain forests, second growth, deciduous forest, along woodland streams to 1000 m. Shy, mostly arboreal, to the treetops. Alone or in pairs or flocks up to 100. Forages on the ground. Call: single, soft, deep- repeated "coooo-oó" with a rising inflection.

## MAROON-CHESTED GROUND-DOVE

*Claravis mondetoura*
PALOMITA PECHIRROJA

Pl. 7

8.5" (22 cm.). Forehead, throat and sides of head white, *forehead* and *breast* dark *reddish purple*, abdomen gray fading to white on belly and under tail coverts. Upperparts, wings and tail dark gray, wings with 3 broad purple bars, edged white posteriorly. Outer tail feathers mostly white, conspicuous in flight. ♀: quite different. Olive brown above, face and rump cinnamon; central tail feathers rufous brown, outer ones black tipped buff, wings marked as in ♂. Below buffy, grayish on breast, whitish on throat and belly.

Subtropical zone. Very local in the Sierra de Perijá, Zulia, sw Táchira, nw Mérida, w Aragua and the Dist. Federal (*mondetoura*). [Mexico to w Panama. Colombia e of the Andes to Bolivia.]

Cloud forests, in open vegetation at highest altitudes, 1300–2600 m. Dense undergrowth, bamboo thickets. Solitary, terrestrial. Difficult to see. Call: "coo-ah, coo-ah," with a rising inflection similar to the Blue Ground-Dove.

## SCALED DOVE

*Scardafella squammata*
PALOMITA MARAQUITA

Pl. 7

8.5" (22 cm.). Tail long, pointed, body feathers conspicuously edged black giving a *scaled appearance*. Above sandy brown, below white, tinged pink on breast, feathers broadly edged with a crescentine black border. Outer web of outer wing coverts white forming a band, primaries black, inner webs rufous. Tail graduated, central feathers like back, outer ones black, broadly tipped white.

Tropical zone. N of the Orinoco in semi-arid regions, including Margarita I., but not recorded from Táchira or Trujillo; Río Meta, Apure; s of the Orinoco only along the s bank of the Orinoco (*ridgwayi*). [Ne Colombia, French Guiana, e Brazil to n Argentina.]

Scrub, xerophytic areas, semi-arid woodland edge, savannas with scattered trees, second growth, pastures, suburban areas, to 1100 m. n of the Orinoco, to 100 m. s of it. Not shy. Feeds on the ground, perches in the lower branches. Pairs or flocks up to 10. The wings make a rattling sound as it flies. The local names, *Maraquita* and *Maraquera,* refer to this sound. Call: "tooc-ᴜoo-coó."

## WHITE-TIPPED DOVE
*Leptotila verreauxi*
PALOMA TURCA

Pl. 7
12" (30 cm.). Head pale pinkish, palest on forehead shading to slightly iridescent light purplish brown on crown; upperparts grayish olive brown, hindneck and upper mantle iridescent, metallic violet green. Central tail feathers like back, outer tail feathers black, broadly tipped white, tail wedge-shaped. Wing lining chestnut. *No spots on wings.* Orbital skin blue.
Tropical and subtropical zones. N of the Orinoco including Margarita, Los Testigos and Patos Is.; s of the Orinoco in e Bolívar from the Río Cuyuni to the Brazilian border; n Amazonas (*verreauxi*). [S Texas to w Peru, Brazil, Uruguay and Argentina. Aruba to Trinidad and Tobago.]
Found in every kind of habitat, to 3000 m. n of the Orinoco, to 1200 m. s of it. Not shy. Alone or in pairs, and in flocks of over 50 near water holes. Perches in low trees. Forages on the ground for vegetable matter. Call: single, deep, hollow, inquiring "cooo-hooo," repeated at intervals. Nest a shallow platform of sticks in thick shrubbery.

## GRAY-FRONTED DOVE
*Leptotila rufaxilla*
PALOMA PIPA

Pl. 7
11" (28 cm.). Forehead grayish white, *crown blue gray,* hindneck and upper mantle iridescent, metallic purple violet (or with almost no metallic reflections, a). Back and wings dark olive brown, *no spots on wings.* Underparts pale pinkish vinous (or vinous buff, a), throat and center of belly and under tail coverts white. Central tail feathers like back, outer ones blackish tipped white, tail wedge-shaped. Orbital skin red. ♀: duller than ♂, iridescent parts of plumage show more green and little purple.
Tropical zone. Zulia, Táchira, Mérida, Barinas and Apure (*pallidipectus*, a). S of the Orinoco in Amazonas, Bolívar and Delta Amacuro, rare n of the Orinoco where known from Aricagua, Distr. Federal; Guanoco, s Sucre

(*dubusi*). Paria Pen., Sucre (*hellmayri*). Se Bolívar at Cerro Roraima (*rufaxilla*). [E Colombia, the Guianas to Bolivia, Paraguay, ne Argentina and Uruguay.]
Found in all types of habitats, but not in arid areas to 550 m. n of the Orinoco, to 1450 m. s of it. Alone or in pairs. Feeds on the ground. More often heard than seen. Sits cooing in thickets, disappears silently when approached. Call: "coo-ooo-oo," middle note higher. Nest a loose structure of small twigs, low in trees and bushes.

[QUAIL-DOVES ARE PLUMP, long-legged short-tailed, forest-inhabiting, terrestrial birds with characteristic *stripes on the sides of the head.*]

## RUDDY QUAIL-DOVE
*Geotrygon montana*
PALOMA PERDIZ CARA ROJA

Pl. 7
9" (23 cm.). Upperparts, wings and tail rufous chestnut, back strongly glossed with purple. Sides of head below eye pinkish white with two purplish chestnut stripes. Throat and foreneck buffy white becoming vinaceous buff on breast and buff on abdomen. Wing lining cinnamon rufous. ♀: forehead and sides of head dull cinnamon; upperparts and central tail feathers brownish olive glossed with bronzy green, outer tail feathers dusky olive brown. Throat and foreneck white, breast cinnamon, belly and under tail coverts cinnamon buff, sides olive brown, center of belly buffy white.
Tropical and subtropical zones. Locally in w Zulia, Táchira, westernmost Apure, Mérida, Lara, ne Carabobo to e Distr. Federal; s of the Orinoco in Bolívar and Amazonas (*montana*). [Mexico to Colombia, the Guianas, Bolivia, Paraguay and ne Argentina. Greater and Lesser Antilles. Trinidad.]
Rain and cloud forests to 1900 m. Second growth, ravines, wooded slopes. Mostly terrestrial, in dense undergrowth alone or in pairs; silent, shy, inconspicuous. Usually seen briefly only when flushed from the ground. Forages for seeds, fruits on forest floor; perches low. Call: velvety, low, resonant, long "cooooo." Nest, a frail platform of sticks placed low on brush, stumps, vines. Eggs creamy buff.

## VIOLACEOUS QUAIL-DOVE
*Geotrygon violacea*
PALOMA PERDIZ VIOLACEA

Pl. 7
9" (23 cm.). Forehead white, sides of head buffy pink with a faint pale stripe below eye, a purple gold patch on nape. Hindneck and back metallic purple becoming olive on lower back, the feathers edged purple, rump, upper tail coverts reddish purple. Tail and primaries chestnut. Throat white, foreneck and breast vinaceous, rest of underparts white. ♀: much duller, the back strongly olivaceous glossed with bronze green, the breast grayer, less vinaceous, patch on nape shining bronzy green.
Upper tropical and subtropical zones. Very local, recorded from the Sierra de Perijá, Zulia, s Táchira, Mérida (La Azulita), Lara (Cerro El Cogollal), Sucre (Cristóbal Colón) and ne Bolívar (Nuria) (*albiventer*). [Nicaragua to n and e Colombia, Surinam (once) to e Brazil, ne Argentina and in n Bolivia.]
Rain forest, dense second growth, 450–1400 m. n of the Orinoco, 450–500 m. s of it. Wooded ravines. Partly terrestrial but also in the middle branches. Call: a double "oo-oo." Places nests on bushes, eggs light buff.

## LINED QUAIL-DOVE
*Geotrygon linearis*
PALOMA PERDIZ ROJIZA

Pl. 7
11" (28 cm.). Forehead rufous, vinous on crown, crown bordered from behind eye by a broad buffy blue gray band which extends to nape, a black stripe across lower part of face. Back, wings and tail brown, back with a bluish purple (or bronze green, a) sheen. Throat white, breast pale buff with a pinkish wash, tawny buff on flanks, belly and under tail coverts.
Subtropical zone. W and n central mountains from Zulia and Táchira through Mérida and Lara, Falcón and Yaracuy to Miranda (*linearis*). Sucre and Monagas (*trinitatis, a*). [Mexico to w Panama. N and e Colombia. Trinidad, Tobago.]
Cloud forests, second growth, 400–2500 m.; at lowest altitudes found only in steep, humid terrain covered by dense undergrowth. Solitary, very shy, stays on or near the ground. Feeds on seeds. Call: a series of coos, morning and evening. Responds to an imitation of its call but is easily alarmed as it approaches, walking on the forest floor. Nest of twigs, on lower to middle branches.

# PSITTACIFORMES

# MACAWS, PARROTS, PARAKEETS: Psittacidae

## GUACAMAYOS, LOROS, COTORRAS, PERICOS

Most parrots are green and noisy. They vary in size from the very large, gaudily colored macaws to the tiny parrotlets, smaller than a sparrow.

Parrots live in forest or wooded savanna, eat nuts, seeds and fruits and nest in holes in trees where they lay round, white eggs. They are found from the lowlands to the temperate zone of the Andes. The sexes are usually similar. Parrots move about in flocks made up of pairs of birds.

Most macaws are very large birds with long, graduated, pointed tails. The cheeks are bare with some narrow lines of bristly feathers. The larger species make their presence known by their earsplitting, raucous calls.

## BLUE-AND-YELLOW MACAW
*Ara ararauna*
GUACAMAYO AZUL Y AMARILLO

Pl. 8
33" (84 cm.). Above bright blue, below bright yellow

Locally in the tropical zone. E Monagas; middle Delta Amacuro; Amazonas (Cerro Yapacana; headwaters of the Río Siapa at the Brazilian border). [E Panama, Colombia, w Ecuador, the Guianas to Bolivia. Paraguay, se Brazil and ne Argentina. Trinidad.]

Often near rivers in rain forest, savannas with scattered trees and palms, llanos, gallery forest, sea level to 500 m. Flocks up to 25.

## MILITARY MACAW
*Ara militaris*
GUACAMAYO VERDE

Pl. 8
28″ (71 cm.). Mainly green. Forehead scarlet; lower back, rump, and upper tail coverts blue; 4 central tail feathers red, distally blue, rest mostly blue; remiges and primary coverts blue. Under surface of wings and tail golden olive.
Tropical zone. Nw Zulia at La Sierra, Sierra de Perijá; Distr. Federal (San José de los Caracas) (*militaris*). [Mexico. Colombia, e Ecuador, nw and central Peru; e Bolivia; nw Argentina.]
Rain forest in hilly areas to about 600 m. Open, sometimes dry woodland. Treetops; cliffs.

## SCARLET MACAW
*Ara macao*
GUACAMAYO BANDERA

Pl. 8
33″ (84 cm.). Mostly scarlet. Lower back, rump and upper tail coverts light blue, central tail feathers scarlet, rest tipped blue increasingly so to outer feathers which are almost all blue. Median and greater wing coverts and scapulars *yellow*, tipped green. Under tail coverts pale blue.
Locally in tropical zone. E and w Apure; ne Monagas; sw Sucre; nw and s central Bolívar; central and s Amazonas. [Mexico to Colombia, e Ecuador, Amazonian Brazil, Bolivia. Trinidad.]
Rain forest, scrubby growth, open woodland, deciduous forest, llanos, near rivers, to 450 m. Flocks of several dozen. Feed high in trees.

## RED-AND-GREEN MACAW
*Ara chloroptera*
GUACAMAYO ROJO

Pl. 8
35″ (89 cm.). Darker red than the Scarlet Macaw with *no yellow on wings,* greater wing coverts blue. Central tail feathers red, tipped blue. Underside of wings and tail red; under tail coverts blue.
Tropical zone. Locally distributed probably throughout, but not recorded from the llanos of Portuguesa to Monagas or in Sucre. [E Panama, Colombia, the Guianas to n and e Bolivia, n Argentina.]
Rain forest, forest edge, to 450 m. n of the Orinoco, to about 1400 m. s of it. Small flocks.

## CHESTNUT-FRONTED MACAW
*Ara severa*
MARACANÁ

Pl. 8
20″ (51 cm.). Mainly green. Forehead chestnut, crown bluish green. Primaries and primary coverts blue, bend of wing and outer under wing coverts red. Tail dull red basally, edged green near base, distal part bluish green; underside of wings and tail dull golden red.
Tropical zone. Zulia, Táchira, w Apure, Mérida, w Barinas, and in Carabobo and Aragua; nw Bolívar; Amazonas along the Orinoco (*severa*). [E Panama, Colombia, the Guianas s to n and e Bolivia.]
Forested regions near rivers to 350 m. Gallery forest, llanos, pastures. In pairs or small groups. Roosts and often nests in palm trees. Feeds in the treetops. Call: higher-pitched than that of the larger macaws, with a complaining tone.

## RED-BELLIED MACAW
*Ara manilata*
GUACAMAYO BARRIGA ROJA

Pl. 8
18″ (46 cm.). Mainly green. Feathers of throat and breast dull pale bluish, edged green; center of abdomen dull red. Forecrown and cheeks blue. Greater under wing coverts golden olive. Tail green. Bare part of cheeks lemon yellow.
Tropical zone. Recorded from extreme e Anzoátegui, ne Monagas and in Ciudad Bolívar and in se Bolívar on Cerros Roraima and Auyan-tepui. [E Colombia, the Guianas to e Peru, central and e Brazil. Trinidad.]
Forested rivers, Moriche swamps, sea level to 500 m. Sometimes in flocks of over 100. Very similar to the larger *Ara-*

*tingas.* Feeds on *Mauritia* palm fruits. When perched very difficult to see. Call: loud but less raucous than that of other parrots.

## RED-SHOULDERED MACAW

*Ara nobilis*
GUACAMAYO ENANO

Pl. 8

14" (35 cm.). *Very small* for a *macaw,* the only one with *green primaries.* Mainly green. Forehead and supraocular region blue. Shoulders, bend of wing and outer under wing coverts scarlet. Tail green. Underside of tail and wings golden olive. Bare area of cheeks less extensive than in other macaws.

Extreme e Monagas (Maturín); Delta Amacuro (Capure); Bolívar along the lower Río Caura and in the Gran Sabana (*nobilis*). [Guyana, Surinam, ne and central to se Brazil.]

Forested areas, savannas with scattered trees and Moriche swamps, second growth, at about 100 m. n of the Orinoco, 1400 m. s of it. Frequently large noisy flocks.

[*Aratingas* DIFFER FROM MOST MACAWS in having feathered cheeks, but like them have long, pointed tails. Almost all are considerably smaller.]

## BLUE-CROWNED PARAKEET

*Aratinga acuticaudata*
CARAPAICO

Pl. 9

14" (35 cm.). Forecrown blue, rest of plumage green, outer tail feathers with *red on inner web.*

Tropical zone. From Zulia, Lara and Falcón e to Anzoátegui, Guárico and Monagas, on the Río Meta in sw Apure, and along the Orinoco in n Bolívar (*haemorrhous*). Margarita I. (*neoxena*). [Ne Colombia, e and s Brazil to Bolivia and central Argentina.]

All kinds of terrain except rain forest. 100–600 m. n of the Orinoco at 100 m. s of it. Pairs, flocks up to 200. Call: a loud scream rapidly repeated.

## SCARLET-FRONTED PARAKEET

*Aratinga wagleri*
CHACARACO

Pl. 9

13" (33 cm.). Green; *forehead,* tibia and a few spots at sides of neck *red.* Tail green.

Subtropical zone. Sierra de Perijá, Zulia, the Andes of w Barinas, Trujillo and central and s Lara (Cubiro) (*wagleri*). W Lara (El Cerrón) and the coastal Cordilleras from Yaracuy to the Paria Pen., Sucre and n Monagas (*transilis*). [Colombia to e and w Peru.]

Cloud forest, second growth, 800–2000 m. but sometimes descends to sea level in humid plantations with fruiting trees and grain. Flocks of 20–200 which maintain a loud, screechy chatter. Nests in inaccessible holes in rocky precipices.

## WHITE-EYED PARAKEET

*Aratinga leucophthalmus*
PERICO OJO BLANCO

Pl. 9

14" (35 cm.). Green; spots on cheeks and sides of neck red, forehead green. Tail green. Lesser under wing coverts *red,* greater ones *yellow.*

Tropical zone. N central Anzoátegui, n Monagas, Delta Amacuro, extreme ne Bolívar and along the lower Río Paragua (*leucophthalmus*). [The Guianas; e Colombia to Uruguay and Argentina. Trinidad.]

Rain forest, mangroves, savannas, Moriche swamps at 100 m. n of the Orinoco, 200–500 m. s of it. Flocks of 10 to 20. Feeds on fruits and *Erythrina* flowers. Call: higher pitched than that of the Blue-crowned Parakeet; also has a distinctive "che-check" note.

## SUN PARAKEET

*Aratinga solstitialis*
PERICO DORADO

Pl. 9

13" (33 cm.). Mainly yellow; sides of head, belly and flanks orange red, under tail coverts yellowish olive. Greater upper wing coverts green irregularly tipped yellow, primary coverts and remiges dark blue, primaries edged green on basal portion, under wing coverts

yellow and orange. Tail olive, tipped blue; outer remiges shaded with blue.
Tropical zone. Se Bolívar (Cerro Roraima) (*solstitialis*). [The Guianas, e Brazil from Roraima s.]
In small flocks in savannas, 1200 m. Nests in holes in *Mauritia* palm trees.

## BROWN-THROATED PARAKEET

*Aratinga pertinax*
PERICO CARA SUCIA

Pl. 9
10″ (25 cm.). Mainly green, paler and quite yellowish on lower breast and belly. Frontal band whitish (or forehead narrowly dark brown, no pale frontal band, a), crown blue. Sides of head dull, pale, or dark brown with a narrow yellow eye ring (or no eye ring, a; or a broad eye ring, b; or with eye ring and cheeks dull yellow, c). Throat and upper breast dull brown, lower breast and belly yellowish green, center of abdomen yellow (or without yellow patch, a). Wing coverts and inner remiges green, outer remiges dark blue, edged green. Tail green, bluish near tip.
Tropical zone. Nw Zulia and Falcón (*aeruginosa*, a). Elsewhere except areas occupied by other races (*venezuelae*). The delta region in extreme se Monagas and in Delta Amacuro (*surinama*, c). Extreme se Bolívar (*chrysophrys*). Margarita I. (*margaritensis*, b). Tortuga I. (*tortugensis*, b). [W Panama. N Colombia, the Guianas, n Amazonian Brazil. Aruba, Curaçao, Bonaire.] It is possible that along the upper Orinoco *A. p. lehmanni* is found, for it occurs at Maipures, just across the river in Colombia.
Found in a wide variety of wooded areas and in gardens, cactus thickets, and corn fields to 1000 m. n of the Orinoco and 1600 m. s of it. The most common parakeet in the lowlands. Tame. Flocks of 4–20; or more. Feeds on fruits, seeds, flowers. Call: loud, clear, sharp, metallic chattering. Nests in holes in arboreal termite nests.

[*Pyrrhuras* ARE RATHER SMALL parakeets with pointed tails, distinguishable from other parakeets by having the breast feathers brownish or olive with pale edges, giving a barred appearance to the breast.]

## BLOOD-EARED PARAKEET

*Pyrrhura hoematotis*
PERICO COLA ROJA

Pl. 9
10″ (25 cm.). Mainly green. Forehead brown, the feathers edged bluish, hindcrown green, the feathers tipped yellowish buff; cheeks green, ear coverts red; an interrupted collar on sides of neck brown with pale edges (or no interrupted collar, sides of neck green, a). Throat and upper breast olive, the feathers with narrow pale edges; belly green with a small, dull red patch in center. Primary coverts and primaries blue, tipped black. Tail dull red narrowly tipped olive green, below coppery red. Bend of wing bluish; lesser under wing coverts green, rest blackish, tinged olive.
Subtropical zone. Se Lara at Cubiro (*immarginata*, a). The coastal Cordillera from Aragua to Miranda (*hoematotis*).
Cloud forest, clearings and open areas with low, scattered trees, 1200–2000 m. Treetops; flocks of 10–100.

## MAROON-FACED PARAKEET

*Pyrrhura leucotis*
PERICO PINTADO

Pl. 9
8″ (20 cm.). Narrow frontlet and sides of head maroon, forecrown and nape blue, hindcrown dark brown, ear coverts whitish or pale brownish. Breast green, the feathers edged with pale, *straight bars*. Nuchal collar blue. Back and inner remiges green, center of lower back maroon red; belly green, extensively maroon red in center. Shoulders red, primaries and primary coverts blue, lesser under wing coverts green, rest blackish with an olive tinge. Tail maroon, the feathers edged green on outer web basally.
Tropical and lower subtropical zones. The n Cordilleras from Yaracuy to Miranda (*emma*). The n Cordilleras from Anzoátegui to Sucre and Monagas (*auricularis*). [E Brazil from Ceará to São Paulo.]
Rain and cloud forest, to 1700 m. Flocks of 15–20 in treetops.

## PAINTED PARAKEET
*Pyrrhura picta*
PERICO CABECIRROSADO

Pl. 9
9″ (23 cm.). Very like Maroon-faced Parakeet but at once distinguishable by having the *bars* on the breast *V- or U-shaped* instead of straight, and the basal part of the breast feathers blackish brown instead of green, the pale edges also are much more prominent.
Tropical and subtropical zones. The Perijá Mts., Zulia (*pantchenkoi*). Amazonas; generally in Bolívar; s Delta Amacuro (*picta*). [N Colombia, the Guianas, e Peru, n Bolivia n, sw and e Brazil.]
Rain and cloud forest, sea level to 1800 m. Flocks in treetops along rivers. Call: a single note, "eek."

## FIERY-SHOULDERED PARAKEET
*Pyrrhura egregia*
PERICO COLIMORADO

Pl. 9
10″ (25 cm.). Mainly green. Narrow frontlet maroon, crown mixed dark brown and green, ear coverts green, basally maroon, breast feathers narrowly edged pinkish buff; center of abdomen and tail maroon. Shoulder scarlet, bend of wing orange yellow, under wing coverts yellow suffused with scarlet and mixed with green.
Tropical and subtropical zones. Vicinity of Cerro Roraima (*egregia*). The Gran Sabana on the tepuis except Roraima (*obscura*). [Guyana.]
Forest on the slopes of the tepuis, 700–1800 m. Usually in pairs, also small groups. Treetops.

## MAROON-TAILED PARAKEET
*Pyrrhura melanura*
PERICO COLA NEGRA

10″ (25 cm.). Very like Fiery-shouldered Parakeet, but under wing coverts green instead of yellow and no maroon patch on abdomen. Tail dark maroon.
Tropical zone. S central Bolívar along the upper Río Paragua; Amazonas s of the Río Ventuari (*melanura*). [Colombia to Peru and w Brazil.]
Rain forest, 150–300 m.

## ROSE-HEADED PARAKEET
*Pyrrhura rhodocephala*
PERICO CABECIRROJO

Pl. 9
10″ (25 cm.). *Rosy red crown* distinguishes it from all other species of the genus. Mostly green, feathers of breast with only faint pale edges. Ear coverts and center of belly maroon red. Primary coverts white. Tail light red.
Subtropical zone. The Andes from n Táchira, n Barinas and Mérida to n Trujillo.
Cloud forest, páramos, 800–3050 m. Second growth. A local name is *Perico Ronco* (Hoarse Parakeet).

## BARRED PARAKEET
*Bolborhynchus lineola*
PERICO BARRETEADO

Pl. 9
7″ (18 cm.). Olive green above, crown brighter and greener, *upper parts barred with black,* the bars widening toward tail coverts; feathers of rump and upper tail coverts with black tips; lesser upper wing coverts black, rest green, tipped black, forming 2 bars. Tail green, feathers black along shaft, central ones black on distal half. Below yellowish green with narrow black bars on sides. Tail pointed but short.
Subtropical zone. Locally in open country of the Andes in Táchira and Mérida (*tigrinus*). [Mexico to w Panama. Central and w Andes of Colombia. Central Peru.]
Open woodland, 900–1500 m. Clearings. Usually in small flocks, also flocks of 50 or more. Difficult to see in treetops. Flies very high. Call: a musical chatter.

[*Forpus* IS RECOGNIZABLE BY ITS MINUTE SIZE.]

## GREEN-RUMPED PARROTLET
*Forpus passerinus*
PERIQUITO

Pl. 9
5″ (13 cm.). Bright green, underparts paler. Greater upper and under wing coverts blue, rump bright emerald green. Bill whitish. ♀: like ♂ but forecrown yellowish and plumage generally duller.

Tropical, occasionally subtropical zone. N of the Orinoco from Zulia and Táchira to Sucre and Monagas; n Bolívar; Delta Amacuro (*viridissimus*). [E Colombia; the Guianas; n Amazonian Brazil. Curaçao. Trinidad.] All kinds of habitats except rain and thick forest, but including suburban areas, up to 1800 m. In pairs or flocks of 50 or more. Forages in shrubs and trees. Roosts in flocks. Feeds on fruits, grass and other seeds, flowers. Call: penetrating twitter. Nests in holes, often in arboreal termite nests.

### SPECTACLED PARROTLET

*Forpus conspicillatus*
PERIQUITO OJIAZUL

5″ (13 cm.). Green, breast and upper mantle tinged olivaceous; wing coverts and rump cobalt blue; ocular region bright greenish blue. ♀: green, rump and ocular region tinged blue.
Tropical zone. Along the Río Meta in Apure (*metae*). [E Panama, central and e Colombia.]
Llanos, gallery forest, 100 m. In small flocks, feeds on grass seeds. Nests in holes in trees.
Note: New record since publication of Lista Av. Venez.

### DUSKY-BILLED PARROTLET

*Forpus sclateri*
PERIQUITO OBSCURO

5″ (13 cm.). Dark green, darker than the other species. Rump, primary coverts and outer web of inner remiges blue. Mandible dusky. ♀: dark green above, forecrown and cheeks yellowish green in contrast, rump brighter green than back; below much paler and more yellowish than back. *Mandible dusky.*
Tropical zone. W Bolívar on the lower Río Caura (La Unión) and in the e on the Río Cuyuni (*eidos*). [Guyana and French Guiana; se Colombia to n Bolivia and Amazonian Brazil.]
Rain forest, 150–250 m.

### ORANGE-CHINNED PARAKEET

*Brotogeris jugularis*
CHURICA

Pl. 9
7.5″ (19 cm.). Green, top of head bluer (or slightly tinged brown, a), cheeks bluish, *chin spot bright orange. Inner wing coverts bronzy brown,* primary coverts deep blue, *Under wing coverts and axillaries bright yellow,* rest bluish green (or all under wing coverts bright yellow, a). Tail pointed, green, central feathers bluish.
Tropical zone. Zulia in the Perijá and Maracaibo region; n Táchira; w Mérida (*jugularis*). The coastal Cordillera in Yaracuy and Carabobo, and the llanos of Barinas, Apure, Portuguesa, Cojedes e and Guárico (*exsul,* a). [Mid. Amer., n Colombia.]
All sorts of forested areas except rain forest; llanos, semi-arid areas, along streams, towns, to 1000 m. Tame. In small flocks. Rapid flight, alternating wing beats with sails. Feeds on fruits, nectar, seeds. Harsh, rasping chatter while feeding. Very noisy when a flock takes flight.

### COBALT-WINGED PARAKEET

*Brotogeris cyanoptera*
PERIQUITO AZUL

8″ (20 cm.). Dark green, paler below, forecrown yellowish. *Chin spot orange.* Upper wing coverts olive green, *under wing coverts verditer blue,* primary coverts and primaries cobalt blue, latter edged green. Central tail feathers blue edged with green, remainder green, inner webs yellowish green. Tail pointed.
Tropical zone. N Amazonas s to the Río Negro (*cyanoptera*). [Se Colombia to w Amazonian Brazil and n Bolivia.]
Rain forest, 100–180 m. Treetops and upper parts of trees in small flocks.

### GOLDEN-WINGED PARAKEET

*Brotogeris chrysopterus*
PERIQUITO ALA DORADA

Pl. 9
7.5″ (19 cm.). Much like the Orange-chinned and Cobalt-winged Parakeets but forehead and *chin spot brown, primary coverts bright orange.* Under wing coverts verditer blue. Tail pointed, outer feathers olive on inner web.
Tropical zone. Sucre, Monagas and ne Bolívar (*chrysopterus*). [Guianas, e and central Amazonian Brazil.]
Cloud forest, to 1200 m. n of the Orinoco, to 950 m. s of it. Noisy flocks in the

treetops. Call: chil-chil-chil. Nests in holes in trees and in arboreal termite nests.

## TEPUI PARROTLET
*Nannopsittaca panychlora*
CHIRICA

Pl. 9
5.5″ (14 cm.). Tail short, square. Green, darker above; forehead, ocular region and under tail coverts yellowish green. Superficially like *Forpus* from which it differs by its much straighter and more slender bill, without a pronounced tooth.
Uppertropical and subtropical zones. N of the Orinoco only in Sucre (Cerro Papelón, Paria Pen.); Bolívar in the mountains of the Gran Sabana; Amazonas on Cerros Duida and Marahuaca). [W Guyana.]
Cloud forest, 750–950 m. n of the Orinoco, 750–1850 m. s of it. Noisy flocks, up to 100; fly very high and very fast above the treetops, ascend the talus slopes of the tepuis and cross the summits to descend precipitously on the other side and feed silently on fruiting trees. In the frequent fogs of their tepui habitat, they fly low, noisily skimming the treetops.

[*Touit* IS DISTINCTIVE FOR its small size and short, square, brightly colored tail.]

## LILAC-TAILED PARROTLET
*Touit batavica*
PERICO SIETE COLORES

Pl. 9
6″ (15 cm.). Forecrown and face yellowish green, hindcrown, ear coverts, sides of neck bright green; nape yellowish green, the feathers edged dusky giving a scaled appearance. Back black; wings mainly black with a conspicuous yellow green bar formed by wing coverts and tertials, outer edge of greater wing coverts vivid blue, bend of wing rosy red. Tail rosy violet, outer feathers reddish violet, black band near tip. Throat and belly bright green, breast powdery blue. Under wing coverts blue green.
Upper tropical and subtropical zones. The serranías of the n from Aragua to the Paria Pen., Sucre; ne Bolívar on the Río Cuyuni. [Guyana, Surinam. Trinidad.]

Cloud forest, 900–1700 m. Occasionally descends in humid localities to 400 m. Gregarious, flocks of 10–30, usually in the treetops. Feeds on flowers and fruits in the morning. Continually screams nasal calls when flying.

## SAPPHIRE-RUMPED PARROTLET
*Touit purpurata*
PERIQUITO RABADILLA PÚRPURA

Pl. 9
7″ (18 cm.). Mainly green, patch at sides of belly olive. Crown and scapulars dusky brown (or crown green, a). Center of lower back cobalt blue. Central tail feathers bright green, rest crimson, narrow terminal black (or green, ♀) band. Under wing coverts green.
Tropical zone. S Bolívar on the tepuis of the Gran Sabana, and along the upper Caura; central Amazonas on the extreme ne portion of Cerro Duida, 1200 m. (*purpurata*). Amazonas along the Orinoco from the Río Ventuari s and on Cerro Yapacana and the se portion of Cerro Duida, 100–250 m. (*viridiceps*, a). [The Guianas, se Colombia; e Ecuador, nw Brazil and s of the Amazon near Belém.]
Rain forest, low, open woodland at higher altitudes. Usually in small flocks.

## SCARLET-SHOULDERED PARROTLET
*Touit huetii*
PERIQUITO AZUL ALIRROJO

6″ (15 cm.). Mostly green, yellower on abdomen, under tail coverts mostly yellow. Forehead and front of face very dark blue. Bend of wing scarlet, greater wing coverts dark blue; under wing coverts, axillars and patch on sides of breast flame scarlet. Central tail feathers green, rest crimson with a narrow terminal black bar. ♀: like ♂ but outer tail feathers green, yellowish on inner web.
Tropical zone. Very local and recorded only from Maturín, Monagas; extreme nw Bolívar on the upper Río Parguaza; Amazonas along the Orinoco at San Fernando de Atabapo. [N Guyana; e Colombia (Macarena Mts.); e Ecuador; e Peru; e Brazil s of the Amazon in Pará. Trinidad.]

Rain forest, 100–200 m. Near rivers. Call: a high-pitched "witch-witch."

## RED-WINGED PARROTLET

*Touit dilectissima*
CHURIQUITA

Pl. 9
7″ (18 cm.). Mainly green, more yellowish below. Crown blue, lores and below eye scarlet, chin and throat yellow. Inner remiges green, secondaries mainly black, primaries black edged green, bend of wing scarlet, feathers tipped yellow, lesser wing coverts and primary coverts black, median and greater wing coverts scarlet tipped yellow, under wing coverts and patch at sides of breast golden yellow. Central tail feathers yellow at base, with a subterminal green band and broad, black tip, rest of tail feathers golden yellow, tipped black. ♀: similar but without scarlet wing coverts, and outer tail feathers greenish yellow, tipped black. Crown olive instead of blue.
Subtropical zone. Sierra de Perijá, Zulia; the Andes of central Mérida and sw Trujillo (*dilectissima*). [Costa Rica to nw Ecuador.]
Cloud forest border; old, open second growth, 1300–1600 m. Small, swift-flying flocks.

## BLACK-HEADED PARROT

*Pionites melanocephala*
PERICO CALZONCITO

Pl. 9, 23
10″ (25 cm.). *Crown and nape black,* spot before eye blue green; cheeks and throat yellow, nuchal collar cinnamon, thighs and under tail coverts orange, *breast and belly white* to buffy white. Back green; tail square, green.
Tropical zone. Se Sucre and generally s of the Orinoco in Delta Amacuro, Bolívar and Amazonas (*melanocephala*). [The Guianas, e Colombia to ne Peru, n Amazonian Brazil.]
Rain forest to 1100 m. Loose, noisy flocks in the upper branches and treetops, lower at forest edge. Loud, musical call, also a whistled "toot."

## CAICA PARROT

*Pionopsitta caica*
PERICO CABECINEGRO

Pl. 9
9″ (23 cm.). *Head black,* collar on hindneck tawny orange, upper breast tawny olive, back and rest of underparts bright green. Primary coverts dark cobalt blue, outer primaries black, edged green. Tail green, inner webs of outer tail feathers yellow, tipped blue.
Tropical zone. Bolívar along the lower Río Caura, upper Río Cuyuni and in the Gran Sabana. [The Guianas; ne Brazil.] Small flocks in rain forest, 50–1100 m.

## ORANGE-CHEEKED PARROT

*Pionopsitta barrabandi*
PERICO CACHETE AMARILLO

Pl. 9
10″ (25 cm.). Head black, *cheeks* and shoulders *orange,* bend of wing and under wing coverts scarlet. Breast olive yellow; back and belly bright green. Primaries black; tail square, green, tipped blue, outer feathers with yellow inner webs.
Tropical zone. S Amazonas; s central Bolívar (*barrabandi*). [Se Colombia to e Peru and w Amazonian Brazil.]
Rain forest, 150–300 m.

## SAFFRON-HEADED PARROT

*Pionopsitta pyrilia*
PERICO CABECIDORADO

Pl. 9
9.5″ (24 cm.). *Head* and shoulders *yellow,* ocular region tinged orange. Breast olive yellow; back and belly bright green. Bend of wing, axillaries and under wing coverts scarlet. Tail square, green, tipped blue, inner webs of outer feathers yellow, tipped dark blue.
Tropical and subtropical zones. Sierra de Perijá, Zulia, Táchira, Mérida, w Lara. [E Panama; n Colombia.]
Rain and cloud forests, 150–1650 m.

## RUSTY-FACED PARROT

*Hapalopsittaca amazonina*
PERICO MULTICOLOR

Pl. 9
9″ (23 cm.). Front of head vermilion (or brownish red, a), forecrown tawny olive,

occiput bluish; feathers of ear coverts somewhat lengthened, olive with yellow shaft streaks. Back green; breast yellowish olive green (or reddish olive brown, a), rest of underparts yellowish green. Shoulders red, under wing coverts verditer blue. Tail square, central feathers green, rest dull red, broadly tipped blue. Primaries black, edged purplish blue.

Subtropical and temperate zones. Sw Táchira on Páramo de Tamá (*amazonina*). N Táchira (Boca de Monte) and the Andes of Mérida (*theresae*, a). [Andes of Colombia and Ecuador.] Cloud and low, open forest near the páramos, 2300–3000 m.

Note: In Lista Av. Venez. this species is followed by *Gypopsitta vulturina*. The record for Venezuela has been found to be based on a slip of the pen by Berlepsch and Hartert who meant to record *Deroptyus accipitrinus!* *G. vulturina* is found only s of the Amazon in Brazil.

[THE FOLLOWING PARROTS (*Pionus*) are medium-sized, square-tailed birds some with colorful bills and red under tail coverts.]

## BLUE-HEADED PARROT
*Pionus menstruus*
COTORRA CABECIAZUL

Pl. 8
11″ (28 cm.). Base of upper mandible red. Whole head, neck and breast bright blue, with a little red at base of feathers of the lower throat. Back, lower breast and belly green, wing coverts yellowish olive, under tail coverts rosy red. Tail green, basel part of all but central feathers rosy red, distal part blue green. Young birds have red forecrowns with little if any blue on throat and breast.

Tropical zone, but not recorded from Delta Amacuro or s Bolívar (*menstruus*). [Costa Rica to Bolivia and s Brazil. Trinidad.] Rain forest, deciduous forest, clearings with scattered trees, plantations, to 1000 m. n of the Orinoco, to 1500 m. s of it. Pairs and small noisy flocks. Flies, perches and feeds in treetops, also in bushes and cornfields. Shallow wing beats like those of *Amazona* parrots. Call:

similar to those of the larger *Amazona* but slightly higher pitched and more shrill.

## RED-BILLED PARROT
*Pionus sordidus*
PERICO PICO ROJO

Pl. 8
9″ (23 cm.) [or 10.5″ (27 cm.), a]. Mandible and tip of maxilla red. Forehead bluish black, crown and sides of head dark green, the feathers edged dark blue, feathers of hindcrown and nape with white bases that show through. Back and wing coverts pale yellowish olivaceous, the feathers with paler, more yellowish edges giving a scaled appearance (or dark green, with inconspicuous grayish edges, a). Primaries bright green in contrast to rest of plumage (or green not in contrast to rest of plumage, a), under wing coverts green. Feathers of throat and upper breast green, broadly edged bright blue (or without blue edges, b; or almost solid purplish blue, a), some feathers of the breast with inconspicuous pink centers (or without pink centers, b), lower breast and belly pale yellowish olive, the feathers conspicuously pale-edged (or dark grayish olive green, a); under tail coverts rosy crimson on basal half of inner web, rest of inner web green, outer web mainly intense ultramarine blue.

Tropical and subtropical zones. The Sierra de Perijá, Zulia (*ponsi*, a). From the mountains of Falcón and Lara through the coastal Cordillera to the Distr. Federal (*sordidus*). The coastal Cordillera in Anzoátegui, Sucre and n Monagas (*antelius*, b). [Colombia to n Bolivia.] Rain and cloud forests, 100–2200 m.; in the lower altitudes, only along the n coast ranges. In pairs or flocks up to 50. Treetops.

## WHITE-CAPPED PARROT
*Pionus seniloides*
COTORRA CABECIBLANCA

Pl. 8
11″ (28 cm.). Bill pale olive yellow. Forecrown white, a few feathers with pinkish orange edges, feathers of rest of head white basally, broadly edged dusky purple giving a scaled appearance. Back,

wings and central tail feathers green. Breast and belly dark plum purple, flanks and tibia green. Tail, except central pair of feathers, dull red on basal half of inner web, green distally. Imm.: mostly dull green on the undersurface. Subtropical and temperate zones. The Andes of s Táchira and Mérida. [Colombia, Ecuador.] Cloud forest and open terrain with scattered trees near the páramos, 1900–3000 m. Alone, in pairs or small, restless, noisy flocks. Forages inconspicuously from low bushes to treetops. Often near streams.

## BRONZE-WINGED PARROT

*Pionus chalcopterus*
COTORRA NEGRA

Pl. 8
11″ (28 cm.). A very dark parrot. Bill yellowish white. Feathers of head, neck and underparts dark, bronzy brown, broadly edged deep violet blue. Throat whitish with a narrow pinkish band on upper breast. Mantle dark bronzy green, rest of upper side deep blue. Wing coverts and inner secondaries bronzy brown, with pale tips to wing coverts. Tail dark blue, inner webs of outer tail feathers and under tail coverts pinkish red. Wing lining verditer blue.
Tropical and lower subtropical zones. Widespread in the Sierra de Perijá, Zulia (*cyanescens*). [Colombia to nw Peru.]
Rain forest, clearings, 120–1200 m.

## DUSKY PARROT

*Pionus fuscus*
COTORRA MORADA

Pl. 8
10″ (25 cm.). A very dark parrot. Bill dusky with a pinkish red spot near nostril. Head and throat dark purplish blue, somewhat streaked whitish on throat. Back bronzy brown, feathers pale-edged; breast violet brown, becoming redder and more purplish on belly. Wings and tail dark blue, inner webs of outer tail feathers and under tail coverts red. Wing lining blue.
Tropical zone. Nw Bolívar along the lower Río Caura and in the ne on the Altiplanicie de Nuria and on upper Río

Cuyuni to the Sierra de Lema. [The Guianas; e Brazil.]
Rain forest, clearings from near sea level to 1000 m.

[THE PARROTS BELONGING TO the genus *Amazona* are what are thought of as typical parrots and are those often sold as talking parrots. They are mostly green, usually with red or yellow in the tail and often a red or yellow wing speculum. Their tails are square, the primaries black or dark blue.]

## RED-LORED PARROT

*Amazona autumnalis*
LORO FRENTIRROJO

14″ (35 cm.). Mainly green. Frontal band and lores crimson, feathers of crown with lilac edges. Wing speculum red; tail green, the feathers with a broad terminal yellowish green band, the outer feathers red basally on the inner web, edged with blue at base of outer web.
Tropical zone. Río Negro, Sierra de Perijá, Zulia, (*salvini*). [Mexico to w Ecuador. Nw Brazil.]
Rain forest and forest borders along rivers, 100–200 m. Clearings, semi-open second growth. Small flocks. Treetops.

## BLUE-CHEEKED PARROT

*Amazona brasiliensis*
LORO CARIAZUL

14″ (35 cm.). Mainly green. Crown yellowish green, lores orange. Cheeks lavender blue. Wing speculum orange. A broad yellowish green terminal band on outer tail feathers, which are tinged orange or reddish on inner web.
Lower subtropical zone. Bolívar in the Gran Sabana (Kabanayén; Cerro Sororopán-tepui) (*dufresniana*). [The Guianas; e Brazil to Rio Grande do Sul.]
Rain and cloud forests, 1000–1700 m. Small flocks in treetops.
Note: Called *Amazona d. dufresniana* in Lista Av. Venez.

## FESTIVE PARROT

*Amazona festiva*
LORO LOMIRROJO

Pl. 8
15″ (38 cm.). Mostly green. Frontal band and lores crimson, superciliary and fore-

part of cheeks light blue, feathers of nape edged black. *Lower back and rump crimson.* No wing speculum. Tail green, tipped yellowish green, no red.
Tropical zone. S Apure along the Río Meta; nw Bolívar opposite the mouth of the Apure to Altagracia; central Delta Amacuro (*bodini*). [Nw Guyana; e Colombia to e Peru and w Amazonian Brazil.]
Rain forest, gallery forest, llanos, savannas with scattered trees near water, to 100 m. Small bands, but like most large parrots, often congregates in large flocks.

## YELLOW-SHOULDERED PARROT

*Amazona barbadensis*
COTORRA CABECIAMARILLA

Pl. 8
13″ (33 cm.). Mostly green, the feathers fringed black, more heavily above. Whole head and throat and sides of neck bright yellow; forehead, space before eye and center of throat tinged buffy (or fore-crown, lores and ocular region yellow, lower part of cheeks blue green, chin yellow, a). Shoulder extensively yellow (or only tip of shoulder yellow, mixed with scarlet, a). Wing speculum red. Tibia yellow. Under tail coverts bluish. Tail broadly tipped yellowish green, inner web of all but central rectrices basally red.
Semi-arid coastal region in Falcón and Anzoátegui (*barbadensis*). La Blanquilla and Margarita Is. (*rothschildi*, a). [Aruba (formerly); Bonaire.]
Xerophytic areas, savannas with scattered trees, thorny scrub, to 100 m. In pairs and small bands, but larger flocks when feeding. Feeds on cactus and other fruits. Heard usually in the morning and in the afternoon as the flocks leave and return to their roosts.

## YELLOW-HEADED PARROT

*Amazona ochrocephala*
LORO REAL

Pl. 8
14″ (35 cm.). Mainly green; center of breast and belly tinged blue. Center of crown yellow. Bend of wing and wing speculum red. Tail with a broad yellowish green terminal band, outer feathers with red at base of inner web. Tibia

yellow. Imm.: lacks the yellow crown patch.
Tropical zone, except Andean region, the mountains along the ne coast, s Bolívar and s Amazonas (*ochrocephala*). [Mid. Amer. and n Colombia, e Peru, n Amazonian Brazil and n Bolivia. Trinidad.]
Lowland rain, gallery, deciduous forests, savannas; corn fields, suburban areas; near rivers, to 500 m. In pairs and noisy flocks, occasionally up to 300 birds. Roosts and feeds in the treetops. Common and considered the best talker, this is the favorite caged parrot.

## ORANGE-WINGED PARROT

*Amazona amazonica*
LORO GUARO

Pl. 8
13″ (33 cm.). Mainly green. Crown and cheeks yellow, forehead and lores blue. Wing speculum orange red, bend of wing orange. Tail with a yellowish green tip, the outer rectrices orange red on the inner web except at tip, crossed by a green band, outermost tail feather with outer web basally blue.
Tropical zone, but not recorded in Zulia or Mérida (*amazonica*). [The Guianas and Colombia to e Peru and Amazonian and e Brazil. Trinidad, Tobago.]
Rain, gallery and deciduous forest edge, open terrain with scattered trees, second growth, mangroves, to 600 m. n of the Orinoco, to 1100 m. s of it. In pairs, noisy bands up to 50 and flocks of 200 and more. Middle heights of forests to treetops.

## SCALY-NAPED PARROT

*Amazona mercenaria*
LORO VERDE

Pl. 8
13″ (33 cm.). Green to yellowish olive green, upper tail coverts usually pale yellowish green, feathers of hindcrown, nape and breast with conspicuous dusky edges. Wing speculum red if present, but usually absent. *Tail distinctive;* central feathers green tipped yellowish, the rest tipped yellowish with green bases and a variable amount of red between, outermost feather with purple blue outer web, this color present in variable amounts on outer web of other feathers.

Subtropical zone. Sierra de Perijá, Zulia; the Andes of Mérida (*canipalliata*). [Colombia to n Bolivia.] Cloud forest, partly open terrain near the higher altitudes, 1800–2900 m.

## MEALY PARROT
*Amazona farinosa*
LORO BURRÓN

Pl. 8

16″ (41 cm.). Green with a mealy, powdery bloom. Center of crown yellow (or without yellow, a), feathers of hindcrown and nape with violet edges. Bend of wing and large wing speculum red. Basal half of tail dark green, distal half yellow green.
Tropical zone. Zulia, Táchira, Barinas and n and central Amazonas (*inornata*, a). N Bolívar from the lower Río Caura to the Río Cuyuni (*farinosa*). [Mid. Amer. to Colombia, the Guianas, and to n Bolivia, and Amazonian and se Brazil.] The largest parrot in Venezuela. Rain forest, to 500 m. Clearings. Forages from the middle branches of trees to treetops. Very noisy flocks. Call: least strident and lowest in tone of all the *Amazona* calls.

## RED-FAN PARROT
*Deroptyus accipitrinus*
LORO CACIQUE

Pl. 8

14″ (35 cm.). Head brown, whitish on forecrown, the feathers at sides of head with pale shaft streaks. Feathers of nape long, crimson, broadly edged blue, erectile to form a broad, fan-shaped crest surrounding head, but usually lying flat. Breast and belly crimson, the feathers broadly edged blue. Back, wings and tail and under tail coverts green, outer tail feathers with blue black inner webs, underside of tail black.
Tropical zone. N Bolívar from the lower Río Caura to the upper Río Cuyuni (*accipitrinus*). [The Guianas, e Colombia to ne Peru and n Amazonian Brazil.] Rain forest, 100–200 m. In pairs or small bands. Call: a wailing, nasal cry.

# HOATZINS: Opisthocomidae

## GUACHARACAS DE AGUA O CHENCHENAS

The curious hoatzin is among the most remarkable birds because of the peculiarities of its young. Recent anatomical studies have shown that the bird is probably most nearly related to the cuckoos.

Hoatzins are found in groups among bushes and low trees along quiet, forested streams in the Amazon and Orinoco basins and the rivers of the Guianas and feed exclusively on vegetable matter.

Hoatzins are poor fliers, using their wings mostly for gliding, landing awkwardly on the chosen perch. They are noisy, their croaking notes being often heard at night. They have a strong, rather disagreeable musty smell. Call loud, chachalaca-like.

They build a platform of sticks, often over water, in which to lay 2 or 3 eggs. The chicks are hatched practically naked, and possess an archaic feature: 2 claws at the bend of the wing. These are used to clamber about the bushes in which the young live. They are excellent swimmers, and should they fall in the water they swim and pull themselves out with the help of their clawed wings. The claws, and the ability to swim, are lost after 2 or 3 weeks.

## HOATZIN
*Opisthocomus hoazin*
GUACHARACA DE AGUA O CHENCHENA

Fig. 36

24″ (60 cm.). Face bare, bright blue, eye red. Head adorned with an upstanding, untidy, fan-shaped crest. Crest, foreneck and breast buff, rest of underparts chestnut. Upperparts mostly bronzy olive brown, streaked on hind neck and upper mantle with buff. Shoulders buff, wing coverts broadly edged buffy white. Tail

MicHel k. 35

Fig. 36. Hoatzin

rather long, spread when flying, dusky brown, broadly tipped cinnamon buff. Tropical zone. Locally distributed in Apure, Portuguesa, Guárico, Monagas and Sucre; Delta Amacuro; n Bolívar; Amazonas along Caño Casiquiare. [E Colombia, the Guianas and Amazonia.]

# CUCULIFORMES

## CUCKOOS, ANIS: Cuculidae

### Cuclillos, Garrapateros, Piscuas

Typical cuckoos are slim, long-tailed birds of skulking habits that live in scrub lands and forest edge. Like other members of the family they are peculiar in having 2 toes directed forward and 2 backwards.

Cuckoos are well known for their habit of laying their eggs in other birds' nests, but most species nest in the conventional manner. In South America only *Tapera* and *Dromococcyx* are parasitic. The anis are peculiar among cuckoos in building bulky, communal nests in which several females lay their eggs, and when the nest is left unattended the eggs are covered with green leaves. Anis leap from branch to branch with their wings closed.

The ground cuckoos are terrestrial, pheasantlike inhabitants of dense forest. Only one species is found in Venezuela.

## DWARF CUCKOO
*Coccyzus pumilus*
CUCLILLO GUSANERO

Pl. 10
8.5″ (22 cm.). Crown gray, back pale ashy gray. Throat and upper breast orange rufous, rest of underparts white. Tail not strongly graduated, ashy gray with a broad, blackish terminal band and narrow white tip. Bill black. Tropical zone. Locally in Zulia, and Táchira e to Anzoátegui, Delta Amacuro and e Monagas; s Apure; nw Bolívar; Amazonas s to the Río Ventuari; Margarita I. [N Colombia, where it occurs occasionally to the temperate zone.]
Rain forest, open woodland, gallery forest, llanos, xerophytic areas, savannas with scattered trees, to 400 m. n of the Orinoco, to 200 m. s of it. Call: a rapidly repeated cuk cuk cuk.

## BLACK-BILLED CUCKOO
*Coccyzus erythropthalmus*
CUCLILLO PICO NEGRO

11″ (28 cm.). Above bronzy brown, below white. Tail long, strongly graduated, like back in color, with an indistinct, small, blackish subterminal area and small white tip. Bare eye ring red, bill black. Tropical zone. Casual fall visitor, Oct.–Nov. Recorded from Táchira and Aragua. [Breeds in N Amer. Winters chiefly in w S Amer. to n Peru. Acc. Paraguay. Trinidad.]
Rain forest, second growth, semi-open woodland, plantations, 350–1100 m. Solitary, keeps low in trees. Call not unlike that of Dwarf Cuckoo.

## YELLOW-BILLED CUCKOO
*Coccyzus americanus*
CUCLILLO PICO AMARILLO

Pl. 10
11″ (28 cm.). Differs from Black-billed Cuckoo principally by having the outer webs of the primaries mostly rufous, well marked in flight, the outer tail feathers black with extensive white tips, the lower mandible mostly yellow, and the bare eye ring yellow.
Tropical and subtropical zones. Winter resident Aug.–early May, accidentally early June. Recorded virtually throughout e to Aragua and Barinas; nw Bolívar; n Amazonas; Los Testigos, La Orchila Is. (*americanus*). [Breeds in N Amer. to Mexico and the Antilles. Winters to Uruguay and Argentina. Curaçao, Bonaire. Trinidad, Tobago.]
Open situations, open woodland, second growth, xerophytic areas, thickets, páramo, usually from 400 m. n of the Orinoco, to 150 m. s of it, but 2 were found dead at the 4200 m. cable railway station near Mérida.

## PEARLY-BREASTED CUCKOO
*Coccyzus euleri*
CUCLILLO VENTRIBLANCO

10″ (25 cm.). Differs from Yellow-billed Cuckoo by having *no rufous* in wing; throat and upper breast pale silvery gray instead of white. Differs from Black-billed Cuckoo principally by black, broadly white-tipped outer tail feathers and yellow instead of black mandible.
Tropical zone. Very local; recorded in Mérida, the Distr. Federal, nw Bolívar and n, e and s Amazonas. [Guyana, Surinam, e Colombia. E and s Brazil; ne Argentina.]
Rain forest, gallery forest, thickets, forest edge from sea level to 700 m. n of the Orinoco, to 350 m. s of it.

## MANGROVE CUCKOO
*Coccyzus minor*
CUCLILLO DE MANGLAR

12″ (30 cm.). Above brownish gray; distinguishable from Yellow-billed Cuckoo by having *ear coverts black,* underparts pinkish buff. Outer tail feathers black, broadly tipped white. Base of lower mandible yellow.
Known in Venezuela from one old record, with no exact locality, and from Capure, n Delta Amacuro (*minor*) [S Florida, Mid. Amer., Colombia ("Bogota"). The Guianas, Brazil. Aruba, Curaçao, Bonaire. Trinidad. The Antilles.]
Forest, mangroves, xerophytic areas, thickets, at sea level. Solitary, silent, not active. Usually in the upper branches. Feeds on insects.

## DARK-BILLED CUCKOO

*Coccyzus melacoryphus*
CUCLILLO GRISÁCEO

Pl. 10
9″ (23 cm.). Crown and hindneck dark gray; ear coverts blackish, cheeks silvery gray; back and wings olive brown; central tail feathers bronzy tipped black, rest black, tipped white. Below mostly rufescent buff, sides of breast pale gray. Much like Gray-capped Cuckoo but *bill entirely black,* size smaller.
Tropical, occasionally subtropical zone. Locally n of the Orinoco from Zulia, Táchira and s Apure e to Sucre and Delta Amacuro; n and se Bolívar, n Amazonas; Margarita and Patos Is. [The Guianas; Colombia to w Peru, Bolivia, Argentina and Uruguay. Trinidad.]
Rain and deciduous forest edge, mangroves, open bushy country, gallery forest, llanos, xerophytic areas, second growth, to 500 m. n of the Orinoco, to 950 m. s of it. Solitary or in pairs, not shy. Forages in the lower thickets. Food: insects. Call: a series of downward, inflecting, cooing notes.

## GRAY-CAPPED CUCKOO

*Coccyzus lansbergi*
CUCLILLO ACANELADO

Pl. 10
9.5″ (24 cm.). Top and sides of head dark gray; back and wings rufescent brown; tail black, tipped white. Below deep rusty buff, darkest on breast.
Tropical, occasionally subtropical zone. W Zulia (Laguna Tulé); Mérida (Páramo de Culata); Lara (Terepaima); Carabobo (Puerto Cabello); Aragua (Rancho Grande); Distr. Federal, Miranda. [N Colombia; sw Ecuador; n Peru.]
Forested areas, dense shrubby undergrowth, to 1400 m.; secretive.

## SQUIRREL CUCKOO

*Piaya cayana*
PISCUA

Pl. 10
17″ (43 cm.). A slender cuckoo with a very long tail and foxy red back. Throat and upper breast pinkish buff, rest of underparts gray darkening to almost black on under tail coverts. Tail very long, graduated, the feathers with a black subterminal band and conspicuous white tip. Bill olive yellow.
Tropical and subtropical zones. N of the Orinoco except area occupied by *circe* (*mehleri*). Zulia s of L. Maracaibo; n and w Táchira; w and central Mérida; w Apure (*circe*). Delta Amacuro and at the se border of Monagas (*insulana*). S Apure along the Río Meta and generally s of the Orinoco in Amazonas and Bolívar (*cayana*). [Mid. Amer. to nw Peru, n Argentina and Uruguay. Trinidad.]
Rain forest, second growth, gallery, deciduous or open forest, mangroves, gardens, plantations, thickets along rivers, forest edge, savannas, to 2500 m. n of the Orinoco, to 1800 m. s of it. Alone or in pairs, forages at all heights but usually in the middle tier. Slips and glides through the branches. Feeds on insects, lizards. Several calls: a 2-note, loud, melodious, repeated whistle, "who-ée"; also a short "pís-cua." Nest is well built of coarse twigs a few meters from the ground.

## BLACK-BELLIED CUCKOO

*Piaya melanogaster*
PISCUA VENTRINEGRA

Pl. 10
14″ (35 cm.). Top and sides of head light gray. Back, wings and tail foxy red, tail feathers with a black subterminal patch, tipped white. Throat and breast orange rufous, belly and under tail coverts black. *Bill red.* Tail shorter than Squirrel Cuckoo.
Tropical zone. Amazonas and Bolívar (*melanogaster*). [The Guianas, se Colombia to e Peru and n Brazil.]
Rain forest to 500 m. Forages for insects from middle to upper heights.

## LITTLE CUCKOO

*Piaya minuta*
PISCUITA ENANA

Pl. 10
9.5″ (24 cm.). A virtual miniature of Squirrel Cuckoo; differs by size, by having the throat and breast chestnut, lower breast and belly brownish gray instead of pure gray and by having the feathers

of the hindcrown rather long; these can be raised to form a bushy crest.

Tropical zone. Locally distributed throughout but not recorded from s Amazonas (*minuta*). [E Panama, Colombia and the Guianas to Bolivia and s Brazil. Trinidad.]

Rain forest, open second growth, gallery forest, llanos, deciduous forest, along rivers, mangroves; to 700 m. n of the Orinoco, to 950 m. s of it. Solitary, forages for insects slowly and quietly in the foliage from low to middle heights.

## GREATER ANI

*Crotophaga major*
GARRAPATERO HERVIDOR

Fig. 37
17″ (43 cm.). A long-tailed, blue black bird with a compressed, curved bill with a high ridge at base of culmen. Feathers edged metallic bronzy green. Tail shiny purplish blue, purple below. Iris white.

Tropical and subtropical zones. Locally but widely distributed n of the Orinoco; s of it in Amazonas and n Bolívar along the Orinoco, and in Delta Amacuro. [Panama to w Ecuador, and e of the Andes to Argentina. Trinidad.]

Rain forest, thickets along river edge, mangroves, sea level to 200 m. Swampy forests, wet pastures, tall grass. Shy, gregarious; pairs or small flocks. Feeds on insects, berries, lizards. Various calls. Local names, *Hervidor, Hervidera,* refer to "boiling," bubbling notes. Nest of twigs may contain 10 or more eggs, presumably laid by several birds.

Fig. 37. SMOOTH-BILLED ANI (left), GREATER ANI (center),
GROOVE-BILLED ANI (right)

## SMOOTH-BILLED ANI

*Crotophaga ani*
GARRAPATERO COMÚN

Fig. 37

13″ (33 cm.). Bill laterally compressed, strongly arched, the culmen with a blade-like, high ridge. Dull brownish black with a slight bluish sheen, feathers of head, neck, mantle and breast edged dull bronzy purple. Tail long, dull blue black. Iris dark brown.

Tropical and subtropical zones, including Margarita and Patos Is. [S Florida. Sw Costa Rica to w Ecuador and Argentina. Antilles. Trinidad and Tobago.]

Rain and cloud forest edge, clearings, second growth, open terrain with trees, xerophytic areas, pastures, thickets, savannas, gardens, to 2400 m. n of the Orinoco, to 1200 m. s of it. Gregarious, not shy, conspicuous, flocks up to 25. Forages for insects in the foliage and on the open ground, often with cattle. Call: whining whistles. The name *Garrapatero* means "tick-eater"; another local name, *Guainiz,* is in imitation of its call. Nest of sticks; many females may lay in the same nest which can contain up to 22 eggs or more.

## GROOVE-BILLED ANI

*Crotophaga sulcirostris*
GARRAPATERO CURTIDOR

Fig. 37

12″ (30 cm.). *Bill* as in Smooth-billed Ani, not as conspicuously ridged but *distinctly grooved at sides.* Dull black, feathers edged with dull bronze. Wings and central tail feathers glossed purple.

Widespread n of the Orinoco, s of the Orinoco in n Amazonas and Bolívar along the Orinoco (*sulcirostris*). [Texas and Mid. Amer. to n Chile and nw Argentina. Aruba to Bonaire. Trinidad.]

Rain forest edge, open terrain, pastures, second growth, deciduous woodland, gallery forest, llanos, suburban areas, to 750 m. n of the Orinoco, at sea level s of it. Gregarious, flocks to 20; associates with cattle, forages for insects on the open ground. Call: "see, see, see." Nest of twigs, in which several females may lay eggs.

## STRIPED CUCKOO

*Tapera naevia*
SAUCÉ

Pl. 10

11″ (28 cm.). Crown with a bushy crest. Above sandy buff to rufescent buff *boldly streaked with black;* upper tail coverts over half the length of the tail, gray with a central dark streak; tail long, graduated, grayish brown, tipped and edged with buff. Below whitish; narrow malar streak black; breast tinged buff. Imm.: much more rufescent than ad., feathers, crown and upper parts terminating in round cinnamon spots.

Tropical, occasionally subtropical zone, including Margarita I., but not recorded in s Amazonas (*naevia*). [Mexico to sw Ecuador, Bolivia and central Argentina. Trinidad.]

Open wet country, gallery forest, llanos, deciduous woodland, swamps, xerophytic areas, second growth, pastures, cloud forest edge, to 2500 m. n of the Orinoco, to 1300 m. s of it. Shy, forages for insects near the ground in thickets. Responds to an imitation of its insistent, melancholy, 2-note whistle. Parasitic in its nesting.

## PHEASANT CUCKOO

*Dromococcyx phasianellus*
CUCO FAISÁN

Pl. 10

14″ (35 cm.). A dark-backed, crested cuckoo with a thin neck and very small head, and long, wide tail. Crown dark rufous, crest rufous, long postocular streak buffy white. Back dark brown with a purplish gloss. Tail feathers very wide, graduated, dark brown, tipped and margined with white, upper tail coverts plumelike, almost as long as tail, dark brown tipped with a white dot. Wing coverts edged buffy, primaries and secondaries like back with a small buffy white dot at tip. Throat and breast buff spotted with dull black, the spots continued on foreneck and becoming drop-shaped on upper breast, rest of underparts white. Under wing coverts and bases of the primaries white, a white bar across center of middle primaries.

Tropical zone. Rare and local. The upper Río Negro, nw Zulia (*rufigularis*). Carabobo (San Esteban); Aragua (Ocumare de la Costa); Guárico (Potrerito, Parmana); Sucre (Cumaná, San Félix); ne Bolívar (*phasianellus*). [S Mexico to n Bolivia, Paraguay and ne Argentina.] Rain and gallery forest, second growth to 100 m. Shy. Forages on the forest floor and in thick undergrowth. Perches in trees. Call: a whistle. Parasitic in its nesting.

## PAVONINE CUCKOO

*Dromococcyx pavoninus*
Cuco Pavón

Pl. 10
10″ (25 cm.). Not unlike the Pheasant Cuckoo but much smaller, back blacker, upper breast uniform rufous brown without spots, instead of buffy white spotted blackish.
Tropical and subtropical zones. Local. Upper Río Negro, nw Zulia (*perijanus*). Aragua (Colonia Tovar); s Bolívar and s Amazonas along the Brazilian border (*pavoninus*). [The Guianas to e and s Brazil, e Peru, Paraguay and ne Argentina.]
Rain and cloud forests, 900–1950 m. n of the Orinoco, 350–900 m. s of it. Parasitic in its nesting.

## RUFOUS-WINGED GROUND-CUCKOO

*Neomorphus rufipennis*
Pájaro Váquiro

Pl. 10
19″ (48 cm.). Not at all like a cuckoo, more like a small pheasant in appearance. Terrestrial, legs rather long, tail feathers broad and very long. Head crested; head, neck, upper breast and upper back deep purplish blue, throat ashy; lower breast and belly ashy brown. Back metallic olive shot with purple; inner remiges purplish maroon, primaries blue black. Central tail feathers metallic purple, rest greenish black. Bare orbital skin pinkish red.
Tropical zone. Locally in Bolívar and n and central Amazonas. [Guyana; Terr. Roraima, Brazil.]
Rain forest, 100–1100 m. Terrestrial forager. Solitary, wary, restless. When startled runs very fast on the ground. Perches in the middle branches of trees. Difficult to see. Local names of *Pájaro Váquiro* and *Vaquirero* given because it is often found near bands of peccaries.

# STRIGIFORMES

# BARN OWLS: Tytonidae

## Lechuzas de Campanario

Barn Owls are virtually of world-wide distribution. They are mostly nocturnal but are sometimes seen at dusk flying low over meadows and clearings in search of small rodents, which form their principal food. They nest in buildings, holes in trees and even burrows. They have long legs and white faces surrounded by a dark, heartshaped ruff. Their weird nocturnal cries consist of hissing sounds, hoarse screeches and clicking sounds made by snapping the bill.

## BARN OWL

*Tyto alba*
Lechuza de Campanario

Pl. IX
15″ (38 cm.). Above gray densely vermiculated black, white and buffy, feathers basally orange rufous showing through. Face white, dusky around eyes, surrounded by a dark heartshaped ruff. Underparts white, with a few dark spots (or buffy dotted with dusky, a). No ear tufts.
Tropical and subtropical zones. Locally in Zulia, Táchira, Mérida, Trujillo and Lara (*contempta*, a). Locally elsewhere including Margarita I. (*hellmayri*). [Cosmopolitan; not in arctic regions.]

Open country with scattered trees, towns, suburban areas, 200–1500 m. Hides during the day in holes in trees, caves, buildings. Alone or in pairs.

## OWLS: Strigidae

### LECHUZAS, MOCHUELOS, PAVITAS, CURUCUCÚES

Most owls are brown with dark streaks, with or without ear-tufts. They are strictly nocturnal, except for *Glaucidium* and *Speotyto,* and are rarely seen; their presence is often revealed by their calls, by which they are best identified. Owls are useful to man in controlling the rodent population.

### VERMICULATED SCREECH-OWL

*Otus guatemalae*
CURUCUCÚ VERMICULADO

Pl. VIII
8.5″ (22 cm.). A small, eared owl with no prominent streaks or bars. Brown above, vermiculated black. Some of the upper wing coverts with white outer webs, scapulars with outer web barred blackish, inner remiges like back, primaries barred narrowly with black and more broadly with cinnamon buff. Tail grayish brown, vermiculated black and narrowly barred buff. Chin dull white, rest of underparts brown mixed with buffy white, narrowly barred and vermiculated dusky, with inconspicuous, narrow, black shaft stripes on lower breast and belly. Flank feathers rather long, white, with narrow black bars. Facial disk brown, vermiculated dusky, outlined with black. Rufous phase: foxy red, markings much less evident, general plumage more uniform.
Tropical and lower subtropical zones. The mountains of the n in Zulia, Táchira, Aragua and Sucre (*vermiculatus*). Amazonas on Cerros Duida and Neblina; Bolívar on Cerro Roraima (*roraimae*). [Mexico to w Ecuador. Adj. Brazil. N Bolivia.]
Rain and cloud forests to 1100 m. n of the Orinoco, 1000–1800 m. on the slopes of the tepuis. Call: a long series of trilled, wavering notes. The eyes do not shine in reflected light. Often erects ear-tufts.

### TROPICAL SCREECH-OWL

*Otus choliba*
CURUCUCÚ COMÚN

Pl. VIII
9″ (23 cm.). A small, eared owl with well-marked, narrow, black streaks on under-parts. Brown above somewhat mottled with buff, and streaked narrowly with black. Below buffy white, streaked blackish, with narrow, wavy cross bars. Outer webs of scapulars white forming a well-marked *white stripe at sides of back,* outer webs of some of greater wing coverts white. Tail narrowly banded cinnamon buff. Facial disk gray with fine, blackish, transverse lines. Underside of primaries barred.
Caribbean littoral in Zulia, Falcón, Anzoátegui and Margarita I. (*margaritae*). Tropical and subtropical zones. Generally distributed except in areas occupied by other races (*crucigerus*). S Amazonas on Cerros Duida and de la Neblina (*duidae*). [Costa Rica to Colombia; e of the Andes to central Argentina. Trinidad.]
A great variety of habitats that includes clearings and pastures to near the páramos n of the Orinoco, to 1850 m. on the slopes and summits of the tepuis s of it. Nocturnal, alone or in pairs. Feeds on insects. Bubbling call: "coo-roo-coo-coo," ending suddenly with a whistled note. The eyes do not shine in reflected light. Often erects ear-tufts.

### RUFESCENT SCREECH-OWL

*Otus ingens*
CURUCUCÚ PÁLIDO

11″ (28 cm.). Crown cinnamon brown banded with blackish, and more narrowly with buff which merges into buffy white forehead and superciliaries. Back tawny olive with fine dusky vermiculations and a partially concealed white nuchal collar. Facial disk and throat buffy barred with brown, rest of underparts buffy white with conspicuous dark brown streaks and narrow light brown

bars. Thighs and under tail coverts plain, pale buff. Tail dusky brown banded with buff. In the rufous phase the general tone of plumage is rufous brown.
Upper tropical and subtropical zones. Nw Zulia on the upper Río Negro; s Táchira (*venezuelensis*). [Central Colombia to n Bolivia.]
Cloud forest, 1250–1700 m.

## TAWNY-BELLIED SCREECH-OWL
*Otus watsonii*
CURUCUCÚ OREJUDO

Pl. VIII
9″ (23 cm.). A very dark owl with long ear-tufts. Dark brown above spotted with black and tawny, nuchal collar buffy. Underparts deep ochraceous tawny streaked and vermiculated black on breast and obscurely barred with white on belly. Facial disk brown, edged black. No white on wings. Primaries dusky notched with bright buff on outer web, inner web barred with dull buff.
Tropical and subtropical zones. Sierra de Perijá, Zulia; s Táchira; extreme nw Bolívar; central and s Amazonas (*watsonii*). [Surinam, e Colombia to n Bolivia and Amazonian Brazil.]
Rain and cloud forest, 2000–2100 m. n of the Orinoco, 100–250 m. s of it.

## WHITE-THROATED SCREECH-OWL
*Otus albogularis*
CURUCUCÚ GARGANTIBLANCO

Pl. VIII
12″ (30 cm.). A dark owl with an *extensively white throat*. Dark brown to blackish brown above spotted and vermiculated tawny and lightly speckled with white. Throat white, breast like back but profusely spotted with white, belly tawny buff sparsely streaked dusky. Outer webs of remiges notched buff. Tail dusky with many sandy bars.
Subtropical to temperate zones. Nw Zulia along the upper Río Negro; the Andes of Táchira and Mérida (*meridensis*). [Colombia, e Ecuador, ne and nw Peru. N Bolivia.]
Low, open cloud forest and open terrain with scattered trees in the higher altitudes, 1300–3100 m.

## CRESTED OWL
*Lophostrix cristata*
LECHUZA COPETONA

Pl. IX
16″ (40 cm.). Recognizable from any other owl by its long, snow white "horns" and eyebrows. Above dark brown finely vermiculated with blackish. Facial area rufescent. Throat and center of upper breast white, mixed and vermiculated with brown; breast dark brown vermiculated with blackish, rest of underparts tawny buff vermiculated with brown. Closed wings dark brown, the wing coverts and scapulars with large, round white spots; primaries barred with buffy white. Central tail feathers like back, rest usually barred with buffy white. Tarsus feathered. Iris brown; bill and legs greenish yellow to grayish white.
Tropical zone s of Lake Maracaibo in n Táchira (*wedeli*) [S Mexico to Colombia, the Guianas, Amazonian Brazil, Peru and Bolivia.]
Second growth in the lowlands, 100 m. It is not improbable that the paler, typical form occurs in s Venezuela.
Note: Specimen in Estación Biológica "Henri Pittieri," Rancho Grande, Aragua. A new record since publication of Lista Av. Venez.

## GREAT HORNED OWL
*Bubo virginianus*
LECHUZÓN OREJUDO

Pl. IX
20″ (51 cm.). The largest S Amer. owl. "Horns" conspicuous. Blackish brown above, mottled with tawny ochraceous and buffy white. Lower throat white, rest of underparts ochraceous narrowly barred with black. Face dull buffy white bordered behind by a distinct black crescent. Remiges broadly barred sooty brown and buffy. Central tail feathers like back, rest barred sooty brown and buffy.
Tropical and lower subtropical zones. Locally distributed in nw Venezuela from Zulia to Apure e to Anzoátegui; s of the Orinoco in n Bolívar and extreme nw Amazonas (*nacurutu*). [From arctic America to Cape Horn.]
Wooded habitats; cloud, rain and deciduous forests; second growth, thickets,

gallery forest in the llanos to 1600 m. Alone or in pairs. Not exclusively nocturnal. Feeds on rats, mice, rabbits and other small mammals; birds. Call: deep "hoo-hoo-hoo-hoo."
Note: Called *scotinus* in Lista Av. Venez.; this has been found not to differ from *nacurutu*.

## SPECTACLED OWL
*Pulsatrix perspicillata*
LECHUZON DE ANTEOJOS

Pl. IX
18″ (46.5 cm.). A large owl without ear-tufts, with a broad, blackish band across light-colored underparts. Upperparts, face, wings, tail and broad breast band sooty brown, upper breast buffy white, lower breast and belly cinnamon buff. Face dusky, feathers at base of bill, continued upward to form a conspicuous eyebrow, white. Wings and tail barred with dark grayish brown bars.
Tropical and lower subtropical zones. Locally n of the Orinoco from Zulia, Aragua and Guárico to Sucre and Monagas. Commoner s of the Orinoco in n Amazonas, Bolívar and Delta Amacuro (*perspicillata*). [Mid. Amer. to w Ecuador, Bolivia, s Brazil and ne Argentina. Trinidad.]
Rain forest and forest edge, swampy woodland, second growth, savannas with scattered trees, gallery forest, llanos, to 200 m. n of the Orinoco, to 1450 m. s of it. Alone or in pairs. Not exclusively nocturnal. Perches in the middle and high branches of tall trees. Feeds on mammals, birds, lizards, insects. Call: "hoo-hoo-hoo-hoo"; responds to an imitation.

## ANDEAN PYGMY-OWL
*Glaucidium jardinii*
PAVITA ANDINA

Pl. VIII
6″ (15 cm.). A small owl without ear-tufts, more apt to be seen in the daytime than other species. Crown brown dotted with white. Hindneck crossed by a partly concealed cinnamon line surmounted by 2 round, black spots resembling eyes, back brown with small whitish spots, inner remiges similar but barred rather than spotted. Throat and patch on breast white, sides of breast

like back, lower breast and belly white conspicuously streaked dark brown or reddish brown. Tail with 4 grayish and dusky bars. A rufous phase exists.
Subtropical to temperate zones. The Sierra de Perijá, Zulia; the Andes of Táchira and Mérida (*jardinii*). [Costa Rica, w Panama. Colombia to Bolivia.]
Cloud and dwarf forest, páramos, 2000–4000 m.
Note: Considered a race of Ferruginous Pygmy-Owl in Lista Av. Venez.

## FERRUGINOUS PYGMY-OWL
*Glaucidium brasilianum*
PAVITA FERRUGINEA

Pl. VIII
6.5″ (16.5 cm.). Much like Andean Pygmy-Owl and like it apt to be seen in daytime, but found at lower altitudes. Differs from Andean Pygmy-Owl by having the crown with shaft-streaks instead of dots and tail with 5 or 6 instead of 4 bars. A bright rufous phase is not uncommon.
Tropical, lower subtropical zones. N of the Orinoco (*medianum*), s of the Orinoco (*olivaceum*). Cerros Camani, Huachamacari and Duida, Amazonas (*duidae*). Margarita Is. (*margaritae*). [Sw US to Colombia, w Ecuador, Guyana to n Chile and central Argentina. Trinidad.]
Habits similar to Andean Pygmy-Owl.

## BURROWING OWL
*Speotyto cunicularia*
MOCHUELO DE HOYO

Pl. VIII
8.5″ (22 cm.). A *long-legged terrestrial, diurnal owl* of open country. No ear-tufts. Above brown conspicuously spotted with white. Throat patch and breast white; a dark band across lower throat, lower breast and belly white, barred brown. Wings and tail barred buffy white and dark brown.
Tropical zone, locally distributed throughout, except in Amazonas and areas occupied by other races; Margarita, La Borracha and Cubagua Is. (*brachyptera*). The llanos of Apure, Barinas and Cojedes (*apurensis*). Bolívar on the Río Uairén along the Brazilian frontier (*minor*). [S Canada to Tierra del Fuego. Aruba. Trinidad.]

Llanos, savannas, xerophytic areas, to 450 m. n of the Orinoco, to 1000 m. s of it. Alone or in pairs; often seen during the day standing on rocks or mounds near the entrance to the nesting burrows, excavated in the ground often to a length of 3 m. or more. Feeds on small mammals, lizards, snakes, amphibians and scorpions.

## BLACK-AND-WHITE OWL
*Ciccaba nigrolineata*
LECHUZA BLANQUINEGRA

Pl. IX
17″ (43 cm.). This species and Black-banded Owl are the only black and white owls. No ear-tufts. Brownish black above, hindneck and upper mantle with narrow white bars; underparts white with many narrow black bars. Tail blackish with 4 or 5 narrow white bars and white tip. Bill and toes orange yellow.
Tropical zone. Rare and local from Zulia and Aragua to Miranda, the llanos of Guárico (Río Grande), and ne of Tucupita, w Delta Amacuro. [Mexico to Colombia and nw Peru.]
Rain forests, clearings, sea level to 900 m. Second growth, ravines, near rivers; flooded and swampy woodland. Nocturnal. Solitary or in pairs, perches in middle and higher branches. Feeds on rodents, bats, insects. Call: loud, prolonged, high-pitched "who-ah," also a repeated, explosive, "bu."

## BLACK-BANDED OWL
*Ciccaba huhula*
LECHUZA NEGRA

Pl. IX
14″ (35 cm.). No ear-tufts. Above black with very narrow wavy white bars; below black with wider white bars. Tail black with 4 narrow white bars. Bill and toes orange yellow.
Tropical zone. El Cambur, lower Río Caura, nw Bolívar; Cerro Guanarí, Caño Casiquiare, s Amazonas (*huhula*). [The Guianas, e Colombia to e Peru, Amazonian Brazil and n Argentina.]
Rain forest, clearings to 200 m. Habits probably similar to the Black-and-white Owl.

## MOTTLED OWL
*Ciccaba virgata*
LECHUZA COLILARGA

Pl. IX
13″ (33 cm.). No ear-tufts. Variable in color. Upperparts blackish brown everywhere finely dotted and barred with white to reddish buff finely waved with blackish. Scapulars spotted with white or buff. Face dark brown outlined in buff. Eyebrow white to buff. Chest brown everywhere dotted and lined with whitish, rest of underparts buff broadly streaked dark brown. Remiges and rectrices dusky with pale bars. Tail black with 4 white to grayish white bars and tip.
Tropical and subtropical zones. The n mountains from Zulia and Táchira to Sucre and Monagas, and in Delta Amacuro (*virgata*). Bolívar in the Gran Sabana (*macconnelli*). [Mexico to Colombia, w Ecuador, the Guianas, Bolivia and n Argentina. Trinidad.]
Rain, cloud and deciduous forest, mangroves, second growth, thickets, plantations, open fields, to 1900 m. n of the Orinoco, to 300 m. s of it. Nocturnal, solitary. Middle-height branches. Feeds on small mammals. Call: whistled screechy notes. May respond to an imitation of its call.

## RUFOUS-BANDED OWL
*Ciccaba albitarsus*
LECHUZA PATIBLANCA

Pl. IX
14″ (35 cm.). No ear-tufts. Above blackish brown liberally spotted and barred with orange tawny. Below bright orange tawny spotted with silvery white giving an ocellated appearance, the white spots divided in the middle by a dark chestnut line. Primaries dusky notched with rufous. Tail banded.
Upper subtropical and temperate zones. The Andes to Mérida and Trujillo (*albitarsus*). [Colombia to w Peru and Bolivia.]
Cloud forest and the intermediate open terrain with scattered trees in the higher altitudes near the páramos, 2000–3000 m. Nocturnal, solitary. The local names *Borococo* and *Surrucuco* are presumably an imitation of its call.

## STRIPED OWL

*Rhinoptynx clamator*
LECHUZA LISTADA

Pl. IX
15″ (38 cm.). A conspicuously striped owl with long ear-tufts. Face buffy white surrounded by a conspicuous black ruff. Back tawny ochraceous striped black on mantle and axillars, barred and freckled on lower back; underparts buffy, striped black. Wings and tail grayish, banded dusky.
Tropical zone. Locally in nw Zulia; Carabobo, to Anzoátegui, Monagas and n Bolívar (Ciudad Bolívar) and the n Gran Sabana (*clamator*). [Mexico to the Guianas, e Colombia, e Peru. Central and e Brazil to Paraguay and central Argentina. Tobago.]
Rain, deciduous and gallery forest edge to 1000 m. n of the Orinoco, to 500 m. s of it. Savannas, xerophytic areas, suburban areas, marshland, open grassy fields. Alone or in pairs, may congregate in scattered groups of a dozen. Perches in undergrowth to treetops. Feeds on small mammals. "Horns" often visible. Call: reported as a long shrill, melancholy cry. Nests in the grass.

## STYGIAN OWL

*Asio stygius*
LECHUZA ESTIGIA

Pl. IX
17″ (43 cm.). Back blackish brown with a few buff spots on crown and hindneck, ear-tufts present but small. Upper tail coverts barred with buffy, inner remiges spotted with buffy. Underparts buffy mottled and clouded dark brown. Central tail feathers blackish with 3 or 4 narrow buff bars, outer feathers with 4 or 5 much wider buff bars.
Tropical and subtropical zones. Pie Nudo, Sierra de Perijá, Zulia; San Fernando de Atabapo, w Amazonas (*robustus*). [Mexico to Nicaragua. Colombia, e Ecuador, spottily in Amazonian and se Brazil to nw Argentina and Paraguay.]
Great altitudinal range in forested areas: recorded at 2600 m. n of the Orinoco and 100–200 m. s of it. Nocturnal. Feeds on bats.

## SHORT-EARED OWL

*Asio flammeus*
LECHUZA OREJICORTA

Pl. IX
15″ (38 cm.). Tawny brown striped dark brown above and below, wings and tail barred dusky, scapulars with white outer webs. In flight a prominent black patch at bend of wing above and below, and a large pale buffy patch at base of remiges on upper sides of wing. Face brown surrounded by a black ruff, area around eyes black, chin and feathers at base of bill white. Ear-tufts very small.
Tropical zone. Known from the mouth of the Río Meta, Apure, and from Cantaura, Anzoátegui (*pallidicaudus*). [N Amer. wintering to Guatemala. E Colombia, the Guianas to Tierra del Fuego. Greater Antilles, Eurasia, Africa, Hawaii, etc.]
Swampy areas, savannas, gallery forest, llanos, at about 100 m. Hunts while flying low over open terrain. Feeds on mammals, birds, frogs. Call: monotonous hoot, also shrill cries. Nests on the ground. Partly diurnal.

## BUFF-FRONTED OWL

*Aegolius harrisii*
CURUCUCÚ BARRIGA AMARILLA

Pl. VIII
8″ (20 cm.). A small owl, chocolate brown above with a broad yellowish buff band across upper mantle; yellowish buff below with a broad chocolate band across breast. Forecrown yellowish buff. Face yellowish buff, ocular region and chin dusky, a blackish ruff encircling cheeks. Throat, lower breast and belly yellowish buff. No ear-tufts. Wing coverts with white spots. Tail blackish with two broken white bars and white tip.
Temperate zone. Mérida on the Páramo de Culata (*harrisii*). [Central Colombia, Ecuador. Paraguay and se Brazil to Uruguay and n Argentina.]
Páramos, cultivated areas and clearings, 3800 m. A local name, Surrucucú, is presumably an imitation of the call.

# CAPRIMULGIFORMES

## OILBIRDS: Steatornithidae

### GUÁCHAROS

Oilbirds are very local, and found only in the vicinity of caves in which they nest and roost colonially.

They are rather like nightjars, but differ from them by their hawklike bills and sharp claws. They are nocturnal, and very noisy when disturbed. They feed on fruits and palm nuts which they pluck off the trees in flight.

**OILBIRD**

*Steatornis caripensis*
GUÁCHARO

Pl. 25

18″ (46 cm.). Rufescent brown above, somewhat barred blackish; pinkish brown below. Crown with small white spots. Wing coverts with round, white, black-encircled spots, outer primaries with white spots. Tail long, very stiff, barred with narrow black bars, outer feathers with white dots.

Tropical and lower subtropical zones. Nw Zulia, Falcón, Mérida, Cojedes, Aragua and Monagas; Bolívar on the Río Paragua and Cerros Roraima and Sarisariñama. [E Panama; Colombia, Guyana, Ecuador, and Peru. Trinidad.]

Caves with completely dark areas, but also in other caves and in large cavelike crevices, to 2000 m. n of the Orinoco, to 1000 m. s of it. A few may roost in the open, often in palm trees.

## POTOOS: Nyctibiidae

### Nictibios

Potoos are strictly nocturnal and are related to nightjars. They nest on tree stumps, lay but a single egg and when incubating or perching assume an erect position, blending with the stump, which makes them difficult to see. They live in open forest and feed on insects which they catch on the wing.

**GREAT POTOO**

*Nyctibius grandis*
NICTIBIO GRANDE

Pl. IX

20″ (52 cm.). White or grayish white to dark brown marbled with closely set wavy lines of black and rufous. Remiges black on inner web. Tail long, much marbled, gray and black, or brown and black and white or buffy, and with 8 or 9 dusky bars.

Tropical zone. Locally in nw Zulia, Táchira, westernmost Apure, Trujillo, Aragua, Monagas, Delta Amacuro, nw Bolívar and central Amazonas. [Guatemala. Panama, Colombia, the Guianas to e Peru, and s Brazil.]

Rain and deciduous forest, second growth, savannas, open fields, sea level to 300 m. n of the Orinoco, near sea level s of it. Nocturnal, during the day sits motionless on trees or stumps. Call: a harsh, grating, guttural sound "wah-h-h oo-oo-oo." Lays 1 egg in a depression of a high tree stump.

**LONG-TAILED POTOO**

*Nyctibius aethereus*
NICTIBIO COLILARGO

Pl. IX

18″ (46 cm.). Rufous brown, the feathers marbled with black, and with black spots on inner wing coverts and breast. Tail strongly graduated, central feathers pointed.

Tropical zone. Recorded in El Dorado, ne Bolívar (*longicauda*). [Colombia and the Guianas to e Peru, Amazonian and se Brazil and Paraguay.] Rain forest, 100 m. Nocturnal, arboreal.

## COMMON POTOO
*Nyctibius griseus*
NICTIBIO GRISÁCEO

Pl. IX

15" (38 cm.). Grayish brown, mottled, streaked and vermiculated black and cinnamon, appearing darkish gray from a distance. Wing coverts somewhat more rufescent than rest of plumage. Center of crown and center of breast with broad, elongated black spots; narrow, black streaks on underparts. Tail long, like back in color. A dark brown color phase is not unusual.

Tropical and subtropical zones. Sw Táchira (*panamensis*). Elsewhere virtually throughout, but not yet recorded from Amazonas where it undoubtedly occurs (*griseus*). [S Mexico to Bolivia, n Argentina and Uruguay. Trinidad. Tobago. Jamaica, Hispaniola.]

Rain, deciduous, and gallery forest, second growth, open fields, along rivers, savannas with islands of trees, to 1800 m. n of the Orinoco, to 1100 m. s of it. Nocturnal, arboreal. Rests on the top of a high, exposed vertical tree stump. At dusk sallies forth for insects and returns to its perch. At night utters a series of loud melodious, descending, melancholy notes ("poor-me-all-alone," *fide* Bond). Lays 1 egg in a depression on a tree stump at medium-height.

## WHITE-WINGED POTOO
*Nyctibius leucopterus*
NICTIBIO ALIBLANCO

15" (38 cm.). Not unlike the dark brown phase of the Common Potoo but crown very heavily spotted with black, and distinguishable from it and any other potoo by its white, black-tipped, inner wing coverts which form a *broad white band on wing*. Tail dark brown with irregular pale brown bands.

Subtropical zone. Extreme e Táchira at Boca de Monte (*maculosus*). [W slope of e Andes, n Colombia. E Ecuador. Coastal Brazil in Bahia.] Cloud forest, 2400 m.

# NIGHTHAWKS, NIGHTJARS: Caprimulgidae

AGUAITACAMINOS

Two groups form this family: the nighthawks, often seen flying at dusk high over open fields and water courses, and the strictly nocturnal nightjars.

Nighthawks have narrower and more pointed wings than the nightjars, and their tails are usually slightly forked, but both share the same habit of laying their eggs on the bare ground. They feed on insects which are caught on the wing. When perching on trees they perch lengthwise on the branch on which they rest.

As most species resemble each other closely, are nocturnal and not often seen, the various species are best identified by voice.

## SEMICOLLARED NIGHTHAWK
*Lurocalis semitorquatus*
AGUAITACAMINO SEMIACOLLARADO

Pl. XI

8.5" (22 cm.) [or 10" (25 cm.), a]. Very short tail and *long, pointed wings depassing tail when folded*. Upperparts black or blackish sprinkled everywhere with gray and rufous dots and rufous rings. Bar across throat white, breast

blackish with rufescent spots and rings (or blackish with gray and whitish spotting, b). Belly barred rufous and blackish (or rufous, unbarred, c). Scapulars, and particularly the tertials, silvery gray vermiculated black. Remiges black notched with rufous, *no white wing bar*. Central tail feathers dark brown, with wide grayish bands marbled with brown, rest barred buff.

Subtropical zone. The Andes of Táchira

and Mérida (*rufiventris*, a, c). Tropical zone, 450–1140 m. Aragua at Rancho Grande (*schaeferi*, a, b). Migrant from the s, Aragua at Rancho Grande (*nattereri*, a). Se Zulia, ne Portuguesa; s Amazonas; se Bolívar (*semitorquatus*). [Nicaragua. Panama to w Ecuador, the Guianas to se Brazil and n Argentina. Trinidad.]
Rain and cloud forests, nearby open terrain and clearings, to 1800 m. n of the Orinoco, at 1000 m. s of it. Crepuscular. Aerial forager, in pairs or small groups, above the treetops and forest edge. Feeds on insects, including beetles. It is possible that 2 species are involved in this complex.

[BIRDS BELONGING TO the genus *Chordeiles* are mostly vespertine and may be active on cloudy days.]

## LEAST NIGHTHAWK
*Chordeiles pusillus*
AGUAITACAMINO MENUDO

Pl. XI
6″ (15 cm.). A minute nighthawk. Grayish brown vermiculated blackish and spotted and speckled with rufous. Upper throat and breast grayish brown, a white V-shaped band across throat, belly regularly barred with white and dark brown, under tail coverts white (or barred with dusky, a). Outer 4 primaries with a white bar, secondaries tipped buff. Tail dark brown, middle feathers with mottled grayish bars, rest barred with buff, all but central and outermost pairs of feathers tipped white.
Tropical zone. N of the Orinoco only at Cantaura, central Anzoátegui; e Bolívar from Altiplanicie de Nuria s; nw Amazonas (*septentrionalis*). Central and se Amazonas (*esmeraldae*, a). [E Colombia, Guyana, ne and s Brazil.]
Rain forest edge, 100–1000 m. Clearings savannas, open terrain. Call: a "beep" sound while flying.

## SAND-COLORED NIGHTHAWK
*Chordeiles rupestris*
AGUAITACAMINO BLANCO

Pl. XI
9.5″ (24 cm.). Upperparts sandy gray, streaked and vermiculated blackish brown, grayish and buffy. Below white, band across breast same color as back. Outer 4 primaries black, rest of remiges white, tipped black, forming a large white area on both upper and underside of wing. Central tail feathers like back, rest white, tipped black with some black on outer web of outermost. Tail somewhat forked.
Tropical zone. Central and s Amazonas. [Se Colombia to Bolivia, w Amazonian Brazil.]
Rain and open forest, second growth, thickets, river bars, marshes, 100–200 m. A local name: Guacurayo Blanco.

## LESSER NIGHTHAWK
*Chordeiles acutipennis*
AGUAITACAMINO CHIQUITO

Pls. X, XI
8″ (20 cm.). Upperparts and chest grayish, speckled and marbled with black, spots on wing coverts and inner remiges buff. Band across throat white, lower breast and belly regularly banded buff and dark brown. Band across 4 outer primaries white (or buff, ♀), *the band near middle of feathers*. Tail blackish, barred sandy, all but central feathers with a white subterminal bar (or no white bar, ♀).
Tropical zone. Probably throughout including Margarita I. and Cayos Sal and Arriba (Falcón) (*acutipennis*). [Sw US to Colombia, the Guianas, w Peru, n Bolivia, Paraguay and s Brazil. Trinidad, Tobago. N Amer. breeders winter to n and w Colombia.]
All open habitats, to 1200 m. n of the Orinoco, to 500 m. s of it. Mangroves, xerophytic areas, towns, ocean beaches and salt lagoons, gallery forest. In pairs and flocks of 30 or more. Largely crepuscular. Call: repeated guttural trill on the ground, twanging note in flight.

## COMMON NIGHTHAWK
*Chordeiles minor*
AGUAITACAMINO MIGRATORIO

9″ (23 cm.). Very similar to Lesser Nighthawk but slightly larger, more coarsely marked, and best distinguished by the position of the white wing bar which is closer to the base of the outer primaries than to the tip of them. Flies high, Lesser Nighthawk flies low.

Transient (in part winter resident?). Recorded in Apr. from Mérida (*minor*). [Breeds in N Amer.; a breeding race in Panama. Winters to Argentina. Trinidad. Curaçao.]

Open country, near water, 1000 m. Largely crepuscular. Often found resting on the tile roofs. Flies rather high, flight somewhat erratic, interrupted by short sails. Call: a rather harsh "tseep," emitted in flight.

## BAND-TAILED NIGHTHAWK
*Nyctiprogne leucopyga*
AGUAITACAMINO COLIBLANCO

Pl. XI

7" (18 cm.). A small nighthawk with a white bar across middle of tail. Above blackish freckled with buff, scapulars with large, black buff-bordered marks. Wing coverts like back but more coarsely marked. Breast blackish spotted with cinnamon buff, a white patch at sides of throat; belly and under tail coverts barred whitish and black. Wings without white, primaries notched with rufous (or plain blackish, a); central tail feathers dark brown, marbled with black, with several rather wide blackish bars, rest of feathers blackish with a *white bar across central part*. Tail somewhat forked.

Tropical zone. Locally distributed in Apure (Guasdualito), (San Fernando de Apure); se Monagas (Las Barrancas, Corozal); Bolívar from Caicara to Ciudad Bolívar and La Paragua (*pallida*). Amazonas s to Caño Casiquiare (*exigua*). Amazonas along the Río Negro and s of Caño Casiquiare (*latifascia, a*). [Guyana, French Guiana, e Colombia, Amazonian Brazil.]

Rain forest to 200 m. Gallery forest, clearings, savannas, ponds, banks of large rivers. Cherrie (1916:303) noted that during the day, they perch crossways on horizontal branches in thickets, 2 to 10 huddled close beside one another, all facing in the same direction.

## NACUNDA NIGHTHAWK
*Podager nacunda*
AGUAITACAMINO BARRIGA BLANCA

Pl. XI

12" (30 cm.). Upperparts ochraceous buff finely vermiculated and freckled with

black; black spots on head, wing coverts and inner secondaries. Chin and sides of neck rusty, barred black; breast finely barred and spotted sandy and buff; V-shaped white band across throat; abdomen and under tail coverts white. Primaries black with a white diagonal bar, wing lining mostly white. Central tail feathers like back with 5 black bars, rest with a subterminal black bar and broad white tip. ♀: lacks the white tips to tail feathers.

Tropical and subtropical zones. Locally throughout (*minor*). [E Colombia, the Guianas to s Argentina. Trinidad, Tobago.]

Open terrain, to 200 m. n of the Orinoco, to 1000 m. s of it. Llanos, xerophytic areas, seashores, rain and gallery forest edge. Partially crepuscular. Alone, in pairs, and flocks of several hundred.

## PAURAQUE
*Nyctidromus albicollis*
AGUAITACAMINO COMÚN

Pl. X

11" (28 cm.). A handsome nightjar with large velvety black spots on scapulars. There are two color phases, mainly affecting the upper surface. Above grayish brown to reddish brown vermiculated black, crown with black spots, handsomely marked on scapulars with large, velvety black spots margined with buff. Primaries black with a white stripe across them, conspicuous in flight. Sides of head rufous; bar across foreneck white, throat black barred with buff, rest of underparts buff lightly barred with black. Outer tail feathers mostly black, next white on inner web, next all white, remainder like back but with dusky bars. ♀: like ♂ but white wing bar much narrower and tinged buff; tail like back, barred black, with only a small patch of white on inner web of second rectrix from without.

Tropical and lower subtropical zones throughout (*albicollis*). [Texas to nw Peru, Bolivia and ne Argentina. Trinidad.]

A variety of habitats, to 1400 m. n of the Orinoco, to 1000 m. s of it. Forested areas, mangroves, xerophytic areas, llanos, second growth, plantations, rocks in rivers. Alone or in pairs. Nocturnal, partly crepuscular. Flutters close to the ground for flying insects. During the day rests on the leafy forest floor. Call: harsh, strongly accented, repeated "whoo-oo-wé-oo"; another call is a repeated "whip whip whip whip."

[BIRDS BELONGING TO the genus *Caprimulgus* are strictly nocturnal and are all superficially very much alike in color. All are grayish brown, or brown finely vermiculated black, crown and scapulars heavily marked with black. Chin, breast and belly are usually buff with fine dusky bars, a white bar across foreneck. The central tail feathers are like the back but usually with a few black bars. The best differentiating characters are the white markings on wings and tail or lack of them. These will be relied upon to distinguish the species in the following descriptions.]

## CHUCK-WILLS-WIDOW

*Caprimulgus carolinensis*
AGUAITACAMINO AMERICANO

11" (28 cm.). A large nightjar with *no white in wing, inner web of outer 3 tail feathers white.* Eyebrow buffy, narrow band across foreneck buffy white. Primaries black, barred with tawny rufous. Outer 3 tail feathers notched rufous and black on outer web, rufescent at tip of both webs, inner webs white, rest of tail feathers rufous, vermiculated black, with about 7 irregular black bars. ♀: tail feathers like ♂, outer ones without any white, 3 outer pairs tipped rusty buff. Rictal bristles in both sexes with lateral filaments.
Casual winter visitor. Lourdes, central Mérida, Sept. [Breeds in central and s US. Winters from Central Amer. to Colombia.]
Open terrain, 1700 m. Spends the day on the forest floor. To be looked for in a variety of forested and open habitats.

## RUFOUS NIGHTJAR

*Caprimulgus rufus*
AGUAITACAMINO RUFO

Pl. X
12" (30 cm.) [or 10" (25.5 cm.), a]. Very similar to Chuck-Wills-Widow but distinguishable from it by having only half of the inner web of the 3 lateral tail feathers white (or tipped white, a). General plumage more rufescent. Rictal

bristles without lateral filaments. ♀: best distinguished from the Chuck-wills-widow by *absence* of *lateral filaments* on the rictal bristles. More rufous in color, with darker buff tips to rectrices.
Tropical and subtropical zones. Very locally distributed in nw Zulia on Cerro Alto del Cedro; Mérida; Distr. Federal; Lara; Sucre (*minimus*). Sierra de Perijá, Zulia (Sept.); Aragua (Sept.); Miranda (May, Aug., Dec.) (*otiosus*, a). N Amazonas at Caño Cataniapo; Bolívar at El Carmen, upper Río Parguaza (*noctivigulus,* b). [St. Vincent, (*otiosus*). N Colombia. The Guianas to Bolivia and Paraguay and n Argentina. Trinidad.]
Rain forest, savanna thickets, to 900 m. n of the Orinoco, at 100 m. s of it. Perches crossways on branches. Call: loud "chuck-wee-wee-oh."
Note: Status of *C. otiosus* uncertain, whether resident or migrant. If resident then probably a distinct species.

## BAND-WINGED NIGHTJAR

*Caprimulgus longirostris*
AGUAITACAMINO SERRANO

Pl. X
9" (23 cm.). Above black with chestnut spots and rings; central tail feathers gray in contrast to back, vermiculated and barred with black. A white (or buff, ♀) bar across 4 outer primaries. A large white terminal patch on all but central tail feathers (smaller patch clouded with gray, ♀), a white (or buff, ♀) spot or bar on inner webs near base.
Subtropical and temperate zones. The serranías of the n from Zulia, Táchira, w Barinas and Mérida, and from Aragua to n Carabobo (*ruficervix*). The tepuis of the Gran Sabana, Bolívar and of central and s Amazonas (*roraimae*). [Colombia to Chile. Se Brazil, Uruguay and s Argentina.]
Cloud forest edge, low, open vegetation, páramos, 1000–3200 m. n of the Orinoco, 1300–2300 m. s of it. Alone or in pairs Call: a sometimes interminable, plaintive "chee-whit-chee-whit-chee-whit."

## WHITE-TAILED NIGHTJAR

*Caprimulgus cayennensis*
AGUAITACAMINO RASTROJERO

Pl. X
8.5" (22 cm.). Sexes very different; ♂ with a great deal of white; ♀: with no

white. Chin, throat and abdomen white. A broad oblique white band across 4 outer primaries, a narrow, incomplete, white band near base, rest of remiges with incomplete bars; secondaries tipped white, inner webs mostly white. Outer pair of rectrices white with blackish outer web and bar across middle, next 3 pairs similar but with blackish tip and outer web, central pair like back. ♀: darker than ♂, the bars and spots on wings ochraceous buff; no white in tail; chin, throat and abdomen buff barred with black and spotted with white. Outer 4 tail feathers barred rufescent and black, central pair like back with about 6 visible, narrow, black bars.

Tropical and subtropical zones. The coast of Falcón including the Paraguaná Pen.; Margarita I. (*insularis*). Ne Barinas, e Apure and from Zulia and Lara e through Guárico, Aragua and Monagas to Delta Amacuro; Bolívar throughout; w and central Amazonas (*cayennensis*). [Costa Rica to Colombia and the Guianas. Aruba to Bonaire; Trinidad and Tobago. Lesser Antilles.]

Gallery, rain and cloud forest edge, llanos, savannas, xerophytic areas, open second growth, to 1200 m. n of the Orinoco, to 1600 m. s of it. Attracted to insects about animals in cattle corrals. By day rests on the ground or low bushes. Call: clear, high, prolonged, liquid whistle "chi-eeeeeeeeuw"; has been compared to escaping steam. A local name, *Bujío*, is onomatopoeic.

### SPOT-TAILED NIGHTJAR

*Caprimulgus maculicaudus*
AGUAITACAMINO COLA PINTADA

Pl. X
8″ (20 cm.). A small, very rufescent nightjar with no white in the wings; *primaries* dark brown *barred* with *rufous*. Central tail feathers like back with 3 or 4 conspicuous black bars, rest black, outer webs notched rufous, with a white terminal bar and 3 or 4 white spots or bars on inner web.

Tropical zone. Sw Barinas; Miranda; s Amazonas along the Río Negro. [Sw Mexico. N and e Colombia; the Guianas. Central and se Brazil. Se Peru, n Bolivia.]

Rain forest, open marshy places, clearings,

second growth, savannas, to 200 m. Spends the day in thickets and on open terrain. It is reported that when it is first seen in the beam of an electric torch it remains motionless, then flies in small circles and returns to the same spot, repeating the performance several times. Call: a high-pitched "pit-sweet."

### LITTLE NIGHTJAR

*Caprimulgus parvulus*
AGUAITACAMINO PÁLIDO

Pl. X
8″ (20 cm.). General tone of plumage grayer than in other species, breast spotted with white. Outermost primary with a white spot on inner web, next 3 with a broad white band across middle. Scapulars and inner wing coverts with conspicuous buffy white spots. All but central tail feathers with a small white patch at tip of inner web, sometimes on both webs of outer pair. ♀: differs from ♂ by dusky outer tail feathers with interrupted buff bars, primaries blackish with interrupted rufous bars on basal portion.

Tropical zone. Zulia to ne Bolívar. [Ne Colombia. Sw Ecuador. Nw and ne Peru. Brazil s of the Amazon to Bolivia and central Argentina.]

Woodland, savannas, thickets, 400–1000 m.

### BLACKISH NIGHTJAR

*Caprimulgus nigrescens*
AGUAITACAMINO NEGRUZCO

Pl. X
8″ (20 cm.). A small, blackish nightjar with a few white spots on breast. White throat band narrow, sometimes broken in the middle. Primaries black with a white spot on the middle of the inner web of the 2nd, 3rd and 4th feather (sometimes indistinct on the 2nd primary). A white tip 0.5″ (12 mm.) wide on both webs of 2nd and 3rd outer rectrix. ♀: has no white in plumage, otherwise like ♂.

Tropical zone. Amazonas and Bolívar (*nigrescens*). [The Guianas, Colombia to Bolivia and Brazil.]

Rain forest, second growth, savannas, rocky places, along rivers, sits on rocks in mid-stream, 100–1100 m. Not shy. Call: churring "purr"; hisses.

## RORAIMAN NIGHTJAR

*Caprimulgus whitelyi*
AGUAITACAMINO DEL RORAIMA

8.5″ (22 cm.). Primaries blackish with a white bar across 3 outer primaries, secondaries spotted with buff on inner web. Outer 2nd and 3rd rectrix with a subterminal white patch on inner web only. ♀: has a narrow buff bar on inner web of the outer wing feather, on both webs of the next two. Rectrices like ♂ but white much reduced in extent.
Subtropical zone. Bolívar on Cerros Ptaritepui, Roraima and Jaua.
An endemic species to Pantepui. Scattered and very dense vegetation in humid terrain on the slopes and summits of the tepuis, 1300–1800 m. Vespertine.

## LADDER-TAILED NIGHTJAR

*Hydropsalis climacocerca*
AGUAITACAMINO GRISÁCEO

Pl. X
♂ 11″ (28 cm.), ♀ 9″ (23 cm.). *Tail shaped like a W,* central and outer feathers longest, central feathers pale sandy, narrowly banded with black, outer feathers slightly longer than central ones, notched sandy and blackish at base of outer web, barred black and white at base of inner web with a broad, diagonal white band on distal portion of feathers; intervening tail feathers considerably shorter than central and outer feathers, white with black base and tip. Two color phases, gray or buffy particularly marked below. Above sandy buff vermiculated black; breast sandy buff or grayish, vermiculated, belly white. Primaries crossed by a white band. ♀: tail shaped as in ♂ but much

shorter, central feathers like back, rest black barred with rufescent brown; primaries marked as in ♂ but band cinnamon rufous instead of white. General plumage more rufescent than in ♂, particularly below; belly cinnamon buff regularly barred dusky.
Tropical zone. Nw Bolívar along the lower Río Caura; Amazonas along Ríos Orinoco, and Ventuari, Caño Casiquiare and Río Negro (*climacocerca*). Bolívar along the upper Río Paragua (*schomburgki*). [E Colombia, the Guianas to n Bolivia and Amazonian Brazil.]
Rain forest, open woodland, second growth, savannas, 100–350 m. River banks, rocks in midstream, thickets. Not shy.

## LYRE-TAILED NIGHTJAR

*Uropsalis lyra*
AGUAITACAMINO COLA DE LIRA

Pl. X
♂ 31″ (79 cm.), ♀ 10″ (25 cm.). ♂ unmistakable; outer pair of *tail feathers enormously lengthened,* 26″ (66 cm.), lyreshaped, black, tapering to a white tip, outer web very narrow. Primaries black, notched rufous on outer web. ♀: quite different from ♂. Tail of normal length but slightly forked, black with interrupted rufous bars on all the feathers. Primaries black, notched rufous on outer web.
Subtropical and temperate zones in the Andes of Mérida (*lyra*). [Colombia to Peru.]
Cloud forest regions, 2500–3000 m. Forest edge, near streams. Solitary, perches in low branches. Calls at dusk; a local name in Colombia is *tres cueros,* in imitation of its call: "tre-cué, tre-cué, tre-cué."

# APODIFORMES

# SWIFTS: Apodidae

## VENCEJOS

Swifts are virtually of world-wide distribution but because they feed exclusively on small insects, which they catch on the wing, they are most common in warm climates where food is always abundant. Species nesting in cool, temperate regions migrate to the tropics from either north or south.

Swifts are especially well adapted to an aerial life and spend more time in the air than any other birds, some even being reputed to sleep on the wing.

Unlike swallows, with which they are sometimes confused, they never alight on wires or rooftops, and in the air are characterized by their very rapid and dashing flight, often in groups, and by their loud twittering or screeching notes. Swifts nest in hollow trees, rock crevices and caves, and perch by clinging with their strong claws to the sides of rocks or hollows in trees.

Species belonging to the genus *Cypseloides* and particularly *Chaetura* are very difficult to tell apart, while those belonging to other genera are more easily identified.

## WHITE-COLLARED SWIFT
*Streptoprocne zonaris*
VENCEJO GRANDE

Pl. XII

8" (20 cm.). A very large, sooty black swift with a white collar around the neck. Tail forked. Imm.: white collar much reduced or lacking.

Tropical and subtropical zones. Generally distributed n of the Orinoco and locally s of it among the cerros of Amazonas and Bolívar (*albicincta*). [Mexico to Colombia, Guyana and Argentina. Trinidad. Greater Antilles.]

Over all types of terrain at various heights, including cities, to 3000 m. Flocks of 30 to 300 and more. Nests in cliffs, crevices; also behind waterfalls, where the birds dash through the curtain of water as they arrive and leave. Hundreds roost in industrial structures.

## TEPUI SWIFT
*Cypseloides phelpsi*
VENCEJO DE LOS TEPUIS

Pl. XII

6.5" (16.5 cm.). Very similar to Chestnut-collared Swift but tail longer, forked instead of square. Sooty black; cheeks, chin, throat, upper breast and broad nuchal collar orange chestnut. ♀: similar to ♂; in some specimens the orange chestnut of breast somewhat mixed with brown.

Tropical and lower subtropical zones. Amazonas on Cerros Yapacana, Duida and Sierra Parima; Bolívar in the Gran Sabana (upper Río Caroní, Cerros Auyan-tepui, Uei-tepui and Jaua); once in Aragua (Rancho Grande, 1000 m.). [Merumé Mts., nw Guyana, Brazil in the mountains along the Venezuelan border.] Vicinity of cliffs, rocky canyons, waterfalls, 400–1300 m.

Note: C. T. Collins, Contrib. in Science

(June 1972), no. 229: 4 (Cerro Auyan-tepui, 1000 m., Bolívar, Venezuela).

## CHESTNUT-COLLARED SWIFT
*Cypseloides rutilus*
VENCEJO CUELLIRROJO

Pl. XII

6" (15 cm.). A medium-sized swift with a *chestnut breast* and *collar* around neck. Tail square, shafts protruding when worn. Mainly sooty, brownish black, including chin and upper throat; lower throat, cheeks, upper breast and collar around hindneck rufous chestnut. ♀: usually uniform in color, without chestnut as are immature birds; or with indications of chestnut; rarely like males.

Tropical and subtropical zones. The Andes of Táchira, Mérida and Barinas n to Carabobo and e in the n Cordilleras to Sucre (*rutilus*). [Mexico to Colombia and n Bolivia. Trinidad.]

Mostly in mountainous terrain, 600–2000 m. n of the Orinoco. Joins flocks of other swifts.

Note: Specimens recorded in Lista Av. Venez. from s of the Orinoco prove to belong to *C. phelpsi*. The subspecies *brunnitorques* appears to be of doubtful validity.

## SPOT-FRONTED SWIFT
*Cypseloides cherriei*
VENCEJO CUATRO OJOS

Pl. XII

5.5" (14 cm.). Uniform dark sooty, slightly paler below. Lores sooty black, a *white spot at each side* of *forehead*, conspicuous in flight, and a smaller spot or streak *behind eye*, tail short, spines protruding. ♀: lacks white spot behind eye.

Subtropical zone. Winter resident or visitor? Aragua at Rancho Grande.

[Irazú Volcano, Costa Rica. Colombia in Santander, Jan.]
Mountainous regions, 1100 m.

## WHITE-CHINNED SWIFT

*Cypseloides cryptus*
VENCEJO CASTAÑO

Pl. XII
5.5″ (15 cm.). Sooty brown; chin spot white, not always present. Lores deep black, feathers at sides of forehead edged grayish white. Tail short, spines protruding.
Tropical and subtropical zones. Resident or migrant? Breeding grounds unknown. Táchira at Burgua; Aragua at Rancho Grande; Bolívar in the Gran Sabana on Cerros Auyan-tepui and Sororopán-tepui. [British Honduras to Panama, Colombia; Guyana. E Peru.]
Forested, mountainous areas, 260–1000 m. n of the Orinoco, near 2000 m. s of it on the upper slopes and summits of the tepuis.

BLACK SWIFT (*Cypseloides niger*) probably reaches e Venezuela occasionally as a casual migrant, for it has been taken in nw Guyana and seen in Trinidad. It is a large swift (7″, 18 cm.), with a slightly forked tail and whitish forehead.

## CHAPMAN'S SWIFT

*Chaetura chapmani*
VENCEJO DE CHAPMAN

Pl. XII
4.7″ (12 cm.). Crown and back black, wings black with a blue gloss; rump and upper tail coverts grayish brown not contrasting very noticeably with back. Below dull grayish brown, darker than rump; throat and foreneck slightly paler than breast.
Probably resident. Known from Alturita, nw Zulia; Aragua; Irapa, Sucre and Caño Cuao, n Amazonas (*chapmani*). [Panama, Colombia, The Guianas, e Peru, ne Brazil. Trinidad.]
Various terrains to 600 m. n of the Orinoco, to 200 m. s of it.

## CHIMNEY SWIFT

*Chaetura pelagica*
VENCEJO DE CHIMENEA

5″ (13 cm.). Upperparts dark grayish brown, rump and tail slightly paler. Throat whitish, rest of underparts ashy gray, much paler than back. Tail short, spines protruding.
Transient. Recorded once in s Táchira in Nov. Probably passes n Mar.–May. [Breeds in N Amer. Winters in w Amazonian Brazil and w Peru.]
The only specimen recorded in Venezuela was taken in open terrain with scattered trees, at 350 m. Call: reported to be louder than those of the resident birds of the genus.

## VAUX'S SWIFT

*Chaetura vauxi*
VENCEJO DE VAUX

Pl. XII
4.2″ (10.6 cm.). A small, short-tailed swift with whitish throat, foreneck and upper breast. Crown and upper back black; lower back and rump light grayish olive in contrast. Lower breast and belly grayish brown. Imm.: darker than ad.; remiges have white tips.
Tropical and subtropical zones. Serranías of the n from Lara and Yaracuy to Sucre and Monagas (*aphanes*). [From Alaska to e Panama.]
From the seacoast to 1800 m. Flocks up to 50. Joins flocks of other swifts. Call: soft shrill chattering "chee-ee," "chee-ee." Nests and roosts in chimneys in Caracas suburbs.

## GRAY-RUMPED SWIFT

*Chaetura cinereiventris*
VENCEJO CENICIENTO

Pl. XII
4.8″ (12 cm.). Crown, mantle and wings glossy blue black; *lower back, rump* and upper tail coverts and underparts *gray*, under tail coverts black. Throat whitish (or gray like underparts, a). Lores velvety black. Tail glossy black, spines protruding.
Tropical and lower subtropical zones. S Táchira and Mérida (*schistacea*). N serranías in Yaracuy, Aragua, Miranda, Anzoátegui, Sucre and Margarita I.

(*lawrencei*). Bolívar on the cerros of the Gran Sabana and on Cerro Guaiquinima, Río Paragua (*guianensis*, a). Sw Amazonas (*sclateri*). [Nicaragua to w Panama. Colombia to sw Ecuador, Guyana. E Peru, w Amazonian and se Brazil, Paraguay, ne Argentina. Trinidad.]
From the seacoast to 1400 m. Flocks up to 30 or more.

## BAND-RUMPED SWIFT
*Chaetura spinicauda*
VENCEJO LOMIBLANCO

Pl. XII
Very like Gray-rumped Swift, best distinguished by having only the rump and upper tail coverts pale gray, in the form of a band. Underparts darker and brown rather than gray. Tail spines long.
Tropical zone. Sucre at the base of the Paria Pen.; Delta Amacuro at Joburc; Bolívar along the lower Río Caura, the lower Río Paragua and in the se on Cerro Paurai-tepui (*latirostris*). Amazonas (*aethalea*). [Costa Rica to n and e Colombia, the Guianas, n and central Brazil. Trinidad.]
Open terrain at sea level n of the Orinoco and in the delta, to 1000 m. s of the river. Light, whitish rump, not duplicated in the other swifts.

## ASHY-TAILED SWIFT
*Chaetura andrei*
VENCEJO GARGANTIBLANCO

Pl. XII
4.5″ (11.5 cm.) [or 5.5″ (14 cm.), a]. Dark smoky brown above, rump and upper tail coverts smoky gray; tail ashy gray with dark shafts, spines protruding, but shorter than in Gray-rumped Swift. Below ashy gray, throat pale grayish. Not unlike Gray-rumped but back smoky brown instead of blue black, darker below with a more contrasting pale throat. Tail shorter. (Or similar but larger, wing 128–135 mm. vs. 114–117 mm., a).
Tropical zone. Locally in Carabobo, Guárico, Sucre, n Bolívar along the middle Orinoco and near the Sierra de Imataca (*andrei*). Migrant from the s, recorded at Rancho Grande, Aragua, Sept. (*meridionalis*, a). [Panama, migrant. N Colombia, migrant? Surinam. E and s Brazil, n Paraguay, Argentina.]
Flies in various terrains to 900 m. Small groups up to 5 or more. Frequently quite low over the ground.

## SHORT-TAILED SWIFT
*Chaetura brachyura*
VENCEJO COLIBLANCO

Pl. XII
4″ (10 cm.). Mostly black, somewhat glossy above; dull and tinged brown below. Lower back, rump, very short tail and *under tail coverts* light *brownish ashy gray*.
Tropical zone. N of the Orinoco from Zulia, Táchira and Mérida to Sucre and Delta Amacuro; n Bolívar from Caicara to the upper Río Cuyuni; San Fernando de Atabapo, n Amazonas (*brachyura*). Amazonas at the foot of Cerro Duida (*cinereocauda*). [Panama once. Colombia to nw Peru, the Guianas, ne and s Brazil. Trinidad.]
Llanos, rain forest, mangroves, beaches, pastures, plantations, to 900 m.

## WHITE-TIPPED SWIFT
*Aeronautes montivagus*
VENCEJO MONTAÑÉS

Pl. XII
5″ (13 cm.). Above, including wings and tail, glossy brownish black with an olive sheen. Tertials tipped white. Tail somewhat forked, no spines, the feathers edged white apically. Throat, breast, line down center of abdomen dirty white, a tuft of silky white feathers on flanks.
Upper tropical and subtropical zones. Locally distributed in the mountains; Zulia; Carabobo to Sucre; Bolívar on Cerro Auyan-tepui; Amazonas on Cerros Duida and Yapacana. [Serra de Imerí, Brazil. Colombia, e Ecuador to w and se Peru and n Bolivia.]
Mountainous regions, 800–2600 m. n of the Orinoco, 700–1900 m. on the tepuis. In flocks of 10–25. Many nest in the Rancho Grande Biological Station, Maracay.

## LESSER SWALLOW-TAILED SWIFT
*Panyptila cayennensis*
VENCEJITO COLLAR BLANCO

Pl. XII
5.5" (14 cm.). Blue black, collar on hind-neck, throat, breast, patch at sides of lower back and a spot at each side of forehead white. *Tail long, forked,* blue black, base of outer feathers white.
Upper tropical zone. Miranda at Rancho Grande, Maracay, and Cerro Golfo Triste, breeding (*cayennensis*). [S Mexico to n Colombia, the Guianas to e Peru and Amazonia and se Brazil. Trinidad, Tobago.]
Mountainous terrain, forest, clearings, open country, 450–1000 m. Alone or in pairs. Joins other swifts in their very high, wheeling flight above the trees. Deeply forked tail visible when spread in flight. Nest, a tube of plant fibers, 20 to 60 cm. long, some 15 cm. wide, with the entrance at the lower end, hanging from a branch, or to the underside of a ledge. The same nest is used over the years.

## PYGMY SWIFT
*Micropanyptila furcata*
VENCEJO ENANO

Pl. XII
4" (10 cm.). A *tiny swift* with a rather long deeply *forked tail,* (usually closed, appearing long and thin in flight). Above

glossy brownish black with a slight green gloss on wings and tail. Below ashy brown, center of abdomen white.
Tropical zone. Known from Alturita and Guachi, Zulia, Las Mesas, Táchira, El Vigía, Mérida, and Betijoque, nearby in Trujillo. [Ne Colombia in Norte de Santander.]
Rain forests, pastures, open fields with scattered trees, clearings, second growth, 100–500 m. Nests in palm trees.

## FORK-TAILED PALM-SWIFT
*Reinarda squamata*
VENCEJO TIJERETA

Pl. XII
5.5" (14 cm.). *Tail long, deeply forked.* Back, wings and tail brownish black with a strong green gloss, feathers of back pale-edged. Throat and center of breast dirty white, sides of body pale brownish. Toes feathered.
Tropical zone. The llanos from Barinas and Cojedes e to Sucre, Monagas and Delta Amacuro; Bolívar; n Amazonas (*squamata*). S Apure along the Río Meta; s Amazonas (*semota*). [E Colombia, the Guianas, ne Peru, Brazil. Trinidad.]
Open fields, savannas, llanos, swamps, rural habitations, pastures, to 300 m. n of the Orinoco, to 1000 m. s of it. Pairs and small flocks. Aerial foraging usually is only a few meters above the ground. Nests in Moriche palms.

# HUMMINGBIRDS: Trochilidae

## COLIBRIES, TUCUSITOS, CHUPAFLORES

Hummingbirds form one of the most remarkable of bird families. Confined to the Americas, a bewildering number of species is found from Alaska to Tierra del Fuego, but mostly in tropical regions, and occupying all sorts of habitats from deserts and lowland forests to the bleak summits of the Andes.

Hummingbirds are unique in the brilliance of their metallic colors; in addition many are decorated with crests, ruffs and tails of remarkable length or form.

Hummingbirds feed principally on the nectar of flowers, hovering in front of the blossoms on wings which beat at the rate of about 60 beats per second and make the humming noise from which their name is derived. They also eat small insects.

The usual hummingbird nest is a cup-shaped affair built of vegetable down, fibers and lichens bound together with cobwebs, placed in a fork of a branch or attached to the top of a limb. However, birds belonging to the genera *Glaucis, Threnetes* and *Phaethornis* build a curious nest in which the broad cup to hold the eggs is closely attached to the underside of a leaf or branch and has a long, conical, pendant tail hanging from below it. The whole is composed of mosses, rootlets and various fibers bound together with cobwebs and is fairly rigid and rough to the touch.

A short explanation of the descriptions of the hummingbirds follows.

The bill and body length are given separately, the bill measurement in square brackets, the two together giving the total length. Some very small hummingbirds have long bills and some large ones have short bills, and so a total length would mean little in relation to the actual size of the bird. Bills in most hummingbirds are black and straight or nearly so: these will, therefore, only be mentioned if they are not. Wings will not be described as they are almost always blackish, blue black or purple black.

As hummingbirds are often seen hovering in front of flowers the upperparts and tail will be described first. The color and shape of the tail is often one of the best diagnostic characters.

## BLUE-FRONTED LANCEBILL

*Doryfera johannae*
PICO LANZA FRENTIAZUL

Pl. 11

3.5 [1.1]″; 9 [2.8] cm. Frontlet glittering violet blue, back dark bronze green, upper tail coverts bluish; tail slightly rounded, blue black. Underparts dusky green to blue black. ♀: forehead shining blue green, occiput coppery, upperparts dusky bronzy green, upper tail coverts bluish, tail blue black, outer feathers tipped gray. Underparts dark grayish glossed with green.

Tropical and subtropical zones. Cerros and tepuis of Bolívar in the Gran Sabana and in Amazonas (*guianensis*). [Guyana, n Brazil in Roraima, Andes of Colombia to se Peru.]

Rain and cloud forest, forest edge, small clearings, scrub, savannas, along streams, 280–1800 m.

## GREEN-FRONTED LANCEBILL

*Doryfera ludoviciae*
PICO LANZA FRENTIVERDE

Pl. 11

4 [1.4]″; 10 [3.5] cm. Both sexes much like the ♀ of Blue-fronted Lancebill but larger, with longer bill and the frontlet glittering green instead of violet blue.

Subtropical zone. Locally in the Andes of Mérida (*ludoviciae*). [Costa Rica, w Panama. Colombia to n Bolivia.]

Cloud forest, 1600–2200 m.

## RUFOUS-BREASTED HERMIT

*Glaucis hirsuta*
COLIBRÍ PECHO CANELA

Pl. 14

4.2 [1.3]″; 10.6 [3.3] cm. Bill curved, *lower mandible yellow*. Above bronzy green, below bright (or dull, a) cinnamon, whitish on belly. Stripe through eye dusky. Central tail feathers like back with narrow white tip, rest cinnamon rufous with a subterminal black band and white tip. Tail rounded.

Tropical zone. W Venezuela in Zulia, Táchira, Apure, Barinas, Mérida and Portuguesa; s of the Orinoco in Amazonas s to Cerro Duida and w Bolívar from the Río Cuchivero to the upper Río Caura (*affinis*, a). N and s of the Orinoco e of the areas occupied by *affinis* (*hirsuta*). [Panama to n Bolivia, Amazonian and se Brazil. The Guianas. Trinidad, Tobago, Grenada.]

Rain forest, second growth, to 1000 m. n of the Orinoco, to 600 m. s of it. Forest edge, near streams, mangroves, pastures, dense shrubbery, *Heliconia* thickets. Alone, perches low, seldom in high branches. Voice: shrill "sweep." Attaches nest to underside of palm leaves.

## PALE-TAILED BARBTHROAT

*Threnetes leucurus*
GARGANTA LANZA COLIBLANCA

Pl. 14

4 [1.3]″; 10 [3.3] cm. Bill slightly curved, lower mandible bluish gray. Above bronze green, the feathers, especially of crown, edged buffy. Central tail feathers greener than back, tipped white, outer feathers pale buff, outermost with a diagonal, subterminal black band and white tip. Throat black, bordered at sides by a white line and below by a broad buff band. Breast dusky bronze green, lower breast buffy white.

Tropical zone. Locally distributed in central Amazonas and nw, ne and s Bolívar (*leucurus*). [The Guianas, e Colombia to n Bolivia, n Brazil.]

Rain forest, new second growth, plantations, near rivers, 100–1000 m. Solitary. Undergrowth, dense shrubbery, lower understory.

## BAND-TAILED BARBTHROAT

*Threnetes ruckeri*
TUCUSO DE BARBA

Pl. 14
4 [1.3]″; 10 [3.3] cm. Very like Pale-tailed Barbthroat, differing principally by having the tail feathers steel blue, tipped white, all but central feathers basally white. Breast and belly gray, rather than buffy. Mandible yellow.
Tropical zone. The basin of L. Maracaibo, Zulia; n Táchira; w Apure; w Mérida (*venezuelensis*). [Guatemala to w Ecuador.]
Rain forest, second growth, 20–300 m. Along streams, alone or in small groups, usually well inside the forest, low in undergrowth and in *Heliconia* thickets. Banana plantations. Vibrates tail, showing the white tip.

[*Phaethornis* IS COMPOSED OF many species distinctive in structure and color. They are medium to very small in size, have long, curved bills (except the Straight-billed Hermit), the lower mandible mostly yellow or red. They are devoid of iridescence, the upperparts bronzy green, below pale buff to cinnamon, and usually with a dark stripe through the eye and a pale stripe down the center of the throat. The very distinctive tail is long, much graduated, with elongated and narrowed central feathers, all the feathers pale-tipped. When the bird hovers before a flower the tail is often spread and appears very wide. The sexes are similar.]

## GREEN HERMIT

*Phaethornis guy*
ERMITAÑO VERDE

Pl. 14
5 [1.6]″; 13 [4] cm. A dark species. Upperparts, sides of throat and breast bronze green, upper tail coverts blue green. Tail blue at base shading to blue black, central feathers long, narrowed, tipped white. Moustacial streak, streak behind eye, line down center of throat

and patch on abdomen rufescent buff, rest of underparts gray. Mandible reddish orange.
Tropical zone. Very local in nw Zulia, n Táchira and Mérida (*apicalis*). The e coastal Cordillera in Sucre and n Monagas (*guy*). [Costa Rica to Colombia and se Peru.]
Rain forest, second growth, open forest, humid areas, forest edge, to 1200 m. In undergrowth, dense thickets, *Heliconia* thickets. Curious, may hover a meter or so from the intruder. Perches low. Assembles in groups, each male on its own perch, close to the ground, and utters a series of monotonous, strong, sharp chirps. Hangs nest from the tips of palm leaves.

## LONG-TAILED HERMIT

*Phaethornis superciliosus*
ERMITAÑO GUAYANÉS

Pl. 14
5.5 [1.7]″; 14 [4.3] cm. Above bronzy green, crown dusky, feathers of back and particularly upper tail coverts edged buff. Tail dark blue green with a broad subterminal black band, central feathers very long, narrowed, distally white, rest tipped buff. Superciliaries and broad stripe below eye buffy white, moustacial streak dusky, underparts grayish buff, gular streak pale buff. Mandible salmon red, tipped black.
Tropical zone. The Sierra de Perijá, Zulia (*susurrus*). Nw Bolívar along the lower Río Caura and Amazonas n of the Río Ventuari (*saturatior*). E Bolívar from the Río Paragua e; Amazonas s of the Río Ventuari (*superciliosus*). Extreme sw Amazonas (*insolitus*). [Mexico to Colombia, the Guianas, w Ecuador, Amazonian Brazil, n Bolivia.]
Rain and cloud forest, 450–1300 m. n of the Orinoco, sea level to 1300 m. s of it. Not shy, solitary, may hover near the observer. Forages in the lower levels of the forest, *Heliconia* thickets. Gathers in groups, perched in low branches where it chirps continuously. Nests at the tip of palm leaves.
Note: *P. s. susurrus* is listed as a subspecies of *P. malaris* in Lista Av. Venez.

## WHITE-BEARDED HERMIT
*Phaethornis hispidus*
ERMITAÑO BARBIBLANCO

Pl. 14
5 [1.4]″; 13 [3.5] cm. Bronzy coppery green above, crown dusky, upper tail coverts fringed grayish white. Tail dark bronzy green with a black subterminal band and narrow white tip, central feathers long, narrowed, distally white. Sides of throat and breast gray, gular streak white, belly whitish. Base of mandible lemon yellow.
Tropical zone. S Táchira; w Barinas; Apure; Amazonas s to Cerro Duida, Caño Casiquiare and the Río Ocamo; Bolivar in the nw along the lower Río Caura and in the extreme se (Sta. Elena). [E Colombia to se Peru, nw and s Brazil.]
Rain and deciduous forest, second growth, *Heliconia* thickets, banana plantations, 100–800 m. n of the Orinoco, to 1000 m. s of it. Perches low in undergrowth.

## PALE-BELLIED HERMIT
*Phaethornis anthophilus*
ERMITAÑO CARINEGRO

Pl. 14
5.3 [1.4]″; 13.5 [3.5] cm. Above bronze green, the feathers edged ochraceous, tail bluish green, with a black subterminal band and narrow white tip, central feathers long, narrowed, distally white. Sides of head black, superciliary and broad moustacial streak buffy white; the throat streaked black, breast pale grayish, rest of underparts dingy white. Base of mandible bright orange red.
Tropical zone. N of the Orinoco from Zulia, Táchira and Apure to Anzoátegui and Monagas (*anthophilus*). [E Panama, n Colombia.]
Rain and deciduous forest, second growth, clearings, pastures, along streams, thorny thickets, cocoa plantations, sea level to 1200 m. Solitary, forages at low levels.

## STRAIGHT-BILLED HERMIT
*Phaethornis bourcieri*
ERMITAÑO DE PICORRECTO

Pl. 14
4.8 [1.4]″; 12 [3.5] cm. Differs from all other Venezuelan species of *Phaethornis* in having a virtually straight bill; lower mandible orange except for black tip. Above bronze green, feathers edged black, those of upper tail coverts fringed buff. Narrow superciliary and inconspicuous malar streak buff, gular streak dull white, rest of underparts dingy grayish buff, paler on belly. Tail bronze green with a broad, black subterminal band and buff tips, central pair long, narrowed, distally white.
Tropical zone. S Amazonas from the Yavita-Pimichín Trail and Cerro Duida s (*bourcieri*). N Amazonas s to the Río Ventuari; se Bolívar from the upper Río Caura e to El Dorado and Cerro Roraima (*whitelyi*). [The Guianas, se Colombia, n Amazonian Brazil, e Ecuador, ne Peru.]
Rain forest, open brushy terrain, 120–1600 m. Perches low in the underbrush, in display assemblies like other *Phaethornis*.

## SOOTY-CAPPED HERMIT
*Phaethornis augusti*
LIMPIACASA

Pl. 14
5 [1.3]″; 13 [3.3] cm. Crown dusky, back bronze green, upper tail coverts orange rufous; streak behind eye, moustacial and gular streak white, rest of underparts dingy gray, under tail coverts buffy. Central tail feathers very long, slightly tapering, coppery green, distally white, next pair coppery green at base, black in center with distal half white, rest mostly black, broadly edged and tipped white. Mandible red.
Tropical and lower subtropical zones. The n mountains from Zulia and Táchira e to the Paria Pen., Sucre (*augusti*). Locally s of the Orinoco in nw Bolívar and in the Gran Sabana; n Amazonas on Cerros Guanay and Yapacana (*incanescens*). [Guyana, ne Colombia.]
Rain and cloud forests, forest edge, second growth, thickets, plantations, 450–2500 m. n of the Orinoco, sea level to 1600 m. s of it. Solitary, in undergrowth; flicks tail constantly and chirps as it hovers. Called Limpiacasa because it often enters suburban houses and forages in the rooms for spiders and insects.

## DUSKY-THROATED HERMIT
*Phaethornis squalidus*
ERMITAÑITO GARGANTIFUSCO

Pl. 14
3.5 [1]″; 9 [2.5] cm. Crown dusky brown, feathers pale-edged, rest of upperparts dull coppery green, tail coverts edged rufous. Tail feathers dull green, the central pair shorter and more pointed than in the Sooty-capped Hermit tipped white, the lateral ones edged buff. Stripe behind eye, and moustacial streak buffy white. Throat black, the feathers edged buff giving a streaked appearance, rest of underparts buffy. Mandible yellow basally.
Tropical zone. S of the Orinoco in Amazonas and Bolívar, to the Río Paragua and in the Gran Sabana on Cerro Auyantepui (*rupurumii*). [E Colombia, Guyana, e Amazonian and se Brazil.]
Rain forest, second growth, semi–open terrain, scrub, clearings, 50–500 m.
Note: Called *P. rupurumii* in Lista Av. Venez.

## REDDISH HERMIT
*Phaethornis ruber*
ERMITAÑITO RUFO

Pl. 14
3.2 [0.8]″; 8 [2] cm. Crown and center of back coppery, rump and upper tail coverts orange rufous. Tail bronzy brown, lateral feathers narrowly tipped and edged rufous, center pair, not conspicuously narrowed or lengthened, with a small white tip. Sides of head black with a whitish postocular stripe. Throat buffy white, rest of underparts rufous buff with an ill-defined black band across breast. Mandible lemon yellow, tip black.
Tropical zone. N parts of Amazonas and Bolívar, in Delta Amacuro, s in Amazonas to the upper Caño Casiquiare and in Bolívar to the lower Río Caura, the middle Río Paragua and the s Gran Sabana (*episcopus*). S of the areas occupied by *episcopus* (*nigricinctus*). [The Guianas, se Colombia to n Bolivia and s Brazil.]
Rain forest, second growth, forest edge, 50–1100 m. s of the Orinoco, forest edge at sea level in the Delta. Solitary, forages in the lower and middle branches. Nest suspended from palm leaves.

## GRAY-CHINNED HERMIT
*Phaethornis griseogularis*
ERMITAÑITO BARBIGRÍS

Pl. 14
3.4 [0.9]″; 8.6 [2.3] cm. Above much like Reddish Hermit but somewhat greener. Sides of head black, broad buffy postocular stripe, throat grayish, rest of underparts dull ochraceous. Tail feathers basally bronzy green then black with broad buff tips, central pair lengthened, but not conspicuously narrowed, mostly black with long white tips. Basal half of mandible lemon yellow, rest black.
Tropical and lower subtropical zones. Spottily distributed. Nw Zulia in the Perijá region; n and s Táchira; nw Mérida; w Barinas; Amazonas along the Brazilian border and Bolívar on Cerro Roraima (*griseogularis*). [E Colombia to w Ecuador, e and central Amazonian Brazil. Trinidad.]
Rain and cloud forests, second growth, thickets, 300–1700 m. n of the Orinoco, 650–1800 m. on the tepuis.

## LITTLE HERMIT
*Phaethornis longuemareus*
ERMITAÑITO PEQUEÑO

Pl. 14
3.6 [0.9]″; 9.1 [2.3] cm. Differs from Reddish and Gray-chinned Hermits by having the throat streaked dusky; underparts cinnamon buff (or buffy white, a). Central tail feathers bronze green, only slightly elongated, not narrowed, tipped white, rest bronze green tipped cinnamon buff. Basal half of mandible lemon yellow, rest black.
Tropical zone. E Zulia e of L. Maracaibo, adjacent w Mérida; n Táchira (*striigularis*). The n serranías from Mérida, Barinas, Trujillo and Carabobo to Miranda (*ignobilis*). The delta region in e Sucre and Delta Amacuro (*longuemareus*). Cerro Tomasote, ne Bolívar (*imatacae*, a). [Mexico to w Ecuador, e Peru, Amazonian Brazil, the Guianas and Trinidad.]
Rain forest, second growth, clearings, thickets, sea level to 1300 m. n of the Orinoco, at 500 m. s of it. Solitary, curious. Perches in the undergrowth, also near the ground, sometimes in singing groups. Call: various squeaks and

hisses. Nests hang a meter or two above the ground from palm leaves.

[IN *Campylopterus* THE MUCH thickened shaft of the outer primary in the ♂ is the principal character. In color the sexes are similar.]

## GRAY-BREASTED SABREWING
*Campylopterus largipennis*
ALA DE SABLE GRIS

Pl. 11

5 [1.2]″; 13 [3] cm. Above, including central tail feathers, shining dark green, rest of tail feathers steel blue, outer feathers white on distal half. Below plain dark gray. Bill slightly curved.
Tropical zone. S of the Orinoco in Amazonas, w and s Bolívar and Delta Amacuro (*largipennis*). [The Guianas, e Colombia to n and e Bolivia and Amazonian and e Brazil.]
Rain forest, second growth, scrub, plantations, clearings, thickets; 100–150 m. Perches very low to middle branches.

## RUFOUS-BREASTED SABREWING
*Campylopterus hyperythrus*
ALA DE SABLE RUFO

Pl. 11

4 [0.8]″; 10 [2] cm. Above shining bronze green, greener on head, 4 central tail feathers golden bronze, rest cinnamon rufous. Below uniform cinnamon rufous. Bill straight.
Subtropical zone. Se Bolívar on the cerros of the Gran Sabana. [Adjacent n Brazil.]
Endemic species on Pantepui. Cloud forest, 1300–2600 m. Open terrain with scattered vegetation. Usually in the lower branches. Nests 2 or 3 m. above the ground.

## BUFF-BREASTED SABREWING
*Campylopterus duidae*
ALA DE SABLE ANTEADO

4 [0.8]″; 10 [2] cm. Differs from Rufous-breasted Sabrewing by drab buff underparts, tinted tawny on sides, and dull bronze basal portion to buff outer tail feathers. Bill straight.
Upper tropical and subtropical zones. Central and s Amazonas on Cerros Yaví, Parú, Huachamacari, Duida and de la Neblina; sw Bolívar on Cerro Jaua (*duidae*). Cerro Guaiquinima, Río Paragua, central Bolívar (*guaiquinimae*). [Adj. Brazil.]
Endemic species on Pantepui. Cloud forest, 1200–2400 m. Open forest, forest edge, brush. Usually in the lower branches. Nests 2–3 m. above the ground.

## WHITE-TAILED SABREWING
*Campylopterus ensipennis*
ALA DE SABLE VERDE

Pl. 11

5 [1.1]″; 13 [2.8] cm. Upperparts glittering green, central tail feathers dark bronze green, next pair blue black, 3 outermost with blue black basal third and white distal two-thirds. Throat glittering dark violet, rest of underparts glittering green. Bill curved. ♀: differs from ♂ by pale gray underparts with green disks; subocular streak white, violet of throat mixed with green.
Upper tropical and lower subtropical zones. Generally distributed in the mountains of Sucre, ne Anzoátegui and Monagas. [Tobago.]
Cloud forests, 700–2000 m. Low to middle branches. Clearings. Call: a repeated chirp. Nests about 2 m. above the ground.

## LAZULINE SABREWING
*Campylopterus falcatus*
ALA DE SABLE PECHIVIOLETA

Pl. 11

4.5 [1]″; 11.5 [2.5] cm. Above glittering green. *Tail chestnut rufous* tipped blue green, narrowly blackish on outer feathers. Throat, center of breast and sides of neck glittering violet blue, sides of breast glittering golden green, center of belly glittering blue green, sides of belly golden green, under tail coverts rufous chestnut, tipped bronze. Bill curved. ♀: shining green above, central tail feathers shining bronze green, *outer feathers chestnut rufous*. Throat glittering blue green, rest of underparts dark grayish with a few green disks at sides.
Upper tropical to temperate zone. Generally distributed from Zulia and Táchira e through Mérida, Trujillo, Lara and Yaracuy to Miranda. [Colombia, e Ecuador.]

Cloud forests, 900–3000 m. Coffee plantations, scrub, shady gardens. Keeps to the shadiest parts of the forests. Visits *Heliconia* thickets, feeds on fluid and insects in flowers.

## WHITE-NECKED JACOBIN
*Florisuga mellivora*
COLIBRÍ NUCA BLANCA

Pls. 12, 13
4 [0.9]″; 10 [2.3] cm. Head and neck blue, a large white patch on upper mantle, rest of back shining bronze green. Upper tail coverts, as long as central tail feathers, bronze green, tail white, feathers with blue black tips. ♀: bronzy to coppery green above; tail feathers bronze green with a subterminal blue black patch, outermost tipped white, rest narrowly fringed white. Feathers of throat and breast dark bronzy green, broadly edged whitish, giving a scaled or spotted appearance; center of abdomen white, under tail coverts dark blue, tipped white.
Tropical zone throughout (*mellivora*). [Mexico to Bolivia and Brazil. Aruba, Trinidad, Tobago and Carriacou.]
Rain forest, second growth, clearings, forest edge, near streams, plantations. *Heliconia* thickets in damp areas. From near sea level to 1300 m. At all heights in the forest. Solitary or in small groups. Gathers in flocks of 100, joining other birds in flowering trees.

[THE VIOLETEARS (*Colibri*) have very long violet tufts from below the eye to the lengthened feathers of the auriculars, a feature which distinguishes them from other hummingbirds. They all have white tibial tufts. Bill very slightly curved.]

## BROWN VIOLETEAR
*Colibri delphinae*
COLIBRÍ OREJIVIOLETA MARRÓN

Pl. 11
4.5 [0.6]″; 11.5 [1.5] cm. General plumage grayish brown. Ear tufts violet, lores and moustacial streak whitish; irregular patch on lower throat glittering golden green turning to violet blue on lower throat, throat however looks dark and dull unless light is strong. Feathers of lower back and upper and under tail coverts fringed buffy or whitish. Tail pale olive bronze with a broad, subterminal purple bronze band. ♀: like ♂ but throat patch smaller. Imm.: feathers of the entire upperparts broadly edged cinnamon rufous making the upperparts appear rufous from a distance.
Tropical and subtropical zones throughout (*delphinae*). [The Guianas, Colombia to w Ecuador, n and e Bolivia and in ne (Roraima) and e (Bahia) Brazil. Trinidad.]
Rain and cloud forests, second growth, 300–2000 m. n of the Orinoco, 750–2000 m. s of it. Forest edge, clearings, coffee plantations. Solitary. Low heights to treetops. Call: monotonous chirping.

## GREEN VIOLETEAR
*Colibri thalassinus*
COLIBRÍ OREJIVIOLETA VERDE

Pl. 11
4 [0.7]″; 10 [1.8] cm. Shining green, throat and upper breast glittering green, the feathers with a small black central disk giving a scaly appearance, rest of underparts shining green. Ear tufts violet. Central tail feathers shining green with a broad, dull black subterminal patch, rest shining bluish green with a broad black subterminal band.
Upper tropical to temperate zones. Widely distributed in the n mountains from Zulia and Táchira through Mérida, Lara and Trujillo to Sucre and n Monagas (*cyanotus*). [Mexico to w Panama, Colombia to w Ecuador and n Bolivia and nw Argentina.]
Cloud forest and open woods to the páramo edge, 900–3000 m. Coffee plantations, open terrain with scattered bushes and trees on mountain slopes. Medium heights to treetops. Call: repeated sharp, metallic, chipping note.

## SPARKLING VIOLETEAR
*Colibri coruscans*
COLIBRÍ OREJIVIOLETA GRANDE

Pl. 11
5.5 [1]″; 14 [2.5] cm. Shining green above (forehead suffused with blue, a). Central tail feathers shining blue green, rest

brilliant dark green with a subterminal deep purplish blue band, tail slightly forked. Chin, throat, cheeks, and lengthened ear coverts and center of abdomen glittering purple blue; lower throat and breast glittering emerald green, the feathers with dark centers giving a scaled appearance; flanks and belly shining green.

Upper tropical to temperate zones. N mountains from Zulia and Táchira through Mérida, Lara, Barinas and Trujillo to n Guárico and Miranda (*coruscans*). N and central Amazonas on Cerros Yaví, Guanay, Huachamacari and Duida (*rostratus,* a). Bolívar on Cerro Guaiquinima and the cerros of the Gran Sabana (*germanus,* a). [Colombia to w Argentina.]

Rain and cloud forest, second growth, thickets, plantations, gardens, open terrain with scattered trees and bushes in the higher altitudes. Forages at all heights: 600–3500 m. n of the Orinoco, 1200–2400 m. s of it. Display consists of vertical flight to 20 m., then down to the perch while uttering various chirping notes. Call: long series of repeated "chips" while perched, also a thin, high whistle; occasional "churr" while feeding.

## GREEN-THROATED MANGO

*Anthracothorax viridigula*
MANGO GARGANTIVERDE

4.1 [1]″ 10.4 [2.5] cm. Above shining bronze green, becoming bronzy gold on rump and upper tail coverts. Central tail feathers blackish, rest shining purple, outer feathers tipped dark blue. Throat glittering emerald green; center of breast and belly velvety black; sides of body shining green. ♀: like ♂ above, but without the golden bronzy sheen on rump and upper tail coverts. Central tail feathers like back, rest shining purple tipped white. Below white with a black band mixed with green from chin to vent.

Tropical zone. N Delta Amacuro. [Trinidad, the Guianas, ne Brazil to Maranhão.]

Open terrain with scattered trees, second growth, near mangroves at sea level.

## GREEN-BREASTED MANGO

*Anthracothorax prevostii*
MANGO PECHIVERDE

Pl. 11

3.9 [1.1]″; 10 [2.8] cm. Above shining bright green; central tail feathers shining olive green, rest purple, edged and tipped blue. Center of throat and upper breast velvety black, margined laterally with shining greenish blue; belly and sides of body shining green; a more or less concealed white patch on flanks. ♀: similar to ♀ Green-throated Mango, possibly distinguishable by bluer, less green feathers mixed with the black ones of the central underparts.

Tropical zone, very local. Recorded from n Zulia (Río Aurare); s Lara (Guarico); Guárico; coastal Carabobo (Borburata); Puerto Cabello); Distr. Federal (Caracas; San José de los Caracas); e Sucre (San Félix) (*viridicordatus*). [Mexico to n Costa Rica. Colombia to nw Peru. Islands of the sw Caribbean.]

Rain forest edge, second growth, open woodland, sea level to 900 m. Clearings, along streams, parks; forages in low trees and bushes. Perches from low branches to treetops.

## BLACK-THROATED MANGO

*Anthracothorax nigricollis*
MANGO PECHINEGRO

Pl. 11

Much like Green-breasted Mango and best distinguished by glittering deep blue instead of bluish green border to black of throat and breast, the black extending over center of belly, ♀: possibly distinguishable from Green-breasted by smaller white tips to outer tail feathers, but mainly by the black band on underparts, plain deep black with no blue or green admixture.

Tropical, occasionally subtropical zone throughout, but not recorded from s Amazonas. [Panama to Colombia and the Guianas and e of the Andes to Bolivia, Paraguay and ne Argentina. Trinidad, Tobago.]

Rain forest edge, second growth, gallery forest, open woodland, sea level to 1400 m. n of the Orinoco, to 900 m. s of it. Plantations, along streams, clearings, gardens. Solitary but often in groups in flowering trees. Nests high in trees; perches in exposed branches.

## FIERY-TAILED AWLBILL
*Avocettula recurvirostris*
COLIBRÍ PICO LEZNA

Pl. 13
3 [0.7]″; 7.6 [1.8] cm. The only Venezuelan hummingbird with *bill upturned at tip*. Above shining emerald green, central 4 tail feathers dull violet, outer feathers shining dull purple, glistening coppery purple below. Throat and breast glittering emerald green; abdomen dark bronzy green with a dull black longitudinal median band, under tail coverts glittering copper. ♀: above like ♂, below white with a median black band on throat and breast; sides of body coppery green. Lateral tail feathers like back, outer feathers steel blue, tipped white. Young ♂ much like ad. but green of throat broadly margined laterally with white.
Tropical zone. Se Bolívar (Cerro Roraima). [Guyana; French Guiana. Brazil along the lower Amazon from Belém to Monte Alegre and Santarém. E Ecuador in the Napo Valley.]
Probably in the forests which cover the lower terrain near Roraima.

## RUBY-TOPAZ HUMMINGBIRD
*Chrysolampis mosquitus*
TUCUSITO RUBÍ

Pl. 12
3.1 [0.5]″; 7.9 [1.3] cm. Crown feathers, covering basal part of bill, to the nape glittering ruby red bordered on nape by blackish; back dark olive brown; tail rufous chestnut, tipped black. Throat and upper breast glittering topaz orange; belly dusky brown, a tuft of downy white feathers on flanks; under tail coverts rufous chestnut. ♀: above pale coppery green; sides of head and underparts pale smoky gray. Central tail feathers greenish olive, rest grayish with a black subterminal band and white tip, or rufous with a black subterminal band and white tip, the amount of rufous variable.
Tropical zone, including the islands off the Caribbean coast, but not recorded in Delta Amacuro and s Amazonas nor on Las Aves and Patos Is. [N Colombia,

the Guianas to central and e Brazil, ne Bolivia. Aruba to Trinidad and Tobago.]
Gallery forest, xerophytic areas, deciduous forest, open fields, second growth, mangroves, savannas, to 1300 m. n of the Orinoco, to 500 m. s of it. Feeds among flowers in the lower vegetation and in high trees. Nests from low to medium heights.

## VIOLET-HEADED HUMMINGBIRD
*Klais guimeti*
TUCUSITO CABEZA AZUL

Pl. 12
3.5 [0.4]″; 9 [1] cm. Whole head shining purple, *small spot behind eye white*. Back and tail shining green, outer tail feathers with dusky subterminal patch and narrow white tip. Underparts dull gray. ♀: like ♂ but no purple on head. Crown bluish green, a white spot behind eye; throat like rest of underparts.
Lower subtropical, occasionally subtropical zone. From Falcón, Zulia and Táchira e through Yaracuy, Carabobo and Miranda to Sucre (*guimeti*). [Nicaragua to Colombia, w Brazil and n Bolivia.]
Semi-open terrain, second growth, clearings, 150–1900 m. Forages at all heights but prefers small and medium-sized trees. Alone or in groups up to 30 in flowering trees. Usually places nest above running water.

## TUFTED COQUETTE
*Lophornis ornata*
COQUETA ABANICO CANELA

Pl. 12
2.7 [0.4]″; 6.8 [1] cm. Forehead, face and throat glittering emerald green; long crest rufous. Very long plumes, springing fanlike from cheeks, ochraceous rufous, each tipped with a glittering green disk. Mantle and underparts shining pale green; rump and upper tail coverts shining violet, a buffy white band across rump. Central tail feathers bronze green, rufous basally, rest rufous, tipped and edged bronze green. ♀: no plumes. Crown and upper parts bronze green, rump band buff; rump and upper tail coverts shining violet. Below uniform rufous. Tail bronzy green basally, purple bronze distally.
Tropical zone. Very locally in Sucre; ne

Apure near the mouth of the Río Meta; s of the Orinoco in Bolívar from opposite the mouth of the Apure to the lower Río Caura, and in the Gran Sabana. [The Guianas, ne Brazil. Trinidad.] Rain forest edge, gallery forest, thickets, savannas, 100–950 m. n of the Orinoco, to 700 m. s of it. The small size and correspondingly rapid wing beat of all *Lophornis* make them resemble bumblebees.

## SPANGLED COQUETTE
*Lophornis stictolopha*
COQUETA CORONADA

Pl. 12

2.5 [0.3]″; 6.4 [0.8] cm. Crown and long crest rufous, the feathers of crest tipped with small bronze green disks. Back bronze green, band across rump buffy white. Upper tail coverts shining purple (or dark bronzy olive, a), tail reddish bronze (or bronzy olive, a). ♀: above plain bronze green with a buffy white bar across rump. Chin, upper throat and area below eye buff, feathers of cheeks somewhat elongated, dull green tipped white; lower throat, breast and belly blackish mixed with buff. Central tail feathers white at extreme base (concealed), basally bronze green, blackish at tip, the rest dusky bronze tipped grayish white.
Tropical and lower subtropical zones. Locally distributed in the serranías of the n from the Sierra de Perijá, Zulia, to Miranda and in the Andes of Mérida, Barinas and Táchira. [E Colombia to ne Peru.]
Deciduous forest, scrub, second growth, open semi-arid wooded areas, sea level to 1300 m.

## PEACOCK COQUETTE
*Lophornis pavonina*
COQUETA ABANICO PAVO REAL

Pl. 12

3.8 [0.5]″; 9.7 [1.3] cm. Sides of crown glittering golden green, center of crown black, cheek tufts and crest shining green, feathers of cheeks wide with large blue black terminal disks; throat black; rest of plumage dark shining green with a buffy white band across rump; tail purple bronze. ♀: above golden bronze, a narrow white band across rump. Tail bronze green, outer pair of feathers

tipped white. Throat white, streaked black, feathers at sides of neck elongated, black and white; rest of underparts mottled black and white, sides of body with golden bronze disks.
Upper tropical and subtropical zones. Amazonas from Cerros Yaví and Paraque to Cerro Duida; Bolívar on Cerro Guaiquinima, Río Paragua and on Cerro Chimantá-tepui, sw Gran Sabana (*duidae*). E Bolívar on the Sierra de Lema and on Cerro Ptaritepui, nw Gran Sabana (*punctigula*). On Cerro Roraima, se Gran Sabana (*pavonina*). [Guyana.]
An endemic species of Pantepui. Rain and cloud forests. 500–2000 m. Forest edge, clearings. Alone or in small groups, high in trees in exposed branches.

## FESTIVE COQUETTE
*Lophornis chalybea*
COQUETA ABANICO PUNTIBLANCO

Pl. 12

3 [0.6]″; 7.6 [1.5] cm. Hindcrown adorned with a small crest of stiff feathers, the shorter ones green, the longer dark bronzy red. Forehead and area below eye glittering green, chin and very narrow line extending backward to under the eye velvety black. A tuft of narrow, elongated feathers springing from cheeks, forming a ruff, shining green, tipped with a white dot. Back shining green, band across rump buffy white. Upper tail coverts and tail shining coppery bronze (or olive bronze, a). Breast and belly violaceous gray, sides of body bronzy green. ♀: above shining bronzy green, rump band buffy white, upper tail coverts and tail as in respective ♂ but outer feathers tipped gray to buffy. Throat grayish white, rest of underparts mixed gray and black.
Tropical zone. Nw Bolívar along the lower and middle Río Caura (*klagesi*). Se Bolívar along the upper Río Caroní (*verreauxii*). [Colombia to ne Peru.]
Rain forest, 100–500 m.

## BLACK-BELLIED THORNTAIL
*Popelairia langsdorffi*
COQUETA COLA DE LIRA

Pl. 12

♂ 5.4 [0.5]″; 13.7 [1.3] cm; ♀: 3″ (7.6 cm). Tail long, peculiar. Crown, throat and breast glittering emerald green, breast bordered below by a band of glittering golden copper, rest of underparts black. Back and upper tail coverts bronzy green with a white band across rump. Outer tail feathers very narrow, very long, 3″ (7.6 cm.), pale grayish, pointed, narrowing to the shaft at tip, central feathers very short, barely longer than the tail coverts, the rest dark blue with white shafts, sharply pointed and progressively longer toward the outside. ♀: differs from ♂ by having the sides of throat white; tail of normal length, deeply forked, bronze basally, deep blue distally, tipped white.

Tropical zone. Recorded only from the confluence of Caño Casiquiare and Río Guianía, s Amazonas. [Se Colombia to e Peru, Amazonian and se Brazil.]

Rain forest along rivers, 100–200 m.

Note: Called *Lophornis langsdorffi* in Lista Av. Venez.

## RACQUET-TAILED COQUETTE
*Discosura longicauda*
COQUETA COLA RAQUETA

Pl. 12
♂ 3.7 [0.5]″; 9.4 [1.3] cm.; ♀ 2.7″ (6.8 cm). Tail forked, purplish, outer feathers much longer than the rest, 2″ (5 cm.), terminating in a *purple black racquet*. Crown, throat and upper breast glittering emerald green, lower breast golden copper, belly whitish. Back shining green with a buffy band across rump. ♀: no glittering feathers. Above like ♂; throat black bordered laterally by white, breast shining green, belly buffy white. Tail compartively long, 1″ (2.5 cm.), forked, gray with a broad subterminal purple band, outer feathers tipped whitish. No racquets.

Tropical zone. Central and w Amazonas (Nericagua on the Orinoco; Cerro Yapacana). [The Guianas, e Brazil s to Bahia.]

Rain forest, along rivers, 200 m.

Note: Called *Lophornis longicauda* in Lista Av. Venez.

## BLUE-CHINNED SAPPHIRE
*Chlorestes notatus*
COLIBRÍ VERDECITO

Pl. 12
3.5 [0.7″]; 9 [1.8] cm. Dark bronzy green above, wings dark purple, tail steel blue.

Chin and upper throat glittering deep bright blue, rest of underparts glittering green. Mandible red, tipped black in both sexes. ♀: like ♂ but white bases of the feathers of the underparts showing through, center of belly white.

Tropical zone. Widely distributed but not recorded from Zulia, Falcón, s Amazonas or s Bolívar (*notatus*). [Se Colombia, the Guianas to ne Peru, n Amazonian and se Brazil. Trinidad.]

Rain, gallery and deciduous forest, forest edge, sea level to 1000 m. n of the Orinoco, to 700 m. s of it. Llanos, second growth, pastures, savannas. Solitary. Forages from undergrowth to tops of trees.

[THE *Chlorostilbon* GROUP which follows comprises very small, dark green hummingbirds with glittering crowns and underparts. The females are bronzy green above, smoky white or gray below.]

## BLUE-TAILED EMERALD
*Chlorostilbon mellisugus*
ESMERALDA COLIAZUL

Pl. 12
2.7 [0.6]″; 6.8 [1.5] cm. Bill all black. Crown glittering golden green, back shining green, tail steel blue, slightly forked. Below glittering emerald green, tinged blue on throat. ♀: shining grass green above, smoky white below. Central tail feathers greenish blue, rest deep blue.

Tropical and subtropical zones. N Cordilleras from w Falcón to Sucre, and across the llanos from Apure to Monagas, n Amazonas, n Bolívar, Delta Amacuro. Margarita I. (*caribaeus*). Locally distributed in e Bolívar from the Altiplanicie de Nuria and the Río Cuyuni s (*subfurcatus*). Cerro Duida, Amazonas, between 1100–1800 m. (*duidae*). [Costa Rica to Colombia, w Ecuador, the Guianas to Bolivia and the Amazon valley. Aruba to Trinidad.]

Rain, gallery and deciduous forest, second growth, gardens, to 1200 m. n of the Orinoco, to 1850 m. s of it. Llanos, xerophytic areas, open fields with scattered trees. Perches low, seldom in exposed treetops; feeds at various heights. Often pierces the sepals to obtain nectar.

The only emerald found s of the Orinoco.

### RED-BILLED EMERALD
*Chlorostilbon gibsoni*
ESMERALDA PICO ROJO

♂ [0.5]″; 7.6 [1.3] cm. Mandible flesh-colored, tipped black. Much like Blue-tailed Emerald in general color but bluer below, tail much longer and much more deeply forked. ♀: differs from ♀ of Blue-tailed by whitish eyebrow and white-tipped tail feathers.
Tropical zone. Along the n coast from n Zulia to Falcón and Yaracuy and in n Lara and Trujillo (*nitens*). Extreme nw Táchira (*chrysogaster*). [N. Colombia.]
Rain and deciduous forest, xerophytic areas, sea level to 1300 m. Thorn thickets. Habits probably similar to Blue-tailed Emerald.
Note: Treated as subspecies of Blue-tailed Emerald in Lista Av. Venez.

### COPPERY EMERALD
*Chlorostilbon russatus*

ESMERALDA BRONCEADA
♂ [0.3]″; 7.6 [0.8] cm. Crown glittering green, back shining green, *tail golden copper* in sharp contrast to back. Below glittering golden green. ♀: coppery green above, tail *greenish copper,* all but central tail feathers with a coppery purple subterminal band and pale tip. Underparts smoky gray.
Upper tropical zone. Upper Río Negro, Sierra de Perijá, nw Zulia. [Ne Colombia.]

### NARROW-TAILED EMERALD
*Chlorostilbon stenura*
ESMERALDA COLA DE ALAMBRE

Pl. 12
♂ [0.7]″; 7.6 [1.8] cm. Crown glittering golden green, back shining golden green. Tail somewhat forked, shining emerald green, the outer feathers *narrow.* Entire underparts glittering emerald green. ♀: shining green above, tail shaped as in ♂, outermost feathers grayish white, becoming coppery green in center with a shining blue subterminal patch and broad white tip. Smoky gray below.
Subtropical and temperate zones. The

Andes of Trujillo, Mérida and n Táchira (*stenura*). [Ne Colombia.]
Cloud forest, low scrub at higher altitudes, 1950–3000 m.

### GREEN-TAILED EMERALD
*Chlorostilbon alice*
ESMERALDA COLIVERDE

♂ [0.7]″; 7.6 [1.8] cm. In color resembles the Narrow-tailed Emerald but tail feathers normal, not narrowed. ♀: like ♀ of the Narrow-tailed Emerald but outermost feathers coppery green with a much smaller white tip.
Subtropical zone. Widely distributed in the n Cordilleras in the Sierra de San Luis, Falcón, and from Lara and Trujillo to Sucre and Monagas.
Rain and cloud forest edge, second growth, plantations; seldom enters deep forest; 750–1800 m. Perches in undergrowth and low trees.

### SHORT-TAILED EMERALD
*Chlorostilbon poortmani*
ESMERALDA COLA CORTA

♂ 3.1 [0.7]″; 7.9 [1.8] cm. Crown and underparts glittering emerald green, back shining grass green, tail very short, slightly forked, shining green. ♀: differs from all other species except Narrow-tailed Emerald by having the central tail feathers green; rest green with a wide blue subterminal band and white tip.
Subtropical, rarely tropical zone 150–2100 m. Táchira (Santo Domingo, 300 m., Páramo de Tamá); Mérida, (El Vigía, 150 m.) (*poortmani*). [Ne Colombia.]
Cloud forests, open woodland, second growth, along streams, forest edge, usually 800–2100 m.; descends to 150 m. In coffee plantations feeds on the flowers of guamos (*Inga*), often used as shade trees.

### FORK-TAILED WOODNYMPH
*Thalurania furcata*
TUCUSITO MORADITO

Pl. 12
♂ 3.5–4 [0.8]″; 9–10 [2] cm. ♀: ♂ 3″ (7.6 cm.). A very black-appearing hummingbird. Crown dark bronze green to blackish (or shining purple, a). Upperparts dark bronze green, brighter on lower back,

band across shoulders violet blue. Tail rather long, much graduated, deeply forked, purple black. Throat and breast glittering emerald green, belly shining purple to violet blue. ♀: shining bronze green above, bluer on lower back and rump. Central tail feathers like back, rest mostly steel blue tipped grayish white, outer feathers to a greater or lesser extent grayish or green basally. Below pale gray, under tail coverts white.

Tropical and subtropical zones. The Sierra de Perijá, Zulia, s to n central Táchira; w Barinas; Mérida; ne Lara (*colombica*, a). S Táchira on Cerro El Teteo (*rostrifera*, a). The Cordilleras of the ne in Anzoátegui and Sucre including the Paria Pen. (*refulgens*). Extreme se Sucre and Delta Amacuro; Bolívar; ne Amazonas (*fissilis*). Nw Amazonas s through w and central Amazonas to the Río Negro (*orenocensis*). [Mexico to w Ecuador, Bolivia, and n Argentina. Trinidad.]

Rain and cloud forests, open portions of forests, open areas, second growth, sea level to 1900 m. Solitary, not shy, curious, hovers near observer. Forages from very low in thickets to middle heights of trees. Perches on exposed bare twigs. Very pugnacious.

## SHINING-GREEN HUMMINGBIRD
*Lepidopyga goudoti*
TUCUSITO PICO CURVO

Pl. 12
3.6 [0.7]″; 9.1 [1.8] cm. Shining golden green above, crown bluer; glittering golden green below, throat tinged bluish (or glittering bluish green below, a). Tail forked, central feathers bronzy green, outer feathers blue black. Mandible flesh color with black tip (♂, ♀). ♀: upperparts including central tail feathers bronzy green, rest of tail feathers blue black, tail slightly forked. Throat and breast glittering green, gray bases of the feathers showing through; belly white.

Tropical zone. N Zulia from the Perijá region e to the ne side of L. Maracaibo (*zuliae*). Sw Zulia, n Táchira through Mérida and w Barinas to nw Trujillo (*phaeochroa*, a). [N Colombia.]

Open woodland, xerophytic areas, second growth, deciduous forest, sea level to

800 m. Forages alone in understory or quite high on trees.

## RUFOUS-THROATED SAPPHIRE
*Hylocharis sapphirina*
ZAFIRO GARGANTIRRUFO

Pl. 12
3.5 [0.8]″; 9 [2] cm. Upperparts, lower breast and belly shining dark green. Chin rufous, foreneck and upper breast glittering sapphire blue; under tail coverts chestnut. Upper tail coverts and central tail feathers purple bronze, outer tail feathers *chestnut* edged all around with black. *Bill broad, reddish flesh color* tipped black (♂, ♀). ♀: above bronzier green than ♂; tail as in ♂ but outer feathers pale-tipped. Throat and under tail coverts rusty buff, rest of underparts white with glittering blue disks on foreneck and upper breast.

Tropical zone. Nw and se Bolívar and from n Amazonas s to the Río Negro. [E Colombia and the Guianas to e Peru, Amazonian and se Brazil, ne Bolivia, Paraguay and ne Argentina.]

Rain forest edge, from near sea level to 500 m.; at 1850 m. on the talus slope of Roraima. Second growth, clearings, semi-open thickets.

## WHITE-CHINNED SAPPHIRE
*Hylocharis cyanus*
ZAFIRO CABECIMORADO

Pl. 12
3.5 [0.8]″; 9 [2] cm. Head, throat and breast glittering violet blue with a small white patch on chin formed by the white bases of the feathers; belly deep shining green. Upper back shining bronze green gradually changing to bronzy purple on upper tail coverts. Tail and under tail coverts steel blue. *Bill broad, reddish flesh color,* tipped black (♂, ♀). ♀: generally similar to the ♀ of Rufous-throated Sapphire but tail steel blue, outer rectrices tipped gray instead of mostly chestnut; under tail coverts gray instead of rusty buff. Chin white.

Tropical zone. Locally distributed from Zulia, n Táchira and Mérida to w Barinas, and in Trujillo and the Distr. Federal; s of the Orinoco in nw Bolívar along the lower and middle Río Caura and in the e from the Altiplanicie de

Nuria s through the Gran Sabana to Cerro Roraima; from n Amazonas s to the Río Negro (*viridiventris*). [Ne and extreme se Colombia, the Guianas to n Bolivia, Amazonian and se Brazil.] Rain forest, forest edge, second growth, shade trees in plantations, scrub, often near streams, to 600 m. n of the Orinoco, to 1250 m. s of it.

## GOLDEN-TAILED SAPPHIRE

*Chrysuronia oenone*
COLIBRÍ COLA DE ORO

Pl. 12
3.7 [0.8]"; 9.4 [2] cm. Whole head, throat and upper breast glittering violet; back shining green, upper tail coverts shining reddish copper. Tail shining *golden copper* both above and below. Lower breast glittering green becoming golden green on belly. Mandible flesh color (♂, ♀). ♀: shining green above, upper tail coverts and tail as in ♂, but outer feathers tipped grayish. Below white with a few shining blue green disks.
Tropical and subtropical zones. N Cordilleras from Zulia, Táchira, Mérida and w Barinas to Falcón thence e to the Paria Pen., Sucre and ne Monagas (*oenone*). [E Colombia to e Peru. Trinidad.]
Rain forest, plantations, second growth, gardens, deciduous forest, sea level to 1500 m. Solitary or in groups of 20 or more. Forages from low heights to treetops. Nests at medium heights.

## WHITE-TAILED GOLDENTHROAT

*Polytmus guainumbi*
COLIBRÍ GARGANTIDORADO

Pl. 12
3.5 [1]"; 9 [2.5] cm. Crown dull grayish brown, narrow stripe above and below eye white; upperparts shining golden bronze. Tail much rounded, rather long, feathers narrow, somewhat pointed, emerald to blue green, outer feathers with increasing amounts of white on outer webs and tip. Throat, breast and abdomen glittering golden green, golden in certain lights, center of belly white. Bill slightly curved, dull reddish. ♀: like ♂ above, below white to dark buff with green disks on throat and upper breast.
Tropical, occasionally subtropical zone.

Spottily distributed n of the Orinoco where known from ne Apure (San Fernando), s Guárico, (Sta. Rita), Distr. Federal (Caracas), central Anzoátegui (Cantaura), e Sucre (La Laguna), n central Monagas (Caicara); Delta Amacuro; s of the Orinoco in ne Amazonas (Manapiare) and in nw and se Bolívar (*guainumbi*). [Ne Colombia, the Guianas to n Amazonian Brazil and from Maranhão to ne Argentina, Paraguay, Bolivia. Trinidad.]
Deciduous and gallery forest edge, grassy savannas, shrubbery near streams, to 100 m. n of the Orinoco, to 1500 m. on the slopes of the tepuis. Keeps low, flies close to the ground.

## TEPUI GOLDENTHROAT

*Polytmus milleri*
COLIBRÍ TEPUI

Pl. 12
4 [1]"; 10 [2.5] cm. Above bronze green, tail greener, all but central feathers with broad white band at base, and white tips. Below glittering golden grass green; under tail coverts white, tipped shining grass green; green part of underside of tail glistening grass green, much brighter than upper side. Bill slightly curved, black. ♀: upperparts and tail like ♂, throat and breast white thickly spangled with shining green, belly grayish mixed with bronze.
Subtropical zone, Amazonas on Cerro Duida; sw Bolívar on Cerro Jaua and on Cerros Auyan-tepui, Ptari-tepui and Roraima in the Gran Sabana.
An endemic species of Pantepui. Cloud forest edge, open terrain with scattered trees and bushes, 1300–2200 m. Solitary. Builds nest in vegetation a few feet above the ground.

## GREEN-TAILED GOLDENTHROAT

*Polytmus theresiae*
GARGANTA DE ORO COLIVERDE

Pl. 12
3.4 [0.8]"; 8.6 [2] cm. Above bronze green, tail rounded, glistening bronze green above, grass green below, only extreme base white, outer feathers tipped white. Below glittering golden green, under tail coverts white with green disks. ♀: differs

from ♂ by white, green-spangled underparts.
Tropical zone. Amazonas from opposite the mouth of the Río Vichada s to Cerro Duida and the Río Negro (*leucorrhous*). [Se Colombia and the Guianas to Amazonian Brazil and ne Peru.] Forest edge, savannas, second growth, scrub, 100–300 m.

## BUFFY HUMMINGBIRD
*Leucippus fallax*
COLIBRÍ ANTEADO

Pl. 12
3.5 [0.9]″; 9 [2.3] cm. Above dull bluish green, the feathers edged gray; central tail feathers pale dull green, rest with a dark subterminal band and broad white tip. Throat, breast and sides of body rusty buff; belly and large, wide under tail coverts white. Mandible flesh color, tipped black. ♀: similar to ♂ but much duller and grayer above.
Tropical zone. Zulia and Falcón (*cervina*). E Lara to the Distr. Federal (*fallax*). N Anzoátegui and ne Sucre and La Tortuga, Margarita, Coche, Cubagua and Chimana Grande Is. (*richmondi*). [Ne Colombia.]
Xerophytic areas, thorny scrubs, mangroves, sea level to 550 m. Solitary, forages in low trees and bushes, often in the flowers of agave and cactus.

[IN *Amazilia* THE SEXES ARE SIMILAR]

## WHITE-CHESTED EMERALD
*Amazilia chionopectus*
DIAMANTE COLIDORADO

Pl. 12
3.2 [0.6]″; 8 [1.5] cm. Crown, cheeks and sides of neck glittering green, back coppery green gradually becoming reddish bronze on rump and upper tail coverts; central tail feathers reddish bronze, lateral feathers duller, reddish bronze with a large subterminal blackish bar. Below white, sides of breast and body coppery green, sometimes with a few spots on breast. Bill black.
Tropical zone. From Miranda e to Sucre, Monagas and Delta Amacuro; n Bolívar from the lower Río Caura e to the upper Río Cuyuni; n Amazonas (*chionopectus*). [The Guianas, Trinidad.]

Rain and deciduous forest, second growth, forest and savanna edge, semi-open, scrub, to 100 m. n of the Orinoco, to 500 m. s of it. Along rivers. Solitary, also congregates in small groups to sing. Call: "diddle-ee, diddle-ee, diddle-ee."

## VERSICOLORED EMERALD
*Amazilia versicolor*
DIAMANTE MULTICOLOR

Pl. 12
3 [0.6]″; 7.6 [1.5] cm. Crown and upper parts shining grass green (or with glittering blue crown, a); central tail feathers dull bronzy olive, rest with a dusky subterminal bar. Below white, throat and upper breast bordered by glittering bluish green disks (or sides of throat and breast extensively spangled light glittering blue, a). Mandible reddish flesh color with black tip.
Tropical zone. N of the Orinoco only in Apure; nw Bolívar; Amazonas s to the Yavita-Pimichín Trail, but mostly n of the Río Ventuari (*milleri*). Amazonas s of the Río Ventuari and in s Bolívar e to Cerro Paurai-tepui (*hollandi*, a). [E Colombia, n Amazonian and se Brazil, ne Argentina to n Bolivia.]
Rain and cloud forests, second growth, forest edge, 100–1700 m. Gallery forest, semi-open savannas.

## GLITTERING-THROATED EMERALD
*Amazilia fimbriata*
DIAMANTE GARGANTIVERDE

Pl. 12
3.2 [0.7]″; 8 [1.8] cm. Above shining green, central tail feathers bronzier (or very dark, blackish, a), rest with progressively larger blackish tips. Throat and breast glittering green, center of abdomen white, flanks shining green. Mandible pink, tip black.
Tropical zone. From Falcón through Yaracuy to Carabobo thence e to Sucre; the llanos from El Sombrero, Guárico, to Monagas; n Bolívar from Caicara e to Delta Amacuro (*elegantissima*). The w llanos from Táchira and Apure to sw Guárico, Portuguesa and Cojedes (*obscuricauda*). N and central Amazonas and e Bolívar from the Sierra de Imataca s (*fimbriata*, a). [The Guianas, e Co-

lombia to s Bolivia and s Brazil.]
Gallery forest, second growth, xerophytic areas, open deciduous woodland, savannas, thorny scrub, gardens, llanos, sea level to 1300 m. Solitary; may congregate in groups of about 20. Forages and builds nest at various heights. Nests almost throughout the year. Call: a chick-like "peep, peep."

## TACHIRA EMERALD
*Amazilia distans*
DIAMANTE DE WETMORE

In size and general appearance like Glittering-throated Emerald but differs by having the forecrown glittering blue green becoming shining darker green and less blue on hindcrown; foreneck and upper breast glittering blue instead of glittering green, the feathers of throat edged white giving a spotted appearance; abdomen pale olive gray instead of white. Bill reddish, tipped black.
Known only from a specimen from Burgua, sw Táchira (300 m.).
Rain forest.

## SAPPHIRE-SPANGLED EMERALD
*Amazilia lactea*
DIAMANTE PECHIZAFIRO

3.5 [0.8]"; 9 [2] cm. Shining green above, darker and less bronzy on crown. Central tail feathers dark, shining olive green, dark glossy blue toward tip, lateral feathers steel blue with olive margins. Throat, breast and sides of neck glittering violet blue, the feathers edged gray reducing the brilliance of these parts. Broad line down center of abdomen and under tail coverts white. Mandible flesh color with dark tip.
Tropical zone. Bolívar on the upper Río Caura (Cerro Sarisariñama, 1400 m.); on the lower Río Paragua (Cerro Perro, 300 m.) and on Cerro Auyan-tepui, 1100 m., in the n Gran Sabana (*zimmeri*). [E Peru, n Bolivia, e Brazil.]
Rain forest.

## PLAIN-BELLIED EMERALD
*Amazilia leucogaster*
DIAMANTE VENTRIBLANCO

4 [0.9]"; 10 [2.3] cm. Above shining golden green, sometimes golden coppery green; crown, sides of neck and breast glittering green, throat and center of underparts white, flanks shining green. Central tail feathers bronze green, lateral ones blue black. Mandible flesh color, tipped black. ♀: similar but outer tail feathers with gray tips.
Ne Delta Amacuro on Tobejuba and Tobeida Is.; Cerro El Trueno, nw Bolívar (*leucogaster*). [The Guianas, e Brazil to Bahia.]
Semi-open forest, second growth, mangrove edge, sea level to 250 m. Feeds and perches low in trees and shrubs.

## STEELY-VENTED HUMMINGBIRD
*Amazilia saucerrottei*
AMAZILIA VERDE-AZUL

Pl. 12
3.5 [0.7]"; 9 [1.8] cm. Above dark shining green, longer upper tail coverts and tail bright steel blue. Below glittering green, under tail coverts bright steel blue edged white. Mandible flesh color, tipped black.
Tropical to temperate zones. Nw Zulia in the Sierra de Perijá (*warscewiczi*). The Andes of Mérida and Trujillo (*braccata*). [Nicaragua, Costa Rica. N and w Colombia.]
Great altitudinal tolerance. Forested areas from sea level to 3000 m. Second growth, cultivated areas, clearings. Forages at low levels and in the flowers of shade trees in coffee plantations.

## COPPER-RUMPED HUMMINGBIRD
*Amazilia tobaci*
AMAZILIA BRONCEADA COLIAZUL

Pl. 12
3.2 [0.8]"; 8 [2] cm. Crown and upper back shining green becoming coppery purple on wing coverts and rest of upperparts; the amount of golden coppery purple is very variable, sometimes the entire upperparts are of that color; tail slightly forked, dark shining blue. Underparts glittering green, under tail coverts reddish brown (or cinnamon rufous, a; or bluish black, b). Mandible flesh color, tip black.
Tropical and lower subtropical zones. The mountains of Falcón, Lara and Yaracuy (*monticola*). The n Cordilleras from Carabobo to Miranda and the llanos from e Apure to Portuguesa and Cojedes

and through Guárico to se Anzoátegui (*feliciae*). The e Cordilleras from n Anzoátegui to the e Paria Pen., Sucre and n Monagas; Patos I. (*caudata,* a). Margarita I. (*aliciae,* a). N Amazonas and generally in Bolívar (*caurensis,* b). [Tobago, Trinidad.] Rain and cloud forest, second growth, deciduous and gallery forests, llanos, to 1800 m. n of the Orinoco, to 1600 m. s of it. Clearings, forest edge, gardens, thorny scrub, savannas with scattered trees. Solitary, extremely pugnacious. Forages at all heights; congregates in flowering trees. Displays by swinging several times in a wide vertical curve in front of a perched bird. Call: a 3-note, soft, melodious whistle.

## GREEN-BELLIED HUMMINGBIRD
*Amazilia viridigaster*
AMAZILIA COLIMORADA

Pl. 12
3.7 [0.6]″; 9.4 [1.5] cm. Crown shining green, upper back bronze green, lower back and rump coppery bronze (or rump and upper tail coverts mainly rufous, a). Tail shining purple (or tail feathers coppery violet, outer 2 pairs rufous chestnut, tipped coppery violet, a). Throat and breast glittering green, belly dull bronzy brown, under tail coverts white. Mandible flesh color, tip black. Tropical and subtropical zones. Táchira, Mérida and sw Barinas (*viridigaster*). Amazonas on Cerro Duida; nw Bolívar along the lower Río Caura (*duidae*). Extreme ne Bolívar s to the Gran Sabana (*cupreicauda,* a). [Ne Colombia, Guyana, Brazil in Roraima.] Rain and cloud forests, semi-open woodland, second growth, coffee plantations, 200–2100 m. n of the Orinoco, near sea level to 1800 m. s of it.

## RUFOUS-TAILED HUMMINGBIRD
*Amazilia tzacatl*
AMAZILIA COLIRRUFA

Pl. 12
3.7 [0.8]″; 9.4 [2] cm. Above shining dark bronzy green, upper and under tail coverts and *tail chestnut,* inconspicuously tipped shining coppery. Throat and breast glittering green, lower breast and belly grayish. Bill flesh color with black tip.

Tropical, occasionally subtropical zone. The nw in Zulia, Táchira through Mérida to Lara and Trujillo (*tzacatl*). [Mexico to Colombia and w Ecuador.] Rain and cloud forest, second growth, savannas, sea level to 1700 m. Forest edge, cultivated fields, open woodland, along streams. Solitary, sometimes in groups. Forages at all heights.

## WHITE-VENTED PLUMELETEER
*Chalybura buffonii*
COLIBRÍ GRANDE COLINEGRO

Pl. 12
4.5 [1]″; 11.5 [2.5] cm. Upperparts shining bronzy green, bronzier on tail coverts and central tail feathers, rest blue black. Below glittering green, under *tail coverts long, plumelike, snow white.* Bill black, rather heavy, slightly curved. ♀: differs from ♂ by dingy gray underparts; under tail coverts as in ♂, outer tail feathers broadly tipped white. Tropical zone. Zulia in the Sierra de Perijá e, s of L. Maracaibo, to e Mérida (*interior*). The serranías of the nw from Táchira, Barinas, Lara and Falcón e to Miranda and Guárico (*aenicauda*). [Panama to w Ecuador.] Rain forest, second growth, deciduous forest, clearings, forest edge, sea level to 1400 m. Plantations, swampy areas. Alone or in groups forages in the undergrowth and to middle heights. Perches on exposed bare twigs; investigates *Heliconias.*

## SPECKLED HUMMINGBIRD
*Adelomyia melanogenys*
COLIBRÍ SERRANO GARGANTIAZUL

Pl. 12
3.3 [0.5]″; 8.4 [1.3] cm. Shining bronze green above. Cheeks blackish, broad postocular streak buffy white. Below buffy gray (or dirty white, a), speckled on throat with bronze green, sides of body buffier, somewhat mixed with bronze green. Central tail feathers dark bronzy olive, rest gray basally, blackish violet distally, tipped buffy white (or bright buff, a). Bill short. Subtropical zone. The nw mountains in Zulia, Táchira, Mérida to Lara, Trujillo and Falcón (*melanogenys*). Ne Lara through Yaracuy and Carabobo to

Miranda (*aeneosticta*, a). [Se Colombia to nw Peru and nw Argentina.]
Cloud forest, coffee plantations, 1200–2500 m. Solitary. Forages actively from the undergrowth to middle heights; prefers humid areas.

## GOULD'S JEWELFRONT
*Polyplancta aurescens*
COLIBRÍ CUELLICASTAÑO

Pl. 13
4.8 [0.8]″; 12 [2] cm. A narrow line from base of forehead to center of crown glittering iridescent purple blue, sides of crown and entire upperparts shining grass green. Central tail feathers bronze green, rest chestnut, tipped and edged bronze green. Lores and upper throat velvety black, sides of head from behind eyes and sides of neck and lower throat glittering golden green, a broad *band* across the breast *orange rufous,* rest of underparts shining green. ♀: lacks purple line on crown. generally duller in color.
Tropical zone. S Amazonas along the upper Río Asisa, on the Yavita-Pimichín Trail and at the headwaters of the Río Siapa on the Brazilian border; Bolívar in the Gran Sabana on Cerro Auyan-tepui. [Se Colombia to e Peru and nw Brazil and n Bolivia.]
Rain forest, forest edge, 150–550 m.

## VIOLET-FRONTED BRILLIANT
*Heliodoxa leadbeateri*
HELIODOXA FRENTIAZUL

Pl. 11
♂ 5 [0.9]″; 13 [2.3] cm.; ♀ 4.3″ (11 cm.). Above bronze green, reddish bronze on nape and hindneck, crown patch glittering blue to violet blue, narrowing on rear portion. Upper tail coverts and central tail feathers reddish bronzy olive, next pair black tipped bronzy, rest black; tail deeply forked. Throat and breast glittering green, abdomen dark bronzy green, under tail coverts olive green narrowly bordered white. ♀: above bronzy green, short moustacial streak and small spot behind eye white. Tail as in ♂ but outer feathers tipped white. Below white, throat and breast densely covered by glittering green disks, belly buffy in center, under tail coverts bronzy green, fringed white.

Upper tropical and subtropical zones. The mountains of the nw in Zulia, Táchira, Mérida, Barinas and Trujillo (*parvula*). The n Cordilleras from Falcón and Yaracuy through Carabobo to Miranda (*leadbeateri*). [Colombia to n Bolivia.]
Rain and cloud forests, coffee plantations, low open woodland, clearings, forest edge, 500–2250 m. Forages alone in the lower and middle height of trees.

## VELVET-BROWED BRILLIANT
*Heliodoxa xanthogonys*
COLIBRÍ FRENTIVERDE

Pl. 11
4 [0.8]″; 10 [2] cm. Crown velvety black, forehead and band on center of crown glittering green; upper parts dark shining green; throat and breast glittering green, a glittering violet blue patch on center of throat. Central tail feathers dusky green, rest black, tail slightly forked. Bill black, base of mandible orange. ♀: green above, lighter than ♂, below green with a short white moustacial streak, white throat and belly. Lower mandible mostly orange.
Subtropical zone. The cerros of Amazonas and in se Bolívar from the Sierra de Lema to the Gran Sabana. [W Guyana; adjacent Brazil.]
A monotypic endemic species of Pantepui. Forested slopes of the tepuis, 700–2000 m. Forest edge, clearings.

## SCISSOR-TAILED HUMMINGBIRD
*Hylonympha macrocerca*
COLIBRÍ TIJERETA

Pl. 13
♂ 7.5 [1]″; 19 [2.5] cm.; ♀ 4.5″ (11.5 cm.). *Tail very long, deeply forked,* blackish purple, outer feathers very much longer than rest. Forehead and center of crown glittering purple, rest of crown black, back shiny dark green. Throat and upper breast glittering emerald green, belly black, sides with green disks. ♀: Tail forked, much shorter than in ♂, central feathers basally green, distally steel blue, outer feathers mostly cinnamon with subterminal dusky area and buffy white tips. Upperparts dark shining green; below white with shining green disks, center of breast white, ab-

domen and under tail coverts rufous chestnut.

Subtropical zone. Extreme e Paria Pen., Sucre on Cerros Azul, Terrón de Azúcar and Humo.

Cloud forest, forest edge, small clearings, 900–1200 m. An endemic genus of the Paria Pen.

## VIOLET-CHESTED HUMMINGBIRD

*Sternoclyta cyanopectus*
COLIBRÍ PECHIAZUL

Pl. 11

4.5 [1.2]″; 11.5 [3] cm. Above shining grass green. Tail bronze, outer feathers tipped white on inner web. Throat glittering emerald green; breast glittering violet; abdomen gray with green discs. Bill slightly curved. ♀: above including tail, like ♂; below grayish white with green disks; center of abdomen unspotted, rufescent.

Lower subtropical, occasionally tropical zone. The Andes of Táchira, Mérida, Barinas and Lara; the coastal Cordillera from Yaracuy and Carabobo to the Distr. Federal; the interior Cordillera in Miranda.

Rain and cloud forest, coffee plantations, old second growth. Sea level to 1900 m. Solitary; forages in the darkest areas of the forest, damp ravines, *Heliconia* thickets.

## CRIMSON TOPAZ

*Topaza pella*
TOPACIO CANDELA COLICANELO

Pl. 13

7 [1]″; 18 [2.5] cm. Top and sides of head and neck and band across upper breast black; nape and upper back glittering fiery purple shading to glittering gold on upper tail coverts. Central tail feathers shining golden bronze, next 2 blackish purple, very narrow, long, curved, *crossing each other, protruding* 2.5″ (6.4 cm.) beyond the rest, *remainder rufous chestnut*. Throat iridescent glittering topaz; breast and belly glittering crimson; under tail coverts glittering golden bronze. Inner remiges and under wing coverts chestnut basally. ♀: above shining green, emerald green on upper tail coverts. Throat with glittering crimson disks, rest of under parts glistening golden bronze.

Tail rounded, central feathers dusky green, blackish near tip, next 2 pairs dusky violet, outer 2 pairs rufous chestnut. Remiges without chestnut, under wing coverts chestnut.

Tropical zone. Bolívar along the upper Río Caura, across the upper Paragua to the Río Cuyuni and the Gran Sabana (*pella*). [The Guianas, ne Brazil. E Ecuador.]

Rain forest, almost always along streams, 250–500 m. Forages in the flowered canopy of tall trees, 30–60 m. high. Often descends to river banks and branches overhanging the water.

## FIERY TOPAZ

*Topaza pyra*
TOPACIO CANDELA COLIMORADO

Much like Crimson Topaz but differing chiefly in the color of the tail, also as follows. Upper tail coverts glittering emerald green instead of glittering gold; central tail feathers dark bronzy green instead of gold, next pair narrow and long, crossed as in Crimson Topaz, *outer feathers shining dark purple* instead of rufous chestnut. Breast and belly glittering orange red instead of crimson; under tail coverts shining emerald green instead of gold. No rufous at base of inner remiges. ♀: differs principally from ♀ of the Crimson Topaz in the shape and color of the tail. Central pair as in the Crimson Topaz; next pair about 0.5 (1.3 cm.) longer than the rest and somewhat pointed, purple black; next 2 purple black, outermost with rufous outer web.

Tropical zone. Central Amazonas along the upper Río Asisa and in the sw on the Caño Pimichín. [Se Colombia to ne Peru and nw Brazil.]

Rain forest, low, open woodland along streams, savanna edge, 100–300 m.

## MOUNTAIN VELVETBREAST

*Lafresnaya lafresnayi*
COLIBRÍ TERCIOPELO

Pl. 11

4 [1.2]″; 10 [3] cm. Upperparts shining grass green. Central tail feathers shining golden olive, the rest *creamy buff* (or *white*, a) tipped bronze. Throat and breast glittering emerald green, rest of underparts velvety black, under tail cov-

erts creamy buff (or white, a) with shinings green tips. Bill curved. ♀: crown dusky grayish, upper surface shining green; tail and under tail coverts like respective ♂. Throat and breast buffy yellowish finely spotted with green disks, rest of underparts buffy white.

Subtropical zone. Páramo de Tamá, sw Táchira (*lafresnayi*). Ne Táchira, Mérida and s Trujillo (*greenewalti*, a). [Colombia to central Peru.]

Cloud forest edge, open fields with scattered bushy vegetation, 2200–3000 m. Forages in the lower branches of forest trees. Solitary, active. Call: a clear whistle.

## BRONZY INCA

*Coeligena coeligena*
COLIBRÍ INCA BRONCEADO

Pl. 11

4 [1.3]″; 10 [3.3] cm. Above shining coppery purple, feathers of rump with a subterminal green bar (or with entire upperparts more shaded with green, a). Tail forked, dark bronze. Throat whitish, the feathers with dusky centers giving a spotted appearance (or throat dusky olivaceous, the feathers edged whitish giving a somewhat barred appearance, b), rest of underparts dusky with a buff wash; under tail coverts rufous buff, edged white. Bend of wing and outer web of outer primary chestnut.

Upper tropical and subtropical zones. Sierra de Perijá, Zulia (*zuliana*, a). Sierra de San Luis, Falcón (*zuloagae*, b). The Andes of Táchira, Barinas and s Lara (*columbiana*, a). N Lara; Sierra de Aroa, Yaracuy, and along the coastal Cordillera to Miranda, where it also is found along the interior chain (*coeligena*). [Colombia to n Bolivia.]

Cloud forest edge; coffee plantations, 1000–2300 m. Open terrain with scattered trees and bushes. Solitary, forages in trees from low to medium height.

## COLLARED INCA

*Coeligena torquata*
COLIBRÍ INCA ACOLLARADO

Pl. 11

4 [1.4]″; 10 [3.5] cm. Above black; patch in center of crown violet blue with green reflections; wing coverts, rump and upper tail coverts dark shining green; longest upper tail coverts and central rectrices very dark bronzy green, rest of rectrices white, tipped black, increasingly toward outer feathers. Throat very dark bluish green; *breast white; belly black* glossed green, under tail coverts shining green. (Or similar in pattern but black portions of plumage replaced by shining green; crown glittering golden green, throat and sides of neck glittering emerald green. Central tail feathers shining golden green, rest white on basal half, golden green on distal half, a). ♀: in pattern like male but above shining dark green, bluer on crown, tail as in respective ♂, throat thickly spangled with blue green, breast white, belly gray with blue green disks.

Subtropical and temperate zones. The Páramo de Tamá, sw Táchira (*torquata*). The Andes of Mérida (*conradii*, a). [Colombia to w Ecuador and n Bolivia.]

Cloud forest edge, 1500–3000 m. Solitary; forages in trees from low to medium height.

## GOLDEN-BELLIED STARFRONTLET

*Coeligena bonapartei*
COLIBRÍ INCA DORADO

Pl. 11

4.5 [1]″; 11.5 [2.5] cm. Crown and nape black, frontlet glittering grass green; upper back shining grass green, rump and upper tail coverts glittering golden orange; tail forked, rufous, tipped golden bronze (or tail all bronze green, a). Upper throat and breast glittering emerald green, a large patch in center of throat glittering violet blue; belly glittering golden orange, a patch of *rufous chestnut on wings*. ♀: generally like ♂ but much duller, with green crown and buff throat. Outer tail feathers tipped white. No rufous chestnut on wings.

Upper tropical to temperate zones. Sierra de Perijá on Cerro Tetarí, Zulia (*consita*, a). Generally distributed in the Andes of Táchira, Mérida, Barinas and Trujillo (*eos*). [Ne Colombia.]

Cloud and dwarf forest, and the open terrain with scattered vegetation near the páramos, 1400–3200 m. Forages in trees from low to medium heights.

## BLUE-THROATED STARFRONTLET

*Coeligena helianthea*
COLIBRÍ INCA VENTRIVIOLETA

Pl. 11
4.4 [1.2]″; 11 [3] cm.  Black above, small frontlet glittering emerald green, back with a slight green gloss, rump and upper tail coverts glittering blue green; tail forked, black with a bronze sheen. Throat and breast black with a slight green sheen, plaque in center of throat glittering violet blue; belly and under tail coverts glittering bluish violet with steel blue reflections. ♀: shining grass green above, rump, upper tail coverts and tail as in ♂. Throat dark tawny buff, breast paler with green disks; belly as in ♂ but with buff bases of feathers showing through. Under tail coverts edged buff.
Upper subtropical and temperate zones. Sw Táchira (*tamai*). [Ne Colombia.]
Cloud and dwarf forest, open terrain with scattered vegetation, 2400–3000 m.

## SWORD-BILLED HUMMINGBIRD

*Ensifera ensifera*
COLIBRÍ PICO ESPADA

Pl. 13
5.2 [4]″; 13 [10] cm. *Bill enormously long.* Head coppery green, back shining green; tail somewhat forked, coppery green. Throat blackish; breast and sides of neck glittering green, rest of underparts grayish buff with green disks. ♀: much like ♂ but less coppery on head, underparts buffy white, throat spotted with bronze, rest with shining green disks.
Temperate zone. Locally distributed in the Andes of Mérida (*ensifera*). [The Andes from Colombia to n Bolivia.]
Dwarf forest, shrubby slopes, 2500–3000 m. Forages in flowers with large corollas (*Datura* sp.). This species has the longest bill of any hummingbird.

## BUFF-TAILED CORONET

*Boissonneaua flavescens*
COLIBRÍ CABECIDORADO

Pl. 11
4.5 [0.8]″; 11.5 [2] cm. Head glittering green to golden green, back shining green, inner webs of tertials rufescent. Central tail feathers bronze, rest *pale buff* tipped and edged bronze. Breast shining green, belly buff with green discs, under tail coverts buff. Under wing coverts and remiges rufous on basal part of inner web. ♀: like ♂ but less solidly green throat and breast, where buff bases of feathers show through.
Subtropical to páramo zone. Locally in the Andes of Táchira and Mérida to s Trujillo (*flavescens*). [Andes of Colombia to w Ecuador.]
Cloud and dwarf forests, forest edge, open shrubby terrain, 2100–3500 m. Sometimes clings like a woodpecker to the vertical surface of tree trunks, probably to glean whatever insects are stuck in the sap.

[SUNANGELS (*Heliangelus*) have a distinctive white or buff crescent across the breast. In Venezuela they are found only in the Andes and the Sierra de Perijá.]

## ORANGE-THROATED SUNANGEL

*Heliangelus mavors*
ANGEL DEL SOL CUELLIOCRE

Pl. 11
3.7 [0.6]″; 9.4 [1.5] cm. Shining green above, central tail feathers golden green, outer feathers bronzy tipped white. Narrow frontlet, throat and upper breast glittering golden orange, *breast band cinnamon buff*, belly cinnamon buff with green disks. ♀: like ♂ but throat brownish black, the feathers edged rufous.
Upper subtropical and temperate zones. The Andes in Táchira, Mérida, Trujillo and s Lara. [Ne Colombia.]
Cloud and dwarf forest, open terrain with scattered trees and bushes, 2000–3200 m.

## MERIDA SUNANGEL

*Heliangelus spencei*
ANGEL DEL SOL DE MÉRIDA

Pl. 11
3.7 [0.5]″; 9.5 [1.3] cm. Bronzy green above, central tail feathers bronze green, rest blackish. Narrow frontlet glittering steely green, throat and upper breast glittering violet, breast band white, belly buff with green discs. ♀: like ♂ but throat dusky, the feathers with a subterminal rufous bar and bronze green tip. Forehead only slightly greener than rest of crown. Lateral rectrices pale tipped.

152 · THE BIRDS OF VENEZUELA

Upper subtropical and temperate zones. The Andes of central Mérida. Cloud and dwarf forest, páramos, 2000–3600 m. Forages from low to middle height.

## AMETHYST-THROATED SUNANGEL
*Heliangelus amethysticollis*
ANGEL DEL SOL AMATISTA

3.7 [0.7]″; 9.4 [1.8] cm. Crown dark coppery purple, frontlet glittering blue (or bluish green, a), back shining green, central tail feathers green to bronzy green, rest blue black. Throat purple, *pectoral band white,* bordered below by a glittering green band, rest of underparts buff with green disks at sides. ♀: like ♂ but throat dull black, feathers edged rusty. Forehead shining blue or green.
Subtropical and temperate zones. The Sierra de Perijá, Zulia (*violiceps*). Sw Táchira (*verdiscutatus,* a). [Colombia to Bolivia.]
Cloud and dwarf forest, forest edge, open, bushy terrain along streams, 1800–3000 m. Forages actively in the trees at middle height. Whistles.

## GLOWING PUFFLEG
*Eriocnemis vestitus*
COLIBRÍ PANTALÓN VERDE

Pl. 11
3.5 [0.7]″; 9 [1.8] cm. Shining dark green above changing to glittering golden green on rump and upper tail coverts. Tail forked, dark steel blue. Throat and upper breast shining blackish green; patch on throat glittering purple, breast and belly glittering *golden green.* Under tail coverts glittering purple. Downy tibial tufts white. ♀: lighter and more golden green above than ♂; throat patch glittering violet blue, line from gape to below eye buff; breast and sides of throat buff sprinkled with glittering, golden green disks, belly grayish white with glittering, golden green disks. Under tail coverts glittering steel blue. Tail forked, dark blue, shorter than in ♂. Tibial tufts white.
Temperate and páramo zones. The Andes from sw Táchira to n Mérida (*vestitus*). [Colombia to e Ecuador.]

Cloud and dwarf forest, open terrain, páramos, 2800–3600 m.

## COPPERY-BELLIED PUFFLEG
*Eriocnemis cupreoventris*
COLIBRÍ PANTALÓN COBRIZO

Pl. 11
3.8 [0.7]″; 9.7 [1.8] cm. Above shining golden green, upper tail coverts bluish green; tail forked, steel blue. Throat, breast, and sides of body glittering emerald green; belly glittering *golden copper;* under tail coverts glittering purple. Downy tibial tufts white. ♀: like ♂.
Temperate and páramo zones. The Andes from sw Táchira to central Mérida. [Ne Colombia.]
Páramos, 3000 m. Low, scattered vegetation.

## BOOTED RACKET-TAIL
*Ocreatus underwoodii*
COLIBRÍ COLA DE HOJA

Pl. 13
♂ 4.8 [0.5]″; 12 [1.3] cm.; ♀ 3″ (7.5 cm.). Central tail feathers shining green, outer feathers dull blackish, outermost feather very long (3.4″, 8.6 cm.) with partially *bare shaft,* ending in a *large* round steel blue *racquet.* Back and belly bronze green, throat and breast glittering green; under tail coverts buff. Downy tibial tufts white. ♀: upperparts shining green. Tail deeply forked, central tail feathers like back, 2 outer pairs longer than the rest (1.3″, 3.3 cm.), mostly dark blue, outermost broadly tipped white. Below white with green disks. Tibial tufts white.
Upper tropical to temperate zones. Nw Zulia and Falcón s to sw Táchira, Mérida, w Barinas and s Lara (*discifer*). The coastal and interior cordilleras from Carabobo to Miranda (*polystictus*). [Colombia to n Bolivia.]
Cloud and dwarf forests, 850–3000 m. Coffee plantations, damp shady ravines in deep forest. Solitary, perches in lower branches, feeds in treetops. Opens and closes tail as it feeds.

## GREEN-TAILED TRAINBEARER
*Lesbia nuna*
COLIBRÍ COLUDO VERDE

Pl. 13
♂ 6.1 [0.4]″; 15.5 [1] cm.; ♀ 4.3″ (11 cm.). Tail *very long* (4.2″ 10.6 cm.), very *deeply forked,* outer feather much longer than the rest, black with a green gloss, tipped shining green, rest of tail feathers very much graduated, shining, almost glittering emerald green. Back shining green. Throat and upper breast glittering emerald green, lower breast shining golden green; belly similar but buff bases of the feathers showing through. ♀: tail much as in ♂ but much shorter (2.7″, 6.8 cm.), evenly graduated, the outermost pair only slightly longer than the next. Upperparts like ♂; underparts buffy white, thickly sprinkled with green disks.
Known in Venezuela from a specimen in the British Museum marked "Sierra Nevada de Mérida" (*gouldi*). [Ne Colombia to n Bolivia.]
A subtropical and temperate zone species. In Colombia it is found near 3000 m. Has not been reported in Venezuela since a single specimen was collected by Goering in 1874 in the Mérida region.

## PURPLE-BACKED THORNBILL
*Ramphomicron microrhynchum*
COLIBRÍ PICO ESPINA

Pl. 11
3.2 [0.2]″; 8 [0.5] cm. *Shining purple above;* tail rather long, deeply forked, shining blackish purple. Throat glittering golden green; breast and belly shining grass green; under tail coverts cinnamon buff with small blackish violet disks. Bill noticeably very short. ♀: above shining grass green, bronzy on upper tail coverts. Below buffy white with shining green disks, under tail coverts tawny. Tail shorter and less deeply forked than in ♂, blackish, outer feathers tipped white.
Temperate zone. Very locally in the Andes of Táchira and Mérida (*andicolum*). [Colombia to w Ecuador and s Peru.]
Cloud and dwarf forest, bushy hillsides, 2500–3000 m. Has the smallest bill of any hummingbird.

## TYRIAN METALTAIL
*Metallura tyrianthina*
COLIBRÍ VERDE COLIRROJO

Pl. 11
3.5 [0.4]″; 9 [1] cm. Bronzy green (or dark bronzy green, a), throat glittering emerald green. Tail shining golden violet purple (or shining purple, a; or golden purple, b) above, below glistening and brighter. ♀: like ♂, but throat and breast tawny ochraceous, white on belly, some dusky spots on throat. Tail shorter than in ♂ but similarly colored (or without dots on throat, a, b).
Subtropical to temperate zones. Locally along the upper Río Negro, Sierra de Perijá, Zulia (*districta*). N Táchira (Páramo Zumbador; Boca de Monte) and in the Andes of Mérida, Trujillo and Lara (*oreopola*, b). Sw Táchira (*tyrianthina*). The coastal Cordillera from Aragua to Miranda (*chloropogon*, b). [Colombia to n Bolivia.]
Cloud and dwarf forest, páramos, 1700–3800 m.

## PERIJA METALTAIL
*Metallura iracunda*
COLIBRÍ DE PERIJÁ

4.2 [0.4]″; 10.6 [1] cm. Mainly black, glossed strongly with coppery greenish gold. Forecrown shining dark green. Throat glittering emerald green. Tail above and below glistening purple red. ♀: back dusky green, below buffy; tail shining coppery violet above, glistening below.
Nw Zulia on Cerros Pintado and Tres Tetas. [Adj. Colombia.]
Open country near the summits of the mountains between Colombia and Venezuela, 1850–3000 m.

## BRONZE-TAILED THORNBILL
*Chalcostigma heteropogon*
PICO ESPINA BRONCEADO

Pl. 11
♂ 5 [0.5]″; 13 [1.3] cm.; ♀ 4″ (10 cm.). Crown shining green, bronzier on back and bronzy purple on rump and upper tail coverts; tail long, deeply forked, bronze. Throat glittering emerald green turning to rosy violet on breast where it terminates in a sharp point, rest of lower

surface dull olive. ♀: similar to ♂ but throat with glittering green disks, no violet on chest. Tail much shorter.
Páramo de Tamá, Táchira. [Ne Colombia.] Páramos and nearby mountain valleys, 3000–3275 m.

## BEARDED HELMETCREST
*Oxypogon guerinii*
CHIVITO DE LOS PÁRAMOS

Pl. 13
4.5 [0.3]″; 11.5 [0.8] cm. Crown and sides of head black, narrow central crown stripe white branching to nostrils, hindpart developed into a *long, thin crest* where mixed with black crest feathers; back shining olive green. Central tail feathers shining olive green, rest purplish bronze, shafts mostly white, tail forked. A narrow line of glittering green disks in center of throat, bordered by black which joins black of sides of head, moustacial streak white; feathers of lower throat, long, pointed forming a bear of white plumes, rest of underparts dark olive green, grayish in center of abdomen. ♀: much like ♂ but without crest or beard feathers; breast white with dusky disks.
Páramo zone. The Andes of Mérida and Trujillo (*lindeni*). [The mountains of n and central Colombia.]
Páramos and nearby valleys, 3500–4500 m. Bushy or grassy slopes. Sometimes walks on matted grass in search of insects.

## LONG-TAILED SYLPH
*Aglaiocercus kingi*
COLIBRÍ COLUDO AZUL

Pl. 13
♂ 7 [0.6]″; 18 [1.5] cm.; ♀ 3.7″ (9.4 cm.). Tail very long, much graduated, deeply forked, glistening violet blue, tinged green near tip (or central tail feathers glistening green, tinged violet blue near base, a; or central feathers glistening blue, tinged green, outermost pair, very long 6″ (15 cm.) and wide 0.4″ (1 cm.), glistening violet tinged glistening green, rest dark violet basally, turning gradually to blue, b). Above bronze green, glittering green patch in center of crown; below dark bronzy green (with a glittering blue gular patch, a, b). ♀: above

shining green, crown glittering blue; throat white, breast and abdomen cinnamon rufous (or white, b), sides bronzy green.
Upper tropical to temperate zone. Locally distributed in the Sierra de Perijá, Zulia, and generally in the Andes of Táchira, Mérida, Trujillo and Lara (*caudatus*). Generally from the Sierra de San Luis, Falcón, the Sierra de Aroa, Yaracuy, and along the coastal Cordillera to Miranda where also in the central chain (*margarethae,* a). The e coastal Cordillera in Sucre and n Monagas (*berlepschi,* b). [Colombia to w Ecuador and n Bolivia.]
Cloud forest, coffee plantations, scrub, 900–3000 m. Alone or in pairs, forages from the low underbrush to the highest treetops.

## WEDGE-BILLED HUMMINGBIRD
*Schistes geoffroyi*
COLIBRÍ PICO DE CUÑA

Pl. 12
3.4 [0.6]″; 8.6 [1.5] cm. Crown and center of throat glittering emerald green, a tuft at each side of throat glittering violet, a *white patch at sides of breast,* breast and belly grayish with green disks. Postocular streak white. Upper back shining green, lower back and upper tail coverts shining reddish bronze. Tail rounded, central feathers with a broad median blue band tipped shining blue green and fringed white. ♀: differs from ♂ by dull green throat and much smaller violet tufts at side of throat.
Upper tropical and subtropical zones. Very local; Sierra de Perijá, Zulia; the Andes of Táchira and Lara and the central coastal Cordillera in Yaracuy, Carabobo and Aragua (*geoffroyi*). [Colombia to Bolivia.]
Cloud forest, shrubs along forest edge and undergrowth, 1200–1800 m. Solitary. Reputed to be the best hummingbird singer.

## BLACK-EARED FAIRY
*Heliothryx aurita*
COLIBRÍ HADA OREJAZUL

Pl. 13
♂ 4 [0.6]″; 10 [1.5] cm.; ♀ 4.7″ (12 cm.). Crown and sides of neck glittering grass

green, *subocular band black terminating in glittering purple on ear coverts.* Above shining green. Tail rounded, central feathers blue black, rest white. Underparts pure white. ♀: *central 4 tail feathers much longer than outer ones, blue black, rest white,* with a basal blue black band. Upperpart shining green, underparts white sometimes spotted with gray on breast.

Tropical zone. N of the Orinoco in e Sucre (Cerro Azul, Guanoco); s of the Orinoco in Bolívar and Amazonas (*aurita*). [E Colombia; the Guianas to n Bolivia and se Brazil.]

Rain and cloud forest, scrub, to 950 m. n of the Orinoco, 100–1300 m. s of it. Hovers in the leafy vegetation picking small insects; investigates water cups of *Heliconias* which contain drowned insects.

## LONG-BILLED STARTHROAT

*Heliomaster longirostris*
COLIBRÍ ESTRELLA PICOLARGO

Pl. 11

4 [1.5]"; 10 [4] cm. Crown glittering blue, *white spot behind eye;* back bronze green; central tail feathers blue green, rest black, outermost tipped white. Chin black, throat glittering violet red, moustacial streak white; underparts bronzy grayish, under tail coverts blackish broadly tipped white. ♀: generally like ♂ but crown like back, moustacial streak broader, throat feathers edged white.

Tropical zone. Locally distributed n of the Orinoco in s Táchira, Carabobo and Sucre; w Apure; generally distributed s of the Orinoco in Bolívar and n Amazonas (*longirostris*). [Colombia and the Guianas to Bolivia and se Brazil. Trinidad.]

Open terrain, forest edge, second growth, plantations, from to 800 m. n of the Orinoco, to 1200 m. s of it. Forages very low in trees to treetops. Perches on bare twigs.

## AMETHYST WOODSTAR

*Calliphlox amethystina*
TUCUSITO AMATISTA

Pl. 12

♂ 2.6 [0.7]"; 6.6 [1.8] cm.; ♀ 2.4" (6 cm.). Shining bronzy olive green above; tail much graduated, *deeply forked,* central feathers very short, like back in color, rest dark purple, outer feathers pointed (1.1", 2.8 cm.). Throat and sides of neck glittering rosy red, a white band across breast; belly gray with green disks. ♀: above like ♂, throat with glittering green disks; band across breast white, rest of underparts rufous. Tail short, square, central feathers green, rest black with cinnamon tips.

Tropical zone. Very locally distributed n of the Orinoco from Mérida, w Barinas, Carabobo and Guárico to Anzoátegui, Sucre and Delta Amacuro; generally distributed s of the Orinoco in Bolívar and Amazonas. [The Guianas, e Colombia to n Bolivia and ne Argentina.]

One of the smallest hummingbirds; its wing beat, 80 beats per second, produces a distinctive buzz. N of the Orinoco to 1000 m., to 1500 m. s of it. Occurs in almost every kind of habitat except rain forest even including arid areas. Solitary; forages in low bushes and small trees.

## GORGETED WOODSTAR

*Acestrura heliodor*
ESTRELLA CUELLIRROJO

Pl. 12

♂ 2.5 [0.5]"; 6.4 [1.3] cm.; ♀ 2.3" (5.8 cm.). Shining bluish green above; tail black, central feathers very short, next 2 pairs much longer, 2 outermost much shorter and very narrow, hairlike. Throat glittering purplish red, feathers at sides much elongated; breast grayish, belly shining blue green. ♀: shining bronze green above, upper tail coverts and underparts cinnamon, a dusky patch at sides of neck and below eye. Tail cinnamon with a broad subterminal black band.

Subtropical and temperate zones. Locally in the Andes of Mérida (*meridae*). [E Panama to nw Ecuador.]

Cloud forest, forest edge, scrub, 2200–3000 m. Like the other small hummingbirds it looks like a large insect as it feeds actively in very small flowers in thick vegetation.

**RUFOUS-SHAFTED WOODSTAR**
*Chaetocercus jourdanii*
Tucusito Garganta Rosa

Pl. 12
2.8 [0.6]"; 7 [1.5] cm. Shining bronze green above; 4 central rectrices like back, next 2 on either side black, shafts and basal portion of inner webs rufous, outermost very narrow, short, purple black. Throat rosy red (or violet red, a), band across breast white, abdomen shining green. ♀: shining bronze green above, below cinnamon, paler in center of belly, a dark patch below eyes, sides of body bronze green. Central tail feathers like back, next purple black, 3 outer pairs cinnamon with a subterminal black band.

Upper tropical to temperate zones. Nw Zulia in the upper Río Negro; Sierra de San Luis, Falcón, very locally along the coastal Cordillera to the Distr. Federal (*rosae*). Locally in the Andes from Táchira to s Lara (*andinus*). The e Cordillera in Sucre and n Monagas (*jourdanii*, a). [Ne Colombia. Trinidad.]

Very small, insectlike. Cloud forest, forest edge, coffee plantations, scrub, 900–3000 m.

# TROGONIFORMES

## TROGONS: Trogonidae

Sorocuaces, Viudas, Quetzales

These beautiful birds, clothed in metallic greens and blues, with red or yellow stomachs, probably come very close to fulfilling one's idea of what a bird of tropical forests should look like.

Trogons have a curious distribution, being found in se Asia and in Africa s of the Sahara, but in tropical America they reach their highest development.

The magnificent quetzals are found in Central America and n South America, while the more typical species are found from sw US to n Argentina.

Trogons are solitary and rather sluggish birds, which feed on small fruits plucked in flight and on insects which they catch on the wing. They lay their eggs in cavities in trees or in arboreal termite nests but build no nest. Their legs are very short, feet small with 2 toes pointing forward and 2 backward. The bill is short, wide and toothed. In species which resemble each other, sometimes rather closely, the pattern on the underside of the tail is diagnostic. The rolling, ventriloquial calls of all the small trogons sound very much alike and are of little use in identifying the various species.

**CRESTED QUETZAL**

*Pharomachrus antisianus*
Quetzal Coliblanco

Pl. 14
12" (30 cm.). Head and short compressed crest from forehead over base of bill shining golden green. Upper surface, lengthened wing coverts and long upper tail coverts, which are slightly longer than tail, shining emerald green. Throat and breast like back, belly crimson. Middle tail feathers black, *3 outer pairs white*. Bill yellow. ♀: head, throat and breast dull grayish brown, feathers of upper breast edged green. Back as in ♂, tail coverts shorter. Belly crimson. Tail black, 2 outer pairs of feathers notched white on outer web, and narrowly tipped white.

Subtropical zone. Sierra de Perijá, Zulia; the Andes of Táchira, Mérida to n Trujillo. [Colombia through the Andes to Bolivia.]

Cloud forests, 1200–3000 m. Alone or in pairs, in dense foliage high in trees. Perches quietly. Flight deeply undulating. Feeds on fruits, berries, insects,

lizards, frogs. Call: loud, rolling; also a velvety whistle. Responds to an imitated call. Nests in holes in dead trees or limbs.
Note: Called *P. mocinno antisianus* in Lista Av. Venez.

## WHITE-TIPPED QUETZAL
*Pharomachrus fulgidus*
QUETZAL DORADO

12″ (30 cm.). Very like Crested Quetzal, with much smaller frontal crest. Best separable by having the 3 outer pairs of *tail feathers black broadly tipped white.* ♀: differs from the Crested by having the outer pairs of tail feathers black tipped white.
Upper tropical and subtropical zones. The coastal Cordillera from Yaracuy to Miranda, the interior Cordillera on Cerro Golfo Triste; the e Cordillera in e Anzoátegui, n Monagas and Sucre e to Cerro Humo (*fulgidus*). [Ne Colombia. Ecuador?]
Cloud forests, clearings, 900–1900 m. Coffee plantations. Alone or in pairs, forages from the middle heights to the treetops. Difficult to see as it perches motionless. Feeds on fruits, berries. Call: booming hoots, not very loud, but to be heard at some distance. Sometimes nests in old woodpecker holes, usually in holes in dead trees or limbs.

## GOLDEN-HEADED QUETZAL
*Pharomachrus auriceps*
VIUDA DE LA MONTAÑA

Pl. 14
13″ (33 cm.). Differs principally from Crested and White-tipped Quetzals by having the *tail feathers entirely black,* head more golden. ♀: differs from other quetzals by entirely black tail.
Subtropical zone. The Sierra de Perijá and the Andes of Táchira and Mérida to n Trujillo (*hargitti*, a). [The Andes from Colombia to nw Peru and n Bolivia.]
Cloud and dwarf forests, open terrain with scattered trees, 2000–3100 m.

## PAVONINE QUETZAL
*Pharomachrus pavoninus*
VIUDA PICO ROJO

13″ (33 cm.). Very like Golden-headed Quetzal but tail shorter; head less crested, greener, less golden. Bill red instead of yellow. ♀: differs from other quetzals by having the 3 outermost tail feathers barred white on both webs and tipped white. Bill dusky with red base.
Tropical zone in s Amazonas and sw Bolívar (*pavoninus*). [Se Colombia, w Amazonian Brazil, e Ecuador to n Bolivia.]
Rain forest, 150–700 m.

## BLACK-TAILED TROGON
*Trogon melanurus*
SOROCUÁ COLA NEGRA

Pl. 14
13″ (33 cm.) [or 11″ (28 cm.), a]. Upperparts and breast metallic blue green, throat and sides of head black, belly crimson, separated from the green of chest by a white band. Wing coverts and outer webs of secondaries finely vermiculated black and white giving a gray look. Central tail feathers like back with a sharply defined black terminal band, next 2 pairs with inner webs black, next mostly black, 2 outermost pairs black, somewhat freckled white on outer web. Bill orange, eye ring orange red. ♀: *upperparts and breast gray, belly crimson.* Central tail feathers gray, rest blackish, wings much as in ♂.
Tropical zone. Nw Zulia (*macrourus*). Amazonas on Caño Capuana, Río Orinoco, and s of the Río Ventuari; Bolívar from the Río Caura e across the upper Río Paragua to the Gran Sabana and the Altiplanicie de Nuria (*melanurus*, a). [Central Panama to Colombia, nw Peru, the Guianas to n Bolivia and s Brazil.]
Rain forest, to 100 m. n of the Orinoco, to 1000 m. s of it.

## WHITE-TAILED TROGON
*Trogon viridis*
SOROCUÁ COLA BLANCA

Pl. 14
12″ (30 cm.). Crown, hindneck and breast shining violet blue, face and throat dull black. Back shining blue green shading to peacock blue on rump and upper tail coverts. Lower breast and belly orange yellow. Wings black. Central tail feathers blue green tipped black, next 2 pairs with black inner webs, outer 3 pairs black, the distal third diagonally white.

Eye ring pale blue. Bill bluish white.
♀: *gray* with *orange yellow belly* (cf.
Violaceous Trogon), wing coverts narrowly barred with white. Tail black,
outer feathers notched and tipped white.
Tropical zone. Generally distributed (except in the nw) from s Táchira, w Apure
to Barinas and from the Distr. Federal
to Sucre, Monagas and Delta Amacuro,
and throughout Amazonas and Bolívar
(*viridis*). [Central Panama to w Ecuador, the Guianas to Bolivia and s Brazil.
Trinidad.]
Rain and deciduous forest, second growth,
clearings, plantations, along rivers to
800 m. n of the Orinoco, to 1300 m. s
of it. Alone or in pairs, perches motionless in the leafy branches for long periods. Feeds on fruits, insects, lizards,
seeds. Call: a repeated "caw," beginning
slowly and accelerating at the end.

## COLLARED TROGON
*Trogon collaris*
SOROCUÁ ACOLLARADO

Pl. 14
10″ (25 cm.). Upperparts, breast and
central tail feathers shining coppery
green (or blue green, a). Face and
throat black. Wing coverts and inner
secondaries finely vermiculated black
and white, looking gray from a distance.
Belly rosy red, separated from green of
breast by a white bar. Three outer tail
feathers black, conspicuously and evenly
barred with white, tipped white. Bill
greenish yellow, no noticeable eye ring.
♀: upperparts and breast sandy brown.
Belly light pinkish crimson, breast band
white. Wing coverts sandy brown finely
vermiculated black. Central tail feathers hazel, next 2 pairs black on inner
web, tipped black, 3 outer pairs blackish
brown, freckled with white on outer web,
with a white terminal bar, edged above
by a black line.
Tropical and subtropical zones. The serranías of the n from the Sierra de Perijá,
Zulia, through Falcón, n Lara, n Guárico
and Yaracuy to Sucre and the Andes in
w Apure and s Táchira (*exoptatus*).
Central and se Amazonas and across s
Bolívar to the Río Icabarú (*collaris*, a).
[Mexico to Colombia, nw Ecuador, w
Guyana, Surinam to Bolivia and se
Brazil. Trinidad, Tobago.]

Rain and cloud forest, to 2300 m. n of
the Orinoco, 250–1200 m. s of it. Along
rivers. Alone or in pairs forages from
the lower heights to near the treetops.
Call: monotonous series of whistled
notes, uttered at intervals. Responds to
an imitation.

## MASKED TROGON
*Trogon personatus*
SOROCUÁ ENMASCARADO

Pl. 14
10″ (25 cm.). Much like Collared Trogon
but separable by shining brassy green
(or shining deep coppery bronze, a)
central tail feathers, 3 outer pairs of
tail feathers black crossed by very narrow, wavy white lines, sometimes indistinct. Wing coverts much more finely
vermiculated than in Collared Trogon.
♀: differs markedly from ♀ Collared
Trogon by black forehead, face and
throat with a conspicuous white crescent
at rear edge of eye; wing coverts black
instead of sandy brown, finely vermiculated white. Outer 3 pairs of tail feathers black with white wavy lines and
white tip (or barred only on outer web,
inner webs mostly black, freckled with
white near tip, tipped white, a).
Upper tropical and subtropical zones. Nw
Venezuela from nw Zulia and Táchira
to Mérida, Barinas and Trujillo (*personatus*). Amazonas and in nw Bolívar
on the lower Río Caura (*duidae*, a).
Se Bolívar on Cerros Auyan-tepui,
Aprada-tepui, Chimantá-tepui, Uei-tepui
and Roraima, and on the middle Río
Paragua on Cerro Guaiquinima (*roraimae*, a). Se Bolívar at Sierra de Lema,
Kabanayén and Cerros Ptari-tepui and
Uaipán-tepui (*ptaritepui*, a). [Colombia
to nw Peru; Guyana, adj. n Brazil to n
Bolivia.]
Rain and cloud forests, open forests in the
higher altitudes, 1500–3000 m. n of the
Orinoco, 700–1850 m. s of it. Habits
similar to those of its congeners. Keeps
well up in trees but not in forest treetops.

## BLACK-THROATED TROGON
*Trogon rufus*
SOROCUÁ AMARILLO

Pl. 14
9.5″ (24 cm.). The only yellow-bellied
trogon in Venezulea with a green head

and breast (instead of purple blue). Upperparts and breast shining, metallic bronzy green, face and throat black. Belly yellow. Wing coverts and inner remiges black coarsely vermiculated white. Central tail feathers shining blue green (or bronzy green, a; or coppery gold, b) tipped black, outer 3 pairs with inner webs mostly black, outer webs broadly barred black and white, broadly tipped white. ♀: the only trogon in Venezuela with brown back, breast, wings and tail and yellow belly.

Tropical zone. Amazonas at Puerto Yapacana and Caño Casiquiare (*sulphureus*, b). Amazonas at San Fernando de Atabapo s to the Yavita-Pimichín Trail and the upper Río Orinoco (*amazonicus*, a). Central and s Bolívar from the upper Río Caura and the Río Paragua to the Gran Sabana (*rufus*). [Honduras to w Ecuador, e Peru, se Brazil and n Argentina.]

The status of *sulphureus* and *amazonicus* in the Duida region remains to be established. The color of the central tail feathers is unstable and has probably led to confusion.

Rain forest, second growth, open woodland, forest edge, 100–900 m. Perches on lower branches, joins flocks of forest birds. Call: a short series of separate descending whistled notes, also a cackling call. Nests in holes in dead trees.

## VIOLACEOUS TROGON
*Trogon violaceus*
SOROCUÁ VIOLETA

Pl. 14

9.5″ (24 cm.). Not unlike White-tailed Trogon but much smaller with outer tail feathers barred instead of mostly white. Head and breast purple blue, face and throat black (or head black, glossed purple blue on hindcrown, a). Back shining, metallic blue green to green blue, central tail feathers violet (or blue, a) tipped black, outer 3 pairs of feathers broadly barred black and white, inner webs with considerable black, tipped white. Belly yellow. Bare eye ring yellow. ♀: very like ♀ White-tailed Trogon but much smaller and at once distinguishable by a conspicuous ring of white feathers around the eye.

Tropical zone. Widespread in the Sierra de Perijá, Zulia; local in sw Táchira, Mérida and w Barinas (*caligatus*). Locally in w, central and s Amazonas (*crissalis*, a). Locally in e and s Bolívar and in n and e Amazonas (*violaceus*). [Mexico to Colombia, w Ecuador, the Guianas to n Bolivia, and s Brazil. Trinidad.]

Rain forests, clearings, second growth, open woodland, to 1200 m., often along streams. Alone or in pairs, forages at medium heights. Habits similar to those of its congeners. Call: repeated single notes, accelerated toward the end.

# CORACIIFORMES

# KINGFISHERS: Alcedinidae

## MARTINES PESCADORES

Kingfishers are of world-wide distribution and are but poorly represented in the Americas: only 6 out of 87 known species are found there.

Kingfishers frequent streams, lakes and swamps and woodland ponds. They live on fish and sometimes insects and nest in tunnels, which they excavate in river banks.

## RINGED KINGFISHER
*Ceryle torquata*
MARTÍN PESCADOR GRANDE

Fig. 38

16″ (41 cm.). Long crest and upperparts blue gray with narrow, black shaft streaks. Spot before eye, throat, sides of neck and nuchal collar white. Breast and belly chestnut, under tail coverts white, more or less barred gray. Primaries black with a large white area on inner webs, inner remiges notched white. Central tail feathers gray, black along shaft where spotted white, rest black, gray on outer web, with broken white bars. ♀: differs from ♂ by having a broad gray band, sometimes mixed with chestnut, across the breast, bordered below by a white band; belly and under tail coverts chestnut.

Tropical zone, including Margarita I. (*torquata*). [Mexico to Tierra del Fuego. Trinidad. Lesser Antilles.]

Along the shores of lowland rivers, large streams, lakes and lagoons, to 500 m. Alone or in pairs, perches quietly, fairly low, along river banks on the lookout for fishes and crabs. In suitable sites like high sandbanks facing large rivers, over 100 pairs may congregate. Call: loud, wooden slow, rattling notes, also a series of "chick" notes.

## BELTED KINGFISHER

*Ceryle alcyon*
MARTÍN PESCADOR MIGRATORIO

Fig. 38

12″ (30 cm.). Head, neck, upperparts, wings and tail like Ringed Kingfisher. Below white, with a gray band across breast and patch at sides of belly. ♀: differs from ♂ by having a narrow chestnut band across breast and chestnut sides to belly.

Casual winter visitor. Falcón; Carabobo; Delta Amacuro, and sighted on many of

the Caribbean islands (*alcyon*). [Breeds from Alaska and Canada to the Gulf states. Winters to Panama and the W Indies, casually to Colombia. Guyana. Trinidad.]

Passage migrant and winter visitor, Oct.–Apr. Sea coasts, rivers, lakes, swamps, mangroves, to 450 m. Alone, wary, silent. Perches on fairly high branches overlooking the water.

## AMAZON KINGFISHER

*Chloroceryle amazona*
MARTÍN PESCADOR MATRAQUERO

Pl. 15

11″ (28 cm.). Upperparts and central tail feathers dark, shining, oily green. Throat white with a sharp, oily green moustacial streak; nuchal collar and belly white; broad band across upper breast chestnut, sides of body streaked oily green. Inner webs of remiges and lateral tail feathers notched with white. ♀: differs from ♂ by having a glossy green instead of chestnut band, often broken in the center, across the breast.

Tropical zone throughout (*amazona*). [Mexico to Colombia and e of the Andes to n Argentina. Trinidad, Tobago.]

Rivers, lakes, ponds in forests, savannas, to 2500 m. n of the Orinoco, to 500 m. s of it. Usually alone, perches at low to medium heights along open streams and wide forest-fringed rivers. Call: a rattle; also a "click" note.

Fig. 38. BELTED KINGFISHER (left, female), RINGED KINGFISHER (right, female)

## GREEN KINGFISHER

*Chloroceryle americana*
MARTÍN PESCADOR PEQUEÑO

Pl. 15

7.5" (19 cm.). Like Amazon but very much smaller, with conspicuous white spots on wings and outer tail feathers mostly white. Belly thickly spotted with oily green. ♀: like Amazon but throat and breast buff with an oily green band across breast and another below it formed by a row of spots which are continued down sides of body. Wings conspicuously spotted, outer tail feathers mostly white.

Tropical zone throughout (*americana*). [Sw US to Chile and central Argentina.] Rivers, lakes, marshes, swamps near woodland edge, to 1000 m. Rain and deciduous forest edge, mangroves. Alone or in pairs, perches near water at low levels, also on rocks in rivers and on telephone wires. Dives below the water for fish. Call: a series of clicking chirps, "trik, trik, trik, trik."

## GREEN-AND-RUFOUS KINGFISHER

*Chloroceryle inda*
MARTÍN PESCADOR SELVÁTICO

Pl. 15

8.5" (22 cm.). Above shining oily green, speckled with white to buffy white on inner remiges, rump and upper tail coverts. Preocular spot cinnamon. Tail feathers dark shining green, inner web spotted with white, except on central pair. Narrow, broken nuchal collar; throat and sides of neck orange buff, deepening to chestnut on rest of underparts. ♀: differs from ♂ by having a band of oily green, white-barred feathers across breast.

Tropical zone. Very local n of the Orinoco where recorded from w Apure, w Barinas, n Aragua, se Sucre and ne Monagas; generally distributed s of the Orinoco in Amazonas, Bolívar and Delta Amacuro. [Nicaragua to Colombia, w Ecuador, the Guianas, to s Brazil, e Peru and n Bolivia.]

Streams and swamps inside forest, mangroves, to 400 m. Solitary, secretive, keeps low. Seldom flies in the open. Feeds on small fish. Call: a rapid "too-too-too-too."

## PYGMY KINGFISHER

*Chloroceryle aenea*
MARTÍN PESCADOR PIGMEO

Pl. 15

5" (13 cm.). A tiny kingfisher. Like Green-and-Rufous Kingfisher but much smaller and differing in color by having center of belly and under tail coverts white.

Tropical zone. Very local n of the Orinoco where recorded in sw Zulia, w Apure, ne Miranda, and se Sucre; generally distributed s of the Orinoco in Amazonas, Bolívar and Delta Amacuro (*aenea*). [S Mexico to w Ecuador, the Guianas, n Bolivia and s Brazil. Trinidad.]

Borders of small streams and ponds inside forests, edges of mangrove swamps. Usually in pairs, not shy, quiet. Feeds on small fish, insects. Call: a dry, weak, "dzit, dzit, dzit, dzit."

# MOTMOTS: Momotidae

## PÁJARO LEÓN

Motmots form a small family of remarkable birds found only in the American tropics. Their plumage is mostly green, the tail long, graduated, and often ending in a racket.

The Brazilian name for the Blue-crowned Motmot, *Hudú,* well expresses the note of this very widespread species.

Motmots feed on fruit and insects, nest in crevices and holes which they tunnel into the ground and live a solitary and rather sluggish life in the lower stages of the forest trees.

There are 4 genera of motmots but only 1 is found in Venezuela.

## BLUE-CROWNED MOTMOT

*Momotus momota*
PÁJARO LEÓN

Pl. 25

16" (41 cm.). Lores and center of crown black, crown encircled by shining turquoise blue band, deepening to ultra marine blue on hindcrown. Sides of head black, the black prolonged backward to ear coverts where bordered narrowly above and below by shining turquoise blue. Upperparts olive green to grass green, (with a well-marked chestnut nuchal collar, a). Throat and breast dull olive, tinged cinnamon on throat (or cinnamon, tinged olive on breast, b; or underparts chestnut, c). An oval black spot on center of breast narrowly bordered with bright turquoise blue. Tail long, graduated, basally green becoming bluer distally, shaft at end of tail bare, terminating in a blue racket which is tipped black, (tail sometimes normal, without bare shaft and racket).

Tropical zone. Extreme n Perijá region, Zulia, w Lara, Carabobo and Aragua (*subrufescens,* b). Central Perijá and L. Maracaibo regions, Zulia, n Táchira, w Mérida (*osgoodi,* c). Extreme s Táchira, extreme w Apure, w Barinas (*microstephanus*). S of the Orinoco in Amazonas and Bolívar (*momota,* a). A doubtful record exists for Sucre, but it is possible that the species occurs there for it is found in Trinidad. [Mexico to nw Peru, nw Argentina, Paraguay and se Brazil. Trinidad, Tobago.]

Rain and gallery forest, second growth, to 600 m. n of the Orinoco, to 1250 m. s of it. Semi-open terrain, forest and river edges. Alone or in pairs, shy, sits quietly, very low in the undergrowth and to middle heights. Swings tail from side to side, like a pendulum. Call: fairly loud "hudú . . . hudú, du, du, du" etc., also cackling calls.

# PICIFORMES

# JACAMARS: Galbulidae

BARRANQUEROS Y TUCUSOS MONTAÑEROS

There are two types of jacamars. One, with its shining, iridescent green plumage and rather long tail, fulfills the ideal of a beautiful bird of the tropics, the other is smaller, rather dull in color and short-tailed. Both types are recognizable as jacamars by their very long and usually very thin and pointed bills, small weak feet with 2 toes pointing forward and 2 backward.

Jacamars inhabit forest clearings and dry, open woodland, perching on exposed branches from which they sally out after insects. They nest in tunnels, which they excavate in banks, or in arboreal termite nests, and lay round, white eggs.

## BROWN JACAMAR

*Brachygalba lugubris*
BARRANQUERO CASTAÑO

Pl. 15

7" (18 cm.). Crown and mantle ashy brown to sooty brown, lower back darker glossed with greenish black. Chin and throat whitish, breast and sides rufescent brown, center of abdomen buffy white. Wings and tail blue black. Bill long (1.8", 4.6 cm), thin, straight. Tail short (2", 5 cm.).

Tropical zone. Nw Bolívar along the lower Río Caura (*fulviventris*). S and e Bolívar along the upper Río Caura and from Ciudad Bolívar and the Río Paragua e to the Sierra de Imataca, Río Cuyuni and the Gran Sabana (*lugubris*). Central and s Amazonas (*obscuriceps*). [E Colombia and the Guianas to Bolivia and s Brazil.]

Rain and cloud forest, second growth, open terrain with scattered trees, thickets, to 1500 m. Perches low, in pairs or in small groups. Call: a single, loud, whistled note.

## PALE-HEADED JACAMAR
*Brachygalba goeringi*
BARRANQUERO ACOLLARADO

Pl. 15
7″ (18 cm.). Crown and upper mantle pale ashy brown; lower back, wings and tail blackish brown glossed with blue green. Throat white, breast band pale ashy brown; sides of body dark brown; line down center of breast and belly white, belly crossed by a chestnut band. General proportions as in Brown Jacamar.
Tropical zone. Locally distributed in Lara, Barinas, and Apure to Carabobo, Aragua and n Guárico. [Ne Colombia.]
Open woodland, second growth, gallery forest, deciduous forest, savanna edge, semi-arid vegetation, thickets, to 1100 m. Call: high, thin "weet, weet."

## YELLOW-BILLED JACAMAR
*Galbula albirostris*
BARRANQUERO PICO AMARILLO

Pl. 15
8″ (20 cm.). Crown and feathers at base of bill metallic purple; sides of head and neck, back and central tail feathers shining, metallic emerald green; outer tail feathers bronzy brown. Throat cinnamon buff, a triangular white patch on lower throat, rest of underparts cinnamon rufous (or chestnut, a). Bill long, straight, slender, 1.6″ (4 cm.). Mandible yellow, maxilla black, basal half yellow (or all blackish except for base of mandible, a). ♀: no white patch on throat.
Tropical zone. Bolívar along the lower Río Caura, the Río Cuyuni and the Gran Sabana (*albirostris*). S Amazonas s of the Río Ventuari (*chalcocephala*, a). [E Colombia, the Guianas to e Peru and ne Brazil.]
Rain forests, forest edge, 100–1300 m. Usually in pairs, in low trees and shrubs.

## GREEN-TAILED JACAMAR
*Galbula galbula*
TUCUSO MONTAÑERO COLIVERDE

Pl. 15
8.5″ (22 cm.). Top and sides of head metallic bluish green, back metallic coppery green, tail much rounded, metallic bluish green. Throat white, pectoral band metallic green, belly and under wing coverts chestnut. Bill black, long and slender, 1.8″ (4.6 cm.). ♀: throat cinnamon.
Tropical zone. Amazonas and Bolívar; recorded once in s Delta Amacuro (Curiapo). [E Colombia, the Guianas, n and central Brazil.]
Rain forests, near water, forest edge, to 450 m. Usually in pairs, perches low in trees and bushes. Call: a repeated, whistled "peep."

## RUFOUS-TAILED JACAMAR
*Galbula ruficauda*
TUCUSO BARRANQUERO

Pl. 15
10″ (25 cm.). Upperparts and breast band shining metallic golden green; central pair of tail feathers like back, considerably longer than the rest which are cinnamon rufous and much graduated. Throat white, belly and under wing coverts chestnut (or buff, a). Bill black, long and thin. ♀: throat cinnamon buff, belly and under wing coverts buff.
Tropical zone. Generally distributed n of the Ríos Meta and Orinoco (except in the L. Maracaibo region); s of the Orinoco in nw Bolívar e to the Río Caura and in s Delta Amacuro (*ruficauda*). Extreme nw Zulia at the base of the Goajira Pen. (*pallens*, a). The forested region s of L. Maracaibo in Zulia, Táchira and Mérida (*brevirostris*). [Mexico to nw Ecuador, Bolivia, Paraguay and se Brazil. Trinidad, Tobago.]
Gallery forest, second growth, deciduous woodland, llanos, xerophytic areas, savannas with scattered trees, sea level to 850 m. n of the Orinoco, to 300 m. s of it. Alone or in pairs, active, not shy. From an exposed perch sallies forth for insects on the wing, especially butterflies. Call: a high-pitched sharp note, also a clear soft trill.

## BRONZY JACAMAR
*Galbula leucogastra*
BARRANQUERO DORADO

Pl. 15
9″ (23 cm.). Shining metallic bronzy purple shot with green; top and sides of

head metallic dark greenish blue, *throat and belly white*. Tail much graduated, bronze green, outer feathers edged and tipped white. Bill black, slender, very slightly arched. ♀: throat and belly white.

Tropical zone. Amazonas s of the Río Ventuari (*leucogastra*). Recorded in error from Delta Amacuro. [Se Colombia, the Guianas to e Peru, n and central Amazonian Brazil.]

Rain forest, old second growth, 100–900 m. In pairs, at medium heights, often along rivers. Nests in holes made in arboreal termite nests.

## PARADISE JACAMAR

*Galbula dea*
BARRANQUERO COLILARGO

Pl. 15

12″ (30 cm.). *Central tail feathers narrow, up to 7″* (18 cm.) long. General plumage metallic black; crown dark brown (or pale ashy gray, a); chin blackish, throat and upper breast white. Wing coverts and inner remiges shining, metallic bronzy blue green. Bill black, straight, long, thin, 2″ (5 cm.).

Tropical zone. Amazonas (*brunneiceps*). Locally in e Bolívar from the upper Ríos Caura and Paragua to the Río Cuyuni and the Gran Sabana (*dea*, a). [E Colombia, e Ecuador, the Guianas to n Bolivia and n Amazonian Brazil.]

Rain forest, forest edge, small clearings,

savanna edge, along water, 100–1100 m. Quiet, not shy. In pairs or small groups, perches on low to high outer branches of trees, often for long periods. Call: a sharp, repeated "pip."

## GREAT JACAMAR

*Jacamerops aurea*
BARRANQUERO GRANDE

Pl. 15

12″ (30 cm.). *Bill thick, long, 1.7″* (4.3 cm.), somewhat curved; unlike the thin bill of other jacamars. Upperparts and sides of head glistening, brassy golden green (or much shot with red and purple, a). Central tail feathers shining coppery green, rest bluer. Upper throat like back, bordered below by white, rest of underparts chestnut rufous. ♀: no white on throat.

Tropical zone. Ne Bolívar on the Altiplanicie de Nuria and the Río Cuyuni (*aurea*). Locally in Amazonas and Bolívar along the lower Río Caura s to its headwaters and along the headwaters of the Río Paragua (*ridgwayi*, a). [Costa Rica to w Ecuador and the Guianas, thence to n Bolivia and Amazonian Brazil.]

Rain forest, second growth, forest edge, 100–500 m., near streams. Solitary or in pairs, perches quietly in undergrowth to upper branches. Very confiding. Call: high-pitched, clear whistles; nasal notes. Nests in arboreal termite nests.

# PUFFBIRDS: Bucconidae

## JUAN BOBOS

Puffbirds form a small family of interesting neotropical birds. Clothed soberly in black and white or shades of brown, they have large heads and thick necks. The sexes are alike. The bill is peculiar in having a cleft hook at the tip; in some species the bill is rather thick and hooked, in others rather slender and curved.

Puffbirds are rather sluggish birds given to sitting quietly on a perch from which they sail out after passing insects or fly down to pounce upon them on the ground. Puffbirds nest in holes in trees or in banks.

## WHITE-NECKED PUFFBIRD

*Notharchus macrorhynchus*
JUAN BOBO

Pl. 15

10″ (25 cm.). Above black, forehead very narrowly (or broadly, a) white, nuchal

collar white. Sides of head and underparts white with a broad black band across breast, sides black barred white. Wings and tail black.

Tropical zone. Throughout, excluding Bolívar, but including n Delta Amacuro (*hyperrhynchus*, a). Locally in s Delta

Amacuro, and in e Bolívar from the Sierra de Imataca s to the n Gran Sabana (*macrorhynchus*). [Mexico to w Ecuador, n Bolivia, Paraguay, s Brazil and ne Argentina.]
Rain forest, open woodland, to 1200 m. n of the Orinoco, 100–250 m. s of it. Forest borders, savannas with trees, *Cecropia* trees in second growth. Alone or in pairs, perches quietly for long periods in vines and low trees and in the treetops on exposed branches. Investigates swarms of army ants. Call: weak, low, twittering notes.

## BROWN-BANDED PUFFBIRD
*Notharchus ordii*
JUAN DE LA SELVA

Pl. 15
8″ (20 cm.). Not unlike White-necked Puffbird but smaller and differing principally by ochre brown lower breast, narrower breast band, sides of body barred ochre brown and white and all but central tail feathers with a white bar on inner web and narrow buffy tip.
Tropical zone. Amazonas s of the Río Ventuari. [Nw and central Amazonian Brazil.]
Rain forest, 150–300 m.

## PIED PUFFBIRD
*Notharchus tectus*
JUANCITO NEGRO

Pl. 15
6″ (15 cm.). A virtual miniature of the White-necked Puffbird, differing by its white-spotted crown and white eyebrow and scapulars, outer rectrices tipped white with a white median bar on inner web.
Tropical zone. Locally distributed in n, central and se Amazonas; Bolívar from the Río Caura e to the upper Río Cuyuni and Cerro Roraima (*tectus*). [Costa Rica to w Ecuador, the Guianas, Amazonian Brazil and e Peru.]
Rain forest, second growth, open terrain with trees, to 1000 m. Forest edge, along streams. Alone or in small groups forages in the foliage, often in the treetops. Confiding. Perches quietly, inconspicuously, in open branches. Nests in holes in arboreal termite nests. Call: a soft, high-pitched note.

## CHESTNUT-CAPPED PUFFBIRD
*Bucco macrodactylus*
BURRITO CABECIRROJO

Pl. 15
5.5″ (14 cm.). Crown chestnut, sides of head black, stripe below ear coverts white. Back brown speckled with white and buff, nuchal collar orange rufous. Throat pale cinnamon, upper breast white, with a broad black band across lower throat, rest of underparts cinnamon buff to grayish (or dusky olive brown, a), lightly barred with blackish.
Tropical zone. Central Amazonas along the Río Asisa and middle Río Ventuari (*macrodactylus*). Western Amazonas along the upper Río Ventuari; Bolívar on the lower Río Caura and the upper Río Paragua (*caurensis*, a). [E Colombia to e Peru, w Amazonian Brazil and n Bolivia.]
Rain forest, 100–550 m. Forest edge. Captures insects on the wing. Nests in holes in arboreal termite nests.

## SPOTTED PUFFBIRD
*Bucco tamatia*
BURRITO MOTEADO

Pl. 15
7″ (18 cm.). Above brown spotted buff, narrow nuchal collar white to pale cinnamon. Forehead, eyebrow, throat and upper breast orange rufous, throat bordered laterally by a wide black band, this bordered above by a white line which runs below ear coverts. Below white, belly thickly spotted with black. Bill black.
Tropical zone. N Amazonas s to the Duida region; s Delta Amacuro on the Río Amacuro; central Bolívar on the Río Paragua e to the Río Cuyuni and upper Río Caroní (*tamatia*). [Colombia, the Guianas to e Peru and w and central Brazil.]
Rain forest, forest edge, shrubbery, 100–1400 m. Very confiding. Usually alone, perches motionless on low, exposed branches. Feeds on insects and berries.

## COLLARED PUFFBIRD
*Bucco capensis*
MUSIÚ

Pl. 15
7.5″ (19 cm.). Rufous chestnut above, brighter on crown, with very narrow,

wavy black cross lines; a plain buff nuchal collar bordered behind by a black one, the black band continued around the breast to form a pectoral band. Sides of head and eyebrow uniform light orange cinnamon, throat white, rest of lower parts buff. Tail rufous with about 7 narrow black bars. Bill orange with black ridge.

Tropical zone. Extreme nw Bolívar near the Colombian border; n and w Amazonas along the Orinoco to the Yavita-Pimichín Trail (*dugandi*). Bolívar from the lower Río Caura e to the Gran Sabana (*capensis*). [E Colombia, the Guianas to ne Peru and the Amazon Valley, Brazil.]

Rain forest, 100–1000 m.

### RUSSET-THROATED PUFFBIRD

*Hypnelus ruficollis*
BOBITO

Pl. 15
9" (23 cm.). Above brown, crown sometimes lightly spotted with whitish, back with large, diffused whitish spots; frontal band, ear coverts and narrow nuchal collar white. Throat cinnamon rufous, bordered laterally by a broad blackish band, the rufous fading to white on upper breast where crossed by a black pectoral band (or upper throat buffy cinnamon, lower throat barred with black suggesting a band, a broad black band across lower throat, a; or lower parts cinnamon buff, with a broad black band across lower throat and a narrower one across breast, b). Belly buffy white (or white, c; or buff, d), lightly (or heavily, a, b, d) spotted with black. Bill thick, black.

Tropical zone. Ne coastal Zulia (Quisiro) e to Dabajuro in w Falcón (*striaticollis*, a). Nw Zulia in the Perijá region and e of L. Maracaibo (Mene Grande) and in n Táchira (*ruficollis*). Nw Zulia at the base of the Goajira Pen. to the Rio Aurare in ne Zulia, s of the range of *striaticollis;* Falcón on the Paraguaná Pen. (*decolor*, c). Zulia s of L. Maracaibo, w Mérida, w Trujillo (*coloratus*, d). Widespread n of the Meta and Orinoco from e Falcón and Lara e to Sucre, Delta Amacuro and nw Amazonas and Monagas; n Bolívar (*bicinctus*, b). Margarita I. (*stoicus*. b). [Ne Colombia.]

Found in almost any kind of habitat including xerophytic areas but not inside rain forest to 700 m. Usually alone, perches quietly in the twigs of isolated trees. A local name, *Aguanta Piedras*, refers to its confiding nature; presumably it will not flush even if stones are hurled at it repeatedly. Nests in arboreal termite nests; may usurp the oven-shaped nests of *Furnarius*.

### WHITE-CHESTED PUFFBIRD

*Malacoptila fusca*
BOLIO PECHIBLANCO

Pl. 15
7.5" (19 cm.). Upperparts, throat, sides of head and neck, breast and wing coverts blackish brown conspicuously streaked with buff; band across breast, lores and moustacial streak white; belly dirty buffy white; wings and tail dark brown. Bill rather slender, somewhat curved, bright orange, ridge and tip black.

Tropical zone. W Amazonas s of the Río Ventuari (*venezuelae*). [E Colombia, e Ecuador, the Guianas to e Peru and w Amazonian Brazil.]

Rain forest, plantations, 100–200 m. From near the ground to mid-heights.

### MOUSTACHED PUFFBIRD

*Malacoptila mystacalis*
BOLIO DE BIGOTE

Pl. 15
9" (23 cm.). Upperparts, wings and tail earthy brown with small white spots on back and wing coverts, upper tail coverts edged buffy white. Throat and breast orange rufous; moustacial streak white; belly buffy white, mixed with brown. Upper mandible black, lower mandible pale blue gray, tipped black.

Upper tropical and subtropical zones. Widely distributed in the Sierra de Perijá, Zulia, and locally in Táchira, w Barinas, Yaracuy and Carabobo to Miranda. [N, ne and w Colombia to e Peru and w Brazil.]

Rain and cloud forests, open woodland, deciduous forests, forest edge, 450–2000 m. Alone, quiet, confiding, sits motionless on exposed branches in the lower heights. Nests in holes in earth banks.

## RUSTY-BREASTED NUNLET

*Nonnula rubecula*
JUAN FEO

Pl. 15
6.5″ (16.5 cm.). Above olive brown, lores and spot at base of mandible pale cinnamon, eye ring white. Throat and breast cinnamon, sides of body reddish brown, belly white. Bill rather fine, somewhat curved, proportionately long, mostly leaden blue.
Tropical zone. Locally in Amazonas s to Caño Casiquiare (*duidae*). S Amazonas s of Caño Casiquiare (*interfluvialis*). [Surinam. Ne Peru. Amazonian and se Brazil. Paraguay, ne Argentina.]
Rain forest, 100–300 m.

## BLACK NUNBIRD

*Monasa atra*
PICO DE LACRE

10.5″ (27 cm.). Grayish black above, grayer on rump, paler below, except on throat. *Inner wing coverts white,* outer ones dark gray edged white. Bill red, slender, curved.
Tropical zone. Generally distributed in Amazonas and Bolívar; in Delta Amacuro (Piacoa). [E Colombia to n Bolivia; Amazonian and e Brazil.]
Rain forest, scrub, gallery forest, near rivers, to 900 m. In pairs or in groups, perches quietly from low to upper heights. Feeds on insects, lizards. Call: surprisingly loud, often uttered by several in company. Nests in holes in level ground.

## WHITE-FRONTED NUNBIRD

*Monasa morphoeus*
MONJA

Pl. 25
12″ (30 cm.). Gray; *forehead, lores and chin white.* Wings and tail black. Bill red, slender, curved.
Tropical zone. Sw Amazonas (*peruana*). [Honduras to n and e Colombia, Bolivia, nw and e Brazil.]
Habits and habitat as in the Black Nunbird, 100–200 m. Call: noisy whistle, uttered by 10 or 12 birds simultaneously.

## SWALLOW-WING

*Chelidoptera tenebrosa*
MIRASOL

Pl. 15
6″ (15 cm.). Quite different from other puffbirds in looks and habits. Wings long, swallowlike. Tail short, square. Mostly glossy blue black; under wing coverts, rump, upper and under tail coverts white. Upper belly gray, lower belly cinnamon chestnut surrounded by a diffused white area. Bill black, slender, curved.
Tropical zone. Zulia s of L. Maracaibo, adjacent Mérida; sw Trujillo (*pallida*). S Táchira, Barinas, Portuguesa and Carabobo to Sucre and Delta Amacuro, and in Amazonas and Bolívar (*tenebrosa*). [The Guianas, e Colombia to n Bolivia and most of Brazil.]
Woodland edge, clearings, gallery and deciduous forest, scrub, savanna with trees, second growth, sea level to 400 m. n of the Orinoco, to 1000 m. s of it. More active than other species. Goes about in small flocks, or alone or in pairs, perches high on isolated trees and protruding branches. Nests in holes dug in sandy, fairly level ground.

# BARBETS: Capitonidae

CAPITANES

Barbets are widespread and numerous in Africa and se Asia, but are poorly represented in the New World, where only 12 species are found, confined for the most part to nw South America. There are only 2 species in Venezuela.
Their song is usually the monotonous repetition of a single note. They subsist mainly on fruit, inhabit forested country and nest in holes in trees.

**BLACK-SPOTTED BARBET**

*Capito niger*
CAPITÁN TURERO

Pl. 16

7″ (18 cm.). Forecrown and throat crimson (or orange, a; or with forecrown orange, throat crimson, b), shading to yellow on hindcrown and nape, where streaked with dusky. Eyebrow straw yellow. Sides of head, back, scapulars and wing coverts black, scapulars edged straw yellow; greater wing coverts with a subterminal straw yellow spot on outer webs forming a bar; upper tail coverts edged laterally with straw yellow; remiges edged olive, inner remiges edged broadly with whitish. Breast and belly pale yellow (tinged orange in center, a). Sides of body spotted with black (or unspotted, a); flanks olive. ♀: similar to ♂ but sides of head black streaked with pale yellow; breast and sides heavily spotted with black (or unspotted, a).

Tropical zone. Amazonas and Bolívar, except for areas occupied by the next 2 (*aurantiicinctus,* a). Extreme sw Amazonas along the Río Negro (*transilens,* b). Bolívar on the upper Río Cuyuni near the Guyana border (*niger*). [The Guianas, e Colombia to n Bolivia and w and central Amazonian Brazil.]

Rain forests, second growth, swampy woods, plantations, forest edge, 100–1300 m. Finchlike, not shy. Forages actively in groups, from treetops to the lower levels. Visits mango groves, *Cecropia* trees. Joins forest flocks. Call: a monotonous "hoot-oot," repeated for long periods; twitches tail as it calls.

**RED-HEADED BARBET**

*Eubucco bourcierii*
CAPITÁN CABECIRROJO

Pl. 16

6″ (15 cm.). Head, throat and breast scarlet, lores and chin black; a narrow, bright pale blue nuchal band; back and inner remiges grass green, primaries black. Sides of breast bright yellow, belly yellow, streaked olive. Bill greenish yellow with yellow tip. ♀: forehead and chin black, a blue bar across forecrown, hindcrown and nape dull gold; short eyebrow blue; ear coverts pale blue; patch behind ear coverts yellow. Throat and breast pale greenish yellow, pectoral band golden yellow, belly whitish yellow streaked olive. Back, wings and tail as in ♂

Upper tropical zone. Locally distributed in extreme sw Táchira, ne Barinas and e Lara (*bourcierii*). [Costa Rica to w Ecuador and ne Peru.]

Rain and cloud forest transition area, second growth, 1000–1300 m. Forest edge. Forages actively from undergrowth to upper levels of trees. Perches quietly, inconspicuously, in the foliage. Joins forest flocks of small birds.

Note: Called *Capito bourcierii* in Lista Av. Venez.

# TOUCANS, ARACARIS: Ramphastidae

## PICOS DE FRASCO, PIAPOCOS, DIOSTEDÉS, TUCANES, TILINGOS

No birds are more characteristic of the American tropics than the toucans—about 37 species ranging from s Mexico to Argentina. They are instantly recognizable by their enormous bills which, in spite of their size, are very light, the thin outer shell being supported internally by a spongy web of bony struts and tissue. In spite of its size, the bill in no way seems to interfere with the bird's actions.

Five groups, comprising 21 species, inhabit Venezuela. These are the green toucanets and the varicolored mountain-toucans, both inhabitants of montane regions; the typical toucans, black with white or yellow throats, and the varicolored aracaris, both inhabitants of tropical forests; and finally *Selenidera,* the only genus in which the sexes differ, inhabitants of lowland forests.

Toucans are mainly frugivorous, but occasionally eat young birds, eggs and other animal life. They nest in holes in trees, and the aracaris are known to sleep in groups in hollow trees. The caudal vertebrae of toucans are so arranged that when the bird is sleeping the tail can be laid flat over the back so as to cover the bill. Toucans are gregarious, and the cries of certain species have been likened to the yelping of a pack of hounds.

## GROOVE-BILLED TOUCANET

*Aulacorhynchus sulcatus*
PICO DE FRASCO ESMERALDA

13″ (33 cm.). Mainly grass green, paler and brighter below. Tail green, bluish at tip. Ocular region and feathers at base of mandible blue, throat grayish white. Bill grooved, 3″ (7.6 cm.). Upper mandible and tip of lower dull red, upper mandible basally blackish, lower with a white patch at base (or base of bill bright red, a).
Subtropical, casually in the tropical zone. From the Sierra de San Luis, Falcón, and the Sierra de Aroa, Yaracuy, to Carabobo and interior Miranda (*sulcatus*). The e Cordilleras from ne Anzoátegui, n Monagas to the e Paria Pen., Sucre (*erythrognathus*, a).
Rain and cloud forest, second growth, woodland edge, clearings, gardens with isolated trees, to 2000 m. Shy. In pairs or small groups, usually silent, sits quietly, inconspicuously, in the foliage of the undergrowth or upper branches. Gathers in small bands and with short heavy flight the birds follow each other in loose single file from tree to tree to forage. Calls: various grunts, croaks, ducklike quacks, barks.
Note: All bill measurements are those of males. Bills of females are considerably smaller.

## YELLOW-BILLED TOUCANET

*Aulacorhynchus calorhynchus*
PICO DE FRASCO ANDINO

Pl. 16
14″ (35 cm.). Grass green, paler and brighter below, patch below eye blue, sides of neck yellowish green, throat bluish gray. Tail bluish green, tipped blue. Bill 3.7″ (9.4 cm.), maxilla, tip and base of mandible olive yellow, mandible and base of maxilla black.
Lower subtropical zone. The Sierra de Perijá, Zulia; Lara, Mérida, n Barinas, Táchira and Cerro Platillón, n Guárico. [The Sta. Marta Mts., Colombia.]
Cloud forests, forest edge, 1200–1900 m.

General behavior and voice similar to the Groove-billed Toucanet.
Note: Due to the fact that populations intermediate between *A. calorhynchus* and *A. sulcatus* have been found on El Cerrón and Cerro El Cogollal, w Lara, and nw Cerro Platillón, se Carabobo, the two should be considered conspecific (cf. P. Schwartz, Bol. Soc. Venez. Cien. Nat., 1972, 29:459–76).

## CHESTNUT-TIPPED TOUCANET

*Aulacorhynchus derbianus*
PICO DE FRASCO GUAYANÉS

15″ (38 cm.). Grass green, paler below. Throat pale gray, orbital region blue, tips of central tail feathers chestnut. Bill 3″ (7.6 cm.), blackish, culmen red, base of lower mandible white.
Upper tropical and subtropical zones. Generally distributed in the mountains of Amazonas; nw Bolívar on Cerros El Negro, upper Río Cuchivero and Tabaro on the upper Río Nichare (*duidae*). Bolívar on the Sierra de Lema, Cerro Guaiquinima and the cerros of the Gran Sabana (*whitelianus*). [Guyana, adjacent Brazil, se Colombia to nw Bolivia.]
Forests on the slopes of the tepuis, rarely on the summits, 800–2400 m. General behavior and voice similar to Groove-billed Toucanet.

## EMERALD TOUCANET

*Aulacorhynchus prasinus*
PICO DE FRASCO GARGANTIBLANCO

Pl. 16
14″ (35 cm.). Crown and mantle olive green, ocular region blue. Throat whitish, underparts light, bright grass green, flanks yellowish green, under tail coverts chestnut. Tail green, bluish toward tip, all feathers broadly tipped chestnut. Bill 3″ (7.6 cm.), black, culmen olive yellow, base of lower mandible dark red, a sharp, narrow white line outlining base of bill.
Subtropical zone. The nw mountains in Zulia, Táchira, Mérida, Trujillo and s Lara (*albivitta*). [Mexico to w Colombia and se Peru.]

Cloud and temperate forests, forest edge, open terrain with scattered trees, 1800–3000 m. General behavior similar to Groove-billed Toucanet. Call: low, repeated "crik, crik, crik."

## CRIMSON-RUMPED TOUCANET
*Aulacorhynchus haematopygus*
Pico de Frasco Lomirrojo

Pl. 16
19″ (48 cm.). Crown dull green, ear coverts pale green in contrast, spot above and below eye and patch at base of mandible blue. Upper back olive green, lower back and upper tail coverts bright grass green, *rump crimson*. Below bright green with a broad blue band across breast. Tail bluish green, 4 outer feathers broadly tipped chestnut. Bill 4″ (10 cm.), dark crimson, part of ridge and central portion of lower mandible black, conspicuous line outlining base of bill white.
Upper tropical and subtropical zones. The Sierra de Perijá, Zulia (*haematopygus*). [The Andes of Colombia and w Ecuador.]
Cloud forests, forest edge, 1200–2200 m. General behavior and voice similar to Groove-billed Toucanet.

## COLLARED ARACARI
*Pteroglossus torquatus*
Tilingo Acollarado

Pl. 16
16″ (41 cm.). Head and neck black, nuchal collar dark chestnut; back, wings and central tail feathers olive, rump and upper tail coverts scarlet. Breast and belly yellow stained with red, a black patch in center of breast and a band across the belly black in the middle, red at sides; thighs chestnut. Bill 4.5″ (11.5 cm.). Maxilla ivory white, ridge and tip black, mandible black narrowly outlined with a white line.
Tropical zone. Zulia and Táchira through Mérida and Yaracuy to Carabobo and Aragua (*nuchalis*). [Mexico to n Colombia.]
Rain forest, second growth, forest edge, open forest, clearings, to 1000 m. Alone or in small groups, noisy, lively, inquisitive. Like *Aulacorhynchus,* the bands actively straggle in single file through the foliage in the upper and middle heights making long leaps from branch to branch with wings closed. Several usually roost together in holes in trees. Call: a high-pitched, 2-syllable whistle; harsh cries.

## BLACK-NECKED ARACARI
*Pteroglossus aracari*
Tilingo Cuellinegro

Pl. 16
18″ (46 cm.). Head and neck black, ear coverts very dark chestnut. Back dark slaty gray, rump scarlet. Breast and belly yellow, band across abdomen scarlet, thighs olive. Bill 4.5″ (11.5 cm.), maxilla ivory white, ridge black, mandible black, line outlining base of bill black.
Tropical zone. From Anzoátegui e to Sucre, Monagas and Delta Amacuro; Bolívar from the Río Paragua to s Delta Amacuro and the Gran Sabana (*roraimae*). [The Guianas, e Brazil to Sta. Catarina.]
Rain forest, open woodland, second growth, near rivers, forest edge, sea level to 550 m. Stands of papaya trees. General behavior similar to Collared Aracari. Call: a soft, high-pitched, "tilín," one of its local names.

## MANY-BANDED ARACARI
*Pteroglossus pluricinctus*
Tilingo Multibandeado

Pl. 16
18″ (46 cm.). Differs from the Black-necked Aracari mainly by having *2 bands on belly* instead of one, the one across the breast black, across the belly crimson, mixed black. Bill 4.5″ (11.5 cm.), colored as in the Black-necked Aracari.·
Tropical zone. N of the Orinoco in s Táchira and s Barinas; Amazonas s to the Duida region; Bolívar from the Río Paragua to Cerro Paurai-tepui. [Adj. Brazil. Colombia to ne Peru.]
Rain forest, 200–300 m. n of the Orinoco, 100–900 m. s of it. General behavior similar to Collared Aracari.

PLATES

# PREFACE TO THE PLATE NOTES

The plates and text figures illustrate about 85% of the total Venezuelan list and nearly 90% of the *resident* birds. Facing-page identification notes opposite the plates discuss *all* the species, including those not shown. Because of the large number of species and the often complex racial variation, it has been necessary to compress this information rigorously. In a few instances, plate notes continue onto following pages (e.g. Hummingbirds, Plate 12; Manakins, Plate 24; Tyrant Flycatchers, Plates 28-30; and smaller Finches, Plate 40).

The illustrations and notes should thus be used in *conjunction*, utilizing a fair amount of discernment. The observer should refer to the main text frequently as the intricacies can be more confusing than the pictures imply. Furthermore, many tropical species can be differentiated on the basis of range, altitude, and habitat. All qualifying remarks are conditional, pertaining only to Venezuela.

## FORMAT AND SYMBOLS

For brevity, illustrated species in *polytypic genera* are listed in the facing-page notes under a heading containing the English group name in boldface, followed by the Latin generic name (e.g., **Tinamous** *Tinamus*). Beneath, each relevant species is abbreviated to the *specific* English and technical names (hence **Gray** *T. tao*).

All *illustrated* species are preceded by a *number* corresponding to the plate. Names of species not depicted are given in capital letters without a number; these usually immediately follow their most similar congener. However, for geographical reasons, they may be adjacent to the bird with which they would be most likely confused within their *range or habitat*, although another allopatric species may be closer in actual appearance.

*Letters* modifying numbers (1a., 2b., etc.) are used to indicate plumage variations other than sexual. These may refer to an *age* difference, a *subspecific* variation or an alternate color *phase*, and are explained in the notes. If *only* the young or one phase is shown the plumage is identified as such without the use of a letter. Remember that a number always denotes a *full* species. If the gender symbol (♂,♀) is lacking, sexes are identical or nearly so in plumage.

An Appendix designates the appropriate *subspecies* or race that has been *illustrated*. Racial differences, if significant to identification, are discussed in the plate notes as fully as possible.

The letters N or S (sometimes modified) after the species' name means that it occurs only *North* or *South* of the *Orinoco River*, an important faunal barrier. Restricted ranges are mentioned if space permits. Consult map for geographical and political terms (Caution: Amazonas is a specific territory S of the Orinoco).

A horizontal *dividing line* on the plate indicates *two different size scales*; otherwise all birds on the same plate are drawn to scale.

## DEFINITIONS

*Juvenal*: first true plumage succeeding natal down.

*Immature*: here indicates a subadult plumage older than Juvenal.

*No. migrant* or *So. migrant*: Non-resident wintering *visitor* from the North (No. Amer., W. Indies) or from the South (southern So. Amer.); latter birds, of course, occur in Venezuela during the summer months.

*overlap*: used here in a *distributional* sense (overlap in range or altitude).

A clarification of avian topographical terms used in plate notes, but not defined or at slight variance with those of chart on page xxi, will be useful. Some are obvious, but note the following glossary:

soft parts: non-feathered portions collectively (bill, legs, etc.)

maxilla: upper mandible of bill

mandible: lower mandible of bill

culmen: dorsal ridge of maxilla

cere: fleshy area at base of maxilla

orbital or ocular: of the eye area

eyebrow: superciliary

supraloral: above lores (superciliary in front of eye)

spectacles: eyering plus supraloral

malar: of the moustachial or lower jaw area

submalar: immediately beneath malar area

coronal: of the crown

nuchal: of the nape

gorget/frontlet: iridescent feathers of throat/forehead in hummingbirds

mantle: back, scapulars and upper wing-coverts

pectoral: of the breast

wing-lining: under wing-coverts

flight-feathers: primaries plus secondaries (remiges)

crissum: under tail-coverts

PLATE I RAPTORES

**1. Osprey** *Pandion haliaetus* p.47
No. migrant; partial to large bodies of water. Not much like any resident hawk; *large* with *white underparts and head*, dark *mask*. Usually flies with deep heavy flaps of *long*, rather *angular* wings (note *black "wrist" marks*).

**2. Black Vulture** p.33
*Coragyps atratus*
Wings broad; tail *short*. Black with *slaty head*; *whitish patches* at base of primaries (quills white from above). Flight more labored, soaring frequently alternated with *rapid flapping*.

**3. King Vulture** p.33
*Sarcoramphus papa*
Wings *very* broad; tail *short. Body white*; flight-feathers and tail *entirely* black; *garishly colored and wattled* head and neck often *project* in flight. Soaring steady and sustained, often at great height. Juvenal *uniformly blackish* (*lacks* primary-patches of 2); white underparts appear first in slow transition to adult plumage.

**Vultures** *Cathartes*
Tail *noticeably longer* than others; colorful head always appears neckless (Plate 4). Usually *tilts* in flight with wings held above horizontal.

**4. Turkey** *C. aura* Upper Wing p.34
*Two-toned under*wing like 5 but primary *quills darker* (light brownish) as seen from above. Brownish-black; *head mainly red* (dusky in Juvenal). Widespread.

**5. Lesser Yellow-headed** p.34
*C. burrovianus* 5a. Upper Wing
From below, *paler* flight-feathers *contrast* with *dark* wing-linings; differs from 4 by *white primary quills* (from *above*). Plumage as 4 but adult head mainly *yellow-and-orange*. Unlike 6, prefers savanna and marshland areas.

**6. Greater Yellow-headed** p.34
*C. melambrotus* S 6a. Upper Wing
Larger than 5 with more "sail area"; flight steadier, less buoyant. Primary *quills also* white from above but *underwing differs*: flight-feathers *less* contrasting, especially around *base of inner primaries* (broad *dusky suffusion*). Quite black; adult head *mainly yellow*. Presumably confined to *forest* regions.

NOTE: Caracaras are medium-to-large *scavengers* (bill and feet *less* aquiline than hawks). Rather *long* wings and tail; *bare facial skin*. Head projects more in flight which is usually rather direct with deep wingbeats; seldom soar, but in open country may glide on wind.

**7. Yellow-headed Caracara** p.50
*Milvago chimachima*
*Smaller* than 8 but with *similar flight pattern*: striking *light wing-patches and basal tail*. Head and below *buffy*.

**8. Crested Caracara** p.50
*Polyborus plancus* 8a. Juvenal
*Long-legged* (often terrestrial) with naked *red* face and *very stout* bill. Black *"crest,"* light breast and *black belly*; Juvenal similar but black areas paler and *browner*; below well *streaked*.

**Caracaras** *Daptrius*
Mainly *glossy-black forest* caracaras with *orange or red* facial skin and legs. Neither resembles any hawk (cf. Pl. III). Juvenals essentially *similar* to adults.

**9. Black** *D. ater* p.49
*White band* across *base of tail*. Extensive bare face *bright vermilion*, much *more conspicuous* than 10; bill dark. Juvenal has yellower face and barring on white tail-band.

**10. Red-throated** *D. americanus* p.50
*Abdomen and crissum white* but tail *all-black*. Facial skin differs in aspect from 9: more *reduced* around eye, *duller* and redder on throat; cere grayish, bill yellowish. In conjunction with bushier crown, rounder wings, more *social* habits and *very raucous voice*, notably dissimilar.

NOTE: The huge Andean Condor *Vultur gryphus* has apparently been extirpated in Venezuelan Andes.

I

PLATE II  RAPTORES

**Hawks**  *Buteo*
In general, rather compactly built with *broad* wings and *moderate-length* tail (see also large *B. albicaudatus*). Typically engage in *prolonged soaring* at some height, particularly longer-winged species which are far more often seen aloft. See text for very rare No. migrant Swainson's Hawk.

**1. Zone-tailed**  *B. albonotatus*  p.40
Juvenal  (Adult-Plate III)
Rangy, *black Buteo* with *long wings* of rather parallel width; *moderately long* tail. Bears resemblance to *Cathartes* in *tilting* flight and *two-toned wings*. Juvenal *spotted white* below; flight-feathers *paler* than adult (patterned like 2a but note *dissimilar contour*).

**2. Short-tailed**  *B. brachyurus*  p.41
2a. Dark Phase
Ample-winged and *short*-tailed. Dark phase has *black body; wing-linings contrast with pale flight-feathers*; predominate Light phase has dark cheeks, *largely white* underwings. In both, note white at base of bill; *narrowly barred tail* (quite *pale* from below). Juvenals *approach respective* adults but Light phase *pale-streaked* about *head and neck*; Dark phase *mottled with white below* (much like 1).

**3. White-throated**  *B. albigula* N  p.41
*Upper altitude* representative of 2 (probably no overlap); tail *somewhat longer*, very *dimly* barred. All plumages quite *streaked below*, especially on *flanks*; thighs *barred* (with rusty in adult). Juvenal most like 6a but flank markings *heavier*.

**4. White-rumped**  *B. leucorrhous* N  p.41
Small, *dark, short*-winged *Buteo* of subtropics. Note *white rump and crissum* plus tail-pattern; *light wing-linings* contrast with *black flight-feathers* and body in adult (*reverse* of 2a). Juvenal differs in being streaked on head, *heavily mottled below with fulvous*; underwing decidedly *barred*; *thighs chestnut* like adult.

**5. Gray**  *B. nitidus*  p.42
Adult (Pl. 5) *finely* barred *silvery-gray* below; tail *broadly banded black-and-white*. Juvenal (Pl. 4) is *buffier* with *paler head*, coarser streaking than allies; above shows *striking light wing-patches* and tail-bars (more contrasty than 6a or 7a). Flight shape nearest 7. Cf. also Plate IV.

**6. Broad-winged**  *B. platypterus*  p.40
6a. Juvenal
No. migrant. Chunky and rather *short*-tailed. *Rusty-barred* underparts; *largely white* flight-feathers; tail shows *two (narrow and wide) white bands* (Pl. 5). Juvenal has *moderately streaked*, whitish underparts; *dimly* barred tail.

**7. Roadside**  *B. magnirostris*  p.41
7a. Juvenal
Small, lightly built *Buteo*; wings a bit shorter, tail longer than 6. *Quite grayish above* and *on breast*; *upper flight-feathers* basally *rich rufous* (only tinged below); tail *evenly* banded black-and-grayish (Pl. 5). Juvenal generally differs from other brownish young by combination of streaked breast with coarsely *barred belly*.

**8. Hook-billed Kite**  p.36
*Chondrohierax uncinatus*
Basic description on Plate III. Barred phases may be confused with various *Buteos*, but note lanky contour, *heavy hooked bill* and *boldly barred* flight-feathers. Also see Plate 4.

**9. Double-toothed Kite**  p.36
*Harpagus bidentatus*  9a. Juvenal
*Smallish*, rather *short*-winged kite; often likened to *Accipiter* although confiding behavior more nearly recalls a little *Buteo*. Usual flap-and-glide flight but often *soars briefly* in tight circles. Besides *coloration* (Pl. 5), note *boldly barred* primaries, *contrasting light wing-linings*, fluffy white *crissum*; pale tail-bands quite *narrow*. Juvenal sooty above, whitish below with *streaked breast* (rarely not at all); always has adult's characteristic *median throat-stripe*.

**10. Sharp-shinned Hawk**  p.39
*Accipiter striatus*
Included to show representative flight shape of genus: *short*-winged and *long*-tailed (both usually well-barred); may soar occasionally in manner of 9 but tends to keep to cover. See species accounts on Plate 5; note that *only streaked Accipiter* is young *striatus*.

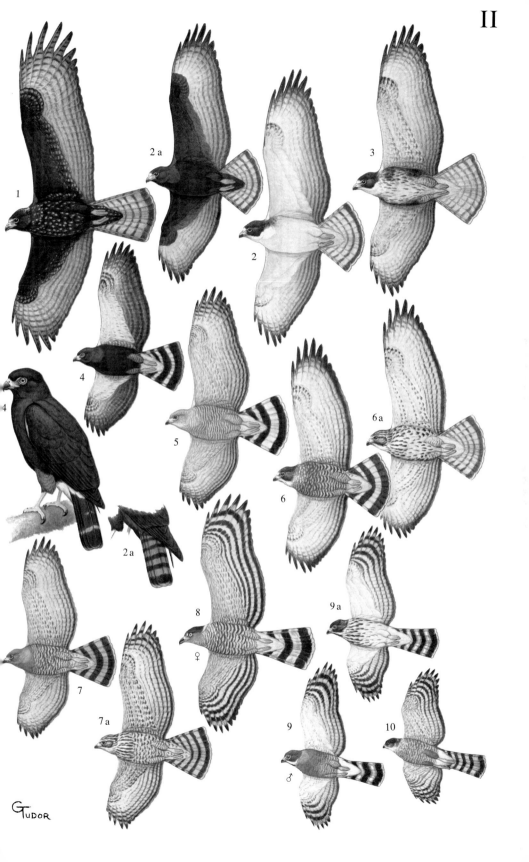

GTUDOR

PLATE III   RAPTORES

NOTE: In general, an array of *medium-sized dark* hawks of rather *long-tailed* aspect. Most figured on color Plate 4.

### 1. Crane Hawk  p.47
*Geranospiza caerulescens*
Active, *lanky, slate-gray* hawk; rounded wings, rather *long* tail. May soar occasionally but usual flight flap-and-glide. Note *weak* bill, *long orange legs* and distinctive *white band across base of primaries* (obscure from above). Adult has *two white* tail-bands. Juvenal differs: streaked *on face* and barred on lower underparts with *white*; white tail-bands tend to be *wider*, but *underwing pattern similar to adult*.

### 2. Hook-billed Kite  p.36
*Chondrohierax uncinatus*  2a. Black Phase
Loosely built with narrow-based wings and longish tail (usually held closed). Often soars, at times prolonged (head *projects* somewhat). Great *plumage variation* complicates analysis but *all* are told by *heavy hooked bill, facial* markings and *short* legs. Adult below either *coarsely barred (rusty or gray)* or *solid gray, slaty or black*. Flight-feathers typically *boldly barred*; tail normally shows *two broad pale* bands. Rarer Black phase has underwing nearly *uniform*; tail with only *one white* band in adult (intermediate wing-barring in adult, *several* tail-bands in younger stage). Normal phase Juvenal mainly *white below*, later becoming *barred* (cf. Pl. V).

### 3. Zone-tailed Hawk  p.40
*Buteo albonotatus*
Basic description on Plate II. Adult normally shows *one narrow* and *one wide white* tail-band from below (*gray* from above). Compare with various stages of 2a and differently-shaped *Buteogallus* (Pl. IV) and *Spizaetus* (Pl. VI).

### 4. Slate-colored Hawk  p.43
*Leucopternis schistacea*
Juvenal   S (Amazonas)
Rather *sturdy*, sluggish, *slate-gray* hawk with *broad rounded* wings; *moderate* length tail. Often soars. Might be confused with *blacker Buteogallus* but cere and long legs *vermilion*. Adult underwing essentially *all slaty*; black tail with *one median white* band (like 2a). Juvenal differs by *under*wing and *lower* underparts *barred* with white; often a *second narrow* band on tail.

### 5. Slender-billed Kite  p.37
*Helicolestes hamatus*   Juvenal
*Chunky, slate-gray* kite associated with *swampy woodland*; often soars for brief periods. Easily told by *slender hooked bill*, reddish cere and legs, and *short square* tail. Adult underwing and tail *without any* pattern; Juvenal has *several narrow* tail-bars.

### 6. Snail or Everglade Kite  p.37
*Rostrhamus sociabilis*   6a. Immature
Social kite given to prolonged quartering, some soaring over *open marshes*. Bill and soft parts as 5. Narrow-based wings somewhat longer than allies; medium-length *squared-off tail* shows *conspicuous white at base* (especially below). ♂ *blackish-slate; dusky-brown* ♀ heavily *mottled* below. Youngest show much *white about face* and appear *streaked below*.

### 7. Gray-headed Kite  p.36
*Leptodon cayanensis*
Juvenal Dark Phase
Basic description on Plate V. Juvenal Dark phase *blackish above* with *boldly* barred *primaries*, banded tail. Note dark head and *very heavy black streaking on throat and chest*. Cf. smaller *Harpagus* and larger *Spizaetus*.

### 8. Bay-winged or Harris' Hawk  p.42
*Parabuteo unicinctus*   Immature
Dark *sooty*, buteonine hawk; *rather long* tail prominently *based and tipped white* (white *rump* above). Sometimes soars. Adult has *chestnut shoulders, thighs* and wing-linings (basal under-primaries white). Young not dissimilar but chestnut *veiled*; face and below *streaked or blotched* with white; tail tends to *barring*. Mainly N. Cf. Pl. IV.

### 9. Long-winged Harrier  p.46
*Circus buffoni*   9a. Dark Phase Juvenal
Typical harrier: *lanky* with *long wings*; *long multibanded* tail; *rump white* (reduced in dark birds). Normally quarters wetlands in *low*, buoyant flight. Variable, but *all* show distinct *gray areas above* on barred *flight-feathers*. Light phase slaty (♂) or sooty (♀) above; *dark chest contrasts with light* underparts. Dark phase has *blackish body*. Juvenals *approach respective* adults but are *heavily streaked below* with dark *or* light *according to phase*. See text for very rare migrant Northern Harrier (Juvenal *rufescent* below).

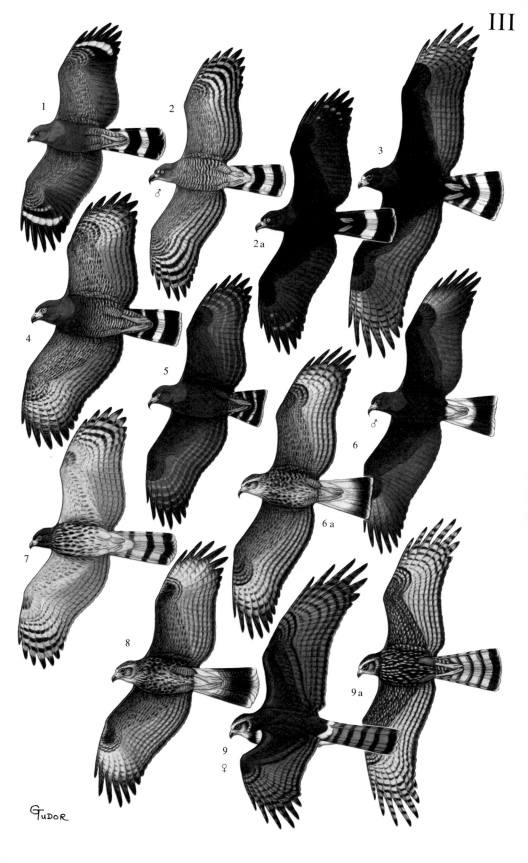

III

1

2

2a

3

4

5

6

6a

7

8

9

9a

GTUDOR

# PLATE IV  RAPTORES

NOTE: In general, a group of *large*, *long*-legged, *heavily built* hawks; *broad*-winged and usually *rather short-tailed*. Sluggish when perched, they often engage in certain amount of soaring; longer-winged species are particularly prone to extended flight aloft.

## 1. Black-chested Buzzard-Eagle  p.39
*Geranoaetus melanoleucus*  N  Juvenal
Basic description on Plate VII. More *ample-tailed* Juvenal rather different from adult but *high* altitudes, *habitat* and *very large* size should identify it (note *longer primaries* than 7). Older stages have *blacker chest*, more barred abdomen and *shorter*, darker tail; gradually take on adult plumage. Bare legs are *heavy but rather short.*

## 2. White-tailed Hawk  p.39
*Buteo albicaudatus*  2a. Juvenal
Robust *Buteo* of open, often semi-arid country. *Long attenuated primaries* and *shortish* tail. Sometimes *hovers*. Light phase *slaty-gray* above (*upper shoulder rufous*); mainly *white below*, dark sides of head often extend *onto throat*. Light wing-linings contrast with *gray flight-feathers*; *tail strikingly white* with *subterminal black band*. Dark phase occurs in *colonus* race: *entirely* slate-gray with *diagnostic tail*. *Pale-tailed* Juvenal *more or less heavily* blotched below, some (dark phase ?) even *solid black*; latter from Plate II allies by *contour* and *gray* underwing.

## 3. Savanna Hawk  p.43
*Heterospizias meridionalis*  Immature
Very common in favored habitat. Wings *long and broad*; tail *rather short*. Distinctive adult *largely rufescent* with *median white* tail-band (Plate 4). Head and underparts of Young streaked and blotched with *buff-and-sepia* but recognizable by *same expanse of rufous* on shoulders and *upper flight-feathers* (tinged cinnamon below); tail *barred*.

## 4. Black-collared Hawk  p.43
*Busarellus nigricollis*  Juvenal
*Pale-headed*, *rufescent* hawk; *broad* wings and *noticeably short* tail. Never very far from *water* (feeds on fish). Adult unique (Plate 4). Juvenal more *streaked and blotched* but always with *enough rufous color and black collar* for recognition. In any plumage, note contrasting *blackish* primaries.

## Hawks  *Buteogallus*
*Sturdy* hawks with *very broad*, *rounded* wings; *short to moderate* tail. Often, but not necessarily found near water. Two most widespread species are *black* with *white tail-band*, *long yellow legs*. Juvenals *very different* from adults.

## 5. Common Black  *B. anthracinus*  N  p.44
Adult has *one median white* tail-band and *extensive yellow* facial skin. Juvenal *very similar* to 6 in pattern but has *fewer tail-bars* and *shorter legs*; tends to *heavier* black blotching on *sides of chest and flanks* than 6 of equivalent age. RUFOUS CRAB *B. aequinoctialis* (Delta): Confined to *coastal region*; tends to replace close ally 5 *east* of Delta (some overlap). Distinctive adult (Plate 4) most likely confused with Savanna Hawk. Juvenal not unlike allies but more *nondescript*; mainly *lacks* large rufous wing-patches of 3, *heavy* black blotching below of 5.

## 6. Great Black  *B. urubitinga*  p.44
6a. Juvenal
Substantially *larger* than 5. Somewhat *longer tail* shows different pattern: *entire basal half white*. Legs *decidedly longer*; *less* yellow on face (basal bill blacker, lores duller *and grayer*). Juvenal *blackish* above, rich *buff* below, *heavily streaked and blotched* (more so in *older* stages); tail with *numerous narrow bars*. Typical calls of 5 and 6 totally dissimilar.

## 7. Solitary Eagle  p.44
*Harpyhaliaetus solitarius*
Much *rarer* ally of *Buteogallus*; chiefly found in *subtropical* forest. Aside from *greater size*, note these characteristics: wings similarly *very broad* and rounded but *proportionally somewhat longer* (more "sail area"); *tail decidedly short* with *median white* band (like 5); aquiline head *projects* more in flight; nearby shows *short* bushy crest, rather *long heavy legs*, slatier (less black) plumage. Juvenal *boldly blotched* with black-and-buffy below; tends to be *more black* on chest and thighs than 6; pale tail is *shorter without distinct barring*. Voice different. Cf. Juvenal 1 and *Oroaetus*.

IV

1 juv

2

2 a juv

3 imm

4 juv

5

6

6 a juv

5

6

7

ꞰUDOR

PLATE V RAPTORES

NOTE: Medium-to-large, generally *longish tailed* forest hawks; sooty-brown or blackish above, usually *immaculate white below*. Most of them soar frequently. Two other genera (which almost *never* soar) may be mentioned here: very distinctive *Herpetotheres* (Plate 4) and *Micrastur* (Plate 5); *M. semitorquatus*, in particular may be confused with some of these but has *short rounded* wings, *long legs and tail*, and dark-capped look enhanced by pointed "*sideburns.*"

**Hawks** *Leucopternis*
Rather stocky, buteonine hawks with *broad, rounded* wings; *moderate*-length tail. Most are *strikingly black-and-white* (but cf. *L. schistacea*); have characteristic *tail-patterns*; note black lores, *white or streaked* crown (never a patch), and fairly long *bare legs*. Juvenals are *much like* adults.

**1. White** *L. albicollis* p.42
Tail of widespread nominate race appears *mostly black* with (especially below) white *base*, and *broad white terminal band*. Juvenal often shows *streaking on crown* like 2 but *tail-pattern* holds. Far N.W. race (Perija) differs mainly by having tail *mostly white* with *narrower black band* in the fashion of *B. albicaudatus* (otherwise dissimilar). Habitually *soars*, often to some height.

**2. Black-faced** *L. melanops* S p.42
*Smaller* ally of 1 that differs as follows: crown *much more streaked* (usually); *cere rich orange* rather than grayish; black tail *crossed* by a *narrow white median* band. Unlike 1, *seldom if ever* soars.

**3. Hook-billed Kite** p.36
*Chondrohierax uncinatus* Juvenal
Basic description on Plate III. Normal Juvenal has *light* underparts, most showing some *indistinct scattered barring* below. Note characteristic *bill and face* (like adult), *dark crown* with *light collar*, somewhat elliptical wings, and *narrow pale* tail-bands.

**4. Gray-headed Kite** p.36
*Leptodon cayanensis*
4a. Juvenal Light Phase
Rather large kite with ample, *blunt-tipped* wings and *long* tail; often prolonged soaring at moderate heights. Distinctive adult (*no* phases) has *dove-gray head contrasting with black upper-parts*, merging into white below. Note *black wing-linings*, *broadly* barred *primaries*; *prominent white* tail-bands (narrower *and grayer* above). Pattern of Juvenal Light phase superficially like 5 but note *yellow lores*, *short legs* and *weaker* feet; flight *contour* differs; *broader banding* on primaries and tail. See Plate III for Juvenal Dark phase (rare *intermediate* phase occurs with *sparse fine streaks* below).

**5. Black-and-white Hawk-Eagle** p.45
*Spizastur melanoleucus*
Scarce, smallish hawk-eagle (though big ♀ may approach size of 6) of *average proportions*: wings *longer and less rounded* than 4 or 6; *tail somewhat shorter*. Quite *black* above with *short black* crest forming *patch*; under-wings *largely white* with *minimal* barring. Compared to 4a it has more aquiline head with *jet-black lores sharply demarcated from orange cere*; much *longer* legs *feathered to base* of powerful feet. Juvenal is similar.

**6. Ornate Hawk-Eagle** p.46
*Spizaetus ornatus* Juvenal
Basic description on Plate VI. Adult quite *distinctive*. Juvenal, with *white head and underparts*, may be confused with several other genera but is commonest large raptore of its type: the *feathered legs*, *blunt rounded* primaries and rather *long tail* (all *boldly banded*) are typical of *Spizaetus*. Differs from 5 thus: *flanks and thighs barred*, wing-linings *usually spotted* black (but *may be white* in youngest); cere *yellower*, lores *much paler*; *expressive occipital crest much longer* (nearly white in very young, later turning blacker). Cf. also Juvenals of *Morphnus* and *Oroaetus*.

G TUDOR

PLATE VI  RAPTORES

NOTE: In general, *large-to-very large* forest eagles; *broad, rounded, blunt-tipped* wings; rather *long* tail. Caution: larger species are seldom encountered.

**1. Collared Forest-Falcon**  p.48
*Micrastur semitorquatus*  Dark Phase
*Not known* to soar but included here to show flight shape of genus: *short rounded* wings and *long, multi-banded* tail. Rare, *sooty* Dark phase should not be confused with 3; cf. also Pl. III.

**Hawk-Eagles**  *Spizaetus*
Rather rangy and large with *occipital crest*; legs *feathered to toes*. In flight note *projecting head* (as with eagles in general); rounded, *heavily barred* wings and *long, broadly-banded* tail. Soaring habitual (often quite *vocal* aloft). Neither species particularly uncommon.

**2. Ornate**  *S. ornatus*  p.46
Adult unmistakable: *long, spiky* black crest (often elevated); *sides of head and neck bright rufous*, sharply set off from white throat by *black malar stripes; lower* underparts and *wing-linings* boldly *spotted and barred* with black. For effect see 12a on Plate 5; (this rare *Accipiter* superficially similar but *smaller, bare-legged, lacks* crest). Youngest have head and below *largely white* (Pl. V); later stages *intermediate*. Overall *proportions* and *heavily barred thighs* should preclude Juvenals of *Oroaetus, Morphnus* et al.

**3. Black**  *S. tyrannus*  3a. Juvenal  p.46
Structurally differs from 2 by *short bushy* crest and (when soaring overhead) by somewhat longer tail and more *narrowly based* wings (these carried quite far forward, appear *indented at rear*). *Largely black* adult distinctive. Juvenal might be confused with 2 but note combination of *white brows and black cheeks*; overall *darker appearance*, especially on *flanks and belly* (never any rufous).

**4. Black-and-chestnut Eagle**  p.45
*Oroaetus isidori*  N  Early Immature
*Very large*; chiefly *subtropical* zone. Like related *Spizaetus* has *long spiky crest* (often elevated) and *feathered legs*. However, it is *bigger*, more robust with slightly different flight contour: wings *as broad* but primaries *somewhat longer*, tail obviously *shorter*. Often soars. *Richly colored* adult distinctive (Pl. VII). Juvenal *mainly white on head and below* with much *pale mottling on mantle*;

gradually matures through *successive stages* (later *washed rusty-brown* with dark *streaking*); tail changes *last*. Cf. *Spizaetus* (*longer* tail; *barred* thighs), *Spizastur* (*much smaller; "cleaner"* plumage), and young *Harpyhaliaetus*, which shares habitat (*very short* tail; *bare* legs).

NOTE: Next two allies are *powerful, long-tailed*, lowland eagles with *very broad* wings; occasionally soar. When agitated, *long occipital crests* are *broadly flared* behind ominous dark eyes (paler in old birds). Note that the *legs are bare*.

**5. Crested Eagle**  p.44
*Morphnus guianensis*  5a. Dark Phase
*Very large*; proportionally *longer tail* than most. More lightly built than 6; *weaker bill* and feet; *longer, more slender legs*; crest *undivided*. Normal adult has *gray head and chest*, white belly and wing-linings; usually some *pale gray marbling* on wing-*coverts*, *faint* tawny barring on thighs. Rarer Dark or Banded phase has *blackish chest, heavy barring on underparts and wing-linings*. Juvenal, as in 6, has *white* head and underparts (later *clouded* grayish); *conspicuous mottling on wing-coverts*; more *finely banded* tail. Smaller *Spizaetus* have feathered *legs*.

**6. Harpy Eagle**  p.45
*Harpia harpyja*  6a. Early Immature
*Huge*, especially ♀; *massive bill* and remarkably *thick and powerful legs*. Crest *divided*; tail *moderately* long. Adult unmistakable: *gray head* contrasts with *black chest* and mantle; below white with *black-barred thighs* and *boldly patterned wing-linings*. Younger stages roughly parallel 5, when they look much alike (however, dark *chest-band* appears rather *early*). Juvenal 4 might cause confusion but is smaller; legs *feathered*, tail *shorter*.

1

2

3

3 a

4

5

5 a

6

6 a

GTUDOR

PLATE VII RAPTORES

**1. Black-chested Buzzard-Eagle** p.39
*Geranoaetus melanoleucus* N (Andes)
Adult unmistakable; *long broad* wings and *extremely short, wedge-shaped tail.* Note *black chest* contrasting with vermiculated *pearly-gray* belly; blackish above with *gray-mottled shoulders.* Highly aerial, *open* country eagle of *temperate and paramo* zones.

**2. Black-and-chestnut Eagle** p.45
*Oroaetus isidori* N
Basic description on Plate VI. Mature adult handsome: *head,* upperparts and *most of thighs black;* wing-linings and *below chestnut* finely streaked with black. Note *pale base of primaries;* light gray tail with *broad black terminal band.* Immature shows enough *black-and-chestnut streaking* by late third year to be recognizable by color.

**3. Swallow-tailed Kite** p.35
*Elanoides forficatus*
Large, elegant kite with *very long, deeply forked tail.* Often quite social; seems continually on the wing. *Head* and below *snowy-white;* upperparts steely blue-black with powdery bloom. Young are similar.

**4. Plumbeous Kite** p.37
*Ictinea plumbea* 4a. Juvenal
Common, highly visible kite. Mainly *deep gray* with *long, pointed primaries basally chestnut* in adult (Plate 4); *dark tail* shows several white bands *from below* in all plumages. Flight graceful, buoyant and sustained; sometimes in *flocks.* Note *oblique posture* and *short* legs when perched. Juvenal head and below *much paler and streaked.*

**5. White-tailed Kite** p.35
*Elanus leucurus* 5a. Juvenal
Medium-sized, *pallid* kite with *pointed wings* and essentially *white tail.* Flight much like 5 though often *hovers.* Juvenal somewhat streaky but has same *black shoulders* and *under*wing *wristmarks* as adult. Unmistakable.

**6. Pearl Kite** *Gampsonyx swainsonii* p.35
Miniature kite, related to *Elanus* but only likely confused with 11. Has similar dashing, falcon-like flight and preference for *open* country. Mainly *slaty and white coloration* render it unmistakable (Plate 5).

**Falcons** *Falco*
Classic falcons characterized by *rapid, direct flight* with steady, rowing beats of the *pointed wings.* All show *dark moustaches* to greater *or* lesser degree; ♂♂ smaller than ♀♀. Residents on Pl. 5.

**7. Peregrine** *F. peregrinus* Juvenal p.51
No. migrant; mainly along coast. Note *large size, heavy moustaches,* big feet. Adult has *black* cap, *bluish-slate* mantle; *light chest* contrasts with *barred-and-spotted lower* underparts. Young *sooty* above, *heavily streaked* below; usually with *indistinct* eyebrows.

**8. Aplomado** *F. femoralis* Juvenal p. 51
Lightly built, *rather long-tailed* falcon of *open* country. Note *prominent light eyebrows, distinct* moustaches and *black "vest."* Juvenal has *sootier* mantle, more *heavily streaked breast, paler* (tawny-buff) abdomen and thighs.

**9. Bat** *F. rufigularis* p.51
*Small; dark.* Often seen perched high at forest edge, or skimming through sky in manner of large swift (resemblance enhanced by *short* tail). Complete *black cap,* extensive *"vest" finely barred with white; rufous* abdomen and thighs in *all* plumages. ORANGE-BREASTED *F. deiroleucus:* Rather *rare, larger* version of 9 (though ♂ may be quite small); similar plumage and habitat but *proportionally much bigger feet.* "Vest" more restricted (*lower* on breast), *more coarsely barred* with white *and rufous.* Juvenal *duller* below with barred *thighs* but basically *close enough* not to be confused with 7 (which *lacks* all-dark cheeks, rufous color, "vested" effect).

**10. Merlin** *Falco columbarius* p.52
No. migrant; often along coast. Note *smallish* size, *very indistinct* moustaches, fairly pale brows, and *well-streaked underparts* in *all* plumages. *Bluish-slate* above in ♂, *sooty-brown* in ♀ and Juvenal; never *any* rufous.

**11. American Kestrel** p.52
*Falco sparverius*
*Longish-*tailed, *colorful little* falcon of *open* country; often *hovers.* Both sexes show ornate face-pattern, *rufous back and tail.* ♂ has *blue-gray* wings; ochraceous below. ♀ has distinct *barring above* and *streaky* breast.

PLATE VIII CURASSOWS and SMALL OWLS

## VII

NOTE: Following genera of *medium to very large* Cracids have plumage principally *glossy black* (except 5). See Plate 1.

### 1. Wattled Guan p.55
*Aburria aburri* N
Enlarged cere light turquoise; *pendulous throat wattle* and short legs yellow. Mainly subtropical zone.

### 2. Blue-throated Piping-Guan p.55
*Pipile pipile* S
*White crest*; large *white wing-patch*. Cere and facial skin *bluish-white*; dewlap dark blue; short legs red.

### 3. Helmeted Curassow p.56
*Pauxi pauxi* N
*White abdomen and tail-tips*. ♀ either like ♂ or (in rarer phase) vermiculated *rufescent-brown* from breast to rump. All have bluish *fig-shaped casque* atop forehead; red bill and legs. Mainly subtropical zone.

### 4. Lesser Razor-billed Curassow p.55
*Mitu tomentosa*
*Rufous-chestnut abdomen and tail-tips*. Bill and legs *red*. Mainly in S.

### 5. Nocturnal Curassow p.55
*Nothocrax urumutum* S (s. Amazonas)
Medium-sized (smaller than 4). Partially *nocturnal*. Plumage generally *rufous-chestnut* with *buff tail-tips*. Black *Crax*-like crest; red *Mitu*-like bill; extensive *facial skin* yellow, greenish-blue and slate.

### Curassows *Crax*
Well-developed, *forward-curling crest*. Abdomen *white*; distal bill *not red*.

### 6. Yellow-knobbed *C. daubentoni* N p.56
*White tail-tips*. ♂ has bright *yellow knob*, cere and wattles. ♀ lacks bill ornamentation, has *light iris* and narrow *white barring* on belly.

### 7. Black *C. alector* S p.56
Tail *all-black* (no white tips). Sexes nearly alike; both have *brightly colored swollen cere*, which *varies* geographically (west to east) from vermilion-red to orange-yellow.

### 8. Burrowing Owl p.118
*Speotyto cunicularis*
*Ground-loving* owl of *open* country; note *long legs*. Often *diurnal*.

### Pygmy-Owls *Glaucidium*
*Very small* with *longish tail*. Habitually *diurnal*. Broadly streaked below; *black patches* on either side of *hindneck*. Rufescent phase exists in both species.

### 9. Ferruginous *G. brasilianum* p.118
Common, widespread at *lower* elevations.

### 10. Andean *G. jardinii* N p.118
Similar to 9 but at *higher altitudes*. Typically, crown *dotted* rather than finely streaked (hard to see); tail contains *one less white* bar. Uncommon.

### 11. Buff-fronted Owl p.120
*Aegolius harrisii* N (Merida)
Temperate zone. *Forehead*, black-rimmed *facial disks* and *unmarked* underparts *rich buff*. Unmistakable but rare.

### Screech-Owls *Otus*
*Small* with *ear-tufts* (more or less). Often difficult to identify visually.

### 12. Vermiculated *O. guatemalae* p.116
Tropical zone in N (overlaps only 13), but in S seems to occur higher than 14. *Weak pattern*: facial disks *dingy*, *rims poorly defined*; shaft-streaks *indistinct*. Also rufous phase. Iris yellow.

### 13. Tropical *O. choliba* p.116
Most widespread and commonest of genus. Light eyebrows; *light outer facial disks conspicuously black-rimmed*. Pronounced *black shaft-streaks* stand out against rather pale underparts (contrasty effect). Iris yellow.

### 14. Tawny-bellied *O. watsonii* p.117
Subtropical in N. Tropical zone in S (where overlaps 13). Rather dark above with crown and *long ear-tufts* blackish. Strongly *rufescent* brows, facial disks and underparts; latter with *fairly distinct* shaft-streaks. Iris usually amber. RUFESCENT *O. ingens* N: Very local or rare, subtropical *Otus*, overlapping most others. Much like 14 in most respects but *tufts* seem *shorter*; also like *rufescent phase* of 12 but at *higher* altitude. Iris labeled brown.

### 15. White-throated p.117
*O. albogularis*
*Upper* altitudes. *Very reduced eartufts* impart puffy-headed aspect. Note *conspicuous white throat* contrasting with *sooty breast*; buff belly *sparsely* streaked. Iris yellow.

PLATE IX  POTOOS and LARGER OWLS

## VIII

**Potoos** *Nyctibius*
*Solitary, nocturnal* birds of cryptic pattern with *huge*, light-reflective eyes (at night). Differ from *smaller* nightjars and gregarious Oilbird by *upright stance when perched.* Note vocalizations.

**1. Common** *N. griseus* p.122
Commonest, *most widespread* potoo; iris *yellow* (in daylight). WHITE-WINGED *N. leucopterus* N (Tachira): Rare, *subtropical* species, rather similar *in size and pattern* to 1 but generally *darker* on crown and breast, *much whiter on lesser wing-coverts* (thus lending a more contrasting effect).

**2. Long-tailed** *N. aethereus* S p.121
Rare. *Large* (near size of 3) but *form and pattern more like* 1. Note proportionally *very long tail*; iris color?

**3. Great** *N. grandis* p.121
*Big and robust*, appearing *much paler and grayer* than others. *Large head lacks* strong crown-markings and dark gape-stripe. Iris *brown* (in daylight).

**4. Barn Owl** *Tyto alba* p.115
*Pale and long-legged. White heart-shaped* facial disks and *dark* eyes; minutely dotted underparts vary from *white to rich buff.*

**5. Spectacled Owl** p.118
*Pulsatrix perspicillata*  5a. Juvenal
Robust. *Chocolate-brown* upperparts and *broad breast-band* contrast with *white eyebrows and throat, immaculate buff* belly. Juvenal has black facial disks, but young of some other owls look quite similar.

**Owls** *Ciccaba*
Medium-large. *Rounded head* (no tufts)

**6. Mottled** *C. virgata* p.119
Most *widespread* of genus. Mainly rich *brown* above; *mottled and streaked below.* Dark facial disks outlined in buff with *brown* eyes.

**7. Rufous-banded** *C. albitarsus* N p.119
Generally similar to 6 but occurs at *higher altitude.* Differs by *bolder* cinnamon mottled-barring on *hindneck and mantle;* light facial markings more prominent; *pearly-white ocellations* on belly. Iris labeled yellow.

**8. Black-and-white** p.119
*C. nigrolineata* N
Uncommon but distinctive. *Blackish facial disks* and upperparts. *Black and white barred* hindneck and underparts; iris color variable.

**9. Black-banded** *C. huhula* S p.119
Scarce, *blackish* owl. *Narrowly barred* (fasciated) with *white* throughout.

**10. Crested Owl** p.117
*Lophostrix cristata* S
Peculiar, scarce owl with *striking* (especially when alertly erect), *partially white ear-tufts.* Note *lack* of streaking or barring below; some are rather *pale and rufescent.* Facial disks *chestnut;* iris color variable.

**11. Striped Owl** p.120
*Rhinoptynx clamator*
Streaky with *prominent ear-tufts;* related to Asio (shows *dark wrist-patches* in flight like 12). Note *boldly striped* underparts; *black-rimmed whitish* facial disks contrasting with rather *dark* eyes. A non-forest species.

**Owls** *Asio*

**12. Short-eared** *A. flammeus* N p.120
Most like 11 but ear-tufts *rudimentary. Less* boldly streaked below; *small yellow* eyes set in blackish ocular disks. Habituates *open country* where usually seen *on wing;* very local.

**13. Stygian** *A. stygius* p.120
*Very dark* appearing, rare owl. *Heavily mottled sooty-and-buff* underparts. Note *closely spaced* ear-tufts with *light forehead blaze; yellow* eyes set in *sooty* facial disks. Very local.

**14. Great Horned Owl** p.117
*Bubo virginianus*
*Larger, much more powerful* than other "eared" owls; tufts *widely spaced apart.* Note *white throat-patch* and *barred* underparts.

1

2

3

4

5a

6

7

8

9

10

11

12

13

14

J.Gwynne 76

PLATE X NIGHTJARS

NOTE: In alert posture to depict underparts; more often flattened on ground. Look for *presence or absence* in ♂♂ of *white band across primaries* and *extent of white* in *outer* tail-feathers; these greatly *reduced* in respective ♀♀, being replaced by *narrower buff or tawny* wing-bands; *minimal or no* tail-tipping. Learn commoner species first; e.g., 1, 3, 4, 5, 8, and 9. See text for vocalizations.

### 1. Lesser Nighthawk p.123
*Chordeiles acutipennis*
*Chordeiles* and *Podager* Nighthawks may be seen on ground in open country. They are separable from similar nightjars by *wing-tips reaching nearly to end of tail.* See Nighthawks, Pl. XI.

### 2. Ladder-tailed Nightjar p.127
*Hydropsalis climacocerca* S
Respective sexes most like commoner 4 but are *sandier* above *without* distinct rufous collar. *Tail somewhat longer* with *diagnostic shape*; this "double-notched" effect *less evident* in ♀.

### 3. Pauraque p.124
*Nyctidromus albicollis*
*Large, widespread* nightjar with *longish* tail; the one whose reflective, fiery eye-shine is most often seen on roads at night. *Black markings* on grayish (or rufescent) crown and mantle *more contrasty* than most others; note *rufous cheeks.* ♂ has *prominent white wing-band*; largely *white middle tail-feathers.* ♀ has *buff* wing-band and *little* white in tail. Calls frequently.

### Nightjars *Caprimulgus*

### 4. White-tailed C. *cayennensis* p.125
Open country; rather common. *Cinnamon nuchal collar.* ♂ has throat, *belly*, *prominent wing-band* and *most of undertail white.* ♀ quite different, more mottled ochraceous below; *tawny-buff* wing-band (or two); *no* white in tail; *smaller* than ♀ 3 with *darker* crown, tawny *collar* (but much like 2, 6, 7).

### 5. Band-winged C. *longirostris* p.125
Commonest *upper altitude* nightjar; quite *dark* with *rufous nuchal collar.* ♂ has *prominent white wing-band* (narrower in S Tepui race); *very large* distal *tail-patches*. These *reduced* in ♀ but wing-band still *rather white.*

### 6. Little C. *parvulus* p.126
*Small* and *dark* with *interrupted rufous collar.* ♂ has *conspicuous white throat*; broad *white wing-band* and *small* distal tail-spots. ♀ throat-patch *reduced* and buffier; in all, much like ♀ 4 but tail *shorter*; at least *several tawny-buff* wing-bars. *Lower* elevation than 5.

### 7. Spot-tailed C. *maculicaudus* p.126
Also *small* with *rufous collar.* ♂ has *several tawny-buff* wing-bars and a *neat white* distal tail-*band*, as well as *several pairs of spots* nearer base. ♀ generally resembles ♀♀ of 4 and 6, but note (in *both* sexes) *blackish crown*, light eyebrow and *dark malar* area. Unlike 6, buffy throat merges into *coarse spotting on breast.*

### 8. Blackish C. *nigrescens* S p.126
*Small* and *very dark*; common in *lowland* forest. *No rufous* collar. ♂ has white *spots* on 3 *inner* primaries and distal *tips* on 2 *inner* tail-feathers (showing in flight). *No* white at all in ♀. RORAIMAN C. *whitelyi* S (Tepuis): *Very local.* Much like 8 (see text) but at *somewhat higher* elevation. More likely confused with ♀ 5 (with which it occurs) but *no* rufous collar. ♂ has *white wing-band* and *small* tail-*tips*, more clean-cut white than ♀ 5.

### 9. Rufous C. *rufus* p.125
Rather *large and dark* with strong *rufescent* tone but *no* collar. Wings *multiply and evenly barred with rufous* (lacking banded effect of ♀♀ 3 and 5). *Large* distal *buff patches* on ♂ *undertail* (but buff-*and*-white *inner* patches above). ♀ tail *tipped* with buff. Loud *distinctive* call heard regularly but seldom seen in open. CHUCK-WILL'S-WIDOW C. *carolinensis* N: Very rare No. migrant. *Not* separable in field except by *bigger* size (but W. I. migrant race of 9 *equally* large).

### 10. Lyre-tailed Nightjar p.127
*Uropsalis lyra* N (Mérida)
*Dark, upper altitude* nightjar, similar to and occurring with 5. *Incredibly long, plume-like tail-feathers* render ♂ unmistakable. ♀ much like ♀ 5 but primaries show *multiple rufous barring* (as in 9) rather than single pale band; tail *slightly longer.*

X

GUDOR

PLATE XI   NIGHTHAWKS and SWALLOWS

NOTE: Nighthawks differ from *rounder*-winged nightjars by *flight*: usually *much more sustained* and *higher* above ground.

### 1. Nacunda Nighthawk  p.124
*Podager nacunda*
Robust; *blunted* wings, *shortish* tail. *Belly*, wing-linings and *broad wing-bar white*. Flight buoyant; open country.

**Nighthawks**  *Chordeiles*
Open country genus. *White wing-markings*; ♀ has *buffier* throat, *less* white in tail.

### 2. Sand-colored  *C. rupestris*  S  p.123
Quite pallid; *belly*, wing-*patches* (*no* bar) and *most of undertail pure white*. Flight odd, "mechanical." Habituates riverine sandbars; Amazonas only.

### 3. Lesser  *C. acutipennis*  p.123
Widespread. *Medium*-sized with distinct *white* (buff ♀) *bar across primaries*. COMMON *C. minor* N: Rare No. migrant. White wing-bar *nearer base* than smaller 3; *higher* flight, different *voice*.

### 4. Least  *C. pusillus*  p.123
*Miniature* edition of 3. Note *pale trailing edge of secondaries* in flight.

### 5. Band-tailed Nighthawk  p.124
*Nyctiprogne leucopyga*
Small and dark. No wing-bar but note *median white band across longish tail*.

### 6. Semicollared Nighthawk  p.122
*Lurocalis semitorquatus*
Dark and short-tailed; *no* white wing-bar. Often in *low bat-like flight* over forest canopy. Other races *larger* than shown; Andean with *plain rufous* belly.

**Martins**  *Progne*
*Larger*, broader-winged than swallows.

### 7. Gray-breasted  *P. chalybea*  p.284
*Throat* and breast *sooty-gray*. ♂ *steel-blue* above; ♀ *duller blue* with *brownish* cast. PURPLE *P. subis*: No. migrant. ♂ *all* steel-blue; ♀ from 7 by *paler gray* forehead (often) and *sides of neck*, enhancing dark lores, cheeks.

### 8. Brown-chested  *P. tapera*  p.284
Above *sooty-brown*. Differs from Juvenal 7 by *whitish throat* contrasting with *obscure breast-band* effect. So. migrant race has more *clear-cut* band, plus dark *spots down center* of belly.

### 9. Rough-winged Swallow  p.286
*Stelgidopteryx ruficollis*
Most widespread *sooty-brown backed* swallow. Throat tawny-buff; belly and crissum pale yellowish. Easily told by *pale rump* (So. migrant race *may* occur).

### 10. Tawny-headed Swallow  p.285
*Alopochelidon fucata*  (Local)
*Lacks* pale rump. Tawny throat *extends* onto upper chest and merges into *rich rufous eyebrow and nuchal collar*.

### 11. Bank Swallow  *Riparia riparia*  p.286
No. migrant. From resident "*brown*-backs" by *clear-cut sooty breast-band*.

### 12. White-thighed Swallow  p.285
*Neochelidon tibialis*  S
Very dark, little forest swallow. *Smoky ash-brown below* with dusky crissum; note *white thighs* when perched.

**Swallows**  *Notiochelidon*
*Steel-blue* upperparts with forked tail.

### 13. Brown-bellied  *N. murina* N  p.284
*Smoky grayish-brown* below with *black crissum*. *Upper* elevations in Andes.

### 14. Blue-and-white  *N. cyanoleuca*  p.285
*Immaculate white* below; *crissum black*.

### 15. White-winged Swallow  p.283
*Tachycineta albiventer*
Glossy *blue-green* above. Underparts, *rump and wing-patches* white. Riparian.

**Swallows**  *Atticora*
Steely *blue-black and white* pattern. Note *long, deeply forked tail*.

### 16. White-banded  *A. fasciata*  S  p.285
*All dark* with *white* lower *breast-band*.

### 17. Black-collared  p.285
*A. melanoleuca*  S
*Pure white* underparts with *breast-band*. Prefers vicinity of mid-river rocks.

### 18. Barn Swallow  *Hirundo rustica*  p.286
Common No. migrant. *Steel-blue* above; throat *chestnut*, belly *buff*. Young *lack long streamers* but all show *white inner* tail-spots. See text for rare No. migrant Cliff Swallow.

NOTE: Juvenals of "blue-backed" swallows are *much browner above* but *basic pattern is indicative* of adult.

XI
1 ♂
2 ♂
3 ♂
4 ♂
5
6
7 ♀
8
9
10
11
12
13
14
15
16
17
18

TUDOR

PLATE XII   SWIFTS

NOTE: Certain *Cypseloides* and *Chaetura* are notoriously *difficult to identify* in field. Thoroughly learn more *gregarious, commoner* species (3, 6, 7, 8, and 11) before attempting others.

### 1. White-collared Swift  p.128
*Streptoprocne zonaris*
*Very large*, common black swift with well-notched tail. *Sharp white collar* (much *reduced or lacking* in Juvenal).

### Swifts  *Cypseloides*
*Larger, more blackish* than *Chaetura*. Rump and tail *always concolor with* back; also throat *as dark as* breast (except when chestnut). Black Swift *C. niger* may occur as No. migrant; size of 4 but with appreciatively *longer, well-notched tail;* forehead usually quite *whitish.*

### 2. Tepui  *C. phelpsi*  S (mainly)  p.128
Differs from 3 by *brighter* (rufous) *collar* extending *to chin* in *both* sexes; longer wings *and tail*, latter *notably forked*. Tepuis (once in N, migrant?).

### 3. Chestnut-collared  p.128
*C. rutilus*  N
In proper light, adult ♂ shows complete *chestnut collar;* reduced *or lacking* in ♀. Note *dark rump and throat;* square or notched tail seems slightly *longer* than *Chaetura.*

### 4. White-chinned  *C. cryptus*  p.129
*Larger* than ♀ 3, but *tail noticeably short;* white chin spot very obscure. Apparently *local or rare;* status?

### 5. Spot-fronted  *C. cherriei*  N  p.128
Another *rare* swift, very similar to 4. *White loral and postocular spots* diagnostic if seen. Very local (Aragua).

### Swifts  *Chaetura*
*Small*, short-tailed, generally *sooty-brown* with *paler throats and/or rumps.*

### 6. Band-rumped  *C. spinicauda*  p.130
Note rather *narrow but well-defined light band* across rump; *throat paler* than underparts. Occurs mainly in S.

### 7. Gray-rumped  *C. cinereiventris*  p.129
*Entire rump gray* set off against black back and tail. Below gray; *not as dark* as others and with *less contrasting* throat but *crissum black*. Lacks brownish tone, appearing *black-and-gray.*

### 8. Vaux's  *C. vauxi*  N  p.129
Rump more *brownish*-gray than 7, merging into *short* dark tail; *throat paler* than underparts. CHIMNEY *C. pelagica*: No. migrant; *rare* but status uncertain. Size of 9. *Very little contrast* between rump and back (*least* of genus); *throat paler* than underparts.

### 9. Chapman's  *C. chapmani*  p.129
Local or scarce. Similar to 8 but slightly *larger* and fuller-tailed; *rump* somewhat *less* contrasting; *throat rather dark, barely paler* than breast. Generally the most *uniform Chaetura.*

### 10. Ashy-tailed  *C. andrei*  p.130
Resembles both 8 and 11 but much *rarer;* rump vs. tail effect *intermediate*. Best told by *strong contrast* between *pale throat* and *very dark sooty* underparts. So. migrant race is *larger.*

### 11. Short-tailed  *C. brachyura*  p.130
Noticeably *stumpy, short-tailed Chaetura. Very dark,* almost blackish fore parts (*throat barely paler* than breast) contrast strongly with *much paler rump, crissum and tail.*

### 12. White-tipped Swift  p.130
*Aeronautes montivagus*
Note *white throat*. Rump dark; *moderate* tail slightly notched (shows *white tipping* from above). Gregarious; normally occurs at *higher* elevations than 13.

### 13. Lesser Swallow-tailed Swift  p.131
*Panyptila cayennensis*
Differs mainly from 12 by complete white *collar* and *much longer, deeply forked* tail (usually held *closed*). Solitary or in pairs at most.

### 14. Fork-tailed Palm-Swift  p.131
*Reinarda squamata*
Slender and *streamlined*, low-flying swift with *very long, forked* tail; *mottled with dirty-white* below. Llanos and savanna with palms.

### 15. Pygmy Swift  p.131
*Micropanyptila furcata*  N
*Miniature* edition of 14; much more *local and scarce. Habitat* somewhat *dissimilar;* ranges to *higher* elevation. Subtly differs in underparts pattern and faster wing-beats, but most reliable (if seen when banking) are *white spots* showing at *base of upper tail.*

XII

1

2

3 ♂

3 ♀

4

5

6

7

8

11

7

8

10

11

9

12

13

14

15

15

GUDOR

## PLATE XIII TYRANTS and ICTERIDS (in part)

NOTE: Tyrants of *black/white/gray* hue.

**1. Long-tailed Tyrant** p.246
*Colonia colonus* S
*Blackish* Juvenal *lacks tail-streamers.*

**2. Black Phoebe** p.246
*Sayornis nigricans* N
*Blackish*; obvious *white wing-edgings.*
*Wags tail.* Invariably near water.

**3. Greater Pewee** p.259
*Contopus fumigatus*
*Larger* and much *darker* than *Contopus* on
Pl. 29, especially *below*; coloration
*smoky-gray*. Like 4, often prefers high ex-
posed perches.

**4. Olive-sided Flycatcher** p.258
*Contopus borealis* N
No. migrant. *More olive* than 3. Best told by
*dark sides* contrasting with *white throat* and
narrow *median* breast-stripe.

**5. White-headed Marsh-Tyrant** p.247
*Arundinicola leucocephala*
♂ unique. ♀ *quite pale* with *whitish face*
and black *tail.* Note habitat.

**6. Fork-tailed Flycatcher** p.249
*Muscivora tyrannus*
Juvenal tail *nearly normal* (cf. Pl. 28).

**7. Pied Water-Tyrant** p.247
*Fluvicola pica*
*Boldly pied* pattern diagnostic.

**8. Riverside Tyrant** p.246
*Knipolegus orenocensis*
♂ *dull blackish-slate.* ♀ similar but *paler*
*smoky-gray.* Note *range, habitat.*

**9. Amazonian Black-Tyrant** p.247
*Phaeotriccus poecilocercus* S (mainly)
Wings *short* (narrow pointed primaries). ♂
*glossy blue-black* (cf. *Xenopipo*). ♀ resembles Bran-color Flyc. but back more
*olive*; rump, tail-edging *rufous.*

NOTE: Following Icterids have plumage *all or*
*mostly black.* See also Plate 38.

**10. Crested Oropendola** p.308
*Psarocolius decumanus*
Only *blackish* oropendola (*larger* than
caciques, especially ♂). *Dark chestnut*
lower back, rump and crissum; *entire*
*under*tail yellow; iris blue.

**Caciques** *Cacicus*
Sharply pointed *pale bill.* Many have *colorful*
*rump*, blue iris. ♀♀ smaller.

**11. Scarlet-rumped** p.310
*C. uropygialis* N
Rump *flame-scarlet.* RED-RUMPED *C.*
*haemorrhous* S: Rather like 11 but rump-
patch *larger, intense scarlet.*

**12. Yellow-rumped** *C. cela* p.309
*Golden-yellow* inner wing-coverts, *lower*
*back, crissum and basal tail.*

**13. Mountain** *C. leucoramphus* N p.310
Mainly differs from 12 by *crissum* and
*longer* tail *entirely black.* Occurs at *higher*
elevations; s.w. Tachira.

**14. Yellow-billed** *C. holosericeus* N p.310
*All black.* Bill *and iris pale yellow.*

**15. Solitary Black** *C. solitarius* N p.310
*Lower* altitude than somewhat smaller,
commoner 14. Differs chiefly by *brown iris*;
bill pale greenish, shading to bluish basally. E. of Andes only.

**16. Golden-tufted Grackle** p.311
*Macroagelaius imthurni* S (Tepuis)
*Rather long* bill and tail. Semiconcealed
*golden pectoral-tufts.*

**17. Velvet-fronted Grackle** p.311
*Lampropsar tanagrinus*
Sexes alike. Bill somewhat *more pointed*,
plumage *much less glossy* than 19 (reflec-
tions *dull* steel-blue). *Social.* (Cf.
*Tachyphonus rufus*). Note range.

**18. Carib Grackle** p.311
*Quiscalus lugubris* 18a. Juvenal
Note *grackle bill, wedge-shaped* tail,
*straw-colored* iris. Smaller ♀ *sooty-choco-*
*late; paler* throat, *dark* iris in young.
GREAT-TAILED *Cassidix mexicanus* N
(Zulia): ♂ *twice as large* and *much longer*
*tail.* ♀ from 18a by *size, much paler* eyebrow, breast; *light* iris.

**19. Shiny Cowbird** p.308
*Molothrus bonariensis*
♂ *highly glossed: purple* on head and
body, *blue-green* on wings. ♀ *dull*
*grayish-brown*, eyebrow and throat *paler*;
note typical *cowbird bill.*

**20. Giant Cowbird** p.308
*Scaphidura oryzivora*
Noticeably *large* with *small-headed* aspect,
especially ♂ which often displays *swollen*
*neck ruff.* Note *bill shape.* Juvenal (host
mimic) has *pale bill and iris* but tail shorter
and face grayer than similar caciques.

PLATE 1 TINAMOUS, QUAIL and GUANS

**1. Highland Tinamou** p.4
*Nothocercus bonapartei* N
*Medium*-sized. *Deep brown* above, *rear-parts dotted* buff; *slaty cap, fulvous throat*. Below *strongly rufescent*. Subtropical. TAWNY-BREASTED *N. julius* S.w. Tachira. Slightly smaller than 1. *Chestnut* cap; *contrasting white* throat.

**Tinamous** *Tinamus*
*Medium-to-large.* Mostly tropical zone.

**2. Gray** *T. tao* N p.3
*Large and grayish*; neck *speckled* white.

**3. Great** *T. major* p.3
Rather common. *Olive-brown* above with *broken black barring*; throat and belly *whitish.* WHITE-THROATED *T. guttatus* S (Amazonas): Similar to larger 3 but *rear-parts spotted with buff.*

**Tinamous** *Crypturellus*

**4. Brown** *C. obsoletus* N p.5
*Larger*, much *rarer* than 5. Rufescent below with *gray throat, barred flanks.*

**5. Little** *C. soui* p.4
*Small*; common. *White throat*; virtually *un-barred* flanks. ♂ *less rufous* below than ♀. TEPUI *C. ptaritepui* S (Tepuis of Bolivar-local): Much like 4. *Higher elevation* than others in range.

**6. Undulated** *C. undulatus* S p.5
Amazonas. *Grayish olive-brown* with *white throat, pale* belly; above *lacks* distinct barring or spotting of *larger Tinamus.* CINEREOUS *C. cinereus* S (Amazonas): Almost *uniform smoky-brown; lacks* contrasting throat or belly.

**7. Red-legged** *C. erythropus* p.5
Common. Typically *barred above* but may be *much reduced* in ♂ or some races. *Upper* breast *gray*, below *buff to cinnamon*; flanks *barred*; legs *reddish.* GRAY-LEGGED *C. duidae* S (Amazonas): Rather similar to *lightly-barred* forms of 7 (*no* overlap) but *entire neck and breast rufous*; legs grayish.

**8. Variegated** *C. variegatus* S p.5
Rather common. *Boldly barred* black-and-cinnamon above; neck and breast *rufous, cap blackish.* BARRED *C. casiquiare*: Very local in Amazonas. *Barred mantle* like larger 8 but cap *chestnut*; foreneck and breast *clear gray.*

**9. Crested Bobwhite** *Colinus cristatus* p.57
*Variable*: some races *lack* cinnamon on face; ♀ less ornate with *short* crest. Only quail in *open* country.

**Wood-Quail** *Odontophorus*
Robust, shy, *forest* quail with puffy crest and *heavy* bill.

**10. Venezuelan** *O. columbianus* N p.58
*White throat*; obvious *spotted* breast.

**11. Marbled** *O. gujanensis* p.57
*Lacks* distinct pattern below; bare *orbital area vermilion.* Widespread at *lower* elevations. BLACK-FRONTED *O. atrifrons* N (subtropical S. de Perija): *Black* forecrown, *face and throat*; breast speckled.

**12. Rufous-vented Chachalaca** p.53
*Ortalis ruficauda* N
Rather *plain.* Widespread nominate race has *chestnut tail-tips* (tips *white* in N.w. Zulia). LITTLE *O. motmot* S: Much like nominate race of 12 but *entire head* is *chestnut*; legs reddish.

**Guans** *Penelope*
Generally *dark olive-brown*, forest guans with *white-streaked fore*parts. Crest bushy; note *bare red dewlap.*

**13. Band-tailed** *P. argyrotis* N p.53
Widespread. *Conspicuous silvery-white* streaking *on face. Tail tipped* with rufous (buff in Perija race). CRESTED *P. purpurascens* N (plus Delta): Only *very large Penelope* in range (size of 15). Well-developed crest; *no gray streaking on face.*

**14. Andean** *P. montagnii* N p.54
*Higher* elevations. *Some* overlap with 13 but *streaking duller and grayer*, especially on face; dewlap *very small.*

**15. Spix's** *P. jacquacu* S p.54
Only *very large Penelope* in range; Amazonas race somewhat *smaller.* Voice loud. MARAIL *P. marail* S: Confined to Bolivar where it occurs with *large grantii* race of 15 (shown). Similar *in color* but looks *noticeably smaller* (size nearer 13) with proportionally slightly shorter legs and tail.

NOTE: See Plate VIII for other Cracids.

1

# PLATE 2  HERONS

NOTE: See also large *Ardea* and various "white" herons in text figs.

## 1. Yellow-crowned Night Heron  p.19
*Nyctanassa violacea*
Gray body in adult. Juvenal much like shorter-legged 2a but *slatier*, *crown* darker, spotting *finer*, bill *blunter*.

## 2. Black-crowned Night Heron  p.19
*Nycticorax nycticorax*  2a. Juvenal
*Blackish* crown and back, *white* belly. Juvenal *drab grayish-brown* with whitish spots on back and wings.

## 3. Boat-billed Heron  p.21
*Cochlearius cochlearius*
*Broad, massive bill*; *long* black crest, *rufous-and-black* belly, pale primaries. Juvenal *tawny-brown*, paler below with black crown. Mainly nocturnal.

## 4. Capped Heron  p.18
*Pilherodius pileatus*
Appears *very pale*; likely to be taken for an egret (but becomes buffy in breeding condition). Note *small* black cap and *bright blue* facial skin.

## Tiger-Herons  *Tigrisoma*
Bittern-like herons that mature through many stages from *very bolded banded* Juvenal to more *finely barred* Immature to distinctive adult. Juvenals are *inseparable*, but later stages gradually approach adult plumage.

## 5. Rufescent  *T. lineatum*  p.19
5a. Juvenal
Adult has *chestnut* foreparts. Unlike 7, ground color of Juvenal strongly *rufescent*. Widespread.

## 6. Fasciated  *T. fasciatum*  N  p.19
Adult has *slaty neck* and body, *very finely barred* with buff; *black* cap. Much scarcer than 5, ranging to higher elevations; prefers forested streams.

## 7. Pinnated Bittern  p.20
*Botaurus pinnatus*
Told from immature *Tigrisoma* by *fine barring* on *decidedly buffy* ground color, and especially the distinct *streaked effect on mantle*; note also dark crown and long toes. Confined to marshes.

## 8. Stripe-backed Bittern  p.20
*Ixobrychus involucris*  N
Tiny. *Contrasting pattern* in flight; *very buffy* with *boldly striped back*, wings tipped with tawny. ♀ similar but duller. LEAST *I. exilis* N: Differs by *rich rufous face and hindneck*, all-dark primaries and *solid back* (black in ♂, chestnut in ♀).

## 9. Striated Heron  p.18
*Butorides striatus*
Small; common and widespread. *Gray face and neck*. Juvenal has *streaked foreneck*. GREEN *B. virescens* N: Darker with rich *maroon-chestnut* face and neck; Juvenal like 9 but *suggests* adult coloration. Resident and No. migrant races occur.

## 10. Zigzag Heron  p.19
*Zebrilus undulatus*
*Ample crest* imparts bull-headed look. *Foreparts variable* (phases or age stages): may be as shown, or *unbarred chestnut-and-buff* or *intermediate*. Note *small size* and *very dark, fasciated mantle*. Seldom encountered.

## 11. Reddish Egret  Dark Phase  p.17
*Dichromanassa rufescens*  N
Large; *shaggy neck*, *long* legs. Body *ash-gray*, adult bill basally *flesh-color*. Cf. White Phase. Coastal.

## 12. Little Blue Heron  p.17
*Florida caerulea*
Quite dark (*slate-blue* body, *maroon* neck); bill basally bluish-white. Juvenal *white*, subadult piebald.

## 13. Whistling Heron  p.18
*Syrigma sibilatrix*
*Buffy neck*, large *wing-patches*, *white* rump and tail. Llanos mainly.

## 14. Tricolored or Louisiana Heron  p.17
*Hydranassa tricolor*  N
Bill *long*, neck very slender. Note *white* belly and wing-linings, pale rump. Juvenal neck chestnut. Coastal.

## 15. Chestnut-bellied Heron  p.18
*Agamia agami*
Note *extremely long bill* and unique *color* pattern. Juvenal mainly *dark brown*; underparts *buffy* with heavy *streaking*. Forests; scarce.

2

PLATE 3  LIMPKIN, IBISES, and DUCKS

**1. Limpkin**  p.58
*Aramus guarauna*
Brown; neck *streaked white*. Basally yellowish bill *straighter* than ibises, wingstroke *shallower* with upward flick. *Voice* distinctive; legs long.

**2. Glossy Ibis**  2a. Immature  p.23
*Plegadis falcinellus*  N
Only ibis *extensively maroon-chestnut*. Facial skin *never* red; legs *long*. Young and winter adult *duller*, head and neck *flecked* with whitish.

**3. Scarlet Ibis**  Juvenal  p.23
*Eudocimus ruber*
Younger stages have *white rump and belly* (as in White Ibis), later becoming *patched with pink* (cf. Fig. 9).

**4. Buff-necked Ibis**  p.22
*Theristicus caudatus*
Buff neck and bold *wing-pattern*.

**5. Green Ibis**  p.23
*Mesembrinibis cayennensis*
*Stocky build*, longish tail, *short* legs and bushy nuchal crest. Facial skin *greenish-gray*.

**6. Bare-faced Ibis**  p.23
*Phimosus infuscatus*
Bare facial skin *red*. Smaller than 7 with *shorter* tail.

**7. Sharp-tailed Ibis**  p.23
*Cercibis oxycerca*
*Large* and husky; bushy nuchal crest and *unusually long tail*. Facial skin *red*. Less numerous than 5 or 6.

NOTE: See other Ibises in text Figs.

**8. Orinoco Goose**  *Neochen jubata*  p.28
Rather large (size of ♀ Comb Duck). *Buff foreparts*, *chestnut* belly, reddish legs; wing-speculum *white*. Note erect posture when walking.

**9. Masked Duck**  p.32
*Oxyura dominica*
Secretive little duck with stubby build and *spiky tail*. Note ♂ and ♀ *face-patterns*; white wing-patches.

**10. Brazilian Duck**  p.31
*Amazonetta brasiliensis*
*Contrasting* iridescent *black wings* with *white* speculum; pale brown tail-coverts. Note *red* bill of ♂ and *face-patterns* (but cf. darker brown ♀ Southern Pochard, text Fig. 13).

**11. Blue-winged Teal**  p.29
*Anas discors*  N
No. migrant. ♂ has bold *white crescents front and rear*; ♀ foreface *whitish*, flanks *patterned*. Note *chalky-blue* shoulders. Other No. Amer. ducks may winter irregularly.

**12. Speckled Teal**  p.28
*Anas flavirostris*  N
*Darker, puffier* head than ♀ 11. *Gray-brown* shoulders; dark wing-speculum edged tawny-and-buff; flanks *unpatterned*. Paramo zone.

**13. White-cheeked Pintail**  p.29
*Anas bahamensis*  N
Clear-cut *white cheeks*. *Buffy*, pointed tail; narrow dark speculum broadly edged with tawny. Bill *basally bright red*. Coastal region.

**14. Torrent Duck**  p.30
*Merganetta armata*  N
*Shape, color pattern and habitat* diagnostic. Juvenal patterned like ♀ but cinnamon replaced by white.

**Whistling-Ducks**  *Dendrocygna*
Typically upright posture; long legs.

**15. Black-bellied**  *D. autumnalis*  p.28
*Black belly* and *rosy-red* bill (lacking in Juvenal); *extensive white patch* along forewing in any plumage.

**16. White-faced**  *D. viduata*  N  p.28
Striking *white face* diagnostic.

**17. Fulvous**  *D. bicolor*  N  p.27
Mostly *tawny-fulvous* with creamy *flank stripe*; white upper tail-coverts.

NOTE: See pochards and large perching ducks in text figs.

# PLATE 4  RAPTORES

NOTE: Refer to Plates I-VII for flight diagrams, Juvenals, similar species, etc.

**1. Yellow-headed Caracara**  p.50
*Milvago chimachima*  1a. Juvenal
*Head* and underparts *buff*; compare, especially Juvenal, with various hawks; note *less aquiline* bill and feet, *conspicuous buff wing-patches*.

**2. Plumbeous Kite**  p.37
*Ictinea plumbea*
*Short*-legged, *gray* kite with *slaty mantle*. *Long, pointed primaries* have chestnut bases; undertail banded.

**Vultures**  *Cathartes*
Blackish with *colorful* naked head.

**3. Turkey**  *C. aura.*  p.34
Head *deep red* (occasionally pinker) with creamy *nape*; never looks yellow.

**4. Lesser Yellow-headed**  p.34
*C. burrovianus*
Yellowish head variable but usually *rich suffusion of orange* fore and aft.

**5. Greater Yellow-headed**  p.34
*C. melambrotus*  S
Head like 4 but yellower, *very little* orange (contrasts with black plumage).

**6. Laughing Hawk** or **Falcon**  p.48
*Herpetotheres cachinnans*
Underparts and *large head buff* with broad, conspicuous *black mask*.

**7. Gray Hawk**  Juvenal p.42
*Buteo nitidus*
Juvenal is one of most prevalent of many *streaked* young *Buteos*, etc. It is also one of *buffiest* with conspicuous *wing-patches* in flight (thus resembling 1a). See adult, Pl. 5.

**8. Slate-colored Hawk**  p.43
*Leucopternis schistacea*  S
Rather stocky and stolid *slate-gray* hawk with black tail crossed by *one median white* band; *cere* and *long legs reddish-orange*, iris *golden*.

**9. Crane Hawk**  p.47
*Geranospiza caerulescens*
Active, *lanky*, weak-billed *slate-gray* hawk with *long orange* legs, *crimson iris*. *Rather long* black tail crossed by *two white* bands. Note distinctive *underwing pattern*, Plate III.

**10. Collared Forest-Falcon**  p.48
*Micrastur semitorquatus*  Juvenal
See Plate 5 for generic and specific characters; occurs also in *tawny* (rich buff replacing white) and *dark phases*. Juvenal *buff-to-tawny* below with various amount of *coarse* barring.

**11. Snail** or **Everglade Kite**  p.37
*Rostrhamus sociabilis*  11a. Immature
Marsh kite with *slender, deeply* hooked bill; orange or red cere and legs, *red* iris. Square tail *basally white*. ♂ *dark slate;* ♀ and young brownish, heavily *mottled or streaked* below.

**12. Slender-billed Kite**  p.37
*Helicolestes hamatus*
Forest-based ally of commoner 11 with *similar face and bill* except iris is *yellow*. Adult slate-gray with *short, unmarked tail* (but cf. Juvenal).

**13. Hook-billed Kite**  13a. Black Phase p.36
*Chondrohierax uncinatus*
*Highly* variable; note rather *massive* hooked bill, *weak legs, odd visage* enhanced by *light* iris. Gray phase (mostly ♂ ♂) *coarsely* barred or, less commonly, *solid gray* below. Brown phase (mostly ♀ ♀) *coarsely* barred *rusty* below with *tawny collar*. Tail typically has one or two *narrow white* and one *broad gray* band (*but* cf. Black Phase).

**14. Rufous Crab-Hawk**  p.43
*Buteogallus aequinoctialis*
Much more local (Delta) than larger 16. *Head and mantle* are *slaty*; tail band more obscure. *Coastal.*

**15. Bay-winged or Harris' Hawk**  p.42
*Parabuteo unicinctus*
Mostly *sooty* with *chestnut shoulders* and thighs; conspicuous *white at base* of longish tail.

**16. Savanna Hawk**  p.43
*Heterospizias meridionalis*
Rather stolid, *long*-legged, *dull cinnamon-rufous* and grayish hawk. One median white band across rather short black tail. Common in llanos.

**17. Black-collared Hawk**  p.43
*Busarellus nigricollis*
Heavy-footed, short-tailed, mostly *rufous-chestnut* hawk with *creamy head* and *black upper-chest crescent*.

GTUDOR

PLATE 5  RAPTORES

NOTE: Gender symbols on plate denote *plumage* dimorphism, not size differential.

**Falcons**  *Falco*
Note *pointed* wings and black *moustaches*; ♀♀ larger. 3 neotropical species all have black *"vest,"* tawny or rufous *abdomen*.

**1. Bat**  *F. rufigularis*  p.51
*Dark* and *rather small* (although ♀ nearly size of ♂ 2); black vest *finely* barred with *white*.

**2. Orange-breasted**  *F. deiroleucus*  p.51
Larger and rarer than 1; *much bigger feet* proportionally. Reliably told by *coarser, more rufescent* barring on vest.

**3. Aplomado**  *F. femoralis*  p.51
Paler and longer-tailed than above; *narrow* moustaches and *light eyebrows*.

**4. American Kestrel**  *F. sparverius*  p.52
Small; *no vest. Back and tail rufous.*

**5. Pearl Kite**  p.35
*Gampsonyx swainsonii*
Distinctive *little* kite; *slaty* cap and upperparts, *buff forehead and cheeks*; mainly *white* below. Juvenal duller.

**Hawks**  *Buteo*
Smaller woodland *Buteos* with *barred underparts* and *wide*-banded tail *in adult*.

**6. Gray**  *B. nitidus*  p.42
*Silvery-gray*, barred below; one wide and (often) one narrow *white* tail-band.

**7. Roadside**  *B. magnirostris*  p.41
Upperparts and *unbarred* breast quite *grayish*; several gray tail-bands. Best told by *contrasting rufous in wings*.

**8. Broad-winged**  *B. platypterus*  p.40
No. migrant. *Browner* above than 7; *rusty-barred* breast, 2 *white* tail-bands.

**9. Double-toothed Kite**  p.36
*Harpagus bidentatus*
Smallish. *Gray head* and *rufous chest*. Note rather *blunt* bill, dark *throat-stripe*; legs *not* long. 3 narrow pale tail-bars. Juvenal differs (Pl. II).

**Hawks**  *Accipiter*
*Short*-winged, *long*-legged bird hawks; ♀♀ much larger. Typically look *dark-capped*; *longish* tail crossed by three *wide gray* bands (*more* in young).

**10. Bicolored**  *A. bicolor*  10a. Juvenal p.38
*Never* barred. Adult some shade of *gray below*; thighs *rufous*. Juv. varies from *creamy-white to rufous* below, thighs often *rusty*; may show *"collared"* effect.

**11. Sharp-shinned**  *A. striatus*  p.39
11a. Light Phase   11b. Dark Ph. Juvenal
Variable. Adult either *clear-breasted* (light to dark) or *coarsely mottled rusty*, *not* finely barred or gray below; thighs usually rusty. Young *overlaid* below with *streaking*. Upper altitudes.

**12. Gray-bellied**  *A. poliogaster*  p.38
Larger (esp. ♀), rarer than 10. Underparts *paler* (whitish to light gray), *cheeks usually darker*; thighs *never* rufous. Juvenal (12a) *very different*, resembles undersized Ornate Hawk-Eagle.

**13. Tiny**  *A. superciliosus*  13a. Juvenal p.38
*Small*, esp. ♂. *Finely barred below* in *all* plumages; a *rufous* phase of Juvenal has rusty wings, black-banded rufous tail. SEMICOLLARED *A. collaris* N: Much rarer, *upper* altitude ally of 13; plumages quite similar, see text.

**Forest-Falcons**  *Micrastur*
Rounder-headed than *Accipiter* with *enlarged area of bare facial skin*; tail crossed by several *narrow* white or pale gray bars. Highly *vocal*.

**14. Collared**  p.49
*M. semitorquatus*  Light Ph.
Large; *long-tailed*. Above *blackish* with light *collar, sharply tapered "sideburns"*; cere olive. Thighs *not* rusty.

**15. Slaty-backed**  *M. mirandollei*  S p.49
Much like Juv. of commoner 16 but *clear white below*, tail with 3 bars. Told from 12 by *generic* characters and (usually) *paler* cheeks. Juvenal breast *streaked or mottled* gray, never barred.

**16. Lined**  *M. gilvicollis*  S p.49
Typically *clear white belly* and 2 tail-bars; best told from 17 S by *white iris, red-orange* cere (in adult). Juvenal a bit grayer than 17; *never* fulvous below.

**17. Barred**  *M. ruficollis*  17a. Juvenal p.49
*Well barred* below. S birds more like 16 but *tend* toward 3 tail-bars and barred belly; iris *ochre to brown*, cere *yellow-orange*. Juvenal *brownish* above, white to fulvous below with *scattered barring*; may show *collar*.

5

# PLATE 6   LAPWINGS, RAILS and ALLIES, JACANA

**1. Pied Lapwing** p.67
*Hoploxypterus cayanus*
*Medium*-sized plover with *bold pattern* on mantle and wings; *long, bright red legs*. Unmistakable (cf. Fig. 19).

**2. Southern Lapwing** p.67
*Vanellus chilensis*
*Large, crested* plover. *Flashy pattern in* flight; wings *broad and rounded*.

**Rails** *Rallus*
Medium-sized with *long bill*.

**3. Spotted** *R. maculatus* N p.60
Heavily *spotted, streaked and barred*.

**4. Plain-flanked** *R. wetmorei* N p.60
Flanks *plain*, not barred; occurs along coast in same habitat as next. CLAPPER *R. longirostris* N: Smaller mainland race very similar to 4 but flanks are *lightly barred*.

**Wood-Rails** *Aramides*
*Large*; *long legs, fairly long* bill. Soft parts colorful. *Slaty-to-black rearparts*, rufous primaries.

**5. Gray-necked** *A. cajanea* p.61
*Entire neck gray*. Juvenal duller.

**6. Rufous-necked** *A. axillaris* N p.61
*Smaller*, less widespread than 5. Head and foreneck *rufous-chestnut* (this grayish-brown in Juvenal but rufous patches show later). UNIFORM CRAKE *Amaurolimnas concolor* N: Entirely *rufescent brown*, brighter below; *rather short greenish* bill, red legs. Larger, longer-billed 6 has *blackish* rearparts; smaller 14 has *gray* cheeks and shorter *dark* bill.

**Crakes** *Porzana*

**7. Sora** *Porzana carolina* p.61
No. migrant. *Gray breast, black face* and *yellow* bill; all lacking in Juvenal which is only *medium-sized* crake with *buffy-white* underparts.

**8. Ash-throated** *P. albicollis* p.62
Rather large crake with *gray* breast and *streaked mantle*; leg color dull.

**9. Yellow-breasted** *P. flaviventer* p.62
*Creamy-buff* below; note *facial stripes*, *barred* flanks, *yellow* legs. Very small.

**10. Ocellated Crake** p.63
*Micropygia schomburgkii*
*Ochraceous* below and *ocellated above*. Flanks *plain*; bill and feet small. SPECKLED CRAKE *Coturnicops notata* N: Built like 10. *Very dark* brownish-slate, *speckled and barred* overall with *white*.

**11. Paint-billed Crake** p.63
*Neocrex erythrops*
*Gray* breast; *uniform* olive-brown above. Adult bill basally *orange-red*.

**Crakes** *Laterallus*

**12. Gray-breasted** *L. exilis* N p.62
*Gray* breast; *median* underparts *paler* than 11; broad *chestnut nuchal patch*.

**13. Rusty-flanked** *L. levraudi* N p.62
*Rufous and white* below; flanks *plain*. RUFOUS-SIDED *L. melanophaius* N: Flanks *barred* black-and-white unlike 13.

**14. Russet-crowned** *L. viridis* S p.63
*Entirely rufous* below with *plain* flanks; crown chestnut, *cheeks gray*.

**Gallinules** *Porphyrula*
*Completely white* crissum; large, *bright yellow* feet. Cf. *Gallinula*, text Fig. 16.

**15. Azure** *P. flavirostris* p.64
*Pale blue* on foreparts; bill *greenish*. Juvenal like 16a but *smaller*, mantle more streaked, rump blacker (similar crakes, e.g. 8, *lack* yellow legs).

**16. Purple** *P. martinica* p.64
16a. Juvenal
Note *vivid colors* of adult. Juvenal is *buffy and white* below (drab young *Gallinula* is much *grayer* below).

**17. Sunbittern** *Eurypyga helias* p.65
Distinctive *shape* and *ornate pattern* unmistakable; spread wings display a "sunburst" effect. Often terrestrial.

**18. Sungrebe** *Heliornis fulica* p.65
A Finfoot—note *long "stern"* and *lobed* toes; normally *aquatic*, but seclusive. Upperparts olive-brown, head *and neck boldly striped*.

**19. Wattled Jacana** 19a. Juvenal p.66
*Jacana jacana*
In any plumage note *extremely long toes*, *lemon-yellow* flight feathers.

6

PLATE 7 PIGEONS

**Pigeons** *Columba*
*Large*; typically arboreal, *high*-flying.

**1. Bare-eyed** *C. corensis* N p.93
Rather pale. Extensive *white wing-patch*; bare *orbital skin blue*. SCALY-NAPED *C. squamosa* N (offshore islands): Only *large dark* pigeon in range.

**2. Pale-vented** *C. cayennensis* p.94
Vinaceous *and gray* color with *pale* crissum; bill *dark*.

**3. Scaled** *C. speciosa* p.93
*Scaly neck*, underparts; *pale* crissum. Bill *red* and yellow. ♀ mantle browner.

**4. Ruddy** *C. subvinacea* p.94
Rather *slender*, longish-tailed, *brown*-and-vinaceous forest pigeon. *Slightly ruddy cast* in good light; crissum *dark*, short bill *black*. PLUMBEOUS *C. plumbea: Extremely similar* to 4 but much more local; difficult to separate in field. *Lacks* ruddy cast, tends to be a bit more grayish-pink below.

**5. Band-tailed** *C. fasciata* p.93
*White nuchal-crescent*, yellow bill, *two-toned* gray tail; *upper* altitudes.

**6. Scaled Dove** p.96
*Scardafella squammata*
*Heavily scaled*, pale dove. *Long*, white-edged tail; *russet* in primaries.

**Ground-Doves** *Columbina*
*Small*. *Short* tailed; *russet* in primaries.

**7. Common** *C. passerina* p.95
Both sexes show *spotted-scaling on breast*; bill basally pinkish unlike 9.

**8. Ruddy** *C. talpacoti* p.95
♂ *small* and *rufous*-brown; note wing-spots, *blue-gray* crown. ♀ much *duller*.

**9. Plain-breasted** *C. minuta* p.95
*No* breast spotting. ♀ much like 8 but *obviously smaller*, wings less russet.

**10. Eared Dove** p.94
*Zenaida auriculata*
Note *black wing-spots* and *cheek marks*. Underparts uniform; graduated tail broadly *edged with buff*.

**Ground-Doves** *Claravis*
*Larger*, tail a bit longer than *Columbina*

**11. Blue** *C. pretiosa* p.94
♂ *all bluish-gray*; ♀ has chestnut wing-spots and *contrasting russet* rump and tail. Tails of both sexes edged with black (*no* white).

**12. Maroon-chested** p.96
*C. mondetoura* N
♂ has *maroon breast* and *white-edged* tail; ♀ differs from 11 by fulvous forehead, *purple* wing-spots, *dull* tail with *white tips*. Much scarcer and at *higher* elevations than 11.

**Doves** *Leptotila*
*Uniform* mantle (no spots); *pale forehead* and *belly*; dusky primaries (wing-linings rufous). Outer tail-feathers noticeably *tipped with white*. Often terrestrial.

**13. White-tipped** *L. verreauxi* p.97
*Grayer*, more pallid than very similar 14; crown *lacks* blue tone. Orbital skin blue in N, perhaps (?) red in S.

**14. Gray-fronted** *L. rufaxilla* p.97
Told with care from 13 by more *blue*-gray *crown* and *cinnamon tint* on *cheeks*; mantle a *shade richer* brown. Orbital skin red. Less often seen than 13.

**Quail-Doves** *Geotrygon*
*Plumper* shape than *Leptotila*; *shorter tail without* white tips. Much scarcer or more retiring than others generally.

**15. Ruddy** *G. montana* p.97
More or less distinct *malar stripe*. ♂ *rufous-chestnut*; ♀ and Juvenal are olive-brown above, *fulvous below* with a little chestnut in primaries.

**16. Violaceous** *G. violacea* p.98
Differs from much commoner 15 by combination of *whitish forecrown* and *belly without* a malar stripe. Primaries and tail deep chestnut; note *violet* sheen on back in good light. ♀ duller and darker (cf. *Leptotila*).

**17. Lined** *G. linearis* N p.98
Quite *large*. Note *crown* colors and *narrow*, *black malar stripe*. Juvenal dingy but suggestion of malar stripe.

PLATE 8 MACAWS and LARGER PARROTS

## 7

**Macaws** *Ara*
Very large to rather small in size; note *bare facial skin*.

**1. Blue-and-yellow** *A. ararauna* p.98
*Coloration* unique; unmistakable.

**2. Red-and-green** *A. chloroptera* p.99
Quite similar to 3 but *median* wing-coverts *green*, face *more lined*, red color a bit deeper; often difficult to separate when flying *overhead*.

**3. Scarlet** *A. macao* p.99
*Bright yellow median* wing-coverts.

**4. Military** *A. militaris* N p.99
Only *very large green* macaw.

**5. Chestnut-fronted** *A. severa* p.99
Forehead chestnut, facial skin *white*; underwrist *scarlet*, under surface of flight-feathers and tail *dull red*.

**6. Red-bellied** *A. manilata* p.99
Facial skin *yellow*, abdomen dark red; underside of wings and tail *brassy-gold*.

**7. Red-shouldered** *A. nobilis* p.100
Underwrist *scarlet*, underside of wings and tail *brassy-gold*; most like *A. leucophthalmus* (Plate 9) but note *facial skin*, blue forecrown, *darker bill*.

**Parrots** *Pionus*
*Medium*-sized; rather dark. Note *red crissum*. Wing beats *deeper* than *Amazona*.

**8. Bronze-winged** p.107
*P. chalcopterus* N
*Very dark* body with *bronzy* shoulders; *yellow bill*. Underwings cerulean blue.

**9. Red-billed** *P. sordidus* N p.106
Mantle and underparts more bronzy than 11, often *white* markings on head; best told by *entirely red bill*.

**10. White-capped** *P. seniloides* N p.106
*Rosy-white* forecrown; upperparts *green*.

**11. Blue-headed** *P. menstruus* p.106
*Blue head* and green body; pink spot on bill. Juvenal *mostly green*. Widespread.

**12. Dusky** *P. fuscus* S p.107
*Darker* than 11, *lacking* green; usually some *irregular white markings* about head. Underwings cobalt blue.

**13. Red-fan Parrot** p.109
*Deroptyus accipitrinus* S
*Pale forecrown* and *shaggy nape* (red and blue fan-like ruff usually depressed); note *long dark tail*. Flight distinctive, wing beats alternating with *short sails*.

**Parrots** *Amazona*
*Large*; mainly bright green. Wing beats quite *stiff and shallow*.

**14. Orange-winged** *A. amazonica* p.108
*Yellow cheeks*, yellow *and blue* crown; wing-speculum *orange-red*. Most widespread *Amazona*. BLUE-CHEEKED *A. brasiliensis* S (S.e. Bolivar): *Golden lores* and *blue cheeks*; *light orange* speculum (less reddish than 14).

**15. Yellow-headed** *A. ochrocephala* p.108
More *apple-green*. *Forecrown yellow*; wing-speculum and *shoulder-edge scarlet*.

**16. Yellow-shouldered** p.108
*A. barbadensis* N
From 14 and 15 by yellow *cheeks and lores*, yellow *shoulder-edge*, more scaly effect; note range and habitat.

**17. Mealy** *A. farinosa* p.109
*Largest Amazona*; lacks positive characters. Generally more *glaucous*-green, with *or* without yellow crown-spot; tail more two-toned; *very prominent orbital-ring*; speculum red. RED-LORED *A. autumnalis* N (S. de Perija): Only *Amazona* in range with *red forehead* (*no* yellow); speculum scarlet.

**18. Scaly-naped** *A. mercenaria* N p.108
Occurs at *higher altitude* than other Amazons (but cf. *Pionus*). Mainly *all-green*; wing-speculum normally *lacking*; red median band across outer tail.

**19. Festive** *A. festiva* p.107
Only *Amazona* in range (along Orinoco) with *red forehead*; *lacks* wing-speculum. Look for diagnostic *scarlet lower back*.

NOTE: In Plates 8 and 9, "*underwrist*" denotes the lesser *under* primary-coverts, while "*primary-coverts*" is retained for the *upper* surface.

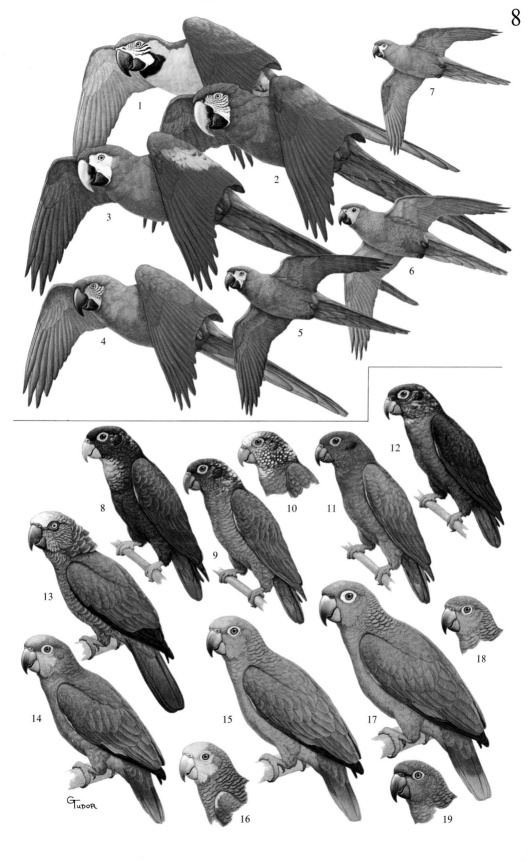

8

GTUDOR

PLATE 9  SMALLER PARROTS

**Parakeets**  *Aratinga*
*Long*, pointed *greenish* tail.

**1. Brown-throated**  *A. pertinax*  p.101
Smallish.  Face  and  chest  *brownish*;
*golden-tawny* ocular area and abdomen.

**2. Sun**  *A. solstitialis*  S  p.100
*Flame-orange* head, *yellow* back. Local.

**3. Blue-crowned**  *A. acuticaudata*  p.100
Forecrown  *azure-blue*;  basal  undertail
tinged with reddish unlike 4 or 5.

**4. White-eyed**  *A. leucophthalmus*  p.100
Underwrist *scarlet* plus yellow; head often
flecked with red. Juvenal *all-green*. *Pale* bill
(cf. *Ara nobilis*).

**5. Scarlet-fronted**  *A. wagleri*  N  p.100
Forecrown more or less *scarlet*.

**Parakeets**  *Pyrrhura*
*Long, dark crimson* tail; blue primaries.

**6. Blood-eared**  *P. hoematotis*  N  p.101
*Less* ornate than 7; *auriculars red.*

**7. Maroon-faced**  *P. leucotis*  N  p.101
Best told from 6 by *whitish auriculars.*

**8. Painted**  *P. picta*  S  p.102
Ornate head with *pale auriculars, scalloped*
breast; belly and rump crimson.

**9. Fiery-shouldered**  *P. egregia*  S  p.102
Tepuis. Mostly *dark green*; tail deep maroon.  Note  *flame-orange  underwrist.*
MAROON-TAILED  *P. melanura*  S: Differs
mainly from 9 by *green* underwrist and
*scarlet primary-coverts.*

**10. Rose-headed**  *P. rhodocephala*  N  p.102
Smaller than 5 with *maroon-red tail*; note
striking *white primary-coverts.*

**Parrotlets**  *Forpus*
*Tiny.* ♂♂ have *blue* in wings; ♀♀ much alike,
*all-green* with *brighter* rump.

**11. Green-rumped**  *F. passerinus*  p.102
*Azure*-blue on ♂ wings; ♀ *brighter* green
than  12,  especially  *rump.*  Most  widespread. SPECTACLED  *F. conspicillatus*  N
(Apure): *Cobalt*-blue on ♂ wings *and rump.*
DUSKY-BILLED  *F. sclateri*  S: *Deep cobalt-
blue* on ♂ wings *and rump.* Rather *dark*
green, forest-based *Forpus* with *dusky*
maxilla (*lower* altitude than 12).

**12. Tepui Parrotlet**  p.104
*Nannopsittaca panychlora*
Darkish green above *including rump*; ocu-
lar area yellowish. Note *range.*

**13. Barred Parakeet**  p.102
*Bolborhynchus lineola*  N
Tail short and pointed; *barring* diagnostic if
seen. *Subtropical* zone.

**Parakeets**  *Brotogeris*
*Pointed* tail; orange chin-spot.

**14. Orange-chinned**  *B. jugularis*  N  p.103
*Brownish shoulders*; underwrist yellow.

**15. Golden-winged**  *B. chrysopterus*  p.103
*Orange  primary-coverts.*  COBALT-WINGED
*B. cyanoptera*  S  (Amazonas): *More and
brighter blue* (no orange) on flight-feathers;
*noticeable* chin-spot.

**Parrotlets**  *Touit*
Note *black on wings*; colorful, *square* tail.
Often much scarcer than *Brotogeris.*

**16. Sapphire-rumped**  *T. purpurata*  S  p.104
*Dusky* crown and *scapulars*; lower back
deep cobalt; outer tail mainly *magenta.*
SCARLET-SHOULDERED  *T. huetii*: Local. No
similar parrot *in range* with *scarlet underwrist*; *fore*face blackish.

**17. Lilac-tailed**  *T. batavica*  p.104
*Yellowish patches* on *black wings.*

**18. Red-winged**  *T. dilectissima*  N  p.105
*Scarlet* on ♂ upper wings; ♀ *shares yellow
underwrist* and yellow in tail.

**19. Rusty-faced Parrot**  p.105
*Hapalopsittaca amazonina*  N
*Face and bend of wing more or less rusty-
red. Upper* altitudes.

**Parrots**  *Pionopsitta*

**20. Saffron-headed**  *P. pyrilia*  N  p.105
*Golden-yellow head*; scarlet underwrist.

**21. Caica**  *P. caica*  S  p.105
*Black head* and tawny *nuchal* collar.

**22. Orange-cheeked**  p.105
*P. barrabandi*  S
*Pionus*-sized. Colorful; note large *orange
malar-patch, scarlet* underwrist.

**23. Black-headed Parrot**  p.105
*Pionites melanocephala*
Black *cap* and *creamy-white* breast.

PLATE 10 CUCKOOS and JAYS

## 9

**Cuckoos** *Coccyzus*

**1. Yellow-billed** *C. americanus* p.111
Widespread No. migrant. *Whitish* below; *rufous in primaries*; *mandible* mostly *yellow*. PEARLY-BREASTED *C. euleri*: Local. *Very similar* to 1 but *no* rufous in wings. BLACK-BILLED *C. erythropthalmus* N: Rare No. migrant. Below *whitish*, mandible *black*, orbital-ring *red*; *obscure* spots on *gray* undertail.

**2. Dark-billed** *C. melacoryphus* p.112
*Rich buff* below. *Blackish auriculars*; mandible *black*; fairly widespread. MANGROVE *C. minor* N (Rare or local; *coastal*): Similar to 2 but somewhat larger; *mandible* mostly *yellow*.

**3. Gray-capped** *C. lansbergi* N p.112
*Browner* above, more *fulvous* below than other *Coccyzus*. Note *slaty cap*, black mandible, blackish tail. Local.

**4. Dwarf** *C. pumilus* p.111
Smallest; tail quite *short*. Contrasting *rufous throat and chest*.

**5. Striped Cuckoo** p.114
*Tapera naevia*
Only cuckoo boldly *streaked above*, including rusty crest and long upper tail-coverts. Note *bill shape* and black *whisker-mark*; common.

**Cuckoos** *Dromococcyx*
*Small head* and *thin* bill; *pointed crest* rusty. *Dark* upperparts *scaled* and very long upper tail-coverts *spotted* with whitish; generally uncommon.

**6. Pavonine** *D. pavoninus* p.115
Configuration *less* distinctive than 7. *Fulvous* breast *lacks* spotting.

**7. Pheasant** *D. phasianellus* p.114
*Larger* than 6 with long and *very broad, graduated* tail; note *spotting on chest*.

NOTE: See Anis (*Crotophaga*), text Fig. 37.

**Cuckoos** *Piaya*
Largely *rufous-chestnut* in color.

**8. Little** *P. minuta* p.112
*Noticeably smallest Piaya* with proportionally *much shorter tail*; bill greenish-yellow, bare orbital-ring red.

**9. Squirrel** *P. cayana* p.112
Bill and orbital-ring *greenish-yellow* in N; orbital-ring *red* in S (cf. 8).

**10. Black-bellied** p.112
*P. melanogaster* S
*Gray cap* and black belly. Note *crimson bill* and bare, *yellow loral-spot*.

**11. Rufous-winged Ground-Cuckoo** p.115
*Neomorphus rufipennis* S
*Very large, terrestrial* forest cuckoo; expressive crest and general behavior recall No. Am. Roadrunner. Note *color pattern* (cf. Cracids). Scarce.

**12. Collared Jay** p.287
*Cyanolyca viridicyana* N
Mostly *deep blue*, crown and throat *brighter*; occurs at *higher* elevations than other "blue" jays.

**Jays** *Cyanocorax*
*Black throat and chest*. Three species with *white tail-tips* do *not* overlap.

**13. Black-chested** p.288
*C. affinis* N
Only jay in range (Maracaibo basin) with *white belly* and *tail-tips*.

**14. Green** *C. yncas* N p.288
*Yellow* belly and *outer* tail-feathers.

**15. Violaceous** *C. violaceus* p.287
Tail *not* white-tipped; *no* malar streak. Belly *violaceous*. AZURE-NAPED *C. heilprini* S (Amazonas): *White tail-tips*. Patterned like 16 but hindcrown and malar streak pale *chalky blue*, belly *violaceous*.

**16. Cayenne** *C. cayanus* S p.288
*White belly*, hindcrown and *tail-tips*.

PLATE 11 HUMMINGBIRDS

## 10

**Sunangels** *Heliangelus*
Note *short* bill; *light chest-band*. ♀♀ have *dark, rusty-flecked* gorgets. Andes.

1. **Orange-throated** *H. mavors* N p.151
   Rich buff breast-band; gorget *orange*.

2. **Merida** *H. spencei* N (Merida) p.151
   *White* breast-band; gorget *violet-rose*.
   AMETHYST-THROATED *H. amethysticollis* N:
   Much like 2 but *no* overlap.

3. **Tyrian Metaltail** p.153
   *Metallura tyrianthina* N
   Very short bill; ample tail metallic coppery-purple. ♂ gorget emerald; ♀ throat fulvous. PERIJA *M. iracunda*: Very local in S. de Perija; see text.

4. **Bronze-tailed Thornbill** p.153
   *Chalcostigma heteropogon* N (s. Tachira)
   *Very short* bill; *ample* tail *bronzy*.

5. **Purple-backed Thornbill** p.153
   *Ramphomicron microrhynchum* N (Andes)
   Tiny bill. ♂ purple above; ♀ see text.

**Pufflegs** *Eriocnemis*
Straight bill. *Large* white thigh *puffs*.

6. **Coppery-bellied** *E. cupreoventris* p.152
   N (Andes). *Glittering belly orange-gold*; crissum violet. ♀ similar.

7. **Glowing** *E. vestitus* N (Andes) p.152
   Rump more glittering than 6. Emerald belly; small violet gorget. ♀ duller.

**Brilliants** *Heliodoxa*
♂ gorgets *emerald*. Ample, notched black tail. ♀♀ heavily disked green below.

8. **Violet-fronted** *H. leadbeateri* N p.148
   ♂ frontlet violet (cf. *Thalurania*).

9. **Velvet-browed** *H. xanthogonys* S p.148
   Tepuis. ♂ frontlet *emerald*.

**Lancebills** *Doryfera*
Long straight bill. Plumage *quite dark*.

10. **Blue-fronted** p.132
    *D. johannae* S (Tepuis)
    ♂ blackish; frontlet violet. ♀ like 11.

11. **Green-fronted** *D. ludoviciae* N p.132
    Merida. *Very dull*; ♂ frontlet *green*.

**Violetears** *Colibri*
Violet *auriculars*. Dark distal *tail-band*.

12. **Brown** *C. delphinae* p.137
    Bill *shortish*. Dingy. *Dull* gorget outlined by whitish (cf. 17); rump *rusty*.

13. **Green** *C. thalassinus* N p.137
    Tail-tips *aquamarine*; *smaller* than 14.

14. **Sparkling** *C. coruscans* p.137
    Glorified version of 13: *larger* with *chin and belly* also violet.

**Mangos** *Anthracothorax*
Bill *a bit* decurved. Tail *deep magenta*. ♀♀ all alike: with *black median breast-stripe*.

15. **Black-throated** *A nigricollis* p.138
    ♂ extensively black below. GREEN-THROATED *A. viridigula* N (Delta): ♂ differs by *large emerald gorget*.

16. **Green-breasted** *A. prevostii* N p.138
    ♂ black throat narrower with wider green border. Much more local than 15.

17. **Long-billed Starthroat** p.151
    *Heliomaster longirostris*
    Long bill. Violet-red gorget outlined with whitish; ♀ similar but duller.

18. **Mountain Velvetbreast** p.149
    *Lafresnaya lafresnayi* N (Andes)
    Decurved bill. Tail mostly white or (s.w. Tachira) buff; ♂ has black belly.

**Sabrewings** *Campylopterus*

19. **Lazuline** *C. falcatus* N p.136
    Decurved bill. Tail mainly chestnut. Violet-blue of ♂ much reduced in ♀.

20. **Gray-breasted** *C. largipennis* S p.136
    Uniformly gray below; large white tail-tips. BUFF-BREASTED *C. duidae* S: Tepuis. Drab buff below; tail coppery with large buff tips.

21. **White-tailed** p.136
    *C. ensipennis* N (east)
    Huge white tail-tips; ♀ duller.

22. **Rufous-breasted** p.136
    *C. hyperythrus* S
    Tepuis; ally of duidae but no overlap. Uniform rufous below including tail.

23. **Violet-chested Hummingbird** p.149
    *Sternoclyta cyanopectus* N
    Bill quite long. Tail bronzy olive. ♂ chest-patch violet; ♀ belly rusty.

24. **Buff-tailed Coronet** p.151
    *Boissonneaua flavescens* N (Andes)
    Short bill. Ample tail mostly buff.

25. **Collared Inca** p.150
    *C. torquata* N
    Long bill. Bold white breast-plate in ♂ ♀. Andes (plumage blacker in Tachira).

26. **Bronzy Inca** p.150
    *C. coeligena* N
    Long straight bill. Dark purplish bronze above; throat streaky.

**Starfrontlets** *Coeligena*
Long straight bill. Fulvous throat in ♀.

27. **Golden-bellied** *C. bonapartei* N p.150
    Distinct wing-patch and most of tail (in Andes) rufous. Belly orange-gold.

28. **Blue-throated** *C. helianthea* N p.150
    S.w. Tachira. ♂ very dark; belly rose (duller in ♀). Rump glittering green.

GTUDOR

PLATE 12  HUMMINGBIRDS (Nos. 23-34 cont'd next page)

**Coquettes**  *Lophornis*
*Small. Pale rump-bar. ♂♂* ornamented.

**1. Spangled**  *L. stictolopha*  N  p.140
♂ crest and much of tail *rich rufous; short red* bill. ♀ *forehead* rufous.

**2. Tufted**  *L. ornata*  p.139
Like 1 but ♂ has *long cinnamon cheek-plumes.* ♀ mainly *rufescent* below.

**3. Peacock**  *L. pavonina*  S (Tepuis)  p.140
♂ *green* cheek-plumes *boldly spotted black.* ♀ throat and breast *streaked.*

**4. Festive**  *L. chalybea*  S  p.140
♂ *green* plumes *dotted white;* ♀ like 5.

**5. Black-bellied Thorntail**  p.140
*Popelairia langsdorffi*  S
♂ distinct. ♀ has *rump-bar; white malar* area set off by *black throat.*

**6. Racket-tailed Coquette**  p.141
*Discosura longicauda*  S
♂ distinctive. ♀ much like 5.

**Woodstars**
*Calliphlox, Chaetocercus, Acestrura*
*Small. Chest-band;* ♂ gorgets *violet-rose.* ♀♀ *rufescent* below. *No rump-bar.*

**7. Amethyst**  *C. amethystina*  p.155
♂ tail *deeply forked.* ♀ throat *flecked.*

**8. Rufous-shafted**  *Ch. jourdanii*  N  p.156
Bill and ♂ tail *(different shape) shorter* than 7; gorget often *rose-red.*

**9. Gorgeted**  *A. heliodor*  N  p.155
♂ deeper green than 8, tail *shorter;* gorget *streamered.* ♀ *rump* rufous.

**Emeralds**  *Chlorostilbon*
*Small; glittering green.* Many difficult to separate. ♀♀ *pale grayish* below with tail-tips; note *dark facial "mask."*

**10. Blue-tailed**  *C. mellisugus*  p.141
Tail *steel-blue;* shortish bill *all*-black. RED-BILLED *C. gibsoni* N: ♂ tail more forked; *mandible reddish.*

**11. Narrow-tailed**  *C. stenura*  N  p.142
Tail *green* (outer feathers very narrow). GREEN-TAILED *C. alice* N and SHORT-TAILED *C. poortmanni* N: Both *green-tailed* like 11. None safely told apart but see *ranges.* COPPERY *C. russatus* N (S. de Perija): Tail *coppery-gold.*

**Emeralds**  *Amazilia*
*Variable amount of white* mixed with green on underparts; another difficult group.

**12. White-chested**  *A. chionopectus*  p.145
*Throat sharply white,* tail *bronze-olive;* mandible *all*-black (unlike next two). PLAIN-BELLIED *A. leucogaster* N (Delta): *Outer* tail blacker.

**13. Versicolored**  *A. versicolor*  p.145
Mainly S. One race has *blue crown.*

**14. Glittering-throated**  *A. fimbriata*  p.145
Best told by white abdomen *penetrating narrowly into median* breast; common. SAPPHIRE-SPANGLED *A. lactea* S (Bolivar): Like 14 but gorget *dull violet-blue.* TACHIRA *A. distans* N (s.w. Tachira): Very rare, see text.

**15. Blue-chinned Sapphire**  p.141
*Chlorestes notatus*
*Unforked, steel-blue* tail; note *blue chin, reddish* mandible. ♀ disked with green below, *lacks* tail-tipping.

**16. Shining-green Hummingbird**  p.143
*Lepidopyga goudoti*  N
Tail rather *forked,* steel-blue with *middle* feathers *green. Bluish cast* to bright green underparts. ♀ duller.

**17. Wedge-billed Hummingbird**  p.154
*Schistes geoffroyi*  N
*White pectoral-patches; coppery* rump, *Colibri*-like tail. Note *bill shape.*

**18. Speckled Hummingbird**  p.147
*Adelomyia melanogenys*  N
*Hermit-like* face pattern, *speckled* throat. *Buffy* underparts, tail-tips.

**Hummingbirds**  *Amazilia*
Green with *contrasting* rump and tail.

**19. Rufous-tailed**  *A. tzacatl*  N  p.147
Rump *and tail rufous;* bill basally pink.

**20. Green-bellied**  *A. viridigaster*  N  p.147
Much like 22 but tail *purple* or (in e. Bolivar) *purplish-chestnut.*

**21. Copper-rumped**  *A. tobaci*  p.146
Tail *steel-blue;* conspicuous, *coppery lower back* and rump.

**22. Steely vented**  *A. saucerottei*  N  p.146
Tail *steel-blue* with *dull rusty tinge* on *rump.* ♀ duller, tail *untipped.*

*Plate 12   (Cont'd)*

**23. Fork-tailed Woodnymph**  p.142
*Thalurania furcata*
Note *emerald* gorget, *violet belly* (and *crown* in N.w.); *ample well-forked* tail. ♀ *grayish* below (*belly dark* in N.w).

**24. Golden-tailed Sapphire**  p.144
*Chrysuronia oenone*   N
*Coppery-golden rump and tail.* ♂ has *violet head;* ♀ green-disked below.

**Sapphires**  *Hylocharis*
♂ bills *bright red.* ♀♀ much duller.

**25. Rufous-throated**  *H. sapphirina*  S  p.143
♂ has *purple* gorget. ♀ *shares* rusty *chin* and *coppery-chestnut tail.*

**26. White-chinned**  *H. cyanus*  p.143
♂ has *purple hood* and *blue-black* tail. ♀ much like 22 but tail *tipped gray.*

**27. Buffy Hummingbird**  p.145
*Leucippus fallax*   N
Rather *grayish cast* above, decidedly *buffy* on underparts. Arid coastal area.

**28. Ruby-topaz Hummingbird**  p.139
*Chrysolampis mosquitus*
♂ unique. *Rufous tail* reduced in ♀; *grayish* below with *coppery sheen* above.

**29. Violet-headed Hummingbird**  p.139
*Klais guimeti*   N
♂ has *deep violet hood.* Note *white post-ocular spot* (not streak) in ♂♀.

**Goldenthroats**  *Polytmus*
Above more *bronzy* green, below more *golden* green, tail more *emerald*-green.

**30. Green-tailed**  *P. theresiae*  S  p.144
Some *white* below and on tail-*tips* in ♀.

**31. White-tailed**  *P. guainumbi*  p.144
Most golden. Bill *reddish. Facial stripes, edges and tips* of ample tail *white.* ♀ rather *buffy* below (cf. 27).

**32. Tepui**  *P. milleri*  S (Tepuis)  p.144
Much like a *large* 30 but with *broad, white basal undertail band;* bill black.

**33. White-vented Plumeleteer**  p.147
*Chalybura buffonii*   N
Rather *large* and dull; bill *longish.* Told by *prominent snowy-white crissum.*

**34. White-necked Jacobin**  p.137
*Florisuga mellivora*
♀ throat *noticeably scaly;* belly white.

# PLATE 13  HUMMINGBIRDS

**1. White-necked Jacobin**  p.137
*Florisuga mellivora*
♂ has *nuchal-patch,* belly and *almost entire tail* snowy-white; ♀ on Pl. 12.

**2. Gould's Jewelfront**  p.148
*Polyplancta aurescens*  S
Broad *rufous breast-band;* much *chestnut* in tail. ♀ duller (cf. *Threnetes*).

**3. Crimson Topaz**  p.149
*Topaza pella*  S (Bolivar)
*Very large,* colorful. ♂ has *tail-streamers;* green ♀ has *fiery red* gorget. Note *rufous* in tails. FIERY TOPAZ *T. pyra* S (Amazonas): Rather like 3 but *lacks* rufous in tail.

**4. Booted Racket-tail**  p.152
*Ocreatus underwoodii*   N
♂ distinct. Emerald-like ♀ has tail *forked,* more *blue*-green, tips *white.*

**5. Bearded Helmetcrest**  p.154
*Oxypogon guerinii*   N
*Very short* bill. Duller ♀ differs from Thornbills by *white on throat and chest.*

**6. Fiery-tailed Awlbill**  p.139
*Avocettula recurvirostris*   S
*Recurved* bill. ♂ *undertail fiery copper.* ♀ resembles *small* ♀ Mango.

**7. Scissor-tailed Hummingbird**  p.148
*Hylonympha macrocerca*   N
Told from *shorter*-billed 11 by *lack of glitter* on ♂ *upper-tail; longer forked* tail of ♀. Paria Pen., Sucre.

**8. Green-tailed Trainbearer**  p.153
*Lesbia nuna*   N
*Short* bill. *Smaller* than 11, *long tail emerald.* ♀ from similars by *noticeably long* tail (½ length of ♂).

**9. Sword-billed Hummingbird**  p.151
*Ensifera ensifera*   N
*Amazingly long* bill unmistakable.

**10. Black-eared Fairy**  p.154
*Heliothryx aurita*
*Underparts* and most of *rather long, graduated* tail immaculate snowy white. Note *short* bill and dark auriculars.

**11. Long-tailed Sylph**  p.154
*Aglaiocercus kingi*   N
♂ tail all or partially *glittering violet-blue;* crown *emerald.* ♀ has *cinnamon belly* (usually) and *longish,* shining *blue*-green upper-tail.

K.D. de Phelpe

PLATE 14 HERMITS and TROGONS

**Hermits** *Phaethornis*
*Long decurved* bill, strong *facial pattern* (except 6). Two types: *Larger* with *very elongated white tail-tips*; and *small* with *much shorter* buff or white *tips*.

**1. Pale-bellied** *P. anthophilus* N p.134
*Lacks dark submalar* area, thus accentuating *auriculars*; median throat *dusky*.

**2. Green** *P. guy* N p.133
*Dark green* above (not bronzy olive); below quite dingy. Light facial lines and median throat-streak *rufescent*.

**3. White-bearded** *P. hispidus* p.134
*Sharp white throat-streak* (face-lines weaker). Quite *gray including rump*.

**4. Sooty-capped** *P. augusti* p.134
Facial-lines *strong. Rump rufous;* base of decidedly *long* tail *bronzy*.

**5. Long-tailed** *P. superciliosus* p.133
Facial-lines and median throat-streak *buffy.* Rump *rusty* but *basal* tail *dark*.

**6. Straight-billed** *P. bourcieri* S p.134
Face-pattern weaker than 5. Best told from allies by *nearly straight bill*.

**7. Dusky-throated** *P. squalidus* S p.135
*Throat very dusky; lacks* obvious rufescence even on rump (8 very local in S).

**8. Little** *P. longuemareus* p.135
*Rufescence variable* but *all* races have *dusky-streaked throat* (unlike 9 or 10).

**9. Gray-chinned** *P. griseogularis* p.135
In N see 8. In S, *very similar* to ♀ 10.

**10. Reddish** *P. ruber* S p.135
Quite *rufous.* ♀ *paler* than ♂, *black breast-band* reduced to *indistinct* patch.

**11. Rufous-breasted Hermit** p.132
*Glaucis hirsuta*
*Long decurved* bill. Dull *russet below*; basal tail largely *chestnut* (cf. Pl. 11).

**Barbthroats** *Threnetes*
Hermit-like head but note *blackish chin* bordered below by *cinnamon-buff*.

**12. Pale-tailed** *T. leucurus* S p.132
*Under*tail appears *largely buffy white.*

**13. Band-tailed** *T. ruckeri* N p.133
*Under*tail has *wide white base* and *tips*.

**Quetzals** *Pharomachrus*
*Larger, more robust* than (red-bellied) trogons; green *lanceolate plumes* above, *no* white chest-band. ♀♀ are mixed green-and-brown on breast. Note ranges.

**14. Golden-headed** *P. auriceps* N p.157
♂ frontal crest *less* developed than 15 (bill more exposed). *Undertail black* or nearly so in *both* sexes. PAVONINE *P. pavoninus* S: Only quetzal *in range.* Very similar to 14 except ♀ undertail shows *some* barring; maxilla usually daubed with red.

**15. Crested** *P. antisianus* N p.156
♂ shows *bushy frontal* crest. Undertail *white* in ♂, *noticeably barred* in ♀. Occurs with 14. WHITE-TIPPED *P. fulgidus* N: Only quetzal *in range.* Undertail *broadly tipped* with white in ♂, much like 15 in ♀.

**Trogons** *Trogon*

**16. White-tailed** *T. viridis* p.157
Larger. ♂ crown and breast *violet*, undertail *broadly tipped* with white; ♀ mostly *slate-gray* with *barred* undertail. Bare eye-ring *pale blue* in both sexes.

**17. Violaceous** *T. violaceus* p.159
♂ differs from 16 by *barred* undertail, bright *yellow* eye-ring. ♀ much like 16 (white chest-band diffused); best told by *smaller size* and *broken white* (feathered) eye-ring.

**18. Black-tailed** *T. melanurus* p.157
Larger. Undertail *blackish-slate.* ♀ only *red*-belly with *slate-gray* foreparts; tail may show *faint* barring.

**19. Masked** *T. personatus* p.158
♂ *very similar* to 20 but *white* barring on undertail *very fine* (uppertail quite *bronzy* in S races); ♀ more easily told by *well-demarcated black* facial mask and *all-yellow* bill.

**20. Collared** *T. collaris* p.158
♂ undertail *noticeably barred.* ♀ foreparts *brown*; tail *chestnut above*, freckled below. Note *dusky maxilla.*

**21. Black-throated** *T. rufus* S p.158
♂ crown and breast *metallic green* (violet-blue in 17); eye-ring *pale blue.* ♀ only *yellow*-belly with *brown* foreparts; uppertail *chestnut.*

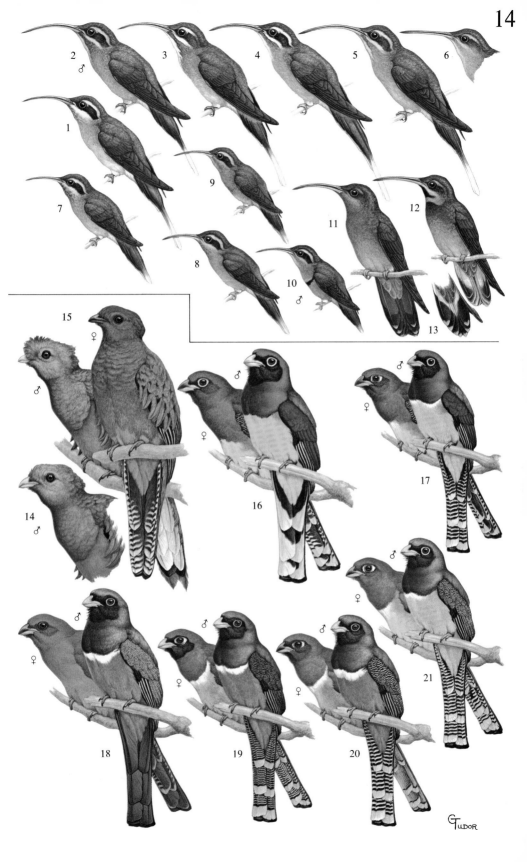

14

PLATE 15 PUFFBIRDS, JACAMARS and KINGFISHERS

**1. Swallow-wing** p.167
*Chelidoptera tenebrosa*
Unmistakable, *blackish* puffbird with *white rump* and *short tail*. Social; conspicuous, often aerial.

**Puffbirds** *Notharchus*
Boldly patterned in *black and white*.

**2. White-necked** *N. macrorhynchus* p.164
*Large*; narrow forecrown in far e. race.

**3. Brown-banded** p.165
*N ordii* S (Amazonas)
*Medium*-sized. *Narrow* white forehead (no overlap with e. race of 2); *lower part* of breast-band *brown*. Rare.

**4. Pied** *N. tectus* S p.165
*Small*. White *eyebrow*, *scapular patches* and spotted crown.

**5. Russet-throated Puffbird** p.166
*Hypnelus ruficollis*
Two "types": widespread *bicinctus* only *double-banded* puffbird. More *russet*-throated N.w. races are *single-banded* (lacking upper); none similar in range.

**Puffbirds** *Malacoptila*
Characterized by more pointed bill encircled with *puffy white* "whiskers." Underparts more or less *streaky*.

**6. Moustached** *M. mystacalis* N p.166
No similar puffbird in range.

**7. White-chested** p.166
*M. fusca* S (Amazonas)
Heavily *streaked*; *white chest-crescent*.

**8. Rusty-breasted Nunlet** p.167
*Nonnula rubecula* S (Amazonas)
*Very small and plain*, unlike any other. Note large head with white eye-ring.

**Puffbirds** *Bucco*

**9. Spotted** *B. tamatia* S p.165
Throat *cinnamon*; black *malar patch*. Coarsely *spotted or barred* black below.

**10. Chestnut-capped** p.165
*B. macrodactylus* S
*Smaller*. Crown *chestnut*; note *single*, well-defined *black chest-band*.

**11. Collared** *B. capensis* S p.165
*Cinnamon-rufous face*, mostly *rich orange bill*; *single* black chest-band.

NOTE: See also *large, slaty* Nunbirds (*Monasa*) on Plate 25.

**Jacamars** *Brachygalba*
*Small* with rather *short tail*.

**12. Pale-headed** *B. goeringi* N p.163
Occurs only with very different 16.

**13. Brown** *B. lugubris* S p.162
*Brownish*; throat *clouded*, belly white.

**Jacamars** *Galbula*
♀♀ (except 18) differ by *buffy* throat.

**14. Bronzy** *G. leucogastra* S p.163
*Dark* (metallic purplish bronze); note *clear-cut white/buff throat* and *belly*.

**15. Green-tailed** *G. galbula* S p.163
Belly deep *rufous*; undertail *blackish*.

**16. Rufous-tailed** *G. ruficauda* p.163
Much like 15 but longer tail is *rufous underneath*. Rather local in S.

**17. Yellow-billed** *G. albirostris* S p.163
Note mainly *bright yellow bill* (mandible only in s. Amazonas race). *Lacks* metallic green breast-band.

**18. Paradise** *G. dea* S p.164
*Dark* body; *very long, tapering tail*.

**19. Great Jacamar** p.164
*Jacamerops aurea* S
*Larger* and huskier; much more *massive*, *slightly arched bill*. *Lacks* metallic breast-band; no white crescent in ♀.

**Kingfishers** *Chloroceryle*
Dark metallic *green* above (cf. *Ceryle*). Note *sizes*; ♀♀ have *green chest-band*.

**20. Amazon** *C. amazona* p.160
Bill and crest somewhat more developed than 21. Almost *no* wing-spots, tail *only notched* with white. ♀ has *single, broken* green band (no rufous).

**21. Green** *C. americana* p.161
Much *smaller*. White *spotting on wing*; outer *tail-bases white* (often evident in flight). ♀ has *double* bands below.

**22. Pygmy** *C. aenea* p.161
*Tiny*. *Rufous-chestnut below* merges into paler throat; note *white abdomen*.

**23. Green-and-rufous** *C. inda* p.161
Much *larger* edition of 22 but rufous *extends to crissum* (♂ lacks chest-band); wing-spotting *minute*.

J. GWYNNE

PLATE 16 BARBETS and TOUCANS

**1. Red-headed Barbet** p.168
*Eubucco bourcierii* N
Small (6″) and *colorful*. Both sexes have *green mantle* and *black ocular area* encircling *stout yellowish bill*.

**2. Black-spotted Barbet** p.168
*Capito niger* S 2a. N.e. Bolivar race
Ornate. ♂ has *clear* breast, ♀ *heavily spotted* with black below. *Head colors differ* among 3 races (S.w. Amazonas race has orange forecrown, red throat).

**Toucanets** *Aulacorhynchus*
Small, *grass-green* toucans. Subtropical.

**3. Yellow-billed** *A. calorhynchus* N p.169
Maxilla mainly *yellowish*. *Throat much grayer* than 4. *Lacks* chestnut. (Race of *sulcatus*, see text.) GROOVE-BILLED *A. sulcatus* N: Maxilla mainly *deep reddish*; no overlap with other "red-billed" *Aulacorhynchus*.

**4. Emerald** *A. prasinus* N p.169
*Crissum and tail-tips chestnut*. Maxilla mainly *yellow*; throat *much whiter*, more contrasting than 3.

**5. Crimson-rumped** p.170
*A. haematopygus* N
No other *in range* (S. de Perija) has maxilla mainly *deep reddish*. Greenish throat, chestnut tail-tips, crimson rump-patch. CHESTNUT-TIPPED *A. derbianus* S (Tepuis): *No other in range*. Bill most like 5; body nearest 3 but tail tipped with chestnut.

**Aracaris** *Pteroglossus*
*Dark hood*. Yellow *belly* usually *banded* with red and/or black; rump crimson.

**6. Collared** *P. torquatus* N p.170
Chest with black *spot or patch*.

**7. Many-banded** *P. pluricinctus* p.170
Chest with *complete* black *band*, not patch (*double*-banded). E. of Andes.

**8. Black-necked** *P. aracari* p.170
Breast *clear yellow* (no black); belly-band *pure red* unlike 6 and 7.

**9. Green** *P. viridis* S p.170
*Small*. Underparts *clear yellow without* bands; bill *more colorful* (red, etc.).

**10. Ivory-billed** *P. flavirostris* S p.171
Yellow confined to *belly*. *Entire bill* appears largely *ivory white*.

**Toucanets** *Selenidera*
Sexes *differ*; throat and breast of ♂♂ are *black*. Both have *golden ear-tufts*.

**11. Guianan** *S. culik* S p.171
Bill *quite dull*. ♀ largely *gray* below.

**12. Tawny-tufted** *S. nattereri* S p.171
*More colorful* bill ornately *blotched*. Also differs by *golden-orange flanks* (♂) or *chestnut* underparts (♀).

**13. Black-billed Mountain-Toucan** p.171
*Andigena nigrirostris* N
*Powder-blue below* with white throat. Bill *black*; mantle olive-brown. Local.

**Toucans** *Ramphastos*
*Large* with *big bill*. Note bill pattern, color of bib (i.e., throat and chest) and rump (i.e., upper tail-coverts).

**14. Black-mandibled** *R. ambiguus* N p.173
Maxilla *diagonally bisected* black-and-yellow. Bib uniformly *sulphur-yellow; rump white*. KEEL-BILLED *R. sulfuratus* N (N.w. Zulia): Body like 14; vivid *greenish bill* with orange wedge and *crimson tip* unlike any other.

NOTE: Following 3 forms are *closely related*. Ranges for most part do not overlap, but some hybrids occur.

**15. Channel-billed** *R. vitellinus* p.172
Bib suffused with *rich golden-orange; rump red*. Bill largely black *including ridge and tip*. Mainly in S.

**16. Citron-throated** p.172
*R. citreolaemus* N
Bill largely black with *yellowish ridge and tip*. Bib and rump *pale sulphur-yellow*. Maracaibo basin.

**17. Yellow-ridged** *R. culminatus* p.172
Bill *much like* 16. Bib white; rump golden-yellow. Southeast of Andes.

**18. Cuvier's** *R. cuvieri* S (Amazonas) p.173
Although allied to 19, *very similar to* and occurs with somewhat smaller 17. Bill usually *larger and proportionately longer*; voice different.

**19. Red-billed** *R. tucanus* p.173
Differs from similars by main portion of bill being *dark wine-red* rather than black; *rump yellow*. ORANGE-BILLED *R. aurantiirostris* S: Apparently a local variant of 19.

16

PLATE 17 WOODPECKERS

NOTE: Most ♀♀ differ from ♂♂ only in *lack* of red·forecrown and/or moustaches.

**Woodpeckers** *Celeus*
"*Chestnut*-colored" genus with prominent *bushy crest*, *pale ivory-yellow bill*.

**1. Chestnut** *C. elegans* p.176
*Large* and dark *without* barring; rump buff-yellow. Crest color *varies* among races from chestnut to cinnamon.

**2. Scale-breasted** *C. grammicus* S p.177
*Medium*-sized. Rather *uniform, barred* chestnut; rump *unbarred* buff-yellow.

**3. Waved** *C. undatus* p.177
*Medium*. Head appears *paler* than body, contrasts with *dark breast*; *bold barring* extends onto *rump and tail*.

**4. Ringed** *C. torquatus* S p.177
*Large* with paler head, *sharply black breast*; Amazonas race *heavily barred* on mantle and belly (*twice* size of 3).

**5. Cream-colored** *C. flavus* p.177
Mostly *yellow-buff* coloration.

**6. Spot-breasted Woodpecker** p.175
*Chrysoptilus punctigula*
*White cheeks*; barred *back* and *finely spotted*, yellowish underparts.

**Woodpeckers** *Piculus*

**7. Golden-olive** *P. rubiginosus* p.176
*Whitish cheeks*; gray forecrown (red nape in ♀). Completely *barred below*.

**8. Golden-green** *P. chrysochloros* p.176
S race has barred throat (and olive crown in ♀); N race (8a) has plain, brassy-gold throat (and crown in ♀). All told by well-defined *yellow gape stripe below olive cheek*.

**9. Yellow-throated** *P. flavigula* S p.176
*Golden-yellow cheeks* and throat, *scalloped* rather than barred effect below. ♀ forecrown brassy gold; ♀ (and Amazonas race ♂) lacks moustache.

**10. Crimson-mantled** *P. rivolii* N p.175
*Cheeks white*. Mantle *crimson*; belly buff-yellow; crown may be blacker.

**Woodpeckers** *Veniliornis*
*Smaller* than *Piculus*. Face pattern usually *weaker*; ♀♀ lack red on crown.

**11. Yellow-vented** *V. dignus* N p.180
*Pronounced face pattern* (cheeks *dark*); barred breast, *yellowish belly*. Local.

**12. Smoky-brown** *V. fumigatus* N p.178
*Unbarred* brownish with *paler cheeks*.

**13. Red-rumped** *V. kirkii* p.179
Extensive *red rump* in both sexes.

**14. Little** *V. passerinus* p.179
Quite small. *No* golden nape. *Narrowly* pale-barred below (grayer in Orinoco race); *indistinct* whitish *malar-stripe*.

**15. Golden-collared** *V. cassini* S p.179
*Golden nape* and *wing-dots*; *strongly barred* below (black and buffy-white). RED-STAINED *V. affinis* S (Amazonas): *Very similar* to 15: duller golden nape, darker face and *bill*, fairly heavy barring (dark olive-brown and buff); *lacks* yellow wing-dots (but red staining obscure). Cf. also 14.

**Woodpeckers** *Melanerpes*
Distinctive patterns with *white rump*.

**16. Red-crowned** *M. rubricapillus* p.178
Black-and-white "*zebra*" barring above.

**17. Yellow-tufted** *M. cruentatus* p.178
Only smallish "*black*" species. A local color variant in S *lacks* yellow brow.

**18. Lineated Woodpecker** p.178
*Dryocopus lineatus*
Scapular stripes do *not meet* on back; *white* gape-stripe *narrow*.

**Woodpeckers** *Campephilus*
Throat *solid black*/red (*streaked* in 18).

**19. Crimson-crested** p.180
*C. melanoleucos*
White scapular stripes normally *meet* on back to form "V." Note ♂ *cheek spot*, *broad white gape-stripe* of ♀.

**20. Powerful** *C. pollens* N p.181
Scapular stripes *converge* into *extensive white rump*. ♂ face not unlike ♀♀ of 18 or 19; ♀ has *crown entirely black*. Bill *blackish*. S.w. Táchira.

**21. Red-necked** *C. rubricollis* S p.180
Back *entirely black*. Underparts and inner primaries *pale rufous*; *head and neck red* or nearly so in both sexes.

17

PLATE 18 PICULETS and WOODCREEPERS

**Piculets** *Picumnus*
Easily told by *color or pattern below*; ♀
crowns *all* white-dotted. Also note *ranges*.
Rare *P. nigropunctatus* in text.

**1. Chestnut** *P. cinnamomeus* N p.174

**2. Olivaceous** *P. olivaceus* N p.174

**3. Scaled** *P. squamulatus* N p.174

**4. White-bellied** *P. spilogaster* p.174

**5. Golden-spangled** *P. exilis* S p.175

**6. Olivaceous Woodcreeper** p.183
*Sittasomus griseicapillus*
*Small. Short* bill; *olive-gray* foreparts.

**7. Wedge-billed Woodcreeper** p.183
*Glyphorhynchus spirurus*
*Small. Very short, wedge-shaped* bill.

**8. Long-tailed Woodcreeper** p.182
*Deconychura longicauda* S
*Rather short, straight bill. Indistinct* buffy
*eyebrow* and *chest spotting.* SPOT-
THROATED *D. stictolaema* S Barely separa-
ble in field; see text.

**Woodcreepers** *Dendrocincla*
Bill *straight.* Essentially *unpatterned.*

**9. Plain-brown** *D. fuliginosa* p.181
Commonest of genus. In S (notably e.
Bolivar race) tends to *paler throat,* indistinct
*postocular streak;* all show *dusky malar*
smudge. TYRANNINE *D. tyrannina* N (w.
Tachira): *Larger* than 9; vague pale throat
streaks. Occurs at *higher altitudes.*

**10. White-chinned** *D. merula* S p.182
Like 9 but *deeper, more uniform* brown on
*face;* upper throat *sharply white.*

**11. Ruddy** *D. homochroa* N p.182
Warmer brown than 9 with *tawnier throat;*
decidedly *rufous-chestnut* tone on *crown*
and shoulders.

**Woodcreepers** *Lepidocolaptes*
*Rather pale* bill more *slender, decurved* than
allies. Back appears *unstreaked.*

**12. Streak-headed** *L. souleyetii* p.186
Crown *profusely streaked.* LINEATED *L. albolineatus* S: Much like 12 but crown *plain*
or, in n.e. Bolivar, *finely spotted* (overall not
unlike 13).

**13. Spot-crowned** *L. affinis* N p.187
Crown *spotted. Higher altitude* than 12; *distinct white streaks* below (cf. 14).

**Woodcreepers** *Xiphorhynchus*

**14. Olive-backed** *X. triangularis* N p.186
More *olivaceous. Unstreaked* back; obviously *spotted below.* Subtropical.

**15. Buff-throated** *X. guttatus* p.186
Widespread. *Longish, dark* bill. *Back* appears *streaked, throat* buffy; in n.e. breast
streaks much more *guttate.*

**16. Chestnut-rumped** p.186
*X. pardalotus* S
Much like 15 but slightly smaller; *throat
deeper fulvous* and *vaguely streaked.*
OCELLATED *X. ocellatus* S (Amazonas): Similar to allies (15-17) but *back* streaking *almost nonexistent.*

**17. Striped** *X. obsoletus* p.185
*Entire back streaked;* throat *whitish.* Culmen *not* as straight as S races of 18.

**18. Straight-billed** *X. picus* p.185
Bill *quite pale, culmen straight.* In N races,
*broad white throat* and *eyebrow;* S races
*less* distinctive, nearer 17.

**Woodcreepers** *Dendrocolaptes*
*Large. Sturdy* bill *nearly straight.*

**19. Barred** *D. certhia* p.184
*Finely barred* below, *crown* appearing *spotted.* S race bill may look *reddish.*

**20. Black-banded** *D. picumnus* p.184
*Crown, throat* and *chest streaked. Lower
underparts barred,* variably from *light* (race
shown) to *heavy* (S race).

**21. Strong-billed Woodcreeper** p.184
*Xiphocolaptes promeropirhynchus*
*Very large. Massive* bill *slightly decurved.*
Note *clear upper* throat and *dark malar;
belly streaked* (cf. 20).

**22. Red-billed Woodcreeper** p.183
*Hylexetastes perrotii* S (e. Bolivar)
*Lacks* barring of 19. *Well-defined light
gape stripe;* bill *dark red.*

**23. Long-billed Woodcreeper** p.183
*Nasica longirostris* S (Amazonas)
*Large. Very long, straight* bill.

**Scythebills** *Campylorhamphus*
Long, *sickle-shaped* bill. Note ranges.

**24. Red-billed** *C. trochilirostris* p.187
Bill decidedly *rusty-red.* BROWN-BILLED *C.
pusillus* N: Bill *brown;* streaking *deeper*
buff, crown darker.

**25. Curve-billed** *C. procurvoides* S p.188
Bill brownish; *less* streaking than 24.

18

PLATE 19 FURNARIIDS (SPINETAILS, etc.)

**1. Bar-winged Cinclodes** p.188
*Cinclodes fuscus* N (Paramo)
*Terrestrial. Prominent eyebrow*, mottled throat *whitish*; *bold* cinnamon *wing-band*.

**2. Streak-backed Canastero** p.193
*Asthenes wyatti* N (Paramo)
Often terrestrial. *Upperparts streaked.* Buffy eyebrow; *dull* rufous *wing-band*.

**3. Ochre-browed Thistletail** p.192
*Schizoeaca coryi* N
*Narrow tail pointed* and frayed. *Tawny eyebrow* and chin-spot. WHITE-CHINNED *S. fuliginosa* N (w. Tachira paramo): Warmer above; eyebrow *gray*, chin *white*.

**4. Andean Tit-Spinetail** p.189
*Leptasthenura andicola* N (Paramo)
Bill *small*; central tail-feathers *very pointed. Conspicuous pale streaking.*

**5. White-whiskered Spinetail** p.191
*Poecilurus candei* N (Arid N.w.)
*Bright rufous* upperparts. *Black cheeks* and *throat-band*; *dusky* distal tail.

**Spinetails** *Synallaxis*

**6. White-browed** *S. gularis* N p.191
*Short-tailed*, rather wren-like *Synallaxis*; *eyebrow, lores* and chin *white*.

**7. Rufous** *S. unirufa* N p.190
*Uniform rufous*; *lores* black. W. races *lack* black throat (cf. Rufous Wren).

**8. Stripe-breasted** p.190
*S. cinnamomea* N
Entire *underparts streaked* with black.

**9. Pale-breasted** *S. albescens* p.189
Widespread. *Tail brown*; Juvenal much duller. AZARA'S *S. azarae* N: *Higher* altitude than 9; *more rufous* above, *including longer tail*.

**10. Dusky** *S. moesta* S (Tepuis) p.189
*Darker below* than 9; *forehead* and *tail* deep rufous. Note *dusky throat* (cf. 17).

**11. Plain-crowned** *S. gujanensis* S p.190
Wings and *tail rufous*, but *not* crown.

**12. Ruddy** *S. rutilans* S p.191
*Chestnut* foreparts; *black throat*, and *tail*.

**13. Plain-fronted Thornbird** p.193
*Phacellodomus rufifrons* N
*Very plain, lacking* obvious rufous of allies. Note *rounded* tail.

**14. Yellow-throated Spinetail** p.191
*Certhiaxis cinnamomea*
*Uniform dull rufous* above, *buffy white below*; *dark bill and lores*. Near water.

**Spinetails** *Cranioleuca*

**15. Crested** *C. subcristata* N p.191
*Crown* appears *dull* (not rufous) with *vague streaking*; bill *pale*. Arboreal.

**16. Rusty-backed** *C. vulpina* p.192
*Dingier below* than 14; *mandible pale*.

**17. Tepui** *C. demissa* S (Tepuis) p.192
Tail rufous (*brighter* than 10). *Lacks* dark throat-patch; eyebrow *grayish*.

**18. Speckled** *C. gutturata* S p.192
Only spinetail in S *speckled below*.

**19. Orinoco Softtail** p.193
*Thripophaga cherriei* S (Amazonas)
Note *orange chin, pale streaks* below.

**Xenops** *Xenops*
Small; note *wing-pattern*. Most have *upturned* mandible, *white malar streak*.

**20. Plain** *X. minutus* p.200
*Back plain.* STREAKED *X. rutilans* N: Like 20 but *more streaked* (as in 21).

**21. Slender-billed** *X. tenuirostris* S p.199
More *streaked, bill slenderer* than 20.

**22. Rufous-tailed** *X. milleri* S p.199
Much *less* typical but note *Xenops* wings. Tail *entirely rufous* (no black).

**23. Pearled Treerunner** p.193
*Margarornis squamiger* N
Above *rich rufous*. Eyebrow, throat and *distinct guttate spotting creamy-white*.

**Barbtails** *Premnoplex*

**24. Rusty-winged** *P. guttuligera* N p.194
Local. Note *finely streaked brown back; buffy, squamate* throat and chest; rusty on wings, and *rich rufous tail*.

**25. Spotted** *P. brunnescens* N p.194
*Darker* brown above, *especially tail*. Throat and *spotting* below *ochraceous*. WHITE-THROATED *P. tatei* N (east): Above like 25 (*no* overlap), below like 26.

**26. Roraiman** *P. adusta* S (Tepuis) p.194
*Breast streaked*; unlike any *in range*.

PLATE 20  FURNARIIDS (FOLIAGE-GLEANERS, etc.)

## 19

**1. Streaked Tuftedcheek**  p.195
*Pseudocolaptes boissonneautii*   N
Large. *Prominent, puffy white cheek-tufts* diagnostic; tawny wing-bars.

**Treehunters**  *Thripadectes*
*Larger* than *Syndactyla* with stouter bill; *throat more or less streaked*. Note the ranges (all 3 occur in s.w. Tachira).

**2. Streak-capped**  *T. virgaticeps*  N  p.199
Streaking *very light, almost none on back*; *streaky fulvous throat*.

**3. Striped**  *T. holostictus*  N  p.199
Much *less* boldly streaked *below* than 4.

**4. Flammulated**  *T. flammulatus*  N  p.198
Tachira race (shown) *very boldly, extensively* streaked below; rather *less* so in Merida (but *none* similar here).

**5. Pale-legged Hornero**  p.189
*Furnarius leucopus*   N (Maracaibo basin)
*Bright cinnamon-rufous* above with *short tail*; white eyebrow and throat.

**6. Lineated Foliage-gleaner**  p.195
*Syndactyla subalaris*   N
Heavily *streaked* with *contrasting buffy throat*. GUTTULATED *S. guttulata* N: Similar but with plain crown, *prominent* buff eyebrow (*no* overlap). More *streaked* than 2 but *not* on throat.

**7. Montane Foliage-gleaner**  p.196
*Anabacerthia striaticollis*   N
Virtually *unstreaked*. Dark face enhances *buffy spectacles*; throat pale. W. races *lack* rufous on wings.

**Foliage-gleaners**  *Philydor*
Note *pronounced eyebrow* (cf. *Automolus*).

**8. Buff-fronted**  *P. rufus*  p.197
*Rich tawny buff* eyebrow and throat. *Ochraceous* below; wings rufous.

**9. Cinnamon-rumped**  p.196
*P. pyrrhodes*  S
Underparts and tail *cinnamon*; *wings blackish*. NEBLINA *P. hylobius*  S (Tepuis—*very* local): See text.

**10. Rufous-tailed**  *P. ruficaudatus*  S  p.197
*Yellow-buff* eyebrow and throat. *Wings concolor* with back; only tail rufous.

**11. Chestnut-winged**  p.197
*P. erythropterus*  S
Much like 10 but *wings mainly rufous*. Duller below than 8, *back much grayer*.

**Foliage-gleaners**  *Automolus*
Somewhat stockier, more *somber hued* than *Philydor*; most rather similar.

**12. Chestnut-crowned**  *A. rufipileatus*  p.198
Crown chestnut; throat only *slightly paler* than underparts. Local in N. RUDDY *A. rubiginosus*: Similar to 12 but *deeper* brown; chin pale but *throat becomes light rufous contrasting* with *darker* breast. Only w. Apure in N.

**13. Buff-throated**  *A. ochrolaemus*  S  p.198
Note *well-developed eyering* and *extensive,* contrasting *bright buffy* throat.

**14. Olive-backed**  *A. infuscatus*  S  p.197
*Grayer* below than others; throat quite *white*. One of commoner *Automolus*.

**15. White-throated**  *A. roraimae*  S  p.198
*Blackish cheeks* with *white eyebrow; very* contrasting throat. Tepuis.

**16. Striped Woodhaunter**  p.195
*Hyloctistes subulatus*  S
Rather like *Automolus* but differs by *pale fine streaking* on *foreparts*.

**Leafscrapers**  *Sclerurus*
Mainly *terrestrial. Dark* with *slender bill,* chestnut rump and *blackish tail*; 3 quite similar species occur in S.

**17. Gray-throated**  *S. albigularis*  N  p.200
*Upper* throat *pale ash-gray*. Widespread.

**18. Tawny-throated**  *S. mexicanus*  p.200
Local, uncommon *Sclerurus* throughout range. *Face darker* and throat *richer rufous* than others in S.

**19. Black-tailed**  *S. caudacutus*  S  p.201
Throat *rusty buff* (*whitish* with *scaled* effect in s.w. Amazonas); suggestion of *rusty around* eye. SHORT-BILLED *S. rufigularis* S: Similar to slightly larger 19 (race shown) but *bill perceptibly shorter* (⅔ as long). Cf. 18.

**20. Sharp-tailed Streamcreeper**  p.201
*Lochmias nematura*
*Sclerurus*-like but profusely *spotted with white below*; very local in N.

**21. Point-tailed Palmcreeper**  p.195
*Berlepschia rikeri*  S (Amazonas)
Woodcreeper-like but *boldly* streaked *black-and-white*; *rufous-chestnut* mantle and tail. Note habitat.

PLATE 21 ANTSHRIKES, ANTWRENS, etc.

**1. Black-throated Antshrike** p.202
*Frederickena viridis* S
*Very large*; crested. ♂ *slate-gray* with *blackish hood, no* wing-spots (cf. Pl. 22). Note *size, color pattern* of ♀.

**2. Great Antshrike** *Taraba major* p.202
*Large.* Black or chestnut above and *white below*; iris *red*.

**3. Fasciated Antshrike** p.202
*Cymbilaimus lineatus*
*Very finely* barred; iris *red*. Note *chestnut crown* and barring *above* in ♀.

**4. Barred Antshrike** p.203
*Thamnophilus doliatus*
♂ rather *coarsely barred* (w. race ♂ *more like* 3 but iris *yellow*). ♀ *rufous* and *tawny-buff*; sides of head *streaked*. BAR-CRESTED *T. multistriatus* N (Subtrop. Perija): ♂ barring *coarser* than *w. race* of 4. ♀ *like* 4 *above* but underparts *barred black-and-white*.

**Antshrikes** *Sakesphorus*
*Prominent crest*, esp. 5. *Black-hooded* effect (♂ ♂). *Boldly margined* wings.

**5. Black-crested** *S. canadensis* p.203
♂ back *brownish*; much *white on face* of w. races. ♀ *crest rufous*, breast more or (w.) less streaked; *tail black*.

**6. Black-backed** *S. melanonotus* N p.203
♂ has *black back* (face *always* black). ♀ has *blackish crest, chestnut tail*.

**Antwrens** *Herpsilochmus*
*Black* crown (♂) with *white eyebrow*. *Boldly* white-spotted wings and *tail*.

**7. Rufous-winged** *H. rufimarginatus* p.212
Only *Herpsilochmus* with *rufous on wings*.

**8. Todd's** *H. stictocephalus* S p.211
♀ crown *white-spotted*. SPOT-TAILED *H. sticturus* S: ♂ *very similar* to 8; ♀ crown *streaked* with *chestnut*.

**9. Spot-backed** *H. dorsimaculatus* S p.211
Black and white *back-patch more extensive* than 8. White *crown-spots* of ♀ *become buffy* on *fore*head and lores.

**10. Roraiman** *H. roraimae* S (Tepuis) p.211
*Higher* altitude, *longer* tail with *more spots* than others. ♀ crown white-spotted.

**11. Ash-winged Antwren** p.213
*Terenura spodioptila* S
*Small.* Note *bright chestnut back*, *very pale* eyebrow and underparts, white wing-spots; ♂ *crown black*. RUFOUS-RUMPED *T. callinota* N: see text.

**Antwrens** *Myrmotherula*
*Small.* Many ♀ ♀ *confusing*, not analyzed.

**12. Pygmy** *M. brachyura* S p.207
*Streaked above* and *pale yellow* below; ♀ crown buffier. YELLOW-THROATED *M. ambigua* S (Amazonas): see text.

**13. Streaked** *M. surinamensis* S p.208
♂ *entirely streaked*. ♀ crown streaky *rufous*, throat tawny (*streaked* black *below* in n. Amazonas). CHERRIE'S *M. cherriei* S (Amazonas): ♂ *very similar* (see text); ♀ *streaked below* but crown *buffier* than 13

**14. Rufous-bellied** *M. guttata* S p.208
Rufous *abdomen*; bold *tawny wing-bars*.

**15. Brown-bellied** *M. gutturalis* S p.209
Back *brown*. ♂ throat *checkered*.

**16. Stipple-throated** p.209
*M. haemotonota* S
Similar to 15 but back *chestnut*; wing-coverts *blackish* with *larger* spots.

**17. Slaty** *M. schisticolor* N p.210
♂ throat *black*; wings *spotted* white.

**18. White-flanked** *M. axillaris* p.209
*White flank-plumes*. ♂ quite blackish.

**19. Gray** *M. menetriesii* S p.210
♂ throat *gray*; wings *margined* white.

**20. Plain-winged** p.210
*M. behni* S (Tepuis)
♂ *throat black*; wings *plain gray*. LONG-WINGED *M. longipennis* S: ♂ throat *black*; wing-coverts *black* with white *margins* (effect much like 17).

**21. White-fringed Antwren** p.211
*Formicivora grisea* 21a. s. Amazonas
*Black underparts* of ♂ outlined *with white*. *Pale-browed* ♀ spotted, streaked or cinnamon below. Tail *not* short.

**22. Plain Antvireo** p.206
*Dysithamnus mentalis*
*Smaller*, stubbier than gray antshrikes; best told by *darker auriculars*. Note *russet* crown, *yellowish* belly of ♀.

**23. Russet Antshrike** p.206
*Thamnistes anabatinus* N (Tachira)
*Heavy bill, pale* eyebrow; *rufous tail*.

**24. Long-tailed Antbird** p.212
*Drymophila caudata* N
*Streaked*; rump *rufous*. Tail very *long*.

**25. Warbling Antbird** p.215
*Hypocnemis cantator* S
*Streaky head and breast*; yellowish (white in east) below, *flanks rusty*.

PLATE 22 ANTSHRIKES, ANTBIRDS, etc.

## 21

**1. Pearly Antshrike** p.206
*Megastictus margaritatus* S
Wing-spots *large and round*. Underparts
and spots *bright buff* in brownish ♀.

**Antshrikes** *Thamnophilus*

**2. Slaty** *T. punctatus* p.204
*Bold white* wing-markings. ♂ crown *black;*
♀ crown *chestnut* (less so in w.)

**3. Amazonian** *T. amazonicus* S p.205
Amazonas race ♂ smaller than 2, *crown
gray;* e. Bolivar race ♂ *much like* 2 but *back
blacker.* ♀ *head and breast bright rufous;*
wing-markings *white.*

**4. Streak-backed** p.205
*T. insignis* S (Tepuis)
*Longer-tailed* version of Bolivar ♂ 3. ♀ *simi-
lar to* ♂ but crown *chestnut.*

**5. Mouse-colored** *T. murinus* S p.204
Note *lightly dotted, brownish wings* of ♂. ♀
*drab* brownish (cf. Antvireo).

**6. White-shouldered** *T. aethiops* S p.204
♂ wings *dotted* white (nearly *identical*
Caura Antbird ♂ is *larger* with *longer, slenderer bill*). ♀ *uniformly chestnut.*

**7. Blackish-gray** *T. nigrocinereus* S p.204
♂ like 6 but wings *narrowly margined* white.
♀ much like ♀ 9 but crown *slatier, bill
stouter; no* wing-spots.

**8. Spot-winged Antshrike** p.206
*Pygiptila stellaris* S
Note *large bill* and *very short tail.*

**Antbirds** *Percnostola*
Bill *more slender* than *Thamnophilus.*

**9. Spot-winged** *P. leucostigma* p.215
♂ wings *spotted or dotted* white, but *paler
below* than 6 (local N race *as dark*). ♀
shows *tawny buff wing-spots.* CAURA *P.
caurensis* S: *Large version* of 9. ♂ *darker*
below (cf. 6). ♀ of w. race like 9 but *richer
rufous* below; e. race ♀ *adds* chestnut
wash on *head.*

**10. Black-headed** *P. rufifrons* S p.215
♂ *crown and throat* black; wings *margined*
white. ♀ *paler* below than 9; wings *margined tawny buff.* Amazonas.

**Antbirds** *Cercomacra*

**11. Jet** *C. nigricans* N p.214
Wing-coverts, tail *boldly white-tipped.* ♀
*dark*-slate, throat *streaked white.*

**12. Dusky** *C. tyrannina* p.213
♂ wings *margined* white; *no* black on head
(cf. 15). ♀ *all-rufescent* below. GRAY
ANTBIRD *C. cinerascens* S: ♂ *mostly gray*

(wing-dots *minute*). ♀ *dull ochraceous* below. *Longish* tail *boldly white-tipped* in both
sexes (like 11). cf. 16.

**13. Scale-backed Antbird** p.219
*Hylophylax poecilonota* S
Wings *and back scaled;* tail spotted. ♂
head *gray.* ♀ *face rufous,* scaling tawny;
below *gray.* S. Amazonas race ♀ scaled
*white* (as ♂); *all-rufous* below.

**14. Black-chinned Antbird** p.215
*Hypocnemoides melanopogon* S (mainly)
*Slender* bill and *short tail.* Wings *margined*
white. ♂ throat *black,* crown gray. ♀ *mottled* gray-and-white below.

**Antshrikes** *Thamnomanes*

**15. Plumbeous** *T. plumbeus* N p.207
♂ a bit chunkier than 12, *chest blackish.* ♀
*streaked* gray-and-white below.

**16. Cinereous** *T. caesius* S p.207
♂ *all* slate-gray; *no* wing/tail spots. ♀ like
17 but belly *richer rufous.*

**17. Dusky-throated** *T. ardesiacus* S p.207
♂ *all* slate-gray with *black throat.* ♀ throat
whitish, belly *ochraceous.*

**18. Silvered Antbird** p.216
*Sclateria naevia* 18a. Amazonas race
Bill *longish;* legs pale. Above *gray* (♂) or
mainly brown (♀). Races *vary below* from
*extensive* streaking to *reduced streaks to
none* (with white median breast).

**Antbirds** *Myrmeciza*
In most, *upperparts* some shade of *brown;*
♂♂ with black throat. Some have a bare
*pale blue orbital-patch.*

**19. Black-throated** *M. atrothorax* S p.217
Wings *white-dotted.* ♂ dark brown above,
throat black. ♀ has *white* throat and *rufous*
breast. YAPACANA *M. disjuncta* S
(Amazonas-local): Atypical, see text.

**20. Gray-bellied** p.217
*M. pelzelni* S (Amaz.)
♂ near 19 but wings with *buff spots;* cheeks
mottled grayish. ♀ mainly whitish below;
breast scaled with black.

**21. White-bellied** *M. longipes* p.216
Bright *rufous-chestnut upper*parts.

**22. Dull-mantled** *M. laemosticta* N p.217
♂ recalls 19; ♀ throat *checkered.*

**23. Immaculate** p.218
*M. immaculata* N (Local)
*Large;* unpatterned. *Orbital-patch big.* ♂
*jet*-black; ♀ *chocolate-brown.*

PLATE 23   ANTTHRUSHES, ANTPITTAS, etc.

**1. Ocellated Tapaculo** p.226
*Acropternis orthonyx*   N
Size, *shape* and *ornate* pattern unique.

**2. Recurve-billed Bushbird** p.206
*Clytoctantes alixi* N (S. de Perija)
Best told by peculiar, *stout recurved bill* (cf. Pl. 22). ♀ mainly *chestnut*.

**Antthrushes** *Chamaeza*
Proportions, behavior rather similar to *Formicarius* but *pattern* different.

**3. Short-tailed** *C. campanisona* p.220
*Streaked* below; *tail narrowly pale-tipped*. S races washed fulvous below.

**4. Rufous-tailed** *C. ruficauda* N p.220
Similar to 3 but breast more *heavily* marked (more *scalloped effect*); eyebrow whiter. Tail *lacks* pale tipping.

**Antpittas** *Grallaria*
Large-headed, *bob-tailed, very long legged*. Terrestrial, normally hopping.

**5. Plain-backed** *G. haplonota* N p.223
Among *larger* antpittas, *overlaps only* very different 9 and 10.

**6. Scaled** *G. guatimalensis* p.222
*Scaled* effect above. *Dark throat* with conspicuous buffy-white malar-stripe and transverse lower *throat-patch*. VARIEGATED *G. varia* S (Amazonas): Much like 6. Perceptibly larger; pale lower throat-patch *restricted laterally*, *not reaching* malar-stripe. At *lower* altitude. TACHIRA *G. chthonia* N (s.w. Tachira only); see text.

**7. Rufous** *G. rufula* N p.223
Entirely *rufous-chestnut*, paler below. Perija race much *duller*, browner (but at higher altitude than little 13).

**8. Gray-naped** *G. griseonucha* N p.223
Like 7 but *nape* decidedly *dark gray*.

**9. Chestnut-crowned** p.223
*G. ruficapilla* N
*Large* size; distinctive *color pattern*.

**10. Great** *G. excelsa* N p.222
*Very large*. Tawny underparts *boldly barred* black. UNDULATED *G. squamigera* N: Large size—between 9 and *very similar* 10. *Grayer back merges* into crown; *black submalar streak* separates barred malar area from white median throat.

**11. Spotted Antpitta** p.223
*Hylopezus macularius* S
No other antpitta in range with *bold black* "*necklace*"; *large eye-ring* buff.

**12. Thrush-like Antpitta** p.224
*Myrmothera campanisona* S
Mainly *white* below, breast *streaked brownish*. BROWN-BREASTED *M. simplex* S (Tepuis): Rather like 12 but breast and sides *unstreaked brownish gray*, only *throat and median belly* remaining white. Normally *higher* altitudes.

**Antpittas** *Grallaricula*
Non-terrestrial antpittas in *miniature*.

**13. Rusty-breasted** p.224
*G. ferrugineipectus* N
Like 14 but *crown concolor* with back; tawny underparts *paler, more ochraceous* (Perija race darker below).

**14. Slate-crowned** *G. nana* p.224
All races are largely *rich rufous* below with *slate-gray crown*.

**15. Hooded** p.225
*G. cucullata* N (s. Tachira)
*Rufous-chestnut head*; grayish below.

**16. Scallop-breasted** *G. loricata* N p.225
Heavily *scalloped breast* diagnostic.

**Antthrushes** *Formicarius*
Terrestrial; *walk* with cocked tail twitching. Mantle *uniform, unpatterned*.

**17. Black-faced** *F. analis* p.221
*Crown brown*; black face and throat contrasts with *gray breast*.

**18. Rufous-breasted** *F. rufipectus* N p.221
Breast rich *rufous-chestnut*. Local.

**19. Rufous-capped** *F. colma* S p.221
Note *rufous crown* and *blackish chest*. ♀ has lores and throat *white*, often spotted or barred with black.

**20. Reddish-winged Bare-eye** p.220
*Phlegopsis erythroptera* S (Amazonas)
Large. *Bare red eye-patch*. ♀ *rich brown* above, rufous-chestnut below; *double* wing-bars, *primary-band* tawny.

**21. Wing-banded Antbird** p.220
*Myrmornis torquata* S
*Ornate*. Longish bill, *stubby tail* (cf. longer-tailed *Myrmeciza*). ♀ has *throat and chest rufous*.

23

TUDOR

PLATE 24 ANTBIRDS and MANAKINS (Nos. 21-30 cont'd next page)

**Antbirds** *Myrmoborus*
Note *prominent pale eyebrow* (cf. Pl. 22).

**1. White-browed** *M. leucophrys* p.214
♂ eyebrow *broad and white*; black face, *dark gray* underparts. ♀ white below; black *cheeks*, broad *cinnamon eyebrow*.

**2. Black-faced** *M. myotherinus* S p.214
♂ face *well-defined* from *pale gray breast* and narrow eyebrow; wings *margined* white. ♀ has *black cheeks*, *plain back*, white throat; tawny underparts, wing-*margins*; *sparse* chest-spotting.

**3. Rufous-throated Antbird** p.218
*Gymnopithys rufigula* S
Black *lores*, *rufous throat* and buffy breast. Bare *bluish-white eye-patch*.

**Antbirds** *Hylophylax*
Breast *black-spotted*; lower *back pale-dotted*. Sexes similar *above;* ♀♀ *lack* black throat but show dark malar-stripe.

**4. Spot-backed** *H. naevia* S p.219
Back-spots *buff*, more *restricted*. ♀ *buff below*; breast-spotting *moderate*.

**5. Dot-backed** *H. punctulata* S p.219
Back-spots *white, extending over rump*; lores and cheeks *pale* gray. ♀ underparts *white, heavily spotted* as ♂.

**6. Banded Antbird** p.211
*Dichrozona cincta* S (s. Amazonas)
Small. *Long bill*, *stubby* tail. Black *breast spots*; obvious *wing-bars and band* (buff in ♀) across *lower back*.

**7. White-plumed Antbird** p.218
*Pithys albifrons*
Decorative *white plumes*. Local in N.

**8. Lance-tailed Manakin** p.240
*Chiroxiphia lanceolata* N
♂ back *azure-blue*. Note *lanceolate* inner tail-feathers in *both sexes*. ♀ legs pale dull orange. BLUE-BACKED *C. pareola* S: ♂ like 8 but tail *normal*. ♀ much like 10 but legs *flesh-yellow* (*shorter* tail than 15).

**9. Wire-tailed Manakin** p.240
*Teleonema filicauda*
Tails of *both sexes* end in *long wiry filaments*; ♀ belly *brighter* yellow than most others. No overlap with 14.

**10. White-bearded Manakin** p.241
*Manacus manacus*
Note *black and white* ♂. ♀ best told from all others by *bright orange legs*.

**11. Golden-winged Manakin** p.240
*Masius chrysopterus* N
♂ has *bright yellow* inner webs and linings of *wings*. ♀ differs from rest by *well-defined yellow chin and throat patches* and yellow belly. Subtropical.

**Manakins** *Pipra*
All ♂♂ distinctive, not analyzed. ♀♀ often *difficult*, even from some *other* genera; Immature ♂♂ are intermediate.

**12. White-crowned** *P. pipra* p.239
♀ decidedly *gray on crown*; soft parts quite *dark*. N race is *brighter* olive above and *yellower* below (cf. 18 N).

**13. Golden-headed** p.238
*P. erythrocephala*
♀ small and dingy; legs *flesh-color*.

**14. Crimson-hooded** *P. aureola* p.239
♀ more *orange*-yellow below than others.

**15. Scarlet-horned** *P. cornuta* S p.239
Tepuis. ♀ rather *large, dingy*; tail *longish*. Soft parts *paler* than 19, 20.

**16. White-fronted** *P. serena* S p.239
This and 17 only ♀♀ *pure green above*, lacking olive tone. Tepuis mainly.

**17. Blue-crowned** *P. coronata* S p.239
♀ much like 16 but belly *paler* yellow.

**18. White-throated Manakin** p.240
*Corapipo gutturalis* S
♂ black with *snowy-white bib*. ♀ has throat and belly *whiter* than similars. WHITE-RUFFED *C. leucorrhoa* N: ♂ pattern comparable but *no* overlap. ♀ *brighter* olive above, *much yellower* below than 18 (much like N race of 12).

**19. Black Manakin** p.242
*Xenopipo atronitens* S
*Longer* tail than *Pipra*. ♂ all *glossy black* with *black* wing-linings (cf. *Volatinia*). ♀ similar to 20.

**20. Olive Manakin** p.242
*Chloropipo uniformis* S (Tepuis)
Both sexes *dingy olive* with *longish* tail, *dark* soft parts (cf. 15). Normally inseparable in field from ♀ 19 but ranges to *higher* elevations.

*Plate 24 (Cont'd)  Manakins*    PLATE  25  COTINGAS, et al.

**Manakins**  *Machaeropterus*
Small. ♂♂ streaky rose-chestnut below.

**21. Striped**  *M. regulus*  p.242
♂ crown crimson, back olive; boldly
streaked below. ♀ best told by vague rufous streaking on lower underparts.

**22. Fiery-capped**  *M. pyrocephalus*  S  p.241
♂ crown golden with vermilion stripe; back
rufous. ♀ like *Tyranneutes*. Local.

**Tyrant-Manakins**  *Tyranneutes*
Very small. Either may resemble various ♀ or
pale-eyed young ♂ *Pipra*, etc. Note lack of
wing-bars (cf. Pl. 30).

**23. Dwarf**  *T. stolzmanni*  S  p.243
No crown-patch. Iris pale (buff, straw-color,
grayish-white). More widespread.

**24. Tiny**  *T. virescens*  S (e. Bolivar)  p.242
Semiconcealed yellow coronal-patch (♂);
vestigial (♀). Iris gray to brown.

**25. Cinnamon Manakin**  p.242
*Neopipo cinnamomea*  S (s. Amazonas)
Recalls *Terenotriccus* but bill narrower; no
rictal bristles; semiconcealed yellow/rufous
crown-patch. Much rarer.

**26. Saffron-crested Tyrant-Manakin**  p.243
*Neopelma chrysocephalum*  S
Tyrant-like; sexes alike. Note broad, golden
median-crest (flared in display). *Myiopagis*
have wing-bars or spectacles.

**27. Wing-barred Manakin**  p.243
*Piprites chloris*
Only manakin with noticeable wing-bar (cf.
various tyrants). Note stubby bill and yellow
suffusion on foreface.

**Manakins**  *Schiffornis*
Large and longish-tailed. Sexes alike, without
olive-green coloration.

**28. Thrush-like**  *S. turdinus*  p.244
Rather uniform dingy olivaceous-brown.

**29. Greater**  *S. major*  S (Amazonas)  p.244
Note cinnamon belly, rump and tail.

**30. Yellow-crowned Manakin**  p.242
*Heterocercus flavivertex*  S (Amazonas)
♂ has silky-white ruffed bib; below variably
rich rufous. ♀ told from other large olive
♀♀ by slaty cheeks, gray throat and fulvous wash on belly.

**1. Blue-crowned Motmot**  p.162
*Momotus momota*
Large Coraciiform (cf. *Jacamerops*). Note
color and racket-tipped tail.

**2. Amazonian Umbrellabird**  p.234
*Cephalopterus ornatus*  S
Very large. Black; ♀ crest less developed,
no wattle. Solitary; scarce.

**3. Purple-throated Fruitcrow**  p.234
*Querula purpurata*  S
Rather large. Black; ♂ throat magenta-
crimson. Usually in family parties; vocal.
Not uncommon (cf. *Gymnoderus*).

**4. Black Nunbird**  p.167
*Monasa atra*  S
Large, dark slaty puffbird. Note decurved
red bill; white wing-markings. WHITE-
FRONTED *M. morphoeus*  S (Amazonas):
Body grayer than 4; wings plain. Forehead,
lores and chin white.

**5. Guianan Cock-of-the-Rock**  p.237
*Rupicola rupicola*  S
Largish. Spectacular ♂ bright orange. Dark
♀ uniform ashy-brown with rudimentary
frontal crest. ANDEAN *R. peruviana*  N
(Tachira): ♀ mainly dark orangy-brown.
See text for ♂.

**6. Capuchinbird**  p.235
*Perissocephalus tricolor*  S
Very large; big-billed. Rufescent with naked
bluish-gray crown and face.

**Red-Cotingas**  *Phoenicircus*
Piha-sized. Rosy-crimson on ♂♂. ♀♀ mainly
olive-brown with dull maroon-red crown and
tail, rose-red belly.

**7. Guianan**  *P. carnifex*  S (Bolivar)  p.237
Maroon breast of ♂ merges into red belly;
wings brownish. ♀ throat paler and rosier
than next; rump mixed with red. BLACK-
NECKED *P. nigricollis*  S (Amazonas): ♂
wings, throat blacker; well-defined from red
breast. ♀ has throat, rump olive-brown like
back.

**8. Red-ruffed Fruitcrow**  p.234
*Pyroderus scutatus*
Very large. Throat broadly flame-red. N
race belly black, dappled chestnut.

**9. Oilbird**  *Steatornis caripensis*  p.121
Large; nocturnal. Social; differs from potoos
in almost all aspects. Note rufescence and
white spotting.

1

2 ♂

3 ♂

4

5 ♂

6

7 ♂

8

9

KD Phelps

PLATE 26  COTINGAS and ALLIES

**1. Pompadour Cotinga**  p.228
*Xipholena punicea*  S
♂ raspberry-purple; *wings mostly white.* ♀ gray; wings *broadly edged* with *white*; young ♂ intermediate. Note *white iris.*

**Cotingas**  *Cotinga*
♂♂ some shade of *brilliant blue* with *red-purple* throat. ♀♀ *dusky-brownish*, more or less *scaled and spotted.*

**2. Purple-breasted**  *C. cotinga*  S  p.227
♂ *deep cobalt*-blue; purple *extends over breast.* ♀ *conspicuously scaled.*

**3. Spangled**  *C. cayana*  S (mainly)  p.227
♂ black-spangled *light turquoise.* Scaling in ♀ *far less evident* than 2, mostly on *breast*; wings *finely* edged *fulvous.* E. of Andes. BLUE *C. nattererii* N (w. of Andes): ♂ *deeper* turquoise; *less* spangles. ♀ *much as* 2.

**4. Red-crested Cotinga**  p.228
*Ampelion rubrocristata*  N
*Slate-gray* cotinga of *higher* altitudes. Note maroon *crest*, *two-toned* bill and *white-banded tail.* Juvenal streaked.

**5. Cinereous Mourner**  p.255
*Laniocera hypopyrrha*  S
Gray with dull *cinnamon wing-spots*; Juvenal also *adds* variable amount of *spotting on belly.* Look for *obscure* rufous (♂) to yellow (♀/young♂) *pectoral-tufts.* Much scarcer than 6, 7.

**6. Grayish Mourner**  p.255
*Rhytipterna simplex*  S
Size of 5 but essentially *plain gray.* Some (young?) have fulvous wing and tail *edging*, but never distinct spots.

**Pihas**  *Lipaugus*

**7. Screaming**  *L. vociferans*  p.230
Noticeably *larger*, rather huskier than very similar 6; throat *somewhat paler.* Best told by *loud, often heard call.*

**8. Rose-collared**  *L. streptophorus*  S  p.230
Tepuis: ♂ gray; *magenta-pink collar* and crissum. Size between 6 and 7; ♀ similar to either but *crissum rufous.*

**9. Shrike-like Cotinga**  p.227
*Laniisoma elegans*  N (local)
♂ crown *black*; below *mainly yellow.* ♀ crown *mixed with olive*; more *heavily barred* below. *Lower* elevation than 10.

**10. Scaled Fruiteater**  p.229
*Ampelioides tschudii*  N (local)
Complex pattern. Both sexes *scalloped above and below; pale loral and malar stripes.* ♀ differs by *olive* crown, *bolder* black-edged scalloping below.

**Bellbirds**  *Procnias*
Quite large. Dark olive ♀♀ are broadly *streaked with yellowish* below. Juvenal ♂ resembles ♀, progressing through stages to maturity. *Voice unmistakable.*

**11. Bearded**  *P. averano*  p.236
♂ has *coffee-brown cap*, pale *tail* and cluster of *black wattles*; ♀ similar to next. WHITE *P. alba* S: ♂ see Fig. 40. ♀ told from 11 by *less slaty* crown and face (more concolor with back), *broader* pale streaking on *throat.*

**Fruiteaters**  *Pipreola*
Mantle *olive to grass-green.* Note *plump* shape and brightly colored *bill.*

**12. Green-and-black**  *P. riefferii*  N  p.228
*Dark hood* of ♂ extends over breast, *margined* more or less with yellow. ♀ shows same *hooded effect* in *olive.*

**13. Barred**  *P. arcuata*  N  p.229
Both sexes *heavily black-barred* below. ♀ lacks black hood, is *barred to chin.*

**14. Handsome**  *P. formosa*  N  p.229
This and 15 are small, *bright green Pipreola.* ♂ has *black head* and *fiery orange chest*; ♀ appears *barred with yellow below*, coupled with a *small golden patch* on upper breast.

**15. Golden-breasted**  p.228
*P. aureopectus*  N
♂ *golden* underparts *extend onto throat.* ♀ *uniformly streaked* with yellow below.

**16. Red-banded**  p.229
*P. whitelyi*  S (Tepuis)
♂ has *vermilion breast-band.* ♀ similar above but *tawny-gold head patches* and *orange-brown wing-edging* of ♂ replaced by *olive-yellow*; below yellowish white, *boldly streaked black.*

**17. Sharpbill**  *Oxyruncus cristatus*  S  p.283
Tepuis mainly. Olive above, *profusely spotted* below. Note *pointed conical bill*; black-edged *flame-colored* crest normally recumbent.

TUDOR

PLATE 27 COTINGAS and ALLIES

**Tityras** *Tityra*
Bull-headed. *Very pale* (*browner* cast on ♀)
with *black* on head, wings and tail.

**1. Masked** *T. semifasciata* N p.233
*Bill and face* like 2 but ♂ has *black mask*
only. ♀ similar to 2 but *lacks* streaking.
Basal tail and tips *white*.

**2. Black-tailed** *T. cayana* p.233
*Basal bill* and *facial skin red*. ♂ with *full*
black *cap*; ♀ browner, *streaked* above and
below. Tail *entirely* black.

**3. Black-crowned** *T. inquisitor* p.234
*Solid black* bill and black *cap* in both
sexes; ♀ has *chestnut cheeks*.

**Becards** *Pachyramphus*
First 3 have wings and tail-tips *boldly marked*
with white (♂) or cinnamon (♀).

**4. White-winged** *P. polychopterus* p.232
♂ *dark gray to blackish* below; back *black*.
♀ crown *grayer-to-browner* olive.

**5. Black-and-white** *P. albogriseus* N p.233
♂ *light gray* below; back *plain gray*. ♀ has
white eyebrow and *black-margined
chestnut* crown. *Higher* altitude than 6.

**6. Black-capped** *P. marginatus* p.232
♂ *light gray* below; back *mixed with black*.
♀ much as 4 but crown *chestnut*.

**7. Cinereous** *P. rufus* p.231
♂ wing-markings *finer, less contrasty* than
5 or 6; back *plain gray*, tail *not* tipped. *Rufous* ♀ *very similar* to 8 but *lores paler*, contrast *less* with white supraloral stripe. Also
see 13 N.

**8. Cinnamon** p.232
*P. cinnamomeus* N (west)
Sexes alike. *Well-defined slaty lores* contrast with buffy supraloral stripe.

**9. Chestnut-crowned** *P. castaneus* p.231
Sexes alike. From 8 and ♀ 7 by crown
being *clearly margined with gray*.

**10. Barred** *P. versicolor* N p.231
*Compact* little becard, *lightly barred* below.
♂ wings *boldly* marked but *face obviously
yellowish*. ♀ has *slaty* crown, and wings
broadly edged *rich rufous*.

**11. Green-backed** p.231
*P. viridis* S (Bolivar)
Only becard *plain olive-green* above (*no*
white in wings). ♀ has grayish-olive crown
and *chestnut shoulders*.

**12. White-naped Xenopsaris** p.230
*Xenopsaris albinucha*
♂ smaller than 7, bill more *slender*. *Nape*
white; below whiter with *wings* decidedly
*brownish*. ♀ has crown mixed *brown*, belly
*yellowish*. Quite local.

**13. Pink-throated Becard** p.233
*Platypsaris minor* S
♂ dark slate-gray, blacker above; *rosy*
throat-patch. Rufescent ♀ has *gray crown
and back*. ONE-COLORED *P. homochrous* N
(Maracaibo basin): ♂ like 13 *without*
throat-patch. *All-rufous* ♀ *very similar* to 8
and especially ♀ 7 (*little* contrast in lores)
but is *larger* with *heavier bill*.

**Attilas** *Attila*
This genus (also *Pseudattila*) told from becards, et al. by *distinctive straight, hooked bill*.
Most quite *rufescent* with slightly to very contrasting rumps.

**14. Bright-rumped** *A. spadiceus* p.254
Variable *color phases*: streaky-breasted
olivaceous to plain rufescent (intermediate
shown). All told by *wing-bars*, very contrasty *tawny-yellow rump*.

**15. Citron-bellied** *A. citriniventris* S p.255
Amazonas. Similar to *rufous* phase of 14
but *cap grayish; no* wing-bars. Rump
somewhat *less* contrasting. RUFOUS-TAILED
*Pseudattila phoenicurus* S (Amazonas-local): From 15 by slightly shorter bill; *clear
gray* cap *sharply demarcated* from *rich rufous* back. Rump only *slightly paler* than
back.

**16. Cinnamon** *A. cinnamomeus* p.255
*Entirely rufescent* including *crown; no*
wing-bars. Rump only *slightly* paler.

**17. White-browed Purpletuft** p.230
*Iodopleura isabellae* S (Amazonas)
*Small and stubby;* bill *short. White face*
markings, median underparts and *rump-band;* ♂ has purple flank-tufts. DUSKY *I.
fusca* S (e. Bolivar): White *reduced* to *mid-belly,* crissum and rump-band. (cf. larger
*Chelidoptera*).

**18. Ringed Antpipit** p.282
*Corythopis torquata* S
Normally *terrestrial,* pumping *longish tail.*
Note broad black *breast-band* and *lack* of
wing-bars (cf. Plate 24).

PLATE 28   TYRANT FLYCATCHERS   (Nos. 22-28 cont'd following Plate 30)

**1. Cattle Tyrant** p.248
*Machetornis rixosa*
Often *terrestrial*; note *long legs*. Yellow below with *brownish* upperparts.

**Bush-Tyrants** *Myiotheretes*
*Upper* altitude genus. Striking *rufous primary-patches* show on spread wings.

**2. Smoky** *M.* fumigatus N p.245
Dark *smoky-brown*. W. race has *pale eyebrow* (cf. much smaller *Ochthoeca*).

**3. Streak-throated** p.245
*M. striaticollis* N
*Large. Cinnamon below; throat streaked.*

**4. Cliff Flycatcher** p.262
*Hirundinea ferruginea*
*Chestnut underparts* and patches on *long wings*; freckled face, broad bill. *Behavior and habitat* distinctive.

**5. Yellow-browed Tyrant** p.248
*Satrapa icterophrys*
So. migrant. Note conspicuous *yellow* brows and *gray wing-bars* (unlike 11).

**Kingbirds** *Tyrannus*
Note *dusky auriculars* and notched tail.

**6. Gray** *T. dominicensis* p.249
Bill *large*. Grayish above; *dirty-white* below. EASTERN *T. tyrannus*: No. migrant. Unlike others. *Slaty* above; *white terminal tailband.*

**7. Tropical** *T. melancholicus* p.249
Back *olive-gray; lower* underparts yellow. *Throat whiter* in N race.

**8. White-throated** *T. albogularis* S p.250
Very similar to much commoner 7 but *back paler and greener*; throat *white* (S race of 7 has *grayer* throat). Local.

**Flycatchers** *Tyrannopsis*

**9. Sulphury** *T. sulphurea* p.250
Darker above than 7 with *shorter* bill. Duskier ˌface *extends onto malar area*; suggestion of *streaky "divider"* between *extensive* white throat and rich yellow belly (cf. *also* 14). Local in N.

**10. Dusky-chested** *T. luteiventris* S p.250
Rather *small* with short bill. Note *dark* head, *dusky breast*, rich yellow belly; *lack of* wing-bars. Very local.

**Flycatchers** *Conopias*
*Longer bill* than *Myiozetetes*; throat *yellow*

**11. Lemon-browed** *C. cinchoneti* N p.251
Eyebrow *yellow*; cheeks *olive*. Subtrop.

**12. White-ringed** *C. parva* S p.251
White brows extend narrowly *across forehead.* THREE-STRIPED *C. trivirgata* S (local): *Small* edition of 12. White brows *fail to meet* across forehead; back paler. Lacks crown-patch.

**Flycatchers** *Myiozetetes*
*Short bill.* Dark cheeks; *white* throat; semiconcealed coronal-patch in most.

**13. Social** *M. similis* p.253
N race *crown* quite *gray*. S race much *more similar* to S race of 16 but crown *retains grayer tone* (patch vermilion).

**14. Gray-capped** *M. granadensis* S p.253
White eyebrow *much less evident*. Not unlike larger 9 but forehead and *malar area whiter*, dark cheeks more *obvious*, white throat *more restricted.*

**15. White-bearded** *M. inornatus* p.253
From *overlapping races* of 13 and 16 by *combination* of *black* crown (no patch) with *lack of rufous* in wing. Mainly N.

**16. Rusty-margined** *M. cayanensis* p.253
Crown *blackish* (patch golden). W. and S races show *much less rufous* in wing.

**Flycatchers** *Myiodynastes*

**17. Streaked** *M. maculatus* p.252
*Large bill* and conspicuous *streaking.*

**18. Golden-crowned** p.252
*M. chrysocephalus* N
*Large* bill. *Dark malar streak; buffy* throat and *clouded* breast. Subtropical.

**19. Boat-billed Flycatcher** p.252
*Megarynchus pitangua*
*Large* bill *very broad*, culmen *curved. Much less* rufous in wings than 20.

**Kiskadees** *Pitangus*

**20. Great** *P. sulphuratus* p.254
*Large. Prominent rufous* in wings, tail.

**21. Lesser** *P. lictor* p.254
Told from 16 and *larger* 20 by *rather long, slender bill*. Favors *wet* areas.

28

PLATE 29 TYRANT FLYCATCHERS (Nos. 25-34 cont'd following Plate 30)

**1. Cinnamon Flycatcher** p.261
*Pyrrhomyias cinnamomea* N
Entirely *rich cinnamon-rufous* below.

**Chat-Tyrants** *Ochthoeca*
*Striking long eyebrow. Upper* altitudes.

**2. Brown-backed** *O. fumicolor* N p.245
Eyebrow and breast *rufous*. Brow *buffy-
white*, below *dingier* in s.w. Tachira.

**3. Rufous-breasted** p.245
*O. rufipectoralis* N
Eyebrow *white* (cf. 4). S. de Perija.

**4. Yellow-bellied** *O. diadema* N p.246
Eyebrow *yellow*. Below *yellow-olive*.

**5. Slaty-backed** p.246
*O. cinnamomeiventris* N
*Dark slaty*; shorter *white* eyebrow. Belly
*chestnut-red* in s.w. Tachira.

**6. Vermilion Flycatcher** p.247
*Pyrocephalus rubinus*
♂ unmistakable; ♀ has *rose-red* belly.

**7. Drab Water-Tyrant** p.248
*Ochthornis littoralis* S
*Sandy*-brown, especially *pale on rump*;
white supraloral, chin. Along *rivers*.

**Flycatchers** *Myiobius*
*Sulphur rump* and expressive *black tail*.

**8. Tawny-breasted** *M. villosus* N p.260
*Deep ochraceous* below. Subtropical.

**9. Sulphur-rumped** *M. barbatus* S p.260
Breast *grayish-olive*; belly sulphur. BLACK-
TAILED *M. atricaudus* S (local): *Very* similar,
differing only in warm *ochraceous-buff* tone
on breast, flanks.

**10. Agile Tit-Tyrant** p.272
*Uromyias agilis* N (Tachira-local)
*Profusely streaked*. White *eyebrow*; *long-
ish*, notched tail (cf. *Leptasthenura*).

**11. Rufous-tailed Tyrant** p.247
*Knipolegus poecilurus*
*Ashy* above, vague wing-bars; *fawn-buff
abdomen*. Rufous on *inner* tail-webs
(*vestigial* in S Tepui races). *Iris red.*

**12. Tropical Pewee** p.258
*Contopus cinereus*
Grayish cast above; *narrow whitish* wing-
bars. *Weak* eye-ring. See text for No. migrant *C. virens*.

**13. Euler's Flycatcher** p.259
*Empidonax euleri*
Washed more olive on breast, more yellow
on belly than 12; *wider, buffier wing-bars*.
No. migrant *Empidonax*: see text.

**14. Fuscous Flycatcher** p.260
*Cnemotriccus fuscatus*
Obvious *brownish cast* above; conspicuous *tawny-buff* wing-bars. *Long pale eyebrow*; black bill (cf. *Phaeomyias*).

**Flycatchers** *Myiophobus*
Prominent *buffy-to-rufescent* wing-bars.

**15. Flavescent** *M. flavicans* N p.261
*Olive* above; *bright yellow wash* below.

**16. Roraiman** p.262
*M. roraimae* S (Tepuis)
*Warm-brown* above; *cinnamon* wing-bars.

**17. Bran-colored** *M. fasciatus* p.261
*Reddish-brown* above; *streaked* below.

**Flycatchers** *Tolmomyias*
Difficult genus. *Rather wide* bill (*pale* mandible). Wing-margins *sharply yellow*.

**18. Yellow-olive** *T. sulphurescens* p.264
*Crown* more or less *grayish* with narrow
*spectacles*; iris *pale gray*. YELLOW-
MARGINED *T. assimilis* S: Almost identical,
see text; iris *may* be brown?

**19. Gray-crowned** p.264
*T. poliocephalus* S
*Smallest* and *grayest*-crowned; unlike
others, only *basal* mandible is pale.

**20. Yellow-breasted** *T. flaviventris* p.264
Different. *Bright olive-green* above; *rich yellow* below. Note *ochre lores*.

**21. Olivaceous Flatbill** p.265
*Rhynchocyclus olivaceus*
Bull-headed. *Bill very broad* (pale *mandi-
ble*); narrow *eyering*. Dark olive above;
*streaky grayish-olive* breast. FULVOUS-
BREASTED *R. fulvipectus* N (s.w. Tachira):
Similar but *tawny-fulvous* wing-edgings,
*wash on breast*.

**Flatbills** *Ramphotrigon*
Bill *fairly wide* (mandible pale *basally*).

**22. Large-headed** *R. megacephala* p.265
Smallish. Recalls *commoner* 15 (of subtropics) but *bill* somewhat *larger and wider*;
*supraloral* more *accentuated*.

**23. Rufous-tailed** *R. ruficauda* S p.265
Dark olive above with *streaky* breast. Note
*rich rufous* on wings *and tail*.

**24. Scrub Flycatcher** p.277
*Sublegatus modestus*
Similar to various *Elaenias* (*no* crown-
patch); below *more contrasty, clearer gray
and yellow*. Note short *all-black* bill; *narrow*
but *distinct supraloral*.

GUDOR

PLATE 30 TYRANT FLYCATCHERS (Nos. 25-48 cont'd following page)

**1. Black-chested Tyrant** p.269
*Taeniotriccus andrei* S
♀ *paler* but *face and wings* like ♂.

**Spadebills** *Platyrinchus*
Very *broad* bill and *stubby tail.*

**2. White-crested** *P. platyrhynchos* S p.262
*Dark gray* crown (white patch) *contrasting
with brown* back; breast *ochraceous.*
CINNAMON-CRESTED *P. saturatus* S: *Weak*
face-pattern; *all-brown* above (rufous
patch). *Whitest below* of genus.

**3. Golden-crowned** *P. coronatus* S p.263
*Strong face-pattern;* black-bordered *rufous*
crown (golden patch in ♂).

**4. White-throated** *P. mystaceus* p.263
*Strong face-pattern;* olive-brown crown
(golden patch in ♂). Breast rich *buffy.*

**5. Yellow-throated** *P. flavigularis* N
Crown *reddish-brown* (white patch). *Much
yellower below* than 4. Subtropics.

**6. Rufous-crowned Tody-Tyrant** p.268
*Poecilotriccus ruficeps* N (Tachira)
Tody bill. *Bright rufous* crown, *bold face-
pattern.* Underparts "*divided.*"

**Tody-Flycatchers** *Todirostrum*
Rather *long flat* bill; perky narrow tail.

**7. Ruddy** *T. russatum* S (Tepuis) p.267
*Face, breast* and wing-bars *rufous.*

**8. Common** *T. cinereum* p.266
Hindcrown *and back slaty-gray;* below *all-*
yellow. SHORT-TAILED *T. viridanum* (Arid
N.w.): Differs mainly by *whitish* lores and
*much shorter* tail.

**9. Black-headed** *T. nigriceps* N p.266
Very small. *Black crown* contrasts with
*olive-yellow* back. Throat *white.*

**10. Painted** *T. chrysocrotaphum* S p.266
Like 9 but breast *boldly black-spotted.*

**11. Spotted** *T. maculatum* N p.267
Throat and breast *finely streaked with
black;* belly yellow. Delta region.

**12. Slate-headed** *T. sylvia* p.266
*Slaty* crown, white *spectacles; grayish-
white* below. *Strong golden* wing-bars.

NOTE: Nos. 14-17 are *vaguely streaked below.* Two scarce allies, *Idioptilon zosterops*
and *Snethlagea minor* occur only in
Amazonas; both recall 16 (but *not* crested).
See text.

**Tody-Tyrants** *Idioptilon*
Bill *less flat* than *Todirostrum.*

**13. Black-throated** *I. granadense* N p.268
Upper throat *blackish* with *prominent
buffy-white spectacles;* no wing-bars.

**14. Pearly-vented** p.266
*I. margaritaceiventris*
Bill *quite long.* Brownish tone above; iris
*orange.* S Tepui races *much darker* above
and (in Amazonas) *below.*

**15. Pale-eyed Pygmy-Tyrant** p.269
*Atalotriccus pilaris*
Bill *shorter* than 14. *Grayish* crown; *olive*
back. *Less* streaky; iris *straw.*

**16. Helmeted Pygmy-Tyrant** p.269
*Colopteryx galeatus*
Black-streaked, *spiky crest* (not conspicu-
ous); *weak* wing-bars. Local in N.

**17. Scale-crested Pygmy-Tyrant** p.269
*Lophotriccus pileatus* N
Broad, *rufous-and-black crest* (often incon-
spicuous); note *streaky* breast.

**18. Short-tailed Pygmy-Tyrant** p.270
*Myiornis ecaudatus*
*Tiny* with almost *nonexistent tail.*

**19. Bearded Tachuri** p.272
*Polystictus pectoralis*
*Brown* above; breast *ochraceous.* ♂ has
short, *streaky crest* and *mottled chin.*

**20. Tawny-crowned Pygmy-Tyrant** p.272
*Euscarthmus meloryphus*
Quite *brownish* above; *obscure* wing-bars.
Note *orange-rufous* crown-patch.

**21. Mouse-colored Tyrannulet** p.278
*Phaeomyias murina*
*Brownish* tone above. Note *pale eyebrow*
and *buffy wing-bars.* Smaller 22 more *olive*
above with *yellower* belly.

**22. Southern Beardless Tyrannulet** p.278
*Camptostoma obsoletum*
*Bushy-crested* crown slightly *duskier* than
allies; wing-bars *whiter* than 21.

**Tyrannulets** *Inezia*

**23. Slender-billed** *I. tenuirostris* N p.273
*Very* similar to 22. Look for slightly browner
upperparts (*crown concolor*); somewhat
*thinner* bill. Arid N.w.

**24. Pale-tipped** *I. subflava* p.273
*Sharp white* wing-bars. *Blackish tail,* outer
webs and tips *white;* iris pale.

*Plate 28 (Cont'd)    Tyrant Flycatchers    Plate 29 (Cont'd)*

**22. Piratic Flycatcher** p.251
*Legatus leucophaius*
*Small.* Head-pattern. *Streaked below*; *no rufous at all*, wings rather plain.

**Flycatchers** *Empidonomus*

**23. Variegated** *E. varius* p.250
Bill *smallish. Streaked below*, more (So. migrant race) or less (resident race shown). *Larger* than 22 with *longer, rufous-edged tail*; more *pronounced* wing-margining.

**24. Crowned Slaty-** p.251
*E. aurantioatrocristatus*
Rare So. migrant. *Smoky-gray below* with *black* crown (semiconcealed patch).

**25. Sirystes** p.248
*Sirystes sibilator*    N (local)
Blackish crown, *gray* back; *whitish under-parts*. Easily told from various allies by *contrasting white rump*.

**Flycatchers** *Myiarchus*
*Very difficult* genus, some species entirely or nearly indistinguishable *by appearance*; see text for detailed analysis and vocalizations.

**26. Brown-crested** *M. tyrannulus* p.257
Common, *large Myiarchus* with *inner* webs of tail-feathers *extensively rufous*. GREAT CRESTED *M. crinitus*: No. migrant. Similar to 26, see text.

**27. Venezuelan** *M. venezuelensis* p.256
*No* noticeable rufous on inner tail-webs. A *typical medium*-sized *Myiarchus* but nearly identical to some of the following. PANAMA *M. panamensis* N (Maracaibo basin): See text. SHORT-CRESTED *M. ferox*: Race from e. and s.e. much like 27; race from w. Venez. has *buffier crissum*. SWAINSON'S *M. swainsoni*: Resident race (S) much like 27. So. migrant race differs by *brownish* (not black) *mandible*.

**28. Dusky-capped** *M. tuberculifer* p.257
Common, *small Myiarchus* with *blackish* crown and *no* rufous in tail. PALE-EDGED *M. cephalotes* N: *Upper* altitude species, overlapping only 28. Larger. Crown *not* blackish; *outermost* webs of tail-feathers *whitish*.

**Elaenias** *Myiopagis*
Rather *dark-capped* look with (often) *more obvious coronal-patch* than *Elaenia*. Bill *smaller* than *Tolmomyias*.

**25. Greenish** *M. viridicata* p.277
Differs from others by *very obscure wing-bars*. Coronal-patch *yellow*.

**26. Forest** *M. gaimardii* p.276
Crown *slaty* (patch *white*). *Prominent yellow* wing-bars. YELLOW-CROWNED *M. flavivertex* S: Crown-patch *yellow* like 25 but wing-bars *nearly as strong* as 26; spectacles quite obscure.

**27. Gray** *M. caniceps* S (mainly) p.277
♂ *gray; bold wing-edgings*; ♀ see text.

**28. Royal Flycatcher** p.262
*Onychorhynchus coronatus*
Note *long bill* and "*hammerhead*" aspect (spectacular *fan-shaped crest* seldom displayed). Rump and *tail chestnut* (pale *cinnamon* in N race). Cf. *Attila*.

**Elaenias** *Elaenia*
*Very* difficult genus. Bill *quite small*; typically look *cresty* (semiconcealed crown-patch). *Conspicuous* wing-bars.

**29. Yellow-bellied** *E. flavogaster* p.274
One of larger Elaenias. *Very pronounced shaggy* crest; belly pale sulphur.

**30. Small-billed** *E. parvirostris* p.274
So. migrant. Smaller; crest *weaker*. LESSER *E. chiriquensis*: Almost identical (belly *a bit* yellower); crest *also* weak (unlike 29). PLAIN-CRESTED *E. cristata*: From two above by *lack* of white coronal-patch. MOUNTAIN *E. frantzii* N: *Dingier* above *and below* than others with *greenish* tone on sides of head; crest *very weak* (*no* patch). Generally *higher* elevations.

**31. Rufous-crowned** *E. ruficeps* S p.275
Darker and *browner* above; crown-patch *rufous*. Breast *vaguely streaked*.

**32. Sierran** *E. pallatangae* S (Tepuis) p.276
Note *weak* crest, distinct *yellow wash* below and generally *higher* altitudes.

**33. Great** *E. dayi* S (Tepuis) p.276
*Very large* and *dark. Upper* altitudes.

**34. Slaty** *E. strepera* p.275
So. migrant. Only *slaty-gray Elaenia*.

*Plate 30 (Cont'd)   Tyrant Flycatchers*

**25. Torrent Tyrannulet** p.273
*Serpophaga cinerea* N
*Grayish and black.* RIVER TYRANNULET S.
*hypoleuca* (Orinoco-Apure): *Smaller.* More
*uniform brownish* above; *blackish* crest-
feathers. Note *habitat of both.*

**Tyrannulets** *Mecocerculus*

**26. White-banded** *M. stictopterus* N p.274
*Medium*-sized. *Prominent white eyebrow*
and *wing-bars*; *pale grayish* below.

**27. White-throated** *M. leucophrys* p.273
Note *distinct white throat* (even in Tepuis).
SULPHUR-BELLIED *M. minor* S.w. Tachira. *Different*; more like 33 but crown *gray*, wing-
bars *buffy.*

**Tyrannulets** *Ornithion*
Distinct *white eyebrow*; *stubby tail.*

**28. Yellow-bellied** *O. semiflavum* N p.281
Crown *sepia.* Below *yellow*; *no* wing-bars.

**29. White-lored** *O. inerme* S p.280
Distinctive *white-"spotted"* wing-bars.

**30. Yellow Tyrannulet** p.271
*Capsiempis flaveola*
Quite *greenish* above; eyebrow and *entire*
underparts *bright yellow.*

**Tyrannulets** *Tyranniscus*
*Dusky* crown, *short eyebrow*; bill *short.*

**31. Golden-faced** *T. viridiflavus* N p.280
Brow *rich yellow.* Wings *edged* like 32.

**32. Paltry** *T. vilissimus* N p.279
*Bold white* eyebrow. Wings *edged* yellow.

**33. Black-capped** *T. nigrocapillus* N p.279
Contrasting *sepia or black* crown. Underparts *yellow*; note *wing-bars.* TAWNY-
RUMPED *T. uropygialis* N Mérida. Differs by
*brownish* back, *whitish* belly and *ochraceous rump.*

**34. Slender-footed** *T. gracilipes* S p.279
Crown *slaty.* Wings show yellow bars *and
edges.* See text for confusing and scarce
*Acrochordopus burmeisteri.*

**35. Yellow-crowned Tyrannulet** p.280
*Tyrannulus elatus*
*Dark crown* often reveals *golden median-
stripe. Bold* wing-bars; *small* bill.

**36. Sooty-headed Tyrannulet** p.278
*Phyllomyias griseiceps*
From 22, 34, 35 etc. by *very weak* wing-
bars. *Dusky* crown often has bushy look.

**37. Greenish Tyrannulet** p.278
*Xanthomyias virescens* N.e. Mts.
Few similars within *range and elevation*;
note *small* bill, *bold* wing-bars.

**Bristle-Tyrants** *Pogonotriccus*
*Bold dark patch* on auriculars. *Shorter* bill;
more spritely than *Leptopogon.*

**38. Yellow-bellied** *P. flaviventris* N p.271
*Rufous* spectacles. *Bright yellow* below.

**39. Venezuelan** *P. venezuelanus* N p.270
*Yellower* face, somewhat *bolder* wing-bars
than larger 40; *mandible pale.*

**40. Marble-faced** *P. ophthalmicus* N p.270
Face grizzled *with white.* Wing-bars more
*"edged."* VARIEGATED *P. poecilotis* N (local): Not unlike 40 but with *prominent cinnamon wing-bars*; nothing really similar
within range.

**Tyrannulets** *Phylloscartes*
*Face-pattern* recalls *Pogonotriccus.*

**41. Chapman's** p.271
*P. chapmani* S (Tepuis)
Breast *yellowish*; wing-bars *tawny-buff.*

**42. Black-fronted** *P. nigrifrons* S p.271
Tepuis. Note *black forehead*; below
*grayish.* See text for *P. superciliaris* (S. de
Perija): Short *rufous* eyebrow.

**43. Olive-striped Flycatcher** p.281
*Mionectes olivaceus* N
*Dark* olive, *finely streaked yellow* below;
note white *postocular* spot.

**44. Ochre-bellied Flycatcher** p.282
*Pipromorpha oleaginea*
Olive-gray breast; *rich ochraceous belly.*
MCCONNELL'S *P. macconnelli* S: *Very* similar
but *lacks any evidence* of wing-bars or
edging on tertials.

**Flycatchers** *Leptopogon*
*Dark patch* on *auriculars*; bill narrow.

**45. Rufous-breasted** *L. rufipectus* N p.281
S.w. Tachira. *Rufous* throat and breast.

**46. Slaty-capped** *L. superciliaris* p.281
*Slate-gray* crown; *yellowish* wing-bars.

**47. Sepia-capped** p.281
*L. amaurocephalus*
*Dark brown* crown; *tawny-buff* wing-bars.
Breast *dingier* than 41 (46 mainly N).

**48. Ruddy-tailed Flycatcher** p.260
*Terenotriccus erythrurus*
Very *small. Cinnamon* breast; *wing-edging,
rump and tail bright rufous.*

PLATE 31 TAPACULOS, WRENS and GNATWRENS

**Tapaculos** *Scytalopus*
*Confusing* genus of *higher* altitudes. *Very dark* with *short* bill. Young are much *browner*, more or less *barred below*.

**1. Unicolored** *S. unicolor* N p.225
*Uniformly blackish slate-gray.*

**2. Rufous-vented** *S. femoralis* N p.226
*White crown-spot*; faint rusty *barring* on flanks. ♀ often *paler* gray below.

**3. Brown-rumped** *S. latebricola* N p.226
Dark *mouse-gray* below; *barred flanks and rump* a bit brighter rusty-brown than 2. (3a. Young.) ANDEAN *S. magellanicus* N (local): Rather *paler*; *plain bright rusty* rump and flanks.

**4. Rufous Wren** p.290
*Cinnycerthia unirufa* N
Most like w. races of Rufous Spinetail but tail *shorter*; wings *lightly barred*. *Family groups* may contain young with *whitish forecrown*. Local.

**Wrens** *Campylorhynchus*

**5. Bicolored** *C. griseus* p.289
All races *very large* and *white below*.

**6. Stripe-backed** *C. nuchalis* p.289
*Boldly striped* above and *spotted* below.

**Wrens** *Thryothorus*
*Cheeks* more or less *striped*; tail normal.

**7. Rufous-breasted** *T. rutilus* N p.291
Bright rufous *breast*; *black* face *and throat speckled* with white.

**8. Moustached** *T. genibarbis* N p.290
*Lower mantle* chestnut; *below* rather *dingy*. Prominent *black submalar stripe*.

**9. Coraya** *T. coraya* S p.291
*Much more black on face* than 11 and belly dingier (breast rufescent in e.).

**10. Rufous-and-white** *T. rufalbus* N p.291
*Bright rufous-chestnut* above. Median underparts *white*; crissum *barred*.

**11. Buff-breasted** *T. leucotis* p.292
*Warm brown* above. Races vary below: from *very rich* to *nearly whitish buff*.

**Wood-Wrens** *Henicorhina*
*Heavily striped cheeks* with *stubby tail*. Note breast coloration. *No overlap*.

**12. Gray-breasted** *H. leucophrys* N p.293

**13. White-breasted** *H. leucosticta* S p.293

**Wrens** *Troglodytes*
Smallish; tail *not short*. *Cheeks plain* but with *moderately evident eyebrow*.

**14. Mountain** *T. solstitialis* N p.292
*Ruddier* than 15 with *broader* eyebrow.

**15. House** *T. aedon* p.292
Widespread. Crissum *not barred like* 14.

**16. Tepui** *T. rufulus* S (Tepuis) p.292
*Chestnut-brown* above. Below *very rufescent* or (Amazonas) more *grayish-white*.

**Wrens** *Cistothorus*
Small with *striped back*. Note *habitat*.

**17. Grass** *C. platensis* p.290
Tachira race has more and richer *buff*.

**18. Paramo** *C. meridae* N (local) p.290
*Higher zone* than 17 when in *same* range. Back-striping *extensive*; flanks *barred*.

**19. Musician Wren** p.294
*Cyphorhinus arada* S (Bolivar)
*Rufous face* and breast; *striped nuchal collar*. Note *bill shape*; *bare orbital* patch.

**Wrens** *Microcerculus*
Longish bill; *stubby tail*. Face *plain*.

**20. Nightingale** *M. marginatus* p.293
Variable: *squamulatus* race often *well-scaled* below. Amazonian race (20a) much more *white-breasted*, esp. adult.

**21 Flutist** *M. ustulatus* S (Tepuis) p.294
Rather *uniform rich brown*, faintly barred on belly. Note *lack* of eyebrow.

**22. Wing-banded** *M. bambla* S p.294
Conspicuous *white wing-band*.

**23. Collared Gnatwren** p.301
*Microbates collaris* S
*Long* bill; *short tail*. Bold *face-pattern*; black *chest-band* (cf. *Dichrozona*).

**24. Long-billed Gnatwren** p.301
*Ramphocaenus melanurus*
*Very long bill* and rather *long* tail (tipped white in N.w.). *Cheeks* fulvous.

**Gnatcatchers** *Polioptila*
*Blue-gray* above. Long, *bicolored tail*.

**25. Tropical** *P. plumbea* p.302
♂ cap *black*. ♀ cap gray; *cheeks white*.

**26. Guianan** *P. guianensis* S p.302
Breast and cheeks *darker and grayer* than 25; note narrow *white eyering*.

PLATE 32 DIPPER, MIMIDS and THRUSHES

## 31

**1. White-capped Dipper** p.289
*Cinclus leucocephalus* N (Mt. streams)
*Shape, pattern, behavior* diagnostic.

**2. Tropical Mockingbird** p.295
*Mimus gilvus*
Slender; mainly *pale gray*. White-*edged*
wings; *long*, broadly *white-tipped tail*.

**3. Black-capped Mockingthrush** p.295
*Donacobius atricapillus*
*Black* cap; *coffee-brown* above; *rich buff*
below. White in *wings* and long tail; iris *yellow*. Always near *water*.

**4. Gray-cheeked Thrush** p.297
*Catharus minimus*
No. migrant. *Grayish*-brown above; *breast
spotted*. Two allies, Swainson's and Veery,
also winter; see text.

**Nightingale-Thrushes** *Catharus*
Medium-size. *Bright orange bill and legs*.

**5. Orange-billed** p.296
*C. aurantiirostris* N
*Warm-brown* above; *grayish* below.

**6. Slaty-backed** *C. fuscater* N p.296
*Dark slaty-gray* above; iris *white*.

**7. Spotted** *C. dryas* N p.296
*Apricot-yellow* below with *spotted breast*;
iris dark. Local.

**Solitaires** *Myadestes*
Arboreal; *short* legs. *Upright carriage*; longish
tail held *vertically* (not cocked).

**8. Andean** *M. ralloides* N p.296
*Warm-brown* above; *leaden-gray* below.
*Silvery-white* on *outer* tail-feathers.

**9. Rufous-brown** *M. leucogenys* S p.296
Tepuis (Bolivar). No *Turdus* has *short bill*
and *orange-rufous median throat*.

**Thrushes** *Platycichla*
*Larger* than *Catharus*; *bill, legs yellow*.

**10. Yellow-legged** *P. flavipes* p.297
♂ *black* with *gray back, rump* and (usually)
belly. ♀ quite *dingy*, best told from similar
*Turdus* by *brighter yellow* on bill and *particularly legs*.

**11. Pale-eyed** *P. leucops* p.298
♂ plumage *black*; iris *white. Dingy*-throated
♀ like 10 or 15 but somewhat *darker, especially breast*; soft parts quite *brownish*.
Tepuis in S.

**Thrushes** *Turdus*
A familiar genus; sexes usually alike. Several,
especially *lower elevation* species, are quite
*confusing*.

**12. Great** *T. fuscater* N p.298
Obviously *much larger* than others.

**13. Glossy-black** *T. serranus* N p.298
Rather large. ♂ plumage *black*; iris *dark*. ♀
quite *dingy*, much like 10 or 15 but *larger*
with *grayer belly*; bill and legs amber-color.
In N.e., ♀ more distinct: *sootier*; bill *bright
yellow*.

**14. Chestnut-bellied** *T. fulviventris* N p.299
From all others by bright *rufous belly*. ♀
head *sooty*, less black than ♂.

**15. Black-hooded** *T. olivater* p.298
♂ *black-hooded* (S Tepui races have black
greatly *reduced* and *confined to head*). ♀
*dingy*-throated; *paler and tawnier on belly*
than *Platycichla* or 13; bill dark, legs amber.

NOTE: All remaining species have *pale throats*
which are more or less *streaked*.

**16. Bare-eyed** *T. nudigenis* p.300
Most like 19 but easily told from all by *conspicuous* bare ochraceous eyering.

**17. White-necked** *T. albicollis* p.300
*Thickly streaked* throat bordered *below* by
*distinct white crescent*; note contrast of
deep brown back, *gray* breast.

**18. Black-billed** *T. ignobilis* p.299
*Grayer* above than 17 or 19. Bill *entirely
sooty-black. Throat* of smaller N race *approaches effect* of 17 but streaking *finer*,
white crescent *much reduced*. Mainly
Tepuis in S.

**19. Pale-breasted** *T. leucomelas* p.299
*Mantle decidedly browner*, bill *paler* than
18; throat *generously* streaked.

**20. Cocoa** *T. fumigatus* p.300
*Much more rufescent* above and below
than any of preceding. PALE-VENTED *T. obsoletus*: Barely differs from 20 by somewhat
*paler, whiter crissum; no overlap* likely.
LAWRENCE'S *T. lawrencii* S (very local): *Less*
rufescent; look for *pure white crissum* and
*black-tipped, bright yellow* bill.

PLATE 33  VIREOS and WOOD-WARBLERS

## 32

**1. Rufous-browed Peppershrike**  p.304
*Cyclarhis gujanensis*
Very *stout, hooked bill*. Grayish head with prominent, *broad rufous eyebrow*.

**Shrike-Vireos**  *Smaragdolanius*
Heavy hooked bill. *Golden eyebrows*.

**2. Slaty-capped**  *S. leucotis*  S  p.304
Note *striking face-pattern*.

**3. Green**  *S. pulchellus*  N (local)  p.304
*Bright grass-green* above; yellow below.

**4. Red-eyed Vireo**  *Vireo olivaceus*  p.305
*Gray crown*; strong *white eyebrow outlined by black*. Two allies occur in winter: Black-whiskered (also breeds offshore islands) and Yellow-throated Vireos; see text.

**5. Warbling Vireo**  *Vireo gilvus*  N  p.305
*Dull brown* crown; *whitish brows*.

**Greenlets**  *Hylophilus*
*Small* vireos; bills tend to look *pale*. Many, especially in S, are *very similar*.

**6. Tawny-crowned**  p.307
*H. ochraceiceps*  S
Browner above. *Forecrown contrasting rufous*; iris *pale*. E. Bolivar race nearer 7 but tail *russet*; iris dark?

**7. Brown-headed**  *H. brunneiceps*  S  p.306
Amazonas. Crown *dull brown*. Mainly *buffy-grayish* below; iris?. DUSKY-CAPPED *H. hypoxanthus* S (Amazonas): Similar above to 7; *all buffy-yellow* below.

**8. Buff-cheeked**  *H. muscicapinus*  S  p.306
*Rearcrown gray*. Face and breast *brightly buff*; iris dark.

**9. Gray-chested**  *H. semicinereus*  S  p.306
Similar to 10 (iris *pale*) but crown *olive-gray*. Breast *gray*, tinged olive-yellow *at sides only*. Both uncommon.

**10. Lemon-chested**  *H. thoracicus*  S  p.305
No. Bolivar. *Rearcrown gray*. Olive-yellow *pectoral band*; iris *pale*. ASHY-HEADED *H. pectoralis* S (Delta): Crown *gray*. More extensive, *brighter yellow* on breast than 10; iris dark.

**11. Tepui**  *H. sclateri*  S (Tepuis)  p.306
*Crown and wings* contrastingly *gray*. Breast yellowish; iris *pale*.

**12. Rufous-naped**  p.306
*H. semibrunneus*  N
S. de Perija. Rich *rufous crown and nape*. Face and throat *pale gray*.

**13. Golden-fronted**  p.307
*H. aurantiifrons*  N
*Tawny-gold forehead* with brown crown. Underparts *buffy-yellow*; iris dark.

**14. Scrub**  *H. flavipes*  p.307
Crown *concolor* with back. Buffy wash on breast. *Legs* and mandible *flesh-color*; iris brown-to-gray.

Migrant No. Am. **Warblers** (winter plumage):

**15. Black-and-white**  *Mniotilta varia*  p.315
**16. Tennessee**  *Vermivora peregrina*  p.316
**17. Blackpoll**  *Dendroica striata*  p.319
**18. Blackburnian**  *D. fusca*  p.318

**19. Yellow Warbler**  p.317
*Dendroica petechia*
*Very yellow*. Chestnut *varies* on ♂ head in N *resident* races (19a. *paraguanae*). All show breast streaking.

**20. Tropical Parula**  *Parula pitiayumi*  p.316
*Dull blue* above; yellow below. Note *black* for       face; *wing-bars*.

**Warblers**  *Basileuterus*

**21. Gray-headed**  *B. griseiceps*  N  p.325
*Head* appears *slate-gray* with *white loral* spot. Northeastern mts.

**22. Russet-crowned**  *B. coronatus*  N  p.325
*Black-bordered rufous* coronal-stripe. *Throat gray*.

**23. Gray-throated**  *B. cinereicollis*  N  p.325
*Black-bordered yellow* coronal-patch. *Gray* throat extends down *over breast*.

**24. Rufous-capped**  *B. rufifrons*  N  p.325
W. Zulia. *Chestnut* cap; *white* eyebrow.

**25. Black-crested**  p.323
*B. nigrocristatus*  N
Like 26 but *mid*-crown, lores *jet-black*.

**26. Flavescent**  *B. flaveolus*  N  p.324
*All-olive* above. *Distinct* yellow *supraloral* stripe. Pale legs; *expressive* tail (cf. ♀ 30). CITRINE *B. luteoviridis* N: Duller than 26; legs *darker*. Much *higher* altitudes.

**27. Three-striped**  *B. tristriatus*  N  p.324
Yellow-*buff* below. *Contrasting* coronal-stripe and brows *olive-buff*. In so. Tachira and Perija, *black cheeks added*.

**28. Golden-crowned**  *B. culicivorus*  p.324
Coronal-stripe *golden-orange*; brows *grayish-white*. Mantle *grayer* in N race.

**29. Two-banded**  *B. bivittatus*  S  p.324
Tepuis. Rather like a *larger* edition of 28 but note *yellow-olive* eyebrows.

**30. Masked Yellowthroat**  p.321
*Geothlypis aequinoctialis*
♂ black *masked*. ♀ grayer above; supraloral *weak* (cf. 26). Note habitat.

**31. Northern Waterthrush**  p.320
*Seiurus noveboracensis*  No. migrant

**32. River Warbler**  p.325
*Phaeothlypis rivularis*  S (and Delta)
Brownish above, *cinnamon face*; *buffy-white* below. *Fans tail*. Near ground.

**33. Rose-breasted Chat**  p.321
*Granatellus pelzelni*  S
Distinctive; note *rosy crissum of* ♀.

33

PLATE 34   REDSTARTS, HONEYCREEPERS, CONEBILLS, etc.

**Redstarts**  *Myioborus*
Expressive tail, outer-feathers white.

**1. Golden-fronted**  *M. ornatus*  N  p.322
Bright *yellow crown*. S.w. Tachira.

**2. White-fronted**  *M. albifrons*  N  p.323
*Black crown* with rufous patch; *white facial mask*. Andes.

**3. Slate-throated**  *M. miniatus*  p.322
From other *Myioborus* by *slaty-black throat*. Widespread in N; Tepuis in S. YELLOW-FACED *M. pariae* N (Sucre): Much like 4 but with *yellow spectacles*.

**4. Brown-capped**  *M. brunniceps*  S  p.323
*Yellow-to-orange throat*. Widespread on Tepuis but occurs only with 3.

**5. White-faced**  *M. albifacies*  S  p.323
*Orange* below; *face white*. Tepuis (n. Amazonas); overlaps 3. *M. cardonai* occurs only on *one* Tepui in c. Bolivar. Like 5 but only *spectacles* white.

**6. American Redstart**  p.322
*Setophaga ruticilla*  No. migrant
Large salmon (♂) or yellow (♀) *tail-patches*.

**7. Green Honeycreeper**  p.331
*Chlorophanes spiza*
♂ shining *blue-green* with *black cap*. ♀ *all bright green*; mandible *yellow*.

**Honeycreepers**  *Cyanerpes*
Bill slightly *decurved*. ♂♂ some shade of *violet-blue*. ♀♀ green; *streaky* below.

**8. Red-legged**  *C. cyaneus*  p.331
Bill *long*. ♂ crown turquoise; legs *red*. ♀ *vaguely* streaked with *pale eyebrow*.

**9. Purple**  *C. caeruleus*  p.331
Bill *long* but *tail short*. ♂ throat black; legs *bright yellow*. ♀ *strongly* streaked with *buff* lores and throat.

**10. Short-billed**  *C. nitidus*  S  p.331
*Bill* and tail *short*. ♂ brighter than 9, black throat *more extensive*; legs *pinkish*. ♀ like 9 but face *less* buffy.

**Dacnis**  *Dacnis*
*Sharply pointed* bill as in *Conirostrum*.

**11. Blue**  *D. cayana*  p.332
♂ *turquoise*-blue; black *throat*. ♀ *grass-green*; *blue cap*, grayish throat.

**12. Black-faced**  *D. lineata*  p.332
♂ *lighter* turquoise than 11; *black mask*, golden iris. ♀ *brownish-olive* above; *olive-buffy* below. Mainly S.

**13. White-bellied**  *D. albiventris*  S  p.332
♂ deeper, *more cobalt*-blue than other Dacnis (cf. *Tangara*). ♀ *green* above; *yellowish* below. Local in Amazonas.

**14. Yellow-bellied**  *D. flaviventer*  S  p.332
♂ *black and yellow*. ♀ similar to 12.

**15. Bananaquit**  *Coereba flaveola*  p.327
*White eyebrow*, *gray* throat; *yellow* below;

often a white wing-speculum. Some Island races *all-black* (15a. *laurae*).

**Conebills**  *Conirostrum*

**16. Bicolored**  *C. bicolor*  N  p.326
*Blue-gray* above; *grayish-buff* below. ♀ may breed in *grayish-olive*/yellowish Immature plumage (16a). Coastal.

**17. Chestnut-vented**  p.326
*C. speciosum*  N
♂ *darker blue-gray* than 16; *crissum chestnut*. ♀ near 18 but back *greener*; underparts *less* buffy. Llanos.

**18. White-eared**  *C. leucogenys*  N  p.326
Smallest. ♂ *crown black*; *auriculars white*. ♀ *blue-gray* above; face and underparts *bright buff*; *rump whitish*.

**19. Capped**  *C. albifrons*  N (local)  p.327
♂ dull *purplish-black*; *crown white* (s.w. Tachira) or *dark blue* (Aragua; D.F.). ♀ *olive-green* above; crown *dull blue*, throat *and breast grayish*.

**20. Blue-backed**  *C. sitticolor*  N  p.326
*Mantle blue*. Lower underparts rich *rufous*; lacks eyebrow in s.w. Tachira.

**Flower-piercers**  *Diglossa*
Slightly *upturned* bill *hooked* at tip.

**21. Rusty**  *D. sittoides*  N  p.331
♂ bluish-slate above; *cinnamon below*. ♀ very dull but note *Diglossa* bill, *streaking* below. VENEZUELAN *D. venezuelensis* (N.e. mts.): ♂ like a *larger, blacker* 22; tufts vestigial (*no overlap*). ♀ dingier than 21.

**22. White-sided**  *D. albilatera*  N  p.331
♂ dark slaty; *white flank-tufts* and wing-linings. ♀ *buffy* below *without* streaking; flank-tufts less than ♂.

**23. Greater**  *D. major*  S  p.329
Tepuis of *Bolivar*. *Quite large*; mainly bluish-slate with black *face*. SCALED *D. duidae* S (Tepuis of Amazonas): *Smaller* than 23. *Whole head* blackish; breast scaly; crissum *gray*.

**24. Coal-black**  *D. carbonaria*  N  p.329
Note *chestnut belly*. *Mantle black* with gray shoulders (cf. 20).

**25. Glossy**  *D. lafresnayii*  N  p.329
*Glossy-black* with *blue*-gray shoulders.

**26. Black**  *D. humeralis*  N  p.329
S.w. Tachira race *smaller* than 25; shoulders *ashy*-gray. S. de Perija race *black* with gray *rump* (not shoulder).

**27. Bluish**  *D. caerulescens*  N  p.328
Dusty *grayish-blue*. Bill more normal, *lacking* strong hook; iris dull orange.

**28. Masked**  *D. cyanea*  N  p.329
Rich *ultramarine*-blue with well-defined *black mask*; iris red.

PLATE 35 TANAGERS and ALLIES

**Chlorophonias** *Chlorophonia*
*Bright grass-green. Plump; short-*tailed.

**1. Chestnut-breasted** p.338
*C. pyrrhophrys* N
*Deep cobalt crown* and dark brow in ♂♀. ♂
*median* belly *chestnut*; *rump* yellow.

**2. Blue-naped** *C. cyanea* p.338
♂ belly *clear yellow*. Amount of *blue* above
variable but always on *nape and rump* (*not
crown*). ♀ belly *olive-yellow*; blue confined
to *nape*. Tepuis in S.

**3. Swallow-Tanager** p.328
*Tersina viridis*
♂ *turquoise*; black *mask*, *barred flanks*,
*white* median belly. ♀ differs from green
tanagers by *barring on flanks*.

**Tanagers** *Tangara*
Rather small, brightly colored genus; sexes
usually alike. Cf. Plate 34.

**4. Golden** *T. arthus* N p.334
Rich *yellow head* with large *black cheek-
patch*. S. de Perija race *entirely golden* below, lacking chestnut.

**5. Flame-faced** *T. parzudakii* N p.335
Most like 6 but *face fiery-red*; back black;
below *opalescent*. S.w. Tachira.

**6. Saffron-crowned** p.334
*T. xanthocephala* N
*Golden head* with black *mask*. *Turquoise-
green*; belly and crissum fawn.

**7. Blue-and-black** *T. vassorii* N p.337
Only *Tangara* in range predominantly *pure
blue*; wings and tail *black*.

**8. Rufous-cheeked** *T. rufigenis* N p.335
Rather dull. *Turquoise-green* crown, breast
and rump; from ♀♀ of 9 and 13 by *rufous
cheeks* and *fawn* crissum.

**9. Black-capped** *T. heinei* N p.337
♂ has *black crown* and *streaky opa-
lescent-green cheeks*, throat and breast. ♀
duller and greener above but retains *darkish crown, streaky-faced* effect.

**10. Beryl-spangled** *T. nigroviridis* N p.336
Note *spotted effect* due to *opalescent-blue
spangles*; mask and back black.

**11. Blue-necked** *T. cyanicollis* N p.335
Solid black mask, back and *underparts*
contrasting with *bright turquoise head* and
*bronzy-gold* wing-coverts.

**12. Burnished-buff** *T. cayana* p.336
Largely *opalescent-buff* with *coppery
crown*, black *auriculars*, greenish-blue
wings and tail. ♀ similar but duller.

**13. Black-headed** *T. cyanoptera* p.337
♂ *opalescent* with *black head*, wings and
tail. ♀ much like 9 but *crown* and under
parts *paler and grayer*. S Tepui race generally *darker and dingier*, pale areas more
mottled with dusky.

**14. Bay-headed** *T. gyrola* p.336
Mainly *bright green* with *rich red-chestnut
head*. Underparts green (N) or with varying
amount of *blue* (S races).

**15. Turquoise** *T. mexicana* p.336
Much black above, somewhat spangled on
*cobalt-blue face* and breast; *belly creamy
yellow*; flanks black-*spotted*.

**16. Speckled** *T. guttata* p.333
Most *widespread* of 3 similar "speckled"
*Tangara*. Face, principally *orbital area*, *yel-
lower* than 17, especially in S.

**17. Spotted** *T. punctata* S p.333
Slightly smaller than 16. *Lacks any bright*
yellow on face; *wing-edgings pure green*
without turquoise tone.

**18. Green-and-gold** *T. schrankii* S p.333
From "speckled" types by *bold black*
cheek-patch, lack of spotting *below*. ♀
similar, crown and rump *less* golden.

**19. Masked** *T. nigrocincta* S p.335
Head *pale lavender-blue*. Back and *breast*
black; median belly *white*.

**20. Yellow-bellied** *T. xanthogastra* S p.334
Much like 16 or 17 but breast much
*greener*; *median belly bright yellow* rather
than white. Commonest on Tepuis.

**21. Dotted** *T. varia* S p.334
Essentially *all-green*. ♂ has *vaguely speckled* aspect (*far less* than 20, etc.) and *bluish*
wings; both lacking in ♀.

**22. Paradise** *T. chilensis* S p.333
Note brilliant *apple-green face*, yellow and
*scarlet* lower back and rump.

**23. Opal-rumped** *T. velia* S p.332
*Deep purplish-blue* below; *rufous* abdomen
and shining *opalescent* rump.

wynne

PLATE 36  TANAGERS and ALLIES

**Euphonias** *Euphonia*
Bill and tail *stubby*. ♀♀ difficult (*not* analyzed); best told by attendant ♂.

**1. Thick-billed** *E. laniirostris* N p.340
This and 2 are only blue-black Euphonias with *yellow throats*. Forecrown *extends well past eye*.

**2. Violaceous** *E. violacea* p.340
*Richer* yellow below than 1; forecrown more *restricted*, reaching *only to eye*.

**3. Orange-bellied** *E. xanthogaster* p.338
Breast *much richer* yellow than similars. Forecrown *rufous* (N) or *deep* yellow and *extensive* (S). FINSCH'S *E. finschi* S (e. Bolivar): Differs from S race of 3 by *rich* yellow below merging into *fulvous belly and crissum*.

**4. Trinidad** *E. trinitatis* p.339
*Extensive* forecrown and underparts (including *crissum*) *bright yellow*. PURPLE-THROATED *E. chlorotica*: Mainly S. Probably inseparable in field from 4; throat and nape gloss *slightly* more *purplish*. Note ranges.

**5. White-vented** *E. minuta* p.339
Forecrown reaches *only to eye*. *White crissum* diagnostic.

**6. Blue-hooded** *E. musica* p.338
*Both sexes have blue crown and nape*. ♂ *deep* yellow below with yellow *rump*.

**7. Golden-sided** *E. cayennensis* S p.338
Golden *pectoral-patches*. E. Bolivar.

**8. Rufous-bellied** *E. rufiventris* S p.340
*Lacks* yellow forecrown (as 7). Note *rufous belly*.

**9. Plumbeous** *E. plumbea* S p.341
Glossy *steel-gray* upperparts; *chest sharply defined* from *rich* yellow belly.

**10. Golden-bellied** *E. chrysopasta* S p.341
Somewhat *glossier olive* above than similar ♀ Euphonias; best told by *pale gray lores* in both sexes.

**Tanagers** *Hemithraupis*

**11. Guira** *H. guira* p.348
♂ has *black face outlined* by yellow; *breast and rump orange-rufous*. ♀ warbler-like but note *yellowish rump*.

**12. Yellow-backed** *H. flavicollis* S p.348
♂ *black* above; *yellow throat* and *lower back*. ♀ similar to 11 but much *darker* above, *dingier* below (crissum yellow).

**13. Hooded** *Nemosia pileata* p.348
Mantle *grayish-blue*; underparts *white*. ♂ has *black cap*; ♀ buffy-tinged below. In both note white *lores*, *golden* iris and flesh-yellow legs.

**14. Fulvous-headed Tanager** p.349
*Thlypopsis fulviceps* N
Grayish; *entire head rufous-chestnut*. ORANGE-HEADED *T. sordida* (Orinoco): Recalls 14. Head *orange-cinnamon*; ocular area, throat *yellow*. Below buffier.

**Bush-Tanagers** *Chlorospingus*
Note *olive-yellow pectoral band*.

**15. Common** *C. ophthalmicus* N p.351
Cap *brownish*-gray to *sooty-brown* (in s.w. Andes). Note *white postocular orbital-spot* and *speckled* throat.

**16. Ashy-throated** *C. canigularis* N p.351
Cap *grayer* than 15; *no* eye-spot. Throat *plain gray*. S. Tachira.

**17. Gray-hooded Hemispingus** p.350
*Cnemoscopus rubrirostris* N (s.w. Tach.)
*Entire hood* clear *gray*; bill *pinkish*.

**Hemispinguses** *Hemispingus*

**18. Gray-capped** *H. reyi* N p.349
Olive above; *yellow* below. *Crown gray*.

**19. Superciliaried** *H. superciliaris* N p.349
Olive above; *eyebrow* and *underparts yellowish*. Andes only.

**20. Oleaginous** *H. frontalis* N p.350
Differs from 19 by *ochraceous-buff* eyebrow and underparts, especially so in *area of overlap*.

**21. Black-capped** *H. atropileus* N p.349
Similar to 20 but *crown and cheeks black*; eyebrow *whiter*. S.w. Tachira.

**22. Black-eared** *H. melanotis* N p.350
*Back and crown gray*, only *hint* of eyebrow; *cinnamon* below. Much like ♀ 25 but *no* trace of *blue*. S.w. Tachira.

**23. Slaty-backed** *H. goeringi* N p.350
Back *gray*; crown *black*; eyebrow *long and white*. Underparts *rufous*. C. Andes.

**24. Black-headed** *H. verticalis* N p.350
*Distinct black head* with *clay-colored coronal-stripe* and iris. S.w. Tachira.

**25. Fawn-breasted Tanager** p.337
*Pipraeidea melanonota*
Black *mask*. ♂ has *blue crown* and rump; ♀ *duller* above but *rump still bluish*. Underparts *fawn-buff*; iris red.

**26. Rufous-crested Tanager** p.347
*Creurgops verticalis* N (s.w. Tachira)
Bill *stout*. *Gray above* (*no* ear-patch); *below cinnamon* (also ♂ *crown-patch*).

**27. Plush-capped Finch** p.352
*Catamblyrhynchus diadema* N
Note *thick stubby bill*; graduated tail. Forecrown *golden*; below *chestnut*.

PLATE 37 TANAGERS

## 36

**Tanagers** *Thraupis*

**1. Blue-gray** *T. episcopus* p.342
*Head always paler than back.* Variable: in e. and S, wings bluer or also with white shoulders.

**2. Glaucous** *T. glaucocolpa* N p.343
From 1 by *grayer* head *concolor* with back; *light turquoise* flight-feathers contrast with dark primary-coverts; whiter median belly. Mainly coastal.

**3. Palm** *T. palmarum* p.343
Dull *grayish-olive.* Note lighter and darker *two-toned pattern on wings.*

**4. Blue-capped** *T. cyanocephala* N p.343
4a. central Coastal Cord. race
Variable; all races have *blue crown, bright olive* upperparts. Below *gray or blue*; pale malar in e. Cf. Mt.-Tanagers.

**Tanagers** *Piranga*
♂♂ mostly some shade of *bright red.* ♀♀ *olive* above; bright *yellowish* below.

**5. Hepatic** *P. flava* p.344
Bill *dark*; *auriculars* slightly *grayer, duskier* than *rubra.* S Tepui race ♂ is *deeper, richer* red. SUMMER *P. rubra*: No. migrant. *Paler* bill. ♂ somewhat *rosier* red; ♀ has *tawnier-orange* tone below, especially on *crissum.*

**6. White-winged** *P. leucoptera* p.345
Small. Blackish wings with *bold white wing-bars* in *both* sexes. Tepuis in S.

**7. Black-faced Tanager** p.351
*Schistochlamys melanopis*
*Gray body* with *black face and chest.* Non-forest species; cf. Grosbeaks.

**8. Red-crowned Ant-Tanager** p.345
*Habia rubica* N (mainly)
♂ throat and contrasting *crown-stripe rosy-red.* ♀ *olive-brown* above, *dingy buff* below; throat a bit brighter; *concealed crown-stripe tawny.*

**Tanagers** *Ramphocelus*
Deep crimson and black ♂♂ have swollen, *silvery mandible.* Bills of *dusky-maroon* ♀♀ recall ♂ but much less striking.

**9. Silver-beaked** *R. carbo* p.343
Slightly variable. *No* overlap with 10?

**10. Crimson-backed** *R. dimidiatus* N p.344
Belly and *especially rump* much *redder and brighter* than respective sexes of 9. Maracaibo basin.

**11. Rose-breasted Thrush-Tanager** p.348
*Rhodinocichla rosea* N
*Dark gray* above with *rose-red* (♂) or *orange-rufous* (♀) underparts. Note rather *long* bill and *eyebrows.*

**Tanagers** *Tachyphonus*
Black ♂♂ have varying amount of *white on inner*-shoulder, and *white wing-linings.*

**12. White-lined** *T. rufus* p.346
♂ normally appears *all-black* (mandible *bluish*); white inner-shoulder and linings *noticeable in flight.* ♀ uniform *rufous*, paler below with *conical* bill.

**13. Red-shouldered** *T. phoenicius* S p.347
♂ differs from larger 12 by *half scarlet* inner-shoulder. ♀ most like 15 but *entirely grayish* above (no olive); underparts *much less* buffy.

**14. White-shouldered** *T. luctuosus* p.347
Small. *Extensive white* on ♂ shoulder. ♀ back *olive*; head *gray*; throat *whitish*, underparts *yellow* (cf. *Eucometis*).

**15. Fulvous-crested** *T. surinamus* p.346
♂ *rump* and *small* crown-patch *golden-buff* (throat *black*); chestnut flank-patches. ♀ *darker* above than 14; quite *buffy below* (not yellow). S plus Delta.

**16. Flame-crested** *T. cristatus* S p.346
♂ *rump* and narrow *throat*-patch *golden-buff; conspicuous* crown-patch *golden-orange or vermilion.* ♀ *warm-brown* above; *rich ochraceous* below.

**17. Gray-headed Tanager** p.347
*Eucometis penicillata* N (mainly)
*Bright olive* above; *rich yellow* below. *Well-demarcated gray head* (weak crest).

**18. Olive-backed Tanager** p.347
*Mitrospingus oleagineus* S (Tepuis)
Dull *olive* above including *crown; olive-yellow* below with *gray face and throat.* Note bill shape and *gray iris.*

**19. Fulvous Shrike-Tanager** p.346
*Lanio fulvus* S (very local in N)
Solid *black head* contrasts with *tawny-yellow and fulvous back* in ♂. ♀ quite similar to ♀ 16 but *rump and crissum richer rufous.* Note *shrike-like* bill.

**20. Blue-backed Tanager** p.345
*Cyanicterus cyanicterus* S (e. Bolivar)
Superb ♂ *cobalt-blue* and *bright yellow.* ♀ duller; differs by blue being *paler*, more greenish; *face and throat buffy-yellow.* Note *heavy* bill. Rare.

PLATE 38 LARGE TANAGERS, and ICTERIDS (In part)

## 37

**1. Buff-breasted Mountain-Tanager** p.342
*Dubusia taeniata* N
*Silvery-blue eyebrow* and *buffy chest.*

**Mountain-Tanagers** *Anisognathus*

**2. Lachrymose** *A. lacrymosus* N p.341
*Mustard*-yellow *facial spots* and *underparts*; *less* blackish on head in far w.
SCARLET-BELLIED *A. igniventris* N (S.w. Tachira). Pattern recalls 2 except throat *to chest black*, and yellow is *replaced by scarlet*; rump azure-blue.

**3. Blue-winged** *A. flavinucha* N p.342
Large *yellow crown-patch*; bright blue on wings. Moss-green *back* in Tachira.

**4. Golden-crowned Tanager** p.341
*Iridosornis rufivertex* N (s.w. Tachira)
Mostly *rich, deep blue*. Head black with *golden crown*; crissum *chestnut.*

**Mountain-Tanagers** *Buthraupis*
Larger and huskier than *Anisognathus.*

**5. Black-chested** *B. eximia* N p.342
*Black* of face extends over *upper breast* (unlike 6). *Crown dusky-blue*; mantle *moss-green.* S.w. Tachira.

**6. Hooded** *B. montana* N p.342
*Entire head* black; iris *red.* Mantle *dusky-blue.* S. de Perija; s.w. Tachira.

**7. Magpie Tanager** p.351
*Cissopis leveriana*
Size, *pattern, long* tail diagnostic.

**8. White-capped Tanager** p.351
*Sericossypha albocristata* N
*Large and black* with *snowy-white cap*; throat crimson-to-maroon. S.w. Tachira.

**Oropendolas** *Psarocolius*
Giant icterids (♂ much larger than ♀) with *undertail* typically *all-yellow.* This genus has *feathered* cheeks. See *blackish P. decumanus* on Plate XIII.

**9. Russet-backed** *P. angustifrons* N p.309
Only *"olive"* species in range. *Smaller* than 10; undertail *partially* yellow.

**10. Green** *P. viridis* S (plus N.e.) p.309
*Basal bill pale greenish.*

**11. Olive Oropendola** p.309
*Gymnostinops yuracares* S
Brighter, more *yellow*-olive foreparts; *much more chestnut* on rearparts than 10. Note *black basal bill, bare cheeks.*

**12. Oriole Blackbird** p.314
*Gymnomystax mexicanus*
Quite *large. Entire head and underparts yellow* except for bare *black* areas on *face.* Immature crown black.

**13. Troupial** *Icterus icterus* p.312
Large oriole. Note *bare blue eye-patch*; black *head* and *lanceolate* breast-feathers; extensive *white in wing.*

**Orioles** *Icterus*
Note sharply pointed bill. Juvenals usually *olive* above and *lemon*-yellow below with black bibs in older stages.

**14. Baltimore** *I. galbula* N p.313
No. migrant. White *wing-bars.* ♂ *head and back* black; undertail yellow; ♀ *grayer-*backed than resident juvenals; below washed with *orange.* See text for Orchard Oriole, rare no. migrant.

**15. Yellow** *I. nigrogularis* p.313
15a. Immature
*Back yellow.* Only resident *black-bibbed* oriole with *white wing-edgings.*

**16. Yellow-backed** *I. chrysater* N p.313
*Back yellow.* Wings and tail *all-black.*

**17. Yellow-tailed** *I. mesomelas* N p.313
Back *black.* Wing-*coverts* and *undertail yellow.* Maracaibo basin.

**18. Orange-crowned** *I. auricapillus* p.312
Head *fiery-orange.* Back and tail *black.*

**19. Moriche** *I. chrysocephalus* p.312
Mostly *black*; note *yellow crown*, etc.

**20. Yellow-hooded Blackbird** p.311
*Agelaius icterocephalus*
Black ♂ has *yellow hood.* ♀ somewhat *streaky* with *yellow on face and throat.*

**21. Red-breasted Blackbird** p.314
*Leistes militaris*
♂ distinctive. *Heavily streaked* ♀ often *tinged pink* below. BOBOLINK *Dolichonyx oryzivorus*: No. migrant. Fall ♂ and ♀ similar to ♀ 21 but bill *blunter*; more *yellowish-buff* tone (no pink); spiky tail *unbarred.*

**22. Eastern Meadowlark** p.314
*Sturnella magna*
Long bill. Yellow below with *black crescent*; *white outer* tail-feathers.

NOTE: Mainly *black* Icterids, Plate XIII.

38

PLATE 39 LARGER FINCHES

**1. Red-capped Cardinal** p.356
*Paroaria gularis* (Llanos, rivers)
Sexes alike. Amazonas-s. Bolivar race has crimson *cheeks*, black *lower* throat.

**2. Vermilion Cardinal** p.355
*Cardinalis phoenicius* N
Unmistakable. *Long rosy-vermilion crest* in *both* sexes. Arid coastal area.

**3. Slate-colored Grosbeak** p.354
*Pitylus grossus* S
Heavy *coral-red bill. Duller slate* ♀ (without black) retains *white throat.*

**4. Red-and-black Grosbeak** p.354
*Periporphyrus erythromelas* S
Size of 3. ♂ distinctive; ♀ *dingier olive-and-yellow* than 8 with *complete black head.* E. Bolivar; very scarce.

**Grosbeaks** *Pheucticus*
Wings boldly *marked with white.*

**5. Rose-breasted** *P. ludovicianus* p.355
No. migrant. Note *rosy breast* of ♂ even in *winter plumage* (shown). ♀ has *white eyebrow, brown cheeks,* and *streaked* back *and breast.*

**6. Yellow** *P. chrysopeplus* N p.355
♂ distinctive. ♀ heavily *streaked above;* eyebrow and underparts *yellow.*

**7. Black-backed** *P. aureoventris* N p.355
Mérida. ♂ *black-hooded.* ♀ differs from 6 (*no* overlap) by *sooty* face and upperparts; *speckled* throat and breast.

**8. Yellow-green Grosbeak** p.355
*Caryothraustes canadensis* S
All *yellow-olive* with well-defined *black face.* Usually in flocks.

**Saltators** *Saltator*
Large; *stout bill.* Note *pale supraloral, dark submalar* stripes (*none on crown*).

**9. Streaked** *S. albicollis* N p.354
*Grayish-olive* above; *profusely streaked below.* More lightly-built than 10.

**10. Grayish** *S. coerulescens* p.353
Most nondescript. *Gray* above (in e. Bolivar *shade more olivaceous* overall).

**11. Buff-throated** *S. maximus* p.353
Bright *olive* upperparts. *Lower* throat *buff* (paler-to-absent in ♀ and young).

**12. Orinocan** *S. orenocensis* N p.354
Gray above; *sides of head black* with *long* eyebrow. Mostly *buffy* below.

**13. Rufous-collared Sparrow** p.366
*Zonotrichia capensis* 13a. Juvenal
Common. Note black crown-stripes, *rusty nape, wing-bars* and *streaked brown* back. Mainly Tepuis in S.

**Sparrows** *Arremonops*

**14. Black-striped** *A. conirostris* p.358
*Black stripes* on *gray* head; *brownish*-olive back. Overlaps 15 in e. Falcon.

**15. Tocuyo** *A. tocuyensis* N p.358
Arid N.w. Somewhat smaller and paler than 14. *Eyebrow* and coronal stripe *much lighter*, more *clay*-colored.

**Sparrows** *Arremon*
*Golden shoulder;* black *pectoral-patches.*

**16. Pectoral** *A. taciturnus* p.359
*Bold* head-stripes. N race (e. of Andes) has black *patches; yellow mandible.* S race (16a) has *full breast-band* and *all-black* bill. ♀♀ of both *buffier below* with *faint "echo"* of breast marks.

**17. Golden-winged** *A. schlegeli* N p.359
Unstriped *black cap;* pronounced golden shoulder. *Entire bill bright yellow.*

**Brush-Finches** *Atlapetes*
Most (18-21) have *black sides of head* with *rufous on crown.* Mainly subtropical.

**18. Pale-naped** *A. pallidinucha* N p.358
*Slaty* back; *yellow* below. Broad coronal stripe blends from *cinnamon into buffy-white at rear.* S.w. Tachira.

**19. Moustached** *A. albofrenatus* N p.358
*Olive* back; *yellow* below with *white malar stripe.* E. Tachira and Mérida.

**20. Slaty** *A. schistaceus* N p.358
*Slaty* back; *gray below.* Head similar to 19. Perija; Andes (occurs with 19). RUFOUS-NAPED *A. rufinucha* N (S. de Perija): Slaty above; *yellow* below. *Black* sides of head *extend onto malar.*

**21. Chestnut-capped** p.357
*A. brunneinucha* N
*Dark olive* back; black *forehead. Extensive white throat;* black *breast band* (lacking in one local race).

**22. Stripe-headed** *A. torquatus* N p.357
Underparts like 21 but *crown striped* black *and gray.* Coastal Cordillera races have *white eyebrow* (cf. 16 N).

**23. Ochre-breasted** *A. semirufus* N p.357
*Entire head and breast* cinnamon-*rufous.*

**24. Tepui** *A. personatus* S (Tepuis) p.357
Races *vary* in amount of *chestnut on head;* limits shown (e.g., 24a. *duidae*).

**Grosbeaks** *Cyanocompsa*
♂♂ *dark* slaty-*blue;* ♀♀ *rich cocoa-brown.*

**25. Blue-black** *C. cyanoides* p.353
N race *quite dark.* Blue areas *brighter* in ♂ of S race (meets 26 in Sucre), except for *rump* which *remains dark.*

**26. Ultramarine** *C. cyanea* N p.353
*Less husky* than 25. ♂ *rump* always contrasting *brighter blue;* ♀ obviously *lighter* brown *below* (cf. ♀ *Oryzoborus*).

39

PLATE 40 SMALLER FINCHES (Nos. 21-34 cont'd following page)

**Seed-Finches** *Oryzoborus*
Bill *very thick*, culmen almost *straight*. ♀♀ are *richer brown* than *Sporophila*.

**1. Large-billed** *O. crassirostris* p.361
Uncommon. *All-black* ♂ has *whitish*-horn bill; (often) white wing-spot. ♀ bill *darker* (like 2 but more *massive*); brown tones a *shade less rich and warm*. Also, more *olivaceous above* than ♀ *C. cyanea*. Almost identical *O. maximiliani* occurs S (along Orinoco); see text.

**2. Lesser** *O. angolensis* p.360
♂ has black hood, *chestnut belly*; ♀ *deep brown* above, *cinnamon*-brown below.

**3. Blue-black Grassquit** p.363
*Volatinia jacarina*
Adult ♂ *glossy blue-black*; ♀ only *tiny* finch distinctly *streaked below*.

**Grassquits** *Tiaris*
♀♀ *tend* to be stubbier, more pointy-billed, more *dingy-olive* than *Sporophila*.

**4. Yellow-faced** *T. olivacea* N p.360
Note *black and golden face* of ♂. ♀ usually shows *trace of same pattern*.

**5. Black-faced** *T. bicolor* N p.359
♂ ashy-olive; *face, breast dull black*.

**6. Sooty** *T. fuliginosa* p.359
♂ *dull sooty-blackish*. Form and bill recall *Sporophila* but ♀ *dingier below*.

**7. White-naped Seedeater** p.360
*Dolospingus fringilloides* S (Amazonas)
Bill more *conical*. Otherwise suggests *Sporophila* but ♂ *head all-black*. ♀ *deep brown; throat, mid-belly whitish*.

**Seedeaters** *Sporophila*
Bill thick, *stubby*; culmen *curved*. ♀♀ all *much alike*: olivaceous-brown above; *dingy buff below*, some washed yellow on belly; see text. Young ♂♂ intermediate.

**8. Lined** *S. lineola* p.362
8a. "Lined" type
Broad *malar-patch* and rump *white*. Two variants occur; those *without white coronal-stripe* have been known as "S. bouvronides." VARIABLE *S. americana*: N.east. Recalls 7 (white *semi-collar, wing-bars*) but *chin to throat white*, bordered by untidy black *chest-band*.

**9. Black-and-white** *S. luctuosa* N p.362
*Mostly glossy-black; clear white belly.*

**10. Yellow-bellied** *S. nigricollis* p.363
Black *hood* and *pale sulphur belly*.

**11. Ruddy-breasted** *S. minuta* p.363
*Ashy*-gray above; *rump and below rufous*.

**12. Gray** *S. intermedia* p.361
Most widespread of 3 "gray" *Sporophila*. Rather nondescript, but *some may* look more like 13 (*with* submalar patch). Bill *pinkish*-yellow; legs *blackish*.

**13. Slate-colored** *S. schistacea* p.361
Subtly differs from 12 by: a bit more white in wing, often *whitish submalar patch*, more demarcated belly, *rich yellow* bill (no pink tinge), *green-gray* legs. Local; usually at forest edge.

**14. Plumbeous** *S. plumbea* p.362
Slightly *paler* gray below than 12 or 13; easily told by *dark bill*. Mainly S.

**15. Dull-colored** *S. obscura* N p.363
Adult ♂ hen-plumaged. Rather *grayish Sporophila* (*Tiaris?*) *without noticeable buff below*; *mandible flesh*-color.

**16. Chestnut-bellied** p.363
*S. castaneiventris* S
*Bluish-gray* above including *rump and flanks*; median underparts *chestnut*.

**Seedeaters** *Catamenia*
*Upper* altitude genus. Smallish *pale* bill; *rich rusty crissum* and longish tail.

**17. Paramo** *C. homochroa* p.360
♂ *dark gray* with *blackish foreface*; grayish-brown ♀ *streaked inconspicuously* above *and below*. Browner S Tepui race has *dark-tipped* bill.

**18. Plain-colored** *C. inornata* N p.360
*Paler, grayer* than 17. *Back streaking more obvious*; bill more *reddish*. ♂ foreface *not* dark; ♀ *unstreaked below*.

**19. Plumbeous Sierra-Finch** p.364
*Phrygilus unicolor* N (higher Andes)
*Conical* bill. ♂ *slate-gray, paler below*; narrow *eye-ring*. ♀ *heavily and conspicuously streaked* above and below.

**20. Slaty Finch** *Haplospiza rustica* p.365
*Conical pointed* bill. ♂ *bluish-slate*, notably *darker* than 19 (cf. *Diglossa*). ♀ *brown; paler* below, *obscure streaks* on breast (recalls 3). Subtropical. Scarce; only on *one* Tepui in S.

*Plate 40 (Cont'd)   Smaller Finches*

**21. Pileated Finch**  p.356
*Coryphospingus pileatus*  N (mainly)
Gray ♂ has *black crown* with semiconcealed *scarlet center*.  ♀ *plain grayish*
above; note *whitish eyering* and lores,
dimly streaked breast. See text for rare No.
migrant Indigo Bunting; ♀ most like 21 but
*browner* above.

**22. Wedge-tailed Grass-Finch**  p.365
*Emberizoides herbicola*
*Long spiky tail* diagnostic; *upper*parts
*streaked*, wing-edging olive. *Lower* elevations (except *duidae*). Cf. Pl. 19

**Sparrows**  *Ammodramus*
Nondescript. *Streaked above*; *grayish-white*
underparts (streaked in Juvenal).

**23. Grassland**  *A. humeralis*  p.366
Only *lores* yellow. Streaking *blacker* (especially on crown) with subtle *chestnut edging*. Less local than 24.

**24. Yellow-browed**  *A. aurifrons*  p.365
*Yellow extends* onto eyebrow, eyering and
base of malar; streaking *browner*.

**25. Dickcissel**  *Spiza americana*  p.356
No. migrant; gregarious. Note *streaked*
back, *rusty shoulder*, *yellowish* eyebrow
*and breast*.  ♂ has *black patch* on lower
throat (*veiled* in winter).

**26. Saffron Finch**  *Sicalis flaveola*  p.364
Extensively *bright yellow*; *golden-orange*
forecrown. Adult ♀ *duller*. Prevalent older
stages (26a. Immature) of *streaky* young
show *yellowish collar* and crissum. Local in
S.

**Yellow-Finches**  *Sicalis*
As 26, more or less *bright yellow below*. Often
occur in *flocks* in *open* country.

**27. Orange-fronted**  *S. columbiana*  p.364
♂ *smaller*, dingier than 26; *lores darker*, reduced forecrown *burnt*-orange. ♀ like 26a
but *lacks all streaking*, yellowish collar.
Scarcer than 26 in N.

**28. Stripe-tailed**  *S. citrina*  p.364
♂ olive above; *dull citrine* forecrown, *indistinct back streaks*; breast clouded olivaceous. ♀ mostly *streaked below* (unlike
29); belly yellow. Note *white inner tail-
patches* (reduced in ♀).

**29. Grassland**  *S. luteola*  p.364
*Conspicuously streaked above* including
crown. Clear *yellow lores* and throat *en-
hance darker cheeks* in ♂; ♀ similar but facial area much *buffier*; clouded breast and
yellow belly *not* streaked.

**30. Dark-backed Goldfinch**  p.368
*Carduelis psaltria*  N (mainly)
♂ *glossy-black* above; *yellow below*; ♀
from siskins by *small white* wing-spot.

**Siskins**  *Carduelis*
Typical siskins show *conspicuous patch of
yellow* on blackish wing; *olive-and-yellow* ♀ ♀
are *much alike* but *wing-pattern* and *bright-
ness of rump* more or less *duplicate* respective ♂ ♂.

**31. Yellow-bellied**  p.367
*C. xanthogastra*  N
Black *hood and back* in ♂; ♀ shows "*echo*"
of *hooded* effect; rump is *dark*.

**32. Andean**  *C. spinescens*  N  p.367
Black *crown* in ♂; ♀ rump *somewhat yellowish*, wing markings *more extensive* than
31. YELLOW-FACED *C. yarrellii* N (Carabobo):
Similar but *face, breast and rump much
brighter yellow*; less so in ♀ but rump still
*yellower* than 32.

**33. Hooded**  *C. magellanica*  S  p.367
Only siskin in range (Tepui region). Note
*black head* in ♂.

**34. Red**  *C. cucullata*  N  p.367
♂ unique. ♀ also *unlike* others; wing-patch,
rump and sides of breast *salmon-vermilion*.
Now quite rare.

## GREEN ARACARI
*Pteroglossus viridis*
TILINGO LIMÓN

Pl. 16
12″ (30 cm.). Head and neck black. Back, wings, upper tail coverts and tail dark, slaty green, rump crimson. Underparts yellow, thighs olive. Bill 3.2″ (8 cm.), ridge orange yellow, wedge-shaped red mark at sides of maxilla, mandible black, base of bill dull orange; skin before eye blue, behind it red. ♀: head and neck bright chestnut.
Tropical zone. Nw Bolívar along the lower Río Caura and in the e from the Sierra de Imataca s to the n Gran Sabana (*viridis*). [The Guianas, n Brazil.]
Rain forest to 600 m. General behavior similar to Collared Aracari. Call: a rattling "tika, tika, tika, tika."

## IVORY-BILLED ARACARI
*Pteroglossus flavirostris*
TILINGO PICO AMARILLO

Pl. 16
18″ (46 cm.). Crown and nape glossy black; hindneck and mantle maroon red; center of back, wings and tail olive; rump scarlet. Throat and sides of head chestnut, narrow band across base of throat black margined below with a wide scarlet band, broad band across lower breast black, narrowly margined below with scarlet, belly and under tail coverts lemon yellow; thighs olive. Bill 4″ (10 cm.), ivory white, "teeth" black, nostril orange.
Tropical zone. S of the Orinoco in Amazonas and w Bolívar e to the Río Paragua (*flavirostris*). [Se Colombia to sw Amazonian Brazil and e to the Rio Negro.]
Rain forest, forest edge near savannas, plantations to 350 m. Near streams and humid areas. General behavior similar to Collared Aracari.

## GUIANAN TOUCANET
*Selenidera culik*
TUCANCITO PICO NEGRO

Pl. 16
13″ (33 cm.). Head, neck, throat and most of underparts glossy black; ear coverts long, bright yellow. Band across upper mantle orange yellow, back olive green, flanks greenish gray, thighs chestnut, under tail coverts crimson. Wings and tail olive, with a bluish tinge. Bill 3″ (7.6 cm.), black with red base. ♀: differs from ♂ by silvery gray nuchal collar and underparts; flanks and belly yellowish green.
Tropical zone. Se Bolívar. [The Guianas, central n Brazil.]
Rain forest, 250–900 m. Shy. Alone or in small groups. Call: rattling note.

## TAWNY-TUFTED TOUCANET
*Selenidera nattereri*
TUCANCITO PICO ROJO

Pl. 16
13″ (33 cm.). Head, hindneck, throat, breast and upper abdomen black; cheeks, and band across upper mantle yellow; long ear tufts yellow tipped chestnut. Back, wings and tail olive green, tail narrowly tipped chestnut. Lower belly olive yellow, flanks orange, thighs chestnut, under tail coverts crimson. Bill 2.5″ (6.4 cm.) reddish brown with several black vertical stripes and black base. ♀: differs from ♂ by black portions of plumage replaced by chestnut.
Tropical zone. Locally in Amazonas (Cerro Yapacana; base of Duida) and Bolívar (Río Carún, an affluent of the upper Río Paragua) and possibly the lower Río Caura. [The Guianas, se Colombia, nw Amazonian Brazil.]
Rain forest, 300 m. General habits similar to those of Guianan Toucanet. Like it, found at various heights in trees.

## BLACK-BILLED MOUNTAIN-TOUCAN
*Andigena nigrirostris*
TUCÁN AZUL

Pl. 16
20″ (51 cm.). Crown, nape and upper mantle glossy black; back and outer remiges olive brown, tertials gray; rump lemon yellow, upper tail coverts greenish. Tail gray, tipped chestnut. Cheeks, ear coverts and throat white; breast and belly pale blue, flanks chocolate. Skin before eye bright blue, behind it light yellow. Bill 4″ (10 cm.), mainly black, ridge at base of maxilla and base of both mandibles dark red.

Upper tropical zone. The Andes of Táchira and n Trujillo (*nigrirostris*). [Colombia; ne Ecuador.] Cloud forest, thickets, open terrain with scattered trees, 1800–2700 m. In pairs or small bands forages in the treetops and in the low trees at the higher altitudes. Near water. Call: whistle.

## CHANNEL-BILLED TOUCAN
*Ramphastos vitellinus*
DIOSTEDÉ PICO ACANELADO

Pl. 16
19″ (48 cm.). Upperparts, wings and tail black, upper and under tail coverts crimson. Breast bright orange yellow; throat, sides of neck white, broad breast band crimson, belly black. Bill 5.5″ (14 cm.), black, base of maxilla yellow, of mandible blue.
Tropical zone. N of the Orinoco in e Sucre (Cerro Papelón); s of the Orinoco in Delta Amacuro and Bolívar. [The Guianas, e Brazil s to Santa Catarina. Trinidad.]
Rain forest to 1100 m., often near water. Usually in small bands, forages in the higher branches and treetops of the tall trees; moves with great agility, hopping from branch to branch. Undulating flight. Conspicuous, noisy, when calling from highest exposed branches; loud, repeated, single, yelping notes "kiok, kiok" in a high, shrill tone. Nests in natural hollows high in forest trees.

## CITRON-THROATED TOUCAN
*Ramphastos citreolaemus*
DIOSTEDÉ GARGANTICITRÓN

Pl. 16
19″ (48 cm.). Upperparts, wings and tail black; upper tail coverts lemon yellow, under tail coverts crimson. Throat and breast bright sulphur yellow, ear coverts white, breast band crimson, belly black. Bill 5.5″ (14 cm.), black, ridge pale yellow, greenish in middle, base of bill light blue with a yellow patch at juncture with head.
Tropical zone. The basin of L. Maracaibo, Zulia, and the n slopes of the Andes in Táchira and Mérida. [N Colombia.]
Rain forest to 500 m. Voice and general behavior similar to Channel-billed Toucan.

Note: This and the next species were treated as races of *R. vitellinus* in Lista Av. Venez. Until more is known of voice and range it is best to treat them as distinct.

## YELLOW-RIDGED TOUCAN
*Ramphastos culminatus*
DIOSTEDÉ RABADILLA DORADA

Pl. 16
19″ (48 cm.). Upperparts, wings and tail black; upper tail coverts orange yellow, under tail coverts crimson. Throat and breast white, breast band crimson, belly black. Bill 5.5″ (14 cm.), black, ridge, tip and base of maxilla yellow, base of mandible blue (cf. Cuvier's Toucan).
Tropical, occasionally subtropical zone. Nw Lara; the s slopes of the Andes in Barinas and Táchira, and generally distribued in Amazonas. [E Colombia to n Bolivia, w Amazonian Brazil.]
Rain and cloud forest, 300–1700 m. n of the Orinoco, 100–200 m. s of it. Voice and general behavior similar to Channel-billed Toucan.

'R. Osculans' is the name given to 4 specimens in the Phelps Collection that are generally regarded as hybrids between *R. culminatus* and *R. vitellinus*. They are from Caño Cataniapo and the Río Asisa in n and e Amazonas.

## KEEL-BILLED TOUCAN
*Ramphastos sulfuratus*
PIAPOCO PICO VERDE

19″ (48 cm.). Mantle dark maroon, rest of back, wings and tail black; upper tail coverts white, under tail coverts yellow. Throat and breast yellow, breast band crimson, belly black. Bill 5.5″ (14 cm.), maxilla pea green with a longitudinal, wedge-shaped orange mark along cutting edge, tip crimson, mandible mostly light blue with crimson tip and pea green patch near base, "teeth" dusky.
Tropical zone. The Perijá region in nw Zulia (*brevicarinatus*). [Mexico to n Colombia.]
Rain forest, forest edge, clearings, second growth, to 450 m. Scattered tall trees. General behavior like the other large toucans, see Channel-billed Toucan.

Call: a dry, sharp, steadily repeated grunting call, "we-trek, we-trek."

## BLACK-MANDIBLED TOUCAN
*Ramphastos ambiguus*
DIOSTEDÉ PICO NEGRO

Pl. 16
22″ (56 cm.). Blackish maroon above, wings and tail black; upper tail coverts white, under tail coverts crimson. Throat and breast deep yellow, breast band crimson, belly black. Bill 7″ (18 cm.), maxilla mainly yellow, tinged green near base of ridge and black basally, mandible black with a slight reddish tinge near base. Orbital skin greenish yellow or green.
Tropical and subtropical zones. Generally distributed in the Sierra de Perijá and locally in Táchira and w Barinas through Mérida and Yaracuy to Carabobo and Miranda (*abbreviatus*). [Colombia to central Peru.] The species does not occur in e Panama (*fide* Wetmore).
Rain and cloud forests, 100–1800 m. General behavior like the other large toucans, see Channel-billed Toucan. The local name, *Dios-te-dé*, a transcription of its call, more or less fits all *Ramphastos*.

## RED-BILLED TOUCAN
*Ramphastos tucanus*
PIAPOCO PICO ROJO

Pl. 16
21″ (53 cm.). Upperparts, wings and tail black; upper tail coverts yellow, under tail coverts crimson. Throat and breast white, tinged sulphur yellow, breast band crimson, belly black. Bill 6.5″ (16.5 cm.), mainly dark red, ridge, tip and base of maxilla yellow, base of mandible blue.
Tropical zone n of the Orinoco, and s of it in Bolívar (*tucanus*). [The Guianas. Ne Colombia, ne Brazil.]
Rain forest, forest edge, clearings, along rivers, to 500 m. n of the Orinoco, to 1100 m. s of it. General behavior like the other large toucans; see Channel-billed Toucan.

## ORANGE-BILLED TOUCAN
*Ramphastos aurantiirostris*
PIAPOCO PICO DORADO

Similar in pulmage and size to Red-billed Toucan. Bill differently colored, the dark red being replaced by light orange red.
Tropical zone. S Delta Amacuro (Manoa), ne Bolívar in the Río Cuyuni. [Guyana.]
Rain forest to 250 m. General behavior like the other large toucans, see Channel-billed Toucan. This "species" is currently considered a phase of *vitellinus* with no taxonomic standing.

## CUVIER'S TOUCAN
*Ramphastos cuvieri*
PIAPOCO PICO CURVO

Pl. 16
23″ (58 cm.). Similar in plumage to Red-billed Toucan, but bill black, tinged red basally, ridge and base of bill yellowish pea green. Looks also much like Yellow-ridged Toucan but is very much larger with a somewhat differently colored bill.
Tropical zone. Amazonas. [Se Colombia to n Bolivia and w Amazonian Brazil.]
Rain forest, plantations, clearings, along rivers, 100–500 m. General behavior like other large toucans, see Channel-billed Toucan.
Note: Treated as a race of *R. tucanus* in Lista Av. Venez., which it probably is.

# PICULETS, WOODPECKERS: Picidae

## TELEGRAFISTAS, CARPINTEROS

South American woodpeckers do not differ in general appearance or habits from woodpeckers from elsewhere. Their tree-climbing propensities, undulating flight, and tapping on tree trunks help to identify them.
The tiny piculets, 3.5″ (9 cm.), look more like nuthatches than woodpeckers, and like these have unstiffened tails. They usually clamber about on the small twigs

on the end of branches and among bamboos. They inhabit dense scrub and open woodland in the tropical zone. Piculets tap like woodpeckers and if tapping on a hollow branch or seed pod make a remarkably loud tapping sound for their size—hence their name in Venezuela. Piculets are found in tropical Africa and se Asia as well as in South America.

## CHESTNUT PICULET
*Picumnus cinnamomeus*
TELEGRAFISTA CASTAÑO

Pl. 18
4″ (10 cm.). General plumage rufous chestnut; forehead yellowish white (or rufous chestnut shading to buff posteriorly, a). Crown black, forecrown spotted with yellow in front, with white behind (or without white spots posteriorly, a). Tail black, inner webs of central pair of tail feathers white, a diagonal white band across both webs of outer 2 pairs. ♀: like ♂ but forecrown plain black, hindcrown spotted with white (or whole crown spotted with white, b).
Arid tropical zone. Nw Zulia on the Goajira Pen. (*cinnamomeus*). Zulia nw and ne of L. Maracaibo (*perijanus*, b). Humid forest s of L. Maracaibo, Zulia (*venezuelensis*, a). [Ne Colombia.]
Rain forest, deciduous forest and xerophytic areas, to 100 m. Open terrain with scattered trees, very active, not shy, inconspicuous: forages in dense thickets and thickly tangled vines. All piculets, *telegrafistas*, are usually first located by the sound of their pecking, reminiscent of the sound of the primitive hand-telegraph key.

## WHITE-BELLIED PICULET
*Picumnus spilogaster*
TELEGRAFISTA PÁLIDO

Pl. 18
3.5″ (9 cm.). Crown scarlet, bases of feathers black, hindcrown black dotted with white; back brown indistinctly barred, upper tail coverts whitish; inner remiges broadly edged with buffy white. Underparts whitish. Tail as in Chestnut Piculet.
Tropical zone. Se Apure along the Río Meta; from Altagracia e along the Orinoco to Delta Amacuro (*orinocensis*). [Surinam, French Guiana, ne Brazil.]
Rain, gallery and deciduous forest, clear-ings, forest edge, open woodland, thickets, to 100 m.

## SCALED PICULET
*Picumnus squamulatus*
TELEGRAFISTA ESCAMADO

Pl. 18
3.5″ (9 cm.). Crown black, forecrown speckled with orange, with white on hindcrown. Back pale olive brown, below white, the feathers both above and below margined with black giving a scaled appearance, (or with the dark margins very much less marked, a). Tail as in Chestnut Piculet. ♀: forecrown speckled with white.
Tropical and subtropical zones n of the Orinoco e to w Sucre and Monagas (*rohli*). Ne Sucre (*obsoletus*, a). [Ne Colombia.]
Gallery forest, second growth, deciduous woodland, open terrain with scattered trees, forest edge, xerophytic areas, pastures, to 1800 m. Alone or in pairs, inconspicuous, forages in dense scrub, tangled undergrowth and small trees, examining the thin branches and twigs.

## OLIVACEOUS PICULET
*Picumnus olivaceus*
TELEGRAFISTA OLIVA

Pl. 18
3.5″ (9 cm.). Crown brownish black dotted with orange in front with white behind. Back pale grayish olive (or with a yellowish tinge, a); throat whitish, breast olive brown, (or olive, feathers edged pale yellowish, a), rest of underparts yellowish, streaked dusky. Tail as in Chestnut Piculet. ♀: crown dotted with white.
Upper tropical and subtropical zones. Generally distributed in the Sierra de Perijá, Zulia (*eisenmanni*, a). The Andes of sw Táchira (*tachirensis*). [Honduras to w Ecuador.]
Rain and cloud forest, second growth, open woodland, forest edge, clearings, cultivated lands, 800–2300 m. In pairs

or family groups, actively forages in the thin dead branches of the undergrowth, open thickets, low tangles; also in the treetops. Call: a twitter or trill.

## BLACK-DOTTED PICULET
*Picumnus nigropunctatus*
TELEGRAFISTA PUNTEADO

3.5" (9 cm.). Crown black, finely streaked red. Back greenish yellow, feathers with a dusky subterminal bar giving a scaled appearance. Below pale yellow, barred on throat, and with round black spots on breast and sides. Tail as in Chestnut Piculet. ♀ unknown.
Known only from Misión Araguaimujo and Capure, Delta Amacuro.
Rain forest, second growth, sea level.

## GOLDEN-SPANGLED PICULET
*Picumnus exilis*
TELEGRAFISTA VERDOSO

Pl. 18
3.5" (9 cm.). Nasal plumes whitish, forehead narrowly black, crown black dotted orange scarlet on forecrown, white on hindcrown. Back grayish olive (or brownish olive, a), barred yellowish white and blackish, giving a spotted appearance. Wing coverts with small, white, black-encircled spots. Underparts yellowish white (or yellowish, a) barred with black. Tail as in Chestnut Piculet. ♀: entire crown dotted white.
Tropical and subtropical zones. Ne Bolívar from the lower Río Paragua to the Sierra de Imataca and the Río Cuyuni (*clarus*). Elsewhere in Bolívar and in Amazonas (*undulatus*, a). [The Guianas; n and e Brazil to Espírito Santo.]
Rain and cloud forests, second growth. Open woodland, savanna edge, to 1900 m. Alone or in pairs forages in the small lower branches.

## SPOT-BREASTED WOODPECKER
*Chrysoptilus punctigula*
CARPINTERO PECHIPUNTEADO

Pl. 17
9" (23 cm.). Forecrown black, hindcrown, nape and moustacial streak crimson. Lores and sides of head white. Back olive, barred dusky; rump saffron with a few black spots. Throat black, spotted with white. Breast olive sometimes stained with crimson, fading to mustard yellow on belly, where spotted (or dotted, a) with black. ♀: lacks moustacial streak.
Tropical zone. Zulia, sw and e of L. Maracaibo; n Táchira (*zuliae*). Locally n of the Orinoco from Carabobo to Sucre and across the llanos from s Táchira and Apure to Delta Amacuro; s of the Orinoco in Bolívar from Caicara to Ciudad Bolívar, and in nw Amazonas (*punctipectus*, a). [E Panama, Colombia, the Guianas to Bolivia and Brazil.]
Rain, deciduous and gallery forest, second growth, open woodland, mangroves, to 600 m. n of the Orinoco, to 150 m. s of it. Llanos, forest edge, open terrain with large trees, scrub, clearings, Moriche palm groves. In pairs or family groups; descends to the ground to forage in ant hills. Call: loud series of whistles.

## CRIMSON-MANTLED WOODPECKER
*Piculus rivolii*
CARPINTERO CANDELA

Pl. 17
11" (28 cm.). *Above crimson;* upper tail coverts mustard yellow, barred black (or black, sometimes with a few yellow bars on lateral feathers, a), tail black; primaries edged olive. Sides of head yellowish white, moustacial streak crimson, throat black more to less spotted with white. ♀: differs from ♂ by having a black crown, no moustacial streak; feathers of upper breast black with white crescentic bars and crimson fringe, rest of underparts mustard yellow, sometimes barred or spotted with black at sides.
Subtropical and temperate zones. Locally in the Sierra de Perijá, Zulia, and in extreme sw Táchira (*rivolii*). The Andes of n Táchira, Mérida and Trujillo (*meridae*, a). [Colombia, the Guianas through the Andes to Bolivia.]
Rain, cloud and dwarf forests, páramos, 950–3700 m.; among scattered trees, also in low bushes at the higher altitudes; conspicuous, forages in the thicker branches, alone, in pairs or family groups. Call: loud, sonorous.

## GOLDEN-OLIVE WOODPECKER
*Piculus rubiginosus*
CARPINTERO DORADO VERDE

Pl. 17
8″ (20 cm.). Forecrown gray, sides of crown, hindcrown and moustacial streak crimson; sides of head white, throat checkered black and white. Back olive to golden olive. Breast and belly whitish yellow regularly barred with dusky olive. Central tail feathers olive with black along shaft and black apical portion, outer feathers pale olive brown. Inner remiges like back, rest uniform dusky with olive outer web. Under wing coverts and wing lining creamy white. ♀: only nape crimson.

Mostly upper tropical and subtropical zones. The Sierra de Perijá, Zulia, and the Andes from Táchira to Lara, n to Falcón and e in the coastal and interior Cordilleras to Miranda (*meridensis*). The e Cordillera from Anzoátegui to the e Paria Pen., Sucre, and Monagas (*rubiginosus*). S Delta Amacuro (Caño Tipuro, 20 m.) (*deltanus*). Generally in the mountains of Bolívar and Amazonas (*guianae*). On the summit of Cerro Auyan-tepui, Bolívar (*viridissimus*). [Mexico to w Panama. Colombia to nw Peru and nw Argentina. N Brazil, Guyana. Trinidad, Tobago.]

Rain and cloud forests, to 2800 m. n of the Orinoco, at sea level in the delta of the Orinoco, and from 350–2000 m. s of the river. Forest edge, clearings with trees. Alone or in pairs, forages in large trees. Various loud rolling calls, churrs and trills.

## YELLOW-THROATED WOODPECKER
*Piculus flavigula*
CARPINTERO CUELLIAMARILLO

Pl. 17
8″ (20 cm.). Crown, nape and moustacial streak crimson, (no moustacial streak, a); throat, foreneck and sides of head golden yellow. Back bright olive, tail olive. Breast olive, spotted with white; belly barred olive and white. Under tail coverts ochraceous buff; wing lining cinnamon chestnut. ♀: differs from ♂ by lacking the crimson malar stripe; forecrown old gold instead of crimson.

Tropical zone. Locally in Amazonas (*magnus*, a). Locally in Bolívar from the Río Caura e to the Río Cuyuni and the Gran Sabana (*flavigula*). [Colombia and the Guianas to e Peru and n and se Brazil.]
Rain forest to 700 m. Forages in the treetops.

## GOLDEN-GREEN WOODPECKER
*Piculus chrysochloros*
CARPINTERO DORADO

Pl. 17
9.5″ (24 cm.). Crown, nape and malar streak crimson. Sides of head olive with a golden yellow band below eye. Above bright olive green, tail olive. Throat whitish banded with olive, rest of underparts banded greenish white and olive. Wings like back, under wing coverts and wing lining cinnamon chestnut. ♀: differs from ♂ by having the crown, nape and moustacial streak olive green.

Tropical zone. The basin of L. Maracaibo in Zulia and Trujillo; e Falcón (Tucacas); w Táchira (San Cristóbal) (*xanthochloros*). Locally through Amazonas (*capistratus*). [E Panama, n Colombia and the Guianas to se Bolivia and n Argentina.]
Rain forest, xerophytic areas (in Zulia), deciduous forest, to 450 m. n of the Orinoco, 100–650 m. s of it. Tall trees in clearings and pastures, often near water or marshy ground.

## CHESTNUT WOODPECKER
*Celeus elegans*
CARPINTERO CASTAÑO

Pl. 17
11″ (28 cm.). Long crest dark chestnut (or cinnamon to ochraceous cinnamon, a; or light reddish brown, b). General color chestnut with rump, flanks and under wing coverts cinnamon to yellowish buff; inner webs of inner remiges barred black and buff. Moustacial streak crimson. Tail black. ♀: no moustacial streak.

Tropical zone. Amazonas and Bolívar e to the upper Río Paragua and the Gran Sabana (*jumana*). N Bolívar from the lower Río Paragua e to the Sierra de Imataca n through Anzoátegui to Sucre (*hellmayri*, a). Ne Monagas and Delta

Amacuro (*deltanus*, b). [E Colombia, the Guianas to n Bolivia and Amazonian Brazil. Trinidad.]
Rain forest, 450–1000 m. n of the Orinoco, at sea level in the delta, and to 1100 m. s of the river. Cocoa plantations. Alone or in pairs; forages inconspicuously from low to medium heights, feeds on ants. Rattling, screechy calls.

## SCALE-BREASTED WOODPECKER
*Celeus grammicus*
CARPINTERO ROJIZO

Pl. 17
9″ (23 cm.). Crown and crest uniform chestnut. Back chestnut, barred black, underparts darker with crescentic black bars giving a scaled appearance. Sides of body and under wing coverts pale yellow; primaries black, unbarred. Moustacial streak crimson. Tail black. ♀: no moustacial streak:
Tropical zone. Amazonas and s Bolívar from the Río Caura e (*grammicus*). [Se Colombia and the Guianas to n Bolivia and w and central Amazonian Brazil.]
Rain forest, forest edge, savannas with scattered trees, second growth, 100–900 m. Forages inconspicuously, feeds on ants.

## WAVED WOODPECKER
*Celeus undatus*
CARPINTERO ONDULADO

Pl. 17
8.5″ (22 cm.). Head and crest cinnamon rufous with not too many dusky dots; moustacial streak crimson. General color rufous with broad wavy black bars above, regularly barred below, breast more heavily barred, rump paler than back, tinged yellowish green. Tail and closed wing rufous barred black, tail tipped black. ♀: no moustacial streak.
Tropical zone. Extreme e Paria Pen., Sucre (Cristóbal Colón); locally in ne Bolívar on the Altiplanicie de Nuria and Río Cuyuni (*undatus*). E Delta Amacuro near the main mouth of the Orinoco (*amacurensis*). [The Guianas, ne Brazil.]
Rain forest, forest edge, to 500 m., near rivers. Forages inconspicuously in the treetops. Feeds on ants. Call: soft, quiet.

## CREAM-COLORED WOODPECKER
*Celeus flavus*
CARPINTERO AMARILLO

Pl. 17
11″ (28 cm.). Yellowish buff including long crest, moustacial streak crimson. Wing coverts blackish brown to rufous brown (or brown, broadly tipped yellowish buff, a), secondaries chestnut (or pale sandy brown, a), primaries brownish black. Under wing coverts yellowish buff, wing lining rufous chestnut (or cinnamon, a). Tail blackish brown. ♀: no moustacial streak.
Tropical zone. Apure, nw Bolívar, n and w Amazonas (*flavus*). Locally in Sucre and Monagas, generally in Delta Amacuro (*semicinnamomeus*, a). [The Guianas; e Colombia to n Bolivia and Amazonian and se Brazil.]
Rain forest, gallery forest, mangroves, deciduous woodland, second growth, to 200 m. Near water. Not shy, forages in the lower parts of trees. Call: high, laughing.

## RINGED WOODPECKER
*Celeus torquatus*
CARPINTERO PECHINEGRO

Pl. 17
11″ (28 cm.). Long crest, head, chin and upper throat pale cinnamon rufous, broad moustacial streak crimson. Neck all around, upper mantle and breast black (or with no black on hindneck and upper mantle, these parts uniform with back, a). Back plain light chestnut (or heavily barred with black, a). Lower breast and belly plain cinnamon buff (or heavily barred with black, a). Wing coverts mostly plain chestnut, inner remiges with a few black bars, primaries barred black and chestnut (or wing coverts and remiges heavily barred black, a). Tail light chestnut barred and tipped black. ♀: no moustacial streak.
Tropical zone. Amazonas s to Cerro Duida (*occidentalis*, a). Generally distributed along the lower Río Caura, locally in the Gran Sabana (Cerro Chimantá-tepui) and Delta Amacuro (Jobure) (*torquatus*). [The Guianas; Colombia to n Bolivia, and w and central Amazonian Brazil and in Bahia.]
Rain and gallery forest, 100–500 m. Forages in the lower parts of trees.

## LINEATED WOODPECKER
*Dryocopus lineatus*
CARPINTERO REAL BARBIRRAYADO

Pl. 17
14″ (35 cm.). Crown, bushy crest and moustacial streak crimson. Lores golden yellow; line running below eye and down sides of neck and breast white, bordered by a black line in front. Ear coverts dark gray; throat finely streaked black and white. Upperparts, wings and tail black, rest of underparts buffy white barred with black, under wing coverts and wing lining white (cf. Crimson-crested Woodpecker). ♀: like ♂ but anterior part of crown and malar streak black instead of crimson.
Tropical zone. From the L. Maracaibo region in Zulia s to s Táchira and w Apure and through w Barinas to w Mérida (*nuperus*). Generally distributed elsewhere, including Delta Amacuro but in Amazonas only in the north (*lineatus*). [Mexico to nw Peru, Bolivia, ne Argentina and s Brazil. Trinidad.]
Inhabits a wide variety of habitats including Moriche groves, but does not occur in xerophitic areas or marshes, to 1200 m. Alone, in pairs, or family groups. Active, noisy, forages at all heights on limbs and trunk. Loud drumming. Rattling calls.

## YELLOW-TUFTED WOODPECKER
*Melanerpes cruentatus*
CARPINTERO NEGRO AZUL

Pl. 17
8″ (20 cm.). Head, breast, back, wings and tail shining blue black, center of crown crimson. Broad eyebrow yellowish white, becoming golden yellow posteriorly, the eyebrows joining across the nape to form a golden yellow band. Lower back and upper tail coverts white. A broad band down center of lower breast and belly scarlet, sides of underparts barred black and yellowish white. ♀: lacks crimson on crown.
Tropical zone. Sw Táchira, the base of the Andes in s Barinas; nw and s Amazonas, across Bolívar to the lower Río Paragua and the Gran Sabana (*extensus*). [E Colombia, the Guianas to Bolivia and Amazonian Brazil.]
Rain forest, second growth, clearings with isolated trees to 1200 m. In pairs or groups, forages in the upper parts of tall, dead trees.
Note: *M. rubrifrons* of Lista Av. Venez. and Sp. Bds. S Amer. is here considered a color variant of *M. cruentatus,* differing by the absence of the eyebrow.

## RED-CROWNED WOODPECKER
*Melanerpes rubricapillus*
CARPINTERO HABADO

Pl. 17
8″ (20 cm.). Forehead yellowish white, crown and nape scarlet (or crown scarlet only in center, a). Back evenly barred black and white (or with white bars broader than black ones, a); rump and upper tail coverts white. Sides of head, throat and underparts pale olive grayish to dark brownish olive, scarlet in center of belly. Tail black, central feathers barred and spotted with white, 2 outer pairs narrowly barred and tipped white; primaries black, tipped and barred across middle with white, inner remiges barred black and white. ♀: nape only scarlet (or nape pale dull brown, tinged orange, a).
Tropical zone. Falcón on the Paraguaná Pen. and the Sierra de San Luis; n Lara (probably w coastally to the Goajira Pen., Zulia, for its occurs at the e end of that peninsula in Colombia (*paraguanae,* a). N of the Orinoco except areas occupied by *paraguanae;* extreme n Amazonas; n Bolívar from the Río Cuchivero e to the Altiplanicie de Nuria; w Delta Amacuro; Margarita and Patos Is. (*rubricapillus*). [Bay Is., Honduras; sw Costa Rica, Panama to n Colombia. Guyana, Surinam. Tobago.]
Gallery and deciduous forest, open woodland, xerophytic areas, second growth, to 1900 m. n of the Orinoco, to 500 m. s of it. Open country, tall trees along streams, forest edge, clearings, gardens. Usually in pairs, not shy, forages at various heights. Calls: soft long churrs, shrill chattering and rattling. Nests high in holes in trees, including dried giant cactus.

## SMOKY-BROWN WOODPECKER
*Veniliornis fumigatus*
CARPINTERO AHUMADO

Pl. 17
6.2″ (15.7 cm.). Crown crimson. General plumage olive brown somewhat stained

with crimson and yellow on lower back, throat dark grayish. Wings dull brown, feathers barred white on inner web, innermost barred on both webs. Tail blackish. ♀: crown dark brown.
Upper tropical and subtropical zones. Zulia in the Sierra de Perijá; the Andes of Táchira and w Barinas; the coastal Cordilleras from Carabobo, Miranda and the interior of Aragua to Anzoátegui, Sucre and Monagas (*fumigatus*). [Mexico to w Ecuador, Bolivia and nw Argentina.]
Phelps & Phelps, after careful study of Venezuelan series of this woodpecker, came to the conclusion that neither race described from Venezuela is valid.
Cloud forest, forest edge, second growth, coffee plantations, 800–2700 m. Solitary, forages at medium tree heights. Call: a rapid, wooden rattle.

## LITTLE WOODPECKER
*Veniliornis passerinus*
CARPINTERO OLIVÁCEO

Pl. 17
6.5″ (16.5 cm.). Forecrown and sides of head brownish olive, hindcrown scarlet. Above bright yellowish olive, below dark olive (or grayish olive, a), breast slightly spotted, belly narrowly barred with dull yellowish white. Wing coverts with triangular yellowish spots, the tips of the feathers sometimes tinged red. Tail blackish. ♀: differs by having the crown olive, dotted with whitish, and the tail obscurely barred olive.
Tropical zone. Locally in w Táchira, s Barinas, w Apure and extreme n Amazonas (*fidelis*). Locally along the Orinoco from s Guárico and Caicara, Bolívar, to Delta Amacuro (*modestus, a*). [The Guianas, e Colombia, to Bolivia, Brazil, Paraguay and n Argentina.]
Cloud forest edge, gallery forest, deciduous woodland, mangroves, second growth, along rivers, to 850 m. n of the Orinoco, to 400 m. s of it. Alone, in pairs or small groups, forages from low in the undergrowth to upper heights in trees.

## GOLDEN-COLLARED WOODPECKER
*Veniliornis cassini*
CARPINTERO ZEBRA

Pl. 17
7.5″ (19 cm.). Crown crimson, nuchal band yellow, tail blackish barred with dusky olive. Entire underparts barred black and white. Wing coverts with a few yellowish white spots; remiges notched white on inner web. ♀: has forecrown olive brown, nape dull yellow, tail less barred.
Tropical zone. Generally distributed in n and central Amazonas, in Bolívar and in w Delta Amacuro (*cassini*). [The Guianas and n Brazil.]
Rain forests, clearings, open terrain with trees, shrubbery, to 1500 m. Solitary, low to treetops.

## RED-STAINED WOODPECKER
*Veniliornis affinis*
CARPINTERO BARRETEADO

7.5″ (19 cm.). Much like Golden-collared Woodpecker, differing mainly by crimson-tipped wing coverts and olivaceous white instead of white ground color of underparts. Crown and nape crimson, nuchal band golden yellow, back golden olive tinged red. Below olivaceous white banded with dark olive. Wing coverts crimson at tips; outer webs of primaries notched with buff, those of inner remiges with faint yellow notches. Tail blackish banded with olive. ♀: crown olive brown, feathers of nape ochraceous yellow.
Tropical zone throughout Amazonas (*orenocensis*). [E Colombia to n Bolivia, and Amazonian and se Brazil.]
Rain forest, scrub, 100–500 m.

## RED-RUMPED WOODPECKER
*Veniliornis kirkii*
CARPINTERO RABADILLA ROJA

Pl. 17
6.5″ (16.5 cm.). The only species of the genus in Venezuela with a *red rump* and upper tail coverts. Crown scarlet, nuchal band golden yellow. Back golden olive, rump and upper tail coverts scarlet. Underparts evenly banded yellowish white and dark olive (or white banded with blackish, a). Remiges notched with white on inner web. Tail blackish barred olive on outer web. ♀: crown slaty brownish black indistinctly spotted brown.
Tropical and subtropical zones. N of the Orinoco from Zulia, Táchira and Apure e through Falcón and Guárico to An-

zoátegui and Monagas (*continentalis*, a). Extreme e Sucre (*kirkii*). Nw Amazonas (Cerro Paraque) and the se Gran Sabana, Bolívar (*monticola*). [Sw Costa Rica to w Ecuador, Trinidad and Tobago.]

Gallery forest, xerophytic areas, second growth, deciduous woodland, tall open woodland, along rivers, to 1000 m. n of the Orinoco (found at the higher altitudes only in Táchira and Barinas), at 1500–1750 m. s of it. Savannas, plantations; probably in the mangroves of the Orinoco delta. Alone, in pairs or small groups, forages at all levels, joins forest bands. Calls: low, shrill, ventriloquial call; noisy rapid drumming.

## YELLOW-VENTED WOODPECKER

*Veniliornis dignus*
CARPINTERO BARRIGA AMARILLA

Pl. 17

7″ (18 cm.). Crown and nape crimson, *eyebrow and moustacial streak white*. Back golden olive somewhat stained with crimson; upper tail coverts somewhat barred with yellow; wing coverts spotted yellowish white. Throat and breast barred yellowish white and blackish, *belly plain lemon yellow*. Central tail feathers black, outer ones black, barred with olive. ♀: crown black with a crimson nuchal band.

Subtropical zone. Río Chiquito, sw Táchira (*abdominalis*). [Colombia to central Peru.]

Cloud forest, 1800 m.

## CRIMSON-CRESTED WOODPECKER

*Campephilus melanoleucos*
CARPINTERO REAL PICO AMARILLO

Pl. 17

14″ (36 cm.). Crown, crest and sides of head crimson; spot on cheek black above, white below; area at base of bill white edged black above (or without black edge, a). A white stripe down sides of neck continuing down sides of mantle and joining on back to form a V. Back, throat and breast, closed wings and tail black, belly buffy white (or cinnamon buff, a) barred black. Under wing coverts and wing lining white. Can be confused with Lineated Woodpecker but throat black instead of finely streaked

black and white, cheeks white or red instead of gray, and bill lighter in color. ♀: differs from ♂ by a broad white stripe from gape across the lower part of cheeks joining stripe down sides of neck.

Tropical and subtropical zones. Zulia in the Perijá region and in the sw along the Río Catatumbo and in the L. Maracaibo drainage in n Táchira and in Mérida (*malherbi*, a). E Zulia, s Táchira and Apure e through Guárico and Lara to Sucre, Carabobo and Delta Amacuro; n Amazonas s to Cerro Yapacana; n Bolívar (*melanoleucos*). [Panama to Bolivia, Paraguay and n Argentina. The Guianas. Trinidad.]

Cloud, rain, gallery and deciduous forests, second growth, to 2000 m. n of the Orinoco, to 950 m. s of it. Clearings, forest edge, semi-open country plantations, pastures, along rivers, swampy areas. In pairs or small groups, actively and conspicuously forages in tall, dead tree trunks in the forest or in isolated trees. Calls: high-pitched, sonorous call; loud, slow, deliberate, brief drumming or pounding.

Note: In Lista Av. Venez. and Sp. Bds. S Amer., this and the next 3 species were referred to the genus *Phloeoceastes*, now considered inseparable from *Campephilus*.

## RED-NECKED WOODPECKER

*Campephilus rubricollis*
CARPINTERO PESCUECIRROJO

Pl. 17

14″ (36 cm.). Entire head, neck and upper breast crimson. Back, wings and tail black. Lower breast, belly and wing lining rufous. Primaries with basal half rufous forming a *prominent patch in flight*, ♀: like ♂ but has forehead white, and broad, wedge-shaped stripe below eye white, margined with black.

Tropical, occasionally lower subtropical zone to 1600 m. N Amazonas s to Cerro Yapacana and the Yavita-Pimichín Trail; generally distributed in Bolívar (*rubricollis*). [E Colombia and the Guianas.]

Rain and cloud forests, forest edge, semi-open woodland. In pairs, conspicuous, actively forages from middle to upper heights on trunks and limbs of tall trees. Calls: loud explosive; brief drumming.

## POWERFUL WOODPECKER

*Campephilus pollens*
CARPINTERO GIGANTE

Pl. 17
14.5″ (37 cm.). When climbing can be confused with Lineated or Crimson-crested Woodpeckers but is easily distinguishable from either by its white, buff-tinged, lower back and rump. Forehead and sides of head black, crown and bushy crest scarlet. Stripe below eye white, continuing down sides of neck, breast and sides of mantle, joining on back to form a V. Center of upper back black, lower back white, tinged buff, upper tail coverts and tail black. Throat and upper breast black, rest of underparts buff, barred black. Remiges black, barred white on inner web and tipped white. ♀: no scarlet on head, underparts darker, cinnamon rufous, barred black.
Subtropical zone. Extreme sw Táchira on Páramo de Tamá and the Río Chiquito (*pollens*). [The Andes of Colombia to Peru.]
Cloud forest, 1800–2250 m. Loud, brief drumming. Inconspicuous except when it drums.

# PASSERIFORMES

## WOODCREEPERS: Dendrocolaptidae

TREPADORES

Woodcreepers are tree-climbing birds found in forested regions from s Mexico to n Argentina.
   In color many are much alike, being clothed in shades of brown, with rufous wings and tail, sometimes streaked or spotted on backs and underparts. Bills are often a handy means of distinguishing the species, for these vary from short and straight to very long and curved. The bills are used to probe cavities in trees or under the bark in search of insects and never to hammer as do woodpeckers. When feeding, woodcreepers usually start climbing from the base of the tree, working their way upward aided by their stiffened tails found in most species. Natural cavities in trees or holes made by other birds are used for nesting. Two or 3 greenish white, unspotted eggs are laid.
   Woodcreepers are usually solitary birds, but sometimes form mixed bands of birds foraging through the forest. Although hardly looked upon as songbirds, they have rather musical voices, their notes often consisting of ringing notes and trills, as well as rattling or buzzing sounds. (Also see note to Furnariidae, p. 188.)

## TYRANNINE WOODCREEPER

*Dendrocincla tyrannina*
TREPADOR PARAMERO

10″ (25 cm.). More or less uniform dull brown, less rufescent, more olivaceous below; feathers of throat and breast with inconspicuous pale shaft streaks. Wings, tail, upper and under tail coverts rufous chestnut. Iris dark brown; maxilla black, mandible blue gray. Bill straight, 1.3″ (3.3 cm.).
Subtropical zone. Known only from w Táchira on the Páramo Zumbador and along the Río Chiquito (*hellmayri*). [Colombia; e Ecuador; n Peru.]
Damp, mossy cloud forests, 1800–2300 m.

## PLAIN-BROWN WOODCREEPER

*Dendrocincla fuliginosa*
TREPADOR MARRÓN

Pl. 18
8″ (20 cm.). Reddish brown to olivaceous brown, paler and grayer on the throat and ear coverts (with a pale postocular streak, a). Wings, tail, upper and under tail coverts rufous chestnut. Iris brown

to grayish brown. Maxilla black, mandible blue gray. Bill straight, 1" (2.5 cm.).
Tropical and subtropical zones. Nw Zulia and the Andes in Táchira and Mérida (*lafresnayi*). The n Cordillera and interior chain from Falcón and w Lara to the Paria Pen., the llanos of Guárico and Monagas (*meruloides*). The w llanos in Táchira, Apure, Barinas and Portuguesa (*barinensis*). Amazonas and nw Bolívar (*phaeochroa*). The delta of the Orinoco (*deltana*). E Bolívar from the Altiplanicie de Nuria s to Cerro Roraima (*fuliginosa*, a). [Honduras to w Ecuador, Bolivia, Paraguay, s Brazil and ne Argentina. Trinidad, Tobago.]
Mostly in the lowlands. Ranges from sea level in mangroves, rain forests and high second growth to, occasionally, 1800 m. The most common and widespread species of the family in Venezuela. Forest dweller, gregarious, seldom alone but in pairs or small flocks, or with other birds. Forages from the base to the tops of trees. Follows army ants.

## WHITE-CHINNED WOODCREEPER
*Dendrocincla merula*
Trepador Barbiblanco

Pl. 18
7" (18 cm.). Wood brown; upper *throat white;* wings, tail, upper and under tail coverts dark chestnut. Bill straight, 0.9" (2.3 cm.).
Tropical zone. W Amazonas from Caño Cataniapo s to the Río Negro; n Bolívar in the lower Caura region (*bartletti*). [The Guianas; se Colombia; Peru, ne Bolivia; Amazonian Brazil.]
Rain forests, 100–200 m. Often near watercourses. Call: typical woodcreeper call, a chattering of many single notes, rather soft, falling in scale.

## RUDDY WOODCREEPER
*Dendrocincla homochroa*
Trepador Rojizo

Pl. 18
7.5" (18 cm.). Mainly dark olive brown, shoulders chestnut. Crown dark chestnut, feathers of forehead with pale centers and shaft streaks giving a slightly streaked appearance; *chin and upper*

*throat tawny ochraceous.* Bill straight, 1" (2.5 cm.).
Tropical, occasionally subtropical zone. Zulia and Táchira to Lara, Barinas and Cojedes (*meridionalis*). [Mexico to n Colombia.]
Cloud and dense rain forests, open forest and high second growth, occasionally to 1800 m. Shy, secretive. Follows army ants and forages in the lower parts of the tree trunks using the tail as a prop, constantly flicking its folded wings. Call: reedy, scratchy, squeaky notes, also a chattering and a rattle.

## LONG-TAILED WOODCREEPER
*Deconychura longicauda*
Trepador Colilargo

Pl. 18
7.7–8.5" (19.5–22 cm.). Above reddish brown, crown and nape with buff shaft streaks; lores, sides of head and superciliary whitish. Throat dirty white, rest of underparts olivaceous brown, breast feathers with buffy white centers. Lesser wing coverts tinged rufous. Wings, tail, upper and under tail coverts dull chestnut. Bill straight, 1" (2.5 cm.).
Tropical zone. S Amazonas; central and s Bolívar (*connectens*). [The Guianas; w and se Colombia to e Peru and Amazonian Brazil.]
Rain forests to about 400 m. Forages on tree trunks. Call: very light rattle, up and down scale.

## SPOT-THROATED WOODCREEPER
*Deconychura stictolaema*
Trepador Pechipunteado

7.5" (19 cm.). Very like the Long-tailed Woodcreeper but somewhat smaller and easily distinguishable by *rufous instead of brown rump.* Bill straight, 0.8" (2 cm.).
Tropical zone. S Amazonas n to Cerro Yapacana (*secunda*). [French Guiana; e Ecuador; nw and e central Peru; central and w Amazonian Brazil.]
Low, open rain forests near watercourses at about 150 m.

## OLIVACEOUS WOODCREEPER
*Sittasomus griseicapillus*
TREPADOR VERDÓN

Pl. 18
6.5" (16.5 cm.). *Head, neck* and *underparts gray*, tinged olivaceous. Mantle olivaceous brown; lower back, rump, upper and under tail coverts and tail rufous. Under wing coverts and bases of inner webs of inner remiges white or cinnamon, forming a wing band. Bill short, straight, 0.6" (1.5 cm.).
Tropical and subtropical zones. Sw Táchira (*tachirensis*). The Sierra de Perijá, Zulia (*perijanus*). From sw Barinas, Mérida and Lara through Yaracuy e along the n Cordillera to Carabobo and Sucre (*griseus*). W and s Amazonas (*amazonus*). N and central Amazonas; Bolívar from the Ríos Cuchivero and Caura e to the Sierra de Imataca and Cerro Roraima (*axillaris*). [Mid. Amer. to se Brazil, ne Argentina, Paraguay and Bolivia. Tobago.]
Deep shady forests, forest edge, open woodland and tall second growth, to 2300 m. n of the Orinoco and to 1600 m. on the tepuis. Usually solitary, inconspicuously forages on tree trunks from low to medium heights, plucking insects from the soft bark. Active, sometimes captures insects in the air. Joins flocks of other species. Call: a woodpeckerlike, very sharp, fine, rapid, rattling trill.

## WEDGE-BILLED WOODCREEPER
*Glyphorynchus spirurus*
TREPADOR PICO DE CUÑA

Pl. 18
5.5" (14 cm.). Crown and mantle brown (forecrown tinged grayish in some races); lower back, rump, upper and under tail coverts and tail rufous chestnut. Throat buffy white to cinnamon buff; underparts pale olivaceous brown with conspicuous, arrow-shaped, buff marks on breast, and less conspicuous shaft streaks on lower breast. Wings like back, inner webs of inner remiges buffy white to cinnamon buff forming a wing band. *Bill short, 0.4; (1 cm.); lower mandible curved upwards* for distal half.
Tropical and lower subtropical zones. The Sierra de Perijá, Zulia, s to s Táchira, w Barinas and n Mérida (*integratus*). S

and central Amazonas e across s Bolívar (*rufigularis*). Extreme s Amazonas on Cerro de la Neblina (*coronobscurus*). E Bolívar from the Altiplanicie de Nuria s to the Gran Sabana in the Ptari-tepui area (*spirurus*). In Sucre and Delta Amacuro (*amacurensis*). [Mid. Amer. to w Ecuador, Peru, Bolivia and s and e Brazil.]
Rain forests, second growth, plantations, open areas and brush. Ranges from sea level in the Orinoco delta and the shores of L. Maracaibo to 1800 m. in the n mountains and the tepuis. Usually seen alone, but others are likely to be present. Inconspicuous. Forages on tree trunks through the lower level of the forest, also creeps along the branches. Aided by its tail climbs in agile spurts and pecks into decayed wood. Call: a series of shrill, metallic squeaks.

## LONG-BILLED WOODCREEPER
*Nasica longirostris*
TREPADOR PESCUECILARGO

Pl. 18
14" (35 cm.). Crown and hindneck dark brown with buff shaft streaks, these broadening on hindneck and becoming white. Conspicuous white postocular streak. Back, wings and tail rufous chestnut. Throat white. Underparts light olivaceous brown with conspicuous white, black-bordered stripes reaching upper belly. Bill very slightly curved, very long, 3" (7.6 cm.).
Tropical zone. Amazonas in Puerto Ayacucho, the lower Río Ventuari and Cerro Duida. [French Guiana; e Colombia to e Amazonian Brazil and Bolivia.]
Rain forests, 100–200 m.

## RED-BILLED WOODCREEPER
*Hylexetastes perrotii*
TREPADOR PICO ROJO

Pl. 18
12" (30 cm.). Crown dark olive brown, lores and stripe below eye whitish, sides of throat olive brown, center of throat grayish white. Mantle olive brown, rump and upper tail coverts rufous chestnut. Lower parts grayish olive brown, center of belly lightly barred white and grayish. Under tail coverts slightly barred ochraceous and blackish. Wings and tail

rufous chestnut. Bill heavy, slightly curved, *wine red*, 1.5″ (4 cm.).
Tropical zone. Ne Bolívar (Río Yuruán only) (*perrotii*). [The Guianas, central Amazonian Brazil.]
Rain forests in the lowlands. Forages in the higher levels of the trees.

## STRONG-BILLED WOODCREEPER

*Xiphocolaptes promeropirhynchus*
TREPADOR PICO NEGRO

Pl. 18
11–12″ (28–30 cm.). Crown dusky brown, pale-streaked. Back brown, the streaks of crown continuing narrowly to upper back; lower back, rump and upper tail coverts rufous chestnut. An ill-defined pale subocular streak, and dusky moustacial streak. Throat whitish (somewhat streaked dusky, a), rest of underparts brown, broadly (or narrowly, b) streaked buffy white. Center of abdomen buffy somewhat spotted with dusky (not constant). Wings and tail rufous chestnut. Bill somewhat curved, dusky (or almost straight and pale horn, c), 1.5–2″ (4–5 cm.).
Mostly subtropical zone. The Sierra de Perijá, Zulia, and in the Andes of Táchira, Mérida and Trujillo, 450–2800 m. (*promeropirhynchus*). Nw Zulia, n Mérida to Sucre, Monagas and the e llanos of Guárico, to 2000 m. (*procerus*, b). Tropical zone in the Orinoco Valley from Puerto Ayacucho s (*orenocensis*, c). Amazonas on Cerro de la Neblina, 1800 m. (*neblinae*, a). S Bolívar on Cerros Chimantá-tepui and Roraima and in the Gran Sabana, 700–1200 m. (*tenebrosus*, a). [Colombia to nw Peru, n Bolivia and Amazonian Brazil.]
Rain and cloud forests, open forest and forest edge; coffee plantations. N of the Orinoco to 3000 m., s of it to 1800 m. on the slopes of the tepuis. Not shy nor very active. Climbs the trunks of trees, sometimes in spirals, starting at base, examining epiphytes, but also frequents tree tops. Solitary, sometimes in pairs, does not mix with other species. At dawn and in the evening emits a loud song decreasing in pitch; another call is a series of repeated, monotonous whistle-like notes.

## BLACK-BANDED WOODCREEPER

*Dendrocolaptes picumnus*
TREPADOR TANGUERO

Pl. 18
10″ (25 cm.). Much like the Strong-billed Woodcreeper but smaller with a shorter, straighter bill, and easily distinguishable by its *banded lower breast*, belly and under tail coverts (banding not as evident, a). Bill straight, 1.4″ (3.5 cm.).
Tropical and subtropical zones. The Sierra de Perijá, Zulia, the Andes from Táchira and Mérida and in n Barinas (*multistrigatus*). N coastal mountains from Falcón to Sucre and Monagas (*seilerni*, a). W Amazonas e to e Bolívar on the Río Cuyuni (*picumnus*). [Guatemala to w Panama. Colombia to w Ecuador, nw Argentina, Paraguay, Amazonian Brazil.]
Rain and cloud forests, forest edge and plantations. N of the Orinoco 450–2700 m., s of it to 500 m. on the Sierra de Imataca. Follows army ants. Alone or in pairs, climbs trees to various heights. Preys on invertebrates and small cold-blooded vertebrates. Call: a simple, repeated note "oi," falling in pitch.

## BARRED WOODCREEPER

*Dendrocolaptes certhia*
TREPADOR BARRETEADO

Pl. 18
11″ (28 cm.). Crown olivaceous brown, the feathers barred black. Upper back olivaceous brown obscurely barred black; lower back, wings and tail bright rufous chestnut. Underparts pale brownish buff *lightly barred* with *black* (or breast olivaceous with oval buff spots outlined in black, rest of underparts broadly barred warm buff and black, less strongly so on crissum, a). Bill slightly curved, 1.5″ (3.8 cm.), basal part flesh color.
Tropical zone. The base of the Sierra de Perijá, Zulia, and in n Mérida (*punctipectus*, a). Amazonas, Bolívar and Delta Amacuro (*certhia*). [The Guianas; Colombia to nw Ecuador, n Bolivia, Amazonian and e Brazil.]
Rain forests, tall second growth, forest edge. N of the Orinoco from the lowlands to 150 m., s of it to 1400 m. on the slopes of the tepuis. Follows army ants regularly, actively flying from tree to

tree looking for insects. Not shy. Solitary.

## STRAIGHT-BILLED WOODCREEPER

*Xiphorhynchus picus*
TREPADOR SUBESUBE

Pl. 18
8.5″ (22 cm.). Back, wings and tail rufous chestnut; crown dark brown with numerous small, dropshaped buff marks, these extending to the extreme upper mantle (becoming wide and conspicuous on hindneck and upper mantle, where they are white outlined in black, a). Throat and extreme upper breast white, rest of underparts reddish brown to olive brown, breast with white, black-bordered streaks which merge into the white of throat. Bill, 1–1.2″ (2.5–3 cm.), very straight, maxilla dusky horn, mandible flesh.
Tropical zone. Extreme n Zulia e to the e side of the mouth of L. Maracaibo (*picirostris, a*). Zulia around the middle and s Maracaibo region to n Táchira and n Mérida (*saturatior*). Arid w coastal Falcón from Casigua e to the Paraguaná Pen. and the Serranía de San Luis and s to n Lara (*paraguanae*). Extreme e coastal Falcón e of the Río Tocuyo along the coast of Carabobo to Miranda (*choica*). The e coast in Anzoátegui and Sucre and the llanos from w Apure to Guárico and e Anzoátegui and along the s bank of the Orinoco in w Bolívar e to Altagracia (*phalara*). Both banks of the lower Orinoco between Ciudad Bolívar and Barrancas, Monagas (*picus*). Delta Amacuro (*deltanus*). Nw Bolívar on the upper Río Cuchivero; Amazonas s to the Duida region (*duidae*). Margarita I. (*longirostris, a*). [Panama to n Bolivia and Amazonian Brazil. Trinidad.]
Rain forests n of the Orinoco to 1400 m., s of it in the lowlands to about 200 m. Forest edge, swamp forests, mangroves and dry scrub, clearings, gallery forests, gardens, parks, Alone or in pairs, forages in the tree trunks; joins mixed flocks. One of the most common woodcreepers. Call: a series of loud whistles descending the scale, more rapid at the end.

## STRIPED WOODCREEPER

*Xiphorhynchus obsoletus*
TREPADOR LOCO

Pl. 18
7.5″ (19 cm.). Crown blackish with numerous dropshaped, buff, black-bordered marks. Back reddish brown with white, black-bordered streaks, extending further down back than in Straight-billed Woodcreepers, rump and upper tail coverts rufous. Throat buffy white, rest of underparts grayish olive brown with linear, white, black-bordered streaks on breast and upper belly. Crissum plain grayish olive. Bill straight, 0.8″ (2 cm.).
Tropical zone. The Orinoco valley in Bolívar from Caicara e to Altagracia (*caicarae*). N of the Orinoco in sw Táchira, Barinas and w Apure; Amazonas; Bolívar from the lower Río Caura e across the Río Caroní to the Río Cuyuni (*notatus*). Delta Amacuro (*obsoletus*). [E Colombia and the Guianas to ne Peru, Amazonian Brazil and ne Bolivia.]
Rain forests n of the Orinoco, 300–500 m., s of it to 400 m. Frequently in damp areas and near water. Creeps along the upper or under side of horizontal branches. Nests in holes in trees and in arboreal termite nests.

## OCELLATED WOODCREEPER

*Xiphorhynchus ocellatus*
TREPADOR DE OCELOS

8″ (20 cm.). Above rather like Striped Woodcreeper but marks on back very much narrower, more like shaft streaks. Below much darker and browner, less gray, the throat much darker buff, the feathers narrowly edged black, the breast marked with dropshaped spots rather than linear streaks, and much buffier in color. Bill straight, considerably longer than in Striped Woodcreeper, 1.1″ (2.8 cm.).
Tropical zone. Sw Amazonas (*ocellatus*). [Se Colombia to n Bolivia; w and central Amazonian Brazil.]
Rain forests, 120–150 m. Frequently near rivers. Common in the Yavita-Pimichín Trail.

## CHESTNUT-RUMPED WOODCREEPER
*Xiphorhynchus pardalotus*
TREPADOR SILBADOR

Pl. 18
8.5″ (21.6 cm.). Not unlike Striped Woodcreeper but streaks on mantle more prominent. Crown blackish with dropshaped, buff markings; mantle reddish brown with long, prominent dropshaped marks; rump, wings and tail chestnut; shoulders olive brown. Throat cinnamon buff; breast olive brown, streaked cinnamon buff; belly dull cinnamon buff, browner on sides of body. Bill straight, 1.3″ (3.3 cm.).
Tropical and lower subtropical zones. Amazonas from Caño Cataniapo s to Sierra Imerí and generally in Bolívar (*caurensis*). [The Guianas; e and n Amazonian Brazil.]
Rain forests in Pantepui above 100 m., ranging to 1800 m. on the slopes of the tepuis. Follows army ants. A medium-sized woodcreeper, similar to but smaller than Buff-throated Woodcreeper.

## BUFF-THROATED WOODCREEPER
*Xiphorhynchus guttatus*
TREPADOR PEGÓN

Pl. 18
10″ [25 cm.] (8.5″ [21.6 cm.], a). There are two types, one with stripes on breast and upper belly, the other with spots on breast and upper belly. Above reddish brown, crown blackish with dropshaped, buff marks, these broadening, becoming linear on upper back (or with streaks smaller, much reduced in number, b). Rump, wings and tail rufous chestnut. Throat plain buff (or the feathers narrowly edged black, c); underparts buffy brown to grayish brown with broad, black-edged buff stripes (or with round, buff spots on breast virtually disappearing on belly, b).
Tropical, occasionally subtropical zone. From Zulia, Táchira and Apure w through Falcón, Barinas, Portuguesa and Yaracuy to e Miranda (*nanus*, a). N Amazonas across n Bolívar and s Anzoátegui to Delta Amacuro (*polystictus*, b). W and s Amazonas (*guttatoides*, b). Ne Anzoátegui and n Monagas e through the Paria Pen., Sucre (*jardinei*). Se Sucre (*susurrans*, c). Margarita I.

(*margaritae*). [The Guianas, e and central Colombia, to n Bolivia and Brazil. Trinidad, Tobago.]
Rain forests, n of the Orinoco to 1900 m., s of it to 500 m. Humid forest edge, second growth, cocoa plantations, mangroves and arid areas. Forages alone or in pairs in medium-sized trees; not conspicuous but very noisy, usually heard before it is seen. Joins forest flocks. Follows army ants.

## OLIVE-BACKED WOODCREEPER
*Xiphorhynchus triangularis*
TREPADOR LOMIACEITUNO

Pl. 18
8.5″ (22 cm.). Olive brown above, crown with pale shaft streaks, these expanding into small spots on hindneck, back unmarked; upper tail coverts chestnut. Throat and foreneck buff, the feathers conspicuously edged black giving a scaled appearance. Breast and belly spotted with buff. Outer webs of remiges olive, inner webs rufescent chestnut, the wing when closed differing from that of most other species by being less obviously chestnut. Tail chestnut. Bill very slightly curved, 1.2″ (3 cm.).
Upper tropical and subtropical zones. Zulia, Táchira and Mérida (*triangularis*). Yaracuy; e along the coastal and interior Cordillera from Carabobo to Miranda (*hylodromus*). [Colombia to w Bolivia.]
Cloud forest, 1000–2300 m., seldom at the lower altitudes. Alone or in small groups. Joins flocks of other birds. Forages in the highest branches, creeping up the trees and thick lianas and vines probing in crevices. Loud calls.

## STREAK-HEADED WOODCREEPER
*Lepidocolaptes souleyetii*
TREPADORCITO LISTADO

Pl. 18
7″ (18 cm.). Crown and hindneck dark brown streaked buff, back reddish brown, rump and upper tail coverts rufous chestnut. Throat whitish buff to buff, rest of underparts olive brown, broadly and profusely streaked buffy white, the streaks conspicuously edged blackish. Wings and tail rufous. Bill very slightly curved, 1″ (2.5 cm.).
Tropical zone. Zulia to Sucre and the llanos from Apure to Monagas n of the

Orinoco, s of it in n and se Bolívar (*littoralis*). The Andes in w Táchira, w Barinas and w Mérida (*lineaticeps*). Extreme se Bolívar along the Río Uairén (*uaireni*). [Mexico to Colombia, e of the Andes to Meta, w of them to nw Peru. Guyana, Brazil in Roraima. Trinidad.] Rain forests n of the Orinoco to 1600 m., s of it to 1100 m. Open forest, second growth, cocoa plantations, brush and small scattered trees in savannas. Explores trees actively from low to medium heights alone or in pairs. Joins other species. Not shy. Call: a descending musical trill; also piercing staccato notes, highly pitched.

**SPOT-CROWNED WOODCREEPER**
*Lepidocolaptes affinis*
TREPADOR GAMUSITA

Pl. 18
7.5″ (19 cm.). Rather like Streak-headed Woodcreeper but crown spotted instead of streaked and stripes of underparts pure white, rounded terminally and more conspicuously margined with black. Bill more curved and slightly longer.
Subtropical zone. The Sierra de Perijá, Zulia, and the Andes of Mérida (*lacrymiger*). The coastal Cordillera from Carabobo to Sucre (*lafresnayi*). [S Mexico to w Panama. Colombia through the Andes to n Bolivia.]
Open as well as dense, humid cloud forests, high second growth, 1500–2900 m. Alone or in pairs. Behaves in typical woodcreeper fashion. Joins other species. Prefers the higher parts of trees. One of its calls is a series of reedy squeaks.

**LINEATED WOODCREEPER**
*Lepidocolaptes albolineatus*
TREPADORCITO GOTEADO

7″ (18 cm.). Rather like Spot-crowned Woodcreeper but crown minutely dotted with buff (or plain, a). Back darker and underparts grayer, the stripes truncate rather than rounded terminally. Wings duller and darker. Bill curved, shorter, 0.9″ (2.3 cm.).
Tropical zone. Amazonas and s Bolívar (*duidae*, a). Ne Bolívar (*albolineatus*). [The Guianas, e Ecuador to n Bolivia, Amazonian Brazil.]

Rain forest, plantations, open woods, scrub, 150–1300 m. Forages in the undergrowth.

**RED-BILLED SCYTHEBILL**
*Campylorhamphus trochilirostris*
TREPADOR PICO DE GARFIO

Pl. 18
8″ (20 cm.). Bill long, sickleshaped, chord 2.4″ (6 cm.), very slender, light reddish brown. Crown dark brown, rest of plumage light reddish brown, streaked on crown, mantle, throat, breast and upper belly with buffy white. Wings, upper tail coverts and tail rufous.
Tropical and subtropical zones. From Zulia, Táchira and Apure, n of the Orinoco to Sucre and the llanos of Anzoátegui; nw Bolívar and across s Bolívar from the upper Río Caura to the headwaters of the Río Caroní (*venezuelensis*). [Central and e Panama to n Bolivia, Paraguay and Argentina.]
Deciduous and humid forests, n of the Orinoco to 2000 m., s of it from 350 m. to 950 m. near the tepuis. Alone or in pairs, sometimes joins other species. Forages mostly from medium heights to tree tops. Shy, inconspicuous. Probes inside Bromeliads and other epiphytes. Call: one begins with 4 or 5 spaced notes followed by a series of monotonous, staccato notes.

**BROWN-BILLED SCYTHEBILL**
*Campylorhamphus pusillus*
TREPADOR PIQUICURVADO

9″ (23 cm.). Bill very long, sickleshaped, light brown, chord 2″ (5 cm.). Dark olivaceous brown, darkest on head; crown, sides and back of neck, mantle, breast and upper belly streaked buff. Throat dark buff. Rump rufous chestnut. Wings and tail dark chestnut brown.
Subtropical zone. Sierra de Perijá, Zulia; sw Táchira (*tachirensis*). [Costa Rica and w Panama. Colombia, w Ecuador, Guyana.]
Cloud forests, 1800–2175 m., joins mixed bird parties. Forages in trees at all heights.

**CURVE-BILLED SCYTHEBILL**

*Campylorhamphus procurvoides*
TREPADOR PICO DE HOZ

Pl. 18
8.5″ (22 cm.). Bill very long, sickleshaped, light reddish brown, chord 2.2″ (5.6 cm.). Differs from Red- and Brown-billed Scythebill in that streaks of the upperparts only reach the extreme upper mantle. In general color most like Red-billed. Crown dark brown with buff shaft streaks; back reddish brown; rump, upper tail coverts, wings and tail rufous chestnut. Throat buffy white, the feathers edged all around with dusky giving a scaled appearance; rest of underparts pale brown, the upper breast with pointed, buffy white spots, these becoming shaft streaks on lower breast and belly.
Tropical zone. S Amazonas n to the Yavita-Pimichín Trail; e Bolívar from the Altiplanicie de Nuria to the Río Cuyuni (*sanus*). [The Guianas. E Colombia. Central Amazonian Brazil.] Rain forest to 450 m. on Nuria. Probes for insects in epiphytes.

# HORNEROS, SPINETAILS, FOLIAGE-GLEANERS, ETC.: Furnariidae

ALBAÑILES, GÜITÍOS, RASPA HOJAS, ETC.

This large family of typically neotropical birds comprises many groups of widely differing appearance and habits. Almost all, however, are clothed in shades of brown, rufous or buff, some streaked, others not. Some species are terrestrial, others climb trees like woodcreepers and inhabit forests, some are found in hot desert areas, while others inhabit the cold páramos.

Nests are as varied as the birds. Some species nest in holes in trees or banks, others build domed mud nests or enormous round structures of sticks and still others weave basketlike nests of grass.

Food consists mainly of insects and vegetable matter, the tree-climbing species finding their food in the bark of trees by prying rather than digging it out in the manner of woodpeckers.

They are not noted as songbirds, but some emit a rather pleasant trilling song.

Note: Two revisions of this family have been proposed recently. They are: A. Feduccia, "Evolutionary Trends in the Avian Families Furnariidae and Dendrocolaptidae," Ph.D. diss., University of Michigan, 1969; and C. E. Vaurie, "A Revised Classification of the Ovenbirds (Furnariidae)" (London: H. F. and G. Witherby, 1971). Here the traditional treatment of the family is adhered to.

**BAR-WINGED CINCLODES**

*Cinclodes fuscus*
MENEACOLA

Pl. 19
7″ (18 cm.). Reddish brown above; prominent postocular streak buffy white. Throat white, the feathers edged black, bordered below by a blackish band. Upper breast and sides of body pale buffy brown, center of belly dull white. Lesser upper wing coverts like back, but broadly edged dull buffy white forming a wing bar, greater wing coverts with a median cinnamon band. Remiges black-ish, primaries with a broad, cinnamon basal band conspicuous in flight, tertials broadly edged medially with cinnamon. Central tail feathers like back, 3 outer pairs all or mostly cinnamon.
Rocky páramos. The Andes of Mérida, Trujillo and s Lara (*heterurus*). [E Colombia to Tierra del Fuego. In winter in s Brazil and Uruguay.]
Terrestrial, near water in rocky places with low bushes, 3800–5000 m. Not shy, flicks tail. Often in pairs restlessly searching for insects. Ranges up to the glaciers. Nests in holes in banks and among rocks.

## PALE-LEGGED HORNERO
*Furnarius leucopus*
ALBAÑIL

Pl. 20
6.5" (16.5 cm.). Crown and nape ashy gray. Broad eyebrow buffy white. Back, wings and tail bright cinnamon rufous. Throat and center of underparts white, breast and sides of body tawny buff. Primaries blackish with a broad basal band of cinnamon rufous, conspicuous in flight. Bill comparatively long; tail short.
Tropical zone. Nw Lara, nw Falcón and the Sierra de Perijá region, nw Zulia (*longirostris*). S Zulia (*endoecus*). [Guyana; ne and e Colombia to w Peru, n Bolivia and Amazonian and e Brazil.]
Open, brushy country to 600 m. Largely terrestrial. Constructs a domeshaped mud nest 8–10" (20–25 cm.) in diameter with a side entrance. Call: one of its songs consists of a series of high-pitched descending notes.

## ANDEAN TIT-SPINETAIL
*Leptasthenura andicola*
SIETECOLAS

Pl. 19
5.8" (14.7 cm.). Crown dark rufous chestnut, streaked black, eyebrow white. Back dark brown broadly streaked white. Throat and breast white, streaked dusky, abdomen pale grayish. Wings blackish; tail long, graduated, central feathers sharply pointed, blackish, the outer feathers pale-tipped.
Andes of Mérida and Trujillo (*certhia*). [Andes of n and central Colombia s to n Bolivia.]
Páramos, forest edge, 3500–4100 m. Near small, even tiny, streams and lakes, hides in shrubby, matted vegetation. Although agile and shy often will not flush from cover until almost stepped on.

## AZARA'S SPINETAIL
*Synallaxis azarae*
GÜITIÓ DE AZARA

6.5" (16.5 cm). Crown, nape, shoulders and margins of remiges bright rufous; tail long, pointed, graduated, bright rufous. Forehead, back and flanks olive brown. Upper throat white, lower throat black, feathers tipped white giving a spotted appearance. Breast and sides of head and neck grayish, center of abdomen white.
Subtropical zone. The Andes of Táchira, Mérida and Trujillo, (*elegantior*). [Colombia s through the Andes to n Bolivia.]
Cloud forest, clearings, coffee plantations, 1600–2300 m.

## DUSKY SPINETAIL
*Synallaxis moesta*
GÜITÍO GARGANTIHABADO

Pl. 19
6.5" (16.5 cm.). Much darker than Azara's Spinetail with a proportionately shorter tail, the forehead the same color as the rest of the crown. Top of head, nape, shoulders and edges of remiges rufous chestnut, back dull reddish brown. Tail rufous chestnut. Throat black, the feathers edged gray, rest of underparts dark, smoky olivaceous brown (or much paler, light olivaceous, a).
Upper tropical and subtropical zones. Ne Amazonas on Cerro Yaví (*yavii*, a). Ne Amazonas on Cerro Camani; nw Bolívar on Cerro El Negro and the tepuis of the Gran Sabana in the se (*macconnelli*). [Surinam; French Guiana; Amazonian Brazil; e Ecuador; e Peru and n Bolivia.]
Cloud and rain forest in the undergrowth and lower vegetation on the talus slopes of the tepuis, ranging from 1000 m. near Kabanayén to 1900 m. on Ptari-tepui.
Note: Zimmer, in Mayr and Phelps, Bull. AMNH, 1967, *136*, no. 5, reports that the supposed overlap in the ranges of *S. cabanisi* and *S. moesta* was due to the misidentification of a specimen. *S. cabanisi* was treated as a distinct species in both Sp. Bds. S Amer. and Lista Av. Venez. Both *yavii* and *macconnelli* were treated as races of *cabanisi*.

## PALE-BREASTED SPINETAIL
*Synallaxis albescens*
GÜITÍO GARGANTIBLANCO

Pl. 19
6.5" (16.5 cm.). Much like Azara's Spinetail but paler and at once separable by olive brown instead of bright rufous tail; rufous on wings confined to shoulders.
Tropical and lower subtropical zones. The

Caribbean littoral from the Goajira Pen. to w Falcón and in Lara (*perpallida*). Nw Zulia to Táchira through Mérida to e Falcón and Yaracuy and through Carabobo to Miranda (*occipitalis*). From s Táchira, Apure and Barinas e to Anzoátegui, Sucre and Monagas; extreme nw Amazonas and n Bolívar (*trinitatis*). Margarita and Cubagua Is. (*nesiotes*). N and central Amazonas; s Bolívar from La Paragua and Cerro Perro on the Río Paragua to the tepuis of the Gran Sabana; Delta Amacuro at Misión Araguaimujo (*josephinae*). [Colombia; Brazil, to Argentina. Trinidad.] From sea level to 1700 m. in many different habitats from the edge of high virgin forests, coffee plantations and mangroves to thickets, savannas, arid areas and reedbeds. Alone or in pairs forages noisily and actively in low bushes. Flies from branch to branch chattering "güitío." Jerks tail up and down.

**PLAIN-CROWNED SPINETAIL**

*Synallaxis gujanensis*
GÜITÍO ESPINOSO

Pl. 19
5.8″ (14.7 cm.). Much like Azara's Spinetail but paler and at once separable by lacking the rufous crown and black on throat. Crown grayish brown, this color gradually changing to brownish on back. Wings and tail rufous. Below white clouded on breast and flanks with grayish brown.

Tropical zone. The s Orinoco delta in Monagas and Delta Amacuro, widely distributed in Bolívar and Amazonas (*gujanensis*). [Generally distributed e of the Andes to n Bolivia, Paraguay and Brazil to Mato Grosso and Goiás.] Rain forest, high second growth and forest edge, in shrubbery and thick undergrowth, from near sea level in the Orinoco delta to 550 m. in Pantepui. Forages in low bushes. Call: a 2-note "güitío."

**STRIPE-BREASTED SPINETAIL**

*Synallaxis cinnamomea*
GÜITÍO CANELO

Pl. 19
6.5″ (16.5 cm.). A comparatively short-tailed species distinguishable from other members of the genus by its streaked breast. Upper parts dark brown to dark olive brown. Postocular streak and rear part of auriculars dark rufous. Shoulders and margins of remiges chestnut. Tail blackish, the feathers edged chestnut basally. Throat black spotted with white. Breast and upper abdomen cinnamon brown with dark-bordered, pale streaks, sides of body brown.

Upper tropical and subtropical zones. The Sierra de Perijá, Zulia; n Táchira, Mérida, Lara, Falcón and Trujillo (*aveledoi*). E Falcón (Mirimire), the coastal Cordillera from Yaracuy and Guárico (Cerro Platillón) to Miranda and the interior chain from Carabobo to Miranda (*bolivari*). The coastal Cordillera from Anzoátegui to w Sucre (*striatipectus*). The ne coast of Sucre and the Paria Pen. (*pariae*). [Colombia on both slopes of the e Andes s to Cundinamarca. Trinidad, Tobago.] Rain and cloud forest, high second growth, low, open forest, coffee plantations from 700 m. (rarely below) to 2000 m. Forages actively in thickets alone or in pairs. Low, short flights and jerky motions, flirts tail and clings to stems. Call: high-pitched series of squeaking or rattling chirps; song, a shrill "curtío." Builds a round nest of sticks similar to that of *Phacellodomus* but smaller, resting on the fork of a branch.

**RUFOUS SPINETAIL**

*Synallaxis unirufa*
GÜITÍO RUFO

Pl. 19
6.7″ (17 cm.). Uniform rufous chestnut, somewhat paler below. Lores black, forehead somewhat buffy, a faint, pale eyebrow. Tail long, pointed, barbs somewhat ragged. Chin like rest of underparts (or with a suggested black chin patch, a; or with a well-defined black chin patch and 8 instead of 10 rectrices, b). See pl. 31, fig. 4.

Subtropical to temperate zones. The Sierra de Perijá, Zulia (*munoztebari*). The Andes of Táchira, Mérida and Trujillo (*meridana*, a). The coastal Cordillera in Aragua, the Distr. Federal and Miranda (*castanea*, b; now regarded as a distinct species—Vaurie and Schwartz, in prep). [The Andes of Colombia to s Peru.]

Cloud forest from 1300 m. (rarely) to 2900 m. Prefers low, thick, tangled bushes and bamboo thickets near forest edge and clearings. Active, not shy, occasionally in small flocks of 4 to 10.

## RUDDY SPINETAIL
*Synallaxis rutilans*
Güitío ROJIZO

Pl. 19
5.7″ (14.5 cm.). Forehead and sides of head dark rufous chestnut; top of head and back dark reddish brown, rump and upper tail coverts dark gray; tail black. Wings mostly chestnut. Breast and sides of body dark rufous chestnut, center of belly and under tail coverts dark grayish brown.
Tropical zone, s of the Orinoco (*dissors*). [The Guianas, Colombia e of the Andes. E Peru, n Bolivia, Amazonian Brazil.] Rain forests in Pantepui above 100 m. to 900 m. on the slopes of the tepuis. Open second growth. Alone or in pairs, forages actively on the forest floor in the leaf litter, usually near the bases of large tree trunks and in the low vegetation.

## WHITE-BROWED SPINETAIL
*Synallaxis gularis*
Güitío PARAMERO

Pl. 19
4.7″ (12 cm.). Tail sharply pointed but much shorter than in other species, about 2.2″ (4.6 cm.). Forehead, eyebrow and throat white. Above brown (or rufous, a). Below grayish (or brownish gray, a). Tail auburn (or rufous, a).
Subtropical and temperate zones. The Sierra de Perijá, Zulia (*brunneidorsalis*). To the temperate zone in the Andes of Táchira, Mérida and Trujillo (*cinereiventris, a*). [The Andes of Colombia to w Ecuador. Central Peru.] Cloud forest, open woodland, areas with small, scattered trees, 2300–3200 m. Forest undergrowth, frequents the most impenetrable cover, usually near the ground.

## YELLOW-THROATED SPINETAIL
*Certhiaxis cinnamomea*
Güitío DE AGUA

Pl. 19
5″ (13 cm.). Not unlike Plain-crowned Spinetail, but smaller, browner above, whiter below, tail shorter, the shafts of the feathers protruding as bare spines. Above reddish brown, rufescent on crown (with grayish olive forehead, a). Eyebrow white (or dusky, a). Throat very pale yellow, rest of underparts white, clouded grayish or buffy on breast and sides. Wings and tail rufous brown.
Tropical zone. Zulia around L. Maracaibo (*marabina, a*). N Apure and Barinas e to Portuguesa, Guárico and Aragua (*valenciana, a*). S. Apure, se Guárico, n Bolívar e to s Sucre and Delta Amacuro (*orenocensis*). N Sucre and n Anzoátegui (*cinnamomea*). [Colombia, the Guianas to n Bolivia, Uruguay and central Argentina. Trinidad.]
A small, noisy bird. Shy. Usually in pairs, always near water, in thick undergrowth and reeds to 500 m. The nest is a large ball of thorny sticks with an entrance tunnel 10″ (25 cm.) long, sometimes placed as much as 30′ (10 m.) from shore on aquatic vegetation. Call: a trill; harsh notes like a miniature rattle.

## WHITE-WHISKERED SPINETAIL
*Poecilurus candei*
Güitío BARBIBLANCO

Pl. 19
6.2″ (15.7 cm.). Crown ashy, the feathers dark-centered; sides of crown from behind eye, back, wings, breast and sides of body cinnamon rufous; cheeks grayish black; lower throat deep black, chin and upper throat and line separating black of throat from blackish cheeks, white. Center of abdomen white. Tail basally rufous, distally black.
Arid tropical regions. N Zulia, Lara and coastal Falcón (*venezuelensis*). [N Colombia from Cartagena e.]
Ranges to 1100 m. on arid mountain slopes, but more common near sea level. Frequents arid regions with low, thorny scrub, cují trees and cacti. Often hops and scratches on the ground.

## CRESTED SPINETAIL
*Cranioleuca subcristata*
Güitío COPETÓN

Pl. 19
6″ (15 cm.). Crown dull olive brown, the narrow and pointed feathers with black shaft streaks, back lighter olive brown.

Upper tail coverts and tail bright orange rufous. Shoulders and inner remiges rufous, outer ones black on inner web, rufous on outer. Below light smoky grayish brown. Under wing coverts bright ochraceous orange. Imm. shows some rufescent at sides of crown.

Tropical and subtropical zones. The coastal Cordillera from Falcón and Lara to Sucre; the interior chain in Guárico (Cerro El Platillón), the forested region around L. Maracaibo in Zulia and the s slopes of the Andes in Barinas (*subcristata*). W Apure and s Táchira (*fuscivertex*). [Ne Colombia.]

Rain and cloud forests 1950 m. Climbs trees, like a Dendrocolaptid, to the highest branches. Also frequents thick, tangled vines near edge of dense scrub. Often found in pairs. Nest, a mass of straw and leaves hanging from the end of a high branch.

## TEPUI SPINETAIL

*Cranioleuca demissa*
Güitío de Pantepui

Pl. 19

5.5″ (14 cm.). Forehead olivaceous, rest of crown bright rufous chestnut, back olivaceous brown. Tail and upper tail coverts rufous. Shoulders and scapulars chestnut. Remiges dusky, edged chestnut brown. Throat whitish, rest of underparts gray with olivaceous under tail coverts.

Subtropical zone. The tepuis in Bolívar and Cerros Parú, Duida and de la Neblina in Amazonas. [Guyana on Mt. Ayanganna; n Brazil in Roraima.]

Endemic to Pantepui. Rain and cloud forest and in the low vegetation on the upper slopes of the tepuis; ranges to 2450 m., seldom as low as 1100 m.

Mayr & Phelps, Bull. AMNH, no. 5, *136*, 1967, regarded *C. demissa* as a very distinct race of *C. curtata;* Vaurie, Ibis, 1971, no. 4, considers it a distinct species.

## RUSTY-BACKED SPINETAIL

*Cranioleuca vulpina*
Güitío de Cejas Blancas

Pl. 19

5.5″ (14 cm.). Upperparts, wings and tail bright umber brown, forehead narrowly grayish, crown rufous red. Throat whitish, rest of underparts light smoky grayish brown much as in Crested Spinetail.

Tropical zone. The Orinoco valley from Caño Cataniapo, n Amazonas, e to Delta Amacuro and along the lower Río Apure in Guárico and the lower Río Meta in Apure (*alopecias*). The upper Ríos Apure and Arauca, w Apure (*apurensis*). [E Colombia. E Peru, n Bolivia, most of Brazil. Coiba I., Panama.]

Near rivers and lagoons, reedbeds, savannas, to 100 m. Forages near shore, hops in low, brushy, tangled vegetation where it also prepares a crude nesting cavity or reconditions abandoned nests of other birds.

## SPECKLED SPINETAIL

*Cranioleuca gutturata*
Güitío Pechipunteado

Pl. 19

5.5″ (14 cm.). Forehead olivaceous with buff shaft streaks; crown chestnut with pale shaft streaks. Back olivaceous brown becoming lighter and more rufescent on rump. Inner remiges like back, outer ones broadly edged chestnut, shoulders chestnut. Tail rufous chestnut. Upper throat very pale yellow. Underparts fulvous white speckled on breast and sides of head with blackish, belly obscurely mottled with dusky.

Tropical zone. Amazonas w to the headwaters of the Río Caroní, Bolívar (*hyposticta*). [Surinam; French Guiana, Amazonian Brazil in the Río Negro region and generally s of the Amazon. E Ecuador, e Peru, n Bolivia.]

Rain forest from 100 m. ranging to 750 m. on the slopes of the tepuis. Alone or in pairs in thickets or other low vegetation; very noisy, not shy.

[Thistletails somewhat resemble a large *Synallaxis* but are found at higher altitudes than most species of the latter. Their tail feathers are long, sharply pointed, much narrower than in *Synallaxis,* the webs thin and ragged.]

## OCHRE-BROWED THISTLETAIL

*Schizoeaca coryi*
Piscuiz Frentiocre

Pl. 19

7″ (18 cm.). Above earthy brown. Long superciliary, forehead and upper throat ochraceous. Chin spot tawny. Underparts grayish, whiter in center of abdomen. Central tail feathers like back, outer ones dull rufous.

Subtropical and temperate zones. The Andes of Táchira, Mérida and Trujillo. Mossy, low forest, shrubs and fields of *Espeletia* (Frailejón). Usually between 3000 and 4100 m., rarely to 2300 m.

## WHITE-CHINNED THISTLETAIL
*Schizoeaca fuliginosa*
PISCUIZ BARBIBLANCO

7″ (18 cm.). Above rufous brown. Long superciliary gray. Chin white, underparts gray, abdomen paler. Tail rufous. Temperate zone. Páramos de Tamá, El Cristo, w Táchira, (*fuliginosa*). [E and Central Andes of Colombia to nw Ecuador and Amazonas and San Martín, n Peru.]

Addendum, p. 368, gives additional species.

Mossy, low woodland and open páramo, 3000–3300 m.

## STREAK-BACKED CANASTERO
*Asthenes wyatti*
GÜITÍO COLUDO

Pl. 19
5.5″ (14 cm.). Above grayish brown streaked dusky, sparrowlike; upper tail coverts plain olivaceous gray. Remiges basally rufous, distally blackish, the rufous forming a wing patch on closed wing. Chin spot orange rufous; breast grayish brown, finely but indistinctly streaked dusky, rest of underparts paler, unstreaked. Central tail feathers like back, outer ones mostly dull rufous, tail feathers pointed. Imm.: chin and upper throat white, tail feathers less pointed than in ad.

Páramo de Mucuchíes and Laguna Grande, Mérida, and Teta de Niquitao, Trujillo (*mucuchiesi*). The Perijá Mts., Zulia (*perijanus*). [The Sta. Marta Mts. and the ne Andes, Colombia; Ecuador to s Peru.]

Páramos with low, bushy vegetation, 3500–4150 m. Sparrowlike in appearance, often attracts attention by running swiftly over the open ground rather than keeping to the bushes and low trees. Also found in marshy areas. Nest dome-shaped, made of grass, which gives rise to the local Chilean name, *Canastero*, given to similar congeneric species.

## ORINOCO SOFTTAIL
*Thripophaga cherriei*
RABIBLANDO DEL ORINOCO

Pl. 19
5″ (13 cm.). Olivaceous brown above with a slight rufescent tinge, upper tail coverts and tail rufous chestnut. Wings rufous brown. Upper throat bright orange rufous, rest of underparts light olive brown, sides of head and neck, and upper breast with conspicuous buffy white shaft streaks.

Tropical zone. Known only from the forests near Capuana, 30 km. above the mouth of the Río Vichada, Col., on the upper Orinoco, Amazonas.

Rain forests and clearings along river banks and small caños of the upper Orinoco, at 150 m. Active, clambers about in bushes and brush.

## PLAIN-FRONTED THORNBIRD
*Phacellodomus rufifrons*
GÜAITÍ

Pl. 19
7″ (18 cm.). Feathers of crown narrow, pointed and rather stiff. Entire upperparts dull olivaceous brown, wings and tail slightly rufescent. Lores, eyebrow, cheeks and underparts dirty white; flanks crissum and under tail coverts rufescent olive. Under wing coverts pale cinnamon.

Tropical zone. From Barinas and Apure to Sucre and Monagas (*inornatus*). [E Colombia. N Peru. Bolivia, nw Argentina, Paraguay, e Brazil.]

The llanos, forest edge, open fields with scattered trees, to 950 m. on the drier mountain slopes. Makes a large nest of sticks about 6′ (2 m.) tall and 16″ (41 cm.) wide, which are frequently seen along roadways hanging from branches.

## PEARLED TREERUNNER
*Margarornis squamiger*
MARGARORNIS PUNTEADO

Pl. 19
5.7″ (14.5 cm.). Crown chestnut brown. Back, tail and inner remiges rich rufous chestnut, outer remiges and upper wing coverts black, edged chestnut. Conspicuous eyebrow and throat yellowish white. Underparts olive brown, conspicuously

and profusely marked with yellowish white, black-margined, dropshaped spots. Tail feathers with protruding spines. Subtropical and temperate zones. Sierra de Perijá, Zulia; the Andes of Táchira, Mérida and Trujillo (*perlatus*). [The Andes from Colombia to n Bolivia.] Cloud and dwarf forests consisting of mossy, twisted trees, 1800–3200 m. Forages actively on tree trunks and outer branches, and in the underbrush and low bushes. Builds closed nest of moss under limb or rock.

## RORAIMAN BARBTAIL
*Premnoplex adusta*
PIJUÍ PECHIRRAYADO

Pl. 19

6″ (15 cm.). Crown dark olivaceous brown, back rufous brown (or bay, the feathers edged black, a), closed wings and tail like back. Sides of head black; eyebrow, nuchal collar and area behind ear coverts rich reddish chestnut. Throat white, breast and upper belly white, the feathers conspicuously edged black giving a streaked appearance. Lower belly olivaceous mottled with buffy, under tail coverts rufous, barred buff. Tail feathers pointed, spines protruding. Subtropical zone. The tepuis of Bolívar (*adusta*) except Cerro Jaua (*mayri*). Cerros Duida, Huachamacari and Parú in Amazonas (*duidae*). Cerro Paraque, extreme w Amazonas (*obscurodorsalis*, a). [Nw Guyana. Adjacent Brazil.] Endemic to Pantepui. Rain and cloud forest on the slopes and summits of the tepuis, 1000–2500 m. Common on the Sierra de Lema at 1000 m. near the highway leading to the Gran Sabana. Note: Placed in the genus *Roraimia* in Sp. Bds. S Amer. and Lista Av. Venez.

## RUSTY-WINGED BARBTAIL
*Premnoplex guttuligera*
SUBEPALO PUNTEADO

Pl. 19

5.5″ (14 cm.). Crown olivaceous brown, back somewhat more rufescent with buffy shaft streaks on mantle; upper tail coverts and tail chestnut rufous. Wing coverts brown with buff spot at tip of feathers. Wings dusky, broadly margined rufous. Eyebrow and throat dirty white.

Feathers of breast buffy white edged all around with dusky. Belly olive brown, under tail coverts rufescent. Imm.: more rufescent above with broad, black-edged, buff streaks. Below much buffier and more heavily marked than ad. Subtropical zone. Nw Zulia and sw Táchira (*venezuelana*). [The Andes of Colombia to s Peru.] Cloud forest, 1800–2300 m. Note: Placed in the genus *Premnornis* in Sp. Bds. S Amer. and Lista Av. Venez.

## SPOTTED BARBTAIL
*Premnoplex brunnescens*
FAFAO PUNTEADO

Pl. 19

5.8″ (14.7 cm.). Crown dark olivaceous, back dark rufous brown, wings like back, tail brownish black. Throat ochraceous, the feathers narrowly margined black, rest of underparts brownish olive conspicuously and profusely spotted with ochraceous, dusky-bordered dropshaped marks. Upper tropical and subtropical zones. The Sierra de Perijá, Zulia, and from Táchira e to Mérida (*brunnescens*). Lara and Yaracuy to Aragua and Miranda (*rostratus*). [Costa Rica to n Bolivia.] Cloud forests, 1000–2500 m. Inconspicuous in the dark, damp, mossy, exuberant vegetation, near the ground or in the understory of humid, heavy forests, often in ravines. It actively climbs trees to medium heights and creeps along branches, sometimes on their undersides. Usually alone, may join groups of small birds foraging for insects through the lower levels of the forest.

## WHITE-THROATED BARBTAIL
*Premnoplex tatei*
FAFAO GARGANTIBLANCO

6″ (15 cm.). Rather like Roraiman Barbtail but much darker with sides of head and neck blackish, streaked buff. Tail proportionately shorter, blackish instead of rufous brown. Crown dusky olive, back dark chestnut brown, the feathers with black centers. Wings like back, tail brownish black. Throat and center of breast white, the feathers narrowly edged black (or plain buffy, a), sides of

breast and rest of underparts dusky olivaceous, broadly streaked white.
Upper tropical and subtropical zones. The coastal Cordillera from Anzoátegui to Sucre and Monagas (*tatei*). The Paria Pen. on Cerros Humo and Azul (*pariae*). A species endemic to ne Venezuela. Cloud forest and forest edge, 1200–1700 m. on the costal Cordillera and between 900–1200 m. on the Paria Pen. In pairs and sometimes in groups in the underbrush and lower vegetation. Very confiding, approaches readily to an imitation of its call.

## STREAKED TUFTEDCHEEK
*Pseudocolaptes boissonneautii*
Cotí Blanco

Pl. 20
8.5″ (22 cm.). Crown blackish with sharp, buffy shaft streaks. Eyebrow buffy white, ear coverts dusky, a tuft of silky, white, lengthened feathers at sides of neck. Mantle cinnamon brown, streaked buffy white. Lower back, rump and upper tail coverts orange rufous. Wings olive brown, wing coverts pale-tipped forming a double wing bar. Tail orange rufous. Throat and breast white (feathers edged dusky giving a streaked appearance, a), gradually shading to cinnamon on belly and under tail coverts.
Subtropical and temperate zones. The Sierra de Perijá, Zulia, and the Andes of Táchira, Mérida and Trujillo (*meridae*, a). The coastal Cordillera from Miranda to Carabobo, the interior chain in Yaracuy and Miranda (*striaticeps*). [The Andes from Colombia to n Bolivia.]
Cloud and dwarf forest, 1450–3000 m. One of the largest Furnarids. Forages actively on thick, mossy tree trunks. Often joins other smaller species, forming large, mixed flocks. Prefers the higher levels of the forest, from medium heights to the treetops. Often puffs out the white whiskers.

## POINT-TAILED PALMCREEPER
*Berlepschia rikeri*
Cotí de Palmeras

Pl. 20
8.5″ (22 cm.). Head, nape and hindneck black, finely streaked white; throat rather finely, and *breast coarsely, streaked black and white*, belly black spotted white. Under wing coverts and axillaries barred black and white. Back, inner remiges and tail rufous chestnut, outer remiges black.
Tropical zone. S Amazonas at the base of Cerro Duida. [Guyana; Surinam; Amazonian Brazil.]
Locally distributed in thickets, open fields and savannas with *Mauritia* and other palms, at about 150 m. In pairs or small groups forages for insects on tree trunks and in the treetops. Unmistakable because of its sharp black and white streaking.

## STRIPED WOODHAUNTER
*Hyloctistes subulatus*
Hyloctistes Rayado

Pl. 20
7.5″ (19 cm.). Feathers of crown buffy brown edged blackish, with pale shaft streaks, giving a streaked appearance; back dark brown, rump and upper tail coverts and tail rufous chestnut. Throat and foreneck buff, streaked dusky, center of underparts buffy, sides of body brown to olive brown, under tail coverts rufescent. Wings like back.
Upper tropical zone. Central and s Amazonas; sw Bolívar at the headwaters of the Ríos Caura and Paragua (*subulatus*). Se Bolívar on the Sierra de Lema (*lemae*). [Nicaragua to e Peru and n and w Amazonian Brazil.]
Rain forests in the lowlands of Pantepui, above 300 m. to 1000 m. on the slopes of the tepuis. Forest border. Alone or in pairs, forages from low to medium heights. Joins mixed bands.

## LINEATED FOLIAGE-GLEANER
*Syndactyla subalaris*
Tico-tico Estriado

Pl. 20
7″ (18 cm.). Crown, nape and upper mantle blackish brown with fine, buffy white shaft streaks, these widening on upper mantle. Back brown (or blackish brown, a) with narrow, buffy white shaft streaks. Rump, upper tail coverts and tail rufous chestnut. Wings reddish brown. Throat plain buff. Sides of neck streaked buffy white and brown. Breast

brown (or olive brown, a), striped with white; belly reddish brown, finely streaked buffy white. Under tail coverts rufescent streaked buffy white. Young birds are strongly rufescent below.

Upper tropical and subtropical zones. Sw Táchira (*olivacea*, a). The Andes of sw Barinas and s Lara (*striolata*). [Mountains of Costa Rica to s Peru.]

Cloud forest, forest edge, 800–2000 m. Actively searches for insects, alone or in pairs, in the lower branches of tall trees and in the undergrowth. Joins mixed flocks.

## GUTTULATED FOLIAGE-GLEANER
*Syndactyla guttulata*
Tico-tico Goteado

7.5″ (19 cm.). Rather like Lineated Foliage-gleaner but differing by plain, almost unstreaked crown, prominent buff eyebrow and more coarsely streaked underparts. Crown dark brown with minute, pale shaft streaks, eyebrow buff. Mantle olivaceous brown streaked buffy white; rump, upper tail coverts and tail rufous chestnut. Wings reddish brown. Throat buff, rest of underparts olivaceous brown broadly streaked white. Imm.: underparts rusty buff streaked black, eyebrow orange ochraceous.

Upper tropical and subtropical zones. The coastal Cordillera from Yaracuy to the Dist. Federal and the interior chain in Aragua (*guttulata*). The e part of the coastal Cordillera in Anzoátegui, Sucre and Monagas (*pallida*).

Rain and cloud forests, 900–2100 m. Prefers the more humid areas in the densest mossy thickets with low vegetation like *Heliconias*, but also forages actively and noisily quite high in the trees. In pairs or small groups. Endemic to Venezuela.

## MONTANE FOLIAGE-GLEANER
*Anabacerthia striaticollis*
Tico-tico Pico de Cuña

Pl. 20

6.5″ (16.5 cm.). A rather plainly colored bird. Crown and sides of head olivaceous, darker than back, eyebrow buffy. Back olivaceous brown to reddish brown, somewhat tinged cinnamon on rump and upper tail coverts (or rump and upper tail coverts like back, a; or cinnamon,

like tail, on these parts, b). Tail bright cinnamon rufous. Wings like back. Throat white to buffy white, rest of underparts olivaceous buff, feathers of throat with darker edges, feathers of breast indistinctly streaked whitish.

Upper tropical and subtropical zones. The Sierra de Perijá, Zulia (*perijana*, a). The Andes of Táchira, Mérida, Barinas, Trujillo and Lara (*striaticollis*). The coastal Cordillera from the Sierra de Aroa, Yaracuy, to the Distr. Federal and the interior chain in Aragua and Miranda (*venezuelana*, b). [Colombia to n Bolivia.]

Rain and cloud forests, 950–2300 m. Strictly arboreal, usually alone or in pairs, frequents the middle or upper parts of the forest. Actively scrambles and hops about among the twigs and leaves of outer branches noisily investigating the epiphytes; sometimes clings upside down. Joins flocks of other birds. Calls: a scratchy rattle; a sharp squeak.

## NEBLINA FOLIAGE-GLEANER
*Philydor hylobius*
Tico-tico de La Neblina

7″ (18 cm.). Crown and hindneck blackish brown, sides of head dark brown, eyebrow tawny. Back warm cinnamon brown. Tail sepia brown in imm., (unknown in ad.). Below ochraceous tawny shading to cinnamon brown on flanks and under tail coverts.

Subtropical zone. Known from 2 specimens from Cerro de La Neblina, se Amazonas.

Endemic to Pantepui. Cloud forest on the upper slopes of La Neblina at 1800 m. Known from an adult specimen with tail lacking and an immature bird.

## CINNAMON-RUMPED FOLIAGE-GLEANER
*Philydor pyrrhodes*
Tico-tico Rabadilla Acanelada

Pl. 20

6.5″ (16.5 cm.). Crown and upper back rufescent olive, wings blackish. Lower back and tail, eyebrow, sides of head and entire underparts bright cinnamon. Tail rather short, feathers rounded.

Tropical zone. Generally in Amazonas and Bolívar. [The Guianas, e Colombia to ne Peru and Amazonian Brazil.]

Undergrowth in the rain forests of Pantepui above 100 m., to 500 m. on the slopes of the tepuis.

## BUFF-FRONTED FOLIAGE-GLEANER

*Philydor rufus*
TICO-TICO ROJIZO

Pl. 20

7.2″ (18.2 cm.). Above brown, paler on rump; outer tail feathers bright rufous. Below yellowish ochre shading to dull brown on sides of body. Crown olive brown inconspicuously pale-streaked, forehead and eyebrow ochraceous (or buff, a). Shoulders and outer margins of remiges tawny rufous, central feathers duller and browner. The only Venezuelan species of the genus with pointed tail feathers.

Upper tropical and subtropical zones. Sierra de Aroa, Yaracuy and the coastal Cordillera from Carabobo to Miranda (*columbianus*, a). N Amazonas and nw Bolívar (*cuchiverus*). [Colombia to n Bolivia, Paraguay, ne Argentina and e Brazil.]

Rain and cloud forest, forest edge and clearings, 1000–1800 m. Strictly arboreal and seldom seen. Frequents the middle height of trees to treetops. Usually alone, but joins mixed flocks of birds. Actively sweeps its tail and twists its body while searching for insects.

## CHESTNUT-WINGED FOLIAGE-GLEANER

*Philydor erythropterus*
TICO-TICO ALICASTAÑO

Pl. 20

7″ (18 cm.). Upperparts gray with an olivaceous tinge particularly on rump. Wings and tail rufous chestnut. Lores bright cinnamon, ocular region and throat pale cinnamon, streak below eye dusky; breast and belly grayish buff.

Tropical zone. E Amazonas in Simarawochi; s Bolívar in the upper Caura region and in the vicinity of Cerro Paurai-tepui (*erythropterus*). [E Colombia to n Bolivia; w Brazil s of the Amazon.]

Rain forest above 400 m.; to 900 m. on the slopes of the tepuis.

## RUFOUS-TAILED FOLIAGE-GLEANER

*Philydor ruficaudatus*
TICO-TICO RABIRRUFO

Pl. 20

6.3″ (16 cm.). Dull olive above, conspicuous eyebrow yellowish buff. Below yellowish buff indistinctly pale-streaked, throat uniform and yellower, sides and under tail coverts tinged grayish. Wings like back; tail cinnamon rufous.

Upper tropical zone. Amazonas in the Cerro Duida region (*ruficaudatus*). Amazonas along the upper Ríos Ventuari and Asisa and in the s along the upper Río Siapa; Bolívar along the upper Ríos Cuchivero and Caura and in the vicinity of Cerros Auyan-tepui, Ptari-tepui and Paurai-tepui (*flavipectus*). [The Guianas; e Colombia to n Bolivia; adj. Brazil and s of the Amazon e of the Rio Juruá.]

Rain forest above 300 m.; to 1300 m. on the slopes of the tepuis. Usually in the undergrowth.

## OLIVE-BACKED FOLIAGE-GLEANER

*Automolus infuscatus*
TICO-TICO GORRA ACEITUNA

Pl. 20

7.3″ (18.5 cm.). Upperparts reddish brown (or crown and hindneck olive brown contrasting with back, a); rump, upper tail coverts and tail chestnut. Wings like back. Throat white, rest of underparts grayish, flanks and under tail coverts olive brown.

Tropical zone. Amazonas e across Bolívar (*badius*). In ne Bolívar on the Altiplanicie de Nuria to the Río Cuyuni (*cervicalis*). [Guyana, Surinam, se Colombia to e Peru. Amazonian Brazil.]

Rain forest above 100 m. to 1100 m. on the slopes of the tepuis. Usually in the undergrowth. Associates with mixed flocks of birds.

## RUDDY FOLIAGE-GLEANER

*Automolus rubiginosus*
TICO-TICO GARGANTICASTAÑO

7″ (18 cm.). Above reddish brown, upper tail coverts chestnut brown. Throat cinnamon brown, breast and abdomen duller, sides of body darker and browner, under tail coverts cinnamon rufous.

Inner remiges and outer webs of outer ones bright reddish brown. Tail dull chestnut brown.

Tropical zone. W Apure along the upper Río Arauca; s Amazonas; nw and se Bolívar (*venezuelanus*). [Mexico to n Bolivia, w Ecuador, the Guianas, n Brazil.]

Rain forests above 250 m., to 1300 m. on the slopes of the tepuis. Large, solitary and confiding; chiefly in the undergrowth and forest floor of dense humid forests. Locally common but inconspicuous.

## WHITE-THROATED FOLIAGE-GLEANER

*Automolus roraimae*
TICO-TICO GARGANTIBLANCO

Pl. 20

7" (18 cm.). Crown and sides of head dark brown, long eyebrow white. Back and wings reddish brown. Upper tail coverts and tail rufous chestnut. Throat and sides of neck light yellowish buff, rest of underparts dull cinnamon brown (or grayish olive, a; or ochraceous olive, b); under tail coverts rufous chestnut.

Subtropical zone. Amazonas on Cerro Paraque (*paraquensis*, a). Amazonas on Cerros Duida, Parú, Jaua, de la Neblina and Yaví (*duidae*, b). The tepuis in the Gran Sabana, Bolívar (*roraimae*). [Adjacent mountains in Brazil.]

Endemic to Pantepui. Cloud forest, 1300–2500 m., on the slopes of the tepuis. Forages chiefly in the undergrowth.

## BUFF-THROATED FOLIAGE-GLEANER

*Automolus ochrolaemus*
TICO-TICO GARGANTIANTEADO

Pl. 20

7.5" (19 cm.). Upperparts and wings olive brown, rump and upper and under tail coverts and tail rufous chestnut. Throat pinkish buff, rest of underparts brownish ochraceous, indistinctly streaked paler on breast.

Tropical zone. S and central Amazonas; n and central Bolívar (*turdinus*). [The Guianas, Amazonian Brazil; Colombia to w Ecuador and n Bolivia.]

Rain forests in the lowlands of Pantepui above 100 m., to 1000 m. on the outlying mountains in n Bolívar. Thick, tangled

undergrowth and forest edge. Forages in the lower branches and on the ground, rummaging noisily among epiphytes and debris. Confiding and not especially shy; often in pairs or small parties. Food includes lizards.

## CHESTNUT-CROWNED FOLIAGE-GLEANER

*Automolus rufipileatus*
TICO-TICO GORRA CASTAÑA

Pl. 20

7.5" (19 cm.). Back reddish brown; crown, upper tail coverts and tail chestnut. Underparts pale brownish, buffy on throat. Wing coverts dark chestnut.

Tropical zone. Extreme sw Táchira, nw Apure and nw Barinas; Bolívar; s Amazonas (*consobrinus*). [The Guianas; e Colombia to n Bolivia and Amazonian Brazil.]

Rain forest to 550 m. n of the Orinoco, to 350 m. s of it. Frequents undergrowth and forest floor. Makes nesting tunnels.

## FLAMMULATED TREEHUNTER

*Thripadectes flammulatus*
TREPAPALO ROJIZO

Pl. 20

9" (23 cm.). Crown and mantle black, striped narrowly on crown, more widely on mantle, with buff; lower back brown striped with buff. Rump and tail plain chestnut. Throat virtually uniform deep buff (or heavily streaked with black, a); breast and abdomen buff, the feathers broadly edged olive brown (or edged blackish, a) giving a striped appearance; under tail coverts ochraceous (or rufescent, a), the feathers edged black. Wings chestnut brown.

Temperate zone. The Andes of Mérida on Páramos La Culata, Conejos and Escorial (*bricenoi*). Sw Táchira (*flammulatus*, a). [The mountains of Colombia and w Ecuador.]

Low, dense, humid forest, 2700–3000 m. Forages chiefly in the undergrowth, often in deep ravines and near streams but also in the higher branches. Nests in tunnels underground.

## STRIPED TREEHUNTER

*Thripadectes holostictus*
TREPAPALO LISTADO

Pl. 20
7.5" (19 cm.). Rather like Flammulated Treehunter but much smaller and less conspicuously striped. Crown black narrowly streaked buff; mantle blackish brown streaked buff; rump, upper tail coverts and tail rufous chestnut. Throat and breast buff, the feathers edged blackish giving a streaked appearance; belly brown with pale shaft streaks on upper belly; under tail coverts somewhat rufescent. Wings reddish brown.
Subtropical zone. Sw Táchira along the Río Chiquito (*holostictus*). [The Andes from Colombia to n Bolivia.]
Cloud forests, 1800–2000 m. Habits similar to Flammulated Treehunter.

## STREAK-CAPPED TREEHUNTER

*Thripadectes virgaticeps*
TREPAPALO PECHIRRAYADO

Pl. 20
8.5" (22 cm.). The least streaky member of the group. Crown grayish olive, the feathers edged black with white shaft streaks; back amber brown, the feathers of the upper mantle with whitish shaft streaks; rump, upper tail coverts and tail chestnut. Ear coverts dusky with sharp, white shaft streaks. Throat cinnamon buff, the feathers with dusky edges giving a streaked appearance, rest of underparts cinnamon brown, breast washed dusky. Wings reddish brown.
Subtropical zone. Sw Táchira (*tachirensis*). The coastal Cordillera from Carabobo to the Distr. Federal (*klagesi*). [S Colombia; e and w Ecuador.]
Cloud forests, 1250–2000 m. Habits similar to Flammulated Treehunter.

## RUFOUS-TAILED XENOPS

*Xenops milleri*
PICO LEZNA RABIRRUFO

Pl. 19
4" (10 cm.). Crown blackish, conspicuously pale-streaked; mantle olivaceous brown striped buffy white; rump cinnamon rufous; upper tail coverts and tail rufous. Below pale buffy, streaked blackish olive. Primaries black, inner remiges with an ochraceous bar, secondaries basally and tertials mostly rufous.
This species differs from Slender-billed and Streaked Xenops as follows: tail feathers are *plain rufous* without black, lacks silvery white moustacial streak, has straight instead of upcurved mandible.
Tropical zone. S Amazonas; s Bolívar along the upper Ríos Paragua and Caroní (*milleri*). [Surinam; French Guiana; se Colombia to ne Peru. Brazil between the Rios Purús and Juruá.]
Rain forest in the lowlands of Pantepui, 150–400 m., near streams, forest edge and savannas.

## SLENDER-BILLED XENOPS

*Xenops tenuirostris*
PICO LEZNA MENOR

Pl. 19
4.2" (10.6 cm.). Crown brown with white shaft streaks, eyebrow buffy white. Mantle cinnamon rufous streaked buff (or streaked white, a); rump and upper tail coverts plain cinnamon rufous; central and two outer pairs of tail feathers rufous, intermediate ones largely black. Throat white, stripe across lower cheek silvery white; breast and belly grayish olive streaked with white; under tail coverts grayish buff. Outer remiges black with a basal cinnamon band, innermost tertials cinnamon. Bill somewhat upturned.
Tropical zone. Nw Bolívar along the lower Río Caura; extreme nw Amazonas along Caño Cataniapo (*tenuirostris*). Sw Amazonas from Cerro Yapacana s (*acutirostris,* a). [Surinam; French Guiana; se Colombia to nw Bolivia; Amazonian Brazil s of the Amazon.]
Lowland rain forest near 100 m. Forages on the outer branches of treetops; clings to twigs.

## STREAKED XENOPS

*Xenops rutilans*
PICO LEZNA RAYADO

5" (13 cm.). Very like Slender-billed Xenops but larger, back less conspicuously streaked and mandible sharply upturned. Above rufous brown, crown with pale shaft streaks, upper mantle lightly streaked buffy white, rump and upper tail coverts orange rufous. Band across wing cinnamon rufous. Tail mostly rufous, third and fourth feathers from without with black inner webs. Below like Slender-billed (or with breast and belly brownish olive streaked white, a). Tropical and subtropical zones. The Sierra de Perijá, Zulia, and sw Táchira (*perijanus*). The n Cordilleras from Mérida and Lara to Sucre and the llanos of Portuguesa and n Guárico (*heterurus*, a). [Costa Rica to Colombia, the Guianas, w Peru, Bolivia, n Argentina, Paraguay and s Brazil. Trinidad.] Rain and cloud forest and deciduous woodland to 2200 m.; seldom below 1000 m. in Zulia and Táchira. Forages actively, alone or in pairs, along small branches, sometimes upside down. Joins mixed bird parties. Call: a metallic trill.

**PLAIN XENOPS**
*Xenops minutus*
PICO LEZNA PECHIRRAYADO

Pl. 19
4.7″ (12 cm.) [or 5.2″ (13 cm.), a]. Plain, unstreaked back distinguishes it from other members of the genus. Above brown to reddish brown; long eyebrow buffy white, streak across cheek silvery white. Throat white, rest of underparts olivaceous brown (with indications of pale streaks on upper breast, b). Wings much as in other species of the genus. Central tail feathers cinnamon, next pair black, outermost pair cinnamon, intervening feathers with varying amounts of black according to race. Mandible sharply upturned. Tropical and subtropical zones. Nw Zulia, n Mérida and s Táchira (*olivaceus*). Se Zulia, sw Táchira, the w llanos in w Barinas and w Apure and from Lara to e Miranda (*neglectus*). Amazonas except the Río Negro region; Bolívar generally e to Delta Amacuro and the Paria Pen., Sucre (*ruficaudatus*, b). Amazonas along the upper Ríos Negro and Orinoco (*remoratus*). [The Guianas, Colombia, e and w Ecuador to Bolivia, Paraguay, s Brazil and ne Argentina.] Rain and mossy cloud forest to 2200 m. n

of the Orinoco and to 1450 m. in Pantepui. High second growth, clearings and haciendas. Forages actively and conspicuously at low levels in shrubs, *Heliconias* and thick undergrowth, also in high trees. Searches in the bark and under epiphytes, moving sideways or hanging upside down from leaves. Usually alone but joins mixed bands of small birds. Call: a chipping note or rapid trill.

[BIRDS BELONGING TO the genus *Sclerurus* are mainly terrestrial and are reminiscent of a small, long-billed thrush.]

**GRAY-THROATED LEAFSCRAPER**
*Sclerurus albigularis*
RASPA HOJA GARGANTIGRÍS

Pl. 20
6.5″ (16.5 cm.). Above umber brown, upper tail coverts rich chestnut, tail grayish black (or pure black, a). Throat white becoming gray on lower throat, band across breast dull chestnut, rest of underparts dark, grayish brown (or olivaceous brown, a). Wings like back. Upper tropical and subtropical zones. Nw Zulia in the Sierra de Perijá (*kunanensis*, a). S Táchira, Mérida and Lara, thence along the n Cordillera to Sucre (*albigularis*). [Costa Rica, w Panama. Colombia in the Santa Marta Mts. and e of the Andes in Meta. Se Ecuador. Ne Peru. Nw Bolivia. Trinidad, Tobago.] Rain and cloud forests in mountainous regions in the n from 450 m. to 1500 m. in the Andes; to 2200 m. in Perijá; above 800 m. in Paria. Rummages jerkily in the debris tossing leaves and probing the soil. Sometimes in family parties. The stiff posture is reminiscent of a small thrush with short legs. Call: a quick chatter, also a sharp "chick-chick" and squeaks. Song is usually a 5-note sequence. Nests of leaves in holes in banks; flies out when disturbed.

**TAWNY-THROATED LEAFSCRAPER**
*Sclerurus mexicanus*
RASPA HOJA PECHIRROJIZO

Pl. 20
6″ (15 cm.). Dark reddish brown above and below, rump and upper tail coverts brighter and more rufescent. Throat

rusty buff, breast tinged rufescent. Wings and tail like back.

Tropical and subtropical zones. Zulia in the Sierra de Perijá; n Amazonas (Cerro Guanay); s Bolívar from Cerro Guaiquinima e (*andinus*). [Mexico to nw Ecuador; Amazonian and se Brazil; n Bolivia.]

Rain forest in the lowlands of Pantepui above 300 m., to 1100 m. on the slopes of the tepuis; in cloud forest at 2000 m. in the Sierra de Perijá. Terrestrial; forages in the dense undergrowth and the lower levels of the forest.

## SHORT-BILLED LEAFSCRAPER
*Sclerurus rufigularis*
RASPA HOJA PECHIANTEADO

6" (15 cm.). Not unlike Tawny-throated Leafscraper. Above dark reddish brown, upper tail coverts dark chestnut, tail black. Chin white, throat dull cinnamon buff, rest of underparts dull earthy brown, washed with chestnut on breast. Wings like back.

Tropical zone. S Amazonas; Bolívar from the lower Río Caura to the Gran Sabana (*fulvigularis*). [The Guianas, e Colombia and Amazonian Brazil.]

Rain forests and high second growth in the lowlands of Pantepui above 150 m.; to 900 m. on the slopes of the tepuis. Usually alone. Forages in the undergrowth and on the forest floor.

## BLACK-TAILED LEAFSCRAPER
*Sclerurus caudacutus*
RASPA HOJA RABIAGUDO

Pl. 20

7" (18 cm.). Crown dull cinnamon brown, lighter on forehead (or crown and forehead like back, a). Back dark brown becoming rufescent on rump; upper tail coverts dark, dull chestnut; tail black. Chin and center of upper throat light ochraceous buff (or chin and entire throat white, the feathers dusky-edged, a). Below dark brown washed with chestnut on breast. Wings like back.

The white-throated form is much like the Gray-throated Leafscraper but distinguishable by much duller upper tail coverts.

Tropical zone. N (Río Manapiare), central (Cerro Parú) and se (upper Río Siapa) Amazonas; generally in Bolívar (*insignis*). Sw Amazonas along the Yavita-Pimichín Trail (*brunneus,* a). [The Guianas and e Colombia to n Bolivia, Amazonian and se Brazil.]

Rain forest in the lowlands above 150 m., ranging to 460 m. in Nuria and to 1100 m. on the slopes of the tepuis. Terrestrial. Forages in the lower level, in the underbrush and smaller trees.

## SHARP-TAILED STREAMCREEPER
*Lochmias nematura*
MACUQUIÑO

6" (15 cm.). Upperparts and wings sepia brown (or rich chestnut brown, a); tail blackish. Below dark brown heavily spotted with white.

Upper tropical and subtropical zones. The Sierra de Aroa, Yaracuy, and the Distr. Federal (*sororia*). Extreme sw Amazonas; Bolívar on the lower Río Caura (Cerro Tabaro) and in the Gran Sabana on Cerros Chimantá-tepui, Sororopán-tepui, Aprada-tepui and Auyan-tepui (*chimantae*). Bolívar in the extreme se Gran Sabana on Cerros Cuquenán, Roraima, Uei-tepui and Jaua (*castanonota,* a). [E Panama to Bolivia, Argentina and Uruguay.]

Cloud forest, along mountain streams and rivulets overgrown with thick, mossy vegetation, 1000–2500 m. Prefers deep ravines. Active, usually alone or in pairs, generally on the ground or in low bushes. Very shy and secretive; wrenlike. Builds a compact, globular nest with the entrance on the side, placed on the ground.

# ANTBIRDS: Formicariidae

## HORMIGUEROS

One of the largest Venezuelan bird families is that of the antbirds, no less than 89 species being found there. Their name derives from the fact that some species follow army ants to feed on the insects disturbed by them.

Antbirds are for the most part forest dwellers living near the ground in the undergrowth and substage of the forest, some even living on the forest floor. They feed chiefly on insects but take berries and small fruits as well.

Most are soberly colored, shades of gray or brown predominating, but quite a number are black, often with white-dotted wing coverts and white tail tips. A characteristic feature of many species is a semi-concealed white patch in the center of the back. Males of many species are difficult to tell apart but females have more distinctive plumage, and when seen with the male, often help in identification.

Many antbirds have a pleasant song but could not be rated as songbirds. Antbird nests are usually cupshaped but some species use natural tree cavities and others build nests of twigs.

## FASCIATED ANTSHRIKE

*Cymbilaimus lineatus*
HORMIGUEROTE BARRETEADO

Pl. 21

7″ (18 cm.). Bill thick, hooked. Crown black, sometimes lightly barred white. Back and tail black, profusely but narrowly barred white. Sides of head and entire underparts evenly barred black and white. ♀: crown chestnut. Back and tail black, barred buff. Sides of head and entire underparts buffy white with narrow black bars.

Tropical, occasionally lower subtropical zone. The Sierra de Perijá, Zulia, the foothills of the Andes in Táchira, Barinas, w Apure and s Mérida; w Bolívar and generally in Amazonas (*intermedius*). E Bolívar (*lineatus*). [The Guianas; Colombia; e Ecuador to n Bolivia. N Amazonian Brazil.]

Rain forests and high second growth to 1300 m. n of the Orinoco and to 700 m. s of it. Thickets, shrubbery, undergrowth and lower tier of forest trees. Often in pairs near the ground, sedentary and sluggish, moves about in hops and short leaps. Not shy. Call: include 4 or more descending, cooing notes.

## BLACK-THROATED ANTSHRIKE

*Frederickena viridis*
HORMIGUERO RAYADO COPETÓN

Pl. 21

9″ (23 cm.). Bill heavy, hooked. Head crested. Head, throat and upper breast black, rest of plumage dark bluish gray; tail indistinctly barred. ♀: crested. Crown chestnut, back chestnut brown; upper tail coverts and tail black, barred gray. Lores, sides of head and neck, throat and breast barred black and white, belly and under tail coverts barred gray and white. Iris red.

Tropical zone. Nw Bolívar from the lower Río Caura e to the Río Paragua and the upper Río Caroní. [Guianas; ne Brazil n of the Amazon.]

Rain forest in the Pantepui region, 300–500 m. Usually in pairs in the lower bushes.

## GREAT ANTSHRIKE

*Taraba major*
BATARA MAYOR

Pl. 21

8″ (20 cm.). Bill thick, hooked. Crested. Top and sides of head, entire upperparts and wings black; a concealed white dorsal patch; wing coverts conspicuously tipped white forming 3 bars. Below white. Tail black, outer feathers barred white (or black, unbarred, a). Iris light red. ♀: crested. Upperparts, wings and tail chestnut, sides of head darker. Below white, sides of body grayish, flanks rufescent, under tail coverts rufous (breast usually with black shaft streaks, b). Iris light red.

Tropical, occasionally subtropical zone. Nw Zulia, Táchira, w Apure, nw Barinas extending e to Aragua and ne Miranda (*granadensis,* a). From se Miranda e through Guárico and Anzoátegui to the Paria Pen., and the delta of the Orinoco in Monagas; tropical zone in Amazonas generally (*semifasciata*). Subtropical zone of Cerros Jaua in Bolívar and Duida in Amazonas (*duidae,* b). [Mid. Amer. to the Guianas, e and w Colombia to nw Peru, Uruguay and Argentina.]

A large antshrike of varied habitats including rain, cloud and shady, humid forests, second growth, tangled brush, open fields, thick grass and arid areas, to (occasionally) 2200 m. Shy; found alone or in pairs near the ground and sometimes in small trees. May respond to squeaking, approaching in hops and

chattering. Calls: include a loud, bound-
ing, rolling series of identical notes,
weakening as it accelerates, reminiscent
of *Thamnophilus;* also a throaty "churr."

[*Sakesphorus* DIFFERS FROM MOST ANTBIRDS
by its very conspicuous crest.]

## BLACK-CRESTED ANTSHRIKE
*Sakesphorus canadensis*
HORMIGUERO COPETÓN

Pl. 21
6″ (15 cm.). Crested. Entire head black
(or with considerable admixture of white
on forecrown, sides of head and upper
throat, a); breast black, black continued
in a narrowing point over upper belly;
sides of breast and rest of underparts
light gray (or mostly white, a). Nuchal
collar white to grayish white. Back
reddish brown (or cinnamon brown, a;
or grayish brown, b). Wings black, wing
coverts conspicuously edged white forming 3 bars, inner remiges broadly edged
white. ♀: crested. Crown bright rufous
chestnut, back reddish brown (or cinnamon brown, a). Throat and breast cinnamon, lighter on throat, conspicuously (or
only lightly, a) streaked black, sides of
body pale grayish brown (or bright cinnamon, a), paler, almost white in center
of abdomen. Wings and tail as in ♂.
Tropical zone. The Goajira Pen., nw Zulia
e to coastal Falcón, extending s to n
Lara (*paraguanae*). W Zulia from the
Río Socuy s (*pulchellus*). N of the
Orinoco from e Falcón and Apure to
Miranda and the llanos of s Anzoátegui;
s of the Orinoco in n Amazonas and
Bolívar e to the Río Cuyuni (*intermedius*). The e coastal Cordillera from
Anzoátegui to Sucre, s Monagas and
Delta Amacuro (*trinitatis*). S Amazonas
(*fumosus*). [The Guianas, n and e
Colombia. E Peru, n and s central
Brazil. Trinidad.]
Common from sea level to 300 m., very
seldom above. In varied habitats from
open, damp forest to arid cactus lands,
savannas, mangroves and pastures. In
pairs or small flocks, usually chattering
noisily; crest prominent. Call: a series
of low, bubbling notes descending and
rising in pitch.

## BLACK-BACKED ANTSHRIKE
*Sakesphorus melanonotus*
HORMIGUERO ESPALDA NEGRA

Pl. 21
6″ (15 cm.). Much like Black-crested
Antshrike but at once separable by *black*
upper *back* and *white flanks;* lower back
gray, interscapular patch white. ♀:
crested. Crown black, the feathers edged
tawny brown; back tawny brown with a
white interscapular patch which shows
through. Below buffy. Wings as in
Black-crested but brown instead of black.
Tail chestnut brown, with a dark subterminal area and narrow buffy white
tip, outer web of outermost feather buffy
white.
The Caribbean coast from Zulia to Falcón
and Miranda and in nw Táchira. [Coastal
ne Colombia to Norte de Santander.]
Alone or in pairs in the undergrowth of
open forest, second growth and arid
areas, from near sea level rarely to above
500 m.

[IN THE GENUS *Thamnophilus* the bill is
heavy and hooked.]

## BARRED ANTSHRIKE
*Thamnophilus doliatus*
PAVITA HORMIGUERA COMÚN

Pl. 21
6″ (15 cm.). Upperparts, wings and tail
black, barred white. Throat streaked
and underparts evenly barred black and
white (or white bars below only half as
wide as black ones, a). Crown black,
feathers basally white. ♀: upperparts,
wings and tail rufous chestnut. Nape,
sides of head and neck streaked black
and buff. Underparts cinnamon buff;
throat whitish streaked black.
Tropical, casually subtropical zone. Zulia
in the Perijá and L. Maracaibo regions, n
Táchira and w Mérida (*nigrescens*, a).
S Táchira, n Barinas and Apure n and
e to Falcón and Sucre; s of the Orinoco
in n Amazonas and n Bolívar to Ciudad
Bolívar; Margarita I. (*fraterculus*). Ne
Bolívar from the lower Río Paragua to
Delta Amacuro (*doliatus*). [Mid. Amer.
to Bolivia, Paraguay and ne Argentina.
Trinidad, Tobago.]
A common bird in the most varied habitats
from dense undergrowth in forest to

low, brushy areas, savannas and even mangroves and gardens, usually in the lowlands, rarely to 2000 m. Local in distribution, generally heard before being seen. In pairs, within 4 or 5 m. of the ground. Almost always carries crest partially erected. Call: rhythmical song, sometimes a duet, a series of rolling notes rapidly accelerating and descending; also a "churr" constantly repeated for several minutes.

## BAR-CRESTED ANTBIRD

*Thamnophilus multistriatus*
PAVITA HORMIGUERA CORONIPINTADA

6" (15 cm.). Much like Barred Antshrike but crown barred black and white; white dorsal bars not quite as wide. ♀: like Barred Antshrike above; underparts white streaked black on throat, barred black on rest of underparts.
Subtropical zone. Sierra de Perijá, Zulia (*oecotonophilus*), [Colombia.]
Cloud forest at 1650 m.
Note: *Oecotonophilus* called *T. m. multistriatus* in Lista Av. Venez.

## BLACKISH-GRAY ANTSHRIKE

*Thamnophilus nigrocinereus*
CHOCA CENICIENTA

Pl. 22
6" (16 cm.). Crown blackish; back gray with a slight admixture of black on mantle, concealed interscapular patch white. Wings black, wing coverts narrowly fringed white; tail black, very narrowly edged white terminally. Below gray, darkest on throat and breast, paler on belly and under tail coverts where the feathers are inconspicuously edged white. ♀: crown, nape and sides of head blackish gray; back, wings and tail sepia brown. Underparts and under wing coverts orange rufous, becoming brown on flanks and under tail coverts.
Tropical zone. Amazonas; nw Bolívar on the lower Río Caura (*cinereoniger*). [French Guiana; Colombia e of the Andes to e Peru and Amazonian Brazil.]
Rain forest to 400 m.

## WHITE-SHOULDERED ANTSHRIKE

*Thamnophilus aethiops*
CHOCA LOMIBLANCA

Pl. 22
6" (15 cm.). Much like Blackish-gray Antshrike, but wing coverts with small, terminal white dots, no white interscapular patch and tail *all* black. ♀: above uniform chestnut including wing coverts, below paler, tail chestnut brown.
Tropical zone. Amazonas; Bolívar from the middle and upper Río Caura e to the headwaters of the Río Caroní (*polionotus*). [Se Colombia to n Bolivia, Amazonian and e Brazil.]
Rain forest, also near clearings and in open second growth, 100–400 m. Forages alone or in pairs in the lower levels of the forest.

## MOUSE-COLORED ANTSHRIKE

*Thamnophilus murinus*
PAVITA GRIS

Pl. 22
5" (13 cm.). Above gray with a small, concealed white interscapular patch, feathers of crown with black centers, feathers at sides of head with silvery white shafts. Wing coverts with *inconspicuous* gray tips. Tail black *narrowly* tipped white. *Throat* and *center* of *abdomen white*, rest of underparts light gray. ♀: above reddish brown with an olive tinge, crown and wings dull chestnut brown, wing coverts with pale, *buffy* tips. Tail dark chestnut brown. *Throat and abdomen white*, breast and sides of body olive brown.
Tropical zone. Widespread in Amazonas and Bolívar (*murinus*). [The Guianas; se Colombia to ne Peru; n and w Amazonian Brazil.]
Rain forest, savannas, 100–1300 m. Forages alone or in pairs in the undergrowth. Note thick bill.

## SLATY ANTSHRIKE

*Thamnophilus punctatus*
TIOJORITA PUNTEADA

Pl. 22
6" (15 cm.). Crown black, forehead grizzled with gray. Back gray with a concealed white interscapular patch, the

feathers broadly tipped black. Wings black, the wing coverts conspicuously tipped white, the outer remiges narrowly the inner ones broadly, edged white. Under wing coverts white. Upper tail coverts black, tipped white, tail black, conspicuously tipped white, outer feather with a median white patch on outer web. Underparts gray, paler than back, under tail coverts with white tips. ♀: crown bright orange rufous (or dull, dark rufous, a), sides of head light olivaceous, back dull reddish brown with a concealed white interscapular patch; wings reddish brown, the wing coverts with conspicuous pure white (or buff, a) tips, edged dusky above, inner remiges edged white (or buff, a). Upper tail coverts chestnut with white (or buff, a) tips. Tail chestnut with white marks as in ♂.
Tropical and lower subtropical zones. Nw and e Zulia, n Táchira, extreme n Mérida (subcinereus, a). Extreme sw Táchira, w Apure and w Barinas (interpositus). N Amazonas s to the Río Negro; n and e Bolívar; e Sucre and Delta Amacuro (punctatus). [Guatemala to w Ecuador, n Bolivia and Amazonian and e Brazil.] Rain forest, to 1500 m. on some of the more sparsely wooded slopes of the tepuis. Forages in pairs, joins forest flocks in the undergrowth of humid forest, second growth and pastures. A stocky bird which vibrates its short tail up and down while singing.

## AMAZONIAN ANTSHRIKE
*Thamnophilus amazonicus*
CHOCA GORRO GRIS

Pl. 22
6" (15 cm.) [or 5" (13 cm.), a]. Very similar to Slaty Antshrike and perhaps distinguishable in the field by more black on mantle (or much smaller than Slaty with feathers of crown gray with black centers instead of all black, a). ♀: crown and nape rufous chestnut (or orange rufous, a); back olivaceous with a concealed white interscapular patch. Wings and tail as in ♂. Underparts uniform bright cinnamon rufous, (or belly buffy white, sharply defined, a).
Tropical zone. Amazonas (cinereiceps, a). E Bolívar along the upper Río Cuyuni (paraensis). [The Guianas, e Colombia to n Bolivia and Amazonian Brazil.]

Rain forest, open forest and open second growth, mostly in the lowlands from 100 to 400 m., but has been found up to 1300 m. on Cerro Yapacana. Forages alone or in pairs in the middle tier of forest trees.

## STREAK-BACKED ANTSHRIKE
*Thamnophilus insignis*
CHOCA INSIGNE

Pl. 22
6.2" (15.7 cm.). Crown black, the feathers of hindcrown with semiconcealed white subterminal spots; mantle black, streaked white; rump gray; upper tail coverts black, tipped white. Wings and tail as in Slaty Antshrike. Underparts gray, somewhat darker on throat and breast. ♀: forehead barred gray and black (or immaculate black, a), rest of crown chestnut, the feathers of hindcrown with white subterminal spots; rest of plumage as in ♂.
Subtropical zone. The tepuis of Bolívar and Amazonas (insignis). On Cerro Paraque, Amazonas (nigrofrontalis, a). Endemic to Pantepui. Humid forest on the slopes of the tepuis, 900–2000 m., usually above 1200 m. Alone or in pairs in tall vegetation or in thick stands of *Bonnetia* on the summits.

## SPOT-WINGED ANTSHRIKE
*Pygiptila stellaris*
CHOCA ALIPUNTEADA

Pl. 22
5" (13 cm.). Crown black; back, wings and tail blue gray; a concealed white interscapular patch, the feathers tipped black, making a blackish area on mantle. Tail very short, 1.7" (4.3 cm.). Below blue gray, paler than back. Wing coverts with round, white apical spots, inner remiges partially cinnamon on inner web. ♀: forehead ochraceous olive, rest of crown, back, inner remiges and tail blue gray, interscapular patch white. Throat cinnamon buff, gradually darkening over breast and belly. Wing coverts mostly olivaceous brown, remiges reddish brown, innermost tertials like back.
Tropical zone. Amazonas; Bolívar along the course of the Río Caura, the upper Paragua and headwaters of the Río Caroní (occipitalis). [The Guianas, se Colombia to e Peru; Amazonian Brazil.]

High, virgin rain forest in the lowlands above 100 m., rarely as high as 700 m. on the slopes of the tepuis. Forages with mixed groups of birds from the treetops to the lower bushes.

## PEARLY ANTSHRIKE
*Megastictus margaritatus*
HORMIGUERO MARGARITA

Pl. 22

5″ (13 cm.). Blue gray above, no white interscapular patch. Wings and upper tail coverts and tail black, *wing coverts, axillars, inner remiges,* and *upper tail coverts* with large, very *conspicuous, round, white tips,* tail feathers tipped white. Pale gray below, whitish gray on throat and center of abdomen. ♀: crown grayish, back brown; wings, upper tail coverts and tail as in ♂ but spots buff instead of white; outer margins of remiges brown. Throat whitish, rest of underparts dull cinnamon, darkest on breast.

Tropical zone. S Amazonas, s Bolívar along the upper Ríos Caura and Paragua. [Nw Brazil, se Colombia to e Peru.] Rain forest, often near rivers, 100–400 m.

## RECURVE-BILLED BUSHBIRD
*Clytoctantes alixi*
HORMIGUERO PICO DE HOZ

Pl. 23

6.7″ (17 cm.). Dark, slaty gray; lores, throat, breast and sides of neck, wings and tail black; concealed interscapular patch white. *Bill compressed, high, mandible sharply upturned.* ♀: forehead, sides of head and body chestnut; wings and tail blackish; rest of plumage brown. Concealed interscapular patch white. *Bill as in ♂.*

Upper tropical zone. Sierra de Perijá, Zulia. [N Colombia.]

High rain forest, 900–1000 m., also frequents the most impenetrable second growth, always close to the ground. Very shy and secretive.

## RUSSET ANTSHRIKE
*Thamnistes anabatinus*
HORMIGUERO BERMEJO

Pl. 21

6.2″ (15.7 cm.). Bill thick, strongly hooked. Olivaceous brown above; lores

and eyebrow buff; concealed interscapular patch *cinnamon orange* basally, the feathers with a black subterminal patch. Upper tail coverts rufescent, wings and tail rufous brown. Throat ochraceous, breast ochraceous olive, rest of underparts olivaceous grayish, the colors merging. ♀: similar to male, but lacks interscapular patch.

Lower subtropical zone. Extreme s Táchira (*gularis*). [Colombia to n Bolivia.] Dense, humid forests near 1300 m. Second growth, forest edge and semi-open terrain. Alone or in small, loose flocks, forages actively from the ground to the treetops. Joins mixed parties of birds. Call: a rasping note.

## PLAIN ANTVIREO
*Dysithamnus mentalis*
BURUJARA PEQUEÑA

Pl. 21

4.5″ (11.5 cm.). Above pale to dark gray, darkest on crown (or with rump and lower back tinged olive, a; or with crown gray, back light olivaceous gray, b). Wings and tail dark gray, wing coverts narrowly edged white. Throat grayish white, breast and sides of body gray, center of abdomen white (or center of abdomen pale yellow, flanks grayish olive, b). ♀: crown and nape chestnut; eye ring white; back brown (or grayish olive, a; or olive, b). Throat and center of belly whitish, breast and sides of body clay color (or white, sides of body grayish brown, a; or center of belly pale yellowish, b). Wings and tail reddish brown (or grayish brown, a); wing coverts with conspicuous rusty buff edges (or inconspicuous grayish edges, a, b).

Tropical and subtropical zones. The Sierra de Perijá, Zulia, s to sw Táchira and Barinas (*viridis*, b). The n Cordillera from Lara e to Miranda and the Paria Pen. (*cumbreanus*, ♀, a). Extreme s Sucre in the delta region, s in Bolívar to the Sierra de Imataca and upper Cuyuni (*andrei*, a). Bolívar on Cerros Ptaritepui and Sororopán-tepui (*ptaritepui*). Nw Bolívar from the lower Río Caura and the upper Río Cuchivero e to the tepuis of the Gran Sabana; Amazonas (*spodionotus*). [Mid. Amer. to Bolivia, Paraguay, ne Argentina and se Brazil.] Shady, high rain and cloud forests to 2200

m. Prefers the lower trees but seldom on the ground or in undergrowth, also in humid areas with scattered trees and second growth. A small, stout-bodied, curious, confiding bird with a short tail. Usually in pairs or in small groups which frequently join forest flocks. Call: descending, rolling, cackling notes.

## DUSKY-THROATED ANTSHRIKE
*Thamnomanes ardesiacus*
BURUJARA PIZARREÑA

Pl. 22
5″ (13 cm.). Leaden gray, paler on abdomen; chin and throat black. Wing coverts *plain gray;* tail very narrowly fringed white. ♀: above olive brown, slightly grayer on crown, somewhat rufescent on upper tail coverts. Below ochraceous, washed grayish on breast, throat and sides of neck paler and somewhat mottled with dusky. Under wing coverts orange ochraceous. Margins of remiges dull reddish brown.
Tropical zone. Amazonas and Bolívar, and central Delta Amacuro (*obidensis*). [The Guianas, n and central Brazil, se Colombia, e Ecuador.]
Undergrowth and edge of dense forest in the lowlands to 1100 m. On the slopes of the tepuis it is found in open areas with low bushes and small trees, also in second growth. In pairs or with mixed flocks of other birds.
Note: This species and the next were placed in the genus *Dysithamnus* in Lista Av. Venez.

## PLUMBEOUS ANTSHRIKE
*Thamnomanes plumbeus*
BURUJARA PLOMIZA

Pl. 22
5″ (13 cm.). Leaden gray, paler on abdomen, flanks slightly tinged olivaceous. Wing coverts black, edged white. A small white interscapular patch. ♀: crown rufous chestnut, the feathers with pale shaft streaks, back wings and tail reddish brown, wing coverts tipped reddish ochraceous. Eye ring white, sides of head and neck streaked gray and white, throat white, breast broadly streaked gray and white, below white mixed with gray. No interscapular patch.
Subtropical zone. The Andes of s Lara

through Yaracuy along the Cadena del Litoral e to Miranda thence along the Cordillera de la Costa to Monagas (*tucuyensis*). [E Colombia and e Ecuador. Se Brazil.]
Dense, humid cloud forests, 1300–1900 m. Forages in the lower branches of trees and close to the ground but occasionally in the treetops. Active, restless, usually in pairs or in family groups. Joins other antbirds. The dark color and rapid movements of this species makes it difficult to identify.

## CINEREOUS ANTSHRIKE
*Thamnomanes caesius*
CHOCA GUAYANESA

Pl. 22
5.8″ (14.7 cm.). Slaty gray, paler below. *Wing coverts plain slaty gray.* Under tail coverts narrowly fringed white. ♀: rather like Dusky-throated Antshrike but much darker. Above dark brown, darkest on crown, somewhat tinged gray on lower back. Upper tail coverts, wings and tail reddish brown. Throat whitish, upper breast olivaceous gray, rest of underparts bright cinnamon rufous darkening to chestnut rufous on under tail coverts. Under wing coverts cinnamon. A large white interscapular patch.
Tropical zone. Amazonas from Caño Cataniapo s and e in Bolívar across the whole Caura Valley and upper Río Paragua to the Altiplanicie de Nuria and headwaters of the Río Caroní (*glaucus*). [The Guianas; n Brazil, e Colombia, e Ecuador, e Peru, n Bolivia.]
Rain forest, also open forest and open second growth to 850 m. Forages usually alone and near streams from the thick undergrowth to the branches and lianas in the middle tier.

[THE GENUS *Myrmotherula* forms a large group of very small, short-tailed, wren-like birds which inhabit the undergrowth and lower stages of the forest. Most species are inhabitants of the tropical zone.]

## PYGMY ANTWREN
*Myrmotherula brachyura*
HORMIGUERITO PIGMEO

Pl. 21
3.5″ (9 cm.). Crown and mantle black streaked white; moustacial streak black;

rump gray mixed with black. Wing coverts black, median and greater ones broadly tipped white forming 2 bars, remiges black, edged white; tail *very short,* black, narrowly fringed white. Throat white, rest of underparts pale yellow, streaked black at sides of breast. Interscapular patch white. ♀: like ♂, but streaks on crown cinnamon buff, yellowish buff on mantle. Throat and breast pale buff, streaked black on sides of breast, rest of underparts pale yellow.
Tropical zone. Central and s Amazonas; Bolívar on the lower Río Caura, upper Paragua and upper Cuyuni (*brachyura*). [The Guianas, nw Brazil, Colombia to n Bolivia.]
Rain forest from near sea level to, occasionally, 940 m. in savannas and on the slopes of the tepuis. Found also in low, thick brush and undergrowth at forest edge or in clearings, often near rivers, where it forages actively and often joins mixed flocks of birds.

## YELLOW-THROATED ANTWREN
*Myrmotherula ambigua*
Hormiguerito Gargantiamarillo

3.5″ (9 cm.). Top and sides of head black, streaked white; back black streaked pale yellow; moustacial streak black; rump olive grayish. Wings as in Pygmy Antwren, but feathers edged pale yellow instead of white; tail black, tipped pale yellow. Below pale yellow, unstreaked. Interscapular patch pale yellow. ♀: above like ♂ but streaks on head and neck light tawny olive. Below pale yellow, sides of breast somewhat buffy. Interscapular patch hardly present.
Tropical zone. S Amazonas from Cerro Duida s to the confluence of the Casiquiare and the Río Negro. [Nw Brazil; Colombia along the Río Guainía.]
Virgin rain forest at about 100 m.

## STREAKED ANTWREN
*Myrmotherula surinamensis*
Hormiguerito Rayado

Pl. 21
3.7″ (9.4 cm.). Above black, streaked white; rump gray. Wings black, shoulder, double wing bar and edges to remiges white. Below white, streaked black. Interscapular patch white. ♀: crown and

nape chestnut rufous (or orange cinnamon, a); back, wings and tail as in ♂. Throat and breast cinnamon buff, rest of underparts white (or below all creamy white, streaked black, a). Interscapular patch white.
Tropical zone. E Amazonas along the upper Orinoco and lower Río Ventuari (*multostriata,* a). Sw Amazonas (Caño Casiquiare); Bolívar from the Caura and Paragua Valleys to the Ríos Cuyuni and upper Caroní; central Delta Amacuro (*surinamensis*). [Panama to w Ecuador, the Guianas and Amazonian Brazil.]
High rain forests to about 400 m. Undergrowth at forest edge, also clearings, second growth. Forages actively, usually in pairs. Near rivers and wet terrain. ♂ indistinguishable in the field from Cherrie's Antwren.

## CHERRIE'S ANTWREN
*Myrmotherula cherriei*
Hormiguerito de Cherrie

4.1″ (10.4 cm.). Tail longer than in Streaked Antwren. Above black, crown narrowly, back broadly streaked white. Wings and tail as in Streaked Antwren but shoulders black. Below white rather coarsely streaked black. No interscapular patch. ♀: above much like Streaked Antwren, but crown streaks paler, buffy cinnamon. Below buffy cinnamon, streaked black, paler and lightly streaked on abdomen. Wings and tail as in ♂. No interscapular patch.
Tropical zone. Amazonas in the Orinoco Valley, along the Río Ventuari s to the Río Yatúa. [E Colombia at Maipures; upper Rio Negro, Brazil.]
High, dense rain forest from about 100 m. to 550 m. on the slopes of the tepuis. Often in pairs and family groups near rivers and marshy areas. ♂ indistinguishable in the field from Streaked Antwren.

## RUFOUS-BELLIED ANTWREN
*Myrmotherula guttata*
Hormiguerito Vientre Rufo

Pl. 21
3.7″ (9.4 cm.) Head, back, throat, breast and upper belly gray, throat palest; lower belly and under tail coverts cinnamon rufous. A concealed white interscapular

patch, the feathers black subterminally; lower back olivaceous brown. Wings and tail black, median and greater wing coverts, inner remiges, scapulars, upper tail coverts and tail all with large, round and conspicuous cinnamon tips. ♀: crown and upper mantle grayish brown becoming brighter and slightly redder on rump; concealed interscapular patch white. Throat whitish gray, olivaceous gray on breast, cinnamon rufous on belly and under tail coverts. Wings and tail as in ♂.

Tropical zone. Central and s Amazonas e across Bolívar from the Caura Valley and upper Río Paragua to the upper Río Cuyuni and Cerro Roraima. [The Guianas; n Brazil.]

High, dense rain forest, 100–700 m. Often in pairs in the undergrowth and forest edge. Follows army ants and forages on the ground among leaves and under bushes.

## BROWN-BELLIED ANTWREN
*Myrmotherula gutturalis*
HORMIGUERITO ESPALDA MARRÓN

Pl. 21

4.3″ (11 cm.). Tail comparatively long. Above olivaceous brown, wings and tail reddish brown. Wing coverts with rather small round white tips, inner remiges inconspicuously tipped buff. No interscapular patch. Tail reddish brown. Throat black, spotted white, sides of neck and rest of underparts pale gray becoming brownish on flanks and under tail coverts. ♀: above dull olivaceous brown, below pale buffy brown. Wings and tail russet brown tipped buff.

Tropical zone. E Bolívar from the Sierra de Imataca s to Cerro Roraima. [The Guianas, n Brazil.]

High, dense rain forest in the lowlands above 150 m., ascending to 1000 m. on the slopes of the tepuis. Forages in the undergrowth and lower tree branches, often joining groups of other antbirds.

## STIPPLE-THROATED ANTWREN
*Myrmotherula haematonota*
HORMIGUERITO ESPALDA RUFA

Pl. 21

4″ (10 cm.). Tail comparatively long. Crown and nape olivaceous brown, rest

of upperparts chestnut. No interscapular patch. Wing coverts black, lesser and median tipped white, greater tipped buff. Remiges brown, edged russet; tail russet brown. Throat black spotted with white, breast and belly gray, flanks and under tail coverts olivaceous brown. ♀: upperparts, wings and tail much like ♂, but wing coverts not as black and all tipped cinnamon buff. Underparts cinnamon brown becoming darker on flanks and under tail coverts.

Tropical zone. Amazonas generally, e across Bolívar to the tepuis of the Gran Sabana (*pyrrhonota*). [E Ecuador to s Peru and w Amazonian Brazil.]

High, dense rain forest ascending the slopes of the tepuis to 1300 m. Forages in the undergrowth.

## WHITE-FLANKED ANTWREN
*Myrmotherula axillaris*
HORMIGUERITO COSTADOS BLANCOS

Pl. 21

4″ (10 cm.). Gray (or slaty gray, a) above. Wings black, shoulders white, wing coverts black conspicuously tipped white; tail black, feathers with small white tips. Throat, breast and center of abdomen black, *long, silky white plumes at sides of body*. ♀: olivaceous brown above. Wings and tail browner, wing coverts inconspicuously tipped buff. Below buff, white plumes at sides shorter than in ♂.

Tropical zone. From the foothills of the Andes of Táchira, Mérida, Barinas and w Apure s to s Amazonas and e to nw Bolívar along the upper Río Cuchivero (*melaena*, a). E Amazonas along the upper Río Ventuari near the border of Bolívar, and elsewhere s of the Orinoco including Delta Amacuro (*axillaris*). [Generally distributed e of the Andes to n Bolivia and Amazonian and se Brazil.]

High rain forest and open second growth from sea level to, occasionally, 1000 m. on the slopes of some tepuis. Frequents thick, tangled undergrowth at ground level and in the middle tier of forest trees; also forest edge, clearings and in the neighborhood of rivers. Common, restless, inconspicuous; usually in pairs or small parties and in mixed forest flocks. Follows army ants. Flicks its wings showing the white flanks and axillars. Calls: include a series of squeaky, thin, nasal whines.

## SLATY ANTWREN

*Myrmotherula schisticolor*
HORMIGUERITO APIZZARRADO

Pl. 21
3.7″ (9.4 cm.). Slaty gray; throat and foreneck black. Wings black, remiges edged slaty, wing coverts conspicuously tipped white. Tail slaty, very narrowly fringed white. ♀: upperparts grayish olive, wings and tail slightly browner. Throat and breast dirty buff becoming olivaceous drab on belly. Wing coverts plain.
Tropical and subtropical zones. Nw Zulia in the Sierra de Perijá, the Andes of Táchira, Mérida and Lara and e along the coastal Cordillera and interior chain to the mountains of Sucre and n Monagas (*sanctaemartae*). [Mid. Amer. to w Ecuador and se Peru.]
A bird of mountainous terrain with great altitudinal tolerance. From seal level (seldom) to 2250 m. Found in heavy rain forest and dense second growth. Active, forages in the thick undergrowth and lower trees among masses of creepers, sometimes with other birds. The white axillaries are visible as it flicks its wings. Calls: several squeaky, metallic sounds.

## LONG-WINGED ANTWREN

*Myrmotherula longipennis*
HORMIGUERITO ALILARGO

4.2″ (10.6 cm.). Much like ♂ of Slaty Antwren but shoulders conspicuously black and white. Slaty gray; throat and foreneck black. Remiges and tail as in Slaty Antwren. Wing coverts black conspicuously fringed (rather than spotted as in Slaty) with white. ♀: upperparts, wings and tail olive brown, wing coverts plain. Eye ring, throat and upper breast buff, lower breast and belly white, sides of body olive gray.
Tropical zone. Central and s Amazonas e across Bolívar to the Sierra de Imataca, the Río Cuyuni and Cerro Roraima (*longipennis*). [The Guianas, se Colombia to central and e Peru and Amazonian Brazil.]
Dense, high rain forest above 100 m., to

1300 m. on the forested slopes of the tepuis. Forages from the lowest tier to the treetops in pairs and small groups with other species.

## PLAIN-WINGED ANTWREN

*Myrmotherula behni*
HORMIGUERITO DE BEHN

Pl. 21
3.7″ (9.4 cm.). Much like Slaty and Long-winged Antwrens but differs from both by *plain gray wing coverts* and *no white tip to tail*. Throat, foreneck and center of upper breasts black, rest of plumage slaty gray. ♀: rufous brown above (or olivaceous brown, a); throat whitish, rest of underparts olivaceous brown (or dark olive buff, darkest on flanks, a), under tail coverts tawny olive.
Lower subtropical zone. Amazonas on Cerros Yaví, Calentura, Parú and de la Neblina; nw Bolívar on Cerro Tabaro, lower Río Caura, and El Negro, upper Río Cuchivero (*yavi*, a). Cerro Camani, Río Ventuari (*camanii*). Se Bolívar from the Sierra de Lema and the Gran Sabana to the Roraima region (*inornata*). [Guyana, n Brazil, e Colombia.]
High, humid cloud forest on the slopes of the tepuis, 1000–1800 m. In undergrowth, small trees and clearings. Not shy.

## GRAY ANTWREN

*Myrmotherula menetriesii*
HORMIGUERITO GARGANTIGRIS

Pl. 21
3.7″ (9.4 cm.). The only Venezuelan gray *Myrmotherula without a black throat patch*. Above slaty gray, below pale gray. Wings and tail gray, wing coverts black fringed white, tail narrowly fringed white. ♀: above bluish gray, tinged olivaceous on crown; below dull cinnamon buff. Wings light olivaceous brown; tail olivaceous gray.
Tropical zone. From Amazonas e across e Bolívar through the upper Ríos Caura and Paragua to Cerro Paurai-tepui (*pallida*). E Bolívar from the lower Río Paragua to the Sierra de Imataca and the Río Cuyuni s to the Gran Sabana (*cinereiventris*). [The Guianas and se Colombia to Amazonian Brazil and n Bolivia.]

High rain forest and open forest to 1000 m. on the slopes of the tepuis. Forages alone, or with other species of antbirds, from the lowest tier to the treetops.

## BANDED ANTBIRD

*Dichrozona cincta*
HORMIGUERITO BANDEADO

Pl. 24

4.6″ (11.7 cm.). Crown and mantle umber brown; lower back and rump black, rump crossed by a *conspicuous white band.* Wing coverts black tipped by large, round buff spots; margins of remiges umber brown. Below white, breast crossed by a *band of black spots,* flanks umber brown. Tail very short (1.3″, 3.3 cm.). ♀: like ♂ but rump band buff instead of white.
Tropical zone. Sw Amazonas from the Yavita-Pimichín Trail s. [E Colombia to n Bolivia; nw and central Brazil.]
High rain forest at about 150 m. Forages in trees of medium height.

## SPOT-TAILED ANTWREN

*Herpsilochmus sticturus*
TILUCHI RABIPUNTEADO

4″ (10 cm.). Crown and postocular streak black, eyebrow and small shaft streaks on forehead white. Back gray, interscapular patch white, the feathers with some black subterminally. Wings black, wing coverts conspicuously spotted white, remiges margined with white. Tail black, *central feathers with large white spots,* rest tipped white, outermost white on outer web. Throat and center of belly white, rest of underparts pale gray. ♀: much like ♂; differs by dark *chestnut tips to feathers of crown* which have longer whitish shaft streaks, and gray of underparts tinged olive.
Tropical zone. Bolívar on the lower Río Caura (Maripa), in the Gran Sabana in the Cerro Auyan-tepui region and on the Río Cuyuni (*sticturus*). [The Guianas, ne Brazil. Se Colombia, e Ecuador.]
High, dense rain forest to about 300 m. Undergrowth near large rivers and streams.

## TODD'S ANTWREN

*Herpsilochmus stictocephalus*
TILUCHI DE TODD

Pl. 21

4.3″ (11 cm.). Very similar to Spot-tailed Antwren but distinguishable by darker gray back, more black on interscapulum and less white on underparts; forehead dotted white. ♀: differs from ♀ Spot-tailed by darker back, grayish throat and darker and more buffy breast and sides of body. Crown spotted with white.
Tropical zone. Ne Bolívar on the Sierra de Imataca and along the upper Ríos Cuyuni and Yuruán. [The Guianas.]
Dense, high rain forest, 150–300 m. Joins flocks of other antbirds in the treetops.

## SPOT-BACKED ANTWREN

*Herpsilochmus dorsimaculatus*
TILUCHI ESPALDA MANCHADA

Pl. 21

4.3″ (11 cm.). Much like Todd's Antwren, but back broadly striped black and white, upper tail coverts black. ♀: crown black, *forehead spotted deep ochraceous,* rest of crown with large, longitudinal white spots, lores ochraceous, sides of neck and chest bright buff, otherwise like ♂.
Tropical zone. Central and s Amazonas e across Bolívar from the lower Río Caura to the upper Caroní. [Se Colombia, nw Brazil.]
High, dense rain forest, 100–400 m.

## RORAIMAN ANTWREN

*Herpsilochmus roraimae*
TILUCHI DEL RORAIMA

Pl. 21

5″ (13 cm.). Much like Spot-backed Antwren but readily distinguishable by much longer tail, 2.3″ (5.8 cm.) vs. 1.7″ (4.3 cm.). Central tail feathers with *white spots* on *both webs,* outer tail feathers *with white spots* on *inner web.* ♀: differs principally from ♀ Spot-backed by *forehead spotted white* like crown instead of ochraceous.
Upper tropical and subtropical zones. Se Amazonas; w Bolívar along the Río Caura e to the Sierra de Lema, the tepuis of the Gran Sabana and the mountains on the Brazilian border. [Guyana;

Brazilian mountains on Venezuelan border.]
An endemic species of Pantepui. Dense, high rain forest on the slopes of the tepuis above 900 m., occasionally reaching the summits at almost 2000 m. Usually below the mid-level of high trees but found in considerably lower vegetation as the forest diminishes in height with increasing altitude.

## RUFOUS-WINGED ANTWREN
*Herpsilochmus rufimarginatus*
TILUCHI ALIRUFO

Pl. 21
4.5″ (11.5 cm.). Immediately distinguishable from any other *Herpsilochmus* by *chestnut margins* to the *remiges*. Crown and stripe through eye black, long eyebrow white. Back gray, mixed with black down center. Wing coverts, axillaries and inner remiges black, conspicuously edged white, rest of *remiges edged chestnut*. Central tail feathers gray, rest black broadly tipped white. Throat grayish white, rest of underparts creamy white. ♀: differs from ♂ by chestnut crown, back olive gray with little black; throat white, rest of underparts pale, creamy yellow.
Tropical zone. The Sierra de Perijá, Zulia, s Táchira, n Trujillo and Mérida; the llanos of Portuguesa; the n Cordillera from Carabobo to n Monagas; n and central Amazonas; n Bolívar from the Río Caura e to the Sierra de Imataca, s to the lower Ríos Paragua and Cuyuni (*frater*). [E Panama to e Ecuador, n Bolivia, Paraguay and ne Argentina.]
High, dense rain forest to almost 1000 m. Often in pairs near forest edge.

## WHITE-FRINGED ANTWREN
*Formicivora grisea*
COICORITA

Pl. 21
5″ (13 cm.). Smoky brown (or reddish brown, a) above, long eyebrow white. Throat, sides of head and neck, breast and center of abdomen black; sides of body white, flank feathers white, long and silky. Wings black, wing coverts broadly fringed white forming 3 bars. Tail rather long, much graduated, black tipped white, outer web of outer feather white. ♀: above smoky brown (or reddish brown, a). Long eyebrow white (or cinnamon, b). Wings and tail as in ♂. Below white, somewhat spotted with black (or uniform bright cinnamon orange, b; or white, heavily streaked with black on throat, breast and upper belly, a).
Tropical zone. Forested parts of Zulia w and s of L. Maracaibo to n Táchira and e to n Mérida and w Trujillo (*fumosa*). W Venezuela in scrubby and arid areas n of the Ríos Arauca and Orinoco e to Monagas; Margarita I. (*intermedia*). Extreme nw Amazonas e across Bolívar to the Sierra de Imataca and in s Anzoátegui and central Monagas (*orenocensis*, a). Amazonas, s of the range of *intermedia*, to Caño Casiquiare (*rufiventris*, b). [The Guianas, Colombia, Amazonian and e Brazil. Pearl Is., Panama. Trinidad, Tobago.]
Mostly in the lowlands rarely to 1500 m. Common in arid, sparsely wooded areas covered with low, dry scrub, cactus and impenetrable thornbush. Rarely in low thickets in heavily wooded regions, second growth and mangroves. Alone or in family groups, moves about restlessly through the branches near the ground.

## LONG-TAILED ANTBIRD
*Drymophila caudata*
HORMIGUERITO CUCLILLO

Pl. 21
6″ (15 cm.). Tail rather long, 3″ (7.6 cm.). Upperparts streaked black and white, center of crown black, rump rufous. Throat, breast and middle of belly white, sides of breast streaked black, flanks orange rufous. Wings black, remiges edged olive buff, wing coverts broadly tipped white forming 2 bars. Tail much graduated, gray with a subterminal black area and white tip. ♀: very similar to ♂ but back streaked buff and black, flanks paler and tail browner.
Tropical and subtropical zones. The foothills and mountains n of the Orinoco from the Sierra de Perijá to the Paria Pen., Sucre (*klagesi*). [Colombia, e and w Ecuador to n Bolivia.]
Mostly in the mountains to 1800 m., seldom as low as 500 m. Dense as well as open cloud forest, also second growth, clearings and abandoned plantations. Keeps low and in the mid-level of trees.

Forages actively and conspicuously in pairs and family groups in vines, tall bushes, bamboo thickets and braken-covered hills; joins other species.

## RUFOUS-RUMPED ANTWREN
*Terenura callinota*
HORMIGUERITO RABADILLA RUFA

4″ (10 cm.). Crown and nape black, back olivaceous, interscapular patch chestnut, the feathers edged black laterally; rump orange rufous, upper tail coverts olivaceous. Shoulders yellow, wing coverts black, feathers broadly tipped yellow forming 2 bars. Sides of head and neck gray, throat and breast grayish white, rest of underparts greenish yellow. Tail grayish, the feathers with minute yellowish white tips (description of nominate form; ♂ of *venezuelana* unknown). ♀: crown brownish olive; nape and scapulars olivaceous gray, back ochraceous brown, narrow rump band grayish; wing coverts dusky with 2 prominent whitish bars. Throat white with a faint gray tinge, breast grayer, rest of underparts pale yellow. Tail brownish gray, faintly tipped whitish.
Known from a single ♀ from Cerro Pejochaina, Sierra de Perijá, Zulia (*venezuelana*, described as a subspecies of *callinota*, but perhaps belongs to a separate species). [Guyana. Colombia w of the e Andes, e and w Ecuador to s central Peru.]
Dense, humid cloud forest, 1900 m.

## ASH-WINGED ANTWREN
*Terenura spodioptila*
HORMIGUERITO PIOJITO

Pl. 21
4″ (10 cm.). Crown and nape black, eyebrow white, upper mantle and upper tail coverts light gray, rest of back chestnut. Wings gray, coverts crossed by 3 white bars; tail gray, minutely tipped white. Below very pale gray, under tail coverts white. ♀: crown reddish brown, upper mantle and upper tail coverts olivaceous, rest of back chestnut; wings and tail olivaceous marked as in ♂. Throat and breast dull, pale ochraceous, rest of underparts grayish white, under tail coverts white.
Tropical zone. N and central Amazonas

s to Caño Casiquiare and Cerro Duida, e across Bolívar to Sierra de Imataca, Río Cuyuni and the Gran Sabana (*spodioptila*). [The Guianas, se Colombia, Amazonian Brazil n of the Amazon except in the Rio Tapajós region.]
Dense, high rain forest in the lowlands to 1100 m. on the forested slopes of the tepuis. Joins groups of birds moving through the treetops.

## GRAY ANTBIRD
*Cercomacra cinerascens*
HORMIGUERITO GRIS

6.3″ (16 cm.). Tail rather long, 3″ (7.6 cm.). Uniform dark bluish gray, small interscapular patch white (usually missing, a), greater wing coverts very narrowly edged white (or usually without white edges, a). Tail much graduated, conspicuously tipped white, the feathers very indistinctly barred dusky. ♀: upperparts ochraceous brown, tail somewhat grayer. Below ochraceous olive, brighter and paler than back, white markings as in ♂.
Tropical zone. Amazonas; w Bolívar along the lower Río Caura w to the Río Paragua and in the se at the headwaters of the Río Caroní (*cinerascens*). E Bolívar from the Sierra de Imataca to the Río Cuyuni (*immaculata*, a). [The Guianas, e Colombia to n Bolivia and Amazonian Brazil.]
High, dense rain forest in the lowlands to 900 m. on the heavily wooded slopes of some tepuis. Forages from the mid-level of trees to the undergrowth at the edge of the forest and in clearings.

## DUSKY ANTBIRD
*Cercomacra tyrannina*
HORMIGUERITO TIRANO

Pl. 22
5.7″ (14.5 cm.). Much like Gray Antbird but slightly paler and more ashy gray. Wing coverts black, conspicuously edged white. Tail with only a very narrow white tip. White interscapular much larger than in Gray Antbird. ♀: crown and nape grayish brown, back olivaceous brown, interscapular patch white. Wing coverts inconspicuously tipped ochraceous. *Below bright orange rufous.*
Tropical, lower subtropical zones. W Zulia,

Táchira and w Apure e to Mérida and Barinas (*vicina*). Amazonas and Bolívar (*tyrannina*). [The Guianas. Colombia, e and w Ecuador, n Amazonian and ne Brazil.]

High, dense rain forest and second growth, mostly in the lowlands near sea level but occasionally as high as 1800 m. In the Gran Sabana it is also found in thickets and open woods. Alone or in pairs creeps and hops actively in almost impenetrable undergrowth from near the ground to the mid-level of trees. Not shy, easily located, usually heard before being seen. Calls: include a musical, rattling trill consisting of a few slow notes followed by a series of faster ones.

## JET ANTBIRD
*Cercomacra nigricans*
HORMIGUERITO NEGRO

Pl. 22

6″ (15 cm.). Jet black; shoulders, edges to wing coverts, concealed interscapular patch and broad tips to tail feathers white. ♀: dark slaty gray, interscapular patch white. Throat, breast and center of abdomen sooty black, *throat finely streaked white*. Remiges brownish; tail slaty, marked with white as in ♂. Imm.: above slaty gray with or without an interscapular patch. Wings gray, marked as in ad., or brownish without markings. Feathers of throat, breast and center of abdomen white bordered with black, giving a streaked appearance on throat and scalloped on breast and abdomen. Tail as in ad. Below imm. rather resembles ♂ Silvered Antbird.

Tropical zone. S Táchira and w Apure. The n part of the country from the Distr. Federal and the Orinoco Valley from the mouth of the Río Apure e to the Paria Pen. and the delta. [Panama to w Ecuador and se Peru. Ne Brazil.]

Dense rain forest as well as open forest from sea level, seldom to 600 m. Thickets and wet areas in the tangled parts of open woods and second growth. Forages in pairs near the ground.

## WHITE-BROWED ANTBIRD
*Myrmoborus leucophrys*
HORMIGUERO BEJUQUERO

Pl. 24

5.4″ (13.7 cm.). *Forecrown and long, broad eyebrow white*, hindcrown, back, wings and tail blue gray; no interscapular patch; *wing coverts unmarked*. Cheeks, throat and sides of neck black, sharply defined from (or merging with, a) gray of rest of underparts. ♀: *forecrown and eyebrow bright cinnamon*, eyebrow becoming buffy cinnamon behind eye, rest of crown russet brown; back, wings and tail reddish brown, wing coverts with terminal white spots. Lores, cheeks and sides of neck black, throat and rest of underparts white, sides of breast and flanks olivaceous.

Tropical zone. The foothills of the Andes in Mérida, s Táchira, nw Barinas and w Apure (*erythrophrys*, a). Amazonas from Caño Cataniapo s; across n Bolívar to the Río Cuyuni and Delta Amacuro (*angustirostris*). [The Guianas, Colombia e of the Andes to n Bolivia. N and sw Amazonian Brazil.]

Heavy, dense lowland rain forest, occasionally to 1000 m., most frequently below 500 m. Usually in pairs in the undergrowth, in wet, swampy areas and near streams. Often hops on the ground.

## BLACK-FACED ANTBIRD
*Myrmoborus myotherinus*
HORMIGUERO RATONERO

Pl. 24

5″ (13 cm.). Forehead and narrow eyebrow grayish white. Crown and back gray, interscapular patch white. Wing coverts black, edged white, remiges edged gray; tail gray. Lores, throat and sides of head black sharply defined from light gray underparts. ♀: forehead and eyebrow dull buffy brown, crown and back umber brown. Wing coverts black, edged bright cinnamon buff. Margins of remiges and the tail reddish brown. Lores and sides of head black. *Throat white*, rest of *underparts bright pinkish cinnamon*, with *row* of *black spots* at junction of the 2 colors.

Tropical zone. E and s Amazonas, e across Bolívar in the Caura and Paragua Valleys to the headwaters of the Río Caroní (*elegans*). [E Colombia to n and e Bolivia. Amazonian Brazil.]

Dense rain forest above 100 m., rarely to 800 m., mostly below 500 m. Forages in the undergrowth.

## WARBLING ANTBIRD
*Hypocnemis cantator*
HORMIGUERO CANTARÍN

Pl. 21
4.3″ (11 cm.). Crown black, lores and line down center of crown white, sides of head and neck streaked black and white; mantle mixed black, white and olive brown (or gray and black, a), lower back brown, rump and upper tail coverts chestnut rufous (or lower back olive, rump tinged rufescent, a). Wings reddish brown (or olive brown, remiges tipped buffy white, a), wing coverts blackish brown, lesser coverts tipped white, greater tipped buff (or wing coverts black with round, white spots, a). Tail reddish brown, outer feathers with small rusty tips (or dull brown, with a small, blackish subterminal area and white tip, a). Throat and center of abdomen white, breast white streaked black, sides of body bright orange rufous (or below pale yellow, feathers of breast narrowly fringed black, flanks narrowly rufous, a). ♀: much like respective ♂ but crown blackish, streaked brownish, with a buffy white central line; wing coverts tipped cinnamon buff.
Tropical zone. Central and s Amazonas across s Bolívar to the headwaters of the Río Caroní (*flavescens,* a). E Bolívar from the Río Cuyuni to the Gran Sabana (*notaea*). [The Guianas, se Colombia to n Bolivia and Amazonian Brazil.]
Dense, high rain forest, wet forest and savannas to 1200 m. on the slopes of the tepuis, more common at lower elevations. In pairs in open undergrowth, sometimes hops on the ground.

## BLACK-CHINNED ANTBIRD
*Hypocnemoides melanopogon*
HORMIGUERO BARBINEGRO

Pl. 22
4.5″ (11.5 cm.). Uniform blue gray, slightly (or noticeably, a) paler below. Chin and throat black merging into gray of breast (or black of breast more restricted and only reaching upper throat and sharply defined from gray, a). Under tail coverts edged white. Wing coverts grayish black sharply but narrowly fringed white. Tail rather short, dark gray fringed white. Bill slender, comparatively long. ♀: upperparts, wings

and tail like ♂. Below white, feathers of throat and upper breast lightly edged gray (or throat and breast spotted with gray, sides of body gray, a).
Tropical zone. N of the Orinoco in Guárico (Río Zuata); nw Bolívar e to Delta Amacuro and the Gran Sabana (*melanopogon*). Amazonas from Puerto Ayacucho s and across s Bolívar to the Río Icabarú (*occidentalis,* a). [The Guianas, e Colombia to e Peru and the Amazon Valley, Brazil.]
High, dense rain forest to 400 m., in thick undergrowth along streams and in swampy areas, either alone or in pairs.

## BLACK-HEADED ANTBIRD
*Percnostola rufifrons*
HORMIGUERO CABECINEGRO

Pl. 22
5.5″ (14 cm.). Superficially similar to Black-chinned Antbird, but larger with much thicker bill, blackish crown and no white tip to tail. Crown black, the feathers edged gray; chin and throat black, rest of plumage dark bluish gray; no interscapular patch. Wing coverts black, sharply but narrowly fringed white. Tail uniform dark gray. ♀: crown and nape maroon brown; back and tail gray, tinged olivaceous. Wing coverts black, conspicuously edged cinnamon forming 3 bars, remiges olivaceous gray. Throat and breast cinnamon rufous, lower breast and belly light pinkish cinnamon, sharply defined; flanks olivaceous gray.
Tropical zone. S Amazonas from the Yavita-Pimichín Trail and Cerro Duida s (*minor*). [The Guianas. Se Colombia. Ne Peru. N Brazil from the Rio Negro e to Amapá.]
High, dense rain forest in the lowlands near rivers, seldom to 350 m. Forages in pairs in the undergrowth, keeping close to the ground. Follows army ants.

## SPOT-WINGED ANTBIRD
*Percnostola leucostigma*
HORMIGUERO ALIPUNTEADO

Pl. 22
6″ (15 cm.). Above slaty gray, no interscapular patch; below pale gray (or only slightly paler below, a); wing coverts black with prominent, white apical spots

(or dots, a, b). Tail slaty black. ♀: crown and sides of head gray (or crown gray, sides of head brownish olive, b); back dark reddish brown to dark grayish brown, upper tail coverts and tail slaty gray. Wing coverts dusky brown with prominent cinnamon rufous tips. Below orange rufous to rufous chestnut.

Tropical zone. Extreme sw Táchira (*subplumbea*, a). S Amazonas along the upper Orinoco and Caño Casiquiare (*infuscata*, b). E Bolívar in the Gran Sabana and the upper Río Cuyuni (*leucostigma*). [The Guianas, e Colombia to central Peru, n and central Amazonian Brazil.]

High, dense rain forest in the lowlands above 100 m. N of the Orinoco found at about 400 m., s of it in the Pantepui region up to 1500 m.

## CAURA ANTBIRD

*Percnostola caurensis*
HORMIGUEROTE ALIPUNTEADO

7″ (18 cm.). Bill large and heavy, 0.9″ (2.3 cm.). Uniform dark slaty gray, slightly tinged brown above (or slaty blackish without brown tinge, a). Wing coverts dotted white. ♀: crown dark chestnut with pale shaft streaks (or crown sepia, the feathers edged dusky giving a scalloped appearance, a); back dark brown with pale shaft streaks, upper tail coverts dusky olive; tail blackish. Wings dark brown, coverts with conspicuous orange cinnamon tips. Underparts bright rufous chestnut, dark reddish brown on flanks and under tail coverts.

Tropical zone. Nw Bolívar along the upper Río Cuchivero; Amazonas from Caño Cataniapo s (*australis*, a). Bolívar from the Río Caura and upper Paragua to the headwaters of the Río Caroní (*caurensis*). [Nw Brazil.]

High, dense rain forest in the lowlands, seldom as low as 100 m., more frequently on the lower slopes of the tepuis to 1300 m.

## SILVERED ANTBIRD

*Sclateria naevia*
HORMIGUERO TREPADOR

Pl. 22
6″ (15 cm.). Bill slender, long, 0.9″ (2.3 cm.); tail short; legs flesh color.

Upperparts slaty gray to slaty black, wing coverts with round, terminal white spots (or dots, a, b); no interscapular patch. Throat white, feathers of rest of underparts white centrally, broadly fringed gray, giving a scalloped appearance, much like imm. of Jet Antbird (or gray below with only a few white streaks on throat and breast, a; or white below with only a few gray edges to the feathers, b). ♀: upperparts and wings dull reddish brown (or slaty brown, eyebrow rufous, b). Wing coverts with round, cinnamon, apical spots. Below white heavily mottled with brown and dusky (or ochraceous tawny with little or no mottling, a; or white, sides of neck and body bright rufous chestnut, b).

Tropical zone. N and central Amazonas (*argentata*, b). Nw Bolívar along the lower Río Caura and its tributary, the Río Mocho (*diaphora*, a). Central Bolívar on the upper Ríos Paragua and Caroní, in Delta Amacuro and e Sucre (*naevia*). [The Guianas, e Colombia to se Peru and central Amazonian Brazil.]

High, dense forest as well as open woodland in the lowlands, to 500 m. in the Pantepui region. Swampy places and streams; mangroves in the Orinoco delta. In pairs near the ground. Calls: include a series of grating and bubbling notes, also a trill.

[IN *Myrmeciza* the bill is slender and rather long, the tail short, legs rather long. Some species are partly terrestrial.]

## WHITE-BELLIED ANTBIRD

*Myrmeciza longipes*
HORMIGUERO VIENTRIBLANCO

Pl. 22
5.6″ (14 cm.). Upperparts, wings and tail rufous chestnut, interscapular patch white. Forehead and sides of crown gray, lores and sides of head, neck, throat and breast black; lower breast and sides of belly gray, center of abdomen white, flanks and under tail coverts cinnamon brown. Legs flesh color. ♀: crown and nape umber brown, postocular streak gray, cheeks dusky. Back, wings and tail rufous chestnut, wing coverts with a subterminal black bar. Throat and breast cinnamon, paler on throat; belly white, flanks and crissum cinnamon brown.

Tropical zone. Nw Zulia from the Goajira Pen. s to the Río Palmar (*panamensis*). W Zulia s of the Río Palmar to Táchira, w Apure, Barinas and Mérida, Falcón and Yaracuy, thence e along the foothills of the coastal Cordillera to Sucre (*longipes*). Amazonas; nw Bolívar e to the Sierra de Imataca, the Río Cuyuni, Delta Amacuro and central Monagas (*griseipectus*). [Central and e Panama, n Colombia, n Brazil, Guyana. Trinidad.]
Dense rain forests and second growth to 1000 m., occasionally to 1300 m. Forages in low, dense, wet undergrowth, especially near streams. More often heard than seen. Not shy. Walks and runs on the ground, in pairs or several together; investigates leafcutter ants. Calls: include a series of loud flutelike whistles descending in scale, also clicking notes.

## DULL-MANTLED ANTBIRD

*Myrmeciza laemosticta*
HORMIGUERO PECHINEGRO

Pl. 22
5.3″ (13.5 cm.). Crown, nape, sides of head and neck, breast and center of belly iron gray. Throat black. Back, wings and tail olive brown, wing coverts blackish brown with terminal, round, white spots. Large interscapular patch white, feathers edged black. Rump and flanks reddish brown. ♀: differs from ♂ by checkered black and white throat, spots on wing coverts cinnamon buff, tertials with terminal cinnamon spots.
Upper tropical zone. Zulia in the Sierra de Perijá at the headwaters of the Ríos Negro and Apón; w Mérida and s Táchira (*venezuelae*). [Costa Rica to nw Ecuador.]
Shady, humid rain forest and dense, tangled second growth, 400–1000 m. Shy. Alone or in pairs, forages mostly in thick, low undergrowth and in ravines. Hops on the ground.

## FERRUGINOUS-BACKED ANTBIRD

*Myrmeciza ferruginea*
HORMIGUERO LOMIRUFO

Pl. 22
6″ (15 cm.). Above chestnut. Throat, breast and sides of neck black; a long,

white postocular streak. Lower breast white clouded with black, flanks, belly and under tail coverts rufous. Wing coverts black, edged buff. Bare eye patch blue. ♀: like ♂ but throat white. Lores and ocular region feathered, black.
Se Bolívar (*ferruginea*). [The Guianas; Brazil in central and e Amazonia].
Generally similar to Gray-bellied Antbird but does not occur in the same region.

## GRAY-BELLIED ANTBIRD

*Myrmeciza pelzelni*
HORMIGUERO VIENTRE GRIS

Pl. 22
5″ (13.4 cm.). Forehead, lores and sides of head mixed gray and white. Crown dark olivaceous brown, becoming paler and more reddish on back and chestnut brown on rump and tail coverts; tail dark brown tinged chestnut. Wing coverts and tertials blackish with conspicuous, round buff terminal spots. No interscapular patch. Throat and breast black, belly iron gray, flanks and under tail coverts chestnut brown. ♀: above like ♂, but spots on wing coverts and inner tertials larger, tertials like back. Throat and lower breast white, upper breast pure white, lower breast white, the feathers heavily margined with black giving a streaked and scaled appearance; center of belly gray, flanks and under tail coverts brown.
Tropical zone. S Amazonas s of Caño Casiquiare. [Se Colombia; nw Brazil.]
Shady, humid rain forest at about 200 m. Habits like those of Dull-mantled Antbird.

## BLACK-THROATED ANTBIRD

*Myrmeciza atrothorax*
HORMIGUERO GARGANTINEGRO

Pl. 22
5.5″ (14 cm.). Dark reddish brown above, interscapular patch white, rump and upper tail coverts sooty black. Wings dark brown, coverts with small white dots. Forehead, lores and sides of head and neck dark gray, center of throat and upper breast black, lower breast and center of abdomen dark gray, sides of body umber brown. ♀: above like ♂, dots on wing coverts larger and buff instead of white. Throat pure white

sharply defined from rufous chestnut sides of neck and breast, sides of body paler, center of abdomen buffy white. Tropical zone. Amazonas e across Bolívar to the Río Cuyuni, the Gran Sabana to Cerro Roraima and in s Delta Amacuro (*atrothorax*). [The Guianas, e Colombia to n Bolivia and Amazonian Brazil.] High rain forest and edge of savannas from sea level to, occasionally, 1600 m. on the cool slopes of the tepuis. Forages in pairs in the undergrowth near the ground or in very thick shrubbery at forest edge or in clearings.

## YAPACANA ANTBIRD
*Myrmeciza disjuncta*
HORMIGUERO DEL YAPACANA

5.3" (13.5 cm.). Blackish gray above with a large, concealed, white interscapular patch; wing coverts black, lesser and median ones narrowly tipped white. Lores and sides of head gray, chin white, throat and breast white suffused with ochraceous tawny, strongly so on breast and sides of throat, middle of abdomen white, under tail coverts dark gray. Tail sooty black. ♀: differs from ♂ by dark ochraceous buff spots on wing coverts and ochraceous under tail coverts.
Endemic. Known only from the vicinity of Cerro Yapacana, central Amazonas. High rain forest at about 100 m. in undergrowth and low bushes.

## IMMACULATE ANTBIRD
*Myrmeciza immaculata*
HORMIGUEROTE INMACULADO

Pl. 22
7.3" (18.5 cm.). Deep black, no interscapular patch, bend of wing white. Bare orbital skin violet fading to white posteriorly. ♀: forehead, chin and sides of head sooty black, rest of plumage maroon brown, somewhat paler below. Tail sooty black. Facial skin as in ♂.
Upper tropical and subtropical zone. W Zulia in the Sierra de Perijá at the headwaters of the Ríos Negro and Apón (*brunnea*). S Lara (*immaculata*). [Costa Rica to w Ecuador.]
Rain forest and cool, wet, high forest, 950–1700 m. Forages in heavy, low undergrowth and forest border. Joins noisy groups of other antbirds following army ants. Flashes white at bend of wing.

## WHITE-PLUMED ANTBIRD
*Pithys albifrons*
HORMIGUERO PLUMÓN BLANCO

Pl. 24
5" (13 cm.). Head adorned with long white plumes, those springing from forehead and lores forming two "horns," those from chin and throat forming a "beard." Crown, nape, ocular area and sides of throat black, a narrow white postocular streak (or no postocular streak, a). Back and wings gray; nuchal collar, sides of neck, entire underparts, upper tail coverts and tail chestnut. Legs orange yellow.
Tropical zone. Extreme s Táchira (*peruviana*, a). S of the Orinoco in Bolívar and Amazonas (*albifrons*). [The Guianas, n Amazonian Brazil, e Colombia to central Peru.]
High rain forests in the lowlands s of the Orinoco from 100 m. ascending to 1500 m. on the slopes of the tepuis; n of the Orinoco at 500 m. in Burgua, s Táchira. Not shy; forages in the undergrowth and low bushes. Conspicuous as it follows army ants with other antbirds and woodcreepers, sometimes in large noisy groups. Calls: loud, include "churrs" and sharp chips.

## RUFOUS-THROATED ANTBIRD
*Gymnopithys rufigula*
HORMIGUERO GARGANTIRRUFO

Pl. 24
5.7" (14.5 cm.). Umber brown above with a concealed white interscapular patch, wings and tail slightly redder than back. Forehead black, subocular region, chin and sides of throat chestnut, center of throat and breast fading to buffy, rest of underparts olivaceous brown, buffy on center of abdomen. Legs pale brown, bare skin behind eye bluish white. ♀: differs from ♂ only in having a pinkish cinnamon postocular patch.
Tropical zone, s of the Orinoco except in Delta Amacuro (*pallida*). E Bolívar on the upper Río Cuyuni (*rufigula*). Sw Amazonas in the upper Ríos Guainía and Atabapo (*pallidigula*). [The Guianas; n Amazonian Brazil.]
High rain forests in the Pantepui region from 100 m. to 900 m. on the slopes of the tepuis. Always near the ground in the undergrowth. Not shy; conspicuous

as it follows army ants in noisy groups with other antbirds, especially the White-plumed Antbird, and woodcreepers.

## SPOT-BACKED ANTBIRD

*Hylophylax naevia*
HORMIGUERO ESPALDA PUNTEADA

Pl. 24
4″ (10 cm.). Tail short, bill proportionately long. Reddish brown above, interscapular patch white, the feathers terminally black, forming a black patch on center of back, this spotted with buff. Wing coverts black with prominent terminal white spots, tertials black, with large, terminal buff spots. Tail like back, feathers tipped buff. Forehead and sides of head gray. Throat black, rest of underparts white with a band of *large black spots across breast,* flanks reddish brown. ♀: differs from ♂ by white throat, bordered black at sides, rest of underparts cinnamon buff with spots like ♂.
Tropical zone. Amazonas from Caño Cuao s to the Brazilian border; w Bolívar in the Caura valley e across the upper Paragua to the Gran Sabana and Paurai-tepui in the se (*naevia*). [E Colombia, the Guianas to n Bolivia; Amazonian Brazil.]
High rain forests in the Pantepui region from 100 m. to 1100 m. on the slopes of the tepuis. Second growth, undergrowth and low bushes. Probably follows army ants.

## DOT-BACKED ANTBIRD

*Hylophylax punctulata*
HORMIGUERO PUNTEADO

Pl. 24
4.2″ (10.6 cm.). In general pattern much like Spot-backed Antbird. Differs by whitish lores and cheeks, grayish olive crown and mantle; *entire lower back black, dotted with white,* the dots increasing in size toward the tail coverts; wing coverts and tertials black with white terminal spots; tail black, tipped white. Below like Rufous-throated Antbird, but flanks slightly tinged pale grayish. ♀: above like ♂ but somewhat browner. Throat white, heavily bordered with black at sides, breast and upper belly white, heavily spotted with black on breast;

lower belly and under tail coverts pinkish buff.
Tropical zone. Amazonas along the upper Orinoco and the Río Ventuari; w Bolívar along the Río Caura (*punctulata*). [Amazonian Brazil; ne Peru.]
Undergrowth in high rain forest, 100–300 m. Habits probably similar to Spot-backed Antbird.

## SCALE-BACKED ANTBIRD

*Hylophylax poecilonota*
HORMIGUERO LOMO ESCAMADO

Pl. 22
5″ (13 cm.). Gray, paler below, a concealed white interscapular patch; middle of back black, the feathers fringed white giving a *scaled appearance;* upper tail coverts black broadly tipped white. Wings black, coverts fringed white like back, tertials tipped white. Tail black tipped white, with a *band across* the *middle* formed by a white patch on inner web of the feathers. ♀: top and sides of head and upper throat orange rufous, darkest on hindcrown; back reddish brown, the feathers in center of back black, edged cinnamon (or edged white, a) giving a scaled appearance; wings and upper tail coverts as in ♂ but feathers edged cinnamon buff (or edged white as in ♂, a). Tail as in ♂. Lower throat, breast and center of belly light gray, flanks umber brown (or entire underparts ochraceous rufous, most intense on throat and breast, a).
Tropical zone. Nw and central Amazonas s to Nericagua, along the Río Asisa and the se slopes of Cerro Duida; Bolívar from the upper Río Cuchivero e across the Caura to the Gran Sabana (*poecilonota*, a). Amazonas from San Fernando de Atabapo and the w slope of Cerro Duida s (*duidae*). [The Guianas, e Colombia to se Peru; Amazonian Brazil.]
High rain forest from 100 m. in the Pantepui region to 1400 m. on the slopes of the tepuis. Dense undergrowth and low bushes. Forages alone but may congregate in groups of a dozen or more following army ants. Utters sharp, snapping calls as it clings to upright stems.

## REDDISH-WINGED BARE-EYE

*Phlegopsis erythroptera*
HORMIGUERO OJIPELADO

Pl. 23
7" (18 cm.). Mainly black, feathers of
back and lesser wing coverts narrowly
fringed white giving a scaled appearance.
Broad tips of greater wing coverts and
basal portion of remiges extensively
chestnut forming a large patch on wing.
Tail black. Bare ocular skin red. ♀:
chestnut brown above, orange rufous
below. Wings and tail blackish, double
wing bar and patch on outer web of
remiges buff.
Tropical zone. S Amazonas from the
Duida region s (*erythroptera*). [Nw
Brazil, se Colombia, e Ecuador, e Peru.]
High, dense rain forest, 150 m. Undergrowth of thick as well as of more open
forest.

## WING-BANDED ANTPITTA

*Myrmornis torquata*
POLLITO DE SELVAS

Pl. 23
6.5" (16.5 cm.). Bill rather long 0.8"
(2 cm.); tail very short, 1.2" (3 cm.).
Crown deep chestnut, narrow eyebrow
black, feathers edged white giving a
barred appearance, this continued down
sides of neck. Back olivaceous gray, the
feathers broadly margined chestnut; concealed interscapular patch white, the
feathers terminally black, upper tail
coverts and tail chestnut. Wings black
with a double buff bar, the outer remiges
with the outer web buff medially. Throat
and upper breast black, bordered white,
rest of underparts gray, tinged olivaceous on flanks; under tail coverts chestnut. ♀: differs from ♂ principally by
having the throat and center of upper
breast bright orange rufous.
Tropical zone. Central and s Amazonas;
Bolívar from the Río Caura to the
Sierra de Imataca and the headwaters of
the Río Caroní (*torquata*). [The Guianas,
n and e Colombia to e Ecuador and
Amazonian Brazil. E Panama.]
High rain forests from 300 m. in the
Pantepui region to 1200 m. on the slopes
of the tepuis. Undergrowth and low
bushes. Not shy. Difficult to observe.
In pairs, forages quietly in the leaf litter.

Walks and hops on the ground with tail
carried erect.

## SHORT-TAILED ANTTHRUSH

*Chamaeza campanisona*
HORMIGUERO CUASCÁ

Pl. 23
8" (20 cm.). Looks like a thrush with very
short bill, tail and legs. Above uniform
reddish brown to olivaceous brown; postocular streak white; tail with a subterminal black bar and narrow, buffy
white tip. Below white more or less
tinged ochraceous buff on breast, flanks
and under tail coverts; feathers of throat
lightly tipped black, those of rest of
underparts narrowly to broadly edged
laterally with black or brownish black
giving a streaked appearance.
Tropical and subtropical zones. The Andes
of w Táchira e through Yaracuy along
the coastal Cordillera to the Distr. Federal, and the interior chain in Aragua
(*venezuelana*). Amazonas on Cerro
Yaví (*yavii*); on Cerro Huachamacari
(*huachamacarii*); on Cerros Calentura
and de la Neblina, Amazonas, and in
Bolívar on Cerros El Negro and Tabaro
and on the tepuis of the Gran Sabana
(*obscura*); on Cerro Roraima (*ful-
vescens*). [Guyana, e Colombia to n
Bolivia. Se Brazil, ne Argentina.]
Humid, mossy forests as well as more open
ones on the slopes of the mountains,
400–1850 m., very rarely as low as
100 m. Runs along the ground, mouselike, in pairs and family groups, and in
the evening congregates in larger groups
in thick, low bushes. Calls: include a
clear, sonorous whistle not difficult to
imitate.

## RUFOUS-TAILED ANTTHRUSH

*Chamaeza ruficauda*
HORMIGUERO MAZAMORRERO

Pl. 23
7.5" (19 cm.). Much like Short-tailed Ant-
thrush but redder above and much more
heavily marked below; no black band
on tail. Upperparts, wings and tail
russet brown; prominent postocular
streak white. Throat white, rest of underparts buffy white, the feathers of the
underparts heavily margined with black,
those of belly and flanks with a broad

*dusky central stripe.* Under tail coverts cinnamon, barred dusky.
Subtropical zone. The Sierra de Aroa in Yaracuy and the coastal Cordillera from Carabobo to Miranda (*chionogaster*). [The E and Central Andes, Colombia. Se Brazil from Espírito Santo to Rio Grande do Sul.]
Cloud forest, 1500–2100 m. Low bushes and thickets in the most humid areas. Alone or in pairs, frequently runs along the ground, mouselike. Call: single, loud, protracted whistle steadily repeated, slowly at first then accelerating quickly at the end.

## RUFOUS-CAPPED ANTTHRUSH
*Formicarius colma*
POLLITO HORMIGUERO

Pl. 23
7″ (18 cm.). Forehead very narrowly black (or forecrown black, a); lores, sides of head, throat and breast black; rest of underparts dark olivaceous gray, more strongly olivaceous on flanks. Crown and nape chestnut, paler at sides. Back and wings olivaceous brown, tail blackish; outer web of outer greater wing coverts and base of primaries (not visible) cinnamon. ♀: like ♂ but lores and throat white, spotted with black, center of belly buffy white, tail browner.
Tropical zone. Amazonas except the s; Bolívar generally (*colma*). S Amazonas on Cerro Yapacana and Temblador I., upper Orinoco (*nigrifrons*). [The Guianas, e Colombia to e Peru, Amazonian and se Brazil.]
High rain forest in the lowlands from sea level in the Orinoco delta to 1100 m. on the slopes of the tepuis. Thick undergrowth. Lives on the forest floor, actively runs on the ground and over logs, like a small rail with its tail cocked up. An imitation of its low whistle attracts this rail-like bird.

## BLACK-FACED ANTTHRUSH
*Formicarius analis*
GALLITO HORMIGUERO

Pl. 23
7″ (18 cm.). Umber brown becoming chestnut brown on upper tail coverts. Lores and throat black, sides of neck drab grayish olivaceous, ear coverts dusky (or sides of neck and ear coverts rufous chestnut, a), rest of underparts drab grayish olivaceous, lighter in center of abdomen; under tail coverts chestnut. Wings like back, remiges basally cinnamon (not visible). Tail blackish. Imm.: like ad. but throat white, spotted with black.
Tropical zone. Zulia, n Táchira and n Mérida (*griseoventris*, a). Elsewhere n of the Apure and the Orinoco (*saturatus*). E Bolívar from the Sierra de Imataca to the Sierra de Lema and the Gran Sabana (*crissalis*). [S Mexico to n Bolivia, the Guianas and Amazonian Brazil. Trinidad.]
High, humid rain forests to 1700 m. n of the Orinoco, s of it to 800 m. Open, shaded second growth with good canopy. Primarily terrestrial. Forages on and near the ground alone or in family groups. Walks, struts or runs with its tail cocked like a bantam cock or little rail but never hops and seldom flies. Although hard to see and secretive, it is not wary and responds to its easily imitated deep, melodious, ventriloquial whistle, consisting of a loud, explosive note followed by 3 or 4 descending ones.

## RUFOUS-BREASTED ANTTHRUSH
*Formicarius rufipectus*
HORMIGUERO PECHIRROJO

Pl. 23
7.5″ (19 cm.). Lores, throat and sides of head and neck black. Crown, nape and breast chestnut, belly olive gray, buffy in center of abdomen. Back dark olive, upper and under tail coverts chestnut. Tail short, black. ♀: similar to ♂ but crown darker; blackish on forehead.
Subtropical zone. W Zulia; sw Táchira (*lasallei*). [Colombia, e and w Ecuador to central Peru.]
Cloud forest, 1100–2200 m. Terrestrial, forages on the mossy ground, alone or in pairs. Call: 2 sharp whistles, the last a semitone above the first.

[ANTPITTAS FORM A LARGE GROUP of long-legged, short-tailed, thrushlike, terrestrial birds. The majority are found in the subtropical zone and are difficult to see because of their retiring habits.]

## UNDULATED ANTPITTA
*Grallaria squamigera*
HORMIGUERO TORORÓI ONDULADO

9" (23 cm.). Upperparts, wings and tail olivaceous washed with gray, the feathers very narrowly and inconspicuously margined dusky. Moustacial streak black, throat white; rest of underparts light ochraceous heavily spotted with black.
Subtropical and temperate zones. The Andes of Mérida and the Páramo de Tamá, sw Táchira (*squamigera*). [Colombia to n Bolivia.]
Damp, mossy, low forest and open terrain with scattered bushes, 2000–3300 m. Shy and almost always terrestrial, runs quickly over open fields. When perched on a low branch remains silent and immobile and is difficult to observe.

## GREAT ANTPITTA
*Grallaria excelsa*
HORMIGUERO TORORÓI EXCELSO

Pl. 23
11" (28 cm.). Differs from Undulated Antpitta by browner back, hindcrown and nape gray, no moustacial streak and larger size.
Subtropical zone. Nw Zulia, e Táchira, e Mérida, se Trujillo and se Lara (*excelsa*). Colonia Tovar, Aragua (*phelpsi*).
Dense cloud forest, 1700–2300 m., where it is difficult to see. Forages alone in the debris on the highest ridges. Responds to an imitation of its whistle, which sounds like the low, vibrant note created by blowing over the neck of an empty bottle. Endemic.

## VARIEGATED ANTPITTA
*Grallaria varia*
HORMIGUERO TORORÓI CABECINEGRO

8" (20 cm.). Very similar to the gray-naped form of Scaled Antpitta but much larger with larger bill and longer legs. Throat and breast rufous brown, breast more heavily streaked; rest of underparts paler, pale patch on lower throat more in the form of a wide streak than a transverse patch; back browner and brighter.
Tropical zone. Amazonas from Caño Casiquiare south (*cinereiceps*). [The Guianas, Amazonian Brazil to e Paraguay and ne Argentina.]

High rain forest in the lowlands and up to 600 m. on the slopes in higher terrain. Terrestrial, shy and difficult to see.

## SCALED ANTPITTA
*Grallaria guatimalensis*
HORMIGUERO TORORÓI GUATEMALTECO

7" (18 cm.). Above olive (with hindcrown and nape gray, a), the feathers margined with black giving a scaled appearance. Moustacial streak whitish to pale rufous, throat olive brown mottled dusky and buffy, patch at lower throat white; breast olivaceous brown mottled and streaked buffy white, rest of underparts bright buffy ochraceous, paler in center of abdomen.
Upper tropical and subtropical zones. Zulia on the upper Río Negro (*carmelitae*). Extreme s Táchira; central Mérida (*regulus*). N Amazonas; nw Bolívar along the lower Río Caura, and in the se on Cerro Roraima (*roraimae*, a). [Colombia, nw Ecuador. E and central Peru. Trinidad.]
High, very dense, damp forests, as well as more open second growth, 350–2400 m. n of the Orinoco, 650–2000 m. on the slopes and forested summits of the tepuis. Basically terrestrial, and very secretive. It struts about on the ground, tail up like a rail, and hops as it forages in the clearings and thick undergrowth, alone or in family groups. Low, melodious, whistle, repeated several times.

## TACHIRA ANTPITTA
*Grallaria chthonia*
HORMIGUERO TORORÓI TACHIRENSE

7.5" (19 cm.). Above like the gray-naped form of Scaled Antpitta. Differs principally by dull whitish lower breast and sides which are barred lightly with gray.
Subtropical zone. Sw Táchira (Río Chiquito).
Forages alone in the mossy undergrowth of high, dense cloud forest, 1800–2100 m. Basically terrestrial and difficult to see. Endemic.

## PLAIN-BACKED ANTPITTA
*Grallaria haplonota*
HORMIGUERO TORERO

Pl. 23
7" (18 cm.). Above plain olivaceous brown, upper tail coverts and tail rufous

brown. Lores and throat white, moustacial streak dusky olive, separated from the dusky sides of head by a white line, white of throat bordered below by a narrow, irregular black line, rest of underparts buffy ochraceous (or ochraceous, a).

Upper tropical and subtropical zones. The coastal Cordillera from Carabobo to Miranda and the interior chain in Lara, Yaracuy and s Aragua (*haplonota*). On the Paria Pen., Sucre (*pariae*, a). [W Ecuador.]

High cloud forests, 900–1950 m., preferring the more humid terrain along the ridges. Primarily terrestrial and solitary, it walks and runs warily on the ground. Difficult to observe. Responds to an imitation of its song, which consists of a low-pitched, rather hollow-sounding whistle.

## CHESTNUT-CROWNED ANTPITTA
*Grallaria ruficapilla*
HORMIGUERO COMPADRE

Pl. 23
7.8″ (20 cm.). Crown, nape and sides of head and neck cinnamon rufous to rufous chestnut; back, wings and tail olive brown. Below white, lengthened feathers at sides of body edged blackish olive giving a conspicuously streaked appearance.

Subtropical to temperate zones. Nw Zulia (*perijana*). Ne Táchira through Mérida to n Trujillo (*nigrolineata*). The Andes in s Lara; the coastal Cordillera from Aragua to Miranda (*avilae*). [Colombia to e and w Peru.]

High, dense cloud forests and the thin woods and open terrain of the higher altitudes, preferring damp areas, 1300–3000 m. Terrestrial and usually alone. Although difficult to see but not very shy, it is often heard, and responds to an imitation of its whistle, consisting of 3 drawled notes, the first and second 3 tones apart, and the last between the 2. Its onomatopoeic local names are *Adios compadre*, *Seco estoy*, and *Compra pan*. Sometimes emits a prolonged, loud note.

## GRAY-NAPED ANTPITTA
*Grallaria griseonucha*
HORMIGUERO SECO ESTOY

Pl. 23
6.5″ (16.5 cm.). Upperparts, wings and tail rufous brown (or brownish olive, a). Band across nape dark gray. Underparts bright rufous (or with throat noticeably paler, a).

Subtropical zone. Ne Táchira (Boca de Monte) (*tachirae*, a). The Andes of central Mérida (*griseonucha*).

High, dense, humid rain forest, 2300–2800 m. Solitary and terrestrial, and like other species, difficult to see. Endemic.

## RUFOUS ANTPITTA
*Grallaria rufula*
HORMIGUERO PICHÓN RUFO

Pl. 23
6″ (15 cm.). Uniform rufous brown above; below lighter and brighter, center of abdomen buffy (or above uniform olive brown, below grayish brown, a).

Subtropical and temperate zones. Sierra de Perijá, Zulia (*saltuensis*, a). W and e Táchira (*rufula*). [Colombia to n Bolivia.]

High, dense, humid rain forest as well as low, mossy forest and meadows at the higher altitudes, 2000–3100 m. Terrestrial, solitary and difficult to see in the undergrowth. Call: heard more frequently in the early morning and evening, consists of a series of gradually ascending notes.

## SPOTTED ANTPITTA
*Hylopezus macularius*
HORMIGUERO PICHÓN PUNTEADO

Pl. 23
5.7″ (14.5 cm.). Crown and nape dark gray, lores and conspicuous eye ring buff; back and tail olive. Bend of wing ochraceous, wing coverts olive with 2 ochraceous bars, greater coverts black, primaries olive, basal part of outer web ochraceous forming a speculum. Streak below eye and moustacial streak black; underparts white, breast tinged ochraceous and heavily spotted with black; flanks ochraceous. ♀: similar to ♂ but no ochraceous wash on chest.

Tropical zone. S Amazonas (*diversus*). E

Bolívar on the Sierra de Imataca (*macularius*). [The Guianas; se Colombia; ne Peru, Amazonian Brazil; nw Bolivia.]
High, heavy rain forest in the lowlands to about 500 m. Terrestrial and solitary. Common at the base of Cerro Yapacana, Amazonas, on the upper Orinoco. Calls: include a rattle and a series of hoots. Note: Called *Grallaria macularia* in Lista Av. Venez. and Sp. Bds. S Amer.

### THRUSH-LIKE ANTPITTA
*Myrmothera campanisona*
HORMIGUERO CAMPANERO

Pl. 23
5.6" (14 cm.). Upperparts, wings and tail reddish brown; below white, heavily streaked on breast with dark olive brown, flanks grayish. Tail very short 1.5" (4 cm.).
Tropical zone. Central and s Amazonas (*dissors*). Ne Bolívar on the Sierra de Imataca s to Sierra de Lema (*campanisona*). [The Guianas, e Colombia to e Peru, Amazonian Brazil.]
High rain forest from 150 m. to 800 m. on the slopes of the mountains in thick undergrowth. Solitary and difficult to observe. Walks like a rail on the forest floor. Call: a clear, sonorous 2-noted whistle.

### BROWN-BREASTED ANTPITTA
*Myrmothera simplex*
HORMIGUERO FLAUTISTA

5.6" (14 cm.). Upperparts, wings and tail chestnut brown; breast and sides ashy gray (or olivaceous gray, a; or ochraceous brown, b). Throat white, sharply outlined; belly white.
Upper tropical and subtropical zones. Amazonas from Cerro Yaví s (*duidae,* b). Central and se Bolívar on Cerros Guaiquinima and Paurai-tepui (*guaiquinimae,* a). Bolívar in the Gran Sabana s to the Brazilian border (*simplex*). [Adjacent Brazil.]
Endemic to Pantepui. Dense rain and cloud forests from 600 to 2400 m. on the slopes of the tepuis and in the more open vegetation of the summits. Forages alone. Almost entirely terrestrial. Responds to an imitation of its hollow, slow, melancholy whistle, which begins in low tones and continues in 8 ascending semitones.

[GRALLARICULAS RESEMBLE Grallarias in miniature but are less terrestrial, being found mainly in forest undergrowth.]

### RUSTY-BREASTED ANTPITTA
*Grallaricula ferrugineipectus*
PONCHITO PECHICASTAÑO

Pl. 23
4.5" (11.5 cm.). Upperparts, wings and tail light olivaceous brown (or top and sides of head deep rufous brown, back somewhat duller, a); bend of wing and base of remiges cinnamon forming a wing speculum. Underparts orange ochraceous; patch at base of throat and center of abdomen white (or more deeply colored below, practically without white patch at base of throat, a).
Upper tropical and subtropical zones. The Sierra de Perijá, Zulia (*rara*, a). The Andes of central Mérida and w Lara and e through Falcón and Yaracuy to the Distr. Federal (*ferrugineipectus*). [Ne Colombia. N Peru.]
Rain and cloud forest between 800 and 2200 m., rarely as low as 250 m. (Mirimire, Falcón). Open parts of shady forest and woods. Not shy. Alone or in pairs in low bushes, but is not terrestrial. Call: a rhythmic series of soft, whistled notes rising and falling in tone, accelerating and decelerating. Responds to its easily imitated whistle.

### SLATE-CROWNED ANTPITTA
*Grallaricula nana*
PONCHITO ENANO

Pl. 23
4.2" (10.6 cm.). Crown and nape slaty gray. Back, wings and tail dark olivaceous brown to greenish olive. Below much like Rusty-breasted Antpitta but much more deeply colored, chestnut rather than ochraceous. Lores ochraceous chestnut, conspicuous.
Upper tropical to subtropical zones. The Andes of Táchira, Mérida and central Trujillo (*nana*). The coastal Cordillera in the Distr. Federal and Aragua (*olivascens*). The coastal Cordillera in Anzoátegui, Monagas and w Sucre (*cumanensis*). The Paria Pen. on Cerros

Humo and Azul (*pariae*). The mountains of the se Gran Sabana, Bolívar (*kukenamensis*). [Colombia, Ecuador.] High, rain and cloud forests, 700–2100 m. Not very shy. Alone or in pairs, forages actively in low bushes.

## SCALLOP-BREASTED ANTPITTA
*Grallaricula loricata*
PONCHITO PECHIESCAMADO

Pl. 23
4″ (10 cm.). Crown, nape and extreme upper back rufous chestnut. Back, wings and tail light olivaceous brown. Throat white, moustacial streak dusky; breast white, the feathers heavily margined black giving a scaled appearance; belly white, with a few gray streaks.
Subtropical zone. The mountains of Yaracuy e along the coastal Cordillera through Carabobo and Aragua to the Distr. Federal.
Thick cloud forest as well as more open woods, 1440–2100 m. Alone or in pairs, forages actively in low bushes.

## HOODED ANTPITTA
*Grallaricula cucullata*
PONCHITO CABECICASTAÑO

Pl. 23
4.5″ (11.5 cm.). Whole head rufous chestnut. Back and tail dark olivaceous brown, wings browner, base of remiges ochraceous. Patch across lower part of throat white; band across breast, continued down sides of body, olivaceous gray; center of lower breast and belly pale yellowish.
Subtropical zone. Known only from Río Chiquito, sw Táchira (*venezuelana*). [W and Central Andes, Colombia.]
Dense cloud forest, low bushes in more open parts of forest, 1800 m. Forages alone.

[CONOPOPHAGIDAE (G n a t e a t e r s; Chupadientes). Birds belonging to this family, which formerly followed the Antbirds, have recently been placed in other families and the family Conopophagidae eliminated. Thus the Ringed Antpipit (*Corythopis torquata*) is now placed with the Tyrant-Flycatchers. The only other genus in the family, *Conopophaga*, is now considered to be an antbird. It has not been recorded from Venezuela but the Chestnut-belted Gnateater (*C. aurita*) is likely to be found in the s for it occurs commonly in adjacent Brazil, the Guianas and se Colombia. It is a small brown bird with a black face and a silvery white postocular tuft.

# TAPACULOS: Pteroptochidae

## TAPACULOS

Birds belonging to this New World family are for the most part inhabitants of cool, mountain forests from Costa Rica to Cape Horn, but a few also occur on the plateau of se Brazil. Five species belonging to two genera are found in the mountains of n Venezuela. Four of these belong to the genus *Scytalopus*, tiny, mouselike inhabitants of the undergrowth in mossy cloud forests, often near streams, and in ravines in tangled vegetation affording ample cover. The fifth species, the curious Ocellated Tapaculo, is about the size of a small thrush and is peculiar for its conspicuously white-spotted plumage and very long, straight hind claw.

Tapaculos live principally on insects and construct large nests in crevices and under roots of trees. This family was called Rhinocryptidae in Lista Av. Venez.

## UNICOLORED TAPACULO
*Scytalopus unicolor*
TAPACULO UNICOLOR

Pl. 31
4.2″ (10.6 cm.). Uniform slaty gray.
Imm.: differs in plumage from other species by uniform dark brown plumage devoid of markings.
Subtropical zone. The Andes of Táchira and Mérida (*latrans*). [The Andes from Colombia to w Peru and nw Bolivia.]

Cloud forest in damp, mossy undergrowth and low bushes, 1800–2200 m. Shy, alert, agile, usually alone. Difficult to see as it scurries through the undergrowth near the ground.

## RUFOUS-VENTED TAPACULO
*Scytalopus femoralis*
TAPACULO VIENTRIRRUFO

Pl. 31
5.3″ (13.5 cm.). Black, crown patch white; throat grayish mixed with white, a suggestion of rufous barring on belly and under tail coverts. ♀: differs from ♂ by dark gray breast mixed with white. Subtropical zone. Nw Zulia in the upper Río Negro, Sierra de Perijá; sw Táchira (*nigricans*). [E Panama to w Ecuador.] Usually alone in the lower branches of bushes in cloud forest, 1150–1900 m. Shy, elusive, almost invisible in the dark, mossy undergrowth with which it blends.

## BROWN-RUMPED TAPACULO
*Scytalopus latebricola*
TAPACULO RATONA

Pl. 31
4.5″ (11.5 cm.). Above grayish brown (or slaty gray, a); below mouse gray (or slaty gray, a); rump, flanks and under tail coverts cinnamon brown, barred black. Subtropical and temperate zones. The Sierra de Perijá, Zulia; the Andes of Táchira, Mérida, Trujillo on Páramo de Cendé, and Lara at Anzoátegui (*meridanus*). The coastal Cordillera from Aragua to Miranda and in Sucre on

Cerro Turumiquire (*caracae*, a). [The mountains of Colombia and Ecuador.] Cloud forest in the mossy undergrowth and in thickets in more open woodland, 1600–3300 m. Same habitats as other tapaculos.

## ANDEAN TAPACULO
*Scytalopus magellanicus*
TAPACULO CHIRCÁN

4″ (10 cm.). Grayish brown above, light mouse gray below; rump and flanks plain cinnamon rufous; tail dusky brown. Subtropical and temperate zones. S Lara and s Trujillo (*fuscicauda*). [The Andes to Cape Horn. Falkland Is.] Cloud forest in ravines, often near streams, 2500–3200 m. The same secretive habits as Unicolored and Rufous-vented Tapaculos.

## OCELLATED TAPACULO
*Acropternis orthonyx*
TAPACULO DE OCELOS

Pl. 23
8″ (20 cm.). Forecrown, throat, sides of head and neck bright cinnamon rufous; back, wing coverts and underparts black, profusely spotted with white. Lower back, rump, upper and under tail coverts chestnut rufous. Remiges brownish black edged rufous; tail brownish black. Hind claw long, 0.8″ (2 cm.), straight. Upper subtropical and temperate zones. The Andes of Táchira to central Mérida. [Colombia to central Ecuador.] Undergrowth in dense as well as fairly open forest, 2250–3300 m., usually above 3000 m.

# COTINGAS, FRUITEATERS, BELLBIRDS, BECARDS: Cotingidae

## COTINGAS, GRANICERAS

Cotingas form a large family of ill-assorted but most interesting birds, extending s in South America only to n Argentina, n Bolivia and s Brazil. One species reaches n as far as the sw US.

Some of the most beautiful birds, as well as some rather bizarre ones, are found among the cotingas. In size they vary from that of a crow to a small tanager, and even smaller in Brazil. Among the most beautiful are the members of the genus *Cotinga*, clothed in enamel-like plumage in shades of turquoise blue and purple, and the fruiteaters, brilliant green in color varied with shades of yellow, orange and crimson. Curiously adorned are some of the bellbirds whose heads are decorated with fleshy wattles, and the Umbrellabird whose tall crest falls over its head like an umbrella. Among those whose looks are not very prepossessing are the brown, bald-headed Capuchinbird, and the Bare-necked Fruitcrow, mostly black with a bare neck. Plumage is not the only remarkable thing about this fascinating family, for the voice of some almost defies description. The Screaming Piha emits a 3-note cry, "pee-pe-yó," preceded by a low gurgling sound, which can be heard for half a mile and once heard is never forgotten. The well-known note of the Bellbird resembles an anvil being struck, and its ringing sound can be heard for a great distance.

Naturally in such a diverse family habits vary widely, but most species inhabit thick tropical forest and feed largely on fruit.

In Lista Av. Venez. certain genera were included in the family Cotingidae which since have been found to be better placed in other families. These are *Acrochordopus*, *Attila*, *Laniocera* and *Rhytipterna*, which are currently placed in the Tyrannidae, and *Rupicola*, which is placed in a family of its own, Rupicolidae.

## SHRIKE-LIKE COTINGA
*Laniisoma elegans*
COTINGA PIRARI

Pl. 26
6.5″ (16.5 cm.). Top of head black; back, wings and tail olive green. Below yellow with a few black crescentic marks at sides of throat and body.
Tropical zone. S Táchira (*venezuelensis*). [E Colombia; e Ecuador. Peru, nw Bolivia. Se Brazil.]
Rain forest from 200 m. ascending the wooded slopes of the Andes to about 500 m. and probably more.

## BLUE COTINGA
*Cotinga nattererii*
COTINGA AZUL

7.2″ (18.2 cm.). Mostly bright blue, black bases of the feathers showing through here and there on upper parts. Eye ring black. Throat and extreme upper breast dusky purple, center of abdomen brighter purple. Wings and tail black, remiges edged blue. ♀: dusky brown above, the feathers narrowly edged whitish. Eye ring white. Throat sandy buff, feathers of breast dusky brown, edged sandy or cinnamon, center of belly pale cinnamon buff. Wings blackish brown, inner remiges edged cinnamon, under wing coverts pinkish cinnamon. Tail blackish brown.
Tropical zone. The n base of the Andes in Mérida. [Central and w Colombia; w Ecuador.]
Rain forest near L. Maracaibo at sea level. Clearings. Forages in the higher branches of trees.

## SPANGLED COTINGA
*Cotinga cayana*
COTINGA GARGANTIMORADA

Pl. 26
8.5″ (22 cm.). Brilliant turquoise blue, spangled with black above. Throat plum-color. Wings and tail black, wing coverts broadly edged turquoise blue. ♀: much like Blue Cotinga but paler, grayer, feather edgings less distinct; under wing coverts cinnamon buff. Inner webs of outer tail feathers cinnamon brown in contrast to dusky outer webs.
Tropical zone. N of the Orinoco in s Táchira. Amazonas s to Caño Casiquiare; nw and s Bolívar from the lower Río Caura e to the upper Río Paragua, the Gran Sabana and upper Río Cuyuni; s Delta Amacuro at Joubre (*cayana*). [The Guianas. E Colombia to nw Bolivia. Amazonian Brazil.]
Rain forest, open woodland and clearings to 500 m. Forages in small groups in the higher branches and tops of tall, fruiting trees, sometimes associated with other cotingas.

## PURPLE-BREASTED COTINGA
*Cotinga cotinga*
COTINGA PECHIMORADA

Pl. 26
7.5″ (19 cm.). Upperparts, sides of head, flanks and under tail coverts purplish blue, back spangled with black. Throat, breast and center of belly rich reddish purple. Wings and tail black, wing coverts broadly edged purplish blue. ♀: blackish brown above, glossed with greenish blue, the feathers tipped whitish giving a speckled appearance. Below

brownish black, the feathers broadly edged whitish, under tail coverts cinnamon buff. Wings brownish black, wing coverts and inner remiges edged buff and tipped white; under wing coverts light cinnamon buff.

Tropical zone. Amazonas from the Yavita-Pimichín Trail s; e Bolívar from the Río Cuyuni to the Gran Sabana. [The Guianas, n Brazil.]

Rain forest from 150 m. to 600 m. on the slopes of the tepuis. Habits similar to Spangled Cotinga.

## POMPADOUR COTINGA
*Xipholena punicea*
COTINGA VINO TINTO

Pl. 26

7.5″ (19 cm.). Shining purple red, inner upper wing coverts lengthened, stiffened, with white shafts. Wings white, feathers tipped black. Tail light rosy purple. ♀: gray, whitish on center of abdomen, under tail coverts pink. Wing coverts and inner remiges broadly edged white. Iris yellow.

Tropical zone. N Amazonas s; nw Bolívar on the lower Río Caura and across the s from the upper Río Caura to the Gran Sabana and the Río Cuyuni. [The Guianas, se Colombia, e Ecuador, n and central Amazonian Brazil.]

Rain forest above 100 m. ascending the slopes of the tepuis to 1300 m. Small groups often fly in the treetops. Feeds on berries and fruit. The white wings are conspicuous in flight.

## RED-CRESTED COTINGA
*Ampelion rubrocristatus*
COTINGA CRESTA ROJA

Pl. 26

8″ (20 cm.). Gray; long, narrow crest mahogany red, paling toward tip. Feathers of rump and upper tail coverts with black centers and whitish edges; feathers on center of abdomen broadly edged white, under tail coverts black, edged white. Wings and tail black, all but central feathers with a white subterminal patch forming a band across the distal third of the tail.

Upper subtropical and temperate zones. The Sierra de Perijá, Zulia; the Andes of Táchira and Mérida to n Trujillo. [The

Andes from Colombia to w Peru and n Bolivia.]

Low, mossy forest, open woods and isolated trees, bushes, 2500–3250 m. Solitary, not shy; perches quietly in treetops and on bushes. Call: a froglike "rrrhhei," also nasal sounds.

## GREEN-AND-BLACK FRUITEATER
*Pipreola riefferii*
GRANICERA VERDECITA

Pl. 26

7.7″ (19.5 cm.) [or 7″ (18 cm.), a]. Top and sides of head blue black, throat and upper breast greenish black, a yellow edge bordering the blackish breast and sides of head. Lower breast and rest of underparts yellow, streaked with green at sides of body. Back, inner remiges and tail grass green, inner remiges tipped yellowish white, primaries black, edged greenish yellow. Bill red; legs orange yellow. ♀: differs from ♂ by having the head and breast grass green like back.

Subtropical and temperate zones. The Sierra de Perijá, Zulia, s to sw Táchira (*riefferii*). E and central Táchira, ne through Mérida to n Trujillo, and along the coastal Cordillera from Aragua to Miranda (*melanolaema,* a). [The Andes of Colombia to e and w Ecuador and ne Peru.]

Cloud forest, 1750–3050 m., in low, mossy trees at the higher elevations, frequently on the ridges. Solitary, sometimes in pairs, perches quietly and inconspicuously on small limbs in the lower or middle tier of the trees. Forages in the treetops. The wings make a rattling sound. Call: a shrill, ventriloquial whistle prolonged for half a minute, so high in pitch that it is difficult to imitate, "seeeeeee. . . ."

## GOLDEN-BREASTED FRUITEATER
*Pipreola aureopectus*
GRANICERA PECHIDORADA

Pl. 26

7″ (18 cm.). Upperparts, chin, sides of head and neck, wings and tail grass green with a bluish tinge. Throat, breast and center of underparts golden yellow, sides of body green mixed with yellow. Inner remiges tipped white. ♀: upperparts grass green, underparts yellow streaked with green.

Upper tropical and subtropical zones. The Sierra de Perijá, Zulia, s to s Táchira and e through Mérida and Trujillo to w and s Lara (*aureopectus*). The coastal Cordillera from Carabobo to the Distr. Federal, the interior Cordillera in Aragua on Cerro Golfo Triste (*festiva*). [Ne and central Colombia.]

Cloud forest, 800–2300 m., but rarely below 1000 m. Avoids excessively humid areas. Alone or in small groups forages from the middle tier to the treetops.

## HANDSOME FRUITEATER
*Pipreola formosa*
GRANICERA HERMOSA

Pl. 26

7″ (18 cm.). Head glossy black; back, wings and tail grass green. Upper breast orange (or scarlet, a) shading to lemon yellow on lower breast and belly. Flanks and under tail coverts pale green. Inner remiges with large white tips. ♀: above grass green. Throat pale green (or yellowish spotted or barred with dusky, a). A golden yellow patch at lower throat, rest of underparts barred yellow and green.

Upper tropical and subtropical zones. From the Sierra de Aroa in central Yaracuy e along the coastal and interior Cordilleras through Carabobo to Miranda and the Distr. Federal (*formosa*). The coastal Cordillera in Anzoátegui, Sucre and Monagas (*rubidior*, a). Cerros Humo and Azul in the Paria Pen., Sucre (*pariae*, a).

Cloud forests, 800–2200 m. A heavy-bodied bird, difficult to see when at rest. Alone or in pairs, forages actively in the dark, low, heavy underbrush and to the middle tier of the trees. It is the most common of the genus and cannot be confused with any other species in its habitat. Endemic.

## RED-BANDED FRUITEATER
*Pipreola whitelyi*
GRANICERA DEGOLLADA

Pl. 26

6.5″ (16.5 cm.). Upper parts dull moss green, forehead (or forecrown, a) orange, this color continued to form an eyebrow and narrow nuchal collar and spreading over cheeks. Below gray, pec-

toral band scarlet fading to orange at sides of breast, under tail coverts pinkish orange. Remiges and rectrices dusky, conspicuously edged orange brown. Iris orange; bill lacquer red; legs orange. ♀: above green, brighter and much lighter than in ♂, an inconspicuous greenish yellow eyebrow and nuchal collar. Below yellowish white, broadly streaked black. Wings and tail olivaceous green. Iris light ochre; bill dark brown; legs brown, feet ochre.

Subtropical zone. E Bolívar on the tepuis of the Gran Sabana (*kathleenae*); on Cerro Roraima (*whitelyi*). [Adjacent Guyana.]

Endemic to Pantepui. Cloud forest on the slopes of the tepuis, 1300–2230 m. Solitary, not shy. Feeds actively from the upper parts of trees to treetops. Calls include a soft, high whistle.

## BARRED FRUITEATER
*Pipreola arcuata*
GRANICERA REQUINTILLA

Pl. 26

8.5″ (22 cm.). Head, throat and breast glossy black, rest of underparts yellow, evenly barred black. Back bright olive green, upper tail coverts with a broad black subterminal band and yellow tip. Wing coverts black, green on outer web, with a conspicuous yellow spot near tip of outer web; remiges black edged olive, with a conspicuous yellow spot on outer web of inner remiges. Tail green like back with a broad subterminal black band and narrow white tip. ♀: differs from ♂ by top and sides of head like back, throat and breast barred yellow and black like rest of underparts.

Subtropical and temperate zones. From the Sierra de Perijá, Zulia, s to s Táchira and e to Mérida and n Trujillo (*arcuata*). [Colombia through the Andes to n Bolivia.]

Cloud forest, 1800–3100 m. and the low mossy woods with twisted trees found at higher elevations. Usually alone, forages in the upper branches of trees.

## SCALED FRUITEATER
*Ampelioides tschudii*
COME FRUTA TALABARTERO

Pl. 26

7.5″ (19 cm.). Crown, nape and sides of head glossy black, lores yellowish white;

nuchal collar lemon yellow, bordered black. Back black, the feathers broadly edged olive green giving a scaled appearance. Wings black, greater wing coverts broadly edged light olive forming a wing bar, outer remiges edged yellowish white, inner ones tipped olive. Tail coverts long, olive, subterminally black with yellow tip; tail black, tipped white. ♀: generally like ♂ but crown and sides of head green with small black spots.
Subtropical zone. Nw Zulia along the upper Río Negro; sw Táchira on Cerro El Teteo. [Colombia through the Andes to central Peru.]
Cloud forest, 1250–2000 m. Forages, usually alone, in the highest trees and canopy of the forest.

### DUSKY PURPLETUFT

*Iodopleura fusca*
COTINGUITA FUSCA

4.3″ (11 cm.). Above including wings and tail blackish, rump band white. Below smoky brown, center of belly and under tail coverts white. Long pectoral tufts violet. ♀: like ♂ but pectoral tufts white.
Tropical zone. Se Bolívar along the Río Icabarú, an affluent of the upper Río Caroní. [The Guianas.]
Rain forest, forest edge, second growth and clearings in the lowlands, to 500 m. on the slopes of the tepuis. A small dark bird with short bill and tail, difficult to see as it moves about quietly, alone or in pairs, feeding silently on small berries.

### WHITE-BROWED PURPLETUFT

*Iodopleura isabellae*
COTINGUITA FRENTE BLANCA

Pl. 27
4.3″ (11 cm.). Differs principally from Dusky Purpletuft in both sexes by white lores, white patch behind eye and at base of lower mandible.
Tropical zone. S Amazonas s of San Fernando de Atabapo (*isabellae*). [Se Colombia to Amazonian Brazil and n Bolivia.]
Same habits and habitat as Dusky Purpletuft.

### SCREAMING PIHA

*Lipaugus vociferans*
MINERO

Pl. 26
9″ (23 cm.). Gray, paler and somewhat tinged brownish below. Wings and tail brownish gray. Tail rather long, 4.5″ (11.4 cm.).
Tropical zone. Se Sucre at Guanoco; Delta Amacuro and rather generally in Amazonas and Bolívar (*vociferans*). [The Guianas, Colombia and Brazil to n Bolivia.]
Quite common in lowland rain forest from sea level, rarely to 1400 m. on the slopes of the tepuis. Solitary and thrushlike. Its startlingly loud penetrating cry "pee-pe-yó," preceded by a gurgling note (only heard if the bird is nearby) is an extraordinary forest sound. More often heard than seen because of this far-carrying, explosive, call, it is, however, not infrequently discovered perching quietly on an exposed branch in the middle or upper tier of forest trees.

### ROSE-COLLARED PIHA

*Lipaugus streptophorus*
MINERO COLLAR ROSADO

Pl. 26
8.5″ (22 cm.). Dark gray above, pale gray below; a broad rosy pink collar across upper breast, continued as a narrow nuchal collar across hindneck. Under tail coverts rosy pink. Wings and tail black edged gray. ♀: lacks the pink collar; under tail coverts rufous instead of pink.
Subtropical zone. S Bolívar on Cerros Ptari-tepui, Aprada-tepui, Acopán-tepui, Roraima and Uei-tepui. [Adj. Guyana and adj. Brazil.]
Endemic to Pantepui. Dense, high cloud forest on the slopes of the tepuis, 1000–1800 m. Solitary, quiet and inconspicuous. Its song is soft and subdued in contrast to the explosive notes of the Screaming Piha.

### WHITE-NAPED XENOPSARIS

*Xenopsaris albinucha*
XENOPSARIS NUCA BLANCA

Pl. 27
5″ (13 cm.). Crown glossy blue black, forehead, lores and spot on nape white.

Back gray; underparts white. Wings and tail brown. Wing coverts and inner remiges margined white. ♀: similar to ♂ but feathers of crown with brownish edges.

Tropical zone. W Apure, ne Lara and along the s bank of the Orinoco in Bolívar (*minor*). [N Bolivia, n Argentina, Paraguay. E Brazil in Ceará, Piauí and Bahia.]

Deciduous forest in the lowlands near sea level, thickets, pastures, reedbeds and the sedge of riverbanks.

Note: Placed in the Tyrannidae in Lista Av. Venez.

## GREEN-BACKED BECARD
*Pachyramphus viridis*
CABEZÓN GARGANTIGRÍS

Pl. 27
5.5" (14 cm.). Crown and nape black, lores white. Back light olive green. Throat and cheeks light gray, breast lemon yellow, rest of underparts white. Primaries black, inner remiges and wing coverts black margined olive green. Tail much rounded, olive gray. ♀: like ♂, but crown like back instead of black.

Tropical zone. E Bolívar in the Sierra de Imataca and from Cerro Ptari-tepui to Cerro Roraima in the Gran Sabana (*griseigularis*). [Guyana; e Ecuador to e Bolivia, n Argentina and e and s Brazil.]

High rain forest at 450 m. on the Sierra de Imataca ascending to 1000 m. on the slopes of the tepuis. Solitary, forages in the treetops.

## BARRED BECARD
*Pachyramphus versicolor*
CABEZÓN VETEADO

Pl. 27
5" (13 cm.). Above black, upper tail coverts gray. Wings black, inner remiges and wing coverts extensively margined with white. Lores, throat and sides of head pale yellowish green, breast white, these areas lightly barred black; center of abdomen pure white. Tail gray, tipped white. ♀: crown and nape dark gray, back olive. Below pale lemon yellow, lightly barred on throat and breast with black. Wing coverts and margins to secondaries chestnut, tertials margined buff. Tail brownish gray.

Subtropical zone. The Sierra de Perijá, Zulia, n Táchira, central Mérida (*versicolor*). [Costa Rica to n Bolivia.]

Mossy cloud forest, ravines and more open areas, 2000–2900 m. A chunky bird with a large head. Alone or in pairs in low bushes and the higher parts of trees. Actively hunts insects among the leaves and parasitic vegetation. Joins flocks of other birds. Call: a series of insistent "pee" sounds.

## CINEREOUS BECARD
*Pachyramphus rufus*
CABEZÓN CINÉREO

Pl. 27
5.3" (13.5 cm.). Crown and nape lustrous black, forehead and lores pure white. Back light gray. Throat, sides of neck, and rest of underparts whitish gray, under tail coverts white. Greater wing coverts black, middle coverts white on outer web; all but innermost remiges black, margined white; innermost remiges gray, conspicuously margined white. Middle and outermost tail feathers gray edged white, rest gray, black along shaft. ♀: rusty rufous above, darkest on crown. Throat and breast rusty buff, rest of underparts white, tinged buff. Wing coverts, inner remiges and tail like back; outer remiges black margined rusty rufous.

Tropical zone to 1300 m. From Zulia, Táchira and Apure e to Sucre and Delta Amacuro and along the s bank of the Orinoco in Bolívar e of Altagracia. [Panama, Colombia and the Guianas to ne Peru and Amazonian Brazil.]

Found in many types of vegetation from heavy forest to open fields, plantations, mangroves, low, dry bushes etc. Usually in pairs in the lower branches as well as in the crowns of trees. Feeds on berries and insects. Call: a low, bubbling trill like that of a small woodcreeper.

## CHESTNUT-CROWNED BECARD
*Pachyramphus castaneus*
CABEZÓN CASTAÑO

Pl. 27
5.5" (14 cm.). Center of crown chestnut, narrow supraloral streak white; lores, eyebrow continued around hindneck to form a nuchal collar gray. Back, inner

remiges and tail chestnut rufous. Underparts tawny buff. Outer remiges black narrowly edged chestnut rufous.
Tropical and subtropical zone. In the n from Falcón through Yaracuy and Aragua to n Monagas and Cerro Azul, Sucre (*intermedius*). Amazonas on Cerro Parú (*parui*). Bolívar near Santa Elena in the Gran Sabana (*saturatus*). [Se Colombia to n Bolivia, n Argentina and se Brazil.]
Humid and deciduous forest, clearings, open woods, scattered trees, dry vegetation and damp ravines, to 1700 m. In pairs and family groups from the middle tier to the treetops.

## CINNAMON BECARD

*Pachyramphus cinnamomeus*
CABEZÓN CANELO

Pl. 27
5.5″ (14 cm.). Cinnamon rufous above including closed wings and tail; primaries blackish brown, edged cinnamon rufous. Below buffy white, buffiest on breast (or back brownish cinnamon, breast cinnamon buff, belly ochraceous buff, a).
Tropical zone to 1200 m. Zulia in the L. Maracaibo region, n Táchira, n Mérida (*magdalenae*). Extreme s Táchira (*badius*, a). [N and w Colombia, nw Ecuador.]
Rain forest and second growth, in more open areas and the edge of woods in the lowlands and the lower slopes of the mountains. This large-headed, thickbilled bird is found alone or in small, scattered groups in low bushes and also high in trees. Calls: many different calls, from thin squeaks to a soft, wistful 2-note whistle repeated a few times.

## WHITE-WINGED BECARD

*Pachyramphus polychopterus*
CABEZÓN ALIBLANCO

Pl. 27
5.5″ (14 cm.). Crown lustrous blue black, back shiny black, rump and underparts dark gray (or all black both above and below, a). Wings and tail black, wing coverts and inner remiges broadly edged white, tail broadly tipped white. ♀: crown grayish, back brownish gray (or olive brown above, a); below pale yellow. Wing coverts and outer remiges edged cinnamon, inner remiges edged white (or edged cinnamon, a). Central tail feathers like back, rest mostly black, tipped and edged pale cinnamon (or central tail feathers darker than back, rest mostly black broadly tipped and edged bright cinnamon, a).
Tropical and casually subtropical zone. Throughout in suitable localities except for Duida region (*tristis*). Amazonas in the Cerro Duida region (*niger*, a). [Guatemala to Bolivia, n Argentina and Uruguay. Trinidad, Tobago.]
Forest and forest border, second growth, plantations, mangroves, clearings, isolated trees in humid or dry localities, to 1900 m. Alone or in pairs, it forages in hops from the lowest bushes to the treetops. Feeds on fruit and insects. Call: a plaintive series of "chus" descending in pitch, which could be taken for that of a trogon.

## BLACK-CAPPED BECARD

*Pachyramphus marginatus*
CABEZÓN DE CACHUCHA NEGRA

Pl. 27
5.2″ (13 cm.). Crown and nape lustrous blue black, back mixed dark gray and black, rump and tail coverts blue gray. Lores, sides of head and neck and underparts pale gray, almost white on abdomen. Wings and tail black, wing coverts and inner remiges broadly edged white, outer tail feathers broadly tipped white. ♀: crown chestnut, lores gray, back olive green, central tail feathers grayish brown, with a black subterminal patch and narrow cinnamon tip, rest mostly black broadly tipped cinnamon. Underparts pale yellow clouded with olive. Wings black, wing coverts and inner remiges broadly edged cinnamon.
Tropical zone. The mountains of Carabobo; Amazonas s to Caño Casiquiare and the Río Negro; e across Bolívar to the Sierra de Imataca and the Gran Sabana (*nanus*). [The Guianas; e Colombia to Bolivia and Amazonian and e Brazil.]
Forests in the lowlands and lower mountain slopes, to 1000 m. Forages alone or in pairs from the low to the middle tier of trees and forest edge.

## BLACK-AND-WHITE BECARD
*Pachyramphus albogriseus*
CABEZÓN BLANCO Y NEGRO

Pl. 27
5″ (13 cm.). Differs principally from Black-capped Becard by clear gray back, gray central tail feathers and much smaller white tips to rectrices. ♀: differs from Black-capped Becard by having the crown margined laterally with black, lores whiter, underparts clearer yellow and paler cinnamon tips to tail feathers.
Upper tropical and subtropical zones. The Sierra de Perijá, Zulia (*coronatus*). The Andes of Táchira, Mérida and Lara e along the coastal Cordillera through Carabobo, Aragua and the Distr. Federal to Sucre (*albogriseus*). [Nicaragua to n Peru.]
Open forest and clearings in not very humid areas, 1200–2200 m. Alone or in pairs in the middle part of trees. Joins moving parties of mixed birds.

## ONE-COLORED BECARD
*Platypsaris homochrous*
PICO GRUESO GRIS

6.5″ (16.5 cm.). Crown sooty gray, back gray, wings and tail black. Underparts light gray, palest on abdomen. ♀: upperparts, wings and tail rufous. Throat, breast and under tail coverts cinnamon buff, center of abdomen white, tinged buff. Resembles a rufous *Pachyramphus* but is considerably larger with a much larger bill.
Tropical zone. L. Maracaibo region, Zulia (*canescens*). [E Panama to nw Peru.]
Thick forest and open woods in the lowlands to about 500 m. on the slopes of the Sierra de Perijá. Often in pairs, this quiet and silent bird of the treetops is difficult to spot.

## PINK-THROATED BECARD
*Platypsaris minor*
PICO GRUESO GARGANTIRROSADO

Pl. 27
6.5″ (16.5 cm.). Upperparts, wings and tail black; below dark gray, lower throat magenta pink. ♀: crown and nape gray tinged rufous, back gray more strongly tinged rufous and becoming bright rufous on rump and upper tail coverts.

Wings and tail bright rufous. Sides of head and neck rufous, rest of underparts cinnamon buff.
Tropical zone. E Amazonas e to the Caura Valley, Bolívar. [The Guianas, e Colombia to n Bolivia and Amazonian Brazil.]
Rain forest in the lowlands of Pantepui from 100 to 800 m. on the slopes of the tepuis. Clearings, forest borders and shrubbery near rivers. Feeds on berries and insects. Calls: include one described as a series of thin, tinkling, musical, notes.

## BLACK-TAILED TITYRA
*Tityra cayana*
BACACO BENEDICTINO

Pl. 27
8″ (20.3 cm.). Pale silvery gray. Top and sides of head, wings and tail black, inner remiges silvery gray. Bare facial skin and basal part of bill pink, tip of bill black. ♀: like ♂ but black portions of plumage tinged brownish; back narrowly and underparts broadly streaked black. Face and bill as in ♂.
Tropical zone, throughout (*cayana*). [The Guianas. E Colombia to Bolivia, Paraguay and ne Argentina. Brazil.]
From sea level to 1100 m. In a wide variety of forested areas from clearings in high rain forest to open deciduous woods, plantations and savannas with scattered and isolated live or dead trees. Always in the upper half of the trees conspicuously feeding on berries and fruit, often in pairs. An audible wing-clapping when it takes off. Calls: a froglike croak; a weak, toneless, rattling note.

## MASKED TITYRA
*Tityra semifasciata*
BACACO DE ANTIFAZ

Pl. 27
9″ (23 cm.). Differs from Black-tailed Tityra by black of head restricted to forecrown, ocular region and chin. Tail basally white, distally black, broadly tipped white. Facial skin and base of bill purplish red, tip of bill leaden blue. ♀: top and sides of head smoky brown, back paler becoming gray on rump. Below white. Wings and tail as in ♂.
Tropical and lower subtropical zones. The

Sierra de Perijá, Zulia, s to n Táchira and e through Mérida, Yaracuy, Carabobo, Aragua and Miranda to the Distr. Federal (*columbiana*). [Mid. Amer. to w Ecuador, the Guianas and Amazonian Brazil to n and e Bolivia.]

Sparsely forested areas, seldom below 500 m., ascending to 1800 m. Open woods, forest edge, scattered, tall, dead trees. Singly or in small flocks feeds quietly on berries and fruit in the upper half of trees to treetops. A heavy-looking bird, it perches silently for minutes at a time. Calls: buzzy notes compared to the grunting of a pig or croaking of a small frog.

### BLACK-CROWNED TITYRA

*Tityra inquisitor*
BACACO PEQUEÑO

Pl. 27

7″ (18 cm.). Differs from Black-tailed Tityra principally by black of head not reaching nape and by *all black bill*. Flashes white patch on underside of wing. ♀: forehead rusty white, crown black, sides of head rufous. Back, wings and tail as in Black-tailed Tityra. Below white, tinged gray on breast.

Tropical zone. From Zulia e to Guárico and Sucre and s to the llanos of Apure, nw Amazonas and the lower Ríos Caura, Paragua and upper Cuyuni, Bolívar (*erythrogenys*). [The Guianas and Colombia to n Bolivia, Paraguay, ne Argentina and se Brazil. Mid. Amer.]

Wooded areas in the lowlands to 1200 m. Similar in habits and habitat to Masked Tityra except that it keeps lower in the trees.

### PURPLE-THROATED FRUITCROW

*Querula purpurata*
PÁJARO TORO

Pl. 25

10″ (25 cm.). Black; throat and upper breast crimson. Bill slate blue. ♀: all black. Bill slate blue.

Tropical zone. N Bolívar from the lower Ríos Caura and Paragua to the Sierra de Imataca and the Río Cuyuni. [The Guianas and e Colombia to e and w Ecuador, Amazonian Brazil and n Bolivia.]

Rain forest in humid lowlands to 500 m.

Forest borders, scattered trees, plantations, seldom well inside the forest. It frequents medium heights of trees to the canopy of the tallest trees in pairs or small, noisy groups. Bold, it may sit exposed to view, but is often heard before being seen. The flight consists of glides and small dips. Feeds on berries, fruits and large insects. Responds to an imitation of its calls, which include harsh quacking sounds, a series of cooings, a nasal "awow." Called *Mae de Tucano* in ne Brazil because it is said to accompany toucans.

### RED-RUFFED FRUITCROW

*Pyroderus scutatus*
PÁJARO TORERO

Pl. 25

15″ (38 cm.). Glossy black above including wings and tail. Throat, breast and sides of neck orange, the feathers crimped and tipped crimson. Lower breast and belly black, spots on lower breast and the under wing coverts rufous brown (or lower breast and belly virtually solid rufous brown, a).

Subtropical zone in the Sierra de Perijá, Zulia, and the Andes of Táchira e through Mérida, Barinas, Yaracuy, Carabobo and Aragua to the Distr. Federal (*granadensis*). Tropical zone in ne Bolívar on the Sierra de Imataca and along the Río Cuyuni (*orenocensis*, a). [Guyana and Colombia to w Ecuador, central Peru, Paraguay, ne Argentina and se Brazil.]

N of the Orinoco in cloud forest, 1200–1900 m. s of the river in high rain forest, 50–500 m. Clearings and savannas with scattered trees near forest. Alone or in pairs in the highest part of the trees, sometimes in the middle branches of scattered trees. Feeds on fruit. Call: emits a deep, booming, hollow sound resembling the bellowing of a bull.

### AMAZONIAN UMBRELLABIRD

*Cephalopterus ornatus*
PÁJARO PARAGUAS

Pl. 25

18″ (46 cm.). Black. Feathers of forecrown upstanding forming a tall crest of hairlike feathers with white shafts. Feathers of mantle edged metallic steel blue. Lower throat adorned by a tri-angular wattle covered in front by shiny steel blue feathers. ♀: similar but crest much smaller; general color duller and less glossy; no wattle.

Tropical zone. Nw Bolívar opposite the mouth of the Meta; Amazonas s to the lower Río Ventuari (*ornatus*). [Guyana, e Colombia to Amazonian Brazil and n Bolivia.]

Rain forest to 200 m. Near rivers and on islands in big rivers. In spite of its large size difficult to see because it usually keeps to the very tops of the highest trees. Occasionally flies high over open terrain, clearings and rivers. Feeds on fruits and large insects.

## CAPUCHINBIRD

*Perissocephalus tricolor*
PÁJARO CAPUCHINO

Pl. 25

14″ (36 cm.). Crown and sides of head bare, dark blue gray; upper mantle cinnamon brown, darkening to reddish brown on lower back. Throat and upper breast cinnamon brown brightening to chestnut rufous on rest of underparts. Wings dusky brown, under wing coverts white. Tail and upper tail coverts black.

Tropical zone. S Amazonas from the Yavita-Pimichín Trail s. E Bolívar from the Sierra de Imataca to the Gran Sabana and Cerro Guaiquinima. [The Guianas; n Amazonian Brazil.]

Rain forest in the lowlands of Pantepui from 150 m., ascending the slopes of the tepuis, but rarely to 1400 m. A locally abundant forest species found in small groups near the treetops where they perch in pairs sitting close together. Often found near rivers and in flooded forest. Feeds on berries, fruits, palm nuts and insects. The far-sounding call, a long, drawn-out, loud "woooo" has been compared to the lowing of a cow or calf or the bellowing of an ox.

## BARE-NECKED FRUITCROW

*Gymnoderus foetidus*
PAVITA PESCUECIPELADA

Fig. 39

15″ (38 cm.). Neck bare, dark slaty blue, sprinkled with a few short, plushy feathers. Crown, chin and subocular

Fig. 39. BARE-NECKED FRUITCROW
(male)

region covered with short, black, plush-like feathers. Back and underparts black with a powdery gray bloom. Inner wing coverts, inner remiges, and basal part of outer web of primaries silvery gray. Tail black. ♀: differs chiefly from ♂ by plain wings, like rest of plumage, and general plumage grayer, particularly on abdomen.

Tropical zone. Extreme nw Bolívar (Bachaco I.) s through w and central Amazonas. [The Guianas, Colombia to n Bolivia and Amazonian Brazil.]

Rain forest, second growth and clearings in the lowlands at about 150 m. In pairs and small flocks it keeps to the thick foliage of the treetops. Runs over thick branches like a rail. Feeds on berries, fruits and insects.

## WHITE BELLBIRD

*Procnias alba*
PÁJARO CAMPANERO

Fig. 40

11″ (28 cm.). White; a long (3″, 7.6 cm.) thin, black wattle hanging over bill. Iris and bill black. ♀: olive green above, yellowish below heavily streaked olive. Inner remiges like back, outer ones dusky brown; tail dusky brown, outer webs of feathers olive. No wattle.

Tropical zone. E Bolívar from the Sierra de Imataca to the Gran Sabana. [Trinidad. The Guianas; n Brazil in the Rio Negro region.]

High rain forest on the slopes of the tepuis and other highlands between 450 and 1100 m. The males perch in the tree-tops, often on conspicuous dead branches. The females, with plumage that merges with the foliage, flit about silently lower down in the trees. They feed on berries and fruits. From the tops of very tall trees ♂ utters a very loud, penetrating, clear metallic cry, which sounds like the clanging of a medium-pitched bell.

## BEARDED BELLBIRD
*Procnias averano*
CAMPANERO HERRERO

Pl. 26

10″ (25 cm.). Crown, ear coverts and nape snuff brown; body plumage light silvery gray, tail whiter, wings black. Throat bare, adorned with many short, thread-like wattles, forming a sort of beard. ♀: crown dusky green; back, wings and tail yellowish olive; below pale yellow, streaked olive. No wattles.

Tropical and subtropical zones. Forested portions from nw Zulia, Falcón, Lara and Yaracuy to n Carabobo and Aragua, the coastal Cordillera in Sucre; s Bolívar from the Gran Sabana to the Brazilian border and in the upper Río Caura region; extreme se Amazonas (*carnobarba*). [Guyana, ne Colombia. Ne Brazil. Trinidad.]

Fig. 40. WHITE BELLBIRD (male)

In the n inhabits forests from 360 m. to cloud forests at 1600 m., s of the Orinoco found on the foothills of the tepuis from 700 to 1500 m., usually in the highest branches of tall trees, but sometimes in lower trees. A shy bird, often alone or in pairs. Flight consists of a series of wing beats followed by a short glide. Feeds on fruit. Call: loud, penetrating and metallic sounding like a cracked anvil being repeatedly struck with a hammer. ♀: reported to be silent.

## GUIANAN RED-COTINGA

*Phoenicircus carnifex*
COTINGA ROJA

Pl. 25
8″ (20 cm.). Somewhat crested; feathers of crown silky, crimson; short streak behind eye and eye ring black. Back dusky maroon, rump and tail rosy carmine, tail tipped maroon. Throat and breast maroon red, rest of underparts rosy carmine. Inner remiges brown, wing coverts edged dusky maroon. ♀: crown and tail dull red, back and wings dull olive. Throat and upper breast olive streaked red, rest of underparts pinkish red.
Tropical zone. Ne Bolívar along the upper Río Cuyuni. [The Guianas, n and central Amazonian Brazil.]
High rain forest in the lowlands to about 300 m. Solitary or in pairs; feeds on berries and fruits, especially of *Ficus*.

## BLACK-NECKED RED-COTINGA

*Phoenicircus nigricollis*
COTINGA ROJA PESCUECINEGRA

9″ (23 cm.). Somewhat crested, feathers of crown silky, scarlet. Back, wings, throat and sides of neck velvety black; rump and rest of plumage scarlet, tail tipped black. ♀: crown and tail dull red, back and throat olive, rest of underparts rosy carmine.
Tropical zone. Amazonas along the Río Negro. [Se Colombia to ne Peru; Amazonian Brazil e to the Rios Negro and Xingú.]
Habits as in Guianan Red-Cotinga.

# COCKS-OF-THE-ROCK: Rupicolidae

GALLITOS DE LAS ROCAS

This family contains but two species, both of which are found in Venezuela. The Andean species is found only in Táchira and lives in rocky mountain ravines, where it attaches its mud nests to rock faces. The other, widespread s of the Orinoco, is remarkable for clearing areas on which males dance and display during the breeding season. It also builds mud nests which are placed in caves. Cocks-of-the-Rock live on fruit and insects.

## GUIANAN COCK-OF-THE-ROCK

*Rupicola rupicola*
GALLITO DE LAS ROCAS

Pl. 25
13″ (33 cm.). Bright orange. Strongly compressed, orange, fanshaped crest, springing from before eye, falling forward over bill, crest narrowly bordered dark crimson. Wings brownish black, outer webs of inner remiges ending in long orange filaments, inner remiges very broad, pale-tipped, wing speculum white. Tail basally orange, distally dark brown, tipped pale orange. ♀: dark olive gray, crest very small, outer webs of inner remiges filamentous.
Tropical and subtropical zones. Widespread s of the Orinoco in Amazonas and across Bolívar to the upper Río Cuyuni, the Gran Sabana and Cerro Paurai-tepui. [The Guianas, extreme e Colombia, Brazil n of the Amazon.]
High, dense forest and second growth in the lowlands of Pantepui to 2000 m. on low hills and slopes of the tepuis. Widely but spottily distributed; found locally in humid shady ravines with rock outcroppings or large boulders and cliffs near swiftly flowing water.
  In the breeding season groups congregate on or near the ground for courtship display. The females stay in low, nearby branches. Feeds in treetops.

Voice: an unmusical, explosive "wong" and a cawing squawk. The nest of mud and vegetable fibers is attached to a vertical rockface in grottos or under overhanging rocks.

### ANDEAN COCK-OF-THE-ROCK
*Rupicola peruviana*
GALLITO DE LAS SIERRAS

15" (38 cm.). Bright orange. Bushy orange crest springing from before eye and falling forward to cover bill. Wings and tail deep black, inner remiges very broad, gray. ♀: head with small crest; plumage cinnamon brown, gradually turning to orange brown on breast, belly and back. Wings and tail brown.

Upper tropical zone. Known in Venezuela only from San Cristobal, w Táchira (*aequatorialis*). [The Andes from Colombia to Bolivia.]

Heavy, humid cloud forest and second growth near rivers and streams with rocky gorges and precipitous ravines, at about 1000 m. Feeds on fruit and insects, foraging in the trees from the lowest branches to treetops. Nests in rocky ravines covered with moss-hung forest, often in niches behind waterfalls.

# MANAKINS: Pipridae

## SALTARINES

Manakins are rather well represented in Venezuela, about half of the known species being found within its borders.

Manakins for the most part inhabit thick lowland forest and the males of many species are brightly colored. These small birds are remarkable for their dances and displays, accompanied by curious snapping and rasping noises, very loud for their size, produced in some species by the curiously modified wing feathers or by the bill. Manakins feed on fruit and insects. Females usually differ from males, and because many of them are plain green they are difficult to tell apart.

### GOLDEN-HEADED MANAKIN
*Pipra erythrocephala*
SALTARÍN CABECIDORADO

Pl. 24
3.5" (9 cm.). Shiny blue black. Top and sides of head *golden yellow*. Thighs scarlet. Iris white. ♀: upperparts, throat and breast olive, belly pale dull yellowish. Iris gray; legs flesh; bill black above, flesh below.

Tropical and subtropical zones. In wooded areas throughout (*erythrocephala*). [Colombia to ne Peru, n Bolivia and Brazil n of the Amazon. E Panama; The Guianas; Trinidad.]

Rain and cloud forests and second growth n of the Orinoco to 1700 m.; s of it to 1100 m., rarely to 2000 m. Small forest clearings. Forages in the undergrowth to medium heights in trees, sometimes in treetops. Alone or in small groups of males. Not timid. Responds to an imitation of its loud, squeaky, buzzing call. Displays in groups up to a dozen, about 10 m. from the ground. Appears to jump and slide along perch with raised wings.

### SCARLET-HORNED MANAKIN
*Pipra cornuta*
SALTARÍN ENCOPETADO

Pl. 24
4.6" (11.7 cm.). Shiny blue black. Whole head, long, bilobed crest and thighs scarlet. Tail comparatively long. ♀: upperparts dull olive. Below grayish olive, lighter than back. Thighs olive yellow.

Upper tropical and subtropical zones. Amazonas from Cerros Yaví and Paraque southward; Bolívar from the upper Río Cuchivero and Río Caura e to the Sierra de Lema and the Gran Sabana to Cerro Uei-tepui on the Brazilian border. [Guyana, adj. Brazil s to Óbidos.]

Rain forest in the Pantepui area on the slopes of the tepuis, 500–1800 m. Alone or in small groups in the lower bushes or small trees. Very confiding, curious, active.

Note: Called *Ceratopipra cornuta* in Lista Av. Venez.

## WHITE-CROWNED MANAKIN
*Pipra pipra*
SALTARÍN CABECIBLANCO

Pl. 24
3.5″ (9 cm.). Shiny blue black. Crown and nape *snowy white*. ♀: crown grayish green, back dull olive green (or bright olive green, a). Throat and breast gray, tinged green on breast, belly whitish (or bright yellowish olive, center of belly yellower, a).
Upper tropical and lower subtropical zones. The Sierra de Perijá, Zulia, to s Táchira (*coracina*, a). Amazonas from Caño Cataniapo s and e across Bolívar to the Gran Sabana, the Sierra de Imataca and Delta Amacuro (*pipra*). [Costa Rica to n Colombia and generally e of the Andes to e Peru and se Brazil.]
Forest and second growth in the mountains n of the Orinoco, 1200–1600 m.; from sea level in the Orinoco delta to 900 m. on the slopes of the tepuis. Alone or in family groups, forages in the lower or middle part of trees.

## BLUE-CROWNED MANAKIN
*Pipra coronata*
SALTARÍN CORONA AZUL

Pl. 24
3.8″ (9.7 cm.). Dull black with a slight blue tinge on rump. Crown bright cobalt blue. ♀: upperparts and breast bright green. Throat grayish olive, center of belly pale yellow.
Tropical zone. Amazonas from Caño Cuao s and e across Bolívar from the upper Río Cuchivero to the Gran Sabana and Cerro Paurai-tepui (*carbonata*). [Colombia to w Ecuador, w and central Brazil, n Bolivia.]
High, dense rain forest and second growth in the lowlands of Pantepui from 100 m. to 1200 m. on the slopes of the tepuis. In the lower trees, bushes and undergrowth; plucks insects from the foliage or in the air. Joins mixed flocks of birds following army ants. Congregates in courtship groups in low undergrowth, flitting back and forth silently. Call: a rattling trill, also a loud, harsh "kwek" and a low "prrr."

## WHITE-FRONTED MANAKIN
*Pipra serena*
SALTARÍN FRENTIBLANCO

Pl. 24
3.8″ (9.7 cm.). Upperparts velvety black, forecrown *silvery white*. Upper tail coverts bright blue. Throat and breast black, patch in center of breast orange yellow, belly bright yellow. ♀: above bright bluish green. Throat whitish, breast olive with a suggestion of a yellow patch in center, rest of underparts yellow.
Upper tropical and subtropical zones. S Amazonas from Cerro Duida s; nw Bolívar along the Ríos Cuchivero and lower Caura, in the se on the Sierra de Lema and the Gran Sabana s to Cerro Uei-tepui (*suavissima*). [The Guianas, n Brazil from Roraima e to Amapá.]
Rain forest and forest edge in the Pantepui area, on the slopes of the tepuis to 1800 m., not reported below 500 m. Forages in low bushes. Not shy; solitary or in small groups. Responds to an imitation of its squeak.

## CRIMSON-HOODED MANAKIN
*Pipra aureola*
SALTARÍN CABECIANARANJADO

Pl. 24
4.2″ (10.7 cm.). Crown, nape and *upper mantle crimson scarlet,* back velvety black; wings and tail black, wings with a broad basal white band formed by a white patch on inner webs of feathers. Forehead, lores and throat orange, the feathers of throat tipped scarlet and merging into scarlet of breast and center of belly, sides mixed gray and black. ♀: upperparts, wings and tail dull olive. Below paler with a variable amount of orange wash on throat, center of breast and belly.
Tropical zone. Central and s Sucre, e Monagas and Delta Amacuro; se Bolívar near Cerro Roraima (*aureola*). [The Guianas, central and e Amazonian Brazil.]
High, dense, swampy forest and open woodland, in the thick undergrowth mostly in the lowlands in wet places near sea level, seldom to 1200 m. In one display, the bird slides from side to side on a low perch, vibrating its body. Call: a plaintive "peeewww."

## WIRE-TAILED MANAKIN

*Teleonema filicauda*
SALTARÍN COLA DE HILO

Pl. 24
4.5" (11.5 cm.). Very like Crimson-hooded Manakin differing mainly by the tail feathers ending in long filaments (2", 5 cm.). ♀: upperparts, sides of head and wings olive, throat and breast olive, paler than upperparts, belly yellow, tail olive, feathers ending in *long filaments*. Probably better placed in the genus *Pipra*.
Tropical zone. From w Zulia, Táchira and w Barinas e through Mérida, Portuguesa and Lara to Yaracuy and along the coastal Cordillera in Carabobo, Aragua and Miranda; s of the Orinoco in Amazonas s of the Río Ventuari. [E Colombia to ne Peru and w Amazonian Brazil.]
Rain forest, to 1000 m. n of the Orinoco, to about 300 m. s of it. Prefers humid areas, cocoa plantations and edges of clearings. Forages alone from the middle to the tops of trees.

## LANCE-TAILED MANAKIN

*Chiroxiphia lanceolata*
SALTARÍN COLA DE LANZA

Pl. 24
5.5" (14 cm.). Crown crimson, back and sides of head black. *Back light blue,* rump grayish, wings and tail black, central feathers *prolonged* and pointed. Below grayish black, grayest on sides. ♀: olive above including wings and tail, tail pointed as in ♂, below light grayish olive fading to yellowish white in center of abdomen.
Tropical and lower subtropical zones. Virtually throughout n of the Orinoco (not reported from Apure, Barinas, Monagas nor Delta Amacuro); Margarita I. [Costa Rica to n Colombia.]
Forests at sea level on the mainland, to 800 m. on Margarita I., and at 1700 m. on the Sierra de Aroa, Yaracuy. Dry and more humid woods, second growth, open woodland, scrub, cocoa plantations. Alone or in groups up to 12. Displays actively, leaping from branch to branch. Call: a musical "beni-taro-taro-taro," which is responsible for its local name, *Benitaro,* in Anzoátegui.

## BLUE-BACKED MANAKIN

*Chiroxiphia pareola*
SALTARÍN LOMO AZUL

4" (10 cm.). Differs from Lance-tailed Manakin by black forehead, pure black underparts and square instead of pointed tail. ♀: upperparts, wings and tail green, less olive and belly yellower than in Lance-tail.
Tropical zone. N Bolívar from the lower Río Paragua e to the Sierra de Imataca (*pareola*). [The Guianas and Colombia to n Bolivia and Brazil. Tobago.]
Rain forest and second growth in the lowlands to 500 m. Forages in low bushes, often near streams, in pairs or small flocks. A lively, agile and active bird, its dance consists of 2 birds each jumping repeatedly in an arc over the other's back. Calls: a low, melodious whistle and a froglike, repeated "arrr."

## GOLDEN-WINGED MANAKIN

*Masius chrysopterus*
SALTARÍN ALIDORADO

Pl. 24
4.3" (11 cm.). Velvety black, forecrown golden yellow, the feathers forming a crest which curves forward, the yellow turning abruptly to orange on hindcrown where it forms a narrow recumbent crest of rather stiff feathers. *Inner webs of remiges canary yellow,* tipped black. Center of throat pale yellow expanding to form a patch on upper breast. ♀: upperparts, wings and tail, sides of head and neck and band across breast olive. Center of throat and upper breast pale yellow, sharply defined, rest of underparts yellowish olive.
Upper tropical and subtropical zones. S Táchira, s Barinas, s Trujillo and sw Lara (*chrysopterus*). [Colombia, e and w Ecuador, ne Peru.]
Cloud forest and open second growth in the mountains, 100–1800 m. Forages in the lower parts of trees.

## WHITE-THROATED MANAKIN

*Corapipo gutturalis*
SALTARÍN GARGANTIBLANCO

Pl. 24
3.5" (9 cm.). Upperparts including wings and tail shining blue black. Lores and sides of head and neck velvety black.

Throat white, carried down in a point to upper breast, rest of underparts blue black. ♀: throat and belly white, band across breast and sides of body light olive. Upperparts, wings and tail bright olive.

Tropical zone. Central Amazonas on Cerro Marahuaca; w Bolívar from the upper Río Cuchivero and extreme upper Caura e across the upper Río Paragua to the Gran Sabana and upper Cuyuni. [The Guianas, n Brazil in Roraima and Amapá.]

Rain forest in the lowlands of Pantepui above 250 m., on the slopes of the tepuis to 1100 m. Forages alone or in groups from the lower to the middle height of trees. Descends to mossy logs on the ground to display.

## WHITE-RUFFED MANAKIN

*Corapipo leucorrhoa*
SALTARÍN BUCHIBLANCO

3.5″ (9 cm.). Much like White-throated Manakin but white of throat squared off instead of pointed on upper breast; cheeks and sides of throat white, the feathers silky and lengthened to form a ruff. ♀: much yellower below than White-throated Manakin. Throat gray; breast and sides of body olive becoming pale yellow on central underparts.

Tropical zone. Nw Zulia in the Sierra de Perijá, s Táchira, the n foothills of the Andes of Mérida and the s slopes in Barinas (*leucorrhoa*). [Honduras to central and ne Colombia.]

Dense and open rain forest, second growth and clearings with scattered trees, sea level to 1200 m. Forages, usually in small parties, in the lower and middle part of trees. Restlessly active, it flits about plucking insects from foliage, often on the wing. Call: high, thin, weak notes, "seee." Displays on a log, crawling slowly with wings spread.

## WHITE-BEARDED MANAKIN

*Manacus manacus*
SALTARÍN MARAQUERO

Pl. 24
4.5″ (11.5 cm.). Crown, mantle, wings and tail black, rump and upper tail coverts dark gray. Broad collar across mantle and the underparts white, becoming pale grayish on belly, darker gray on thighs and under tail coverts. The intensity of the gray shading varies with the races. ♀: above olive; throat grayish, breast olive, belly whitish tinged green.

Tropical zone. N of the Orinoco from the Sierra de Perijá, Zulia, s to Táchira, Barinas and Apure; s of the Orinoco in n Amazonas e across Bolívar to the Río Paragua and the Río Icabarú in the se (*interior*). Central Amazonas on Cerro Yapacana on the lower Río Ventuari and the Río Asisa (*umbrosus*); s Amazonas along Caño Casiquiare (*manacus*). [Colombia and the Guianas to s Brazil, n Bolivia, Paraguay and ne Argentina. Trinidad.]

Humid and arid forests in the lowlands, from near sea level to 750 m. n of the Orinoco, to 960 m. on the tepuis. Undergrowth of dense and open woods and forest edge. Forages in the foliage at medium height. Solitary or in flocks of more than 20. Call: one sounds like humming noise. Gathers in groups to perform an elaborate courtship dance in which it leaps back and forth, close to the ground, always landing facing the previous perch. This performance has been likened to a fireworks display because of the sharp, dry, rough "cracks" mechanically produced by the wings, and sounding like the breaking of sticks.

## FIERY-CAPPED MANAKIN

*Machaeropterus pyrocephalus*
SALTARÍN CABECIENCENDIDO

Pl. 24
3.5″ (9 cm.). Crown yellow with a golden brown stripe down center, becoming red posteriorly. Ear coverts, shoulders and outer web of secondaries olive green, tertials gray with a black spot toward tip. Underparts pinkish white broadly streaked rosy violet. Under wing coverts white. Iris orange red. ♀: underparts, wings and tail bright olive green, under wing coverts white. Throat grayish, breast yellowish olive, rest of underparts yellowish white. Iris reddish hazel.

Known only from La Prisión, lower Río Caura, n Bolívar (*pallidiceps*). [Brazil in Amapá and s of the Amazon in Pará, Goiás and Mato Grosso. E Peru, nw Bolivia.]

Undergrowth in high rain forest and second growth in the lowlands near sea level. In display the bird hangs upside down and rotates from side to side.

## STRIPED MANAKIN
*Machaeropterus regulus*
SALTARÍN RAYADO

Pl. 24
3.5″ (9 cm.). Crown crimson. Sides of head and neck, back and wings bright olive green (with upper tail coverts washed orange, a), inner webs of inner remiges white, showing as a small white spot on wing. Throat whitish, below chestnut, striped with white, breast with a few crimson streaks (or with a vivid yellow band across breast, a). Tail grayish. In the Fiery-capped Manakin and particularly in the Striped Manakin the shafts of the inner remiges and those of the rectrices are thick and stiffened, white in color. ♀: upperparts, wings and tail bright olive. Throat grayish, upper breast olivaceous, lower breast and belly yellowish indistinctly streaked rufescent on lower breast.
Tropical zone. Nw Zulia in the Sierra de Perijá s to Táchira and Barinas (*zulianus*). Mérida and El Vigía, s of L. Maracaibo (*obscurostriatus*). W Amazonas; se Bolívar and the headwaters of the Río Caroní (*aureopectus,* a). [Colombia, e Ecuador to e Peru, w and central Amazonian and se Brazil.]
Forests n of the Orinoco from 100 to 1200 m.; s of it from 300 m. ranging to 900 m. on the slopes of the tepuis. Usually alone in the lower trees. Produces a rattling sound with its wing feathers. Displays near the ground.

## BLACK MANAKIN
*Xenopipo atronitens*
SALTARÍN NEGRO

Pl. 24
5.5″ (14 cm.). Uniform glossy blue black, wings and tail brownish black, under wing coverts black. ♀: dark olive green above, head tinged grayish, paler, more yellowish below.
Tropical zone. Amazonas e across Bolívar to the Gran Sabana and the upper Río Caroní. [Guianas, ne Colombia, nw Brazil.]
Rain forest in the lowlands of Pantepui from 100 m. to 1200 m. on the slopes

of the tepuis. Alone and in small groups in low bushes near forest edge and the lower parts of large trees.

## OLIVE MANAKIN
*Chloropipo uniformis*
SALTARÍN UNIFORME

Pl. 24
5.3″ (13.5 cm.). More or less uniform olive, paler and grayer on belly, throat tinged grayish, *under wing coverts white.*
Upper tropical and subtropical zones. Amazonas on Cerros Duida and Paraque (*duidae*). S Bolívar from the upper Río Caura to the Gran Sabana and the Brazilian border (*uniformis*). [Guyana, adj. Brazil.]
Endemic to Pantepui. Forest on the slopes and summits of the tepuis, 800–2100 m. Lower branches of trees. Alone or in pairs; not shy.

## CINNAMON MANAKIN
*Neopipo cinnamomea*
SALTARÍN CANELO

Pl. 24
3.5″ (9 cm.). Crown, nape and upper mantle ashy gray becoming gradually browner and turning to bright cinnamon rufous on lower back, rump and tail. Crown stripe yellow, feathers tipped rufous. Remiges and upper wing coverts dusky, broadly edged cinnamon rufous. Throat buffy white, rest of underparts cinnamon. ♀: similar but crown stripe rufous.
Tropical zone. S Amazonas from Cerros Duida and Yapacana s (*cinnamomea*). [The Guianas, se Colombia to se Peru and w and central Amazonian Brazil.]
Rain forest in the lowlands to about 200 m.

## YELLOW-CROWNED MANAKIN
*Heterocercus flavivertex*
SALTARÍN GARGANTIPLATEADO

Pl. 24
5.7″ (14.5 cm.). Upperparts olive green, silky central crown stripe bright yellow, wings and tail grayish brown, tail rounded, outer feathers very narrow. Throat silvery white, the feathers at sides of throat silky, prolonged to form a ruff at sides of neck; lores and sides of head dark gray. Breast dark chestnut becom-

ing cinnamon on belly and under tail coverts. ♀: like ♂ but much duller, without crown stripe and tail normal.

Tropical zone in Amazonas. [Se Colombia; n Brazil.]

Rain forest and second growth to 300 m., frequently near rivers. Forages alone or in pairs in the lower part of trees.

## SAFFRON-CRESTED TYRANT-MANAKIN

*Neopelma chrysocephalum*
SALTARÍN CORONA DE ORO

Pl. 24
4.8″ (12 cm.). Ample, flat crest golden yellow, sides of crown and head olivaceous gray. Back, wings and tail dull olive, no wing bars. Throat whitish, breast grayish, rest of underparts light yellow. Iris orange.

Looks much like a flycatcher of the genus *Myiopagis,* but is distinguishable from the Yellow-crowned Elaenia (*M. flavivertex,* p. 277) with which it probably occurs in s Amazonas, by its plain, unbarred wings, and from the Greenish Elaenia (*M. viridicata,* p. 277) with which it probably occurs in Amazonas and Bolívar, by being considerably smaller, lacking eye ring or white supraloral streak.

Tropical zone. S Amazonas to the Brazilian border; s Bolívar from the headwaters of the Río Caura to the middle Río Paragua, the Gran Sabana and upper Río Caroní. [The Guianas. Se Colombia, nw Brazil.]

Rain forest and uncluttered second growth in the lowlands of Pantepui, and on the slopes of the tepuis to 700 m. In small trees in open undergrowth. Active, solitary. Captures insects on the wing like a flycatcher. Calls: include a nasal "twang."

## TINY TYRANT-MANAKIN

*Tyranneutes virescens*
SALTARÍN ACEITUNO

Pl. 24
3.1″ (7.9 cm.). Semi-concealed crown stripe yellow. Upperparts, wings and tail dull olive. Throat whitish, slightly streaked, breast grayish olive, rest of underparts yellowish white tinged olive. Tail short. ♀: similar but crown patch much smaller or wanting. Iris gray.

Tropical zone. E Bolívar from the Sierra de Imataca to the Gran Sabana. [Guyana, Surinam, n Brazil from the Rio Negro e.]

Forests at about 500 m. in low bushes. Call: utters a far-sounding, melodious, repeated whistle "chuckle-de-dee."

## DWARF TYRANT-MANAKIN

*Tyranneutes stolzmanni*
SALTARÍN ENANO

Pl. 24
3.1″ (7.9 cm.). Very similar to Tiny Tyrant-Manakin but without crown stripe, underparts slightly brighter olive, throat more conspicuously streaked and center of belly canary yellow instead of yellowish white. Iris straw color, white or grayish white.

Tropical zone. S of the Orinoco in Amazonas and Bolívar. [E Colombia through e Ecuador to n Bolivia and Amazonian Brazil.]

Rain forest in the lowlands, 100–300 m. Alone or in ♂ pairs. Forages in the lower parts of trees.

## WING-BARRED MANAKIN

*Piprites chloris*
SALTARÍN VERDE

Pl. 24
5.2″ (13 cm.). Forehead yellowish brown, eye ring yellowish white, forecrown (or whole crown, a) olive, hindcrown and nape gray (or only a poorly indicated gray nuchal collar, a), ear coverts and sides of neck gray. Back olive green. Wings blackish, *lesser coverts broadly edged olive yellow,* greater coverts broadly *edged yellowish white,* bend of wing yellow, tip of inner remiges yellowish white; tail blackish, tipped yellowish white. Throat and under tail coverts yellow, rest of underparts gray, white in center of belly (or throat and breast yellow tinged olive, belly bright yellow, a).

Tropical and subtropical zones. Sierra de Perijá, Zulia; s Táchira (*perijanus,* a). The coastal Cordillera in Carabobo; Sucre (Cerro Humo); n Amazonas s to Cerro Duida and Caño Casiquiare and across Bolívar to the Altiplanicie de Nuria the middle course of the Cuyuni, the Gran Sabana and Cerro Roraima (*chlorion*). S Amazonas on the Sierra Imerí at Salto de Huá (*tschudii,* a). [The Guianas, Colombia through e Ecuador to Bolivia, Paraguay and ne Argentina.] Forests in the lowlands to about 1500 m.; in the Sierra de Perijá recorded only in the subtropical zone to 2000 m. Forages, usually alone, from low branches to the treetops.

## GREATER MANAKIN
*Schiffornis major*
SALTARÍN MAYOR

Pl. 24
6″ (15 cm.). Crown and hindneck dark gray, sides of head paler, back olive brown, upperpart of rump bright, deep cinnamon rufous shading to cinnamon on upper tail coverts. Throat grayish olive, band across breast orange rufous, duller and browner on sides, belly and under tail coverts ochraceous buff. Wings blackish edged olive brown, wing coverts brownish, inner tertials light reddish brown. Tail cinnamon rufous.
Tropical zone. Amazonas from the Río Ventuari s (*duidae*). [W and central Amazonian Brazil, e Peru, n Bolivia.] Rain forest to about 200 m.

## THRUSH-LIKE MANAKIN
*Schiffornis turdinus*
SALTARÍN PARAULATA

Pl. 24
7″ (18 cm.). Upperparts including wings and tail olivaceous brown, crown brighter and more rufescent (or like back, a). Throat and breast olivaceous brown, belly somewhat paler and grayer (or hardly different, a; or throat and breast brownish, sharply defined from pale olive gray belly, b).
Tropical, occasionally subtropical zone. The nw from Zulia and Táchira to Aragua, Yaracuy and Barinas (*stenorhynchus,* b). N Amazonas s to the Brazilian border (*amazonus*). Bolívar throughout and in s Delta Amacuro (*olivaceus,* a). [Mexico to w Ecuador, the Guianas to n Bolivia, s Brazil.]
High rain forests in the lowlands of the Pantepui area frequently near rivers, and also in lower woodland and tall second growth and on the slopes of the tepuis to 1800 m. Not shy, quiet, inconspicuous and solitary, it forages cautiously for insects in the low trees and undergrowth, often close to the ground. Call: a sweet, melodious, 3-note whistle.

# TYRANT-FLYCATCHERS: Tyrannidae

ATRAPAMOSCAS

This enormous family, comprising 384 species, is found from Alaska to Tierra del Fuego. No less than 315 flycatchers are found in South America, 154 of them in Venezuela. Flycatchers inhabit all types of country and occur from coastal mangroves to snow line in the Andes, as well as in deserts, rain forest and open plains country. They feed chiefly on insects, which they catch on the wing, but the terrestrial species which inhabit the Andes catch insects on the ground much in the manner of pipits. Some species also feed on fruit and berries, and some glean among leaves like vireos. Bills are adapted to catching insects and are provided with bristles at the base.

Flycatchers are for the most part dull in color, olive and dull green predominating, but some have brightly colored crest or coronal streaks in shades of yellow and orange, and a number of species have bright yellow underparts. Some species are notable for long or oddly shaped tails, while one, the Royal Flycatcher, has a spectacular red or yellow fanshaped crest, each feather terminating in a round, metallic blue disk. In size flycatchers vary from the Great Kiskadee, 10″ (25 cm.) in length, to the Short-tailed Pygmy-Flycatcher, about 2.5″ (6.3 cm.) long.

Flycatchers rate poorly as song birds, but some emit very distinct calls, so much so that some have been named for them such as Kiskadee: *Qu'est qu'il dit* in French, *Bemteví* in Portuguese, *Cristofué* in Spanish, also *Pewee, Titirijí,* etc.

Nests are usually open and cupshaped, but some build round, closed structures with an entrance hole at side or bottom, while a few nest in crevices in walls or rocks, or holes in trees.

Note: Included in this family are the genera *Attila, Pseudattila, Casiornis, Laniocera* and *Rhytipterna,* which since the publication of Lista Av. Venez. have been found to belong more properly here than in the Cotingidae, and *Corythopis,* formerly placed in the family Conopophagidae.

## STREAK-THROATED BUSH-TYRANT
*Myiotheretes striaticollis*
ATRAPAMOSCAS CHIFLA PERRO

Pl. 28
9" (23 cm.). Dull, earthy brown above, eyebrow white. Throat white, streaked black, rest of underparts and under wing coverts cinnamon. Closed wing and tail dusky, *inner webs of wing and tail feathers mostly orange rufous,* conspicuous in flight.
Temperate zone. Nw Zulia in the Sierra de Perijá; sw Táchira; central and s Mérida (*striaticollis*). [The Andes from Colombia to nw Argentina.]
Dwarf forest, 3000 m. Bushy, wooded areas, shrubby ravines, haciendas. Solitary. Darts from high perches after insects on the wing, the light showing through the rufous in tail and wing. Call: a prolonged whistle from which its Spanish name, "dog whistler," derives.

## SMOKY BUSH-TYRANT
*Myiotheretes fumigatus*
ATRAPAMOSCAS TERRESTRE

Pl. 28
8" (20 cm.). Dark, smoky olivaceous brown, throat streaked with white; a faint, but long, pale eyebrow. Under wing coverts and inner *margins of remiges cinnamon rufous.* Tail like back, outer web of outer rectrix whitish (or similar but with ochraceous instead of olivaceous under tail coverts and no eyebrow, a).
Upper subtropical and temperate zones. Nw Zulia and w Táchira (*olivacea*). The Andes in n Táchira, Mérida and Trujillo (*lugubris,* a). [The Andes from Colombia to central Peru.]
High cloud and dwarf forests, 2200–3600 m., most frequent at the higher elevations in low, open forest and shrubby hillsides. Perches unobtrusively on the lower branches of forest trees; swampy areas, often on the ground.

## BROWN-BACKED CHAT-TYRANT
*Ochthoeca fumicolor*
PITAJO AHUMADO

Pl. 29
5.6" (14 cm.). Smoky brown above, broad eyebrow white (or bright rufous, a). Wings and tail dusky, wings with two broad chestnut rufous bars, outer rectrix pale-edged. Throat grayish white shading to smoky brown on breast; abdomen and under tail coverts pale dull cinnamon mixed with white (or bright rufous, a).
Upper subtropical to páramo zones. Sw Táchira on the Páramo de Tamá (*fumicolor*). The Andes of Trujillo, Mérida and n Táchira (*superciliosa,* a). [The Andes from Colombia to n Bolivia.]
From cloud forests to the páramos, 2400–4200 m., most frequent at the higher elevations in the open páramos, low bushes, thickets, wooded ravines, open woods, second growth and watered valleys. Solitary or in pairs. Forages for insects on the wing. Undulating flight.

## RUFOUS-BREASTED CHAT-TYRANT
*Ochthoeca rufipectoralis*
PITAJO PECHIRRUFO

Pl. 29
5.2" (13 cm.). Crown, nape and sides of head grayish brown; forehead, connected to long eyebrow, white. Back and wings brown, broad wing bar cinnamon rufous, inner remiges margined pale cinnamon, tertials edged white. Throat and belly grayish, breast cinnamon rufous. Tail brown, narrowly tipped white, outer web of outer feathers white.
Temperate zone. Sierra de Perijá, Zulia (*rubicundulus*). [The Andes from Colombia to n Bolivia.]
High, dense cloud forest, 2900 m. Bushy hillsides, often near streams or brooks.

## SLATY-BACKED CHAT-TYRANT
*Ochthoeca cinnamomeiventris*
PITAJO NEGRO

Pl. 29
5″ (13 cm.). Entirely slaty black except for short, white superciliaries (or similar but lower breast and belly dark reddish chestnut, a). Upper tropical and subtropical zones. The Andes of Mérida and n Táchira (*nigrita*). Sw Táchira on the Río Chiquito (*cinnamomeiventris*, a). [The Andes from Colombia to n Bolivia.] High cloud forest, 1900–2900 m. Frequently near streams. Captures insects on the wing.

## YELLOW-BELLIED CHAT-TYRANT
*Ochthoeca diadema*
PITAJO DIADEMA

Pl. 29
4.7″ (12 cm.). Forehead and long eyebrow yellow, crown and ocular region dusky olive. Back olivaceous brown (or reddish brown, a); wings brown, middle and greater wing coverts broadly edged reddish brown; tail dark grayish brown, edged olive. Throat and breast olive, belly pale yellow.
Subtropical and temperate zones. The Sierra de Perijá, Zulia (*rubellula*, a). Sw Táchira (*diadema*). Ne Táchira through Mérida to Trujillo (*meridana*). The coastal Cordillera in Aragua and the Distr. Federal (*tovarensis*). [The Andes from Colombia to n Peru.]
Cloud forest and more open terrain, 1950–3050 m. Most frequent in the higher elevations in thick second growth, lower branches of small trees and shrubbery near forest edge. Thick, brushy tangles of low vegetation. Flits about in low bushes more like a warbler than a flycatcher. Solitary. Captures insects on the wing.

## BLACK PHOEBE
*Sayornis nigricans*
TIGÜÍN DE AGUA

Pl. XIII
7.5″ (19 cm.). Head, throat, breast and sides of belly black, center of belly white. Back dark gray. Wings black, median and greater wing coverts and inner *remiges broadly edged white*. Tail black, outer web of outer rectrix white.
Tropical to temperate zones. Locally distributed in the n mountains from Zulia to Sucre and s through Yaracuy and Trujillo to Barinas and Táchira (*angustirostris*). [From the w US to e Panama and through the Andes to nw Argentina.]
Steep, rocky mountain streams and humid regions from sea level, rarely to 3000 m. Seldom in the forest. Frequents torrents, ponds, lakes, perching on exposed rocks and low bushes. Sometimes on telephone lines and exposed branches. Solitary; active; tame. Sallied forth to snap up insects on the wing. Flicks tail while perching.

## LONG-TAILED TYRANT
*Colonia colonus*
ATRAPAMOSCAS COLUDO

Pl. XIII
5″ (13 cm.), including lengthened central tail feathers 10″ (25 cm.). Unmistakable because of its very long tail. Black; forehead and short eyebrow white, crown and nape ashy gray; rump white. ♀: similar but tail somewhat shorter and belly grayer.
Tropical zone. Bolívar from the middle and upper Río Paragua to the upper Río Cuyuni (*poecilonota*). [S Honduras to n Bolivia, Paraguay and ne Argentina.]
High rain forest, 200–350 m. Frequently in scrub near water and humid areas at forest edge. Open places with tall, dead trees where it perches conspicuously on the highest branches. Dashes out to catch insects on the wing. Call: a soft "peet" or "weet." Nests in holes in trees.

## RIVERSIDE TYRANT
*Knipolegus orenocensis*
VIUDITA RIBEREÑA

Pl. XIII
6″ (15 cm.). *Dark ashy gray* with an olivaceous tinge, top of head and nape blacker. ♀: similar but paler, crown scarcely different from back.
Tropical zone. Apure along the lower Río Apure; Bolívar along the Orinoco from the mouth of the Meta to Ciudad Bolívar; se Anzoátegui in Soledad (*orenocensis*). [Amazonian Brazil s of the

Amazon from the Rio Xingú to the Rio Madeira. Ne Peru.]
Thickets along water courses and ponds in open situations, 100–150 m. A restless bird; acts like a *Sayornis.*

## RUFOUS-TAILED TYRANT
*Knipolegus poecilurus*
VIUDITA DE LAS SERRANÍAS

Pl. 29
5.6" (14 cm.). Upperparts ashy gray, wings grayish brown, double wing bar buffy white, inner remiges edged white. Throat and belly buffy white, breast grayish. Central tail feathers dusky, *rest cinnamon on inner web* (or with only a suggestion of cinnamon, a; or uniform dusky with no cinnamon, b). Many birds have the belly and wing bars pale cinnamon.
Upper tropical and subtropical zones. The Andes of Mérida and Táchira, and the coastal Cordillera in the Distr. Federal (*venezuelanus*). Central Amazonas; the mountains of s Bolívar (*salvini*, a). Nw Amazonas on Cerro Paraque (*paraquensis*, b). [Colombia to n Bolivia. N Brazil e to ne Roraima. Trinidad, Tobago.]
High rain and cloud forest, 900–2000 m., above 1600 m. in the mountains n of the Orinoco, s of it from 900 m. to the higher slopes and summits of the tepuis. Thickets.

## AMAZONIAN BLACK-TYRANT
*Phaeotriccus poecilocercus*
ATRAPAMOSCAS REMOLONCITO

Pl. XIII
5.2" (13 cm.). Glossy blue black; wings brownish black, the 3 outermost primaries very narrow and pointed. Tail dull black. ♀: upperparts and wings dull olive brown, double wing bars and edges of remiges pale buff. Upper tail coverts and inner webs of rectrices cinnamon. Throat and breast dull yellowish buff, streaked gray, center of belly plain, pale yellow. Three outer primaries like ♂ but not quite as narrow.
Tropical zone. Upper Río Arauca, w Apure; n and central Amazonas. [Guyana; e Colombia in Meta; Amazonian Brazil; ne Peru.]
Dense rain forest and high second growth 100–200 m. Usually near rivers.

## PIED WATER-TYRANT
*Fluvicola pica*
VIUDITA ACUÁTICA

Pl. XIII
5.2" (13 cm.). *Black and white.* Forecrown, sides of head and entire underparts white. Hindcrown, nape, wings and tail black. Back mixed black and white, rump and upper tail coverts white. Inner remiges edged and tail tipped white. ♀: like ♂ but black portions of plumage brownish black.
Tropical zone. Marshes and riverbanks n of the Orinoco; s of it in Amazonas n of the Río Ventuari; nw and se Bolívar and Delta Amacuro (*pica*). [E Panama to Bolivia, n Argentina and Uruguay. Trinidad.]
Reedbeds, swamps, along stream banks, marshes, aquatic vegetation in ponds to 500 m. Perches near the ground on low branches over water. Active, not shy, in pairs and families; wags tail.

## WHITE-HEADED MARSH-TYRANT
*Arundinicola leucocephala*
ATRAPAMOSCAS DUENDE

Pl. XIII
4.6" (11.7 cm.). *Black, whole head white,* lower mandible orange. Second primary from outside narrow and pointed. ♀: pale ashy gray above; forehead, sides of head and underparts white, breast slightly streaked ashy gray. Tail black. Wings normal.
Tropical zone. Marshes and riverbanks n of the Orinoco s to n and central Amazonas, n and Bolívar and Delta Amacuro. [The Guianas. Colombia to Bolivia and Argentina. Trinidad.]
Grassy marshes, wet pastures, river banks, edges of ponds, Moriche swamps. Sea level to 450 m. In pairs or family groups.

## VERMILION FLYCATCHER
*Pyrocephalus rubinus*
ATRAPAMOSCAS SANGRE DE TORO

Pl. 29
5" (13 cm.). *Crown,* short crest and *entire underparts crimson;* sides of head, back, wings and tail sooty brown. ♀: ashy brown above, feathers of crown washed pink; throat and breast white, breast streaked dusky, washed pink, rest of

underparts pinkish crimson. Tail blackish, outer web of outer rectrix white.
Tropical zone. Generally distributed in semi-arid areas and open country n of the Orinoco; s of it in n Bolívar (*saturatus*). [Sw US to s Argentina and n Chile. Galápagos Is.]
The race breeding in s S Amer. (*P. r. rubinus*) migrates n in the s winter and reaches Colombia. It may well also reach sw Venezuela. Males are much like Venezuelan birds but females are very different below. The underparts are white, heavily streaked dusky (no red), the undertail coverts are yellow.
Open country with scattered trees. Arid, semi-arid and dry, scrubby regions from sea level to about 800 m. n of the Orinoco, to 460 m. s of it. Alone or in pairs. Vivid color of male unmistakable. Simple soft song, lispy and thin. Flies up, then sings as it floats down.

**DRAB WATER-TYRANT**
*Ochthornis littoralis*
ATRAPAMOSCAS RIBEREÑO

Pl. 29
5.7″ (14.5 cm.). Pale grayish brown, wings and tail darker; supraloral streak, eyebrow, subocular region and chin white.
Tropical zone. Amazonas and Bolívar. [The Guianas, e Colombia to n Bolivia and Amazonian Brazil.]
High rain forest along river edge, 100–600 m. Flies for short distances very low over water, always very close to the forest edge where it perches. Occasionally on sandy river banks.

**YELLOW-BROWED TYRANT**
*Satrapa icterophrys*
ATRAPAMOSCAS CEJAS AMARILLAS

Pl. 28
6.3″ (16 cm.). Bill much narrower than in other more or less similar yellow-bellied flycatchers. Crown dark gray; long, broad eyebrow from nostril bright yellow, lores and cheeks blackish. Back olive green, somewhat mixed with gray, upper tail coverts dark gray; below lemon yellow, a patch of dusky olive at sides of breast, under tail coverts yellowish white. Wings blackish, lesser wing coverts pale gray, greater coverts and inner remiges edged grayish white. Tail black, outer rectrix edged grayish white.

Tropical zone. Resident during the boreal winter. Recorded from Carabobo, Apure, nw Bolívar and Delta Amacuro. [Breeds in e and se Brazil, Uruguay, Argentina and Bolivia.]
Rain and gallery forest, forest edge, second growth, edges of rivers and lagoons, grassy savannas, llanos. Sea level to 500 m. n of the Orinoco, to 150 m. s of it.

**CATTLE TYRANT**
*Machetornis rixosus*
ATRAPAMOSCAS JINETE

Pl. 28
7.5″ (19 cm.). Crown and nape light grayish brown, becoming sandy brown on back and somewhat rufescent on rump. Partially concealed crest scarlet. Wing coverts and remiges pale edged. Below yellow, palest on throat, pectoral tufts and under wing coverts bright, deep yellow. Tail brown, broadly tipped whitish.
Mostly tropical zone from Zulia and n Apure e through n Venezuela to the Orinoco delta; n Bolívar from Caicara e; the llanos from w Apure to Barinas and Cojedes (*flavigularis*). [N and e Colombia. E and Central Brazil to s Bolivia, Argentina and Uruguay.]
Bushy savannas, fields near water as well as open, arid areas with scattered trees, from sea beaches to, occasionally, the altitude of Caracas. In pairs and family groups. Almost entirely terrestrial, follows and often perches on the backs of livestock. Robinlike, runs on the ground and captures insects. Rests near tops of small, isolated trees. Calls: mouselike, squeaky notes, a hissing "seep."

**SIRYSTES**
*Sirystes sibilator*
ATRAPAMOSCAS DE RABADILLA BLANCA

Pl. 28
7.5″ (19 cm.). Head crested; crown and nape black, lores and sides of head dark gray. Mantle gray, lightly spotted with grayish brown, rump white, upper tail coverts dark grayish brown; tail black. Outer remiges black, inner ones brownish black edged white, wing coverts brownish black edged gray. Throat and breast very light gray, rest of underparts white.

Thighs brownish gray. ♀: crown and nape brownish black.

Tropical zone. Extreme s Táchira (albocinereus). [E Panama, Colombia, Surinam through e Ecuador to Bolivia, Paraguay and ne Argentina, Amazonian and e Brazil.]

High rain forest, 300–550 m. From a perch on the tallest forest trees sallies forth to capture insects on the wing.

## FORK-TAILED FLYCATCHER
*Muscivora tyrannus*
ATRAPAMOSCAS TIJERETA

Pl. XIII

14″ (35 cm.). *Tail very long,* (outer feathers up to 10″ [25 cm.] long), graduated, *deeply forked.* Top and sides of head black, concealed crown patch lemon yellow. Back pale gray, tail black, basal half of outer feather white on outer web. Wings brownish black, lesser wing coverts gray, outer blackish margined with gray. Entire underparts white.

Tropical and subtropical zones. Resident. Extreme nw Zulia on the Goajira Pen. (*sanctaemartae*). Elsewhere except forested regions (*monachus*). Summer resident, Mar.–Oct. Locally throughout except forested regions including Los Testigos Margarita and Patos Is. (*tyrannus*). [S Mexico to s Argentina. Birds breeding in S Amer. migrate to Colombia, Venezuela, Trinidad, Tobago. Casually to the W Indies, and accidentally to Bermuda and New Jersey.] The males of the different races are alike in plumage but can be told apart by the notching of the tips of the outermost primaries.

Llanos, savannas, sparsely wooded areas, low second growth from sea level, ranging to 1600 m. in appropriate open country. Conspicuous. Captures insects on the wing, often pirouetting acrobatically. Perches on high trees, shrubs and even close to the ground. Resident individuals often gather in small flocks of less than 100. Migrants, Mar.–Oct., may form flocks of over 1000. They roost in tall trees.

## EASTERN KINGBIRD
*Tyrannus tyrannus*
PITIRRE AMERICANO

8″ (20 cm.). Top and sides of head black, concealed crest orange, wings brownish black, edged, including coverts, grayish white. Tail black with a sharply defined white terminal band. Below white shaded gray on breast.

Subtropical zone. Casual winter visitor. Recorded from Mérida and from Cerro Roraima, Bolívar. [Breeds in N Amer.; winters to Bolivia, Brazil, Chile and nw Argentina.]

Open fields, savannas. The few Venezuelan records are from between 1400–1700 m. A small flock was seen in open woodland.

## TROPICAL KINGBIRD
*Tyrannus melancholicus*
PITIRRE CHICHARRERO

Pl. 28

8.5″ (22.5 cm.). Crown and nape gray, a partly concealed orange crest; back olivaceous gray; wings, tail and upper tail coverts blackish brown, remiges and wing coverts edged light gray. Throat white (or grayish, a). Underparts bright yellow, lightly (or heavily, a) washed with olive on breast. *Tail slightly forked.*

Tropical and subtropical zones. Open country and savanna generally n of the Orinoco; in Delta Amacuro and along the s bank of the Orinoco and the lower Río Cuchivero in nw Bolívar (*chloronotus*). Elsewhere s of the range of *chloronotus* (*melancholicus*, a). [Sw United States to Ica, w Peru, and s Argentina. Grenada. Tobago, Trinidad, Aruba, Curaçao, Bonaire.]

Open areas with scattered trees, second growth, plantations, gardens from sea level to 2200 m. Captures insects on the wing, returning to the same perch in the top of tall trees; also feeds on berries. Alone, in pairs or small flocks, sometimes in groups of 20 or more on electric wires. Chases hawks. Calls: a long, trembling whistle, "peetséerr"; also a rapid "wee-ree-pee-pée."

## GRAY KINGBIRD
*Tyrannus dominicensis*
PITIRRE GRIS

Pl. 28

9″ (23 cm.). Above light gray, semi-concealed crest orange, broad stripe through eye blackish. Wings and tail dark brown, wing coverts and remiges edged white. Below white tinged gray on breast. Under wing coverts and axillaries pale sulphur yellow. Tail slightly forked. Tropical, casually subtropical zone. Winter resident and occasional breeder. Venezuela n of the Orinoco, and along the s bank of the Orinoco from nw Amazonas to Delta Amacuro, found breeding at Ciudad Bolívar. [Se US to Panama, Colombia, the Guianas. The Bahamas, Antilles, Cozumel.]

Open areas, second growth, gallery forest, beaches and mangroves to 1700 m., occasionally in clearings in cloud forest. Not shy. Alone or in small flocks, often on electric wires. Feeds on berries and seeds. Call: a shrill "peet-cheery."

## WHITE-THROATED KINGBIRD
*Tyrannus albogularis*
PITIRRE GARGANTIBLANCO

Pl. 28
7.5" (19 cm.). Almost exactly like Gray Kingbird in color but much smaller. Crown and back somewhat paler and white of throat more restricted. Tail forked.

Tropical zone. Known only from se Bolívar (Sta. Elena de Uairén). [W Guyana, sw Surinam, Amazonian and se Brazil, e Peru.]

Open areas, forest edge, 960 m.

## SULPHURY FLYCATCHER
*Tyrannopsis sulphurea*
ATRAPAMOSCAS SULFUROSO

Pl. 28
7.5" (19 cm.). Top and sides of head gray with a suggested white postocular streak, concealed crown patch lemon yellow; back dull brownish olive. Throat and extreme upper breast dull white, patch at sides gray, rest of underparts bright lemon yellow. Wings and tail brown, feathers edged dull olive.

Tropical zone. W Amazonas from Ratón I. to Caño Casiquiare; nw and se Bolívar; Delta Amacuro; e Sucre. [Colombia, the Guianas to e Peru and Amazonian and e Brazil.]

Clearings and open areas in forested lowlands from sea level in the delta to 500 m. at the base of the tepuis. Near damp places, often in the crowns of *Mauritia* palms. Swamps. Feeds on insects and berries. Call: harsh, loud, repeated whistles.

## DUSKY-CHESTED FLYCATCHER
*Tyrannopsis luteiventris*
PISPIRILLO CRESTA ANARANJADA

Pl. 28
6" (15 cm.). Bill stubby. Crown dark brown with a concealed orange crest; back, wings and tail blackish brown, no olive tinge. Throat grayish white, underparts yellow heavily streaked dark olive on breast. ♀: like ♂ but lacks orange crest.

Tropical zone. Central Bolívar along the middle Río Paragua (*septentrionalis*). [Sw Surinam. Se Colombia, e Ecuador, e Peru, w Amazonian Brazil.]

High rain forest at about 350 m. Forest edge, open fields and clearings usually near water courses. Usually alone, forages from middle branches to near the treetops.

Note: Placed in the genus *Myiozetetes* in Lista Av. Venez.

## VARIEGATED FLYCATCHER
*Empidonomus varius*
ATRAPAMOSCAS VETEADO

Pl. 28
7.5" (19 cm.). Crown brownish black, semi-concealed crest lemon yellow; forehead and long eyebrow white; sides of head black bordered below by a broad white moustacial streak. Back dark brown, the feathers edged gray giving a streaked appearance; upper tail coverts and tail black, the feathers edged bright chestnut rufous. Throat whitish, rest of underparts yellowish white, streaked sharply with black (or less definitely with gray, a). Wing coverts and remiges brownish black, sharply edged with white.

Tropical and subtropical zones. Generally distributed, but not recorded w of Falcón and Portuguesa (*rufinus*, a). Migrant from the s, recorded Mar., Oct. throughout but not recorded w of Yaracuy (*varius*). [S Amer. generally e of the Andes to Uruguay and Argentina. Trinidad.]

Open woodland, deciduous woods, scattered low trees and bushes, clearings to

1900 m. n of the Orinoco and to 1300 m. s of it on the open slopes of the tepuis. Perches at top of low trees. Forages for insects and berries in the middle tier of forest trees.

## CROWNED SLATY-FLYCATCHER

*Empidonomus aurantioatrocristatus*
ATRAPAMOSCAS COPETE
NEGRO Y AMARILLO

Pl. 28

7" (18 cm.). *Gray, crown black, with a semi-concealed yellow crest; back gray, upper tail coverts brownish; wings and tail brown, wing coverts and remiges narrowly edged grayish white.* Chin and subocular region whitish; throat and breast gray, tinged green on lower breast and sides, center of belly white.

Casual winter visitor. Recorded from Aragua and on the upper Orinoco in A m a z o n a s (*aurantioatrocristatus*). [Breeds from e Brazil s of the Amazon to central Argentina. Winters n to n Brazil, ne Peru, casually to se Colombia.]

Only two specimens have been recorded from Venezuela, one from high rain forest s of the Orinoco at the mouth of the Río Ocamo at 150 m., the other from cloud forest in Rancho Grande at about 1400 m. on the n coastal Cordillera.

## PIRATIC FLYCATCHER

*Legatus leucophaius*
ATRAPAMOSCAS LADRÓN

Pl. 28

6.2" (15.7 cm.). Bill rather broad and stubby. Crown dark brown surrounded by a white band, concealed patch in center of crown yellow to orange yellow. Sides of head blackish brown, cheek stripe white. Back dark olive brown, the feathers inconspicuously pale-edged. Throat white, breast yellowish white becoming pale yellow on sides of body and under tail coverts; breast clouded and streaked dusky, sides streaked dusky. Wings dark brown, wing coverts and inner remiges edged paler. Upper tail coverts and tail olive brown, the feathers edged reddish brown.

Tropical zone, virtually throughout. [Mexico to Argentina.]

Open forest and forest edge to 1000 m. n of the Orinoco, s of it to 600 m. on the slopes of the tepuis. Cacao and coffee plantations, clearings and open country with tall, isolated trees and Moriche palms, stream banks. Usually perches on treetops to sally forth for insects but also feeds on berries. Occupies new nests of oropendolas and of other birds. Noisy, active. Call: a whistled "pie-eee."

## THREE-STRIPED FLYCATCHER

*Conopias trivirgata*
ATRAPAMOSCAS TRILISTADO

6" (15 cm.). Crown dark grayish, feathers basally white. Sides of head black; forehead and broad eyebrow white joining on back of neck to form a nuchal collar; back yellowish green. Wings and tail dusky, wing coverts edged yellowish gray. Underparts lemon yellow, somewhat clouded with olive on breast.

Tropical zone. Cerro Taracuniña, upper Río Caura, Bolívar, on the Brazilian border (*berlepschi*). [E Peru, w Amazonian Brazil. Se Brazil, e Paraguay, ne Argentina.]

Open areas of the high rain forest, 950 m. Often with icterids. Appropriates nests of other birds.

## LEMON-BROWED FLYCATCHER

*Conopias cinchoneti*
ATRAPAMOSCAS CINCHÓN

Pl. 28

6" (15 cm.). Chiefly distinguishable from Three-striped Flycatcher by lemon yellow instead of white forehead and eyebrows. Crown and sides of head olive like back. Underparts bright yellow.

Upper tropical and subtropical zones. The Sierra de Perijá, Zulia; La Azulita, Mérida; Escuque, Trujillo (*icterophrys*). [Colombia through the Andes to central Peru.]

Dense cloud forest, 950–2150 m.

## WHITE-RINGED FLYCATCHER

*Conopias parva*
ATRAPAMOSCAS DIADEMA

Pl. 28

6.5" (16.5 cm.). Superficially like a *Myiozetetes* but bill much larger. Crown and sides of head brownish black. Crown, with a semi-concealed yellow crest, completely surrounded by a broad white band. Back dark brown, the feathers broadly edged olive; below entirely bright yellow. Wings and tail dark brown, wing coverts and inner remiges narrowly edged white.

Tropical zone. W Amazonas s to Cerro Yapacana; e Bolívar from the Sierra de Imataca to the Gran Sabana (*parva*). [Costa Rica to nw Ecuador, the Guianas and n Brazil.]

Clearings and sparsely wooded areas in lowland rain forest from about 150 m., up to 460 m. on the Altiplanicie de Nuria and up to 1300 m. on the slopes of the tepuis. In pairs along forest edge and second growth and in tops of tall trees. Call: Dee-di-di-dee.

Note: Called *Coryphotriccus parvus* in Lista Av. Venez.

## BOAT-BILLED FLYCATCHER

*Megarhynchus pitangua*
ATRAPAMOSCAS PICÓN

Pl. 28

8.5″ (22 cm.). Bill very large, broad. Crown and sides of head brownish black, concealed crest orange or yellow. Long eyebrow and interrupted nuchal collar white. Back olive brown, browner in worn plumage. Throat white, rest of underparts bright yellow. Wings and tail dark brown, inner remiges and the rectrices narrowly edged rufous.

Tropical and subtropical zones. Generally n of the Ríos Meta and Orinoco; n Amazonas; Bolívar along the lower Ríos Caura and Paragua and Cerros Roraima and Uei-tepui in the se; Delta Amacuro; Patos I. (*pitangua*). [Mexico to Argentina. Trinidad.]

Occupies a wide variety of habitats from sea level to 1900 m. Prefers fairly open country with scattered trees, near water where it may feed on frogs; forest edge, clearings, plantations, deciduous woods, etc. In pairs and groups, forages actively and noisily for insects and berries from low branches to near treetops. Attacks hawks. Call: a sustained, harsh, high twitter with a scolding quality.

## STREAKED FLYCATCHER

*Myiodynastes maculatus*
GRAN ATRAPAMOSCAS LISTADO

Pl. 28

7.5″ (19 cm.). Above brown, the feathers conspicuously edged cinnamon rufous (or above dark brown, the feathers conspicuously edged yellowish white, a) giving a streaked appearance, upper tail coverts and tail largely rufous (or tail coverts and tail blackish, edged chestnut rufous, a). Below yellowish white streaked dusky (or pale yellow, very heavily streaked blackish, a), center of belly unstreaked. Wings dark brown, wing coverts and outer remiges edged cinnamon rufous, inner remiges broadly edged white (or with little rufous, edges to feathers mostly white, a).

Tropical zone. Widespread n of the Orinoco, except areas occupied by *tobagensis* (*difficilis*). N Anzoátegui, Sucre, Delta Amacuro and Margarita I. (*tobagensis*). Summer resident, Mar.–Sept. Found spottily n and s of the Orinoco, breeds in s S Amer. (*solitarius*, a). [Mexico to central Argentina, accidentally Chile. Trinidad, Tobago.]

Near forests and open, wooded areas in the lowlands to 1900 m. n of the Orinoco, to 1100 m. s of it on the slopes of the tepuis. Mangroves, clearings, forest edge, plantations, near savannas, usually alone, not shy; keeps to the lower parts of trees. Catches insects on the wing. Call: a short series of whistles diminishing in duration.

## GOLDEN-CROWNED FLYCATCHER

*Myiodynastes chrysocephalus*
ATRAPAMOSCAS CORONA DORADA

Pl. 28

8.5″ (22 cm.). Crown and nape ashy gray, semi-concealed crest golden yellow, lores and sides of head blackish bordered above by a white eyebrow and below by a white moustacial streak. Sides of throat blackish, chin white, throat pinkish white, rest of underparts bright yellow, obscurely streaked gray on breast. Back brownish olive, upper tail coverts edged rufous. Wings and tail dark brown, wing coverts and all remiges but tertials edged rufous, tertials edged white, rectrices edged on both webs with rufous.

Upper tropical and subtropical zones. The

n Cordilleras from Zulia and Táchira to Sucre and Monagas (*cinerascens*). [Panama to e and w Colombia, e and w Ecuador, central and e Peru.] Cloud forest and damp gorges, 600–2300 m. Clearings. Alone or in pairs perches quietly and inconspicuously from the lower branches to treetops.

## RUSTY-MARGINED FLYCATCHER

*Myiozetetes cayanensis*
ATRAPAMOSCAS PECHO AMARILLO

Pl. 28
7" (18 cm.). Crown patch orange, sides of crown and head blackish, conspicuous eyebrow white. Above brown with a slight (or strong, a) olive tinge. Throat white, underparts bright yellow. Wings and tail brown, inner primaries with narrow (or conspicuous, b) rufous edges, inner webs of remiges partly (or mostly, b) rufous.
Tropical and lower subtropical zones. The w slope of the Andes in n Táchira, the sw slopes in Mérida; Zulia e and w of L. Maracaibo (*hellmayri*, a). W Apure; the e slope of the Andes in s Táchira and e Mérida; from e Falcón e, n of the Orinoco, to Sucre and Monagas (*rufipennis*, b). Generally in Amazonas, Bolívar and Delta Amacuro (*cayanensis*). [Panama to w Ecuador, Bolivia and s Brazil.]
In a variety of situations but especially open areas with scattered trees; also near streams and ponds, in dense and gallery forest and second growth to 1900 m. n of the Orinoco, to 950 m. s of it. Usually solitary but conspicuous; hunts in loose groups for insects caught on the wing, from middle heights to treetops. Call: noisy, a high, shrill, plaintive trill.

## SOCIAL FLYCATCHER

*Myiozetetes similis*
PITIRRE COPETE ROJO

Pl. 28
6.3" (16 cm.). Crown and sides of head dark gray, semi-concealed crest scarlet, long eyebrow yellowish white. Back dull olive; wings and tail brown, wing coverts and inner remiges edged grayish white. Throat white, rest of underparts bright yellow.
Tropical and lower subtropical zones. From Zulia and Táchira s to the Río Meta and e to Sucre and Delta Amacuro; n Bolívar along the Orinoco e to the Sierra de Imataca, thence s in the e to the Río Icabarú (*columbianus*). Central Amazonas e across central and s Bolívar to the upper Río Caura and upper Paragua (*similis*). [Mexico to w Peru and Argentina.]
Forests n of the Orinoco to 1500 m., to 500 m. s of it. River banks and edges of marshes and ponds, open country with scattered trees, plantations, forest edge, scrubby second growth. Active, noisily conspicuous, forages for insects and berries alone or in small groups from the ground to the middle branches of trees. Call: a loud, shrill whistle.

## GRAY-CAPPED FLYCATCHER

*Myiozetetes granadensis*
PISPIRILLO COPETE GRIS

Pl. 28
7" (18 cm.). Crown and nape pale gray, concealed crest scarlet, tipped yellow; forehead and short eyebrow white. Back olive; wings and tail brownish black, wing coverts, remiges and rectrices edged yellow. Throat white, tinged yellow, rest of underparts bright yellow. ♀: differs from other ♀ *Myiozetetes* by lacking the colored crest. Crown and nape gray, the crown with a semi-concealed olive patch, otherwise like ♂.
Tropical zone. Central Amazonas; Bolívar along the middle Río Caura and the basin of the upper Río Paragua (*obscurior*). [Nicaragua to w Ecuador, Bolivia and s Brazil.]
Humid forested regions in the lowlands, 100–550 m. Semi-open country with scattered trees, plantations, clearings, stream banks. In pairs and family groups, perches at various heights. Flutters noisily. Captures insects on the wing and feeds also on berries and seeds. Call: 2 loud, scolding, rattling notes.

## WHITE-BEARDED FLYCATCHER

*Myiozetetes inornatus*
ATRAPAMOSCAS BARBIBLANCO

Pl. 28
6" (15 cm). Long eyebrow white. Upperparts olivaceous brown, slightly rufescent on upper tail coverts. Wings and tail

dark brown, wing coverts edged grayish, remiges and rectrices edged pale tawny rufous. Throat white, rest of underparts yellow with a dusky patch at each side of breast. Not unlike Rusty-margined Flycatcher but much smaller.

Tropical zone. The n Cordillera from Carabobo to Anzoátegui and s over the llanos to the Ríos Arauca and Apure and the s bank of the Orinoco in Bolívar.

Pastures, swamps, ponds, llanos, open areas with scattered trees, shrubs, from sea level to 450 m. Forages, alone or in pairs, from the lower to the middle branches of small trees.

Note: Called *Conopias inornata* in Lista Av. Venez.

## GREAT KISKADEE
*Pitangus sulphuratus*
CRISTOFUÉ

Pl. 28
8.5″ (21.6 cm.). Bill long (1.2″, 3 cm.), rather narrow. Crown and sides of head black, semi-concealed crest lemon yellow, forehead, broad eyebrows and nuchal collar white. Back rufescent brown, brighter and more rufous on rump and upper tail coverts. Throat white, rest of underparts lemon yellow. Wings largely rufous. Central tail feathers dark brown edged rufous, outer ones mostly bright rufous (or without rufous, a).

Tropical, casually subtropical zone. N of the Orinoco from Zulia, Táchira and w Apure to w Sucre, w Monagas, and s of the Orinoco in n Amazonas, and in n Bolívar along the s bank of the Orinoco to the border of Delta Amacuro and e Monagas (*rufipennis*). E Sucre; e Monagas; Delta Amacuro; Bolívar from the middle Río Paragua to the Altiplanicie de Nuria; central Amazonas; Patos I. (*trinitatis,* a). [Se Texas to Colombia, Chile and Argentina. Trinidad.]

Semi-open country with scattered trees, high second growth, along streams, edges of fields, plantations, gardens, n of the Orinoco to 1600 m., s of it to 500 m. Savannas, arid areas. Abundant, active, conspicuous, very noisy and aggressive. Usually in pairs in the higher branches. Feeds on insects, fruit and occasionally small fishes. Call: "kis-ka-dee" or "cristofué" uttered melodiously or scoldingly, accented on the last syllable.

## LESSER KISKADEE
*Pitangus lictor*
PECHO AMARILLO ORILLERO

Pl. 28
7″ (18 cm.). A miniature of the Great Kiskadee differing by olivaceous brown instead of rufescent brown back.

Tropical zone. N Venezuela e to Anzoátegui and e Monagas, extending s to n Amazonas, n Bolívar and Delta Amacuro (*lictor*). [Panama, n Colombia to s Brazil and n Bolivia.]

Invariably near water. Mangroves, gallery forest, second growth, lake shores, river banks, wet fields, marshes. Perches on branches overhanging water. Solitary, peaceful, not aggressive. Call: a weak, melancholy whistle.

## BRIGHT-RUMPED ATTILA
*Attila spadiceus*
ATTILA POLIMORFO

Pl. 27
7.5″ (19 cm.). Bill strongly hooked. Plumage variable in color but rump always in contrast to back. Olive above, rump yellow, wings brown with two dingy white bars, tail rufous brown. Throat and breast pale olive obscurely streaked yellow, belly white, under wing and tail coverts pale yellow. Or bright foxy rufous above, brighter on head and rump, becoming cinnamon on upper tail coverts, wings brown with two rufous bars, tail bright rufous. Throat and breast like back, rest of underparts light buff. Or any color between the two extremes.

Tropical and subtropical zones. Zulia around L. Maracaibo; n and w Táchira (*parvirostris*). Extreme sw Táchira, w Apure; e Lara; the Paria Pen., Sucre; Delta Amacuro; generally in Bolívar and Amazonas (*spadiceus*). [S Mexico to w Ecuador, the Guianas, Amazonia and se Brazil and Bolivia. Trinidad.]

Rain and cloud forest, high second growth to 2100 m. n of the Orinoco, to 460 m. s of it. Deep within the forest and along forest edge, damp clearings. Forages alone for insects, lizards, frogs and berries from near the ground to treetops, jumping among the branches. Twitches tail. Investigates army ants. Calls: include a loud, melodious, musical trill and "beetit" repeated several times.

Note: See footnote on p. 227.

## CITRON-BELLIED ATTILA
*Attila citriniventris*
ATTILA VIENTRE CITRINO

Pl. 27
7.5″ (19 cm.). Much like the rufous phase of the Bright-rumped Attila but at once distinguishable by gray crown, nape, sides of head and upper throat, and lack of wing bars. Center of belly yellowish buff.
Tropical zone. Central and s Amazonas. [E Ecuador, ne Peru, nw Brazil.]
Dense rain forest, 100–500 m.

## CINNAMON ATTILA
*Attila cinnamomeus*
ATTILA ACANELADO

Pl. 27
8″ (20 cm.). Much like rufous phase of the Bright-rumped Attila but brighter, reddish rufous above, with rump very slightly brighter than back; *no wing bars;* breast paler than in Bright-rumped, thus not in as strong contrast to belly.
Tropical zone. N central Sucre; Delta Amacuro; central Amazonas; s Bolívar along the Río Icabarú. [The Guianas, Colombia to Amazonian Brazil and Bolivia.]
Mangroves, forest, second growth, near water, to 400 m. Quiet, conspicuous, not shy. Forages for insects in lower tree branches, feeds also on small frogs. Call: a fairly loud double whistle.

## RUFOUS-TAILED ATTILA
*Pseudattila phoenicurus*
ATTILA RABICASTAÑO

7.2″ (18.2 cm.). *Top and sides of head grayish brown, sharply defined* from chestnut cinnamon back. Tail rufous. Underparts chestnut cinnamon, paler than back.
Tropical zone. Known only from Cerro Yapacana in central Amazonas. [Central and s Brazil; Paraguay; ne Argentina.]
Dense rain forest at about 150 m.

## CINEREOUS MOURNER
*Laniocera hypopyrrha*
PLAÑIDERA CINÉREA

Pl. 26
8″ (20 cm.). Above gray, wings brownish gray, wing coverts with two rows of cinnamon spots variable in size, inner remiges tipped cinnamon. Tail gray, tipped cinnamon. Underparts gray, pectoral tufts rufous, a few rufous feathers, tipped black in center of breast (not constant), center of breast sometimes strongly tinged yellowish green. Under tail coverts gray tipped buff and obscurely barred, or bright cinnamon with black tips. ♀: differs from ♂ in having lemon yellow pectoral tufts and plain gray under tail coverts.
Tropical zone. Amazonas from Caño Cuao s; Bolívar from the Ríos Caura and Paragua to the Gran Sabana and the Sierra de Imataca; s Delta Amacuro. [The Guianas, e Colombia to Bolivia.]
Dense rain forest and high second growth, often near water, from sea level to 460 m. Alone, forages for berries and insects among the leaves in the lower levels and in the undergrowth.

## GRAYISH MOURNER
*Rhytipterna simplex*
PLAÑIDERA AMAZÓNICA

Pl. 26
8″ (20 cm.). Plain ashy gray, paler below, particularly on belly. Back, breast and belly slightly tinged greenish. Head somewhat crested, the feathers with blackish centers.
Tropical zone. S of the Orinoco, including Delta Amacuro (*frederici*). [E Colombia and the Guianas to Amazonian and se Brazil and n Bolivia.]
Rain forest to 1300 m. Solitary, silent. Forages for insects and berries from lower levels to the treetops in open forest and clearings. Call: has been compared to a yodeling whistle.

[THE GENUS *Myiarchus* includes a group of medium sized flycatchers, many of which resemble each other closely and are difficult to tell apart. Their notes are probably the best means of distinguishing them. They are for the most part brownish or olive above with gray breasts and yellow bellies and are found in a variety of habitats.]

## SHORT-CRESTED FLYCATCHER
*Myiarchus ferox*
ATRAPAMOSCAS GARROCHERO CHICO

7″ (18 cm.). Somewhat crested. Upperparts grayish brown with an olive cast. Greater and median wing coverts broadly edged pale gray, throat and breast pearly gray, with a suggestion of white streaking on throat. Lower breast, belly and under tail coverts pale yellow. Tail dark brown.
Tropical zone. Táchira; Apure; Portuguesa; n Guárico; nw Amazonas; nw Bolívar (*brunnescens*). Amazonas s of the Río Ventuari; e and s Bolívar; Delta Amacuro; e Sucre (*ferox*). [E Colombia and the Guianas to Argentina. Tobago.]
Areas of open vegetation in the rain forests, to about 500 m. n of the Orinoco and to 100 m. s of it. Plantations, savannas, wet woodland. Solitary or in pairs, forages in the foliage of lower branches and on the wing. Perches quietly, not shy. Nods frequently. Call: most diagnostic is a prolonged, loud, rolling series of rattling notes; no plaintive whistled notes (*fide* Lanyon).
Note: *M. ferox australis* has often been recorded n to Venezuela and Colombia as a migrant from s S Amer. Lanyon (pers. comm.) states that this race actually is not migratory and is not found n of the Amazon. He tells us the confusion is based on specimens intermediate between *brunnescens* and *ferox* which morphologically resemble *australis*.

## PANAMA FLYCATCHER
*Myiarchus panamensis*
ATRAPAMOSCAS DE PANAMÁ

7″ (18 cm.). Not distinguishable in the field from Short-crested Flycatcher except by voice. Differs by lighter, more olivaceous back and grayish forehead.
Tropical zone. Lowlands in the L. Maracaibo basin in Zulia and Mérida. [Costa Rica to n Colombia.]
Rain forest to 150 m. Forest edge, open areas with scattered trees. Call: short whistles given in couplets or in rapid series, (*fide* Lanyon).

Note: Regarded as conspecific with *M. ferox* in Lista Av. Venez. and Sp. Bds. S Amer.

## VENEZUELAN FLYCATCHER
*Myiarchus venezuelensis*
ATRAPAMOSCAS DE VENEZUELA

Pl. 28
7.2″ (18.3 cm.). Probably not distinguishable in the field from Short-crested or Panama Flycatchers. Differs from both by having the outer webs of the primaries narrowly margined with cinnamon rufous, rectrices narrowly edged with hazel. Back darker than in Panama Flycatcher, more as in Short-crested Flycatcher.
Tropical zone. W Zulia, e Falcón, n Carabobo, Distr. Federal; ne Bolívar (*venezuelensis*). [Tobago.]
Rain forest to 500 m. Forest edge, open areas with scattered trees. Call: a long, plaintive whistle, but lacking a sharp huit or the roll (*fide* Lanyon).
Note: Regarded as conspecific with *M. ferox* in Lista Av. Venez. and Sp. Bds. S Amer.

## PALE-EDGED FLYCATCHER
*Myiarchus cephalotes*
ATRAPAMOSCAS MONTAÑERO JUÍ

7.5″ (19 cm.). Above dark olive brown, feathers of crown browner with dusky centers. Lores and cheeks white mottled with dusky. Throat and breast clear, light gray, belly and under tail coverts pale yellow. Remiges and rectrices dusky brown, wing coverts with conspicuous grayish white margins, secondaries narrowly edged pale yellow, tertials rather broadly edged white; outermost rectrix edged yellowish white.
Subtropical zone. The n mountains from Trujillo, Lara, Aragua and n Guárico to e Sucre (*caribbaeus*). [Colombia to n Bolivia.]
Cloud forest, 1400–2100 m. In small trees and bushes. Calls: short, sharp whistles as well as longer, plaintive whistles; short whistles sometimes given in series (*fide* Lanyon).

## BROWN-CRESTED FLYCATCHER
*Myiarchus tyrannulus*
ATRAPAMOSCAS GARROCHERO COLIRUFO

Pl. 28
8" (20 cm.). Above brownish olive, crown darker and browner, upper tail coverts lighter with a slight rufescent wash. Lores and cheeks white, mottled with dusky. Throat and breast clear, very light gray; belly pale yellow. Wings and tail dusky brown, wing coverts conspicuously edged grayish white, inner remiges margined yellowish white, primaries edged rufous, all but central *tail feathers largely rufous on inner web.*
Tropical zone. Generally distributed n of the Ríos Apure and Orinoco; n Amazonas; n and central Bolívar; Margarita, Los Testigos, Los Frailes, La Tortuga and Patos Is. (*tyrannulus*). Los Roques Is. (*brevipennis*). La Blanquilla I. (*blanquillae*). [The Guianas and e Colombia to central Argentina and se Brazil. Aruba to Trinidad and Tobago. Sw US to nw Costa Rica.]
Forested lowlands, second growth to 1100 m. n of the Orinoco, to 300 m. s of it. Adapted to many environments. In mangroves as well as in arid, thorny areas but usually in open forest, humid regions, clearings, plantations and scrub. Not shy. Note rufous tail. Calls: short, harsh "wirrp" and sharp "huit," the latter often given in a rapid series; no whistled notes (*fide* Lanyon).

## GREAT-CRESTED FLYCATCHER
*Myiarchus crinitus*
ATRAPAMOSCAS COPETÓN

8" (20 cm.). Very similar to Brown-crested Flycatcher but larger; bill broader. Inner webs of all but central tail feathers entirely instead of only partly rufous; inner remiges brighter and deeper in color, cinnamon rufous instead of buff; back more strongly olivaceous.
Tropical zone. Winter resident, mid-Oct. to end Mar. Recorded from Zulia, Mérida and n Amazonas (*boreus*). [Breeds in e N Amer. Winters from Florida and Texas to Colombia.]
Occupies many habitats to 1200 m. High, dense forest, open woodland, plantations, forest edge, dry forest and semi-arid regions. Silent and solitary, it perches quietly in the high foliage. Seizes prey on wing, in bark crevices and on the ground.

## SWAINSON'S FLYCATCHER
*Myiarchus swainsoni*
ATRAPAMOSCAS DE SWAINSON

8" (20 cm.). The migrant race differs from other similar species by *reddish brown* instead of black *lower mandible.* Dark olive brown above (with top and sides of head blackish, bill black, a). Throat and breast pale gray, belly pale yellow. Outer web of outer rectrix narrowly pale edged.
Tropical and subtropical zones. Resident s of the Orinoco in Amazonas, Bolívar and Delta Amacuro (*phaeonotus*, a). Migrant from the s, summer resident in the tropical zone found virtually throughout (*swainsoni*). [The Guianas, e Colombia to Bolivia, central Argentina and Uruguay. Trinidad.]
It is possible that the pale-backed *M. s. ferocior* occurs as a summer visitor for it is found in se Colombia as a migrant.
Rain forests in the lowlands to 300 m. n of the Orinoco, but ranging up to humid cloud forests on the slopes of the tepuis at 1800 m. Mangroves, savannas and open fields with scattered trees, low bushes; river banks, low second growth. Not shy nor very active. Calls: plaintive, long whistle; also a rapid series of short whistles (*fide* Lanyon). Migrants recorded Mar.–Sept.

## DUSKY-CAPPED FLYCATCHER
*Myiarchus tuberculifer*
ATRAPAMOSCAS CRESTA NEGRA

Pl. 28
7" (18 cm., a), [6.5" (16.5 cm.), a]. Crown and nape sooty blackish, back dusky olive (or bright grayish olive, a), somewhat rufescent on upper tail coverts. Wings and tail blackish brown, wing coverts edged gray, inner remiges edged white; basal portion of shaft of tail feathers brown. Throat and breast pale gray, belly pale yellow.
Tropical and subtropical zones. From Zulia, Táchira and Barinas e through the n Cordilleras to Sucre and in the llanos of Portuguesa, Guárico and Apure

(*pallidus,* a). Amazonas, Bolívar and Delta Amacuro (*tuberculifer*). [Sw US to nw Peru, Bolivia, nw Argentina and e Brazil. Trinidad.]
Rain and cloud forest, to 2000 m. n of the Orinoco, to 1400 m s of it. Open forest, forest edge, second growth; also arid regions, plantations, near rivers. Forages alone or in pair in the lower and middle parts of trees. Joins forest flocks. Raises black feathers of crown. Hunts insects on the wing and among foliage. Nods frequently. Quiet. Call: a plaintive, long whistle "whe-ee-er," also a sharp "huit" and a roll (rapid series of short whistles) (*fide* Lanyon). The smallest *Myiarchus.*

## OLIVE-SIDED FLYCATCHER

*Contopus borealis*
ATRAPAMOSCAS BOREAL

Pl. XIII
7" (18 cm.). A chunky, large-headed, short-tailed flycatcher. Head somewhat crested. Upperparts gray, a white patch, often partly concealed, at each side of lower back. Throat and center of belly white, breast somewhat streaked, sides of body dark olive in contrast to rest of underparts. Wings and tail dusky, wing coverts with inconspicuous gray edges, inner remiges margined white.
Upper tropical and subtropical zones. Winter resident, Oct.–Apr. The Cordilleras of the n from Zulia and Táchira e. [Breeds in N Amer. Winters to n and w S Amer. Bonaire. Trinidad.]
Occupies varied habitats with high trees from, rarely, 400 to 2200 m. Rain and cloud forest, semi-open country with scattered trees, forest borders and clearings. Solitary, perches conspicuously on the most exposed branches of the highest treetops and makes long sallies for insects. Call: said to resemble the syllables "whi-three-beers," also "pip-pip-pip."
Note: Placed in the monotypic genus *Nuttallornis* in Lista Av. Venez. and Sp. Bds. S Amer.

## WOOD PEWEE

*Contopus virens*
ATRAPAMOSCAS DE LA SELVA

5.7" (14.5 cm.). Slightly crested. Above gray with a slight olive tinge, crown somewhat darker. Wings and tail black- ish, wings with 2 grayish white bars, inner remiges edged white. Throat white, breast and sides of body pale gray, center of belly white with a yellowish wash; under tail coverts white. Under wing coverts whitish (or smoky brown, a). Lower mandible pale. Imm.: above somewhat browner than ad.
Tropical zone. Winter resident, Sept.–Apr. Nw Venezuela e to Mérida, Barinas and Falcón, and in n Amazonas and nw Bolívar (*virens*). Once in the Gran Sabana (*saturatus,* a). Once in s Amazonas on the Brazilian border (*veliei,* a). [Breeds from Alaska and Canada to Guatemala and possibly to nw Colombia (*sordidulus*). Winters from Nicaragua to w Brazil.]
Various habitats to 1300 m. n of the Orinoco, to 1000 m. s of it. Open woods, clearings, vicinity of rivers and ponds, brush; also in the high, dense, humid forest. Active, solitary. Darts after insects from high, exposed perches, also frequents lower branches. Call: a plaintive, sad pee-a-weeee with a rising inflection, long drawn out.
Note: Includes *sordidulus,* listed as a separate species in Lista Av. Venez., where also *saturatus* and *veliei* were regarded as races of *sordidulus,* now considered to be the western race of *virens. Sordidulus* has been reported as breeding in Chocó, w Colombia, but the record needs confirmation.

## TROPICAL PEWEE

*Contopus cinereus*
ATRAPAMOSCAS CENIZO

Pl. 29
5" (13 cm.). Very similar to Wood Pewee but smaller, paler, belly yellower, back grayer without the olivaceous tinge, tail feathers narrowly tipped white. Lores and narrow eye ring white.
Tropical and lower subtropical zones. N of the Orinoco; s Amazonas near the Brazilian border (*bogotensis*). Bolívar along the middle Orinoco (*surinamensis*). [S Mexico to s Bolivia, n Argentina and se Brazil. Trinidad.]
Open forest, savannas with scattered trees, near rivers, second growth and arid scrub, forest edge, to 1900 m. Solitary, keeps from low to middle height of trees. Sallies for insects, shakes tail on returning to perch. Call: a short rapid trill.

# GREATER PEWEE
*Contopus fumigatus*
ATRAPAMOSCAS AHUMADO

Pl. XIII
7" (18 cm.). Crested. Above dark gray, below paler gray, center of abdomen whitish. Wings and tail blackish, wing coverts inconspicuously edged dark gray. Lower mandible yellowish horn color. Imm.: wing coverts conspicuously edged buff.
Upper tropical and subtropical zones. Sierra de Perijá, Zulia; the Andes from Táchira to Trujillo (*ardosiacus*). The coastal Cordilleras from Yaracuy to Miranda and the interior Cordillera in Aragua and Miranda (*cineraceus*). The mountains of Amazonas and s Bolívar (*duidae*). [Sw US to nw Peru, and nw Argentina. Trinidad.]
Humid rain and cloud forests from somewhat below 700 m. to 2800 m. n of the Orinoco, from 900 to 1900 m. s of it. Forest edge, clearings, second growth. Perches alone or in pairs on projecting dead branches of tall trees. Call: wicway-tee.

[ALL *Empidonax* are difficult to identify in the field especially in their wintering grounds. They are easily confused with *Contopus*, but the latter are distinctly less greenish on the back and do not have a white eye ring.]

# ACADIAN FLYCATCHER
*Empidonax virescens*
ATRAPAMOSCAS COPETE VERDE

5.5" (14 cm.). Upperparts dull olive green, eye ring white, tail grayish olive. Wings blackish with 2 conspicuous buffy white wing bars, inner remiges edged buffy white. Throat white, underparts yellowish white suffused with olive at sides of breast.
Upper tropical zone. Winter resident, Nov.–Mar. Sierra de Perijá, Zulia, n slopes of the Andes of Táchira. Breeds in N Amer. Winters from Costa Rica to w Ecuador.
Forest edge, clearings, second growth, haciendas, swampy woods, 900–1200 m. Alone, active, sallies forth for insects among low branches of densely foliaged low trees where it is difficult to see. Flits in the thickets. Twitches tail up and down. Call: a plaintive phit-chwee sliding up to the second note.

# TRAILL'S FLYCATCHER
*Empidonax traillii*
ATRAPAMOSCAS PÁLIDO

5.5" (14 cm.). Back more brownish olive, less green than in Acadian Flycatcher, otherwise not distinguishable.
Tropical zone. Winter resident, Aug.–Feb. Zulia and Falcón s to Mérida, Táchira and w Apure (*traillii*). Breeds in N Amer. Winters from S Mexico to n Argentina. Although recorded in Venezuela only from the tropical zone it has been taken as high as the temperate zone in Colombia and the subtropical zone in Peru.
Sea level to 250 m. Mangroves, low bushes, second growth, open areas, edge of forest, thickets. Solitary, perches quietly in low and fairly high branches twitching the tail up and down. Sallies for insects flitting among the branches.

# EULER'S FLYCATCHER
*Empidonax euleri*
ATRAPAMOSCAS DE EULER

Pl. 29
5" (13 cm.). Back dull grayish olive, grayer on crown (or back dull brownish olive, browner on crown, a). Eye ring and throat whitish, breast grayish, belly and under tail coverts yellowish white. Wings dusky brown, two grayish (or buff, a) wing bars, inner remiges margined yellowish white (or buff, a). Tail grayish brown.
Tropical and lower subtropical zones. From Zulia, Táchira, w Apure and nw Barinas and w Falcón on the Paria Pen., Sucre; nw Bolívar from the lower Río Caura to the Río Cuyuni (*lawrencei*). W Amazonas; se Bolívar (*bolivianus*, a). [Surinam; se Colombia to n and e Bolivia, Paraguay, Brazil to central Argentina. Grenada I.]
Rain and cloud forests and plantations, open woodland, stubble fields to 1500 m. n of the Orinoco, to 1000 m. s of it on the slopes of the tepuis. Perches boldly in lower branches of thickets and open low forest. Sallies forth for insects flitting through the twigs. Twitches tail up and down.

## FUSCOUS FLYCATCHER
*Cnemotriccus fuscatus*
ATRAPAMOSCAS FUSCO

Pl. 29
5.5" (14 cm.). Above rufescent brown (or brown, a; or dark grayish brown, b). Wings with 2 buff bars. Throat white, breast band brownish gray, belly pale yellow (yellow, a; or white, b). Tail brownish.
Tropical zone. Zulia e through Portuguesa, Apure and Guárico to Sucre and Patos I.; s of the Orinoco in n Bolívar from the mouth of the Apure e to Delta Amacuro (*cabanisi,* a). S Amazonas (*duidae*). W Apure (*fuscatior,* b). [The Guianas and Colombia to Bolivia and n Argentina.]
Rain forest and high second growth to 920 m. n of the Orinoco, to 250 m. s of it. Dark, dense, wet undergrowth to semi-arid areas with deciduous trees and scrub. Forages for insects from the lowest branches to treetops. Call: a rough, shrill whistle remarkably loud for the size of the bird.

## RUDDY-TAILED FLYCATCHER
*Terenotriccus erythrurus*
ATRAPAMOSCAS COLICASTAÑO

Pl. 30
4" (10 cm.). Top and sides of head pale gray, mantle olivaceous gray gradually turning to rufescent on lower back and bright cinnamon rufous on rump and tail. Remiges and wing coverts broadly margined bright cinnamon rufous. Throat whitish (or olivaceous buff, a), rest of underparts cinnamon buff, somewhat darker on breast (or underparts cinnamon rufous, a).
Tropical zone. Nw Zulia s to the Andes of Táchira and Barinas; central Carabobo (*fulvigularis*). Amazonas from Caño Cataniapo s and across Bolívar to the upper Ríos Paragua and Caroní (*venezuelensis,* a). E Bolívar from the lower Río Paragua and the vicinity of Cerro Auyan-tepui to the Río Cuyuni (*erythrurus*). [Mexico to Amazonian Brazil and Bolivia.]
High, dense rain forest, high, humid second growth to about 600 m. Not shy. Usually alone, this tiny bird forages for small insects from the shady lower levels of the undergrowth to the upper

branches. When perched flits both wings. Call: a low, weak, 2-note whistle, "eee-wee."

## TAWNY-BREASTED FLYCATCHER
*Myiobius villosus*
ATRAPAMOSCAS PELUDO

Pl. 29
5.5" (14 cm.). Upperparts dusky olive, rump bright pale yellow, semi-concealed crown patch bright yellow. Wings blackish, coverts and inner remiges edged brownish olive; tail black. Throat dull white, rest of underparts reddish olive brown. Tail black. Rictal bristles in the genus very long. ♀: crown patch rufous.
Upper tropical and subtropical zones. The Perijá region, Zulia (*schaeferi*). Sw Táchira and Mérida (*villosus*). [E Panama, Colombia, e and w Ecuador to n Bolivia.]
Cloud forest and open woods, 960–1900 m. All levels in the trees. Small forest clearings, second growth.

## SULPHUR-RUMPED FLYCATCHER
*Myiobius barbatus*
ATRAPAMOSCAS BARBUDO

Pl. 29
5.2" (13 cm.). Upperparts olive green, rump bright pale yellow. Semi-concealed crown patch bright yellow. Wings dusky, feathers edged olive. Throat whitish, breast grayish, belly pale yellow, under tail coverts pale brown with indistinct dusky bars. Tail black. ♀: crown patch barely indicated.
Tropical zone. S Amazonas; Bolívar across the Ríos Caura, Paragua and upper Caroní to Nuria, the Río Cuyuni and Cerro Roraima (*barbatus*). [The Guianas, Colombia, e and w Ecuador to e Peru and Amazonian and se Brazil. Mid. Amer.]
High, dense rain forest, high, humid second growth to 1300 m. Alone or in pairs inside the shaded areas of the forest, seldom at the edge. Forages for insects actively and spreads the tail like a *Myioborus.*

## BLACK-TAILED FLYCATCHER
*Myiobius atricaudus*
ATRAPAMOSCAS COLINEGRO

4.9" (12.5 cm.). Much like the Sulphur-rumped Flycatcher but breast buffy gray, back paler and grayer; size smaller. Tropical zone. Nw Bolívar from Caicara to the Río San Félix and the extreme n of the Sierra de Imataca near the borders of Delta Amacuro (*modestus*). [Sw Costa Rica to nw and se Peru, Brazil s of the Amazon to w Amazonas and São Paulo.] Rain forests in the lowlands, near sea level. Forages actively in the thick woods, also near streams. Recognized by its habit of capturing insects by flitting about with great agility. Spreads the tail like many warblers.

## CINNAMON FLYCATCHER
*Pyrrhomyias cinnamomea*
ATRAPAMOSCAS ACANELADO

Pl. 29
5.2" (13 cm.). Above olive brown (or cinnamon rufous, a); large, semi-concealed bright yellow crest; feathers of rump cinnamon buff terminally, forming a narrow band; upper tail coverts blackish, tipped buff (or upper tail coverts cinnamon rufous, a). Tail dusky brown minutely tipped buff (or cinnamon rufous with black subterminal patch, a). Wings dusky with 2 cinnamon rufous bars, outer remiges basally cinnamon rufous on inner web, inner remiges rufous basally on both webs, tertials margined cinnamon buff (or wings mostly cinnamon rufous, a). Underparts cinnamon rufous shading to cinnamon on belly.
Upper tropical and subtropical zones. The Sierra de Perijá, Zulia; sw Táchira; the coastal Cordillera in Miranda and the Distr. Federal, the interior chain from s Lara through Yaracuy to Aragua and Miranda (*vieillotioides*, a). The mountains of Anzoátegui, Sucre and Monagas (*spadix*, a). The Paria Pen., Sucre on Cerro Humo and Azul (*pariae*). [Colombia through the Andes to Bolivia and n Argentina.] Cloud forest, 700–2900 m., rarely below 1000 m. except in Paria. Coffee haciendas, forest, clearings.

## FLAVESCENT FLYCATCHER
*Myiophobus flavicans*
ATRAPAMOSCAS AMARILLOSO

Pl. 29
5.2" (13 cm.). Semi-concealed crown patch yellow. Upperparts olive green; wings dusky brownish, lesser coverts inconspicuously edged olive brown, greater coverts conspicuously edged buff, inner remiges edged olive yellow; tail grayish brown. Below light greenish yellow washed olivaceous on breast (or without olivaceous wash, a), flanks washed ochraceous brown. ♀: similar but without crown patch.
Upper tropical and subtropical zones. The Sierra de Perijá, Zulia; sw Táchira (*perijanus*). Ne Táchira through the Andes of Mérida, Trujillo and Lara and the coastal Cordillera from Yaracuy to Aragua, Miranda and the Distr. Federal (*venezuelanus*). Cerro Negro, Sucre and the Monagas border (*caripensis*, a). Cloud forest, 900–2300 m., rarely below 1500 m. Interior of dense forests, alone or in pairs in the lower branches of thick woods, low bushes and impenetrable bamboo tangles.

## BRAN-COLORED FLYCATCHER
*Myiophobus fasciatus*
ATRAPAMOSCAS PECHIRRAYADO

Pl. 29
4.3" (11 cm.). Semi-concealed crown patch cinnamon orange. Upper parts reddish brown, wings dark brown with two prominent buffy white bars. Tail dark grayish brown. Throat dull white, rest of underparts yellowish white *conspicuously streaked on breast* with grayish brown.
Tropical and lower subtropical zones. The Sierra de Perijá, Zulia, the Andes of Táchira and Barinas e through the coastal Cordillera to Sucre, Patos I., and to the e llanos of Monagas, thence s in e Bolívar to the Sierra de Imataca, the Gran Sabana and s Amazonas (*fasciatus*). [Costa Rica to Colombia, the Guianas to Bolivia, Uruguay and central Argentina.] Open, brushy fields, open woodland to 1700 m. n of the Orinoco, from 950 to 1200 m. s of it. Not very active, inconspicuous. Alone or in pairs flits among low twigs and sallies forth for

insects from perches up to the middle
tier. Call: a low whistle.

## RORAIMAN FLYCATCHER

*Myiophobus roraimae*
ATRAPAMOSCAS DEL RORAIMA

5.2″ (13 cm.). Semi-concealed crown
patch cinnamon orange. Upperparts and
tail olive brown, wings blackish with
two conspicuous rufous bars, inner remiges margined rufous. Throat yellowish white, breast grayish olive, center of
belly bright yellow, thighs reddish
brown. ♀: similar but crest absent or
only slightly indicated.
Upper tropical and subtropical zones.
Amazonas on Cerros Paraque and Yaví
s to Cerro de la Neblina; nw Bolívar on
Cerro Tabaro, lower Río Caura, and on
the tepuis of the Gran Sabana (*roraimae*).
[Nw Guyana, se Colombia. Central Peru.
Adj. Brazil near la Neblina.]
Cloud forest in the lower parts of trees,
900–1980 m. On the Brazilian side of
the border it has been taken at 550 m.

## CLIFF FLYCATCHER

*Hirundinea ferruginea*
ATRAPAMOSCAS DE PRECIPICIOS

Pl. 28
7.2″ (18.2 cm.). Upperparts sooty blackish brown, top and sides of head mottled
with white, chin white, *entire underparts
bright chestnut*. Wings and tail black
(or with inner webs of all but central
tail feathers chestnut, a). In flight wings
are long and swallowlike and show a
*large chestnut patch* formed by the
inner web at base of inner remiges.
Casually tropical, usually subtropical zone.
W Zulia in the Sierra de Perijá (*sclateri,
a*). W Bolívar along the middle Río
Caura, Cerro Jaua, and the tepuis of
the Gran Sabana; w Amazonas s to
Cerro Duida (*ferruginea*). [Generally
e of the Andes to Bolivia, Paraguay, n
Argentina and Uruguay.]
Vicinity of cliffs, precipices, large rocks
and boulders and similar localities in
forested areas, rivers and open situations. From 1600 to 1900 m. n of the
Orinoco, and s of it rarely from 100 m.
(Río Caura), but usually from 700–
1900 m. Swallowlike; hawks for insects.
Call: a twittering whistle.

## ROYAL FLYCATCHER

*Onychorhynchus coronatus*
ATRAPAMOSCAS REAL

Pl. 29
6.5″ (16.5 cm.). Head adorned with a
*very large fanshaped crimson crest*, terminating in shiny steel blue disks, not
usually held erect. Sides of crown and
head and the back brown, upper tail
coverts cinnamon buff, tail cinnamon
rufous. Wings dark brown; wing coverts
with conspicuous terminal buff dots.
Throat whitish, rest of underparts light
buff more to less barred with blackish
on breast and flanks. Bill long, wide and
flat. ♀: crest orange.
Tropical and subtropical zones. The Sierra
de Perijá, Zulia, and the e slopes of the
Andes in nw Barinas (*fraterculus*). N
Bolívar from the lower Río Caura e to
the Río Cuyuni, Delta Amacuro and the
Paria Pen., Sucre; Amazonas from the
Río Ventuari s to Cerro Duida (*coronatus*). Extreme sw Amazonas at the
juncture of Caño Casiquiare and the Río
Guainía, and on the Sierra Imerí
(*castelnaudi*). [Mexico to Colombia and
nw Peru, the Guianas to n Bolivia and
Amazonia n and se Brazil.]
Rain and cloud forests, second growth,
forest edge, to 2000 m. n of the Orinoco,
to 1000 m. s of it. Alone or in pairs,
forages in the undergrowth and lower
branches, for insects caught on the wing.
Often near streams where it usually
nests. The spectacular crest is not ordi-
narily erected. Call: utters a loud,
mellow whistle.

[BIRDS BELONGING TO *Platyrinchus* are very
small, squat flycatchers recognizable by
their remarkably wide and flat bills and
very short tails.]

## WHITE-CRESTED SPADEBILL

*Platyrinchus platyrhynchos*
PICO CHATO CABECIGRIS

Pl. 30
4.2″ (10.6 cm.). *Top and sides of head
gray;* extensive, semi-concealed *crest
white,* feathers tipped gray. Back ochraceous, tail grayish brown, the feathers
edged ochraceous. Inner remiges edged
ochraceous, primary coverts blackish.
Throat white, rest of underparts bright
tawny ochraceous. Legs yellowish flesh.

Tropical zone. N Amazonas s to the Río Guainía; nw Bolívar from the lower Río Caura to the upper Paragua (*griseiceps*). [The Guianas; e Ecuador to Bolivia and Amazonian Brazil.] Undergrowth in rain forest, low bushes at forest edge, 100–300 m. Feeds on insects.
Note: Called *P. senex griseiceps* in Lista Av. Venez.

## WHITE-THROATED SPADEBILL
*Platyrinchus mystaceus*
PICO CHATO GARGANTIBLANCO

Pl. 30
3.8″ (9.7 cm.). Above brown to brownish olive including wings and tail. Eye ring, spot on lores, base of auriculars and small patch behind eye buffy white forming 3 pale spots; semi-concealed *crest golden yellow*. Throat white, underparts pale buffy to yellowish ochraceous with a brownish wash on breast, abdomen paler. ♀: lacks yellow crown patch.
Tropical and lower subtropical zones. The Sierra de Perijá, Zulia (*perijanus*). S Táchira (*neglectus*). Falcón and w Lara e coastally to the Paria Pen., Sucre, and inland in w Barinas, Aragua, Miranda and n Guárico; s of the Orinoco in n Bolívar from Caicara to Delta Amacuro (*insularis*). In ne Bolívar on the Sierra de Imataca (*imatacae*). Cerros Ptaritepui, Sororopán-tepui and Aprada-tepui (*ptaritepui*). In the Roraima region, se Bolívar and in central Amazonas on Cerros Yaví and Duida (*duidae*). Extreme s Amazonas on Cerro de la Neblina (*ventralis*). [Mid. Amer. to Argentina and Bolivia. Trinidad, Tobago.]
Rain and cloud forest, second growth, to 1800 m. Humid deep forest undergrowth, also forest edge and open brush. Solitary, not shy, inconspicuous. Forages actively for insects in the lower branches. Flits wings. Call: a short, harsh chirp.

## GOLDEN-CROWNED SPADEBILL
*Platyrinchus coronatus*
PICO CHATO CORONA DORADA

Pl. 30
3.5″ (9 cm.). Above dull olivaceous, wings and tail browner. *Crown chestnut* partially concealing *golden yellow crest*, sides of crown, moustacial streak and spot at posterior edge of ear coverts black; lores, eye ring and eyebrow buffy white. Underparts buffy white to yellowish, breast more to less washed with brownish. ♀: crown cinnamon rufous, without yellow.
Tropical and lower subtropical zones. N Amazonas from Caño Cuao to Cerros Parú and Yapacana (*superciliaris*). S Amazonas from Caño Casiquiare s (*coronatus*). Central Bolívar from the Río Paragua e to Sierra de Imataca and the Gran Sabana to Roraima (*gumia*). [The Guianas, e and w Ecuador, e Peru, central Amazonian Brazil.]
High, dense rain forest, old second growth to 1500 m. Alone or in pairs, forages for insects from near the ground to upper forest levels. Joins forest flocks. Not shy. Often near streams. Flicks wings. Call: a thin, whistled trill.

## CINNAMON-CRESTED SPADEBILL
*Platyrinchus saturatus*
PICO CHATO COPETE ACANELADO

4.2″ (10.6 cm.). Above dark reddish brown, wings brighter. Semi-concealed *crest orange cinnamon*. Lores and throat white, breast and sides suffused with brown, rest of underparts buffy yellow. ♀: like ♂ but crest reduced in size.
Tropical zone. Amazonas from Nericagua s to the Yavita-Pimichín Trail and e across Bolívar to the Gran Sabana. [The Guianas, se Colombia. Ne Peru, Amazonian Brazil.]
Dense rain forest, old second growth to 900 m., often in shady and damp areas. Alone, forages for insects in the undergrowth and lower tier of trees.

## YELLOW-THROATED SPADEBILL
*Platyrinchus flavigularis*
PICO CHATO GARGANTIAMARILLO

Pl. 30
4″ (10 cm.). Top and sides of head reddish brown, semi-concealed *crest white*, the feathers tipped black. Back olive, underparts yellow with a strong yellowish green wash across breast. Wings and tail dusky, the feathers edged olive.
Upper tropical and subtropical zones. The Sierra de Perijá, Zulia; s Lara; s Táchira (*vividus*). [Central Colombia. Ne Ecuador. Central Peru.]

Dense cloud forest in lower trees and undergrowth, 1250–2100 m.

[BIRDS BELONGING TO the genus *Tolmomyias* resemble each other closely and are very difficult to tell apart in the field. They are large-headed flycatchers with rather broad, flat bills, and tails of normal length. All are for the most part olive green above, yellowish or yellow below with conspicuous yellowish wing bars (except for Gray-crowned Flycatcher).]

## YELLOW-OLIVE FLYCATCHER
*Tolmomyias sulphurescens*
PICO CHATO SULFUROSO

Pl. 29
6″ (15 cm.). Above olive, crown gray (or olive like back, a), lores white. Underparts pale yellow, throat whitish, sides washed olive. Wings blackish, remiges edged olive yellow, double wing bar yellowish white. Tail gray, edged olive.
Tropical and lower subtropical zones. W Zulia, n Táchira n of the Andes e to the Paria Pen. and from Barinas to Monagas (*exortivus,* a). Sw Táchira along the Colombian border and extreme w Apure (*confusus*). N Bolívar from Caicara and the Río Cuchivero across the lower Río Caura and Paragua to the Río Cuyuni and Delta Amacuro (*cherriei*). N Amazonas s; Bolívar from the upper Ríos Cuchivero and Paragua to the s Gran Sabana in the se corner of Bolívar (*duidae*). [S Mexico to Amazonian Brazil and nw Bolivia. Trinidad.]
Rain forest, second growth, forest edge, at sea level, ascending to 1900 m. in cloud forest n of the Orinoco and to 1500 m. s of it. Open terrain with scattered trees, gallery forest. Alone, inconspicuous, forages for insects and berries in the foliage usually at medium heights. Investigates army ants. Call: a high, thin whistle.

## YELLOW-MARGINED FLYCATCHER
*Tolmomyias assimilis*
PICO CHATO ALIAMARILLO

5.5″ (14 cm.). Indistinguishable in the field from the Yellow-olive Flycatcher. In the hand, and possibly in the field if seen close, a small white speculum at the juncture of the primaries and primary coverts is the best distinguishing character. The cap in this species is gray, slightly darker in tone than that of the gray-capped form of the Yellow-olive Flycatcher.
Tropical zone. Amazonas from Caño Cataniapo to Caño Casiquiare and the Río Negro; n Bolívar along the lower Río Caura (*neglectus*). Central and e Bolívar from the Río Paragua e to the Río Cuyuni, and s to Cerro Paurai-tepui (*examinatus*). [Costa Rica to Colombia, nw Ecuador, the Guianas, Bolivia, n and sw Brazil.]
High rain forest to 1200 m. on the slopes of the tepuis. More of a forest bird than Yellow-olive Flycatcher.

## GRAY-CROWNED FLYCATCHER
*Tolmomyias poliocephalus*
PICO CHATO DE CORONA GRIS

Pl. 29
5″ (13 cm.). Differs from the gray-crowned forms of the Yellow-olive Flycatcher by smaller size, and the wing coverts very narrowly edged yellow.
Tropical zone. N Amazonas s to the Río Ventuari, e across Bolívar to the Sierra de Imataca and the Gran Sabana; Delta Amacuro (*klagesi*). S Amazonas from Cerro Duida and Caño Casiquiare s (*poliocephalus*). [The Guianas, Colombia, Amazonian and se Brazil, n Bolivia.]
Dense rain forest, forest edge, clearings, open terrain with scattered trees, humid areas, to 960 m. Frequents lower levels of trees.

## YELLOW-BREASTED FLYCATCHER
*Tolmomyias flaviventris*
PICO CHATO AMARILLENTO

Pl. 29
5″ (13 cm.). Upperparts yellowish olive, brighter and slightly yellower on forehead, lores ochre yellow. Underparts bright yellow with ochre wash on throat and breast, sides slightly tinged olive. Wings blackish, remiges edged yellowish olive, innermost more broadly edged yellowish white; median and greater coverts edged yellow forming two bars. Tail grayish brown, the feathers edged olive yellow.

Tropical zone. Zulia, Falcón and nw Lara to sw Táchira and ne to Carabobo and Miranda (*aurulentus*). Nw Bolívar along the upper Río Cuchivero; Amazonas from the Río Ventuari s to the Cerro Duida region (*dissors*). Apure and nw Amazonas and the Cordilleras and llanos e of the areas occupied by the above two, e to Delta Amacuro; central and e Bolívar (*collingwoodi*). [The Guianas, e and w Colombia. E Peru, Bolivia, Amazonian and se Brazil. Trinidad, Tobago.]

Sea level to 900 m. but rarely above 500 m. s of the Orinoco. Rain forest, high second growth, dry woods, swampy forest and open terrain with scattered trees. Alone or in pairs, forages for insects at medium height in the trees and in the undergrowth. Actions are those of a warbler. Snaps mandibles audibly. Call: a high, thin "tseeeee."

## OLIVACEOUS FLATBILL

*Rhynchocyclus olivaceus*
PICO CHATO ACEITUNADO

Pl. 29

6" (15 cm.). Olive green above, wings dusky, median and greater coverts edged dull yellowish green (or edged olive buff to buff, a), remiges edged yellowish green, these edges becoming buffy toward ends of feathers; tail grayish, edged olive green. Throat and breast olive (or grayish olive, a) obscurely streaked yellow, rest of underparts pale yellow, washed olivaceous at sides. Bill very wide and flat, black above, whitish flesh below.

Tropical zone. Zulia in the Sierra de Perijá and e of L. Maracaibo s to Táchira, w Barinas and w Apure, e through Mérida and Yaracuy to the tip of the Paria Pen., Sucre (*flavus*). S Amazonas and across Bolívar to the Río Cuyuni and the Gran Sabana; extreme s Sucre (*guianensis*, a). [Panama to Bolivia and Amazonian and se Brazil.]

Rain forests to 1000 m. n of the Orinoco, to 500 m. s of it. Often near swampy areas, open terrain with scattered trees, second growth forest edge, plantations. Alone or in pairs usually forages for insects in the medium height of trees.

## FULVOUS-BREASTED FLATBILL

*Rhynchocyclus fulvipectus*
PICO CHATO PECHIFULVO

6" (15 cm.). Upperparts moss green, wings brownish black, greater coverts broadly edged tawny ochre, remiges margined tawny olivaceous; tail brown. Chin grayish, throat and upper breast tawny ochraceous, rest of underparts bright yellow. Bill very wide and flat, black above, flesh below.

Subtropical zone. Sw Táchira. [Colombia, e and w Ecuador to Bolivia.]

Known only from cloud forest near Río Chiquito in a coffee hacienda at 1800 m.

## RUFOUS-TAILED FLATBILL

*Ramphotrigon ruficauda*
PICO CHATO BARBIRRUFO

Pl. 29

6" (15 cm.). Upperparts dark olive, eye ring white; wings dusky, median and greater coverts and remiges broadly edged rufous chestnut, the wings chestnut when closed. *Tail bright rufous.* Throat grayish olive streaked whitish, rest of underparts yellow, streaked grayish olive, under tail coverts rufous. Bill not as flat or wide as in Fulvous-breasted Flatbill, black, base of lower mandible flesh.

Tropical zone. Amazonas; Bolívar from the lower Río Caura and the Río Paragua to the Sierra de Imataca. [The Guianas, n Bolivia and Amazonian Brazil.]

Dense rain forest, 100–200 m. Alone or in pairs, forages for insects and berries in the dark undergrowth and lower parts of trees.

## LARGE-HEADED FLATBILL

*Ramphotrigon megacephala*
PICO CHATO CABEZÓN

Pl. 29

5.3" (13.5 cm.). Upperparts olive green, crown slightly browner than back with inconspicuous dark shaft stripes; narrow eyebrow white. Wings dusky brown, greater and median coverts broadly edged cinnamon buff forming 2 prominent bars, inner remiges edged yellowish olive; tail dull brown, feathers narrowly edged ochraceous. Throat olive ob-

scurely streaked pale yellow, breast olivaceous, strongly washed with ochraceous and obscurely streaked yellow,
belly bright yellow.
Tropical zone. Ne Yaracuy; nw Barinas; w
Apure (*venezuelensis*). The upper Río
Siapa, s Amazonas (*pectoralis*). [E
Colombia to n Bolivia.]
Rain forest to 300 m n of the Orinoco, at
550 m. s of it. Forages in the undergrowth.

[TODY-FLYCATCHERS (Titirijís) form a
group of very small birds with long, flat,
wide bills and narrow tails. They are
found along forest borders, shrubbery,
gardens and plantations, generally low
down in the undergrowth.]

## BLACK-HEADED TODY-FLYCATCHER
*Todirostrum nigriceps*
TITIRIJÍ CABECINEGRO

Pl. 30
3.2″ (8 cm.). Top and sides of head glossy
black; back olive yellow, yellowest on
upper mantle. Wing coverts black, margined yellow, forming 2 wing bars, inner
remiges edged yellow. Tail dusky, feathers edged olive. Throat white, rest of
underparts bright yellow.
Tropical zone. Central Amazonas; Bolívar
in the upper Río Caura e to the upper
Río Cuyuni (*pictum*, a). Extreme sw
Amazonas (*guttatum*). [The Guianas, e
Colombia to Bolivia; n Amazonian
Brazil.]
Open woods and low second growth from
sea level to 960 m. Plantations, open
forest, forest edge. Forages actively and
inconspicuously for insects, alone or in
pairs, from low to medium heights, often
along the thicker branches.
Note: Called *T. chrysocrotaphum nigriceps*
in Lista Av. Venez.

## PAINTED TODY-FLYCATCHER
*Todirostrum chrysocrotaphum*
TITIRIJÍ PINTADO

Pl. 30
3.4″ (8.6 cm.). Crown black; supraloral
streak, cheeks, malar region and throat
white (or with a long yellow eyebrow;
cheeks, malar region and throat yellow,
a). Wings black, the coverts edged

yellow forming 2 bars, inner remiges
edged yellow. Tail blackish, feathers
edged yellowish. Underparts, except
throat, bright yellow, a row of spots
across upper breast, continued to sides of
neck.
Tropical zone. The Sierra de Perijá, Zulia;
n Táchira; w Mérida. [Costa Rica to ne
and w Colombia, w Ecuador, nw Brazil
and ne Peru.]
Rain forest areas, 200–400 m. Scrub forest, second growth, plantations. Shy,
inconspicuous, forages for insects in the
lower tier. Call: a weak series of "chips."

## COMMON TODY-FLYCATCHER
*Todirostrum cinereum*
TITIRIJÍ LOMICENIZO

Pl. 30
3.8″ (9.7 cm.). Forecrown, lores and
ocular region deep black, shading to
gray on hindcrown and to gray on back,
becoming tinged with olive on rump and
upper tail coverts. Tail strongly graduated, outer feathers 0.3″ (8 mm.) shorter
than central ones, outer feathers broadly
tipped white. Wings black, the feathers
edged yellow, 2 yellow wing bars. Underparts all yellow. Very rarely one or two
white feathers on center of crown.
Tropical, casually subtropical zone. Generally n of the Orinoco except nw Zulia
and coastal Falcón; n Amazonas s to
the Río Ventuari; nw Bolívar e to Delta
Amacuro and to the Gran Sabana
(*cinereum*). [S Mexico to nw Peru,
Bolivia, Amazonian and se Brazil.]
Open woods, wet or dry open terrain with
scattered trees to 1650 m. n of the Orinoco, to 1300 m. s of it. Second growth
and low, dense, scrubby growth, bushes,
gardens, near water. Alone or in pairs
actively hops and flits for insects,
warblerlike, usually in the lower limbs.
Not shy, snaps bill, wriggles tail. Call:
a short series of twitters.

## SHORT-TAILED TODY-FLYCATCHER
*Todirotrum viridanum*
TITIRIJÍ DE MARACAIBO

3.4″ (8.6 cm.). Forehead and lores yellowish white, crown gray spotted with
black, patch in center of crown white.
Back pale olive green, lesser wing cov-

erts pale olive, wings blackish, median and greater coverts edged all around with grayish white. Tail black, short, 0.9" (22 mm.), not strongly graduated, outer feathers 0.1" (4 mm.) shorter than central ones, broadly tipped white, the white continuing up on outer web for half its length. Underparts pale yellow, flanks tinged ochraceous.

Coastal Zulia and Falcón.

Semi-arid country. Habits similar to those of Common Tody-Flycatcher. Endemic.

Note: Made a subspecies of Common Tody-Flycatcher in Lista Av. Venez. and Sp. Bds. S Amer. but its very distinctive features seem to warrant specific separation.

## SPOTTED TODY-FLYCATCHER

*Todirostrum maculatum*
Titirijí Manchado

Pl. 30
4" (10 cm.). Crown black, turning to gray on nape, a few feathers in center of forecrown edged narrowly with white, a narrow white supraloral streak. Back light olive green. Wings black, coverts edged olive green, outer remiges narrowly, inner remiges broadly edged greenish yellow. Tail black, outer web of outer tail feathers margined yellowish white. Throat and upper breast white, streaked black; rest of underparts yellow, streaked olive at sides of breast.

The delta of the Orinoco in Sucre, Monagas and Delta Amacuro (*amacurense, Eisenmann* and Phelps, Bol. Soc. Venez. Cienc. Nat., 1971, 29: 187). [The Guianas, Amazonian Brazil, e Peru. Trinidad.]

Mangroves, humid woodland, low trees near water at sea level. In pairs or family groups, actively forages for insects low in trees. Not shy, curious. Call: a strong chirp out of proportion to its small size.

## RUDDY TODY-FLYCATCHER

*Todirostrum russatum*
Titirijí Bermejo

Pl. 30
4" (10 cm.). *Forecrown, ocular region, throat and breast tawny cinnamon,* middle of crown blackish turning to dark gray on hindcrown and nape; back olive

green. Wings blackish, coverts broadly edged with cinnamon rufous forming 2 bars, remiges narrowly edged greenish yellow. Tail black, edged olive. Center of belly white, sides grayish. Tibia black in front, cinnamon behind. Under tail coverts and under wing coverts cinnamon.

Upper tropical and subtropical zones. Se Bolívar on the tepuis of the Gran Sabana. [The Brazilian slopes of Cerro Uei-tepui.]

Endemic to Pantepui. Cloud forest on the slopes and summits of the tepuis, 1400–2500 m. Forages for insects in thickly wooded, damp areas in proximity of streams. Not shy, quiet, inconspicuous. Call: an explosive rasp.

## SLATE-HEADED TODY-FLYCATCHER

*Todirostrum sylvia*
Titirijí Cabecicenizo

Pl. 30
4" (10 cm.). Crown, nape and extreme upper mantle gray, lores and eye ring white. Back olive green, wings black, coverts broadly edged yellowish green to form 2 wing bars, remiges edged bright greenish yellow. Throat and belly white, breast gray indistinctly streaked. Tail brownish, outer web of 2 outer feathers edged pale yellow, rest edged olive green.

Tropical zone. W Zulia s to Táchira and sw Apure and through Barinas to Lara, Portuguesa and w Aragua; s of the Orinoco in n Bolívar from Caicara to the Río Cuyuni (*griseolum*). [S Mexico to Colombia, the Guianas and n and e Brazil.]

Rain forest to 1000 m. Dense thickets, underbrush, low second growth. Alone or in pairs, quiet, not shy, forages for insects close to the ground hopping and flitting inconspicuously. Call: a harsh, weak note.

## PEARLY-VENTED TODY-TYRANT

*Idioptilon margaritaceiventer*
Pico Chato Vientre Perla

Pl. 30
4.2" (10.6 cm.). Upperparts grayish olive (or sooty olive, a). Wings and tail dusky brown, wing coverts edged whitish to

form 2 wing bars, remiges edged whitish, rectrices edged pale olive. Throat and breast white, streaked dusky, belly white (or ochraceous buff, a).

Tropical and subtropical zones. The Caribbean littoral from w Zulia, including the Goajira Pen., to n Lara thence e to central Guárico, Anzoátegui and Sucre; Margarita I. (*impiger*). Amazonas on Cerro Duida (*duidae*, a). Cerro Jaua (*breweri*). The tepuis of the Gran Sabana, s Bolívar (*auyantepui*). [Colombia to Bolivia, Paraguay, s Brazil and Argentina.]

Rain forest, second growth, savannas with scattered trees, arid areas with cacti and thorn thickets, n of the Orinoco from sea level to 1100 m., s of it in high cloud forest and more open woodland on the slopes and summits of the tepuis, 1000–2000 m. Forages in the lower parts of trees, bushes and other low vegetation.

Note: Called *Euscarthmornis margaritaceiventer* in Lista Av. Venez. *Breweri* described by Phelps in Bol. Soc. Venez. Cienc. Nat., 1977.

## BLACK-THROATED TODY-TYRANT
*Idioptilon granadense*
PICO CHATO GARGANTINEGRO

Pl. 30

4″ (10 cm.). Lores and ocular region white (or buff, a). Subocular region, throat and sides of neck black. Crown, ear coverts and back olive green. Wings and tail dusky brown, the feathers edged olive. Patch at base of lower throat white, breast gray, belly white, flanks tinged yellow.

Subtropical and temperate zones. The Sierra de Perijá, Zulia, sw Táchira along the Río Chiquito (*intense*). Sw Táchira on Páramo de Tamá (*andinum*, a). In the Distr. Federal (*federalis*, a). [Colombia to Peru.]

Cloud forest, 1800–3000 m. Forages for insects in the lower levels of trees in humid, mossy areas.

## WHITE-EYED TODY-TYRANT
*Idioptilon zosterops*
PICO CHATO OJIBLANCO

4.3″ (11 cm.). Upperparts olive green, indistinct supraloral streak and narrow eye ring white. Wings dusky brown, the feathers edged yellowish green, 2 yellowish wing bars. Tail pale grayish, shafts of feathers on undersurface white. Throat grayish white streaked dusky, breast yellowish green streaked olive, center of belly yellowish white, sides olivaceous.

Tropical zone. Amazonas s of the Río Ventuari (*zosterops*). [Surinam; French Guiana; se Colombia, Amazonian Brazil to n Bolivia.]

High rain forest, 100–150 m. Forages for insects in the lower level of trees near streams.

## SNETHLAGE'S TODY-TYRANT
*Snethlagea minor*
PICO CHATO DE SNETHLAGE

4″ (10 cm.). Much like White-eyed Tody-Tyrant in general appearance but tail shorter and narrower, feathers of crown longer and narrower with distinct black median line, belly paler; lores without any white admixture; bill broader.

Tropical zone. Central Amazonas at Puerto Yapacana (*pallens*). [Surinam; Amazonian Brazil.]

High rain forest, 100 m.

Note: Called *S. minima* in Lista Av. Venez.

## RUFOUS-CROWNED TODY-TYRANT
*Poecilotriccus ruficeps*
PICO CHATO DE CORONA RUFA

Pl. 30

3.5″ (9 cm.). Crown bright rufous, bordered posteriorly with black, this followed by a small gray area on extreme upper mantle, back and sides of breast olive; wings and tail black; wing coverts with 2 yellow bars, inner remiges bordered yellow. Sides of head cinnamon rufous; throat and upper breast white, upper throat washed with rufous, white of breast extending upward in a band to behind ear coverts, pectoral band mixed black and olive, rest of underparts bright yellow.

Subtropical zone. Sw Táchira on Páramo de Tamá and the Río Chiquito (*ruficeps*). [Andes of Colombia to n Peru.]

High cloud forest, 1800–2400 m.

## BLACK-CHESTED TYRANT
*Taeniotriccus andrei*
ATRAPAMOSCAS PECHINEGRO

Pl. 30
4.6″ (11.7 cm.). Forehead, throat and sides of head chestnut, center of crown black. Back and breast black, belly olive gray, thighs black. Tail dark olivaceous. Wings black, bend of wing and under wing coverts yellowish white; innermost tertial white on outer web. Bill black, base of mandible, feet and legs flesh color. ♀: head, wings and tail as in ♂; back olive; breast gray, center of belly white, sides of belly and under tail coverts yellowish olive.
Tropical zone. Nw Bolívar along the lower Río Caura, the central portion along the Río Carún; Delta Amacuro at Misión Araguaimujo (*andrei*). [Nw Brazil near border of sw Amazonas, Venezuela and s of the Amazon on the lower Rio Tapajós.]
Rain forest to 350 m. Forages for insects in lower branches of trees.

## SCALE-CRESTED PYGMY-TYRANT
*Lophotriccus pileatus*
PICO CHATO DE PENACHO

Pl. 30
4.2″ (10.6 cm.). Forecrown olivaceous brown, feathers of rest of crown broad, elongated to form an *ample flat crest, black, broadly edged with rufous.* Back olive; wings blackish, the feathers edged olive, wing coverts with 2 olive bars. Tail brownish, feathers edged olive. Throat and breast pale yellow, streaked dusky, belly brighter yellow, unstreaked.
Tropical and subtropical zones. Nw Zulia s to s Táchira and w Barinas n through the mountains to Carabobo thence e to Miranda (*santaeluciae*). [Costa Rica to Colombia s through the Andes to s Peru; sw Brazil on the upper Rio Juruá.]
Rain and cloud forest to 2000 m. Scrub, forest clearings, young second growth. In higher altitudes prefers humid, dense underbrush and small trees. Alone or in pairs this tiny, quiet and inconspicuous bird hovers and flits for insects. Call: a constant, metallic, surprisingly loud, sharp note.
   The Double-banded Pygmy-Tyrant, *L. vitiosus* (*guianensis*) probably occurs in Venezuela for it is known from the Guianas and Colombia along the Río Negro. It resembles the Scale-crested Pygmy-Tyrant but is easily distinguished by the narrower black crest feathers which are *edged conspicuously with gray* instead of rufous. In appearance it is still closer to the Helmeted Pygmy Tyrant but again the pale gray rather than olive edges to the crest feathers are distinctive.

## HELMETED PYGMY-TYRANT
*Colopteryx galeatus*
ATRAPAMOSCAS PIGMEO DE CASQUETE

Pl. 30
4″ (10 cm.). Forecrown olivaceous, feathers of rest of crown elongated, narrow, black, inconspicuously edged olive; back olive. Wings and tail brownish black, the feathers edged yellowish olive. Throat, breast and center of belly white, throat and upper breast streaked dusky, sides of body yellowish olive.
Tropical zone. N Amazonas s; n Bolívar; Delta Amacuro, e Monagas and e Sucre. [The Guianas; e Colombia; central and e Amazonas, Brazil.]
Rain forest and high second growth, often near water, to 1100 m. Alone in the undergrowth, captures flying insects on the wing, also forages in flowers and crevices in bark. Call: a sharp, penetrating chirp.

## PALE-EYED PYGMY-TYRANT
*Atalotriccus pilaris*
ATRAPAMOSCAS PIGMEO OJIBLANCO

Pl. 30
3.4″ (8.6 cm.). Above olive green including crown (or with a gray crown, a). Wings and tail dusky, the feathers edged olive yellow, coverts with 2 bars. Underparts white, obscurely streaked; throat with an indefinite blackish area; flanks and under tail coverts pale yellowish green. *Iris white.*
Tropical, occasionally subtropical zone. Extreme nw Zulia s to nw Táchira (*pilaris*). The n from Carabobo to Monagas and e to Sucre, and in the llanos from w Barinas and w Apure through Portuguesa and central Guárico to Monagas (*venezuelensis*). S Guárico; n Bolívar from Caicara e to the lower Río Paragua, the Sierra de Imataca and

Delta Amacuro; n Amazonas s to Puerto Ayacucho (*griseiceps*, a). [Guyana, n and e Colombia. Panama.]
Semi-arid regions with thorn bush, thickets, small trees and bushes near water, commonly to 1000 m. n of the Orinoco, but to 1700 m. in the Sierra de Perijá; s of the Orinoco to 300 m. Alone or in pairs forages for insects from the underbrush to medium tree heights. Call: loud, harsh, out of proportion to size of bird.

## SHORT-TAILED PYGMY-TYRANT
*Myiornis ecaudatus*
PICO CHATO PIGMEO DESCOLADO

Pl. 30
2.5″ (6.4 cm.). *Tail very short,* barely longer than tail coverts. Crown gray, lores and eye ring white. Back bright yellowish green; wings and tail and primary coverts black, rest of wing coverts and inner remiges broadly edged yellowish green, tail feathers edged yellowish green. Underparts white, band across breast pale yellowish, flanks yellow.
Tropical zone. Carabobo; Mérida; sw Barinas; Táchira; n Amazonas s; Bolívar along the Río Caura and in the se Gran Sabana; Orinoco delta region in Sucre (*miserabilis*). [Guyana; French Guiana; Colombia to w Ecuador, Amazonian Brazil and Bolivia. Trinidad.]
Rain forest to 400 m. n of the Orinoco, to 900 m. s of it. Old forest clearings, high open forest, plantations. Alone or in pairs hops and flits actively for insects from the lower levels to the treetops. Not shy. Tiny and inconspicuous, the smallest of the Tyrannidae.

[THE GENUS *Pogonotriccus* has a characteristic black patch at the sides of the head, formed by the black color of the hind part of the ear coverts.]

## MARBLED-FACED BRISTLE-TYRANT
*Pogonotriccus ophthalmicus*
ATRAPAMOSCAS CARIMARMÓREO

Pl. 30
4.5″ (11.5 cm.). Crown and nape gray, face marbled dark gray and white, hind portion of ear coverts black, forming a black spot at side of head. Back olive green. Wings and tail dusky brown, the feathers edged olive yellow, the wing coverts with 2 bars. Upper throat whitish, rest of underparts bright yellow, breast with an olive wash.
Upper tropical and subtropical zones. The coastal Cordillera from Carabobo to the Distr. Federal and the interior chain in Yaracuy and Aragua (*purus*). [Colombia and nw Ecuador to nw Bolivia.]
Cloud forest, 800–1700 m. Forages for insects, hopping in the parasitic vegetation high in the trees, nearly always in dense, deep forest. Joins flocks of small birds.

## VARIEGATED BRISTLE-TYRANT
*Pogonotriccus poecilotis*
ATRAPAMOSCAS CERDOSO PINTARRAJADO

4.5″ (11.5 cm.). Crown and nape dull dark gray (or shiny dark gray, a). Lores and ocular region whitish, posterior part of ear coverts black, bordered above by white; back olive green. Wings brownish black, wing coverts broadly tipped bright cinnamon forming 2 broad bars, inner remiges edged olive green. Tail gray. Chin whitish, rest of underparts yellow, somewhat clouded with olive on breast, abdomen clear yellow (or abdomen clouded with olive, a).
Upper tropical and subtropical zones. Sierra de Perijá, Zulia (*pifanoi*, a). The Andes of nw Mérida (*poecilotis*). [Colombia, nw Ecuador to central Peru.]
Dense cloud forest, 1900–2300 m. Forages at medium height in trees.

## VENEZUELAN BRISTLE-TYRANT
*Pogonotriccus venezuelanus*
ATRAPAMOSCAS CERDOSO VENEZOLANO

Pl. 30
4″ (10 cm.). Crown and nape gray, lores yellowish, ear coverts yellow, tipped black posteriorly, forming a spot. Back olive green. Wing coverts black, tipped greenish yellow forming 2 bars composed of spots, remiges dusky brown edged greenish yellow, innermost broadly so. Tail light gray, webs somewhat ragged. Underparts bright yellow.
Upper tropical zone. The coastal Cordillera in Carabobo; near Puerto La Cruz in the Distr. Federal and on Cerros Golfo Triste and El Negro in the interior chain in Aragua.

High cloud forest, 1000–1400 m. Forages for insects in very humid areas from medium height to treetops. Joins flocks of other small birds.

## YELLOW-BELLIED BRISTLE-TYRANT
*Pogonotriccus flaviventris*
ATRAPAMOSCAS CERDOSO VIENTRE AMARILLO

Pl. 30
4.7" (12 cm.). *Lores, eye ring* and *eyebrow* to above eye *cinnamon rufous* becoming yellowish behind eye, ear coverts pale buff, black posteriorly. Back olive green. Wings blackish, remiges edged olive, 2 well-developed yellowish white wing bars. Tail dark gray, chin whitish, rest of underparts bright, clear yellow.
Upper tropical zone, 750–1000 m. The Andes of central Mérida; the coastal Cordillera in the Distr. Federal; the interior chain on Cerro El Negro, Miranda. [Se Peru.]
Cloud forest. Habits similar to Venezuelan Bristle-Tyrant.

## CHAPMAN'S TYRANNULET
*Phylloscartes chapmani*
ATRAPAMOSCAS DE CHAPMAN

Pl. 30
4.5" (11.5 cm.). Upperparts light olive green, darkest on crown (or more yellowish green, a), forehead gray connecting with a long, grayish white eyebrow, ear coverts pale yellow tipped sooty gray. Wings and tail dusky brown, inner remiges edged ochraceous buff, 2 prominent ochraceous buff wing bars. Tail dusky brown, feathers narrowly edged yellowish green. Chin whitish, throat, breast and flanks greenish yellow becoming lemon yellow on center of abdomen.
Upper tropical and subtropical zones. Cerros Duida and de la Neblina, Amazonas (*duidae*, a). N Amazonas on Cerros Paraque and Parú; Bolívar on the tepuis in the Gran Sabana (*chapmani*). [N Brazil along the Amazonas border.]
Endemic to Pantepui. Cloud forest on the slopes and summits of the tepuis, 1000–2000 m. Forages alone in the upper parts of the trees. Quiet, inconspicuous.

## BLACK-FRONTED TYRANNULET
*Phylloscartes nigrifrons*
ATRAPAMOSCAS FRENTINEGRO

Pl. 30
5.2" (13 cm.). Nasal plumes white, forehead black, bordered behind by a narrow white line, lores black, eye ring black in front of eye, white behind it. Crown and nape gray, back dull olive green. Wings and tail black, median and greater coverts broadly tipped yellowish, forming 2 bars. Base of primaries just below wing coverts edged white forming a speculum, remiges otherwise edged green, innermost tipped white, tail feathers edged olive green. Throat and breast gray flammulated with white; belly white, under tail coverts pale sulphur yellow.
Upper tropical and subtropical zones. The cerros and tepuis of Amazonas and Bolívar.
Endemic to Pantepui. Cloud forest, 900–1800 m. Habits similar to Chapman's Tyrannulet.

## RUFOUS-BROWED TYRANNULET
*Phylloscartes superciliaris*
ATRAPAMOSCAS FRENTIRUFO

5" (12.5 cm.). Nasal feathers white, crown and nape gray, the feathers with dark centers, giving a slightly streaked appearance. *Forehead, lores* and *superciliary rufous*, ear coverts mixed gray and rufous. Back olive green, a narrow whitish band across tail coverts. Underparts grayish white, sides of breast grayer. Lower flanks and under tail coverts sulphur yellow. Tail brownish, edged olive green.
Subtropical zone. Nw Zulia on the upper Río Negro, Sierra de Perijá (*griseocapillus*). [Costa Rica to e Colombia.]
High cloud forest, 1650–2000 m. Often in wet areas and exposed ridges with less dense vegetation. Joins flocks of other small birds.

## YELLOW TYRANNULET
*Capsiempis flaveola*
ATRAPAMOSCAS AMARILLO

Pl. 30
4.5" (11.5 cm.). Above yellowish olive, lores and superciliary whitish. Throat white, rest of underparts bright yellow, breast washed tawny olive. Wings dusky

brownish, wing coverts with 2 buffy yellow bars, remiges edged olive, innermost more broadly with yellowish white. Tail rounded, pale brown, edged olive.
Tropical zone. Zulia at the base of the Sierra de Perijá; n Táchira, w Mérida, sw Lara; e Falcón (*leucophrys*). Coastally from Carabobo to Sucre and across the llanos from w Barinas and w Apure to Monagas and Delta Amacuro; n Amazonas; Bolívar e to the upper Río Cuyuni (*cerula*). [Nicaragua to sw Ecuador, Bolivia, Paraguay and ne Argentina.]
High rain forest, open woodland, mangroves, arid areas, humid places to 600 m. n of the Orinoco, to 300 m. s of it. Thorn thickets, low dense shrubbery. Active, restless, noisy. In pairs or family groups forages for insects in low bushes and small trees. Behaves like a vireo. Call: a trill, also "wit."

## TAWNY-CROWNED PYGMY-TYRANT

*Euscarthmus meloryphus*
ATRAPAMOSCAS COPETE CASTAÑO

Pl. 30
4.2″ (10.6 cm.). Upperparts, wings and tail light brown, wing coverts obscurely edged buffy brown. Crown patch orange rufous, the feathers tipped brown. Throat and center of breast white, sides of breast grayish, belly and under tail coverts creamy white.
Tropical zone. Zulia; n Táchira; Lara; ne Falcón; Distr. Federal; central and s Anzoátegui; nw Sucre; ne Bolívar (*parulus*). [N Colombia; sw Ecuador; w Peru; n and s Bolivia; n Argentina; s and e Brazil; Uruguay.]
Arid, open woodland, dense second growth, brush piles, weedy tangles, bushes and small trees on savanna edge, rarely to 1000 m. Forages for insects actively near the ground. Secretive, inconspicuous, located easily from repeated twittering call and loud chattering song, "chideree."

CRESTED DORADITO (*Pseudocolopteryx sclateri*), a tiny bird, olive above, bright yellow below with a prominent crest of black, yellow-edged feathers should be looked for in e Venezuela. The species

is widespread in s S Amer. and has been taken in Guyana. Specimens in breeding condition taken in Trinidad are in the collection of the Academy of Natural Sciences in Philadelphia.

## BEARDED TACHURI

*Polystictus pectoralis*
ATRAPAMOSCAS PIOJITO

Pl. 30
4″ (10 cm.). Crown dusky grayish brown, the feathers basally white, lores black, supraloral streak white. Back light brown mixed with cinnamon, rump dull cinnamon; wings dull brown, wing coverts with 2 whitish bars, remiges narrowly edged whitish. Tail narrow, dull brown narrowly edged whitish. Cheeks and upper throat blackish, the feathers edged white giving a mottled appearance, lower throat, belly and under tail coverts white; breast, sides of body and tibial feathers cinnamon. ♀: like ♂ above but wing coverts edged broadly with rufous forming 2 bars, no black on throat, entire undersurface light cinnamon, palest on throat and center of belly.
Tropical zone. W Apure; w Barinas; nw Bolívar at Caicara and in the se in the Gran Sabana; ne Amazonas (*brevipennis*). [Guyana; Surinam. Colombia to the temperate zone. Ne and s Brazil; Uruguay; Bolivia; Argentina.]
Swampy places in low, open woodland, forest edge, savannas to 200 m. n of the Orinoco, to 1300 m. on the slopes of the tepuis.

## AGILE TIT-TYRANT

*Uromyias agilis*
ATRAPAMOSCAS AGIL

Pl. 29
5″ (13 cm.). Center of crown and elongated crest feathers brownish black, lores and sides of crown white, mixed with dusky brown. Back ashy brown, *streaked with blackish,* wings dusky brown, inner remiges edged white, tail rather long, graduated, dull brown, outer web of outer feather white. *Throat and breast white, streaked blackish,* belly creamy white.
Subtropical zone. N Táchira on the Páramo Zumbador, 2300 m. [Colombia to the temperate zone, Ecuador.]

Forested areas near the Páramo Zumbador.

## RIVER TYRANNULET
*Serpophaga hypoleuca*
ATRAPAMOSCAS DE LOS RÍOS

Pl. 30
4.2" (10.6 cm.). Crown and sides of head dark grayish brown; crest feathers black with white bases, back gray with a slight brownish cast; wings and tail like back and unmarked. Underparts white, breast tinged gray particularly at sides, flanks pale clay color.
Tropical zone. The banks of Ríos Apure, Meta and Orinoco, from the mouth of the Meta to Anzoátegui (*venezuelana*). Llanos, sparsely wooded savannas, second growth, river banks, 150 m. Flicks tail.

## TORRENT TYRANNULET
*Serpophaga cinerea*
ATRAPAMOSCAS DE LOS TORRENTES

4.5" (11.5 cm.). Top and sides of head black, base of short crest feathers white. Back light gray; lesser wing coverts gray, greater ones black, edged white forming 2 bars; remiges black, inner ones edged white. Tail black. Below very pale gray, white in center of abdomen.
Subtropical zone. Upper Río Negro, Sierra de Perijá, Zulia; the Andes of Táchira, Mérida and central Trujillo (*cinerea*). [Costa Rica, Panama. Colombia to Bolivia.]
Cloud forest, plantations, rocky torrents, 1500–2200 m. Always near fast flowing streams. Alone or in pairs hops restlessly in the rapids on boulders and mossy stones. Flicks tail.

## PALE-TIPPED TYRANNULET
*Inezia subflava*
INEZIA DE VIENTRE AMARILLO
Pl. 30

4.6" (11.7 cm.). Upperparts dull brownish olive to dull grayish olive, lores blackish, supraloral line and narrow patch below eye white. Wings dusky, wing coverts with 2 well-marked white bars, outer webs of inner remiges white. Tail rather long, basal part like back, deepening to dusky at distal end, the feathers tipped dirty white, outer web of outermost pale grayish. Chin white, rest of underparts dull yellow (suffused on throat and breast with buff, a), clouded with grayish olive on sides of breast.
Tropical zone. In n Venezuela recorded from Zulia, Falcón, Táchira, Portuguesa and Cojedes to Carabobo and from Miranda to Sucre and Monagas (*intermedia*). Apure along the course of the Ríos Apure, Arauca and Meta, on the lower Río Caura in Bolívar and along the lower Orinoco from s Guárico to s Monagas (*caudata, a*). N Amazonas from Caño Cuao to Caño Casiquiare and the Río Negro (*obscura*). [The Guianas, n and e Colombia, n and central Amazonian Brazil.]
Low open forest, second growth, llanos, savannas with scattered trees, gallery forest to 400 m. n of the Orinoco, to 200 m. s of it. Thorny thickets, arid regions, clearings. Alone or in pairs, forages inconspicuously for insects in thickets and undergrowth to medium heights. Often cocks tail.

## SLENDER-BILLED TYRANNULET
*Inezia tenuirostris*
ATRAPAMOSCAS DE PICO TENUE

Pl. 30
4" (10 cm.). Upperparts olivaceous light brown, lores dusky, narrow eyebrow white. Wings and tail dull brown, wing coverts with 2 prominent white bars, outer tail feather with tip and outer web dull white. Throat white, rest of underparts tinged yellow, suffused with clay color on breast.
Arid tropical zone. N Zulia; coastal Falcón to the Paraguaná Pen.; n Lara. [Ne Colombia.]
Xerophytic vegetation to 600 m. Shrubbery and low, open woodland.
Note: *Xenopsaris albinucha* which follows this species in Lista Av. Venez. has been transferred to the Cotingidae and will be found before *Pachyramphus*.

## WHITE-THROATED TYRANNULET
*Mecocerculus leucophrys*
MECOCERCULUS FRENTIBLANCO

Pl. 30
6" (15 cm.). Upperparts smoky brown (with an olivaceous tinge, a); wings

dusky, 2 prominent white (or white, tinged ochraceous, b) wing bars, inner remiges edged white, tail like back. Throat white shading to gray on breast, belly white to very pale yellow.

Subtropical to temperate zones. Sierra de Perijá, Zulia, sw Táchira, through Mérida and Trujillo to s Lara (*gularis*). The coastal Cordillera from Yaracuy and Carabobo to Miranda (*palliditergum*). The mountains of Monagas and Sucre (*nigriceps*, a). Bolívar on Cerros Guaiquinima and Jaua e to the tepuis of the Gran Sabana and in Amazonas on Cerros Huachamacari, Yaví, Duida and de la Neblina (*roraimae*, b). Amazonas on Cerro Parú (*parui*, b). [Adjacent Brazil, Colombia to nw Argentina.]

Cloud forest and low, scrubby growth, n of the Orinoco 1400–3700 m., s of it 1300–2450 m. on the slopes and summits of the tepuis. Open fields with scattered trees, forest edge, second growth. Forages for insects in pairs or families near rivers. Restless, noisy, conspicuous. Joins flocks of forest birds.

## SULPHUR-BELLIED TYRANNULET
*Mecocerculus minor*
MECOCERCULUS MENOR

4.3" (11 cm.). Dull olive above, crown and nape grayish, lores dusky, narrow eyebrow and chin dull white. Underparts yellow clouded with olive on breast. Wings dusky, coverts with 2 conspicuous buff bars, inner remiges edged buff. Tail grayish, edged olive.

Subtropical zone. Río Chiquito, sw Táchira. [Ne and central Colombia. Nw Peru.]

Cloud forest, 1800 m.

## WHITE-BANDED TYRANNULET
*Mecocerculus stictopterus*
MECOCERCULUS RABIBLANCO

Pl. 30

4.6" (11.7 cm.). Dull olive above, crown and nape grayish, lores dusky, long broad eyebrow white. Throat and breast pale gray, belly white, washed pale yellow on flanks and under tail coverts. Wings blackish with 2 conspicuous white bars, outer remiges edged silvery white, inner edged ochraceous. Tail grayish

edged olive, outer pair of feathers dull buffy white, next 2 pairs buffy white on inner web.

Subtropical and temperate zones. The Andes of Táchira, Mérida and Trujillo. [Colombia to Bolivia.]

Cloud forest and in lower vegetation at the higher altitudes, 1900–3050 m.

[ELAENIAS ARE VERY DIFFICULT to distinguish from each other. Probably the only sure way is to become familiar with the notes of the various species. Elaenias are somewhat crested, dull in color, usually olive or brownish above, with grayish breasts, whitish bellies and with 2 pale wing bars. They are birds of open country or lightly wooded areas.]

## YELLOW-BELLIED ELAENIA
*Elaenia flavogaster*
BOBITO COPETÓN VIENTRE AMARILLO

Pl. 29

6.5" (16.5 cm.). Head with a prominent crest, concealed white crown patch and white eye ring. Above olivaceous brown. Throat whitish, breast gray obscurely streaked yellowish, belly pale yellow. Wings and tail dusky brown. Two conspicuous white wing bars, inner remiges pale-edged; tail very narrowly tipped white.

Tropical and subtropical zones. Widely distributed throughout, but not recorded from s Amazonas. Margarita and Patos Is. (*flavogaster*). [S Mexico to nw Peru and Argentina. Lesser Antilles.]

Open woodland, second growth, open savannas with scattered trees, gardens, to 1750 m. Conspicuous, very noisy. Forages for insects and berries in pairs or groups from the ground to the treetops. Stance when perched nearly perpendicular, erects pointed crest, wiggles tail. Call: a short, hoarse, churred, harsh whistle.

## SMALL-BILLED ELAENIA
*Elaenia parvirostris*
BOBITO COPETÓN PICO CORTO

Pl. 29

6" (15 cm.). Very like Yellow-bellied Elaenia, but crest shorter and not as prominent, eye ring more pronounced, back more olivaceous, belly white in-

stead of pale yellow, flanks and under tail coverts yellowish. In spite of its name the bill is not conspicuously smaller than in other species.
Tropical and subtropical zones. Migrant from the s, summer resident, Apr.–Sept. Generally distributed including Margarita I. [Breeds from Bolivia and s Brazil to central Argentina. Migrates to Colombia and the Guianas. Trinidad and casually to Aruba.]
Open country, llanos, scattered trees, forest edge, to 2100 m. Usually in small trees or middle branches of larger ones. Sometimes migrates at night.

## SLATY ELAENIA
*Elaenia strepera*
BOBITO ESCANDALOSO

Pl. 29
6.5″ (16.5 cm.). Distinguishable from other species by its *slaty gray coloring*. Upper parts dark slaty gray, concealed crown patch white. Below paler gray, center of abdomen and under tail coverts white. Wings and tail dusky brown, wing coverts with 2 inconspicuous dark gray bars. Imm.: above olivaceous gray, throat whitish, breast brownish gray, belly very pale yellow, slightly streaked on upper breast. Inner remiges pale-edged. Eye ring white.
Tropical zone. Summer resident. From Carabobo and Guárico e to Sucre and Monagas; ne Bolívar. [Breeds in s Bolivia and nw Argentina. Migrates n as far as e Colombia.]
Rain forest, low open forest and low second growth to 900 m. Recorded in Aug. and Sept.

## PLAIN-CRESTED ELAENIA
*Elaenia cristata*
BOBITO CRESTIAPAGADO

5.5″ (14 cm.). Resembles Yellow-bellied Elaenia in its prominent crest but feathers much narrower and more pointed, darker than back and edged grayish. No white crown patch. Size much smaller.
Tropical zone. From Aragua, Barinas and Apure to Anzoátegui; Delta Amacuro; n Bolívar and in the Gran Sabana; nw and s Amazonas (*cristata*). [The Guianas; ne and se Brazil. Se Peru.]
Open woods, savannas, open areas with

scattered, low trees, thickets and bushes, to 320 m. n of the Orinoco, s of it to 1350 m. Forages in low bushes for insects and berries.

## LESSER ELAENIA
*Elaenia chiriquensis*
BOBITO COPETÓN MOÑO BLANCO

5.8″ (14.7 cm.). Dark olivaceous brown above, crown patch white; wings with 2 prominent white bars, inner remiges edged white. Throat grayish white, upper breast olive gray streaked yellowish. Belly pale yellow, much whiter in worn birds.
Tropical and subtropical zones. Generally distributed in drier campos and savannas (*albivertex*). [Sw Costa Rica to Bolivia, Paraguay, Brazil and nw Argentina. Casual in Bonaire and Curaçao.]
Open woods, second growth, savannas, open areas with scattered, low trees and bushes to 3000 m. n of the Orinoco, s of it to 1850 m. Forages for insects and berries, keeping low in the bushes. Shy, inconspicuous; emits a soft whistle.

## RUFOUS-CROWNED ELAENIA
*Elaenia ruficeps*
BOBITO COPETÓN MOÑO ROJO

Pl. 29
6″ (15 cm.). A very distinct species separable from any other by the concealed *rufous crown patch* and conspicuously *streaked underparts*. Above very dark olive brown; wings with 2 prominent olivaceous gray wing bars, inner remiges streaked white. Throat white, streaked gray, breast gray, streaked pale yellow, belly pale yellow. Tail dusky, very narrowly tipped white.
Tropical zone. S Amazonas; s Bolívar in the Gran Sabana. [The Guianas, e Colombia, n and central Brazil.]
Rain forest on the slopes of the tepuis to 1400 m. Open forest, open areas with bushes and low trees. Forages for insects and berries in the dense, lower vegetation.

## MOUNTAIN ELAENIA
*Elaenia frantzii*
BOBITO COPETÓN MONTAÑERO

5.2″ (13 cm.). Upperparts olivaceous brown, crown uniform, very rarely with a few white bases to the feathers in the center. Eye ring white. Two prominent white wing bars, tertials conspicuously edged white. Throat and breast pale olive gray, sides of body greener, center of abdomen yellowish white (or white, a). Tail like back with a very narrow white tip. Bill small.

Subtropical zone. Nw Zulia in the Sierra de Perijá (*browni*, a). The serranías of the n from Lara, Mérida and Táchira e to Sucre and Monagas (*pudica*). [Guatemala to w Panama. Colombia.]

Cloud forest, second growth, plantations, clearings, 1200–2900 m. In the Sierra de Perijá, 1700–2350 m. Open areas in forest, open ridges. Forages for insects and berries from the ground to the middle tier of trees. Solitary, aggressive.

## GREAT ELAENIA
*Elaenia dayi*
BOBITO GIGANTE

Pl. 29

8″ (20 cm.). Crown blackish without white, back dark olive brown. Two prominent whitish wing bars. Throat whitish to grayish, breast and sides light grayish olive, slightly tinged yellow, becoming yellowish white on lower belly. Tail blackish, narrowly tipped whitish. Base of mandible orange.

Subtropical zone. Cerros Huachamacari, Duida and Parú, Amazonas and Jaua, Bolívar (*tyleri*). Bolívar on Cerro Auyan-tepui, above 1850 m. (*auyantepui*). On Cerros, Chimantá-tepui, Ptari-tepui, Roraima and Cuquenán in the Gran Sabana, Bolívar (*dayi*).

Endemic to Pantepui. On the slopes and summits of the tepuis, 1500–2600 m. Notable for its large size. Quiet, confiding, usually in the tops of trees in the open forest, forest edge, low trees and in impenetrable, humid, mossy *Bonnetia* forest.

## SIERRAN ELAENIA
*Elaenia pallatangae*
BOBITO DE LOS TEPUIS

Pl. 29

5.8″ (14.7 cm.). Much like Mountain Elaenia but somewhat larger and considerably darker above, less so below.

Above darker olivaceous brown, a large concealed white crown patch. No white eye ring. Wings blackish with 2 prominent white bars, tertials broadly edged white. Throat and breast pale brownish, darkest on sides of breast; belly pale, dull greenish yellow, darker and greener on sides of breast. Tail like back with no pale tip.

Upper tropical and subtropical zones. The cerros of Amazonas and s Bolívar (*olivina*). [Colombia, the Guianas, n Brazil to n Bolivia.]

Cloud forest, clearings, and low vegetation at higher altitudes, 950–2400 m. Forages actively for insects and berries in the higher branches and treetops.

[*Myiopagis* DIFFERS FROM *Elaenia* by its brighter coloring and yellow crest (except Gray Elaenia). It is sometimes included in *Elaenia*.]

## FOREST ELAENIA
*Myiopagis gaimardii*
BOBITO DE SELVA

Pl. 29

5.3″ (13.5 cm.). Above dull olive, crown grayer and darker with a large semi-concealed yellowish white patch. Two prominent wing bars and edge to remiges pale yellow; under wing coverts yellow. Supraloral streak and eye ring white. Throat whitish, rest of underparts pale yellow, clouded with brownish on breast. Tail dusky brownish, edged olive. A phase exists which is deprived of yellow pigment; crest white, back brownish gray, underparts white.

Tropical zone. Generally distributed n of the Orinoco except along the Ríos Arauca and Apure and in the delta (*bogotensis*). Amazonas, Bolívar and Delta Amacuro (*guianensis*). [Panama, Colombia and the Guianas to n Bolivia and n Brazil. Trinidad.]

Rain forest to 1000 m.; also various habitats such as humid woods, low second growth, clearings, thorny scrub, open fields, marshes, streams. Alone or in pairs actively and quietly forages for insects and berries in middle-sized trees. Calls: include a prolonged, soft whistle.

## GRAY ELAENIA
*Myiopagis caniceps*
BOBITO GRIS

Pl. 29
5″ (13 cm.). Above blue gray, semi-concealed crown patch white. Eye ring white. Wings black, 3 prominent white wing bars, and white edges to inner primaries. Throat and belly white, breast pale gray. Tail gray, darker than back. ♀: crown, nape and upper mantle dark blue gray, semi-concealed crown patch pale yellow. Back bright olive green. Wings blackish with 3 pale yellow wing bars and edges to tertials, secondaries edged olive yellow. Below like ♂ except for pale yellow under tail coverts.
Tropical zone. Nw Zulia; Bolívar from the lower Río Caura to the upper Río Paragua; Amazonas s to the Río Guainía (*cinerea*). [E Panama to w Ecuador. French Guiana to Amazonian and se Brazil. E Peru.]
Open cloud forest to 1200 m. n of the Orinoco in the Sierra de Perijá, and to 300 m. in dense rain forest s of it.

## YELLOW-CROWNED ELAENIA
*Myiopagis flavivertex*
BOBITO CORONA AMARILLA

5″ (13 cm.). Above dull olive green, large semi-concealed crown patch bright yellow. Wings dusky with 2 pale yellow wing bars, and edges to inner remiges. Throat whitish, breast grayish brown, belly pale dull yellowish. A rather dark, dull-colored species except for crest.
Tropical zone. N and central Amazonas; Delta Amacuro. [Surinam, French Guiana, Amazonian Brazil, ne Peru.]
Dense, humid rain forest to about 150 m. Forages for insects in the undergrowth and the lower parts of trees. Cf. p. 243.

## GREENISH ELAENIA
*Myiopagis viridicata*
BOBITO VERDOSO

Pl. 29
5.8″ (14.7 cm.). Above olive green. Large crown patch golden yellow, the feathers tipped grayish, sides of crown grayish olive, eyebrow white. Lesser wing coverts grayish olive, greater coverts pale-edged forming a tolerably well-marked bar. Tail pale grayish brown, edged olive. Throat and upper breast whitish, rest of underparts pale yellow (or bright yellow, a).
Tropical zone. The Sierra de Perijá, Zulia (*zuliae*, a). Táchira at Seboruco and Colón, and from Barinas, Portuguesa and Cojedes across the llanos to Anzoátegui and coastally from Carabobo to Sucre; n Amazonas, n Bolívar (*restricta*). [Mexico to Bolivia, n Argentina and se Brazil.]
Rain forest and deciduous woodland to 960 m. n of the Orinoco, to 300 m. s of it. Semi-open country, low second growth, often near streams. Forages actively for insects, alone or in pairs. Sometimes joins flocks of forest birds in the upper tier of the forest, but also darts for food in the foliage of lower branches and undergrowth. Cf. p. 243.

## SCRUB FLYCATCHER
*Sublegatus modestus*
ATRAPAMOSCAS DE MATORRAL

Pl. 29
5.2″ (13 cm.). Not unlike *Myiopagis* but bill shorter and wider, and no crown patch. Head somewhat crested. Above grayish brown to grayish olive brown, wings with 2 well-defined white bars (or 2 ill-defined gray bars, a). Throat and breast pale gray, lower breast and belly pale yellow (or throat, breast and upper abdomen dark gray, lower abdomen and under tail coverts yellowish white, a).
Tropical zone. From Zulia, Falcón and Lara to e Sucre and across the llanos from Apure and Portuguesa to Monagas; Margarita and Patos Is. (*glaber*). Los Roques I. (*pallens*). Tortuga I. (*tortugensis*). The middle Orinoco from the mouth of the Apure to Ciudad Bolívar and on the n bank in Guárico and Anzoátegui; n Bolívar from the Río Cuchivero to the lower Paragua and upper Cuyuni (*orinocensis*). Probably a migrant from the s to central Bolívar, e and central Sucre and e Delta Amacuro; on Tobeida I. (*sordidus*, a). [Costa Rica to e Peru, Paraguay, se Brazil, Uruguay and central Argentina. Aruba to Trinidad.]
Possibly the southern *S. modestus* is specifically distinct from *S. arenarum*, as was suggested in Lista Av. Venez. If

this is the case then *sordidus* would become a race of *modestus* and *glaber, pallens, tortugensis* and *orinocensis* would be races of *arenarum.*
Xerophytic and thorny vegetation, scrub, deciduous open woods, mangroves, swamps, sparsely wooded savannas, edge of forest to 600 m. n of the Orinoco and to 460 m. s of it. Solitary, usually quiet, shy. Inconspicuously forages for insects from low branches to the ground. Call: churring notes.

## MOUSE-COLORED TYRANNULET
*Phaeomyias murina*
ATRAPAMOSCAS COLOR RATÓN

Pl. 30
4.2″ (10.6 cm.). Above dull brown, eyebrow grayish white. Wings darker brown with 2 grayish white wing bars. Tail brown like back. Throat and upper breast grayish white, lower breast and belly creamy white.
Tropical and lower subtropical zones. Throughout in scrub, except in s Amazonas and s Bolívar (*incompta*). [Panama to w Peru, n and e Bolivia, Paraguay, Brazil and nw Argentina. Trinidad.]
Xerophytic vegetation, thorny scrub, second growth, coffee haciendas, savannas, mangroves, rain and cloud forest to 1900 m. n of the Orinoco, to 950 m. s of it. Alone or in pairs, forages noisily for insects from the low to the middle tier of trees.

## SOUTHERN BEARDLESS TYRANNULET
*Camptostoma obsoletum*
ATRAPAMOSCAS LAMPIÑO

Pl. 30
3.8″ (9.7 cm.). Dull grayish olive above, slightly darker on crown and erectile crest; narrow eye ring white. Wings dusky brown with 2 broad, pale gray wing bars, inner remiges edged white; tail grayish brown. Throat and breast pale gray, tinged olive on breast; belly pale yellow.
Tropical zone. Zulia, Lara and nw Táchira (*pusillum*). Generally n of the Orinoco from Falcón and Aragua to Sucre; through Apure, Barinas, Guárico and Anzoátegui to Delta Amacuro; Ama-

zonas s to the Río Ventuari; Bolívar from the lower Caura to the Sierra de Imataca and the Río Cuyuni and s to the Río Uairén in the extreme se; Patos I. (*venezuelae*). Central Amazonas s of the Ventuari (*napaeum*). [Costa Rica to w Peru, the Guianas to Bolivia, Brazil, Argentina and Uruguay. Trinidad.] Same habitat as Greenish Tyrannulet to 1000 m. Alone or in pairs forages restlessly and conspicuously for insects and berries in the lower branches and shrubs. Erects crest, cocks tail. Calls: various, frequent, chattering trills and soft, high whistles.

## GREENISH TYRANNULET
*Xanthomyias virescens*
ATRAPAMOSCAS VERDOSO

Pl. 30
5″ (13 cm.). Above dull olive, forehead tinged ashy, supraloral streak and eye ring white. Wings blackish, 2 pale yellow wing bars, remiges edged olive yellow, under wing coverts yellow. Chin and throat whitish, rest of underparts yellow, somewhat flammulated with olive on breast. Tail dull brown, edged olive.
Upper tropical zone. The mountains of Sucre, n Monagas and n Anzoátegui (*urichi*). [S and s central Brazil, e Paraguay, n Argentina.]
Open cloud forest and forest edge, 900–1100 m.

## SOOTY-HEADED TYRANNULET
*Phyllomyias griseiceps*
ATRAPAMOSCAS CABECIGRIS

Pl. 30
4.2″ (10.6 cm.). Head crested, crown and nape very dark brown, nasal plumes and conspicuous eye ring, interrupted behind eye, white. Back dull olive, wings brownish black, wing coverts grayish brown with 2 inconspicuous gray bars. Throat whitish, breast olive, flammulated with pale yellow, belly and under tail coverts clear, pale yellow. Tail dark brown.
Tropical zone. From Zulia, n Táchira, Mérida and Portuguesa to Yaracuy and Carabobo, thence e to Sucre (*cristatus*). E Bolívar from the lower Río Paragua e to the Sierra de Imataca and s to the

Gran Sabana; se Amazonas on the Sierra Parima (*pallidiceps*). [E Panama to w Ecuador, Guyana to Amazonian Brazil and central Peru.] Rain and deciduous forest to 1300 m. n of the Orinoco, to 460 m. s of it. Low, open forest, plantations, thickets, clearings. Often near streams; alone or in pairs forages at lower levels.

## BLACK-CAPPED TYRANNULET
*Tyranniscus nigrocapillus*
ATRAPAMOSCAS GORRA NEGRA

Pl. 30
4.6" (11.7 cm.). Crown sooty black (or sooty brown, a), narrow eyebrow white (or yellow, a). Back olive green. Wings black with 2 wide yellowish white bars, outer remiges margined greenish yellow, inner remiges margined ochraceous yellow. Throat yellowish white, rest of underparts yellow (or golden yellow, a). Tail grayish brown, edged olive.
Subtropical to temperate zones. S Táchira on Páramo de Tamá and Río Chiquito (*nigrocapillus*). The Andes of n Táchira, Mérida, Trujillo and s Lara (*aureus*, a). [Colombia to central Peru.] High, dense, cloud forest, old second growth, and more open woodland in the higher altitudes, 1800–3000 m. Forages alone, inconspicuously, in the treetops.

## TAWNY-RUMPED TYRANNULET
*Tyranniscus uropygialis*
ATRAPAMOSCAS DE RABADILLA LEONADA

4.5" (11.5 cm.). Forehead narrowly, and narrow eyebrow white; crown dark brown, back lighter brown shading to *tawny on rump and upper tail coverts*, tail pale brown. Wings black, middle wing coverts broadly tipped ochraceous, greater wing coverts broadly tipped pale ochraceous, fading to white on innermost coverts, remiges edged olive yellow. Throat, cheeks, and upper breast grayish white, rest of underparts dirty yellowish white.
Temperate zone. W Mérida on Páramo La Negra. [Colombia to w Ecuador and Bolivia.] Thickets and low, open vegetation characteristic of humid situations, 3100 m.

## PALTRY TYRANNULET
*Tyranniscus vilissimus*
ATRAPAMOSCAS DE SERRANÍAS

Pl. 30
4.5" (11.5 cm.). Crown sooty brown (or slaty gray, a), forehead, eyebrow and lower eyelid white (or without white on forehead, a), lores black. Back olive green; wings black, wing coverts and inner remiges narrowly edged pale yellow. Throat whitish, rest of underparts pale greenish yellow, grayish on breast.
Upper tropical to temperate zones. Nw Zulia, w Táchira (*tamae*). E Táchira, w Barinas and Mérida (*improbus*). The Andes of s Lara through Yaracuy to Carabobo and e in the coastal and interior Cordilleras to Miranda (*petersi*, a). [S Mexico to n Colombia.]
Open woods, forest clearings, forest edge and second growth as well as cloud forest, 1800–3000 m. in the Sierra de Perijá, 800–3000 m. in the Andes and 400–2000 m. on the n central Cordillera. Alone, forages for insects and berries from middle heights to treetops. Responds to an imitation of its various, soft, repeated "peeps."

## SLENDER-FOOTED TYRANNULET
*Tyranniscus gracilipes*
ATRAPAMOSCAS PATIFINO

Pl. 30
4" (10 cm.). Crown dull olivaceous gray, lores and short, narrow eyebrow dull white; wings dusky, wing coverts and remiges narrowly but sharply edged with yellow; tail brownish, edged olive. Throat whitish yellow, underparts dull yellow, brightening somewhat toward belly and under tail coverts, breast washed with olive.
Tropical and subtropical zones. Amazonas generally; s Bolívar from the upper Ríos Caura and Paragua to the upper Río Caroní and Cerro Roraima (*gracilipes*). Ne Bolívar from the lower Río Paragua e to the Sierra de Imataca and the Río Cuyuni (*acer*). [E Colombia, the Guianas to n Bolivia and e Brazil.]
High rain and cloud forest, second growth to 2000 m. on the slopes and summits of the tepuis. Small, inconspicuous, forages for berries, flitting actively in the

treetops. Joins forest flocks of mixed species. Call: sharp and unmelodious.

## GOLDEN-FACED TYRANNULET

*Tyranniscus viridiflavus*
ATRAPAMOSCAS CARIDORADO

Pl. 30
4.2" (10.6 cm.). Very like Slender-footed Tyrannulet but slightly larger. Lores and short, narrow eyebrow yellow instead of white. Chin and under tail coverts pale yellow, rest of underparts grayish white, grayest on breast, instead of mostly yellow underparts (or with underparts pale yellow, breast tinged olive buff, a).
Tropical and subtropical zones. Sierra de Perijá, Zulia, to Táchira and w Apure and in Mérida and w Barinas (*chrysops*). The mountains of the ne in Anzoátegui, Sucre and Monagas (*cumanensis*, a). [Colombia to nw and central Peru.]
Rain and cloud forest, to 2400 m. Undergrowth in humid areas. Alone, forages for berries from lower levels to treetops.
Note: Called *T. chrysops* in Lista Av. Venez.

## YELLOW-CROWNED TYRANNULET

*Tyrannulus elatus*
ATRAPAMOSCAS COPETE AMARILLO

Pl. 30
3.5" (9 cm.). Partly concealed, ample golden yellow crest, bordered by black laterally, back dull olive. Wings black, wing coverts with 2 conspicuous white bars, inner remiges broadly edged yellowish white. Tail dusky, tipped white. Throat and sides of head grayish white, breast olive yellow, belly bright yellow.
Tropical zone. Nw and e Zulia s to Táchira, Apure, Barinas and Mérida and in Sucre (*panamensis*). Generally s of the Orinoco (*elatus*). [Panama, Colombia, the Guianas to nw Ecuador, n Bolivia and Amazonian Brazil.]
Rain forest, to 1200 m. Clearings, open woodland, second growth, gardens, river borders. Alone or in pairs forages in the undergrowth, lower trees and bushes. Its 2-note whistle, *De día,* is responsible for its sometimes used, Spanish name.

## ROUGH-LEGGED TYRANNULET

*Acrochordopus burmeisteri*
ATRAPAMOSCAS DE PIERNAS ASPERAS

4.7" (12 cm.). Bill short, curved and rather thick. Crown and nape dark gray (or olive becoming gray on forehead, a), lores gray with a white postnasal spot reaching backward narrowly to above eye. Back olive green; wings blackish, inner primaries edged olive, wing coverts and inner remiges broadly edged with yellow, bend of wing and under wing coverts pale yellow. Chin white, throat, breast and sides of body greenish yellow, feathers with slightly dusky centers, center of abdomen and under tail coverts slightly brighter and clearer yellow. Tail brownish, edged olive.
Upper tropical and lower subtropical zones. Sierra de Perijá, Zulia, on Cerro Pejochaina, 1640 m. (*wetmorei*). The coastal Cordillera in central Carabobo; Rancho Grande, n Aragua, Santa Lucía, se Aragua, and Hacienda Izcaragua, nw Miranda (*viridiceps*, a). The Gran Sabana, Bolívar, on Cerro Chimantátepui at 1300 m. (*bunites*). [Costa Rica to sw Ecuador. Se Peru. E Bolivia. Se Brazil. N Argentina.]
Dense rain and cloud forest, 1100–1650 m. Very active, forages alone or in pairs to the treetops, in very humid clearings, forest edge and *Heliconia* thickets. Calls: include a series of "sit" sounds.
Note: The species *A. zeledoni* (*viridiceps*) placed with the Cotingidae in Lista Av. Venez., is now regarded as a race of *A. burmeisteri*.

## WHITE-LORED TYRANNULET

*Ornithion inerme*
ATRAPAMOSCAS DE CEJAS BLANCAS

Pl. 30
3.3" (8.4 cm.). A very narrow but very sharp white line from nostril to posterior edge of eye, lower eyelid white. Crown and nape dark gray, back dull olive. Wings blackish brown, greater and median wing coverts with a white or buffy spot at tip of outer web forming 2 rows of spots across the coverts, inner remiges edged olive. Throat grayish, rest of underparts light olive yellow, purer yellow on center of abdomen. Tail brownish, edged olive, narrowly edged white at tip.

Tropical zone. Central Amazonas; nw and e Bolívar from the lower Río Caura to the Altiplanicie de Nuria thence to the s Gran Sabana. [E Colombia, the Guianas to Bolivia and n Argentina.] Rain forest, 150–950 m. Forest edge, forages alone or in pairs, not shy, inconspicuous. Joins mixed bands of birds.

## YELLOW-BELLIED TYRANNULET

*Ornithion semiflavum*
ATRAPAMOSCAS GORRO PARDO

Pl. 30
3″ (7.6 cm.). Bill thick, curved; tail short. A well-marked white eyebrow from nostril to well behind eye, wider and longer than in White-lored Tyrannulet. Crown sepia brown, back dull olive, wing coverts grayish brown, unmarked, remiges and rectrices brown, inner remiges edged olive yellow. Underparts bright yellow.
Tropical zone. Nw Zulia, nw Barinas, Carabobo and s Miranda (*dilutum*). [S Mexico to w Ecuador and n Colombia.]
Rain forest areas to 1200 m. High forest, open, humid woodland, second growth, forest edge. Alone or in pairs forages from the lower trees to treetops. Joins mixed forest flocks.

## SLATY-CAPPED FLYCATCHER

*Leptopogon superciliaris*
LEPTOPOGON GORRO GRIS

Pl. 30
5.5″ (14 cm.). Crown slaty gray, large preocular patch whitish, eyebrow and sides of head grizzled gray and white. Back olive green, wings dusky brown with 2 prominent olive green bars, tertials broadly edged pale yellow, tail light brownish gray, edged olive. Throat grayish, breast olivaceous, belly pale yellow.
Upper tropical and subtropical zones. Generally from Zulia and Táchira to Monagas; extreme s Amazonas (*venezuelensis*). Extreme e Paria Pen., Sucre (*pariae*). [Costa Rica to w Ecuador and n Bolivia. Trinidad.]
Rain and cloud forest, 400–2000 m. Clearings, damp forest edge, second growth, plantations. Alone or in small groups, actively forages for insects in low or high trees. Joins mixed bands of birds.

## SEPIA-CAPPED FLYCATCHER

*Leptopogon amaurocephalus*
LEPTOPOGON GORRO SEPIA

Pl. 30
5″ (13 cm.). Very like Slaty-capped Flycatcher but at once distinguishable by sepia instead of gray crown, wing bars buff instead of yellow, tail browner and no pale eyebrow.
Tropical and lower subtropical zones. Nw Zulia (*diversus*). The foothills of the Andes of Portuguesa, Barinas, Táchira and Apure; central Amazonas on Cerro Yapacana; nw Bolívar at Sta. Rosalía between the lower Ríos Caura and Cuchivero (*orinocensis*). Amazonas from the extreme ne on Cerros Calentura and Guanay s to Cerros Yaví, Parú and Duida and the upper Río Ventuari; Bolívar on the upper Río Cuchivero (Cerro El Negro) e to the upper Río Paragua and the Gran Sabana (*obscuritergum*). [Mexico to Ecuador, Guyana and Argentina.]
Dense, damp rain and cloud forest, 100–600 m. n of the Orinoco, to 1600 m. s of it. Shady plantations, scrub near rivers. Quiet and inconspicuous, forages alone to the middle tier of forest trees, and in low second growth.

## RUFOUS-BREASTED FLYCATCHER

*Leptopogon rufipectus*
LEPTOPOGON CARIRRUFO

Pl. 30
5″ (13 cm.). Crown olivaceous black; back moss green; lores, cheeks, throat and breast rufous, belly pale yellow. Wings dusky brown with 2 prominent olivaceous bars, under wing coverts rufous, remiges edged moss green. Tail pale sepia brown.
Subtropical zone. Extreme sw Táchira (*venezuelanus*). [Colombia, ne Ecuador.]
Cloud forest as well as the lower, open vegetation at higher altitudes, 1800–2700 m.

## OLIVE-STRIPED FLYCATCHER

*Mionectes olivaceus*
MIONECTES RAYADO

Pl. 30
5″ (13 cm.). Above olive green, wings dusky brown edged yellowish green with

2 interrupted buffy wing bars (or no wing bars, a). Throat and breast olive, streaked narrowly with yellowish white, sides of body olive, streaked yellow, center of underparts yellow. Tail light grayish brown, broadly edged olive.
Upper tropical to temperate zones. Zulia and Falcón through Lara, Mérida and Barinas to Táchira (*meridae*). From Carabobo along the coastal and interior Cordilleras to the Paria Pen., Sucre (*venezuelensis*, a). [Costa Rica to nw Ecuador and central Peru. Trinidad.]
Has great altitudinal flexibility. Rain and cloud forest as well as humid, mossy vegetation at the highest altitudes, 150–3000 m. Infrequent below 900 m. Plantations, old second growth, shrubbery, clearings. Alone or in small groups forages from the undergrowth to treetops. Joins mixed flocks. Not shy; its confiding nature has earned it the local name of *Bobito*.

## OCHRE-BELLIED FLYCATCHER
*Pipromorpha oleaginea*
PIPROMORPHA ACEITUNADA

Pl. 30
5″ (13 cm.). Pale grayish olive green to olive green above, upper tail coverts like back to paler and tinged ochraceous. Wings dusky brown, wing coverts with 2 well- to poorly marked ochraceous wing bars, remiges edged olive green, tertials broadly edged pale buff to ochraceous buff. Throat pale grayish olive becoming darker and more olivaceous on breast, rest of underparts tawny buff. Tail brown, edged olive.
Tropical to lower subtropical zones. Nw Zulia, n Táchira and Mérida (*parca*). The Distr. Federal and Miranda (*abdominalis*). The ne serranía in Anzoátegui, Sucre and Monagas, and in Delta Amacuro (*pallidiventris*). The foothills of the Andes in s Táchira, Barinas and Apure; n Amazonas s across the lower Río Ventuari to the Río Negro; nw Bolívar along the lower Río Caura (*chloronota*). Amazonas along the upper Río Ventuari, and across Bolívar from the upper Ríos Caura to Caroní and Cuyuni (*intensa*). Subtropical zone, 1450–1850 m., on Cerros Chimantátepui and Roraima (*dorsalis*). [S Mexico to w Ecuador, the Guianas to Bolivia

and Amazonian and se Brazil. Trinidad. Tobago.]
Rain and cloud forests to 1400 m. n of the Orinoco and to 1850 m. s of it. Dense or humid open forest, near streams, clearings, ravines, shrubbery, second growth. Alone or in pairs actively forages for insects and berries from the undergrowth to medium levels. May join forest bands. Twitches one wing at a time. Calls: various squeaky sounds— pips and chips.

## McCONNELL'S FLYCATCHER
*Pipromorpha macconnelli*
PIPROMORPHA MERIDIONAL

4.8″ (12 cm.). Very like Ochre-bellied Flycatcher. Differs by having the lower breast and belly tawny ochraceous rather than tawny buff and the under tail coverts deep ochraceous in contrast, but chiefly by having the *wings plain with no markings*.
Upper tropical and subtropical zones. Ne Bolívar on the Altiplanicie de Nuria (*macconnelli*). S Bolívar from the Sierra de Lema s over the Gran Sabana, and in the nw along the lower Ríos Caura and Cuchivero; n Amazonas s to the Brazilian border (*roraimae*). [The Guianas, Amazonian Brazil, e Peru, n Bolivia.]
Rain and cloud forest, 450–2000 m. Mature forest on the Sierra de Imataca and on the slopes of the tepuis, reaches the summits of some tepuis; also second growth and plantations. Alone or in pairs forages quietly and inconspicuously in the foliage for insects and berries from the undergrowth to medium heights.

## RINGED ANTPIPIT
*Corythopis torquata*
CHUPADIENTE

Pl. 27
5.5″ (14 cm.). Above dark olive brown, crown blackish (♂ only), sides of head dark gray. Wings and tail like back but darker. Below white with a broad, irregular black breast band; under tail coverts and sides of body olive brown.
Tropical zone. Generally distributed in Bolívar and Amazonas (*anthoides*). [The Guianas, se Colombia to n Bolivia and Amazonian Brazil.]

High rain forest and open second growth from near sea level to 1400 m. Usually alone, it forages for insects in the foliage of the underbrush close to the ground near small streams and other wet places. Walks on the ground, wags its tail. Call: teep, teep.

Note: This species was formerly placed with the Gnatcatchers. It has recently been suggested that it is closer to the Tyrannidae, but it seems equally out of place here. As its exact systematic position is still uncertain it is placed at the end of the Tyrannidae.

# SHARPBILLS: Oxyruncidae

## Picoagudos

Little appears to be known about these peculiar birds. Their systematic position is uncertain but they are usually regarded as closely allied to Tyrant-Flycatchers. They are solitary inhabitants of humid forest, and feed on fruit. They are remarkable for their curiously discontinuous range. There is only one species in the family.

### SHARPBILL
*Oxyruncus cristatus*
Picoagudo

Pl. 26
6.7" (17 cm.). Long, flat, silky crest in center of crown crimson (or orange, a), feathers at sides of crown olive broadly tipped black. Back bright olive green. Wings blackish, secondaries edged olive, tertials broadly edged yellowish white, wing coverts edged greenish yellow. Tail blackish edged olive like back. Below white everywhere spotted with black, sides of body pale greenish yellow.

Upper tropical and subtropical zones. Bolívar on the Sierra de Lema and the tepuis of the Gran Sabana; n and e Amazonas on Cerro Calentura and Sierra Parima (*phelpsi*). Se Bolívar on Cerro Roraima (*hypoglaucus*, a). [Guyana, Surinam, central Peru in Junín. Brazil in Sierra Parima, Pará, and from Espírito Santo to Santa Catarina. Paraguay. Costa Rica, Panama.] Rain and cloud forest from the base to the upper slopes of the tepuis, 500–1800 m. Forages actively from medium heights to treetops. Not shy.

# SWALLOWS, MARTINS: Hirundinidae

## Golondrinas

Swallows form a family of birds of world-wide distribution. They have long, pointed wings, often forked tails, and are very graceful in flight. They feed on insects, which are caught on the wing, and the birds may often be seen hawking for them over ponds and rivers and fields. Some inhabit mountain slopes high in the Andes. They often perch on wires and other exposed places, and in flight are much slower than swifts, which they only superficially resemble.

The sexes are usually similar, but the female is somewhat duller than the male.

Most swallows make mud nests, which are placed in tree hollows or plastered to buildings.

### WHITE-WINGED SWALLOW
*Tachycineta albiventer*
Golondrina de Agua

Pl. XI
5" (13 cm.). Upperparts shining oily green to shining dark blue, sometimes the 2 colors mixed, base of feathers white. Remiges black, the secondaries and tertials mostly white on outer web forming a large white wing patch. Rump white; tail blackish, forked, outer feathers white on basal part of inner web. Entire underparts white.

Tropical zone in the vicinity of water throughout, including Margarita I. [S Amer. generally e of the Andes to Argentina. Trinidad.]

Open country near lakes and rivers to 450 m. Forests, mangroves, second growth, sand bars, sand beaches. In small groups zigzags tirelessly low over the water hawking for insects. Not shy, perches on overhanging branches, stumps, buoys, wires.

It is possible that the Tree Swallow (*T. bicolor*), breeding in N Amer., reaches Venezuela in winter, for it has been taken in Guyana and recorded off Trinidad. It resembles the White-winged Swallow, but has no white in the wing, and the rump is shining blue like back instead of white. It closely resembles the Blue-and-White Swallow but is considerably larger, 5.5" (14 cm.) vs. 4.5" (11.4 cm.), and the under tail coverts are white instead of black.

## BROWN-CHESTED MARTIN
*Progne tapera*
GOLONDRINA DE RÍO

Pl. XI
6.7" (17 cm.) [7.2" (18.2 cm.), a]. Upperparts, wings and tail sandy brown, wing coverts and inner remiges narrowly edged white. Throat and belly white, broad breast band sandy brown (with drop-shaped dusky marks on lower breast and upper belly, a). Tail forked (cf. Bank Swallow).

Tropical zone, near water. The foothills of the Andes in Trujillo, Mérida, Barinas and Táchira; the Caribbean littoral in Falcón and Carabobo; n Amazonas; n Bolívar from the lower Río Caura e to Delta Amacuro (*tapera*). Summer resident from the s, Mar.–Oct. in Apure, Zulia, Carabobo, Aragua, Monagas and Amazonas (*fusca*, a). [Panama (migrant). Colombia (where migrants reach the temperate zone), and the Guianas s to central Argentina. Trinidad.]

Forest, open country near lakes and rivers, pastures. The resident subspecies (*tapera*) from sea level to 1000 m., the migrant (*fusca*) recorded only to 400 m. Flocks of thousands of *P. t. tapera* roost on industrial buildings, where their droppings create costly cleaning and safety problems. Often perches on wires.

## PURPLE MARTIN
*Progne subis*
GOLONDRINA DE IGLESIAS

7" (18 cm.). Shining purple blue. Wings and tail blackish. Tail forked. ♀: above like ♂ but duller, and forehead gray. Throat, breast and nuchal collar gray, belly whitish, under tail coverts gray, edged white.

Winter resident, Sept.–Apr., in Zulia, Mérida, Portuguesa, nw Bolívar on the lower Río Caura and s Amazonas (*subis*). [Breeds in N Amer. Winters from n S Amer. to Bolivia and s Brazil. Trinidad, Curaçao.]

Open country to 4000 m. Often near water.

## GRAY-BREASTED MARTIN
*Progne chalybea*
GOLONDRINA URBANA

Pl. XI
6" (15 cm.), [or 7.5" (19 cm.), a]. Very much like ♀ Purple Martin but smaller, under tail coverts white and forehead blue like rest of head (or like ♀ Purple Martin, but forehead blue, under tail coverts white and tail much longer and more deeply forked, a).

Tropical zone. Generally distributed including La Borracha, Margarita and Patos Is. (*chalybea*). Casual visitor from the s, May and Oct., Caño Casiquiare, Amazonas (*domestica*, a). [Breeds from Mexico to Bolivia and central Argentina. Curaçao, Trinidad. Southern migrants winter n to Surinam, n Brazil and Curaçao.]

Open and semi-open country, second growth, clearings, mangroves, towns, coasts, rivers to 1200 m. Flocks of 20 to 200. Perches on electric wires. Attacks hawks. Tame, nests in buildings, roosts in pairs.

## BROWN-BELLIED SWALLOW
*Notiochelidon murina*
GOLONDRINA DE VIENTRE CASTAÑO

Pl. XI
5" (13 cm.). Above shining dark blue, below smoky grayish brown, somewhat lighter on throat. Under tail coverts broadly tipped shining dark blue. Wings and tail dark brown, tail forked. ♀: similar, but back duller and under tail

coverts dark brown. (Cf. White-thighed Swallow.)
Upper subtropical zone. The Andes of s Trujillo and Mérida (*meridensis*). [Colombia to Bolivia.]
Open, steep terrain, cliffs, 2200–2800 m. Flies low over fields, usually alone. Nests in holes in rocky areas, precipices and buildings.

## BLUE-AND-WHITE SWALLOW
*Notiochelidon cyanoleuca*
GOLONDRINA AZUL Y BLANCO

4.5″ (11.5 cm.). Above shining dark blue, sides of head and neck brownish black. Wings and tail blackish. Underparts white, under tail coverts black, tipped shining dark blue. Under wing coverts blackish (or light grayish brown, a).
Upper tropical and subtropical zones throughout the mountains (*cyanoleuca*, resident). Summer resident from the s, June–Aug., recorded from Zulia, Carabobo, the Distr. Federal, Miranda and Sucre (*patagonica*, a). [Breeds from Costa Rica to Tierra del Fuego. Trinidad.]
Various terrains near water, from forests to open fields, to 2500 m. The resident race not recorded below 700 m., the migrant *patagonica* not below 400 m. Clearings, pastures, llanos, gardens, low, open, shrubby woodland. Large flocks, some over 1000. Perches on branches, wires. Nests in burrows, in roofs or walls.

## WHITE-BANDED SWALLOW
*Atticora fasciata*
GOLONDRINA CINTURA BLANCA

Pl. XI
5.7″ (14.5 cm.). Glossy blue black; a broad white band across breast. Wings and tail black. Tail long, deeply forked.
Tropical zone. Generally s of the Orinoco including s Delta Amacuro. [E Colombia, the Guianas, Amazonian Brazil, e Peru, nw Brazil.]
Forested rivers, open grassy terrain with bushes; forest edge to 700 m. Skims crisscross over the water for insects, sometimes above the trees. Perches alone or in groups on overhanging branches and buoys. In flocks at dusk.

## BLACK-COLLARED SWALLOW
*Atticora melanoleuca*
GOLONDRINA COLLAR NEGRO

Pl. XI
5.7″ (14.5 cm.). Upperparts glossy blue black, underparts white, broad band across upper breast and under tail coverts blue black. Wings and tail blackish brown, tail long, deeply forked.
Tropical zone. W Amazonas; Bolívar along the Río Orinoco to Delta Amacuro, and s to the lower Río Caura and middle Río Paragua. [Se Colombia. Guyana, Surinam, central and se Brazil.]
Forested rivers, particularly near rocky outcrops and waterfalls, to 300 m. Hawks for insects, zigzagging low over the water. Rests on rocks and sand bars. Nests in crevices in rocks in midstream.

## WHITE-THIGHED SWALLOW
*Neochelidon tibialis*
GOLONDRINA MUSLOS BLANCOS

Pl. XI
5″ (13 cm.). Above brownish black glossed with dark green, rump pale ashy gray. Wings and tail brownish black. Below ashy brownish gray, under tail coverts blackish. Thighs white. Not unlike Brown-bellied Swallow but easily distinguishable by pale rump and brownish black back. Zonal distribution different.
Tropical zone. Se Bolívar in the vicinity of Cerro Auyan-tepui and along the upper Río Paragua; Amazonas along the upper Río Orinoco and e of Cerro Duida (*griseiventris*). [Panama to w Ecuador, Surinam. Amazonian and se Brazil, e Peru.]
Rain forest and scrub, 300–900 m. Hawks for insects near rivers, clearings, low second growth, villages, open terrain with scattered trees.

## TAWNY-HEADED SWALLOW
*Alopochelidon fucata*
GOLONDRINA CABECITOSTADA

Pl. XI
4.7″ (12 cm.). Forehead, eyebrow and broad nuchal band tawny rufous, feathers of crown brownish black edged tawny rufous, lores blackish. Back grayish brown, feathers pale-edged. Wings

and tail dark brown, tail forked. Sides of head, throat and breast tawny buff; belly and under tail coverts white. From below might be confused with Rough-winged Swallow.

Tropical and subtropical zones. Base and uplands of the central coastal Cordilleras in the Distr. Federal, the ne Cordillera near Cumaná, Sucre and the mountains of e Bolívar from the Altiplanicie de Nuria to the Brazilian border. [Ne Colombia along the Río Casanare. Extreme n and s Brazil, Peru, n and e Bolivia, Paraguay to central Argentina.]

Open country and open terrain in the foothills and mountains, 460–1600 m.

## ROUGH-WINGED SWALLOW
*Stelgidopteryx ruficollis*
GOLONDRINA ALA DE SIERRA

Pl. XI

5″ (13 cm.). Above brown, darker on crown, shorter upper tail coverts whitish. Wings and tail dark brown, inner remiges broadly edged white. Tail square. Throat and extreme upper breast tawny buff, breast and sides of body pale grayish, belly pale yellow in fresh plumage, whitish in worn plumage, longest under tail coverts broadly tipped dark brown. The whitish upper tail coverts immediately distinguish this species from Tawny-headed Swallow.

The s breeding race, *S. r. ruficollis,* reaches se Colombia commonly in the s winter and may be found in s Venezuela. It differs from the resident race by being much darker above, the upper tail coverts only slightly paler than the back, the breast and sides of body dark grayish brown.

Tropical and subtropical zones. Virtually throughout near bodies of water (*aequalis*). [Canada to central Argentina. Trinidad.]

Open and semi-open terrain to 1600 m. Llanos, forest clearings; often along watercourses with steep banks and steep roadside cuts where it nests in burrows. Alone or in small groups glides and circles in slow, wavering flight. Perches on low branches, sometimes in hundreds.

## BANK SWALLOW
*Riparia riparia*
GOLONDRINA PARDA

Pl. XI

4.7″ (12 cm.). Above brown, below white with a broad brown band across chest. Wings and tail dark brown. Tail forked. Not unlike Brown-chested Martin but very much smaller with different habits.

Tropical and subtropical zones. Transient, Oct.–Nov., probably some winter residents. Zulia at Encontrados on the Río Catatumbo; vicinity of Cerro Duida and Cerro de la Neblina, Amazonas; sight records from Rancho Grande, Los Roques, La Orchila, L. Valencia, Aragua (*riparia*). [Breeds in the N Hemisphere. In winter s to Tierra del Fuego. Curaçao, Bonaire. Trinidad. S Africa, se Asia.]

Open terrain near water, to 2000 m. Probably coastal marshes during migration.

## BARN SWALLOW
*Hirundo rustica*
GOLONDRINA DE HORQUILLA

Pl. XI

6″ (15 cm.). Shining dark blue above. Forehead, throat and upper breast rufous chestnut, rest of underparts buff to cinnamon buff. Wings and tail blue black, tail deeply forked, all but the central feathers with a large, *white subterminal patch on inner web.*

Tropical to páramo zone. Winter resident throughout including Los Roques, Las Aves, La Orchila, Los Testigos, La Tortuga, Margarita Is. (*erythrogaster*). [Temperature zone of the N Hemisphere. Winters to Tierra del Fuego. Aruba to Trinidad and Tobago, S Africa, se Asia, E Indies.]

Open terrain to 3400 m.; Flies low and at medium heights, zigzagging in small, open groups. Larger groups during the spring and fall migration. Recorded in every month, rare in May, June, July.

## CLIFF SWALLOW
*Petrochelidon pyrrhonota*
GOLONDRINA RISQUERA

5″ (13 cm.). Lores and narrow frontlet black, forecrown white, rest of crown shining blue black; back shining blue

black somewhat streaked with white, rump cinnamon rufous, upper tail coverts dark brown. Wings and tail dark brown, tail square. Cheeks, ear coverts, throat and sides of neck chestnut, collar on hindneck chestnut. Patch on center of lower throat black, breast and belly pale buffy gray, white in center of abdomen. ♀: collar gray.
Tropical to temperate zone. Transient.

Recorded from Mérida in Aug. and from Caracas and La Orchila in Oct. (*pyrrhonota*). [Breeds from Canada to Mexico. Winters in Brazil, Argentina and Paraguay. Recorded in se Colombia in April, and elsewhere in Sept.–Oct.]
In various types of terrain in open country, sometimes near cliffs to the páramos at 3800 m. Rests on wires.

# CROWS, JAYS: Corvidae

## URRACAS, QUERREQUERRES

The members of this family found in South America are all beautiful, brightly colored birds, the typical black crows not being found there.

Jays for the most part inhabit open woodland and wander about in small noisy groups searching for food. They are more or less omnivorous, eating fruit, nuts, eggs, small mammals and reptiles.

## COLLARED JAY

*Cyanolyca viridicyana*
URRACA

Pl. 10
12″ (30 cm.). Bright dark blue (or purplish blue, a) brighter on throat. Crown pale violaceous blue; forehead, face, chin and band around throat deep black. Tail rather long, like back above, black below.
Subtropical and temperate zones. The Andes of Trujillo, Mérida and n Táchira (*meridana*, a). Sw Táchira along the Río Chiquito (*armillata*). [Colombia to w Ecuador and n Bolivia.]
Humid, mossy cloud forest, 1600–3250 m. Not shy. Forages at middle heights in the epiphytic vegetation and in ravines and dense undergrowth, bamboo thickets and tree ferns.

## VIOLACEOUS JAY

*Cyanocorax violaceus*
COROBERO

Pl. 10
15″ (38 cm.). Crested; whole head and breast black, feathers of forecrown and lores stiff, upstanding; nuchal collar milky white. Back, wings and tail violet blue; lower breast and rest of underparts light violet blue.
Tropical zone. The base of the Andes from Táchira and Apure through Barinas to s Anzoátegui; s of the Orinoco in nw Amazonas s to Caño Casiquiare; w Bolívar e to the Río Paragua (*violaceus*). N Anzoátegui (*pallidus*). [Guyana; Colombia e of the Andes to ne Peru and n and w Amazonian Brazil.]
High rain, deciduous, and gallery forest in the llanos, to 400 m., often near water. Forages noisily in the treetops.

## AZURE-NAPED JAY

*Cyanocorax heilprini*
PIARRO NUCA CELESTE

14″ (35 cm.). Feathers of forecrown and lores long, stiff, somewhat curved forming a low frontal crest. Forecrown, sides of head, throat and breast black; malar spot violet blue; hindcrown and nape pale grayish blue; back and wings violet brown, tail darker violet brown, tipped white. Lower parts drab violet fading to whitish on lower belly and to white on under tail coverts.
Tropical w Amazonas. [Se Colombia from the Río Guainía to the Rio Negro and nw Brazil.]
Dense rain forest, savannas, 100–200 m. Bushes and small trees between forest edge and savanna. The basin-shaped nest of sticks, appearing carelessly made, is placed 2–3 m. from the ground.

## CAYENNE JAY

*Cyanocorax cayanus*
PIARRO NUCA BLANCA

Pl. 10

13″ (33 cm.). General pattern much as in Azure-naped Jay. Forecrown, sides of head, throat and breast black, frontal crest shorter than in Azure-naped Jay. Hindcrown and nape white, spot above and below hind part of eye bluish white, malar streak white. Back drab violet; wings and tail dark violet blue, tail tipped white, more extensively than in Azure-naped Jay. Underparts white.

Tropical zone. N and e Bolívar from the lower Río Caura and the Río Paragua e to the Sierra de Imataca, the upper Río Cuyuni and the Gran Sabana. [The Guianas, n Brazil.]

Rain forest to 1100 m. Forages in the treetops for insects, berries and fruit. Calls: various, some fluty and musical but mostly wheezes, caws and other harsh cries.

## BLACK-CHESTED JAY

*Cyanocorax affinis*
URRACA COSQUIOL

Pl. 10

13″ (33 cm.). Crown, sides of head, throat and breast black, large spot above eye and a smaller one below it bright blue, small spot at base of mandible dark blue. Back drab violet; wings and tail dark violet blue, tail with extensive white tip. Underparts white.

Tropical zone. The Perijá region, forested areas s of L. Maracaibo s to the n foothills of the Andes in Táchira, Mérida and Trujillo, n to w Lara and central and e Falcón (*affinis*). [Costa Rica to Colombia.]

Rain and cloud forest to 1700 m. Plantations, second growth. Feeds on fruits, insects; forages from the underbrush to treetops. Shy. Calls: whistles and harsh cries, also a 2-note, metallic call.

## GREEN JAY

*Cyanocorax yncas*
QUERREQUERRE

Pl. 10

11″ (28 cm.). The only green and yellow jay in Venezuela. Upstanding frontal crest and patch at base of mandible sapphire blue, bar across center of crown white, hindcrown and nape violet blue. Sides of head, throat and breast black. Back and wings green, washed with blue, 4 central tail feathers bluish green, rest yellow. Underparts bright yellow.

Tropical and subtropical zones. Nw Zulia and s Lara s through Trujillo, Mérida and w Barinas to Táchira (*andicolus*). The n serranías from Falcón and w Lara to Sucre, the llanos of e Guárico and w Anzoátegui (*guatimalensis*). [S Texas to Honduras. Colombia to n Bolivia.]

Rain and cloud forest and heavy second growth, sea level to 2800 m. Gallery forest, plantations, forest edge, open terrain with scattered trees. Emits a variety of musical as well as harsh calls. Shy. Will respond to imitated notes.

# DIPPERS: Cinclidae

PÁJAROS DE AGUA

Dippers form a small family of very distinctive birds found in North and South America and Eurasia, and are the only truly aquatic passerine birds. They are chunky, short-tailed birds that live along rocky mountain streams, taking short flights from boulder to boulder. They plunge fearlessly into the water, often walking along the bottom of the stream. They live on small molluscs, fish, worms and some vegetable matter.

    The nest is a large, dome-shaped structure with an entrance on the side, and is placed just above the water.

## WHITE-CAPPED DIPPER

*Cinclus leucocephalus*
PÁJARO DE AGUA

Pl. 32
5.5" (14 cm.). Crown, patch on center of back, throat, breast and upper belly white. Broad stripe through eye and rest of plumage dark, sooty brown. Feathers of crown with dark centers. Subtropical and temperate zones, 2000–2600 m. The Sierra de Perijá, Zulia, and the Andes from Lara to Táchira and Mérida (*leuconota*). [The mountains of Colombia to n Bolivia.]

# WRENS: Troglodytidae

## CUCARACHEROS

Wrens are usually thought of as small, brown birds that sing well. This typical American family (only 1 species is found in the Old World), is widespread in South America, living from sea level to the páramo zone. Wrens frequent thickets, forest borders and sometimes the forest itself, and enjoy the vicinity of water but are also found in arid scrub and thorn brush. Wrens vary in size from that of a thrush to the conventional small-sized wren. Both sexes are exceptionally fine singers; their song is often remarkably loud for their size. They feed chiefly on insects and build a globular nest, very often placed near the ground.

## BICOLORED WREN

*Campylorhynchus griseus*
CUCARACHERO CURRUCUCHÚ

Pl. 31
8" (20 cm.). Much the largest Venezuelan wren. Crown and mantle blackish, rest of back dark reddish brown (or crown dark brown, back light reddish brown, a; or back grayish brown, crown and upper mantle sooty brown, b; or back gray, mottled dusky, crown darker than back, c). Long eyebrow, commencing at base of forehead, white; stripe through eye blackish. Underparts white. Central tail feathers like back, rest with a broad white subterminal bar; wings and tail show virtually no to considerable dark barring.
Tropical zone. The Perijá and L. Maracaibo regions, Zulia, extending n through w Lara to n Falcón and s to the n slopes of the Andes in s Lara (*albicilius*). The llanos from Apure and Barinas extending e to Monagas and Delta Amacuro and on the Caribbean coast of Sucre; n Bolívar along the lower Río Caura and upper Cuchivero e to the Altiplanicie de Nuria (*minor*, a). N Amazonas at Puerto Ayacucho e along the Orinoco in nw Bolívar to Altagracia (*griseus*, b). N Amazonas along Caños Cataniapo and Parucito and the Río Manapiare (*pallidus*, c). [Guyana; Roraima, Brazil; n and e Colombia.]
Savannas and scattered bushes, deciduous open woodland, thickets, dry scrub, gardens, gallery forest, second growth from sea level to 1600 m. n of the Orinoco, to 460 m. s of it. Not shy. Active, forages for insects in pairs and family parties. Appropriates large, abandoned nests of other species. Calls: varied, including chattering, scolding, grating sounds and bubbly gurglings.

## STRIPE-BACKED WREN

*Campylorhynchus nuchalis*
CUCARACHERO CHOCOROCOY

Pl. 31
6.7" (17 cm.). Crown ashy gray mottled with black, eyebrow white, stripe through eye blackish. *Back striped black and white* tinged rufescent on upper mantle; upper tail coverts barred black and white; wings and tail black, feathers of tail notched with white on both webs. Throat white, rest of underparts white spotted with black. Wings black; wing coverts and inner remiges barred with white, primaries notched with white.
Tropical zone. Coastal Carabobo to Miranda s to the n llanos in Guárico (*brevipennis*). Along the Orinoco from Caicara to the delta, extending n through

Anzoátegui to the coast and to w Sucre, and from e Guárico and Portuguesa to Barinas and Apure (*nuchalis*). [N Colombia.]

Open fields with scattered trees, deciduous woodland, mangroves, gallery forest, xerophytic vegetation to 500 m. n of the Orinoco, to 100 m. s of it. Forages for insects in thickets and in dense undergrowth to treetops. Partial to isolated trees near water. Probably appropriates large abandoned nests of other species. Calls: similar to Bicolored Wren but more sonorous and melodious.

### RUFOUS WREN

*Cinnycerthia unirufa*
CUCARACHERO BAYO

Pl. 31

7.2″ (18.2 cm.). Uniform cinnamon rufous, lores black. Inner webs of outer remiges blackish, outer webs and all of inner remiges cinnamon rufous lightly barred with black.

Subtropical and temperate zones. Nw Zulia on Cerro Tetarí, Sierra de Perijá (*chakei*). Sw Táchira on the Páramo de Tamá and the Río Chiquito (*unirufa*). [The Andes of Colombia and Ecuador.]

Cloud forest and dense second growth, 1800–3000 m. In small flocks, actively forages on the ground flicking leaves aside while looking for insects. Shy. Call: a loud, sonorous whistle.

### GRASS (OR SHORT-BILLED MARSH) WREN

*Cistothorus platensis*
CUCARACHERO SABANERO
O DE CIÉNAGA

Pl. 31

4.1″ (or 10.4 cm.). [4.4″ (11 cm.), a]. Above brown, *mantle black narrowly streaked white* (or black, broadly streaked buff, a). Eyebrow very narrow, white, sometimes missing (or buff, broad and well marked, a). Wings and tail grayish brown (or reddish brown, a) barred black. Below white, sides of body clay color (or throat white, rest of underparts buff gradually deepening to cinnamon on flanks, lower belly and under tail coverts, a).

Upper tropical and subtropical zones on the Sierra de Perijá, Zulia, the Andes of

Mérida and Lara, the coastal Cordillera in the Distr. Federal and in n Monagas; also in the Gran Sabana, s Bolívar (*alticola*). Subtropical and temperate zones on the Páramo de Tamá, sw Táchira (*tamae,* a). [S Canada to Tierra del Fuego and the Falkland Is.]

Open, grassy savannas, marshes, swampy terrain, 900–3275 m. Secretive, shy, nearly always on the ground, usually alone, disappears, mouselike, into tangled bushes. Call: a series of cheeps and a soft "churr," usually heard before the bird is seen.

### PARAMO WREN

*Cistothorus meridae*
CUCARACHERO TRIGUERO

Pl. 31

4.1″ (10.4 cm.). Differs mainly from the Grass Wren (a) by having wider, longer and whiter eyebrow, extending from the base of the forehead to the sides of the neck. In addition the crown is somewhat spotted dusky; the black- and buff-striped pattern of the back extending to the rump, and the sides and under tail coverts slightly barred.

Temperate and páramo zones. The Andes of Trujillo (Teta de Niquitao) and Mérida (Páramos de La Culata, Mucuchíes, La Negra, Teleférico).

Bogs and humid places in mossy, low, open forest and bushy areas, wheat fields, 3000–4100 m.

### MOUSTACHED WREN

*Thryothorus genibarbis*
CUCARACHERO BIGOTUDO

Pl. 31

6.7″ (17 cm.). Crown, nape and upper mantle brownish gray, eyebrow white (or buff, a) surmounted by a dusky line; back rufous chestnut; tail dull rufous regularly and conspicuously barred black (or uniform bright rufous, occasionally with traces of bars, a). Closed wing like back, primaries edged brown (or rufous, a). Moustacial streak and throat white (or buff, a) with a broad black line at sides of throat. Breast grayish buff, rest of underparts buffy.

Upper tropical and subtropical zones. Nw Zulia in the Río Negro region; Táchira; Mérida and Barinas to s Lara (*conso-*

*brinus*). Yaracuy thence e through the coastal and interior Cordilleras to the Distr. Federal and Cerro El Negro, Miranda (*ruficaudatus*, a). [Colombia through e Ecuador to n Bolivia, most of Brazil.]
Rain and cloud forest, plantations, second growth, clearings, 600–2400 m. Actively and furtively forages near the ground in family groups and small flocks in the humid underbrush, thickets and forest edge, shy, difficult to observe. Joins bands of other small birds. Call: varied, musical, melodious.

## CORAYA WREN
*Thryothorus coraya*
CUCARACHERO DE LLUVIAS

Pl. 31
5.3″ (13.5 cm.). Crown dark brown, sides of head black, superciliary stripe and streaks on ear coverts white. Upperparts chestnut rufous, closed wing like back; tail barred black and grayish buff (or barred black and rufescent, a). Throat and extreme upper breast white, rest of underparts, lower breast and middle of abdomen cinnamon buff, rufous to rufous brown on sides (or breast and center of abdomen light gray, sides of body rufous brown, a); under tail coverts barred buff and black.
Tropical and subtropical zones. Amazonas s of the Río Ventuari; Bolívar from the Río Caura e through the basin of the Río Paragua to the upper Río Caroní (*caurensis*, a). E Bolívar from the Río Cuyuni to the Gran Sabana; the Río Amacuro in s Delta Amacuro (*ridgwayi*). On Cerro Auyan-tepui, Bolívar 1100 m. (*obscurus*). [E Colombia, the Guianas to Amazonian Brazil and e Ecuador.]
Rain and cloud forest, second growth to 2400 m. reaching the summits of some tepuis. Forest edge, undergrowth, savanna edge and thickets. Forages for insects in the bushes. Not shy but difficult to locate. Call: melodious, varied, often in duet.

## RUFOUS-BREASTED WREN
*Thryothorus rutilus*
CUCARACHERO PECHICASTAÑO

Pl. 31
5.5″ (14 cm.). Upper parts brown, somewhat redder on crown. Tail banded black and grayish; wings unbarred. Throat and sides of neck checkered black and white; breast rufous chestnut (or tawny ochraceous spotted black, a), center of abdomen white; under tail coverts barred tawny and black.
Tropical zone. Nw Zulia in the Sierra de Perijá (*laetus*). The basin of L. Maracaibo to northernmost Táchira (*intensus*). Foothills of the Andes in Táchira and Barinas; the llanos in n Portuguesa; the Andes in s Lara to Falcón thence e through the n Cordilleras to Sucre (*rutilus*, a). [Costa Rica to n Colombia. Trinidad, Tobago.]
Rain and cloud forest, 1700 m. Second growth, plantations, deciduous woodland. Never in open country and seldom in dense forest. Forages in pairs in dense, tangled undergrowth and thickets along forest edge. Elusive, difficult to observe. Call: a pleasant, loud, melodious series of notes, often in duet.

## RUFOUS-AND-WHITE WREN
*Thryothorus rufalbus*
CUCARACHERO ROJIZO

Pl. 31
5.7″ (14.5 cm.). Above bright rufous chestnut (or darker with dusky crown, a); below white (tinged gray on breast, a). Wings and tail like back, barred with black. Eyebrow white, ear coverts and sides of neck white, streaked with black.
Tropical and lower subtropical zones. From the Sierra de San Luis, Falcón, and n Yaracuy e along the coastal regions to the Paria Pen., Sucre; the llanos of e Guárico and s Anzoátegui (*cumanensis*). From the Sierra de Perijá to w Táchira and the upper Ríos Arauca, Apure, thence through Mérida and Barinas to the llanos of Portuguesa and Cojedes (*minlosi*, a). [Sw Mexico to n and n Colombia.]
Rain forest, second growth, gallery forest, deciduous woodland, to 1500 m. Alone or in pairs, often near streams, forages for insects in the thick, tangled underbrush, hopping on or near the ground, investigating fallen leaves. Usually heard before it is seen. Responds to squeaks. Song: a versatile, deep, melodious, flutelike, liquid whistle with a bell-like quality.

**BUFF-BREASTED WREN**

*Thryothorus leucotis*
CUCARACHERO FLANQUILEONADO

Pl. 31

5.9" (15 cm.), [or 5.2" (13 cm.) a]. Much like a house wren in general appearance but larger. Above brown to reddish brown, sometimes with traces of narrow black bars on the back. Wings like back, primaries notched with buff, inner remiges barred with black; tail barred black and buffy brown. Eyebrow white, sides of head white, streaked with black. Throat white, rest of underparts light cinnamon brown (to whitish with the cinnamon brown confined to sides, a), under tail coverts darker cinnamon, unbarred.
Tropical zone. The forested regions w of L. Maracaibo and the s Perijá region, Zulia, s to n Táchira and in w Mérida (*zuliensis*). In the n Perijá region, and e of L. Maracaibo in Zulia, Lara and Trujillo n to coastal Falcón and e to Carabobo, n Cojedes, Portuguesa and Barinas (*venezuelanus,* a). The llanos from Cojedes and Apure from the mouth of the Apure e through Guárico to s Anzoátegui and along the banks of the Orinoco in Bolívar to Ciudad Bolívar (*hypoleucus,* a). N Bolívar from the lower Cuchivero, Caura and Paragua e to the Río Cuyuni and the Gran Sabana, and in Delta Amacuro and se Monagas (*albipectus,* a). From s Táchira and sw Barinas s through w and s Apure and Amazonas to Caño Casiquiare and Caño Parucito (*bogotensis*). [E Panama to n Colombia and the Guianas thence to e Peru, Amazonian and se Brazil.]
Rain and gallery forest, second growth, open woodland, mangroves to 750 m. n of the Orinoco, to 950 m. s of it. In pairs, forages for insects near water, creeping rapidly through the tangled, thick undergrowth and the leafy forest floor. Call: loud, brilliant, melodious, liquid notes.

**HOUSE WREN**

*Troglodytes aedon*
CUCARACHERO COMÚN

Pl. 31

4.2" (10.6 cm.). Grayish brown to reddish brown above, narrow postocular streak buffy white. Back with or without traces of narrow dark bars. Outer remiges barred on outer webs, inner remiges barred on both webs with black. Below dull white, sides, lower breast and belly washed with buffy. Tail like back, barred with black.
Tropical and subtropical zones. The nw in Zulia and Táchira e to w Táchira, Trujillo, Mérida and nw Barinas (*effutitus*). Elsewhere throughout (*albicans*). [Canada to Tierra del Fuego and the Falkland Is. Trinidad and Tobago.]
Various habitats including llanos and xerophytic vegetation but not deep forest to 2600 m. n of the Orinoco, to 1700 m. s of it. Actively forages for insects and spiders, often in pairs, in low bushes and thickets, frequently close to the ground. Call: a torrent of pleasant, bubbling notes.

Often nests in houses, but the successful Venezuelan anti-malarial campaign which sprayed DDT in all habitations conspicuously reduced the wren population; now they are infrequently seen in towns.

**MOUNTAIN WREN**

*Troglodytes solstitialis*
CUCARACHERO PARAMERO

Pl. 31

4" (10 cm.). Rather like redder examples of the House Wren but easily distinguished by the broad buffy eyebrow and rufous brown ear coverts. Above reddish brown, wings and tail with narrow black cross bars. Throat, breast, sides of neck pinkish buff; belly white.
Subtropical and temperate zones. W Zulia, n and w Táchira, n through Mérida to Trujillo and s Lara. [Colombia to nw Argentina.]
Cloud forest in humid, mossy shrubbery, open terrain with scattered trees and bushes, 1700–3300 m. Forages in pairs in the lower parts of trees and bushes, and near the ground.

**TEPUI WREN**

*Troglodytes rufulus*
CUCARACHERO DE PANTEPUI

Pl. 31

5" (13 cm.). Much like Mountain Wren but larger and more intensely colored (or with whitish underparts, a; or gray underparts, b).

Upper tropical and subtropical zones. N Amazonas on Cerros Paraque, Guanay and Yaví (*yavii*, a). Central Amazonas on Cerros Duida, Parú and Huachamacare; sw Bolívar on Cerros Jaua and Sarisariñama (*duidae*, a). S Amazonas on Cerro de la Neblina (*wetmorei*, b). Se Bolívar in the tepuis and the central Gran Sabana (*fulvigularis*); on Cerros Roraima and Uei-tepui (*rufulus*). [Adjacent Brazil in Amazonas and Roraima.] Endemic to Pantepui. The slopes and summits of the tepuis, 1000–2800 m. Forages along the forest edge and in low, scattered trees and bushes in open terrain. Keeps low and hops on the ground. Call: a series of melodious notes like its congeners.

## WHITE-BREASTED WOOD-WREN

*Henicorhina leucosticta*
CUCARACHERO GALLINETA

Pl. 31
4″ (10 cm.). *Tail very short. Crown* and sides of head *black;* long narrow eyebrow and streaks on cheeks white. Back, wings and tail rufous brown, inner remiges and tail banded black, more conspicuously on tail. Throat and center of breast pure white, sides of breast pale gray, belly rufous brown.

Tropical and subtropical zones. S of the Orinoco in Bolívar and Amazonas (*leucosticta*). [S Mexico to Colombia, Guyana, w Ecuador and se Peru.]

Rain and cloud forest from sea level and up the slopes of the tepuis to 1800 m. In pairs forages actively for insects in low underbrush and near the ground. Not shy; difficult to observe. Call: a series of pleasant, clear, strong melodious whistles, often a duet.

## GRAY-BREASTED WOOD-WREN

*Henicorhina leucophrys*
CUCARACHERO SELVÁTICO

Pl. 31
4.2″ (10.6 cm.). Very like White-breasted Wood-Wren but crown like back, eyebrows wider, edged black above. Throat and breast dark gray to gray (throat slightly streaked black in some races)

instead of white, bars on wings and particularly on tail less marked.

Upper tropical to temperate zones. Nw Zulia in the Sierra de Perijá (*manastarae*). Sierra de San Luis, Falcón (*sanluisensis*). Trujillo, Mérida and n Táchira (*meridana*). Sw Táchira (*tamae*). Lara and Yaracuy through Carabobo along the coastal and interior Cordilleras to Miranda (*venezuelensis*). [Mexico to Colombia and n Bolivia.]

Cloud forest and the dense, low mossy forest of the higher altitudes, 900–3000 m. Plantations, thick second growth, tangled thickets in clearings and along forest edge. Forages actively in pairs, generally inside the forest, preferring damp, dark ravines. Stays near the ground, investigates under fallen leaves. Call: clear, melodious, surprisingly loud for such a small bird.

## NIGHTINGALE WREN

*Microcerculus marginatus*
CUCARACHERO RUISEÑOR

Pl. 31
4.5″ (11.5 cm.). Bill long, tail very short. Above, including wings and tail dark wood brown, tail and wings unbarred. Throat, breast and upper belly white with a few dark bars, (or white, unbarred, a). Flanks, belly and under tail coverts dark reddish brown. Imm.: underparts closely barred brown and white, these bars gradually disappearing with age until the breast becomes white; every intermediate stage exists.

Tropical and subtropical zones. Sierra de Perijá, Zulia, n Táchira, through Mérida and Yaracuy to Lara and along the coastal and interior Cordilleras to the Distr. Federal (*squamulatus*). S Táchira, w Apure and w Amazonas (*marginatus*, a). [Mexico to Colombia, w Ecuador and n Bolivia.]

Rain and cloud forest to 1700 m. n of the Orinoco, at 150 m. s of it. Keeps to the interior of thick, dark, humid mountain forest. Forages alone for insects in the undergrowth and lower levels of trees. Frequents ravines. Secretive, difficult to locate. Call: sonorous, liquid, with a ventriloquial quality.

## FLUTIST WREN
*Microcerculus ustulatus*
CUCARACHERO FLAUTISTA

Pl. 31
4.2″ (10.6 cm.). Plain-colored; chestnut brown above; throat tawny, breast and belly brown, belly with a few blackish bars (or with bars more prominent and reaching upper breast, a).
Tropical and subtropical zones. N Amazonas s to the Brazilian border; nw Bolívar along the lower Río Caura (*duidae*). Central Bolívar along the Río Paragua to the headwaters of the Río Caroní (*lunatipectus,* a). E Bolívar from the Sierra de Lema and the tepuis of the se near the Brazilian border (*obscurus*). Se Bolívar on Cerro Roraima and Cuquenán (*ustulatus*). [W Guyana, adj. Brazil.]
Dense cloud forest, 860–2100 m. Reaches the summits of the tepuis. Not shy. Alone, forages quietly for insects in the underbrush and on the ground. Call: a very long, flutelike whistle which often lasts for nearly 30 seconds.

## WING-BANDED WREN
*Microcerculus bambla*
CUCARACHERO BANDEADO

Pl. 31
4″ (10 cm.). Recognizable from any other wren by the *white band across* the *wing* formed by a white, subterminal band on the greater wing coverts. Above dark reddish brown, wings and tail blackish. Throat and center of breast gray; belly and sides of body reddish brown, barred dusky (or without bars, a).

Tropical zone. Central and s Amazonas e through Bolívar from the lower Río Caura to the Río Paragua and Cerro Paurai-tepui in the se (*caurensis,* a). Se Bolívar on Cerro Auyan-tepui (*bambla*). [The Guianas; n Brazil; e Ecuador.]
Deep rain forest, 150–1500 m. Forages in the thick, forest undergrowth. Secretive, difficult to observe.

## MUSICIAN WREN
*Cyphorhinus arada*
VIOLINERO

Pl. 31
4.6″ (11.7 cm.). Bill ridged where it joins forehead. Crown and nape chestnut, collar from sides of neck extending across upper back black, striped with white. Back, wings and tail dark reddish brown, wings and tail barred with black. Throat and breast orange rufous, sharply demarcated from the buffy (or buffy white, a) belly; flanks and under tail coverts brown.
Tropical zone. E Bolívar from the Sierra de Imataca to the n Gran Sabana and the upper Río Caroní (*urbanoi,* a). Se Bolívar in the Cerro Roraima region (*arada*). [Honduras to w Ecuador, the Guianas, Amazonian Brazil, n Bolivia.]
Dense rain forest, 280–1000 m. Forages for insects in pairs, usually in dark, impenetrable undergrowth. Keeps close to and hops on the ground. Secretive. Call: beautiful, loud, melodious whistle, often in duet. Its vernacular name attests to its virtuosity. The violin tones of the song may sometimes be only a few feet away but the hidden singers are seldom seen.

# MOCKINGBIRDS, THRASHERS: Mimidae

PARAULATAS, LLANERAS Y DE AQUA

Mockingbirds form a small family of exclusively American birds famous for their song. They are aggressive and conspicuous, have slender bills and long tails, and in the typical species wings and tails are marked with white. They live in bushy areas and edges of woodland, often near human habitations.

The Black-capped Mockingthrush, however, differs radically in habits from its relatives, usually preferring to inhabit swampy woodland near the banks of streams, but sometimes dry scrub.

## TROPICAL MOCKINGBIRD
*Mimus gilvus*
PARAULATA LLANERA

Pl. 32
10" (25 cm.). Above pale ashy gray, below dull white, lores and ocular region dusky. Wings and tail grayish brown, inner remiges and greater wing coverts edged white. Tail much graduated, all but central feathers broadly tipped white. Tropical and subtropical zones. N of the Meta and the Orinoco; n Amazonas; n Bolívar e to Delta Amacuro and extending s in e Bolívar to the Gran Sabana; Los Testigos, Los Frailes, Margarita, Coche and Cubagua Is. (*melanopterus*). La Orchila, La Tortuga, Tortuguilla, La Blanquilla and Los Hermanos (La Horquilla) (*rostratus*). [Mid. Amer. locally, n Colombia, the Guianas, Brazil in Roraima, and from Belém south to Rio de Janeiro. Aruba to Trinidad and Tobago.]
Open, sunny terrain to 2200 m. n of the Orinoco, to 1300 m. s of it. Parks, scattered low trees, cactus and thorn scrub, bushes; never in forest. Feeds on insects and berries. Often on the ground. From exposed perches sings a pleasant series of varied, melodious notes.
It is possible that the Chalk-browed Mockingbird (*M. saturninus*) will be found in s Venezuela for it has been recently recorded from Surinam.

## BLACK-CAPPED MOCKINGTHRUSH
*Donacobius atricapillus*
PARAULATA DE AGUA

Pl. 32
8.5" (22 cm.). Crown, nape, extreme upper mantle and sides of head deep black; back, wing coverts and inner remiges tobacco brown, rump cinnamon. Primaries black, with a broad, basal white band. Underparts light to dark cinnamon buff, throat and center of belly sometimes whitish, a few very narrow wavy black bars on flanks, not always present. Central tail feathers blackish brown, rest black, tipped white, tail graduated.
Tropical zone in swampy areas n of the Ríos Meta and Orinoco; nw Bolívar along the lower Río Caura; Amazonas s to the Río Ventuari; Delta Amacuro (*atricapillus*). [E Panama to Colombia and the Guianas to n Bolivia, Paraguay and ne Argentina.]
Flooded forest areas, rivers, open terrain with low vegetation, swamps, marshes to 750 m. n of the Orinoco, at 200 m. s of it. Active. Song: very loud, varied, liquid, melodious; a pair often sits close together and sings a duet.

## PEARLY-EYED THRASHER
*Margarops fuscatus*
ZORZAL

11" (28 cm.). Looks like a large, coarse thrush. Above dull brown, below white heavily streaked with brown on throat and breast. Wings and tail like back, inner remiges and tail tipped white. Bill straw brown; iris white.
Los Hermanos on La Horquilla I. but not seen there since 1908 (*bonairensis*). [The Bahamas. Puerto Rico, Lesser Antilles. Bonaire.]
Probably extinct on La Horquilla. Frequents arid areas with scattered trees, not shy.

# THRUSHES, SOLITAIRES: Turdidae

PARAULATAS

Thrushes form a large family found virtually throughout the world. In South America they inhabit woodland and open country from sea level to the upper slopes of the mountains. Most species are largely terrestrial and feed on insects and berries as they hop and run on the ground. They are among the best of song birds.

The forest-inhabiting solitaires differ from typical thrushes in their stubby bills, short legs and exclusively arboreal habits. They are very fine singers.

## ANDEAN SOLITAIRE

*Myadestes ralloides*
PARAULATA COTARITA

Pl. 32

7" (18 cm.). Forecrown, sides of head and entire underparts gray. Upper back umber brown gradually becoming rufescent on lower back and dull rufous on upper tail coverts. Remiges white basally on inner webs, otherwise dusky, edged grayish brown, outer web at base of secondaries black forming a dusky spot. Central tail feathers dark grayish brown, rest black, outermost with a long, wedge-shaped white stripe on inner web, next with a much smaller, similar mark, rest minutely tipped white. Bill short and wide; legs short; mandible yellow; legs pale brown.

Upper tropical to páramo zone. The Sierra de Perijá, Zulia; Táchira n through Mérida, Trujillo and Lara to Carabobo and the Distr. Federal (*venezuelensis*). [Costa Rica to w Ecuador and n Bolivia.]

Dense cloud forest in undergrowth to treetops, second growth, dwarf vegetation at the higher altitudes, 900–4500 m., rare near the 2 extremes. Solitary or in pairs, shy, secretive. Song: pure, clear, varied.

## RUFOUS-BROWN SOLITAIRE

*Myadestes leucogenys*
PARAULATA GARGANTIANARANJADA

Pl. 32

8.1" (20.6 cm.). Above rufous brown. Throat orange rufous, sides and lower part of neck and breast reddish brown, belly grayish, sides rusty brown. Under tail coverts ochraceous buff. Bill short, rather wide; legs short.

Upper tropical zone. Se Bolívar in the mountains of the Gran Sabana (*gularis*). [W Guyana. Nw Ecuador. Central Peru. Coastal se Brazil.]

Dense rain forest, 900–1100 m. Solitary; in underbrush in deep forest. Sings from perches in lower tree levels.

Note: Called *Cichlopsis leucogenys* in Lista Av. Venez.

## ORANGE-BILLED NIGHTINGALE-THRUSH

*Catharus aurantiirostris*
MIRLO PICO ANARANJADO

Pl. 32

6.3" (16 cm.). Above somewhat rufescent olive brown (or olive brown without rufescent shade, a). Below white, breast and sides of body washed with gray. Wings and tail slightly more rufescent than back. Bill salmon red; legs orange.

Upper tropical and subtropical zones. The Sierra de Perijá, Zulia (*barbaritoi*, a). W Táchira; s Lara; Falcón in the Sierra San Luis; Carabobo e to Miranda and n Guárico (*aurantiirostris*). The serranías of Sucre and n Monagas (*birchalli*). [Mexico to w Panama. Colombia. Trinidad.]

Low rain forest and cloud forest, 800–2900 m., deciduous forest, dense second growth, bamboo thickets, plantations, ravines. Forages low in trees, in dense scrub and on the ground. Secretive, difficult to observe. Song pleasing, simple, consisting of very high musical notes. Sings chiefly hidden in thickets.

## SLATY-BACKED NIGHTINGALE-THRUSH

*Catharus fuscater*
PARAULATA APIZARRADA

Pl. 32

7" (18 cm.). Upperparts, wings and tail and sides of head slaty gray; underparts pale gray, white in center of abdomen, darker on flanks. Bill and eyelids bright salmon; legs orange yellow.

Subtropical zone. Nw Zulia to sw Táchira and through Mérida and w Barinas to n Trujillo (*fuscater*). [Costa Rica to w Ecuador and n Bolivia.]

Dense cloud forest, 1500–2900 m. Secretive, shy, seldom leaves forest, stays near the ground; occasionally in open fields, fence posts. Call: clear, soft, ventriloquial bell tones while perched near ground.

## SPOTTED NIGHTINGALE-THRUSH

*Catharus dryas*
PARAULATA RUISEÑOR

Pl. 32

7" (18 cm.). Top and sides of head black; back, wings and tail olive. Underparts

apricot yellow, throat and breast spotted dusky. Bill crimson, eyelid red, legs orange red.
Upper tropical and subtropical zones. Nw Zulia; s Táchira; sw Lara (maculatus). [Sw Mexico to w Ecuador and nw Argentina.]
Heavy cloud forest 900–2200 m. Moist, ferny undergrowth, thickets and forest edge. Secretive, shy, difficult to observe. Keeps to lower limbs. Usually heard before being seen. Sings from a low perch, pure, rich, soft flutings.

## VEERY

*Catharus fuscescens*
PARAULATA CACHETONA

7″ (18 cm.). Rusty brown above including wings and tail (or duller, less rusty, a). Lores white, sides of head and sides of neck and band across breast buffy, throat white. Upper breast with small dusky spots, center of underparts white, sides of body grayish.
Tropical zone. Winter resident, Oct.–Apr. Probably throughout (fuscescens). Recorded in Portuguesa, Carabobo and Sucre (salicicola, a). [Breeds in s Canada and the US, winters to s Brazil.]
Rain forest, 200–950 m. n of the Orinoco, 150–350 m. s of it. Forest edge and second growth. Forages alone in the undergrowth and on the ground.
Note: Placed in Hylocichla in Lista Av. Venez.

## GRAY-CHEEKED THRUSH

*Catharus minimus*
PARAULATA DE CARA GRIS

Pl. 32
6.5″ (16.5 cm.). Much the darkest of the very similar N Amer. migrants of this group. Upper parts, wings and tail olive brown. Chin white, *cheeks without buff tinge,* lower throat and breast heavily spotted with large blackish spots. Sides of body gray, center of belly and under tail coverts white.
Tropical and subtropical zones. Winter resident, Sept.–May. Generally distributed in open woodland (minimus). [Breeds in extreme ne Siberia, Alaska, Canada and n US. Winters to Guyana, Colombia and nw Brazil. Trinidad, Curaçao.]

Varied wooded habitats, to 3000 m. n of the Orinoco, to 1500 m. s of it. Shy, solitary, forages in damp thickets, clearings, open woodland, forest edge and in the undergrowth to mid tree levels.
Note: Placed in Hylocichla in Lista Av. Venez.

## SWAINSON'S THRUSH

*Catharus ustulatus*
PARAULATA LOMIACEITUNA

7″ (18 cm.). Very like the Veery, but distinguishable by breast more extensively marked with larger blackish spots, lores and *eye ring buffy;* olivaceous brown upper parts without rufescent tinge.
Tropical and subtropical zones. Winter resident, Nov.–March. Recorded in Zulia, Táchira, Mérida and Barinas, and in Amazonas and Bolívar but probably occurs throughout in open woodland. [Breeds from Alaska to Newfoundland and n US. Winters to Guyana, Colombia and Argentina.]
A variety of wooded habitats 800–2300 m. n of the Orinoco, near 150 m. s of it. Forest, open woodland, second growth, plantations, brushy areas. Solitary, shy, forages from the dark undergrowth to middle heights.
Note: Placed in Hylocichla in Lista Av. Venez. It is probable that the Wood Thrush (Hylocichla mustelina), which breeds in the US, occasionally reaches e Venezuela in winter, for it has been taken in Curaçao and Guyana. It is larger than the other N Amer. migrants (7.5″, 19 cm.), more rufescent above, with foxy red crown, whiter underparts and breast, sides of neck and flanks with large round blackish spots.

## YELLOW-LEGGED THRUSH

*Platycichla flavipes*
PARAULATA NEGRA

Pl. 32
8.5″ (22 cm.) [or 9″ (23 cm.), a]. Head and breast, wings and tail black, back and belly gray, but sometimes with considerable admixture of black (or belly usually mostly black, b). Iris brown; narrow eye ring and bill *orange yellow.* ♀: upperparts, wings and tail olive brown, feathers of rump and upper tail coverts

edged gray. Throat whitish, streaked dusky, a few streaks on upper breast, rest of underparts ashy brown, grayish white in center of abdomen. Under wing coverts and axillars buff. Iris brown, bill blackish with yellow ridge; legs yellow.

Upper tropical and subtropical zones. Virtually throughout, except in the llanos, Cerro Roraima and the mountains of the ne (*venezuelensis*). The serranías of Anzoátegui, Sucre and Monagas (*melanopleura*, b). Cerro Roraima (*polionota*, a). [Ne Colombia. Guyana. Trinidad, Tobago. E Brazil from Paraíba to ne Argentina.]

Rain and cloud forest, deciduous forest, plantations, 500–2500 m. n of the Orinoco, 1000–1800 m. s of it. Gardens. Shy, forages alone or in pairs from middle height to treetops. Strong, clear melodious song from treetops.

## PALE-EYED THRUSH

*Platycichla leucops*
PARAULATA OJIBLANCA

Pl. 32
8.5″ (22 cm.). Entirely glossy blue black. *Iris bluish white, no eye ring;* bill orange; legs yellow. ♀: dark olive brown above, wings and tail darker. Throat and breast and sides of body brown, paler than back, slightly rufescent on sides of body, rest of underparts pale gray. Under wing coverts and axillars cinnamon rufous. Iris brown; bill black; legs yellowish brown.

Subtropical zone. The Andes of s Táchira; the mountains of w and s Lara; the coastal Cordillera in Miranda (Curupao); the mountains of s Bolívar; central and s Amazonas. [Colombia to w Ecuador, Guyana, n Brazil, Peru, n Bolivia.]

Dense, humid cloud forest, damp ravines, 1250–1850 m. n of the Orinoco, 1600–1700 m. s of it. Alone or in pairs in deep forest from middle heights to treetops.

## GREAT THRUSH

*Turdus fuscater*
PARAULATA MORERA

Pl. 32
13″ (33 cm.). Above dark brownish gray (or pale olive brown, a); below paler

and grayer, throat narrowly streaked black (or below light buffy gray, throat heavily streaked light brownish olive, a). Bill bright orange; legs orange yellow.

Subtropical to páramo zone. Nw Zulia on Cerros Tetarí and Pie Cerro (*clarus*, a). The Andes from Lara through Trujillo and Mérida to sw Táchira (*gigas*). [Colombia to n Bolivia.]

Open, grassy terrain with scattered trees and bushes, edge of cloud forest, páramos, 1600–4200 m. Active, forages alone for insects and worms in the morning and evening, seldom in the heat of the day. Frequently utters a weak squeaky song.

## GLOSSY-BLACK THRUSH

*Turdus serranus*
PARAULATA CIOTE

Pl. 32
10″ (25 cm.). Uniform glossy black. *Iris brown;* eye ring and bill orange red; legs orange yellow. Very like Pale-eyed Thrush but easily distinguishable by dark instead of white iris, *orange red eye ring,* and considerably larger size. ♀: dull olive brown above, tail blackish brown; below gray, slightly washed with brown on throat, breast and flanks (or below dark, sooty gray, a). Under wing coverts orange ochraceous (or only fringed orange ochraceous, a). Iris brown; bill yellow with black ridge (or all yellow, a).

Upper tropical and subtropical zones. The Sierra de Perijá, Zulia; e Táchira to Lara and Yaracuy and through the coastal Cordillera to Carabobo and Miranda (*atrosericeus*). W Táchira on the Páramo de Tamá (*fuscobrunneus*). The mountains of the ne in Anzoátegui, Sucre and Monagas (*cumanensis*, a). [Colombia to w Ecuador and n Bolivia and n Argentina.]

Cloud forest, 950–2900 m. Second growth, open fields, gardens, clearings. Alone or in pairs forages on the ground and from middle height to treetops. Song: clear, melodious phrases usually repeated.

## BLACK-HOODED THRUSH

*Turdus olivater*
PARAULATA CABECINEGRA

Pl. 32
9″ (23 cm.). Head, throat and upper breast black (or head and throat black, a; or

top and sides of head and chin black, throat light brownish olive, heavily streaked dusky, b). Back grayish olive brown (or slaty olive, c), tail with shadowy dusk cross bars seen only in certain lights. Below light grayish buff (or light brownish olive, b; or grayish tawny, d). Bill orange yellow; legs brownish yellow. ♀: differs from respective ♂ by lacking the black hood. Bill black, legs brownish yellow.

Upper tropical to subtropical zone. The Sierra de Perijá, Zulia; sw Táchira; nw Barinas; s Lara n to Falcón and Yaracuy e in the coastal Cordillera to n Guárico and Miranda (*olivater*). N Amazonas on Cerros Yaví, Parú, Huachmacare and Duida; Bolívar on Cerro Tabaro on the lower Río Caura (*duidae*, a). N Amazonas on Cerro Paraque (*paraquensis*, a, c, d). S Amazonas on Cerro de la Neblina (*kemptoni*, b). E Bolívar on the Sierra de Lema and the cerros of the Gran Sabana (*roraimae*, a). [Adjacent Brazil, Guyana, Colombia.]

Cloud forests, 800–1950 m. n of the Orinoco, 950–2600 m. s of it. Second growth, open terrain with low trees and bushes, plantations. Shy. Not active during the heat of the day. Sings in the morning and evening.

## CHESTNUT-BELLIED THRUSH
*Turdus fulviventris*
PARAULATA VIENTRE CASTAÑO

Pl. 32

9" (23 cm.). Top and sides of head black, throat black streaked gray. Back dark gray, wings and tail darker. Breast gray, much paler than back; *belly chestnut rufous;* flanks and under tail coverts olive gray. Bill light yellow; legs yellowish brown. ♀: differs from ♂ only by having the head brownish black.

Subtropical zone. Nw Zulia; Táchira n through Mérida to n Trujillo. [Colombia to n Peru.]

Dense cloud forest and in the smaller trees and low bushes at the higher elevations, 1300–2700 m.

[THE FOLLOWING 7 SPECIES are very similar to each other and difficult to tell apart in the field. Each, however, has some diagnostic character not shared by the others.]

## PALE-BREASTED THRUSH
*Turdus leucomelas*
PARAULATA MONTAÑERA

Pl. 32

9.2" (23.4 cm.). Upperparts, wings and tail olive brown. Throat white, streaked dusky; breast and sides of body grayish olive, slightly tinged rufescent at sides of breast; center of belly white. *Under wing coverts and axillars orange cinnamon. Bill dusky horn color.*

Tropical and subtropical zones. N of the Ríos Meta and the Orinoco, s of it in n Amazonas s to Cerro Yapacana; n Bolívar from Caicara e to the Río Cuyuni thence s to the Gran Sabana (*albiventer*). [Colombia and the Guianas to n Bolivia, Paraguay and ne Argentina.]

Open, dry woodland, deciduous forest, to 1900 m. Savannas with scattered trees, clearings, dense thickets, near streams, pastures, gardens. Shy, forages in small groups from the ground to the treetops. Call: clear melodious song and harsh call notes typical of its congeners.

## BLACK-BILLED THRUSH
*Turdus ignobilis*
PARAULATA PICO NEGRO

Pl. 32

9" (23 cm.) [or 7.5" (19 cm.), a]. Like Pale-breasted Thrush but darker and grayer, *under wing coverts and axillars pale buff* (or much smaller and much darker, particularly on breast and sides of body, the white belly very sharply defined, throat whiter with a white patch on lower throat, a; or similar to a but without patch at base of throat, b). Bill black. See White-necked Thrush.

Tropical and subtropical zones. The nw from Zulia, Táchira and Apure to Barinas and Mérida (*debilis*, a). The base and lower slopes of Cerros Duida and Yapacana, Amazonas (*arthuri*, b). Amazonas on Cerros Yaví, Guanay, Camani, Duida (subtropical zone only), and Parú; s Bolívar on the upper Río Caura on the cerros of the Gran Sabana (*murinus*). [Guyana. Colombia to n Bolivia, w and central Amazonian Brazil.]

Forest edge, open low forest, second growth, to 1600 m. n of the Orinoco, 700–1950 m. s of it, to the summits of some tepuis. Near water, plantations, savannas with scattered bushes. Forages for insects, berries, worms, from ground to treetops.

## LAWRENCE'S THRUSH
*Turdus lawrencii*
PARAULATA DE LAWRENCE

Pl. 32
9" (23 cm.). Upperparts, wings and tail dark olivaceous brown. Chin white, throat buffy white, streaked black, underparts olive brown, paler than back, center of lower abdomen white. Under wing coverts and axillars cinnamon. *Bill yellow,* tipped black. The only species in this group with a yellow bill.
Tropical zone. S Amazonas along the Río Negro; s Bolívar along the upper Río Paragua and Cerro Roraima. [E Ecuador, ne and w Amazonian Brazil.]
Dense rain forest, 150–1200 m., usually near water.

## COCOA THRUSH
*Turdus fumigatus*
PARAULATA ACANELADA

9" (23 cm.). Above more *rufescent* than any other member of the group with *no olivaceous tinge.* Upperparts including wings and tail light reddish brown. Throat whitish streaked brown, underparts including under tail coverts, dull cinnamon brown (or bright cinnamon brown, a), center of belly white. Bill dusky.
Tropical, casually subtropical zone. Nw Zulia and s of L. Maracaibo; n Táchira; e Lara and Yaracuy, thence e along the n Cordilleras to Sucre (*aquilonalis*). Delta Amacuro; e Bolívar from the Río Paragua to the Sierra de Imataca (*fumigatus,* a). [The Guianas, ne Colombia; Amazonian and se Brazil; e Bolivia. Trinidad. Lesser Antilles.]
Various forested habitats to 1800 m. n of the Orinoco, to 500 m. s of it. Dense forest, light second growth, deciduous open woodland, cocoa plantations, gardens, gallery forest. Alone or in pairs forages actively from the ground to the treetops. Shy. Often near water. Song: beautiful, very deliberate, melodious.

## PALE-VENTED THRUSH
*Turdus obsoletus*
PARAULATA DEL ORINOCO

9" (23 cm.). Most like Pale-breasted Thrush, but darker and browner with under wing coverts similarly colored. Differs from Cocoa Thrush by darker and more olivaceous coloring, and by having buff-tinged, *white under tail coverts.* Above olive brown, below tawny olive, mixed with whitish on lower abdomen. Throat buffy white, streaked dusky. Under wing coverts and axillars tawny ochraceous.
Tropical zone. The llanos from the base of the Andes in s Táchira to n Barinas; Amazonas along the upper Orinoco from Nericagua to Caño Casiquiare (*orinocensis*). [Costa Rica to w Ecuador, e Peru, w Amazonian Brazil and n Bolivia.]
Rain forest to 850 m. n of the Orinoco, to 160 m. s of it. Dense forest, high second growth, open woodland, plantations. Alone or in small bands forages actively, often near water, from lower branches to treetops. Song: loud, short, melodious.
Note: *T. o. orinocensis* was made a race of *fumigatus* in Lista Av. Venez.

## BARE-EYED THRUSH
*Turdus nudigenis*
PARAULATA OJO DE CANDIL

Pl. 32
9" (23 cm.). Differs from any other member of the group by having a wide, *bare, orange eye ring.* Upperparts, wings and tail grayish olive; throat white, streaked dusky; breast and sides grayish, lighter and slightly browner than back; center of belly white. Bill olive with dusky ridge.
Tropical zone, casually subtropical. Widespread n of the Ríos Meta and Orinoco but not recorded in Zulia, Falcón, Trujillo or Lara; nw Amazonas; Margarita and Patos Is. (*nudigenis*). [The Guianas, e Colombia to nw Peru and ne Amazonian Brazil. Trinidad. Tobago. Lesser Antilles.]
Open rain forest, low open deciduous and xerophytic vegetation to (rarely) 1800 m. n of the Orinoco, to 300 m. s of it. Second growth, plantations, gardens, open country. Shy, forages to lower branches. Excellent singer; from a high

perch emits a pleasing series of loud, melodious notes.

## WHITE-NECKED THRUSH
*Turdus albicollis*
PARAULATA CHOTE

Pl. 32

8″ (20 cm.). Most like Black-billed Thrush but white patch at base of throat very much larger and more conspicuous, underparts much grayer, throat much more heavily streaked and under wing coverts and *axillars gray* instead of buff. Above dark olive brown, rump and *upper tail coverts dark gray;* wings like back, tail dark grayish. Upper throat white heavily streaked dusky, large patch on lower throat, extending to extreme upper breast pure white, rest of underparts light gray, very slightly tinged brown on breast; center of abdomen and under tail coverts pure white. Bill blackish above, mandible leaden olive to pale brown color.

Tropical and subtropical zones. From nw Zulia s to Táchira and w Apure thence n through Mérida and w Barinas to Carabobo and the Distr. Federal (*minusculus*). Sucre and ne Anzoátegui (*phaeopygoides*). Generally distributed through Amazonas and Bolívar (*phaeopygus*). [Mexico to nw Ecuador and the Guianas and e Colombia to n Bolivia, Paraguay, se Brazil and ne Argentina.]

Deep rain forest, damp second growth, to 1900 m. n of the Orinoco, to 1600 m. s of it. Open forest, small clearings, forest edge. Shy, secretive, inconspicuous, forages alone or in pairs in the undergrowth and to middle heights; seldom hops on the ground. A remarkable singer; utters loud, slow, varied, notes, usually in pairs.

# GNATWRENS, GNATCATCHERS: Sylviidae

CHIRITOS

Gnatwrens and gnatcatchers are the only American members of this very large Old World family, but, their affinity to it remains somewhat doubtful.

Gnatwrens for a long time were included in the antbirds, while gnatcatchers formed a family of their own. The former are long-billed, small birds found in humid forest; the latter are small, gray, black and white birds found in thickets and dry forest. Both feed on insects.

## COLLARED GNATWREN
*Microbates collaris*
CHIRITO ACOLLARDO

Pl. 31

4.3″ (11 cm.). Bill long, 0.8″ (2 cm.), legs long; tail very short. Upperparts, wings and tail earthy brown (with a rufescent tinge, a). Eyebrow white, stripe behind eye black, cheeks and ear coverts white, stripe below them from bill black, giving the *sides of head* a *striped* appearance. Below white with a *black band across chest.*

Tropical zone. Amazonas s of the Río Ventuari (*collaris*). Bolívar along the Río Paragua and Cerros Paurai and Chimantá-tepui (*paraguensis*, a). [Se Colombia, Surinam, French Guiana, Amazonian Brazil n of the Amazon.]

Dense rain forest, open low forest and clearings, often near water, 100–900 m. Alone or in pairs forages actively in the undergrowth and lower branches.

## LONG-BILLED GNATWREN
*Ramphocaenus melanurus*
CHIRITO PICÓN

Pl. 31

5.2″ (13 cm.). Bill very long and slender (1″, 2.5 cm.), legs long. Above light brown, rufescent on crown and nape and sides of head. Tail much graduated, black (with all but central tail feathers conspicuously tipped white, a). Below white, (or buff, a), sides of body pinkish buff, bases of throat feathers blackish, showing through as an indefinite dusky patch.

Tropical and lower subtropical zones. Extreme nw Zulia in the Sierra de Perijá

(*sanctaemarthae,* a). Elsewhere n of the Orinoco from Falcón, e Zulia, Mérida, Táchira and Apure to Anzoátegui and Sucre (*trinitatis*). Amazonas generally and Bolívar except area occupied by *albiventris* (*duidae*). Ne Bolívar on the Sierras de Imataca and Lema and the n Gran Sabana (*albiventris*). [S Mexico to Colombia and the Guianas, ne Peru and Amazonian and e Brazil.]
Dense rain and cloud forest, second growth, to 1700 m. n of the Orinoco, to 1000 m. s of it. Forest edge, clearings. Alone or in pairs, elusive, actively forages in thick tangled undergrowth to middle height. Call: utters weak chirps and soft whistles.

**TROPICAL GNATCATCHER**
*Polioptila plumbea*
CHIRITO DE CHAPARRALES

Pl. 31
4.4" (11 cm.). Crown, nape and sides of head to below eyes glossy blue black, lores white (or black, a). Back blue gray. Below white, tinged gray on breast and sides. Wings black, inner remiges broadly edged white. Central tail feathers black, outermost white with black base, next outermost black, outer web and tip white (or 2 outermost pairs white with black base, next basally black distally white, a). ♀: above blue gray, lores and eyebrow white (or lores gray, no eyebrow, a), otherwise like respective ♂.
Tropical zone. N of the Orinoco including

Margarita I. (*plumbiceps*). S Apure; s of the Orinoco except in Delta Amacuro (*innotata,* a). [Mexico to w Peru, the Guianas, n Amazonian and se Brazil.]
Open areas with scattered trees, deciduous as well as dense humid forest edge to 1200 m. n of the Orinoco, to 460 m. s of it. Savannas, scrubby areas, plantations, xerophytic vegetation. Continuously active, not shy, forages alone or in pairs from middle height to treetops. Flicks tail. Call: a pleasant musical trill and insectlike chirps.

**GUIANAN GNATCATCHER**
*Polioptila guianensis*
CHIRITO BRUJITO

Pl. 31
4" (10 cm.). Above blackish gray, narrow eye ring white. Chin and upper throat white, lower throat and breast dark gray, abdomen and under tail coverts white. Wings black, primary coverts and remiges narrowly edged gray. Outer tail feathers white with black base, next pair white with basal half black, next pair black with narrow white tip. ♀: upperparts gray paler than in ♂, superciliary white. Throat, belly and under tail coverts white, breast paler gray than in ♂. Wings and tail as in ♂.
Tropical zone. Amazonas s of the Río Ventuari (*facilis*). [The Guianas, ne and s Brazil.]
Clearings, open woodland at 150 m. Active, flicks tail. Joins other species in the upper levels of the forest.

# PIPITS: Motacillidae

## CAMINEROS, MIRACIELITOS

Pipits are small, brown, terrestrial birds found in open country. They walk and run rather than hop, and although they are somewhat sparrowlike in appearance, they are easily distinguishable from sparrows by their thin bills and long hind claw.
Pipits nest on the ground and live on insects. Usually birds of cool climates, pipits are most numerous in Eurasia and Africa, but a few are found in the Americas.

**YELLOWISH PIPIT**
*Anthus lutescens*
CAMINERO

Fig. 41
5.2" (13 cm.). Above streaked blackish and buff, coarsely so on mantle; below

dull white, tinged yellow in fresh plumage, breast streaked with blackish brown. Tail blackish, 2 outer pairs of feathers largely white.
Tropical zone. The llanos of w Apure and w Barinas; from e Monagas and Delta Amacuro s in Bolívar to the s Gran

Fig. 41. YELLOWISH PIPIT (left), PARAMO PIPIT (right)

Sabana (*lutescens*). [Pacific slope of Panama. E Colombia and the Guianas to central Argentina.]

Open places, damp pastures, llanos, proximity of rivers and lakes, to 200 m. n of the Orinoco, to 1300 m. s of it. Forages for insects in the grass. During the nesting season sings as it makes high undulating flights.

## PARAMO PIPIT

*Anthus bogotensis*
MIRACIELITO

Fig. 41
5.7″ (14.5 cm.). Above reddish buff,

heavily streaked black; below cinnamon buff lightly streaked black on breast. Tail blackish brown, outermost tail feathers mostly buff (or light grayish brown, a).

Subtropical to páramo zone. Páramo de Tamá, sw Táchira (*bogotensis*). The Andes of Mérida and Trujillo (*meridae, a*). [Colombia to nw Argentina.]

Open fields, meadows, 2200–4100 m. Forages for insects and seeds in shrubs and grass; in the higher altitudes in similar low páramo vegetation.

# WAXWINGS: Bombycillidae

## ALAS DE CERA

Waxwings are typical of the northern coniferous and birch forests and rarely reach n South America as winter stragglers.

Waxwings fly in compact flocks uttering a soft, lisping note, and feed on insects and berries. They are named for the small red waxlike appendages to the tips of the inner remiges. Their bills are short, broad and flat.

## CEDAR WAXWING

*Bombycilla cedrorum*
ALA DE CERA

6.7″ (17 cm.). Head crested; mask and throat black, mask outlined in white. General color soft cinnamon brown becoming gray on rump and upper tail coverts, yellowish on belly and white on under tail coverts. Wing coverts like

back, remiges and tail gray, tail with a subterminal black patch and yellow tip. The red, waxlike appendages to the inner remiges are not always present. Imm.: grayer above than ad., only lores black; lower breast and belly whitish with diffused, grayish brown streaks.

Cerro Pejochaina, 1650 m., nw Zulia. [Breeds in e N Amer. Winters to central

Panama and Greater Antilles. W Colombia once, Feb. 8.]
Recorded only once in Feb. in cloud forests. Forages chiefly in the treetops where it rests with crest erected. Call: a thin, high, lisping seeeee.

# PEPPERSHRIKES, SHRIKE-VIREOS, VIREOS, GREENLETS: Vireonidae

## VERDERONES, CHIVÍES

There are 4 distinct types of vireos in South America, all of them found in Venezuela. The peppershrikes are characterized by high and narrow bills and broad chestnut superciliaries. Shrike-vireos are distinguishable by their bright green backs or golden yellow underparts; the ordinary vireos are dull-colored, usually with whitish underparts and dull olive back, and the small, warblerlike greenlets have pointed, slender bills. The sexes are similar in all groups.

Members of this family inhabit forest edge and bushland, and frequent the ends of branches where they feed on insects and berries. They weave prettily constructed nests of bark and grasses which are suspended in the fork of a branch. They have an agreeable, loud, but rather monotonous song.

## RUFOUS-BROWED PEPPERSHRIKE
*Cyclarhis gujanensis*

SIRIRÍ
Pl. 33
6″ (15 cm.). Crown, nape and sides of head bluish gray, forehead and long, broad superciliary orange rufous; back, wings and tail olive green, chin whitish, foreneck, breast and sides of body yellowish green (or bright yellow, a), rest of underparts pale gray (or white with a very slight pink wash in center of abdomen, a; or grayish white, flanks slightly washed clay color, b).
Tropical and central subtropical zones. N of the Orinoco except on the Paria Pen.; s of the Orinoco in n Amazonas, n Bolívar and Delta Amacuro (*parvus, b*). Extreme e part of the Paria Pen., Sucre (*flavipectus, a*). S Amazonas, and s Bolívar (*gujanensis*). [Mexico to Argentina. Trinidad.]
Rain forest, deciduous and xerophytic woodland, second growth, plantations, scrub to 1950 m. n of the Orinoco, to 1600 m. s of it. Alone or in pairs, forages actively for insects in the foliage, from the lower branches to the treetops. Usually heard before being seen. Call: a series of short melodious whistles; the combination, repeated for several minutes, might be rendered as "please, please don't go 'way."

## GREEN SHRIKE-VIREO
*Smaragdolanius pulchellus*
SIRIRÍ REAL GORRO AZUL

Pl. 33
5.5″ (14 cm.). Crown greenish blue, sides of head green, narrow eyebrow and spot below eye yellow; back, wings and tail grass green. Below greenish yellow, under tail coverts yellow.
Tropical and subtropical zones. The Sierra de Perijá, Zulia (*eximius*). [Mexico to n Colombia.]
Rain and cloud forests, 350–1700 m. Forages alone or in pairs from medium heights to treetops. Call: monotonously repeated 3-note song is often heard before the bird is seen.

## SLATY-CAPPED SHRIKE-VIREO
*Smaragdolanius leucotis*
SIRIRÍ REAL OREJIBLANCO

Pl. 33
5.7″ (14.5 cm.). Crown, nape, extreme upper back and sides of head blue gray. Broad eyebrow and spot below eye bright yellow, streak from yellow spot below eye across cheeks and ear coverts grayish white. Back, wings and tail olive green. Throat and breast bright golden yellow, somewhat duller on center of abdomen, sides of body olive green.
Tropical zone. N and central Amazonas e across Bolívar to the Sierra de Imataca

and the Gran Sabana (*leucotis*). [Colombia, the Guianas to nw Ecuador, Amazonian Brazil, e Peru and n Bolivia.] Rain forest, second growth, 200–1300 m., often near streams in damp areas, from medium heights to treetops. Inconspicuous. Joins mixed bands of birds.

## YELLOW-THROATED VIREO
*Vireo flavifrons*
VIREO GARGANTIAMARILLO

5″ (13 cm.). Forehead very narrowly dull yellow, eye ring bright yellow. Crown, mantle and sides of head olive green; lower back, rump and upper tail coverts dark blue gray. Wings blackish with 2 prominent white bars, inner remiges broadly edged white. Tail blackish, the feathers, narrowly edged all around with white. Throat and breast yellow, belly and under tail coverts white, sides of body pale gray.
Tropical and subtropical zones. Winter resident, Nov.–March. The Andes of Lara, Mérida and Táchira; the Distr. Federal; e Sucre. [Breeds in s Canada and the e US. Winters from Mexico to se Colombia. Tobago.]
Rain and cloud forests, 800–1800 m. Second growth, forest edge, coffee plantations. Solitary.

## RED-EYED VIREO
*Vireo olivaceus*
JULIÁN CHIVÍ OJIRROJO

Pl. 33
5″ (13 cm.). Crown slaty gray, broad eyebrow whitish surmounted by a blackish line. Back, wings and tail olive. Below dull white, under tail coverts pale yellow. The resident race is brighter olive green above and has lighter yellow under tail coverts than the migrant races. Mandible leaden blue.
Tropical and subtropical zones. Throughout including Margarita and Patos Is. (*vividior*). Winter resident from the n, Sept.–Mar., mostly in w Venezuela e to Barinas, Portuguesa and Aragua, in Amazonas, and e to the Río Paragua, Bolívar (*olivaceus*). Páramo de Tamá, Táchira, Oct. (*flavoviridis*). Summer resident from the s, Mar.–Aug. nw Bolívar along the lower Río Caura, central and s Amazonas (*chivi*). [E N

Amer. to Colombia, e Peru, n Bolivia, w Brazil. Uruguay, Argentina.]
In a variety of woodland habitats to 1650 m. Rain forest, second growth, plantations, gardens, xerophytic vegetation, mangroves, etc. Forages actively from lower heights to the treetops. Joins mixed forest bands.

## BLACK-WHISKERED VIREO
*Vireo altiloquus*
JULIÁN CHIVÍ BIGOTINEGRO

5.5″ (14 cm.). Not unlike Red-eyed Vireo but with a narrow but prominent dusky malar streak; grayer and duller olive above, crown scarcely different from back (except, a); bill longer and heavier.
Resident on Margarita I. and Los Roques (*bonairensis*, a). Transient, Aug.–Oct., from the Greater Antilles. Recorded from Trujillo, Mérida, s Amazonas; upper Río Paragua, Bolívar; Los Roques (*altiloquus*). Transient, Sept.–Oct. from Cuba. Upper Río Cuyuni, Bolívar (*barbatulus*). [S Florida, Caribbean islands to Surinam, n Brazil and ne Peru.]
Rain forest to 1000 m. Second growth, mangroves, scattered trees, often near water.

## WARBLING VIREO
*Vireo gilvus*
JULIÁN CHIVÍ DE GORRO MARRÓN

Pl. 33
4.4″ (11 cm.). Crown sepia brown, long eyebrow and lores dull white. Back, wings and tail olive brown, paler than back. Throat white, lower breast, belly and under tail coverts yellowish white. Mandible flesh color [cf. Brown-headed Greenlet].
Upper tropical and subtropical zones. The n Cordilleras from Zulia and Táchira to the Paria Pen., Sucre (*mirandae*). [Canada to w Panama. Colombia to w Ecuador and n Bolivia.]
Rain and cloud forests, 700–2500 m. Second growth, open woodland, coffee plantations. Forages actively high in trees, usually in small groups.

## LEMON-CHESTED GREENLET
*Hylophilus thoracicus*
VERDERÓN VIENTRE GRIS

Pl. 33
4.5″ (11.5 cm.). Forecrown, back, wings

and tail olive green; nape and underparts gray, sides of breast tinged yellowish green. Bill slender, pointed in all *Hylophilus*.
Tropical zone. Across n Bolívar from the lower and middle Río Caura e to the Sierra de Imataca and the upper Río Cuyuni (*griseiventris*). [The Guianas, e Colombia to Bolivia, Amazonian and se Brazil.]
Rain forest, 100–700 m. Clearings, gardens, near streams. Forages high in the trees.

## GRAY-CHESTED GREENLET
*Hylophilus semicinereus*
VERDERÓN CABEZA VERDE

Pl. 33
4.5″ (11.5 cm.). Forecrown, back, wings and tail olive green, nape and underparts gray, sides of breast tinged yellowish green.
Tropical zone. Central and s Amazonas; central Bolívar along the Río Paragua (*viridiceps*). [French Guiana, central and e Amazonian Brazil.]
Rain forests, 100–350 m. Second growth. Forages for insects in the foliage, from lower to medium heights.

## ASHY-HEADED GREENLET
*Hylophilus pectoralis*
VERDERÓN CABECIGRIS

4.5″ (11.4 cm.). Hindcrown and nape gray; forecrown, back, wings and tail yellowish olive green. Throat and belly white, breast lemon yellow. Axillars and under wing coverts bright yellow.
Tropical zone. Río Amacuro, Delta Amacuro. [The Guianas; n, e and central Brazil. Ne Bolivia.]
Dense rain forests at sea level, also mangroves, clearings. Forages at medium heights.
Note: A new record since the publication of Lista Av. Venez.

## TEPUI GREENLET
*Hylophilus sclateri*
VERDERÓN DE LOS TEPUIS

Pl. 33
4.7″ (12 cm.). Crown and nape blue gray in sharp contrast to olive green back; wings and tail gray. Throat white, pectoral band dull yellow, sides of body, dull pale green; rest of underparts white.
Upper tropical and subtropical zones. N Amazonas s; nw Bolívar along the upper Río Cuchivero e across the upper Paragua to the Gran Sabana. [Adjacent Brazil; Guyana.]
Endemic to Pantepui. Rain and cloud forests on the slopes of the tepuis, 600–2000 m. Forages in the upper branches.

## BUFF-CHEEKED GREENLET
*Hylophilus muscicapinus*
VERDERÓN ATRAPAMOSCAS

Pl. 33
4.5″ (11.5 cm.). Forehead, cheeks and sides of neck pinkish buff, crown and nape dull gray, back, wings and tail olive green; below dull white tinged pinkish buff on throat and breast.
Tropical zone. N and central Amazonas; n Bolívar s to the upper Río Caroní and the n Gran Sabana (*muscicapinus*). [The Guianas; n Brazil.]
Rain forests and second growth, to 1100 m. In pairs or small groups forages in the high branches and the treetops.

## BROWN-HEADED GREENLET
*Hylophilus brunneiceps*
VERDERÓN CABECICASTAÑO

Pl. 33
4.5″ (11.5 cm.). Not unlike Warbling Vireo but without prominent eyebrow, and upper parts paler and "redder," primaries edged green. Above light reddish brown, becoming pale yellowish olive on upper tail coverts and rump. Wing coverts and edges of remiges light yellowish olive; tail pale grayish olive. Throat and breast very pale buffy brown, belly light grayish; under tail and wing coverts light yellow.
Tropical zone. N Amazonas s to the Río Guainía and Caño Casiquiare (*brunneiceps*). [Se Colombia, n and central Amazonian Brazil.]
Rain forests, 100–200 m. Second growth. clearings.

## RUFOUS-NAPED GREENLET
*Hylophilus semibrunneus*
VERDERÓN GORRO CASTAÑO

Pl. 33
5″ (13 cm.). Crown and nape rufous chestnut, lores and ocular region white.

Back, wings and tail olive green. Throat grayish white, breast pale buff, belly white, under tail and wing coverts and axillars pale yellow.

Tropical and subtropical zones. Sierra de Perijá, Zulia. [Colombia, Ecuador.] Rain and cloud forests, 450–2000 m. Second growth, clearings.

## GOLDEN-FRONTED GREENLET
*Hylophilus aurantiifrons*
VERDERÓN LUISUCHO

Pl. 33

4.5″ (11.5 cm.). Crown and nape dull cinnamon brown (or sepia brown, a), forehead dull yellowish. Upper back paler than nape and gradually changing to pale olive on upper tail coverts. Wings and tail dull citrine. Throat white, sides of head and neck buffy brown, breast washed buffy, rest of underparts very pale yellow, brighter on under tail coverts.

Tropical and subtropical zones. Nw Zulia, n Mérida, n Táchira (*helvinus*, a). Falcón and e Zulia s to s Barinas and s Táchira, thence e across the llanos from Cojedes and Portuguesa to Monagas and Delta Amacuro (*saturatus*). [Central Panama to Colombia. Trinidad.]

A variety of wooded habitats to 1900 m. Humid and deciduous forest, mangroves, second growth, clearings, gallery forest. Alone or in small groups forages actively at all levels. The vernacular name, *Luisucho*, refers to its 3-note chirp.

## DUSKY-CAPPED GREENLET
*Hylophilus hypoxanthus*
VERDERÓN GORRA FUSCA

4.3″ (11 cm.). Above dull sepia brown, darker on crown, rump and upper tail coverts, wings and tail olive. Lores whitish, sides of head like crown, throat whitish washed brownish at sides. Below yellow citrine, center of belly and under tail coverts yellow.

Tropical zone. W Amazonas s of the Río Ventuari (*hypoxanthus*). [E Colombia to Bolivia and Amazonian Brazil.] Rain forests, second growth, plantations, clearings and open fields, 100–200 m.

## SCRUB GREENLET
*Hylophilus flavipes*
VERDERÓN PATIPÁLIDO

Pl. 33

4.5″ (11.5 cm.). Crown and nape dull brownish olive, mantle olive washed with brownish, lower back and rump light citrine; remiges black edged olive, tail grayish citrine. Throat whitish, underparts pale yellow washed buff on breast (or breast buffy, center of abdomen whitish, a). Legs flesh color.

Tropical zone. Nw Zulia to Táchira, n Mérida, w Barinas and n Portuguesa (*galbanus*, a). The n from e Zulia to Sucre, across the llanos from Guárico to Monagas; n Bolívar e to the upper Río Cuyuni; Margarita I. (*acuticauda*). [Costa Rica to Colombia. Tobago.]

Rain forests from sea level to 1200 m. n of the Orinoco, to 500 m. s of it. A variety of habitats including second growth, gallery forests, arid areas, deciduous woodland, thorny thickets, mangroves, etc. Alone or in pairs forages actively in the low thickets and to the middle tier.

## TAWNY-CROWNED GREENLET
*Hylophilus ochraceiceps*
VERDERÓN FRENTE RUFA

Pl. 33

4.7″ (12 cm.). Forehead orange rufous, becoming duller on crown (or forehead tinged dull buffy yellow, crown olive, a). Back and wings olive, tail ochraceous olive (or ochraceous, a). Throat whitish, rest of underparts grayish obscurely streaked with yellow, under tail coverts greenish yellow.

Tropical, occasionally subtropical zone. N Amazonas s to the Brazilian border; Bolívar from the Río Caura to the n Gran Sabana (*ferrugineifrons*). Extreme e Bolívar on the Sierra de Imataca and Cerro Roraima (*luteifrons*). [Mexico to w Ecuador, n Bolivia and Amazonian Brazil.]

Rain forests and cloud forests on the slopes of the tepuis, to 1600 m. Forest edge; second growth. In small groups forages actively and noisily in the understory. Joins mixed forest flocks.

# OROPENDOLAS, AMERICAN ORIOLES, BLACKBIRDS, ETC.: Icteridae

## CONOTOS, TORDOS, TURPIALES, ETC.

This family comprises many groups of species rather unlike each other and includes oropendolas, orioles, blackbirds, marsh birds, meadowlarks, cowbirds etc. and all can be conveniently referred to as Icterids. The bill, however, is characteristic, being rather long, conical and tapering to a sharp point. The New World orioles are brightly colored in contrasting yellow or orange and black, and although resembling Old World orioles in color are not related to them.

Icterids are found in dense or open forest, scrub, llanos and marshes and live on fruit and insects. Some have a pleasant song while others emit harsh disagreeable sounds.

Their nests are often beautifully woven, long, pendant affairs suspended from the ends of branches while others are parasitic on other birds and build no nest.

Males are usually much larger than females and in such cases the measurements of the two sexes are given separately.

## SHINY COWBIRD

*Molothrus bonariensis*
TORDO MIRLO

Pl. XIII

8.5" (22 cm.). Shining, silky purplish blue black above, shining purple black below. Wings and tail black glossed with green. Bill short, conical, black. Iris brown. ♀: 7.5" (19 cm.). Dull grayish brown, paler below, particularly on throat. Wings and tail brown.

Tropical and subtropical zones. N Venezuela s to n Amazonas, n Bolívar and Delta Amacuro (*venezuelensis*). [E Panama to Chile and Argentina. Lesser Antilles. Tobago, Trinidad.]

Rain forest, second growth, farms with scattered trees, marshes, suburban areas to 1600 m. n of the Orinoco, to 250 m. s of it. Usually in small flocks, forages in the trees and on the ground. Feeds on grain, seeds and insects. Calls: warbling, pleasing, musical song and harsh, metallic notes; often sings in flight. A brood parasite, laying its eggs in the nests of other birds, which rear the young.

## GIANT COWBIRD

*Scaphidura oryzivora*
TORDO PIRATA

Pl. XIII

14" (35 cm.). Glossy, silky purplish black, feathers at sides of neck elongated forming a ruff, wings and tail blue black, tail somewhat rounded. Iris orange. ♀: 11" (28 cm.). Dull black, ruff much smaller. Iris brown. Bill black.

Tropical zone. Falcón, Zulia, Táchira, extreme w Apure, Barinas, through Portuguesa to Carabobo and in Sucre; Amazonas along the upper Ríos Ventuari and upper Orinoco; n Bolívar from the lower Caura to the Cuyuni; Delta Amacuro (*oryzivora*). [Mexico to w Ecuador, Bolivia, Paraguay and ne Argentina. Trinidad. Tobago (introduced?).]

Rain forests, but more often in second growth, deciduous woods and open fields to 1600 m. n of the Orinoco, to 300 m. s of it. Near water, cocoa plantations, clearings. Alone or in small groups forages high in the trees and also on the ground in open country. Shy. Feeds on fruits and berries. A brood parasite, laying its eggs in the nests of colonial oropendolas and caciques.

## CRESTED OROPENDOLA

*Psarocolius decumanus*
CONOTO NEGRO

Pl. XIII

16" (41 cm.). Glossy black; lower back, rump, upper and under tail coverts dark chestnut; central tail feathers black, rest *bright yellow*. Head crested, feathers long and very thin. Iris blue, bill pale olive yellow, yellower basally. ♀: 13" (33 cm.). Like ♂ but much smaller, and dull black rather than shiny black.

Tropical zone. Throughout in forested country (*decumanus*). [Panama to n

Bolivia, Paraguay and n Argentina. Trinidad. Tobago.]

Rain forest, second growth, open forest, clearings, plantations, rarely to 1900 m. n of the Orinoco, to 500 m. s of it. Forest rivers, forest edge. Colonial, polygamous, weaves meter-long, purse-shaped nests, many of which hang from outer branches of high trees. Utters a song consisting of hard rasps and liquid gurglings accompanied by an acrobatic contortion. Frequently seen overhead when flying in flocks across wide waterways.

## GREEN OROPENDOLA

*Psarocolius viridis*
CONOTO VERDE

Pl. 38

♂ 17″ (43 cm.); ♀ 14″ (35 cm.). Olive green; lower back, rump, flanks, thighs and under tail coverts dark chestnut; upper tail coverts long, olive, central tail feathers blackish, rest bright yellow. Remiges black. Long crest of threadlike feathers. Bill ivory. ♀: like ♂ but outer web of outer tail feather olive and chestnut parts of plumage lighter.

Tropical zone. Amazonas s of the Río Ventuari; Bolívar from the lower Río Cuchivero e to the Gran Sabana and n through Delta Amacuro to nw Monagas and se Sucre. [E Colombia and the Guianas to ne Peru and the s bank of the Amazon, Brazil.]

Rain and deciduous forest, from sea level to 1100 m. Habitat and habits similar to those of the Crested Oropendola.

## RUSSET-BACKED OROPENDOLA

*Psarocolius angustifrons*
CONOTO ACEITUNO

Pl. 38

♂ 18″ (46 cm.); ♀ 15″ (38 cm.). Head and throat dull olive, forecrown occasionally yellow, (or forecrown always bright yellow, a), upper mantle olive deepening to olive brown on back, brightening to rufous brown on rump and upper tail coverts; underparts olivaceous brown, under tail coverts rufous chestnut. Wings blackish, dusky olivaceous on outer web. Central tail feathers dusky olive, next pair olive on inner web and tip, outer web bright yellow, rest

bright yellow tipped dusky, with dusky outer web on outermost. Crest feathers broader and shorter than in the foregoing species. Bill leaden gray (or ivory, a). ♀: like ♂ but smaller.

Upper tropical and subtropical zones. The Sierra de Perijá, Zulia; s Táchira; central and n Mérida; se Lara (*neglectus*, a). Yaracuy along the coastal Cordillera to the Distr. Federal and the interior chain in Aragua (*oleagineus*). [Colombia to w Ecuador, w Amazonian Brazil and n Bolivia.]

Rain and cloud forests, undergrowth, coffee plantations, from 1200–2500 m. in the w mountains and from 400–2000 m. in the n central mountains. Habits resemble those of the Crested Oropendola.

## OLIVE OROPENDOLA

*Gymnostinops yuracares*
CONOTO PICO ENCARNADO

Pl. 38

♂ 22″ (56 cm.); ♀ 17″ (43 cm.). Head, narrow occipital crest, neck and breast bright olive yellow; back, inner remiges, belly and under tail coverts chestnut. Outer remiges black, edged chestnut. Central tail feathers olive green, rest bright yellow. Bare cheeks pinkish flesh, bill black with salmon red tip. ♀: in color like ♂.

Tropical zone. Nw Bolívar along the lower Río Caura; w and s Amazonas (*yuracares*). [E Colombia to n Bolivia, Amazonian Brazil, n of the Amazon to the Rio Negro, s of the Amazon to the Rio Xingú.]

Rain forest, 100–200 m. Colonial habits like those of the other oropendolas.

## YELLOW-RUMPED CACIQUE

*Cacicus cela*
ARRENDAJO COMÚN

Pl. XIII

♂ 11″ (28 cm.); ♀ 9″ (23 cm.). Glossy black. Inner wing coverts, lower back, rump, upper and under tail coverts bright yellow. Central tail feathers black, basally yellow, rest yellow, broadly tipped black. Iris pale blue, bill greenish white. ♀: like ♂ but duller with belly washed with olive yellow.

Tropical zone. Throughout in wooded country (*cela*). [Central Panama to w

Ecuador, n Bolivia, the Guianas and Amazonian and se Brazil. Trinidad.]
Rain forests, second growth, marshes to 1000 m. n of the Orinoco, to 500 m. s of it. Open country with scattered trees, plantations, river banks, llanos. Nests in colonies, weaves pouchlike nests, placed in high branches near wasps' nests. Forages in the middle tier and near the treetops for berries, fruits and insects. Whistles loud clear melodious notes.

## RED-RUMPED CACIQUE
*Cacicus haemorrhous*
ARRENDAJO RABADILLA ENCARNADA

♂ 11″ (28 cm.); ♀ 9″ (23 cm.). Glossy blue black, lower back and rump scarlet. Iris light blue; bill yellowish green. ♀: like ♂ but dulled, particularly below.
Tropical zone. N and s Amazonas; Bolívar along the lower Río Caura, the Río Paragua and the s Gran Sabana (*haemorrhous*). [E Colombia, the Guianas, e Ecuador, e Peru, n Bolivia, Brazil to Argentina.]
Rain forests, to 900 m. on the slopes of the tepuis. Second growth, forest edge, river banks, clearings. Forages at medium heights in noisy groups. Colonial, it hangs nests from trees like Yellow-rumped Cacique.

## SCARLET-RUMPED CACIQUE
*Cacicus uropygialis*
ARRENDAJO PICO CURVO

Pl. XIII
♂ 11″ (28 cm.); ♀ 10.5″ (26.5 cm.). Much like the Red-rumped Cacique, differing by being black without a blue gloss, only rump orange scarlet and tail rounded instead of square. Iris greenish blue; bill yellow basally, pale pea green apically. ♀: like ♂ but duller.
Upper tropical and subtropical zones. The Perijá region, Zulia, and in Táchira (*uropygialis*). [Costa Rica to central Peru.]
Cloud forests, second growth, forest edge, 1300–2300 m. In small groups forages noisily and actively in the upper branches but may descend near the ground.

## MOUNTAIN CACIQUE
*Cacicus leucoramphus*
ARRENDAJO ALIAMARILLO COLINEGRO

Pl. XIII
♂ 11″ (28 cm.); ♀ 10″ (25 cm.). Black; head somewhat crested. Inner wing coverts and rump bright yellow. Iris bluish gray; bill bluish gray tipped white. Differs readily from Yellow-rumped Cacique by all-black tail. ♀ like ♂.
Subtropical zone. Sw Táchira along the Río Chiquito (*leucoramphus*). [Colombia to n Bolivia.]
Cloud forest, 1900–2800 m. Melodious, whistled song. Feeds on insects and fruit.
Note: Placed in the genus *Archiplanus* in Lista Av. Venez.

## SOLITARY BLACK CACIQUE
*Cacicus solitarius*
ARRENDAJO NEGRO LLANERO

Pl. XIII
♂ 11″ (28 cm.); ♀ 10″ (25 cm.). All black; head somewhat crested. *Iris brown;* bill pale pea green, bluish basally. ♀ like ♂.
Tropical zone. The s base of the Andes in Táchira and Barinas and in w Apure. [Colombia to Bolivia, central Argentina and Uruguay.]
Deciduous forest, woodland, dense scrub, llanos, 50–300 m. Second growth, sugarcane fields. Forages alone or in pairs.
Note: Placed in the genus *Archiplanus* in Lista Av. Venez.

## YELLOW-BILLED CACIQUE
*Cacicus holosericeus*
ARRENDAJO ANDINO

Pl. XIII
♂ 9.7″ (24.7 cm.); ♀ 8.2″ (21 cm.). All dull black. *Iris blue gray or whitish;* bill pale yellow. ♀ like ♂.
Subtropical and temperate zones. Sierra de Perijá, Zulia; the Andes of Táchira and Mérida; the coastal Cordillera in Aragua and the Distr. Federal (*australis*). [Mid. Amer. to nw Peru and Bolivia.]
Dense cloud forest and second growth, bamboo thickets, tangled undergrowth, old clearings, 1800–3100 m. Alone or in small groups, forages noisily at low

levels. Responds to an imitation of its whistles.
Note: Placed in the genus *Amblycercus* in Lista Av. Venez.

## CARIB GRACKLE
*Quiscalus lugubris*
TORDO NEGRO

Pl. XIII
9.5″ (24 cm.). Glossy purple black, wings and tail bluer, tail concave, wedge-shaped. Iris straw white; bill black, long 1″ (2.5 cm.), slender and somewhat curved. Bill in insular birds longer and more slender, up to 1.3″ (3.3 cm.). ♀: above dusky brown with a bronzy sheen, below grayish brown, palest on throat, darkest on abdomen. Iris straw white.
Tropical zone. In the n from Carabobo and Yaracuy to Sucre and Monagas, and across the llanos from Apure and Barinas e to Delta Amacuro (*lugubris*). Margarita and Los Frailes Is. (*insularis*). Los Hermanos Is. (*orquillensis*), Los Testigos Is. (*luminosus*). [E Colombia, the Guianas, ne Brazil in Amapá. Trinidad. Lesser Antilles.]
Open, sparsely wooded areas, gallery forest, from sea level to 850 m., farms, city parks, forest edge. On the islands in thickets and thorny scrub. Noisy, in small groups, often on the ground. Gregarious, gathers in flocks when flying to roosting areas.

## GREAT-TAILED GRACKLE
*Cassidix mexicanus*
GALANDRA

15″ (38 cm.). Head, upper mantle and breast glossy purple black, becoming bluer on back and belly. Tail long, 8″ (20.3 cm.), much graduated, wedge-shaped, glossy black. Wings black with a greenish gloss. Iris straw yellow; bill black, rather long, 1.7″ (4.3 cm.). ♀: 12″ (30 cm.). Above bronzy, crown browner, eyebrow buffy. Throat whitish, rest of underparts light buffy brown deepening to dusky brown on flanks, thighs and under tail coverts. Iris yellow.
Tropical zone. Nw Zulia from the Goajira Pen. to the mouth of L. Maracaibo (*peruvianus*). [Sw US to nw Peru.]
Seashore, river banks, pastures with scattered trees, arid areas at sea level. Its

diet includes fish, birds and insects as well as vegetable matter. Calls: varied, including grunts and soft tinkling notes.

## GOLDEN-TUFTED GRACKLE
*Macroagelaius imthurni*
MORICHE DE LOS TEPUIS

Pl. XIII
♂ 11″ (28 cm.); ♀ 10″ (25 cm.). Glossy blue black, feathers of back with metallic edges; *pectoral tufts golden yellow*. Tail rather long, 5″ (12.7 cm.), rounded. Bill black. ♀: in color like ♂.
Upper tropical and subtropical zones. N Amazonas s to Cerro Duida; n Bolívar along the Río Cuchivero (Cerro Tabaro) and in the tepuis of the Gran Sabana. [Guyana; adj. n Brazil.]
Rain forests on the slopes of the tepuis, 500–2000 m. Gregarious, gathers in noisy flocks as it flies from tree to tree along river banks and forest clearings. Call: emits squeaky, rasping notes.

## VELVET-FRONTED GRACKLE
*Lampropsar tanagrinus*
TORDO FRENTE ATERCIOPELADA

Pl. XIII
♂ 8″ (20 cm.); ♀ 7.5″ (19 cm.). Silky blue black, *feathers of forehead* jet black, stiff, *plushlike*. Bill black, short, 0.6″ (1.5 cm.). ♀: like ♂ but feathers of forehead less specialized. The smallest of all "blackbirds" in Venezuela.
Tropical zone. Nw Amazonas (Munduapo); ne Bolívar (Ciudad Bolívar); e Sucre; e Monagas (*guianensis*). [Guyana; se Colombia; w Amazonian Brazil to n Bolivia.]
Rain forest, mangroves, second growth, near water, to about 200 m. In pairs and small flocks forages for insects low in trees.

## YELLOW-HOODED BLACKBIRD
*Agelaius icterocephalus*
TURPIAL DE AGUA

Pl. 38
♂ 7″ (18 cm.); ♀ 6.5″ (16.5 cm.). Head, neck and upper breast bright yellow, lores and region around base of bill black; rest of plumage silky black. Iris blackish, bill black. ♀: top and sides of head dull brownish olive, eyebrow

yellow; back brownish olive, streaked blackish, wings and tail dark brown. Throat and upper breast bright yellow, lower breast olive yellow shading to gray on belly and dark brown on under tail coverts. The intensity of color on the underparts is rather variable.

Tropical zone. Widespread n of the Orinoco s to n Amazonas, n Bolívar and Delta Amacuro (*icterocephalus*). [The Guianas, Colombia, ne Peru, n and sw Amazonian Brazil, Paraguay. Trinidad.] Marshy areas, rice fields, swampy grassland, bushy river banks, to 600 m. n of the Orinoco, to 250 m. s of it. Gregarious; noisy. Nests in colonies in reeds near shore.

[IN THE GENUS *Icterus* ♀ of the resident species resemble ♂ and there is no significant size difference. In color they are yellow and black except for Orchard Oriole.]

## MORICHE ORIOLE

*Icterus chrysocephalus*
MORICHE

Pl. 38
8.5″ (21.6 cm.). *Black; crown,* wing coverts, rump, thighs and under wing coverts *yellow.*
Tropical zone. Local n of the Orinoco; Apure (San Fernando); se Sucre (Guanoco); e Monagas (Guanipa); s of the Orinoco generally in Amazonas and Bolívar. [The Guianas; e Colombia to e Peru, n and w Amazonian Brazil. Trinidad.]
Forest edge, scrub, llanos, gallery forest, savannas with Moriche palms, swamps to 200 m. n of the Orinoco, to 1200 m. on the slopes of the tepuis. Forages in the treetops and in Moriche palms, where it usually nests. Feeds on insects, fruits and berries. Call: elaborate whistled song is soft and pleasing.

## ORCHARD ORIOLE

*Icterus spurius*
TURPIAL DE HUERTOS

7.2″ (18.2 cm.). Head, neck, and upper back black; lower back, breast and belly chestnut; wings black, upper and under wing coverts, chestnut greater wing coverts narrowly edged white; tail black,

extreme base yellowish white. ♀: above olive, yellower on head and rump, below yellow. Wings brown with 2 white wing bars; tail olive. ♂, 1st year resembles ♀ but has black throat.
Tropical zone. Winter resident, Sept.–Mar. The region around L. Maracaibo in Zulia, Maracay in Aragua (*spurius*). [Breeds in e N Amer., winters from Mexico to w Colombia.]
Thickets and forest edge to about 200 m. Usually forages in low bushes.

## ORANGE-CROWNED ORIOLE

*Icterus auricapillus*
GONZALITO REAL

Pl. 38
7.5″ (19 cm.). Crown, nape, ear coverts and sides of neck orange; forehead, face, throat and upper breast black, rest of underparts rich yellow, deeper at border of black breast. Upper back black; lower back and rump rich yellow. Wings and tail black, inner wing coverts yellow.
Tropical and lower subtropical zones. Generally distributed n of the Orinoco; s of it from Caicara to the lower Río Paragua, Bolívar. [E Panama, n Colombia.]
Rain forest, second growth, semi-arid open woodland, gallery forest, xerophytic vegetation and scrub along streams, cultivated and suburban areas, to 1900 m. n of the Orinoco, to 300 m. s of it. In pairs or small groups, forages in the treetops.

## TROUPIAL

*Icterus icterus*
TURPIAL COMÚN

Pl. 38
9.5″ (24 cm.). Whole head, neck, throat and upper breast black, feathers of throat long, lanceolate, forming a "beard," feathers of breast pointed, encroaching raggedly on yellow of rest of underparts. Collar on hindneck yellow, upper back black, lower back and upper tail coverts yellow (or with back mainly yellow with a black band across upper back, a). Wings and tail black. Lesser wing coverts yellow, median coverts and broad edges to inner remiges white. Bare ocular skin bright blue.
Tropical zone. Arid coastal zone from Goajira Pen., Zulia, e to the Paraguaná

Pen., Falcón, s to e and central Lara; Margarita I. (*ridgwayi*). The Caribbean littoral from Carabobo to Sucre and s across the llanos to the Orinoco and e Apure to the mouth of the Río Meta, and along the s bank of the Orinoco to Cuidad Bolívar (*icterus*). W Apure from Paragüito to the Colombian border (*metae*, a). [Colombia, Amazonian and e Brazil to Bolivia and ne Argentina. Aruba, Curaçao. Trinidad.] Second growth, deciduous woods, gallery forest, to 1300 m. n of the Orinoco, to 100 m. s of it. Llanos, pastures, cactus thickets and other thorny scrub near water. Alone or in pairs forages for fruits, insects and berries at low to medium heights. Call: loud, melodious whistles, usually repeated. The Troupial is the national bird of Venezuela.

## YELLOW ORIOLE
*Icterus nigrogularis*
GONZALITO

Pl. 38
8″ (20 cm.). Yellow; lores, ocular region, center of throat to upper breast black. Wings and tail black; inner wing coverts yellow, greater coverts, inner remiges and base of primaries narrowly edged white (or with outer webs of primaries conspicuously edged white, a).
Tropical and lower subtropical zones. N of the Orinoco except ne Sucre, s to n Amazonas and n Bolívar. Not recorded from Delta Amacuro (*nigrogularis*). The Paria Pen., Sucre, and Patos I. (*trinitatis*). Margarita I. (*helioeides*, a). [The Guianas, n and ne Colombia, n Brazil. Aruba, Curaçao, Bonaire. Trinidad, Monos I.]

## BALTIMORE (OR NORTHERN) ORIOLE
*Icterus galbula*
TURPIAL DE BALTIMORE

Pl. 38
7.2″ (18.2 cm.). Head, neck, upper back and throat black, prolonged in a point to upper breast; underparts, lower back, rump and tail coverts orange. Wings black, lesser wing coverts yellow, greater coverts edged white on outer web, remiges edged white. Central tail feathers

black, rest yellow, basally black. ♀: top and sides of head, and nape dull orange, becoming grayish olive on back where slightly streaked dusky; rump, upper tail coverts and tail dull, light brownish orange. Wings dull brown, white markings as in ♂. Throat whitish, breast and under tail coverts orange yellow, rest of underparts buffy. ♂, 1st winter, like ♀ but throat black and feathers of the upperparts black, edged olive yellow giving a scaled appearance.
Tropical zone. Winter resident, Oct.–Feb. Nw and s Zulia. [Breeds in e N Amer., winters from Mexico to n Colombia.] Second growth, cultivated areas with scattered trees, pastures, thickets, to 150 m. Forages from middle heights to the treetops for insects, fruits and berries.

## YELLOW-BACKED ORIOLE
*Icterus chrysater*
TOCHE

Pl. 38
9″ (23 cm.). Golden yellow; forehead, ocular region, throat and extreme upper breast, wings and tail black; lesser wing coverts yellow.
Tropical and subtropical zones. The Andes from Táchira to s Lara; the Sierra de San Luis, Falcón; the coastal Cordillera to Miranda and in the interior chain on Cerro Negro; the llanos of Portuguesa and w Apure (*giraudii*). [Mexico to n Colombia.]
Rain and cloud forests, to 2900 m. Second growth, thorn scrub, cactus, open woodland, plantations. Forages noisily, alone or in pairs, in the middle height of trees. High melodious whistles.

## YELLOW-TAILED ORIOLE
*Icterus mesomelas*
TURPIAL COLA AMARILLA

Pl. 38
9.5″ (24 cm.). The only resident oriole with yellow in the tail. Yellow; lores, ocular region, throat and extreme upper breast, mantle, wings and central tail feathers black; 3 outer pairs of tail feathers mostly yellow; wing coverts and axillars yellow.
Tropical zone. The region around L. Maracaibo in Zulia, Táchira and Mérida

(*carrikeri*). [Mexico to w Ecuador and n Peru.]
Wooded swamps and marshes, forest edge, second growth, wet clearings, *Heliconia* thickets to 500 m. Forages alone or in pairs. Call: varied, piercing, melodious, whistled song, often repeated.

## ORIOLE BLACKBIRD
*Gymnomystax mexicanus*
TORDO MAICERO

Pl. 38
11″ (28 cm.). Head, neck, upper and under wing coverts golden yellow; back, wings and tail black. Bare orbits and line at sides of upper throat black. Imm.: like ad., but crown black.
Tropical zone. N of the Orinoco from Yaracuy and Carabobo s through Portuguesa to the upper Río Arauca, Apure, thence e to Sucre and Delta Amacuro; nw Amazonas. [The Guianas, e Colombia to ne Peru and n Amazonian Brazil.]
Open fields with scattered trees, gallery forest, deciduous woods, second growth, llanos, suburban areas to 1000 m., in the vicinity of water. Often on the ground, in pairs or small flocks. Feeds on fruits and insects.

## RED-BREASTED BLACKBIRD
*Leistes militaris*
TORDO PECHIRROJO

Pl. 38
7.5″ (19 cm.). Brownish black, including wings and tail; throat, breast and shoulders bright pinkish red. In very fresh plumage all the feathers of the black portions of the plumage are heavily edged sandy buff giving the upperparts a dark, sparrowlike appearance. In this plumage the tail is barred with olive gray. ♀: upperparts brownish black, the feathers edged sandy buff, crown with a median buff line; a broad whitish eyebrow. Bend of wing pink, tail barred black and grayish. Below pale brownish buff, narrowly streaked on breast, broadly on sides of body with dusky; lower breast and belly tinged pink. The pale feather-edges become reduced with wear but are never lost as in very worn ♂.
Tropical zone. N of the Orinoco from s Zulia, s Barinas and w Apure e through Carabobo to Monagas and Delta Amacuro; s of the Orinoco in central Amazonas and nw and e Bolívar. [Panama, Colombia and the Guianas to ne Peru, n and e Brazil. Trinidad.]
Open country, wet savannas, second growth, gallery forest, swampy areas to 600 m. n of the Orinoco, to 950 m. near the tepuis. Forages in bushes and low trees, sometimes on the ground.

## EASTERN MEADOWLARK
*Sturnella magna*
PERDIGÓN

Pl. 38
8.5″ (22 cm.). Lores and most of underparts golden yellow with a black crescent across breast; sides of body sandy buff, streaked dark brown. Sides of crown dark brown, broad central stripe and eyebrows whitish; upper mantle buffy white streaked brown, rest of upperparts dark brown, the feathers margined sandy buff giving a streaked appearance. Inner remiges and central rectrices sandy brown, barred dusky, outer tail feathers white. Bill rather long; tail short.
Subtropical and temperate zones 1700–3000 m. in the Andes of Táchira, Mérida and Trujillo (*meridionalis*). Tropical and subtropical zones to 2000 m., generally distributed but not in the Andes, nor on Cerro Roraima (*paralios*). Upper tropical zone around Cerro Roraima, 1300 m. (*monticola*). [E N Amer. to Colombia, Guyana, Surinam and ne Brazil.]
Llanos, open fields, to 3000 m. n of the Orinoco, to 1350 m. on the open slopes of the tepuis.
Reminiscent of a game bird. Rests low in trees and on fence posts, frequently on the ground. Call: a melodious series of whistled notes.

## BOBOLINK
*Dolichonyx oryzivorus*
TORDO ARROCERO

7″ (18 cm.). ♂ winter plumage and ♀: sparrowlike. Above dark brown, broad coronal streak and eyebrows dark buffy, feathers of back black, edged buffy giving a streaked appearance. Wings and tail brownish black, wing coverts edged buff, remiges and rectrices edged whitish, rectrices sharply pointed, tail unbarred. Underparts yellowish buff, streaked dusky on sides of body. ♂ in breeding plumage: head, neck and underparts black, broad nuchal collar light buff. Upper back black, feathers with some buffy edging, lower back and scapulars white. Tail black. Wing coverts grayish white, wings brownish black, inner remiges edged whitish. Tropical zone. Transient, spring and autumn. Recorded from Mérida, Carabobo and the Distr. Federal, also in Apure and s Bolívar. La Tortuga, La Orchila, Los Roques, Margarita Is. [Breeds in e N Amer. Migrates chiefly through the Antilles, winters from s Peru, to Bolivia, s Brazil and n Argentina.] Open fields, forest edge, rice fields, marshes to 500 m. On the islands in grassy fields and low mangrove bushes. Rests low in trees and in the grass. Walks on the ground. Feeds on grass seeds and insects. Arrives alone or in small flocks during the fall migration.

# WOOD-WARBLERS: Parulidae

## REINITAS, CANDELITAS CANARIOS DE MANGLE

More than half the members of this family found in Venezuela are migrants from North America. Males arrive in their dull winter plumage, which resembles that of females, but assume their colorful breeding plumage in the spring before leaving for their nesting grounds. Females are much duller than males, but usually bear some resemblance, sometimes slight, to males in breeding plumage.

The resident species belong mostly to 2 genera, the redstarts or candelitas (*Myioborus*), arboreal in habits, many of them recognizable by their yellow underparts, and the thicket-inhabiting *Basileuteri,* most of them recognizable by their strongly striped heads.

Warblers feed mainly on insects, and in spite of their name are not particularly good singers.

Birds belonging to the genera *Conirostrum* and *Coereba,* formerly in the Honeycreeper family (Coerebidae), are today included in the Parulidae. Their allocation is still uncertain and here they are placed at the end of the family.

### BLACK-AND-WHITE WARBLER

*Mniotilta varia*
REINITA TREPADORA

Pl. 33

4.5" (11.5 cm.). Black and white, crown with a median white stripe. Can be confused with Blackpoll Warbler but latter has a solid black crown and differs in behavior. Upperparts streaked black and white, rump black. Throat and cheeks black; moustacial streak and eyebrow white. Below white, streaked black on breast and sides. Wing coverts black with 2 white bars. Tail gray, outer feathers with a large white patch at end of inner web. ♀: like ♂ but cheeks, throat and center of breast white. Winter ♂ like ♀.

Winter resident, Sept.–Apr. Tropical and subtropical zones. The n mountains from the Sierra de Perijá and sw Táchira to the Distr. Federal. La Orchila (Oct.). [Breeds in e N Amer. Winters from s US to the Antilles, Colombia and w Ecuador. Trinidad. Curaçao.]

Second growth, coffee plantations, forest edge, clearings to 2500 m. Arboreal, usually forages in open areas in trees and shrubs. Differs from other warblers in habits, behaves like a creeper, climbing treetrunks and branches. Joins forest flocks.

### PROTHONOTARY WARBLER

*Protonotaria citrea*
REINITA PROTONOTARIA

5" (13 cm.). Head and underparts golden yellow, sometimes tinged orange. Back bright yellowish olive. Wings, rump and upper tail coverts gray, central pair of tail feathers gray, rest white on inner web, black on outer and at tip. Under

316 · THE BIRDS OF VENEZUELA

tail coverts white. ♀: like ♂ but duller, top and sides of head only slightly brighter than back. Winter ♂ like ♀.
Winter resident, Sept.–Apr. Tropical zone. Zulia, Falcón and Carabobo, Aragua, Los Roques, and La Orchilas. [Breeds in se US. Winters from the s US to Colombia, Guyana, Surinam, w Ecuador. Trinidad.]
Wooded swamps, mangroves; chiefly near sea level; in cloud forests while crossing the coastal mountains. Forages actively in low bushes, shrubs and thorny thickets, usually near sea and freshwater beaches.

## GOLDEN-WINGED WARBLER
*Vermivora chrysoptera*
REINITA ALIDORADA

4.2" (10.6 cm.). Crown and shoulders golden yellow. Eyebrow and moustacial streak white, cheeks, throat and upper breast black. Back blue gray, below pale gray, white in center of breast and belly. Tail dark gray, 3 outermost pairs of feathers with a large white patch on inner web. ♀: generally like ♂, cheeks and throat gray instead of black. Winter ♂ has back tinged yellowish olive, otherwise like breeding plumage.
Winter resident, Sept.–March. Tropical to temperate zone. The n mountains from Zulia and Táchira through Mérida to Falcón and e to Anzoátegui. [Breeds in the e US. Winters from Guatemala to Colombia.]
Rain and cloud forests, 1000–3000 m.; the dwarf forest in the higher regions; more abundant at high altitudes. Open woodland, damp areas, second growth, forest edge, scattered trees. Alone or with mixed bands, forages at low levels.

## TENNESSEE WARBLER
*Vermivora peregrina*
REINITA GORRO GRIS

Pl. 33
4.2" (10.6 cm.). Crown gray, eyebrow whitish, back olive green. Inner remiges and wing coverts like back with a faint pale bar across tips of greater coverts; tail grayish, outermost feather sometimes with some white on inner web. Underparts white to greenish white. Could be confused with a greenlet (Vireonidae) but distinguishable by its pale eyebrow.

♀: like ♂ but eyebrow and underparts duller and no gray cap. Winter ♂ like ♀.
Winter resident, Sept.–Apr. Tropical and subtropical zones. The n mountains from Zulia, Táchira and Barinas to Sucre. [Breeds in nw and e N Amer. Winters from Mexico to Colombia.]
A variety of wooded habitats to 2200 m. Deciduous, rain and cloud forests, second growth. Alone or in small groups, forages actively from near the ground to the treetops, and in shrubs and trees at forest edge. Joins forest flocks.

## AMERICAN PARULA
*Parula americana*
REINITA AMERICANA

3.7" (9.4 cm.). Lores and forehead black, eye ring white; top and sides of head, lower back and rump blue gray, patch on center of back yellowish olive. Throat yellow, band across base of throat black, this followed by a chestnut band bordered by a wide yellow band, rest of underparts white. Wings dark gray with 2 white bands on coverts. Tail blackish with a white subterminal patch on inner wing of outer feathers. ♀: like ♂ but much duller. Winter ♂ like ♀.
Casual winter visitor. Los Roques I. (Oct.) (*americana*). [Breeds from s Canada to Florida. Winters from Mexico to Costa Rica, the Greater Antilles and Barbados. Casual Curaçao, Jan.–Mar.]
In low mangroves in a scattered flock of other species of warblers.
Note: A new record since publication of Lista Av. Venez.

## TROPICAL PARULA
*Parula pitiayumi*
REINITA MONTAÑERA

Pl. 33
4" (10 cm.). Differs from American Parula by having the entire underparts bright yellow (except the tail coverts) and the breast without the blackish breast band, and only tinged chestnut (or with chestnut breast, a). ♀: like ♂.
Tropical and subtropical zones. The serranías from Zulia and Táchira e to the Paria Pen., Sucre, extending s through Guárico to n Bolívar; Margarita I. (*elegans*). Central and s Amazonas

and tepuis of the Gran Sabana, Bolívar (*roraimae*, a). [Texas to Argentina. Trinidad, Tobago.] Rain and cloud forests to 2500 m. n of the Orinoco, to 2000 m. s of it. Deciduous forest, second growth, forest edge, gallery forest. Alone or in pairs, forages actively from mid-level to the treetops, frequently along streams.

## YELLOW WARBLER

*Dendroica petechia*
CANARIO DE MANGLE

Pl. 33
4.5″ (11.5 cm.). Head and breast chestnut; back olive yellow, lower breast and belly yellow, breast streaked chestnut; remiges dusky and edged yellow; central rectrices dusky olive, outer ones yellow on inner web (or similar but feathers at sides of head *yellow* tipped chestnut, throat and breast with yellow streaking, a; or similar but with crown chestnut, forehead and eyebrow yellow, *throat* and breast yellow *streaked* chestnut, b; or similar, but with crown chestnut, forehead and eyebrow *yellow,* throat yellow, *unstreaked,* breast yellow streaked chestnut, c; or with no chestnut on head, forecrown golden yellow, throat yellow, unstreaked; breast yellow streaked chestnut, d). ♀: above olive yellow, below yellow, wings and tail as in ♂.
Tropical zone. The Goajira Pen. and Punta de Mangle, Zulia (*chrysendeta*). The Paraguaná Pen. in Adícora; Falcón (*paraguanae*, a). The coast of e Falcón and offshore islands, Carabobo and Aragua (*cienagae*, b). The coast of e Anzoátegui and islands in the Bay of Guanta; w Sucre; La Tortuga, Las Tortuguillas and Píritu Is. (*aurifrons*, c). Margarita, Cubagua, La Blanquilla and Los Testigos Is. (*rufopileata*, c). Los Roques, Las Aves, La Orchila Is. (*obscura* c).
Winter resident, mainly inland, Sept.–Apr., throughout (*aestiva*, d). [Breeds from Alaska and Canada to Peru. N migrants winter s to the Amazon.]
Resident. Mangroves, xerophytic vegetation, open grassy fields at sea level. Like the migrants, responds to a squeak and has similar foraging habits but is found usually in pairs or family groups. Frequently hops on the ground. One of its

local names, *Chirito,* refers to its warbling song, "cheeri-cheeri-chiri-chiri." Winter resident. A variety of habitats including mangroves and xerophytic vegetation, to about 1000 m. (rarely to 2000 m.) n of the Orinoco, to 250 m. s of it. Solitary, not shy, forages actively and conspicuously for insects in the low vegetation and to medium heights.

## CAPE MAY WARBLER

*Dendroica tigrina*
REINITA ATIGRADA

5.5″ (14 cm.). Crown black, eyebrow yellow becoming chestnut posteriorly, cheeks and ear coverts chestnut. Patch behind ear coverts and sides of neck bright yellow. Underparts yellow streaked with black, belly whitish. Back olive, the feathers with black centers; rump yellow. Greater wing coverts white. Tail black, the 3 outer pairs of feathers with a large subterminal white patch on inner web. The only warbler with a chestnut ear patch. The throat sometimes washed with chestnut. ♀: upperparts olive, rump olive yellow; conspicuous eyebrow dull white, sides of neck yellowish. Below white, washed with yellow, streaked dusky. Wings with 2 narrow, white wing bars. The 2 outer pairs of tail feathers with a white subterminal patch on inner web, sometimes a small white mark on inner web of third outermost. ♂: winter, like ♀. Imm.: differs from ad. by olive crown, the feathers with black centers like back, no chestnut on cheeks and ear coverts.
Occasional winter visitor. Recorded from Los Roques and La Orchila Is. (Oct.) [Breeds in N Amer. Winters mainly in the West Indies; occasionally in Central America to Panama.] Frequents mangroves.
Note: A new record since publication of Lista Av. Venez.

## BLACK-THROATED BLUE WARBLER

*Dendroica caerulescens*
REINITA AZUL Y NEGRA

5″ (12.7 cm.). Forehead, cheeks, throat, upper breast and sides of body black. Entire upperparts slaty blue gray, belly white. Wing coverts like body, remiges black, basally white, forming a conspicuous white speculum. Central pair of tail feathers black, edged gray, rest black with a large white subterminal patch on inner web increasing in extent toward the outermost. Winter: similar. ♀: upperparts grayish olive. Eyebrow and eye ring white, sides of head dusky olive. Wings grayish olive, base of remiges white forming a *white speculum*, smaller than in ♂. Tail gray without white. Underparts dull light olivaceous, white on center of belly.

Casual winter visitor. El Platillón, Guárico. Sight records from Aragua (Rancho Grande, Ocumare de la Costa) (*caerulescens*). [Breeds in e N Amer. Winters mainly in the Antilles.]

Cloud forest, 1950 m.

Note: New record since publication of Lista Av. Venez.

## MYRTLE WARBLER
*Dendroica coronata*
REINITA CORONADA

5.2″ (13 cm.). Central crown patch, tufts at sides of breast and *band across rump golden yellow*. Upperparts gray, streaked black. Eyebrow white, sides of head black. Throat white, breast black somewhat mottled with white, rest of underparts white, streaked black at sides. Wing coverts with 2 white bars. Tail black, 3 outer pairs of feathers with a large white patch on inner web. ♀: generally like ♂ in pattern but yellow patches smaller, duller; upperparts grayish brown streaked black, supraloral spot and eye ring white. Below white heavily streaked with black on breast. Tail as in ♂. Winter ♂ like ♀.

Casual winter visitor. Recorded from Delta Amacuro (*coronata*). [Breeds from Canada to the ne US. Winters to Panama and the Antilles.]

Rain forest in dense second growth at sea level. Low in the undergrowth.

Note: A new record since publication of Lista Av. Venez.

## BLACK-THROATED GREEN WARBLER
*Dendroica virens*
REINITA GORGINEGRA

5″ (13 cm.). Above bright yellowish olive green; lores, eyebrow and sides of head and neck golden yellow, throat and breast black, rest of underparts white, streaked with black. Wings dark gray with 2 white bars, remiges narrowly edged white. Central 4 tail feathers black, outer 2 pairs almost all white, rest with varying amounts of white. ♀: generally similar to ♂ but throat and breast black, mixed with white. Winter ♂ like ♀. Imm.: throat yellowish white.

Casual winter visitor, recorded in Nov. from coastal Zulia (*virens*). [Breeds in Canada and the US. Winters from s US to Panama and the Greater Antilles.]

Mangroves, open grassy fields with bushes at sea level. Forages actively at low levels. Not shy.

Note: A new record since publication of Lista Av. Venez.

## CERULEAN WARBLER
*Dendroica cerulea*
REINITA CERÚLEA

4.2″ (10.6 cm.). *Above light blue,* crown with 2 ill-defined lateral black stripes, back with a few black streaks, lores and sides of head dusky blue. Below white with a narrow dark blue breast band and blackish blue streaks at sides of body. Wings black with 2 white bars, remiges edged pale blue. All but central pair of tail feathers with a white subterminal patch on inner web. ♀: pale bluish green, bluer on crown, eyebrow white; below buffy white with a greenish tinge. Wings and tail as in ♂.

Winter resident, Sept.–Mar. Tropical and subtropical zones. The n mountain region from Zulia and Táchira to Sucre. [Breeds in s Canada and the e US. Winters from Colombia to Bolivia.]

Rain and cloud forests, second growth, coffee plantations from near sea level (rarely), to 1900 m. Open areas with trees. Alone or in small groups, forages actively in low thickets and in high trees. Joins forest flocks. Not shy.

## BLACKBURNIAN WARBLER
*Dendroica fusca*
REINITA GARGANTIANARANJADA

Pl. 33

5″ (13 cm.). Crown, lores and sides of head black, patch in center of crown, long eyebrow, sides of neck, throat and upper breast orange yellow, rest of underparts yellowish white, streaked on sides with black. Back black, streaked yellowish white. Wings black, greater and median wing coverts mainly white, remiges edged yellowish. Central tail feathers black, rest mainly white. ♀: generally like ♂ but much duller. Winter ♂ like ♀.

Winter resident, Nov.–Apr. Usually subtropical zone. The n Cordilleras from Zulia and Táchira to Anzoátegui and Delta Amacuro (Pedernales) at sea level (once). The mountains of Amazonas and the Gran Sabana in Bolívar. La Orchila Is. (Oct.) [Breeds in Canada and the US. Winters from Guatemala to Peru and n Brazil.]

Rain and cloud forests, 800–3100 m. n of the Orinoco, 1250–2800 m. on the slopes of the tepuis. Coffee plantations, second growth; dwarf forest at the higher altitudes; mangroves at sea level. Forages actively from low to high on trees.

## CHESTNUT-SIDED WARBLER

*Dendroica pensylvanica*
REINITA LADOS CASTAÑOS

4.7″ (12 cm.). Crown yellow, upper back streaked black and white, lower back streaked yellowish green and black. Lores, eyebrow, subocular area and moustacial streak black, the latter abruptly changing to chestnut at sides of neck and continuing down sides of body. Throat and underparts white. Wings black, median and greater wing coverts and edges of remiges yellowish white. Tail black, outermost 3 pairs of tail feathers mainly white. ♀: above bright yellowish green; sides of head and body pale gray, flanks with traces of chestnut. Central underparts white. Wings and tail as in ♂.

Casual winter visitor. Taken once in coastal Aragua (Apr. 15). [Breeds in e Canada and the US. Winters from Nicaragua to Panama and Colombia. Trinidad.]

Cocoa plantations in fairly open country at 200 m. Joins forest flocks.

## BAY-BREASTED WARBLER

*Dendroica castanea*
REINITA PECHO BAYO

5.2″ (13 cm.). Forecrown and sides of head black; hindcrown, throat and upper breast and sides of body chestnut. A large buffy white patch at sides of neck. Center of underparts white. Back grayish olive, streaked black, upper tail coverts and rump grayer, unstreaked. Wings blackish with 2 white bars, remiges edged gray. Tail black, 2 outermost pairs of feathers with a subterminal white patch. ♀: above olive, grayish on upper tail coverts; below dirty white with a slight pinkish cast on belly. Wings and tail as in ♂. Winter ♂ like ♀ but sometimes with some chestnut on flanks.

Winter resident, Nov.–May. Tropical, occasionally to the temperate zone. The Andes of Táchira and Mérida; Aragua; Tortuga I. [Breeds in Canada and the US. Winters from Panama to Colombia. Curaçao.]

A variety of habitats: low thorny bushes and mangroves, at sea level; rain and cloud forests in the middle altitudes, and dwarf forest near the páramos at 3100 m. Usually alone, forages actively at medium heights, often near water. May join forest flocks.

## BLACKPOLL WARBLER

*Dendroica striata*
REINITA RAYADA

Pl. 33

5″ (13 cm.). Crown black, cheeks white; upperparts streaked gray and black. Wings black with 2 white bars, inner remiges edged white. Tail black, 2 outermost feathers with a large white patch on inner web. Underparts white, streaked black on throat and sides. Not unlike Black-and-white Warbler but never creeps on treetrunks. ♀: above olive streaked black. Wings and tail dusky brown, marked as in ♂. Underparts white, tinged olive on sides and breast, streaked black on sides of neck and breast. Winter ♂ like ♀. Imm.: ♂ and ♀ have very little streaking above.

Winter resident, Oct.–Apr. Tropical and subtropical zones, and on Las Aves, Los Roques and La Orchila Is. and cayos offshore in Falcón. [Breeds in Alaska, Canada and the US. Winters chiefly e of the Andes to Brazil and Chile. Migrates through the W Indies. Curaçao to Trinidad and Tobago.]

Deciduous, rain and cloud forests, mangroves to 3000 m. n of the Orinoco, to

1800 on the slopes and summits of the tepuis. Gallery forest, second growth, grassy fields with scattered vegetation. Alone or in groups forages actively low in the trees and bushes, and on the ground.

## OVENBIRD
*Seiurus aurocapillus*
REINITA HORNERA

5″ (13 cm.). Crown orange rufous bordered laterally by black, much as in *Basileuterus*. Upperparts, wings and tail plain, dull brownish olive; underparts white heavily spotted with black on breast and sides.
Winter resident, Oct.–April. Tropical zone. Recorded on the Paraguaná Pen., Falcón, and n Aragua. La Orchila I. (*aurocapillus*). [Breeds in Canada, the US. Winters from Florida and Mexico to Panama, Colombia and W Indies. Curaçao.]
Wooded areas near sea level. Deciduous forest, forest edge. Alone in shrubbery and undergrowth, forages for snails and insects; often walks on the ground. Flicks tail. Call: a 2 note, loud, repeated teacher, teacher, etc. from which one of its common names, Teacher Bird, is derived.

## NORTHERN WATERTHRUSH
*Seiurus noveboracensis*
REINITA DE CHARCOS

Pl. 33
5″ (13 cm.). Upperparts, wings and tail plain dull brown; conspicuous eyebrow creamy white to yellowish buff. Below white with a slight yellowish tinge; throat dotted, breast and sides heavily spotted, with blackish brown.
Winter resident, Sept.–Apr. Tropical zone. Throughout in suitable localities; Los Roques; La Orchila; Los Testigos. [Breeds in Alaska, Canada and the US. Winters from Mexico to ne Peru and the Guianas. Aruba to Trinidad and Tobago. W Indies.]
Always near water to 2000 m. n of the Orinoco, to 900 m. s of it. Streams, lagoons, mangroves, swamps. Solitary, shy, mainly terrestrial. Dips constantly. Responds to a squeak. Call: loud, clear, repeated, whistled single note.

## LOUISIANA WATERTHRUSH
*Seiurus motacilla*
REINITA DE LUISIANA

5″ (13 cm.). Very like Northern Waterthrush but eyebrow and underparts pure white and throat unmarked.
Probably casual winter resident. Recorded from Cubiro, 1600 m., s Lara in Oct. [Breeds in the e and s US. Winters from Mexico to Panama and n Colombia. Trinidad. W Indies.]
Cloud forest near rapid woodland streams. Terrestrial. One Venezuelan record. Call: a loud, metallic "pink."

## KENTUCKY WARBLER
*Oporornis formosus*
REINITA HERMOSA

5.3″ (13.5 cm.). Supraloral streak and ocular area yellow, lores and area below eye and at sides of neck black, crown dark gray, the feathers basally black giving a spotted appearance. Back, wings and tail dark, dull olive; below bright yellow, washed olive at sides (see Mourning Warbler). ♀ like ♂ but crown more olivaceous, less gray.
Winter resident, Oct.–Mar. Tropical zone. The Perijá region, Zulia; n Táchira, w Mérida; Maracay, Aragua; La Orchila I. [Breeds in the e and s US. Winters from Mexico to n Colombia.]
Rain forests, second growth, forest edge. Alone, shy, active, forages for insects low in the humid undergrowth and on the ground. Difficult to observe. Joins forest flocks. Call: not unlike that of the Ovenbird.

## CONNECTICUT WARBLER
*Oporornis agilis*
REINITA DE CONNECTICUT

5″ (13 cm.). Upperparts, wings and tail plain dull olive, *eye ring white*. Throat pale gray deepening to dove gray on breast, rest of underparts dull yellow, clouded with olive at sides. ♀: like ♂ but throat and breast buffy gray; young birds have throat and breast much browner. Winter ♂ like summer.
Probably transient, Oct.–May. Tropical to páramo zone. Recorded from Zulia, Mérida, Lara, Carabobo, Aragua and the Distr. Federal. [Breeds in Canada and n

US. Winters from Colombia to Brazil. Migrates through W Indies, Curaçao.] Rain and cloud forests and páramos, 100–4200 m. n of the Orinoco. In the upper Orinoco recorded Apr. 28 near the Maipures rapids on the Colombian side. Solitary, shy, forages near the ground in dense undergrowth.

## MOURNING WARBLER

*Oporornis philadelphia*
REINITA ENLUTADA

5″ (13 cm.). Crown and sides of head, neck and breast gray, feathers of throat and center of breast black, edged gray, the gray edges disappearing with wear, when throat and center of breast become black. *No eye ring.* Lower breast and belly yellow; back, wings and tail olive. ♀: much like Connecticut Warbler but distinguishable by lacking the white eye ring. Winter ♂ similar to ♀.
Winter resident, Oct.–Apr. Tropical and subtropical zones. The extreme nw from the Perijá region, Zulia, s to w Mérida, Táchira and w Apure; e Amazonas on the Sierra Parima. [Breeds in Canada and the US. Winters from Nicaragua to n Ecuador.]
Rain and cloud forests, second growth, near streams, clearings, coffee plantations, to 1900 m. Alone, secretive, inconspicuous, actively forages in the undergrowth and low shrubbery, also on the ground.

## COMMON YELLOWTHROAT

*Geothlypis trichas*
REINITA GARGANTIAMARILLA

5″ (13 cm.). Forecrown, mask and sides of neck black, the black edged posteriorly by whitish gray. Hindcrown, back, wings and tail dull olive. Throat, breast and under tail coverts yellow, center of belly whitish, sides of belly brownish. Looks rather like Kentucky Warbler but lacks the *yellow eyebrow.* ♀: olive above, throat yellow, bill is buffy yellow, belly white. Eyebrow whitish.
Casual winter visitor. Known from 1 specimen without locality (*trichas*). [Breeds in Alaska, Canada and the US. Winters from Florida and Texas to w Panama

and the Greater Antilles. Casual, n Colombia. Tobago.]
Forages usually in shrubbery close to the ground and frequently near water. Call: a repeated wíchity, wíchity, etc.

## MASKED YELLOWTHROAT

*Geothlypis aequinoctialis*
REINITA EQUINOCCIAL

Pl. 33
5.5″ (14 cm.). Rather like the Common Yellowthroat but *entire underparts bright yellow.* Forehead, lores and cheeks black, crown gray, back, wings and tail olive green. Underparts bright yellow, sides olive. ♀: like ♂ but forehead, lores and cheeks olive.
Tropical zone. Hilly regions in Zulia and Táchira and from Carabobo to Sucre; s of the Orinoco from n Amazonas to Delta Amacuro and in the Gran Sabana, Bolívar (*aequinoctialis*). [Colombia, the Guianas to w Peru, Bolivia and Uruguay, Argentina. Trinidad.]
Savannas, gallery forest, low second growth, near water, to 900 m. Marshes, swampy river banks, low dense underbrush. Forages in pairs near the ground in low dense grass. When flushed flies along the top of the grass then drops out of sight. Song: a series of soft, repeated whistles.

## ROSE-BREASTED CHAT

*Granatellus pelzelni*
REINITA PECHIRROJA

Pl. 33
5.5″ (14 cm.). Crown, sides of head and neck and sides of breast black. Postocular streak and throat white. Back slaty blue. Below rosy pink, sides of body silky white. Wings and tail black, inner remiges slaty blue on outer web. ♀: above slaty blue; eyebrow, throat and sides of head buff; underparts rosy pink, duller than in ♂.
Tropical zone. Amazonas from Caño Cuao southward; Bolívar from the lower Río Caura to the Río Paragua (*pelzelni*). [Guyana, Surinam, Amazonian Brazil, n Bolivia.]
Rain forest, to 850 m. Dense, old second growth, river banks and lagoon edges in deep forest, sloughs. Alone, forages for insects in middle heights.

## HOODED WARBLER
*Wilsonia citrina*
REINITA DE CAPUCHA

5″ (13 cm.). Forecrown and face bright yellow. Crown and nape black, connected to back of throat and upper breast. Back and wings light olive; underparts bright yellow. Tail feathers grayish, edged light olive, outermost 2 pairs white on inner web. ♀: differs from ♂ by having the black on top of head only suggested and the throat yellow like rest of underparts. Imm.: crown olive, forehead yellow, otherwise like ♀.
Casual in n Zulia, Nov. La Orchila I. (Oct.). [Breeds in e US. Winters from n Mexico to Costa Rica, casually to n Colombia and Trinidad.]
Recorded in mangroves. Forages actively among the roots and lower branches. White markings of outer tail feathers visible as it flicks tail.
Note: A new record since publication of Lista Av. Venez.

## CANADA WARBLER
*Wilsonia canadensis*
REINITA CANADENSE

5″ (13 cm.). Forecrown and patch below eye black, lores yellow, feathers of center and hindcrown black, edged gray. Back, wings and tail light gray. Below bright yellow with a *conspicuous row of black spots across breast*. ♀: above olive gray. Eye ring white. Below yellow with a row of gray spots across breast. Winter ♂ like ♀.
Winter resident Oct.–Mar. Subtropical zone. Sierra de Perijá, Zulia, Táchira, Mérida and Aragua; central Amazonas (Cerro Parú and Sierra Parima); e Bolívar on the Sierra de Lema. [Breeds in Canada and the US. Winters from Colombia to central Peru.]
Rain and cloud forests, second growth, 800–2100 m. n of the Orinoco, 1000–1100 m. s of it. Forest edge, clearings. Alone, active, forages in low thickets and in the upper heights. Joins mixed forest bands.

## AMERICAN REDSTART
*Setophaga ruticilla*
CANDELITA MIGRATORIA

Pl. 34
4.5″ (11.5 cm.). Black; lower breast and belly white; sides of breast, large patch in wing and basal two-thirds of tail feathers, except center pair, orange. ♀: above gray, below grayish white, sides of breast and markings in wing and tail yellow.
Winter resident, Aug.–Apr. Tropical and subtropical zone. Throughout including Los Roques and Margarita Is. [Breeds in N Amer. Winters from Mexico to n Peru, the Guianas and n Brazil. Caribbean islands.] No races are currently recognized.
A variety of habitats, to 3000 m. n of the Orinoco, to 1250 m. s of it. Mangroves, savannas, suburban areas, forests thorny thickets, etc. Alone, forages actively in the vegetation at all heights. Flicks tail conspicuously as it flutters after insects.
Note: *S. r. tricolora*, recorded in Lista Av. Venez., is not now considered separable.

## SLATE-THROATED REDSTART
*Myioborus miniatus*
CANDELITA GARGANTIPIZARRA

Pl. 34
5.5″ (14 cm.). Above dark gray, crown patch chestnut; throat slaty black, band across upper breast ochraceous, rest of underparts bright yellow; under tail coverts white. Wings and tail feathers black, outer 2 pairs of tail feathers mostly white, next broadly tipped white.
Upper tropical and subtropical zones. Sierra de Perijá, Zulia, Táchira, Mérida, nw Barinas and Trujillo (*ballux*). Falcón, w Lara, and from Yaracuy through the coastal and interior Cordilleras to Sucre and Monagas (*pallidiventris*). Central and s Amazonas; nw Bolívar on Cerro Tabaro, and the tepuis of the Gran Sabana (*verticalis*). [Mexico to nw Peru, nw Brazil, w Guyana.]
Humid rain forest, cloud forest, second growth, 700–3000 m. n of the Orinoco, 600–1800 m. on the tepuis. In pairs or small groups, forages from medium heights to treetops. Joins forest bands.
The genus *Myioborus* hardly differs from *Setophaga* and probably it should be merged with it.

## GOLDEN-FRONTED REDSTART
*Myioborus ornatus*
CANDELITA COPETIAMARILLA

Pl. 34
5.5″ (14 cm.). Crown and underparts bright yellow, under tail coverts white;

forehead, chin and ocular region white. Broad nuchal collar and sides of neck and breast black; back and wings dark gray. Tail black, 2 outermost pairs of feathers white.
Subtropical and temperate zones. Páramo de Tamá and vicinity, sw Táchira (*ornatus*). [Andes of Colombia.]
Cloud and dwarf forests, 2100–3000 m. In pairs or family groups, forages actively from middle to upper parts of trees.

## WHITE-FRONTED REDSTART
*Myioborus albifrons*
CANDELITA FRENTIBLANCA

Pl. 34
5.2" (13 cm.). Forehead and mask white, crown black with a central chestnut patch. Sides of neck, back and wings gray. Below bright yellow, under tail coverts white. Tail black, outer 2 pairs of feathers mostly white, next partly white.
Subtropical and temperate zones. The Andes of Táchira, Mérida and Trujillo.
Cloud and dwarf forests, 2200–3200 m. Habits similar to Slate-throated Redstart.

## WHITE-FACED REDSTART
*Myioborus albifacies*
CANDELITA CARA BLANCA

Pl. 34
5.5" (14 cm.). Crown black; lores, chin and sides of head white. Back and wings dark gray. Below orange yellow, under tail coverts white. Tail black, outermost feathers mostly white, next 2 pairs broadly tipped white.
Upper tropical and subtropical zones. Amazonas on Cerros Guanay, Yaví and Paraque.
Endemic to Pantepui, 900–2250 m. Rain and cloud forests. Habits similar to Slate-throated Redstart.

## BROWN-CAPPED REDSTART
*Myioborus brunniceps*
CANDELITA GORJEADORA

Pl. 34
5.2" (13 cm.). Crown chestnut; eyebrow white (or eye ring white, a); back dark gray (or grayish brown, a). Below orange (or yellow, tinged chrome on breast, a). Wings like back; tail black, outermost

feather mostly white, next 2 pairs broadly tipped white.
Upper tropical and subtropical zones. Central Amazonas on Cerros Parú, Huachamacari and Duida; s Bolívar on Cerro Jaua (*duidae*). S Amazonas on Cerro de la Neblina (*maguirei*, a). The serranías of the Gran Sabana (*castaneocapillus*, a). [W Guyana; n Brazil. Bolivia; w Argentina.]
Cloud forests on the tepuis, 1250–2200 m. Not shy. Voice: thin, melodious warble. Habits similar to Slate-throated Redstart.

## YELLOW-FACED REDSTART
*Myioborus pariae*
CANDELITA DE PARIA

5.2" (13 cm.). Differs from Brown-capped Redstart by having the front of forehead and eye ring yellow, rest of forehead black; back grayish with a yellowish olive cast, instead of brownish olive, and outer tail feathers more extensively white.
Upper tropical zone. Cerros Humo and Azul, Paria Pen., Sucre.
Humid cloud forests, 800–1200 m. Endemic. Habits similar to Slate-throated Redstart.

## SAFFRON-BREASTED REDSTART
*Myioborus cardonai*
CANDELITA DE CARDONA

5.2" (13 cm.). Crown and preocular region black; eye ring and chin white; eyebrow and back dark gray. Underparts bright orange yellow, under tail coverts white. Wings and tail black, outermost tail feathers mostly white, next tipped white.
Subtropical zone. Cerro Guaiquinima, central Bolívar.
Cloud forest, 1200–1600 m. Endemic.

## BLACK-CRESTED WARBLER
*Basileuterus nigrocristatus*
CHIVÍ GUICHERITO

Pl. 33
6" (15 cm.). Above olive green, below bright golden yellow. Lores and center of crown black, eyebrows golden yellow. Tail olive green, rounded. Iris gray, legs yellowish. ♀: like ♂ but eyebrows duller.

Subtropical and temperate zones. Zulia and Táchira e through Mérida to n Trujillo; the coastal Cordillera from Aragua to the Distr. Federal. [Colombia to n Peru.]
Cloud and dwarf forest 1450–3100 m. Shrubs, bamboo thickets. In pairs, forages in the lower vegetation.

## CITRINE WARBLER
*Basileuterus luteoviridis*
CHIVÍ CETRINO

Pl. 33
5.7″ (14.5 cm.). Above dull olive, below dull yellow, sides olive. Chin white. Lores dusky, supraloral streak yellow. Tail rounded. Iris dark brown, legs yellowish brown.
Subtropical and temperate zones. The Andes of Táchira and Mérida (*luteoviridis*). [The Andes from Colombia to n Bolivia.]
Cloud and dwarf forest, second growth, 2600–3000 m.

## FLAVESCENT WARBLER
*Basileuterus flaveolus*
CHIVÍ AMARILLENTO

5.5″ (14 cm.). Rather like Citrine Warbler but much brighter above and below. Upperparts, wings and tail bright olive green. Below bright yellow, somewhat clouded on breast with olive. Tail rounded. *Bill pale,* legs light yellowish. In the Citrine the bill is black and the legs much darker.
Tropical zone. Along the serranías in extreme w Táchira, Lara, extreme e Falcón, from Carabobo to Miranda and in adjacent Guárico. [Ne Colombia. Ne Bolivia, Paraguay. E Brazil from Maranhão s to São Paulo.]
Deciduous forest, second growth, thorny bushes, 250–1200 m. Alone or in pairs forages low in thickets.

## TWO-BANDED WARBLER
*Basileuterus bivittatus*
CHIVÍ DE LOS TEPUIS

Pl. 33
5.5″ (14 cm.). Above olive, below bright yellow clouded with olive on breast. Center of crown orange rufous bordered on each side by a black band prolonged

over nape, eyebrow olive yellow. Wings and tail like back. Not unlike Citrine Warbler except for crown pattern.
Upper tropical and subtropical zones. The Cerros of Amazonas and Bolívar (*roraimae*). [Guyana; ne Brazil. Se Peru to nw Argentina.]
Rain and cloud forests on the slopes of the tepuis, 900–1800 m. Forages in the upper branches of trees.

## THREE-STRIPED WARBLER
*Basileuterus tristriatus*
CHIVÍ TRES RAYAS

Pl. 33
5″ (13 cm.). Coronal stripe and broad eyebrow buffy olive, a broad black stripe at sides of crown. Sides of head black with a pale patch below eye (or with little or no black on sides of head, a). Back dark olive (or olive brown, a). Below yellowish white to primrose yellow, heavily washed on breast and sides with olive to brownish olive.
Upper tropical to subtropical zone. The Sierra de Perijá, Zulia to sw Táchira (*auricularis*). Ne Táchira, Mérida and s and central Lara (*meridanus,* a). W Lara and from Yaracuy to Carabobo and through the coastal Cordillera to Miranda and Caripe, s Sucre (*bessereri,* a). Sucre on Cerros Azul and Humo, Paria Pen. (*pariae*). [Costa Rica to Colombia, e Ecuador to n Bolivia.]
Rain and cloud forests, 800–2700 m. Coffee plantations, old second growth. In bands up to 30; forages actively in thickets and undergrowth. Seldom leaves the inside of the forest. Joins mixed forest flocks.

## GOLDEN-CROWNED WARBLER
*Basileuterus culicivorus*
CHIVÍ SILBADOR

Pl. 33
5″ (13 cm.). Crown patch yellow (or orange rufous, a) bordered laterally by a broad black stripe. Eyebrow whitish to yellowish white. Back gray (or olive gray, a). Wings and tail brownish gray. Below bright yellow.
Tropical and subtropical zones. Zulia, Táchira, Mérida to Falcón and through the coastal Cordillera to the Distr. Federal (*cabanisi*). The mountains of Anzoátegui, Sucre and n Monagas

(*olivascens*, a). The mountains of w Amazonas and Bolívar (*segrex*, a). [Mexico to w Panama. Colombia, Guyana, to se Brazil, Uruguay and n Argentina. Trinidad.]
Dense rain and cloud forests, second growth to 2100 m. n of the Orinoco, to 1750 m. s of it. Coffee plantations, forest edge, clearings. Alone or in pairs forages in the lower branches and undergrowth. Not shy. Joins forest bands. Call: utters a faint chirping and twittering.

## RUFOUS-CAPPED WARBLER

*Basileuterus rufifrons*
CHIVÍ CORONA CASTAÑA

Pl. 33
4.5″ (11.4 cm.). Crown and ear coverts rufous chestnut, lores and ocular region black, long eyebrow and subocular patch white. Back, wings and tail olive green. Chin white, rest of underparts golden yellow. Legs yellowish flesh.
Upper tropical zone. Nw Zulia (*mesochrysus*). [Mexico to n Colombia.]
Humid rain forests, 1000 m. Second growth, clearings, coffee plantations. Forages actively in low thickets and underbrush.
Note: Called *B. delattrii* in Lista Av. Venez.

## GRAY-THROATED WARBLER

*Basileuterus cinereicollis*
CHIVÍ GARGANTIGRÍS

Pl. 33
5.5″ (14 cm.). Crown patch yellow, bordered laterally by blackish; forehead, eyebrow and sides of head and extreme upper mantle, dull gray. Back, wings and tail dull olive. Throat grayish white, breast light gray, belly yellow, sides olive.
Upper tropical and subtropical zones. The Sierra de Perijá, Zulia and the Andes of Táchira and Mérida (*pallidulus*). [Ne Colombia.]
Rain and cloud forests, 1100–2100 m. low second growth, forages actively in the lower tier. Difficult to observe.

## RUSSET-CROWNED WARBLER

*Basileuterus coronatus*
CHIVÍ CORONA ANARANJADA

Pl. 33
6″ (15 cm.). Differs principally from Gray-throated Warbler by brighter yellow crown patch, which reaches base of bill, bordered laterally by a broad and conspicuous deep black band which extends to nape. Back brighter olive.
Subtropical zone. The Andes of Táchira, Mérida and Trujillo (*regulus*). [The Andes from Colombia to w Peru and n Bolivia.]
Cloud forests, second growth, low open forest, 1800–2800 m.

## GRAY-HEADED WARBLER

*Basileuterus griseiceps*
CHIVÍ CABECIGRÍS

Pl. 33
5.4″ (13.7 cm.). Top and sides of head gray, crown streaked with black. A white spot at each side of forehead. Back and tail olive green; underparts rich, bright yellow. Legs yellow.
Subtropical zone. The coastal Cordillera in Anzoátegui, Monagas and sw Sucre.
Cloud forests, second growth, clearings, 1200–1600 m. Forages in the lower tier of the trees.

## RIVER WARBLER

*Phaeothlypis rivularis*
CHIVÍ CARA ANTEADA

Pl. 33
4.5″ (11.5 cm.). Upperparts, wings and tail umber brown, darkest on head; eyebrow and sides of head cinnamon buff. Below white, cinnamon buff on sides of neck and body.
Tropical zone. The delta region in e Monagas; Delta Amacuro; Bolívar; central and s Amazonas (*mesoleuca*). [The Guianas, through e Brazil to ne Argentina, e Paraguay and Bolivia.]
Rain forest near streams, sea level to 1100 m. Active, terrestrial. Forages in the thick tangled undergrowth.
Note: Separated from *Basileuterus* (following Paynter, Bds. Wld., *14*, 1968), in which genus it was included in Lista Av. Venez. and Sp. Bds. S Amer. Does not include *fulvicauda* and races.

[THE FOLLOWING SPECIES, formerly included in the now supressed family of Honeycreepers (Coerebidae) are tentatively placed with the wood-warblers following Paynter (Bds. Wld., *14, 1968*).

In the genus *Conirostrum* the bill is straight and sharply pointed, in *Coereba* it is rather long and curved.]

## CHESTNUT-VENTED CONEBILL
*Conirostrum speciosum*
MIELERITO AZUL

Pl. 34
4″ (10 cm.). Above blue gray; wings and tail black, edged blue gray, primaries edged light blue, upper tail coverts lighter blue gray than back (with a white wing speculum, a). Below pale blue gray, whitish on abdomen; under tail coverts rufous brown. ♀: crown and nape light blue gray, back yellowish green, wings and tail dark brown, edged yellowish green. Lores, sides of head and entire underparts light buff.
Tropical zone. The llanos of s Apure along the Meta (*amazonum*). The llanos of e Guárico and Anzoátegui (*guaricola,* a). [E Colombia, the Guianas to Bolivia and n Argentina.]
Gallery forest in the llanos, open deciduous woodland, second growth, to about 200 m. In small groups, forages in the treetops, often with other species.

## WHITE-EARED CONEBILL
*Conirostrum leucogenys*
MIELERITO OREJIBLANCO

Pl. 34
3.5″ (9 cm.). Crown and nape glossy black, band from below eye across ear coverts white. Back blue gray, upper tail coverts white. Throat and breast dark gray, lower breast and sides of belly light gray in contrast (or throat, breast and sides of belly uncontrasting pale gray, a), center of belly white; shorter under tail coverts chestnut, longer ones white. ♀: above blue gray, rump white (blue gray with a greenish tinge, rump grayish white, a). Eyebrow and underparts light yellowish buff, flanks grayish.
Tropical zone. The Perijá region, Zulia and the n slopes of the Andes of Táchira and Mérida (*cyanochrous,* a). N and ne Zulia from the lower Río Palmar, w of L. Maracaibo, to Mene Grande e of the lake and through n Falcón to Yaracuy, n Carabobo and Aragua (*leucogenys*). [E Panama, n Colombia.]
Rain forest to 1300 m. Damp woods, second growth, gallery forest, open fields with scattered trees, near rivers. In pairs or small flocks up to 10 forages in the foliage from medium heights to the treetops; often hangs upside down. Frequents fruit trees and Cecropias.

## BICOLORED CONEBILL
*Conirostrum bicolor*
MIELERO MANGLERO

Pl. 34
4.5″ (11.5 cm.). Above blue gray, below light grayish buff, buffy white on center of belly. ♀: crown and nape light grayish olive becoming grayer on rest of upperparts; throat and breast pale yellowish becoming whiter on rest of underparts.
The Caribbean coast from Zulia to Sucre; Margarita I.; coastal Delta Amacuro, Tobeida Is. (*bicolor*). [Coastal n Colombia; the Guianas. Coastal Brazil e along both banks of the Amazon to Peru and Ecuador. Trinidad.]
Almost exclusively in mangroves, but occasionally in adjacent vegetation. Alone or in small groups, forages actively in the trees and undergrowth. Not shy. Responds to a squeak or to an imitation of its soft, repeated call, "tseep, tseep, tseep."

## BLUE-BACKED CONEBILL
*Conirostrum sitticolor*
MIELERO PURPÚREO

Pl. 34
5″ (13 cm.). Head, throat and upper breast black, back blue (with a broad blue eyebrow, a). Underparts chestnut. Wings and tail black.
Subtropical and temperate zones. The Andes of n Táchira and Mérida (*intermedium*). Sw Táchira on the Páramo de Tamá; Zulia on Perijá Mts. (*sitticolor,* a). [The Andes from Colombia to w Peru and n Bolivia.]
Cloud and dwarf forest, 2550–3500 m. Humid open fields with scattered low trees. Forages actively for insects and seeds.

# CAPPED CONEBILL

*Conirostrum albifrons*
MIELERITO GORRA BLANCA

Pl. 34
5.3″ (13.5 cm.). Entire crown snow white (or dark shiny blue with some silvery white streaks on forehead, a). Upper back dull black, turning to dark purplish blue on mantle and becoming bright shiny purple blue on lower back and upper tail coverts. Wings and tail black, edged purplish blue. Below black with a purplish cast. Thighs white. ♀: crown and nape light grayish blue, back olive green. Throat and breast light gray with a bluish cast, rest of underparts yellowish green. Wings and tail brown, edged olive green.
Tropical and subtropical zones. Páramo de Tamá, sw Táchira (*albifrons*). The coastal Cordillera in the Distr. Federal and Aragua (*cyanonotum*, a). [The Andes of Colombia to w Ecuador and n Bolivia.]
Cloud and dwarf forest, open, humid terrain with low, scattered trees, 1850–3000 m.

# BANANAQUIT

*Coereba flaveola*
REINITA COMÚN

Pl. 34
4–4.5″ (10–11.5 cm.). Bill rather long, distinctly curved. Above blackish brown (or paler, grayish brown, a); rump lemon yellow, conspicuous eyebrow white. Throat gray, rest of underparts bright lemon yellow. Wings and tail like back, some races with a white wing speculum. (Or entirely blackish with an ochraceous cast below, no white eyebrow, b).
Tropical and subtropical zones. From n Zulia e to Sucre, s to the Río Apure and through Guárico to Caicara and Altagracia, nw Bolívar (not found in the Maracaibo region or the Andes of Táchira and Mérida); Margarita, Cachicamo and Coche Is. (*luteola*). The Perijá

and Maracaibo regions, Zulia; the n slopes of the Andes of Mérida from La Azulita to nw Táchira (*obscura*). Subtropical zone in the Andes of Mérida and n and sw Táchira (*montana*). N Bolívar from the Río Cuchivero to Delta Amacuro and n to the lower Río Mánamo, the border with Monagas (*bolivari*, a). Nw Bolívar along the lower Río Caura at Suapure to La Prisión (*guianensis*, a). Extreme nw Amazonas from Puerto Ayacucho to Caño Cataniapo, (*columbiana*, a). S Apure along the Río Meta; w Amazonas from San Carlos on the Río Negro and the Sierra Imerí, in central Amazonas s of the Río Ventuari s to the headwaters of the Río Siapa, and e across s Bolívar to the se corner of the Gran Sabana (*roraimae*, a). Extreme sw Amazonas at the Yavita-Pimichín trail and along the Río Guainía to Caño Casiquiare (*intermedia*). The lowlands of Amazonas along the Orinoco from Sanariapo and the Río Ventuari to Caño Casiquiare and the Brazilian border (*minima*). Cayo Sal off the coast of Falcón (*melanornis*, b). Los Roques Is. (*lowii*, b). La Tortuga I. (*ferryi*). Los Hermanos Is. (Morro El Fondeadero) and Los Frailes Is. (Puerto Real) (*frailensis*). Los Testigos Is. (Testigo Grande, Conejo) (*laurae*, b). [The Bahamas, the Antilles, Mid. Amer. to w Peru, Brazil and Argentina. Aruba to Trinidad and Tobago.]
Note: *C. f. intermedia* may represent a population intermediate between *C. f. roraimae* and *C. f. minima*. The genus *Coereba* does not seem to belong in the Parulidae.

A great variety of habitats, sparse, xerophytic, thorny vegetation to luxuriant, humid, mossy virgin cloud forests, mangroves and gardens to 1900 m. n of the Orinoco, to 2000 m. on the slopes and summits of the tepuis. Active, not shy, forages in pairs or family groups from the lowest levels to the treetops. Feeds on nectar, fruits. Visits flowering trees and shrubs. Clings to flowers. Call: a frequent, insectlike, high trill. Builds a large, dome-shaped nest.

# SWALLOW-TANAGERS: Tersinidae

## AZULEJOS GOLONDRINAS

This family, composed of but a single species, is closely related to tanagers but differs from them by having a broad, flat bill, long, pointed and swallowlike wings. It also differs in nesting habits.

Partially migratory, it is found in small flocks in rather open forest.

**SWALLOW-TANAGER**
*Tersina viridis*
AZULEJO GOLONDRINA

Pl. 35

5" (13 cm.). Mainly turquoise blue to purplish blue depending on the incidence of the light. Forehead, mask and throat black; center of lower breast, belly and under tail coverts white, sides of body barred black. Wings and tail black, the feathers edged blue. ♀: mainly grass green. Forehead, mask and throat mottled black and white; center of belly pale yellow, sides of body and under tail coverts yellow, barred with dark green. Wings and tail dusky, the feathers edged grass green.

Tropical and subtropical zones. The Sierra de Perijá, Zulia, s through Táchira to s Amazonas; the Andes of w Barinas and Portuguesa to Carabobo thence through the n Cordilleras to Sucre; Bolívar rather generally (*occidentalis*). [Panama to Colombia, the Guianas, Bolivia, Paraguay, Brazil and n Argentina. Trinidad.] Second growth, clearings, open woodland, suburban areas, 150–1800 m. n of the Orinoco, 100–1050 m. s of it. In pairs or groups; forages in trees from the ground to high branches, feeds on insects on the wing, berries. Nests in tunnels in earth banks. Call: high thin, metallic whistle.

# TANAGERS, EUPHONIAS, DACNIS: Thraupidae

## VERDINES, TANGARAS, FRUTEROS, AZULEJOS

Tanagers form a very large, exclusively American family of birds that are, for the most part, rather small and brightly colored. They are poorly represented in North America but reach their highest development in the forests and woodlands of tropical South America. In Venezuela 100 species are found. Tanagers are nearly devoid of song, and utter high, thin, lisping sounds.

Typical tanagers feed chiefly on fruit, while euphonias eat mainly mistletoe berries. Some tanagers are very finchlike and in some cases it is hard to tell the family to which certain ones should be assigned. Typical of these are *Oreothraupis*, now classified with finches, and *Conothraupis*, still classified as a tanager.

It has been proposed that the tanagers be made a subfamily of the Emberizidae. For notes on the subject see introduction to Fringillidae (p. 352).

Part of the Coerebidae (*Diglossa, Cyanerpes, Chlorophanes,* and *Dacnis*) have been merged, according to current practice, into the Thraupidae.

[THE GENUS *Diglossa* (formerly in the family Coerebidae) is distinguished from other tanagers by its peculiarly shaped bill, in which the lower mandible curves upward and the tip is overhung by the prominently hooked upper mandible. The shape of the bill is useful in piercing the corolla of flowers to reach the nectar on which the birds feed, insects are also taken.

The nomenclature here followed for *Diglossa* is that proposed by F. Vuilleumier (Amer. Mus. Novit., 1969, no. 2381).]

**BLUISH FLOWER-PIERCER**
*Diglossa caerulescens*
DIGLOSSA AZULADA

Pl. 34

5" (13 cm.). Forehead and lores black; back dark slaty blue; underparts paler, center of abdomen whitish, under tail coverts edged white. Bill less strongly hooked than in other species of the genus.

Subtropical to temperate zone. The Sierra de Perijá on the upper Río Negro, Zulia (*ginesi*). The Andes of Táchira, Mérida and Trujillo (*saturata*). The coastal Cordillera from Carabobo to Aragua and the Distr. Federal (*caerulescens*). [The Andes from Colombia to Bolivia.] Cloud and dwarf forest, páramos, 1400–3200 m. Alone or in pairs, forages in wet ravines, at middle height inside forests. At the higher altitudes in open terrain with bamboo, and scattered low vegetation.

## MASKED FLOWER-PIERCER
*Diglossa cyanea*
DIGLOSSA DE ANTIFAZ

Pl. 34
5.5″ (14 cm.). Forecrown, lores and sides of head black, rest of plumage dark blue.
Subtropical and temperate zone. The Sierra de Perijá on the upper Río Negro, Zulia (*obscura*). The Andes of Táchira, Mérida and Trujillo (*cyanea*). The coastal Cordillera in Aragua and the Distr. Federal (*tovarensis*). [The Andes from Colombia to Bolivia.]
Cloud and dwarf forest, 1800–3200 m. Open terrain with scattered low trees and bushes. In cloud forest forages in middle heights, damp ravines, tree ferns.

## GREATER FLOWER-PIERCER
*Diglossa major*
DIGLOSSA MAYOR

Pl. 34
7″ (18 cm.). Forehead, lores and upper throat and sides of head black. Above slaty blue with fine silvery shaft streaks. Below grayish blue, paler than back (with silvery shaft streaks on breast and belly, a; with silvery shaft streaks on breast only, b). Under tail coverts chestnut.
Subtropical zone. The tepuis of the Gran Sabana, s Bolívar; on Auyan-tepui (*gilliardi*, a); on Ptari-tepui, Sororopán-tepui, Uaipán-tepui, Aprada-tepui and Acopán-tepui (*disjuncta*, b); on Chimantá-tepui (*chimantae*); on Roraima,

Cuquenán and Uei-tepui (*major*). [Adj. ne Brazil.]
Endemic to Pantepui, 1650–2800 m. Cloud forest, *Bonnetia* forest on the summits of the tepuis, open terrain with low scattered trees and bushes. Not shy, quiet. Alone or in pairs.

## GLOSSY FLOWER-PIERCER
*Diglossa lafresnayii*
DIGLOSSA LUSTROSA

Pl. 34
5.7″ (14.5 cm.). Glossy black, shoulders blue gray.
Subtropical to temperate zone. The Andes of Táchira, Mérida and Trujillo. [Colombia, Ecuador, and n Peru]. Does not include *D. gloriosa*, see Coal-black Flower-piercer.
Cloud and dwarf forest, 2000–2500 m. Forest edge, open country with isolated vegetation. Usually alone, forages in the middle heights of trees and in the low vegetation of the higher elevations.

## BLACK FLOWER-PIERCER
*Diglossa humeralis*
DIGLOSSA NEGRA Y GRIS

Pl. 34
5.7″ (14.5 cm.). Deep, glossy black, shoulders gray (or deep glossy black, rump dark gray, a).
Subtropical and temperate zones. The Sierra de Perijá, nw Zulia (*nocticolor*, a). Extreme sw Táchira on Páramo de Tamá (*humeralis*). [Ne and sw Colombia to extreme nw Peru.]
Cloud and dwarf forest, 2150–3000 m. Forest edge, open country with isolated trees and bushes. Alone or in pairs, forages actively in the foliage for insects and nectar as do other Diglossas.
Note: Considered a race of *D. carbonaria* in Lista Av. Venez. and Sp. Bds. S Amer.

## COAL-BLACK FLOWER-PIERCER
*Diglossa carbonaria*
DIGLOSSA CARBONOSA

Pl. 34
5.2″ (13 cm.). Head, neck, breast and mantle black; eyebrow, shoulders and rump gray; lower breast, belly and under tail coverts chestnut. Wings and tail black.

Subtropical to páramo zone. The Andes from ne Táchira through Mérida to n Trujillo (*gloriosa*). [N Colombia. Peru, Bolivia.]
Dwarf forest and páramos, 2500–4150 m. Low isolated trees, forest edge, open stretches with bushes. Usually alone, flits nervously. Forages actively in the foliage. Call: a long, thin trill.

## SCALED FLOWER-PIERCER
*Diglossa duidae*
DIGLOSSA MENOR

5.7″ (14.5 cm.). Above blackish gray, blacker on head. Throat blackish becoming dark gray on upper breast, and paler gray on lower breast and belly, feathers of lower breast with pale gray centers giving a scaled appearance. Wings and tail black, greater and median wing coverts edged gray, sometimes edged white.
Subtropical zone. N Amazonas on Cerros Guanay, Yaví and Paraque (*hitchcocki*). Central and s Amazonas on Cerros Parú, Huachamacari, Duida and de la Neblina; extreme sw Bolívar on Cerro Jaua (*duidae*). [Nw Brazil on Cerro de la Neblina.]
Endemic to Pantepui, 1400–2500 m. Cloud forest, *Bonnetia* forest, on the summits of the tepuis, open terrain with low scattered trees and bushes. At the lowest altitude only on Cerro Paraque. Not shy. Quiet. Alone or in pairs. Voice: a short thin whistle.

## WHITE-SIDED FLOWER-PIERCER
*Diglossa albilatera*
DIGLOSSA DE LADOS BLANCOS

Pl. 34
4.5″ (11.5 cm.). Blackish slaty gray (or bluish slaty gray, a); axillars, under wing coverts and pectoral tufts white. ♀: above olive brown, below buffy brown to buffy, pectoral tufts white.
Subtropical to temperate zone. The Sierra de Perijá; Zulia; the Andes from sw Táchira, through Mérida, to n Trujillo (*albilatera*). The coastal Cordillera from Aragua to Miranda (*federalis*, a). [The Andes from Colombia to n Peru.]
Cloud and dwarf forest, páramos, 1600–3200 m. Woodland edge, bushy hillsides, shrubbery, isolated trees, suburban

areas. Usually in pairs, forages actively in the foliage at middle heights. Shy.

## VENEZUELAN FLOWER-PIERCER
*Diglossa venezuelensis*
DIGLOSSA NEGRA

5.5″ (14 cm.). Deep black; axillars, under wing coverts and small pectoral tufts white. ♀: top and sides of head yellowish olive, malar region olive buff. Below dull gray washed with buffy brown on lower throat and upper breast; axillars, under wing coverts and small pectoral tufts white. Back dark brownish gray, browner on rump and upper tail coverts. Wings and tail blackish, feathers edged grayish or brownish.
Subtropical zone. The coastal Cordillera on Cerro Turumiquire, Sucre, and at Caripe and on Cerro El Negro, Monagas.
Cloud forest, forest edge, shrubbery, 1600–2500 m. Forage actively in the foliage at middle heights.

## RUSTY FLOWER-PIERCER
*Diglossa sittoides*
DIGLOSSA PAYADOR

Pl. 34
4.5″ (11.5 cm.). Upperparts slaty blue, blackish on crown and sides of head (paler and bluer with crown blue like back, a). Below cinnamon. Wings and tail blackish edged slaty blue. ♀: above dull olive brown, below dingy white *streaked dusky on breast*.
Upper tropical and subtropical zones. The Sierra de Perijá Zulia (*coelestis*, a). The Andes from sw Táchira, Barinas and Mérida, and s and w Lara (*dorbignyi*). The coastal Cordillera from Yaracuy to Miranda (*hyperythra*). Cerro Turumiquire, Sucre (*mandeli*). [Colombia to nw Argentina.]
Rain and cloud forests, 800–2500 m. Second growth, bushy hillsides, clearings, forest edge, suburban areas. Alone or in groups forages actively in the foliage in shrubs and in the treetops, but usually at medium heights. Call: a thin, weak trill.
Note: Called *D. baritula* in Lista Av. Venez. and Sp. Bds. S Amer.

[IN THE GENUS *Cyanerpes* the bill is comparatively long, slender and distinctly curved.]

## SHORT-BILLED HONEYCREEPER
*Cyanerpes nitidus*
COPEICILLO PICO CORTO

Pl. 34

3.7″ (9.4 cm.). Shiny purplish blue; stripe through eye black; throat black, the black reaching to upper breast; wings and tail black. Legs pink to orange yellow. ♀: above green, brightest on rump. Throat and center of abdomen buff, breast and sides of body green, streaked buff. Ocular region bluish.
Tropical zone. Widespread s of the Orinoco in Amazonas and nw and s Bolívar (*nitidus*). [Se Colombia to ne Peru and nw Brazil.]
Rain forest, 100–400 m. Dense forest, forest edge, clearings. Often near rivers.

## PURPLE HONEYCREEPER
*Cyanerpes caeruleus*
COPEICILLO VIOLÁCEO

Pl. 34

4.2″ (10.6 cm.). Differs from Short-billed Honeycreeper by slightly larger size, black of throat not reaching upper breast, only lores black and legs vivid, pale lemon yellow. Bill much longer, 0.7″ (1.8 cm.) vs. 0.4″ (1 cm.). ♀: differs from Short-billed by buff instead of green lores, buffy sides of head, throat much deeper buff and breast and sides of body blue, streaked pale buff. Patch at base of mandible blue.
Tropical and lower subtropical zones. Zulia and Táchira e to Mérida and w Barinas; n and w Amazonas s to the Brazilian border (*microrhynchus*). The n Cordilleras from Carabobo to Sucre; s of the Orinoco in e Amazonas along the upper Río Ventuari, generally in Bolívar; Delta Amacuro (*caeruleus*). [Colombia to w Ecuador, the Guianas to Bolivia, Amazonian Brazil. Trinidad.]
Rain and cloud forests, mangroves, second growth, to 1500 m. n of the Orinoco, to 1800 m. on the slopes and summits of tepuis. Clearings, plantations, suburban areas, forest edge, wooded swamps. Forages in groups in the canopy of flowering trees.

## RED-LEGGED HONEYCREEPER
*Cyanerpes cyaneus*
TUCUSO DE MONTAÑA

Pl. 34

5″ (13 cm.). General color purplish blue, crown brilliant light turquoise blue; lores, ocular region, mantle, under tail coverts, wings and tail black, inner webs of remiges largely canary yellow. Legs vermilion. ♀: upperparts, wings and tail dull green, inner margins of remiges partly yellow; eyebrow greenish white. Below pale greenish, whitish on abdomen, breast obscurely streaked.
Tropical and subtropical zones. Sierra de Perijá, Zulia, e through Falcón along the coastal areas to Sucre and Margarita I.; in the interior through Portuguesa and Mérida to Táchira (*eximius*). N of the Orinoco in central Monagas; Delta Amacuro (San Francisco de Guayo); generally in Bolívar (*cyaneus*). Amazonas generally (*dispar*). [Mexico to n Bolivia and Amazonian Brazil. Trinidad. Tobago.]
Rain and cloud forests, second growth, to 1500 m. n of the Orinoco, to 2000 m. on the tepuis. Open woods, forest edge, clearings, parks. Feeds on nectar, berries, fruit and insects. Usually in small groups. Forages actively from lower levels to the treetops.

## GREEN HONEYCREEPER
*Chlorophanes spiza*
MIELERO VERDE

Pl. 34

5.5″ (14 cm.). Bill comparatively long, slightly curved, upper mandible black, lower yellow. General color glistening blue green, bluer on central underparts. Top and sides of head black. Remiges and outer tail feathers black, edged blue green. Legs leaden black. ♀: bright green above, yellowish green below (or with throat and center of lower parts yellow to greenish yellow, a).
Tropical zone. The Sierra de Perijá and the Andes in n Táchira and Mérida (*subtropicalis*, a). The s slopes of the Andes in s Táchira and Barinas. The n serranías and savannas from Carabobo to the Paria Pen., Sucre; generally s of the Orinoco in Amazonas and Bolívar (*spiza*). [S Mexico to nw Peru, n Bolivia and se Brazil. Trinidad.]
Rain forest, second growth, plantations from near sea level to 1250 m. n of the Orinoco, to 1400 m. on the slopes of the tepuis. Forest edge, clearings, savannas, near rivers. Feeds on fruit, insects, nectar. Alone or in groups,

frequently inside the forest. Forages actively in lower levels to the treetops, sometimes in large flocks in flowering Bucares (*Erythrina*).

[THE GENUS *Dacnis* differs from other honeycreepers by having a short, conical, sharply pointed bill.]

## BLUE DACNIS

*Dacnis cayana*
MIELERO TURQUESA

Pl. 34
4.5″ (11.5 cm.). General color bright turquoise blue. Throat and interscapular region and tail black. Wings black, wing coverts and remiges edged bright blue. ♀: bright green; top and sides of head blue, throat bluish gray. Wings and tail blackish, the feathers edged green.
Tropical zone virtually throughout (*cayana*). [Nicaragua to w Ecuador, Bolivia, Paraguay and ne Argentina. Trinidad.]
Rain forests, damp open forest, second growth, suburban areas, to 1200 m. n of the Orinoco, to 1400 m. on the slopes of the tepuis. Forest edge, open fields, clearings, haciendas. Feeds on nectar, fruits, insects. Alone or in small groups forages actively mainly near the treetops.

## BLACK-FACED DACNIS

*Dacnis lineata*
MIELERO CELESTE

Pl. 34
4.8″ (12 cm.). Crown, rump and upper tail coverts, throat, breast and sides of body bright blue; center of abdomen, thighs and under tail coverts white. Forehead, sides of head and neck, mantle, wings and tail black. ♀: above dull brownish olive with a green cast in certain lights; throat, breast and sides of body like back but much paler, center of abdomen, axillars and under wing coverts white; under tail coverts buff.
Tropical zone. S Táchira; Amazonas s of the Río Ventuari; generally in Bolívar except the ne (*lineata*). [Colombia and the Guianas to w Ecuador, n Bolivia and Amazonian Brazil.]
Rain forest, forest edge, second growth, at 350–450 m. n of the Orinoco and from near sea level to 1300 m. s of it. Open forest, fruit groves. Alone or with forest

flocks, forages actively in the foliage from medium heights to the treetops, especially in flowering or fruiting trees.

## YELLOW-BELLIED DACNIS

*Dacnis flaviventer*
MIELERO VIENTRE AMARILLO

Pl. 34
4.5″ (11.5 cm.). Crown dull, pale green. Throat, sides of head, mantle, wings and tail black. Sides of back, moustacial streak and underparts bright golden yellow. ♀: very similar to Green Honeycreeper but back browner with green gloss; below browner with no trace of green.
Tropical zone. Central Amazonas in the Río Ventuari region; Bolívar from the lower Río Caura to the upper Río Paragua. [E Colombia to n Bolivia and Amazonian Brazil.]
Rain forest, 100–350 m. Forages actively from medium heights to treetops.

## WHITE-BELLIED DACNIS

*Dacnis albiventris*
MIELERO VIENTRE BLANCO

Pl. 34
4.5″ (11.4 cm.). Mainly cornflower blue; forehead and sides of head black, lower breast, belly and under tail coverts white. Wings and tail black, wing coverts edged cornflower blue. ♀: above green, brighter on rump, underparts greenish yellow, yellow in center of lower belly.
Tropical zone. Amazonas in the vicinity of Cerro Duida and El Carmen, Río Negro. [Se Colombia to e Peru. Brazil in se Pará.]
Rain forest at about 200 m. Forages actively near the treetops.

## OPAL-RUMPED TANAGER

*Tangara velia*
TANAGRELLA

Pl. 35
5.5″ (14 cm.). Forecrown, throat and sides of head glistening purple blue, crown, hindneck and mantle black, rump glistening opalescent silvery green. Underparts shining dark blue, less purplish than throat, an irregular black band across lower throat; center of belly and under

tail coverts chestnut. Lesser and median wing coverts glistening purple blue, greater wing coverts, remiges and rectrices black edged blue. ♀: differs from ♂ by having the sides of head glistening blue green instead of purplish blue.

Tropical zone. Amazonas s of the mouth of the Río Vichada and of the Río Ventuari; Bolívar from the Río Caura to the upper Río Paragua and the Gran Sabana (*iridina*). [E Colombia and the Guianas to central Peru, Amazonian and se Brazil and nw Argentina.] Rain forest, forest edge, second growth, from near sea level to 1200 m. In small groups forages for berries from middle heights to treetops.

Note: Placed in *Tanagrella* in Lista Av. Venez.

## PARADISE TANAGER

*Tangara chilensis*
SIETE COLORES

Pl. 35
5.5″ (14 cm.). Top and sides of head covered with scalelike, shining apple green feathers; mantle velvety black, lower back scarlet, rump and upper tail coverts golden yellow. Throat and upper breast purple blue, rest of underparts shining, bright turquoise blue, center of belly and under tail coverts black. Wing coverts shining turquoise blue, dark purple blue at lower edge; remiges black, edged purple blue; tail black.

Tropical zone. Generally in Amazonas and Bolívar (*coelicolor*). [E Colombia, the Guianas to n Bolivia and Amazonian Brazil.] Rain forest to 1400 m. Confined to forest. With mixed groups of small birds; forages for berries and insects from middle heights to treetops.

## GREEN-AND-GOLD TANAGER

*Tangara schrankii*
TANGARA CARINEGRA

Pl. 35
5.2″ (13 cm.). Forehead, chin and sides of head black, line at anterior edge of eye green. Crown golden yellow; back black, the feathers edged bright shining green giving a streaked look; center of rump yellow. Upper throat, sides of

neck and body bright green, center of underparts yellow. Wing coverts black, edged blue; remiges and rectrices black, inner remiges edged green, outer remiges and tail edged blue. ♀: lacks the yellow crown patch; yellow of rump barely indicated.

Tropical zone. W Amazonas on the upper Río Ventuari and e of Cerro Duida; s Bolívar from the upper Río Caura to the Gran Sabana (*venezuelana*). [E Colombia to n Bolivia and w Amazonian Brazil.] Rain forest, plantations, clearings, 300–900 m. Forages from the undergrowth to medium heights. Joins forest flocks.

## SPOTTED TANAGER

*Tangara punctata*
TANGARA GOTEADA

Pl. 35
4.7″ (12 cm.). Lores black. Upperparts black, the feathers broadly edged grass green giving a scaled appearance, the black centers on the feathers of rump obsolete, this area almost uniform green. Feathers of center of throat and breast black, broadly edged greenish white, those at sides of breast black broadly edged yellow; flanks green; center of abdomen white. Wings dusky, the feathers edged green. Central tail feathers green, outer ones dusky, edged green.

Tropical and subtropical zones. Amazonas s of Cerro Paraque and the Río Ventuari; s Bolívar (*punctata*). [E Ecuador, the Guianas to n Bolivia and n Brazil.] Rain forest, second growth, 250–1600 m. Alone or with other small species forages in fruiting trees from middle heights to treetops.

## SPECKLED TANAGER

*Tangara guttata*
TANGARA PINTADA

Pl. 35
5.2″ (13 cm.). Very like Spotted Tanager but larger, differing principally in color by having the top and sides of head much more yellowish green and the wing coverts and remiges broadly edged pale blue instead of green (or differs additionally by yellow forehead and ocular region, a).

Upper tropical and subtropical zones. The Sierra de Perijá, Zulia and Táchira

through Barinas and Mérida to s Lara (*bogotensis*). The Sierra San Luis, Falcón, and the coastal Cordillera from Yaracuy to Sucre; Amazonas generally; sw Bolívar from the Río Cuchivero to the Río Paragua (*chrysophrys*, a). Se Bolívar in the Gran Sabana (*guttata*, a). [Costa Rica to n Colombia, n Brazil. Trinidad.]
Rain and cloud forest 400–2000 m. Second growth, coffee plantations, suburban areas, forest edge, clearings. Seldom inside the forest. In pairs or in small groups with other species; forages actively in foliage from near the ground to treetops. Eats berries and insects. Call: a series of weak notes.
Note: The name *guttata* has priority over *chrysophrys*, and is therefore used for the species instead of *chrysophrys*, as in Lista Av. Venez.

## DOTTED TANAGER
*Tangara varia*
TANGARA MANCHADA

Pl. 35
4″ (10 cm.). Top and sides of head, rump and upperparts bright grass green, feathers of throat and breast green, basally black, the black showing through giving a somewhat spotted appearance. Mantle, closed wing and tail greenish blue. ♀: mantle green like rest of underparts, center of abdomen greenish yellow.
Tropical zone. Amazonas generally; Bolívar on the upper Río Paragua. [Surinam; French Guiana; Brazil on the Rio Negro and the lower Tapajós.]
Rain forest, 100–300 m. Clearings near rivers.

## YELLOW-BELLIED TANAGER
*Tangara xanthogastra*
TANGARA PUNTEADA

Pl. 35
4.7″ (12 cm.). Much like Spotted and Speckled Tanagers but easily distinguishable by bright yellow center of abdomen which is white in other two. Feathers of crown and mantle black, those of crown edged bright grass green, those of mantle greenish blue; rump grass green, upper tail coverts black edged greenish blue. Feathers of throat and breast black, broadly edged bright grass green, giving a spotted appearance, sides of belly bright grass green; center of belly bright yellow. Wings and tail much as in Green-and-gold Tanager.
Tropical and subtropical zones, 1000–1800 m. Cerros Yaví, Paragua, and de la Neblina and in se Bolívar on the Sierra de Lema and the tepuis of the Gran Sabana (*phelpsi*). 300–750 m. in ne Bolívar near the Río Caura and e Amazonas on the Río Ventuari and the headwaters of the Río Siapa (*xanthogastra*). [E Colombia, nw Brazil to n Bolivia.]
Interior of rain and cloud forests.

## GOLDEN TANAGER
*Tangara arthus*
TANGARA DORADA

Pl. 35
5″ (13 cm.). Crown, nape and ocular region orange yellow (or yellow, a). Lores, chin and auriculars black; mantle black, streaked orange yellow (or greenish yellow, a), lower back and rump yellow; entire underparts cadmium yellow (or throat and center of belly yellow; breast, sides of body and under tail coverts chestnut, a). Wings and tail black, wing coverts and remiges edged yellow (or yellowish green, a).
Upper tropical and subtropical zones. The Sierra de Perijá, Zulia (*aurulenta*). The Andes from Táchira through Barinas and Mérida to w Lara and Yaracuy and the coastal Cordilleras from Falcón to Miranda (*arthus*, a). [Colombia to w Ecuador and n Bolivia.]
Rain and cloud forest, second growth, 700–2000 m. Inside and edge of forest. Alone, or in flocks up to 30, actively forages for berries from the undergrowth to the treetops.

## SAFFRON-CROWNED TANAGER
*Tangara xanthocephala*
TANGARA CORONA AMARILLA

Pl. 35
5″ (13 cm.). Top and sides of head silky golden yellow, forehead, mask and upper throat black. Nuchal collar black; mantle black, streaked blue; lower back, breast and sides of body blue to turquoise green depending on the light; center of lower breast and abdomen and

under tail coverts cinnamon buff. Wings and tail black, the feathers edged blue. Subtropical zone. The Sierra de Perijá and the Andes of Táchira n through Mérida to s Lara (*venusta*). [Colombia to Peru.] Cloud forests, second growth, 1800–2300 m. Forest edge, coffee plantations.

## FLAME-FACED TANAGER
*Tangara parzudakii*
TANGARA CARA DE FUEGO

Pl. 35
6″ (15 cm.). Crown, nape and extreme upper mantle golden yellow, forehead and cheeks flame scarlet, lores, ocular region, ear coverts, chin and upper throat black. Wing coverts, lower back, breast and sides of body glistening silvery opalescent, becoming shining light silvery green in certain lights. Center of belly and under tail coverts cinnamon buff. Wings and tail black, wing coverts, the same color as lower back.
Subtropical zone. Sw Táchira, along the Río Chiquito (*parzudakii*). [Colombia to w Ecuador and e Peru.] Recorded from cloud forest at 1900 m. in humid mossy branches near the treetops. Coffee plantations.

## RUFOUS-CHEEKED TANAGER
*Tangara rufigenis*
TANGARA MEJILLAS RUFAS

Pl. 35
5.7″ (14.5 cm.). Forehead, throat and sides of head cinnamon rufous; crown, nape and extreme upper mantle and rump shining blue green, back and upper tail coverts dark olive green. Lower throat, breast and sides of body shining bluish green; center of belly buffy; crissum and under tail coverts cinnamon. Wings and tail black, wing coverts edged shining bluish green, remiges edged tawny olive, rectrices edged bluish green.
Upper tropical and subtropical zones. Sierra de Aroa, Yaracuy; the Andes of s Lara; the coastal Cordillera from Carabobo to the Distr. Federal.
Rain and cloud forests, 900–2050 m. Often inside the dense, humid parts of the forest. In pairs and small groups forages actively in small and large fruiting trees, from middle heights to treetops. Joins groups of other small birds.

## BLUE-NECKED TANAGER
*Tangara cyanicollis*
TANGARA REY

Pl. 35
5″ (13 cm.). Mainly black. Head and neck bright, light blue; center of throat purple blue, lores and chin black. Rump shining turquoise blue. Lesser and median wing coverts bronzy, opalescent green to burnished gold depending on the light; greater wing coverts, remiges and rectrices edged turquoise blue.
Tropical and subtropical zones. The Sierra de Perijá, Zulia to Táchira, and through w Barinas, Mérida, w Lara and Yaracuy to s Carabobo and n Guárico (*hannahiae*). [Colombia to w Ecuador, n Bolivia and s Brazil.]
Rain and cloud forest, second growth, to 2100 m. Dense woods, open woodland and isolated trees, suburban areas. Alone or in small flocks actively forages for berries in small trees and the high treetops. Call: a high, thin whistle.

## MASKED TANAGER
*Tangara nigrocincta*
TANGARA PECHINEGRA

Pl. 35
5″ (12.7 cm.). Head and throat light lavender blue, ocular region tinged greenish; forehead, lores and chin black. Mantle and breast black, lower back and sides of body cornflower blue, center of abdomen white. Wings and tail black; lesser wing coverts cornflower blue, median and greater wing coverts and inner remiges edged turquoise blue, outer remiges edged cornflower blue. ♀: duller than ♂, the black feathers of breast edged grayish blue; rump and sides of body less purplish, more greenish.
Tropical zone. Amazonas, e and s of the mouth of the Río Vichada; Bolívar from the lower Caura se across the Río Paragua to the Gran Sabana. [E Colombia, Guyana to n Bolivia and central Amazonian Brazil.]
Rain forest, second growth, to 950 m. Clearings, cultivated areas, open woodland. In pairs or small groups forages for berries low levels to treetops.
Note: *T. larvata* of Mid. Amer. to w Ecuador is regarded as a distinct species.

## TURQUOISE TANAGER
*Tangara mexicana*
TANGARA TURQUESA

Pl. 35

5.2″ (13 cm.). Forecrown, throat, breast, sides of head, lower back and rump cornflower blue, the black bases of the feathers showing through here and there; lores and chin black. Hindcrown, nape and mantle, sides of breast, wings and tail black; lower breast, abdomen and under tail coverts pale yellow, sides of body spotted with black. Lesser and median wing coverts shining bright turquoise blue, greater coverts black, edged purple blue, primaries edged turquoise blue.

Tropical zone. Amazonas n of the Río Ventuari; n and se Bolívar; Delta Amacuro n in e Sucre to the base of the Paria Pen. (*media*). [E Colombia, the Guianas to n Bolivia, Amazonian and se Brazil. Trinidad.]

Rain forest, second growth, mangroves to 1000 m. Open woodland, clearings, plantations, isolated trees, forest edge. Usually in small groups, actively forages for fruits and insects from near the ground to the treetops. Call: sharp, twittering chirps.

## BAY-HEADED TANAGER
*Tangara gyrola*
TANGARA CABEZA DE LACRE

Pl. 35

5–5.5″ (13–14 cm.). Top and sides of head and upper throat chestnut red bordered across nape by a more or less distinct golden yellow band. Back grass green, brightest on rump (or center of rump bright blue, a). Below bright grass green, blue in center of breast and belly (or bright blue below except for green crissum and under tail coverts, a; or entirely bright grass green below, b, c); thighs chestnut. Closed wings and tail green (or closed wings golden green, b); shoulders green (or golden yellow, a).

Tropical and subtropical zones. Nw Venezuela from Zulia and Táchira e to Mérida, Barinas, and Portuguesa and from Falcón and Lara to Miranda and n Guárico (*toddi*, c). The e Cordilleras from Anzoátegui to the Paria Pen., Sucre and Monagas (*viridissima*, b). Sw Amazonas along the Río Negro (*parva*,

a). Central Amazonas; w Bolívar e across the Río Paragua to the Gran Sabana (*gyrola*). [Costa Rica to w Ecuador, Bolivia and Amazonian Brazil. Trinidad.]

Rain and cloud forests, second growth, cocoa and coffee plantations, to 1800 m. n of the Orinoco, to 1600 m. on the tepuis. Damp wooded areas, forest edge, clearings. In pairs or small groups forages actively in fruiting trees from low bushes to the treetops. Joins mixed bands of small birds.

## BURNISHED-BUFF TANAGER
*Tangara cayana*
TANGARA MONJITA

Pl. 35

5.2″ (13 cm.). Crown bright coppery rufous, sides of head black. Throat and upper breast dark greenish blue. Back shining opalescent straw color, rather coppery when seen against the light; *rump whitish*. Underparts shining ochraceous with a bluish sheen. Wing coverts greenish blue; remiges and rectrices black, broadly margined greenish blue. ♀: similar to ♂ but much duller.

Tropical and subtropical zones. Generally distributed n of the Orinoco, s of it to central Amazonas, and generally in Bolívar (*cayana*). [E Colombia and the Guianas to n Peru, Amazonian and se Brazil, e Paraguay; n Bolivia, ne Argentina.]

Open rain and cloud forests, second growth, open terrain with scattered trees, low bushes, to 2500 m. n of the Orinoco, to 1800 m. on the tepuis. Deciduous and gallery forest, *Mauritia* swamps, plantations, gardens, pastures. Not inside dense forest. In pairs or small flocks forages actively from low levels to treetops. Joins other species.

## BERYL-SPANGLED TANAGER
*Tangara nigroviridis*
TANGARA MARIPOSA

Pl. 35

5″ (13 cm.). Forehead, mask and mantle black. Feathers of crown, nape, breast and underparts black, broadly tipped shining greenish blue giving a spotted appearance, particularly below; center of abdomen white. Rump virtually uniform shining greenish blue. Wings and tail black, the feathers broadly margined greenish blue.

Subtropical zone. The Sierra de Perijá, Zulia; the Andes from Táchira to s Lara; the coastal Cordillera from Carabobo to Miranda (*cyanescens*). [Colombia to nw Bolivia.] Cloud and dwarf forests, second growth, 1400–3000 m. Forest edge, cultivated areas. In pairs or small groups actively forages in the lower heights and the treetops. Joins flocks of other small species.

## BLACK-CAPPED TANAGER
*Tangara heinei*
TANGARA GORRO NEGRO

Pl. 35

5″ (13 cm.). Cap black. Throat, upper breast and sides of head shining pale green, feathers of breast lanceolate; back and rest of underparts shining grayish blue. Wings and tail black, wing feathers broadly edged dull blue. ♀: feathers of crown and nape blackish basally, broadly edged bluish green; back shining light grass green. Throat, breast and sides of head as in ♂ but duller and greener; central underparts gray, sides green like back. Wings and tail blackish, feathers edged green.

Subtropical zone. The Sierra de Perijá, Zulia; the Andes from Táchira n to Lara; the coastal Cordillera from Yaracuy to n Guárico and the Distr. Federal. [Colombia to ne Ecuador.] Cloud forest, second growth, 1250–2600 m. Open woodland, clearings, isolated trees. Forages for fruit from medium heights to treetops.

## BLACK-HEADED TANAGER
*Tangara cyanoptera*
TANGARA COPINO

Pl. 35

5″ (13 cm.). Head and neck black. Body plumage shining silvery green, with a somewhat brassy sheen (or without brassy sheen, lower parts somewhat mottled with blackish, a). Wings and tail black, wing coverts and remiges broadly margined with dark blue (or plain black, a). ♀: crown grayish green; lores, sides of head, throat and breast gray with a green sheen, rest of underparts pale yellow obscurely mottled

dusky (or buffy, mottled with dusky, a). Above green, paler and yellower on rump. Wings and tail dark brown, the feathers edged green.

Upper tropical and subtropical zones. The Sierra de Perijá, Zulia; the Andes from Táchira to Lara, and from the serranías of Falcón e to Sucre (*cyanoptera*). The tepuis of Amazonas and the Gran Sabana, Bolívar (*whitelyi*, a). [Ne Colombia, Guyana, ne Brazil.] Rain and cloud forest, 450–2200 m. n of the Orinoco, 1100–2250 m. on the tepuis. Second growth. Forages from middle heights to treetops.

## BLUE-AND-BLACK TANAGER
*Tangara vassorii*
TANGARA PIQUIRÓN

Pl. 35

5.5″ (14 cm.). Silky, cornflower blue. Lores, wings and tail black, wing coverts edged blue.

Subtropical and temperate zones. The Andes of Trujillo, Mérida and Táchira (*vassorii*). [Colombia to w Ecuador and nw Bolivia.] Cloud and dwarf forests, second growth, 1800–3200 m. Open terrain with scattered trees and shrubs.

## FAWN-BREASTED TANAGER
*Pipraeidea melanonota*
CHACHAQUITO

Pl. 36

5.5″ (14 cm.). Forehead and sides of head black, crown, nape and rump pale blue; mantle, upper tail coverts very dark blue; entire undersurface pale fawn color. Wings and tail black, lesser wing coverts pale blue, remiges and rectrices edged dark blue. ♀: differs from ♂ mainly by having the mantle dark brown, and blue of crown and rump duller.

Upper tropical and subtropical zones. The Andes of Mérida, w Lara; the coastal Cordillera from Carabobo to the Distr. Federal and in Sucre; n Amazonas; the Sierra Parima along the Brazil border, sw Bolívar (*venezuelensis*). [Colombia to w Peru, Bolivia, s Brazil, Uruguay and n Argentina.] Cloud forest, 1500–2500 m. n of the Orinoco, 950–2100 m. on the tepuis. Second growth, forest borders, wet, open, wooded terrain, clearings, bushy pastures. Alone or in pairs forages for fruits and insects at middle heights.

## BLUE-NAPED CHLOROPHONIA
*Chlorophonia cyanea*
VERDÍN MONTAÑERO

Pl. 35
4.5" (11.5 cm.). Head, throat and breast bright grass green, ocular ring blue (with yellow forehead, a). Nuchal collar, rump and upper tail coverts bright cobalt blue; feathers of back green basally, broadly tipped blue, (or feathers of back all green, b). Lower breast and belly bright yellow. Wings and tail green. ♀: above green, nuchal collar cobalt blue, (forehead yellowish, a). Throat and upper breast like back, rest of underparts olive yellow.
Upper tropical and subtropical zones. The Sierra de Perijá, Zulia. The Andes of Táchira, Mérida and Barinas to s Lara (*longipennis*). The Serranías of w Lara, the Sierra de Aroa, Yaracuy and the coastal Cordillera to the Distr. Federal (*frontalis*, a, b). The e Cordilleras from Anzoátegui to the Paria Pen., Sucre; n Monagas (*minuscula* a, b). The cerros of Amazonas and Bolívar (*roraimae, a*). [Colombia, Guyana to Bolivia, Paraguay, se Brazil and ne Argentina.]
Rain and cloud forests, second growth, 700–2500 m. n of the Orinoco, 500–1800 m. on the tepuis. Clearings, coffee plantations. In pairs or small flocks forages actively for berries from low heights to treetops. Joins forest flocks.

## CHESTNUT-BREASTED CHLOROPHONIA
*Chlorophonia pyrrhophrys*
VERDÍN VIENTRE CASTAÑO

Pl. 35
4.7" (12 cm.). Crown and nape purplish blue, nuchal collar cobalt blue; forehead narrowly green, margined with black, the black continued to form a long eyebrow. Back dark green, rump bright yellow. Sides of head, throat and breast bright grass green, green of breast bordered below by a black line, followed by a chestnut band. Center of underparts chestnut, sides bright yellow. ♀: head much as in ♂ but black of forehead and eyebrow replaced by reddish

chestnut; rump green; sides of head, throat and upper breast grass green, rest of underparts yellowish olive. Wings and tail green.
Subtropical and temperate zones. The Sierra de Perijá, Zulia; the Andes of Táchira, Mérida and Trujillo. [The Andes of Colombia and Ecuador.]
Cloud and dwarf forests, 1800–3300 m. Open damp terrain with scattered trees and shrubs.

[EUPHONIAS FORM A LARGE GROUP of very distinct, small, chunky tanagers, many characterized in the ♂ sex by glossy blue black to purplish black backs and yellow underparts. Their bills are rather heavy, hooked, wide and short. Most have a pleasant, warbling song.]

## BLUE-HOODED EUPHONIA
*Euphonia musica*
CURRUÑATÁ CORONA AZUL

Pl. 36
5" (11.4 cm.). Crown and nape blue, forehead and lores black. Throat, sides of head, mantle, wings and tail glossy blackish purple; lower back, rump and underparts cadmium yellow. ♀: forehead yellow, crown and nape blue; back, sides of head, wings and tail green. Below olive, throat yellowish.
Tropical and subtropical zones. The n serranías from Zulia and Táchira to Sucre and n Monagas; se Bolívar on Cerros Roraima and Uaipán-tepui (*intermedia*). [Mexico to w Panama. Colombia and the Guianas to s Bolivia and n Argentina. Trinidad. The Antilles.]
Rain and cloud forests, low second growth, xerophytic vegetation, to 2500 m. n of the Orinoco, from 500–1500 m. on the tepuis. Coffee plantations, open deciduous forest, suburban areas. Often in pairs, forages for fruits in the middle heights. Not shy.
Note: *Euphonia* replaces *Tanagra* used in Lista Av. Venez. and Sp. Bds. S Amer.

## ORANGE-BELLIED EUPHONIA
*Euphonia xanthogaster*
CURRUÑATÁ AZULEJO

Pl. 36
4.2" (10.6 cm.). Cap bright yellow (or rufous, a). Throat, upper breast, sides of head and neck, upperparts, wings and

tail glossy purple black, more purplish on nape. Below cadmium yellow, tinged rufescent on breast. Outer tail feather with a white patch on inner web; remiges basally white. ♀: olive green above, forehead yellow (or rufous, a), nape tinged gray. Throat and breast grayish, belly and under tail coverts pinkish buff (or center of underparts dark pinkish buff, under tail coverts cinnamon, a); sides of body yellowish olive.

Tropical and subtropical zones. The Sierra de Perijá, Zulia; s Táchira; s and w Mérida; Lara, and from Carabobo to the Distr. Federal (*exsul,* a). The tepuis of s Bolívar and Amazonas (*brevirostris*). [E Panama to w Ecuador; Guyana to Bolivia and se Brazil.]

Rain and cloud forests, second growth, 350–2250 m. n of the Orinoco, 150–1700 m. s of it. Clearings, but usually inside the forest near damp areas. Alone or in pairs forages for berries from low to medium heights. Often roosts in dense mistletoe.

## WHITE-VENTED EUPHONIA

*Euphonia minuta*
Currunatá Menudito

Pl. 36

3.5″ (9 cm.). Forecrown, breast and belly golden yellow, under tail coverts white. Hindcrown, throat and sides of head purplish black becoming steel blue on back, wings and tail. Inner webs of 3 outer tail feathers white; remiges basally white. ♀: above mossy green; throat, center of abdomen and under tail coverts gray; breast and sides of body olive yellow. Wings and tail dusky, edged olive.

Tropical zone. S Táchira (Burgua); e Sucre (Guanoco); Delta Amacuro (Jobure); Amazonas s to Cerro Duida; Bolívar along the lower Río Caura e across the Río Paragua to Cerro Roraima (*minuta*). [Mexico to Bolivia and Amazonian Brazil.]

Rain forest to 500 m. n of the Orinoco, to 900 m. s of it. Second growth, scrub, clearings. In pairs or small groups forages high on trees. Feeds on mistletoe berries.

## TRINIDAD EUPHONIA

*Euphonia trinitatis*
Currunatá Saucito

Pl. 36

3.5″ (9 cm.). Very like White-vented Euphonia, best distinguishable by yellow instead of white under tail coverts and white on 3 outer pairs of tail feathers more restricted, tips of these feathers black on inner web. Upperparts purple black instead of steel blue. ♀: quite different from ♀ White-vented Euphonia. Above light olive green; throat and sides of body bright greenish yellow, center of breast and belly grayish white.

Tropical zone. From Zulia across n Venezuela to the Paria Pen., Sucre, and the delta of the Orinoco, and s across the llanos to n Amazonas and n Bolívar. [N Colombia. Trinidad, Tobago.]

Various types of wooded areas to 600 m. n of the Orinoco, to 300 m. s of it. Rain forest, second growth, open woods, arid scrub, savannas, gallery forest clearings, suburban areas. In pairs or small flocks forages from low levels to treetops. Feeds mostly on insects but also on mistletoe berries. Call: clear high whistle; one of its local names, *Fin-fin,* refers to its song.

## FINSCH'S EUPHONIA

*Euphonia finschi*
Currunatá de Finsch

3.5″ (9 cm.). Very like Trinidad Euphonia, best distinguished by no white in tail and very much darker underparts, deep cadmium yellow on breast shading to tawny yellow on rest of underparts. ♀: quite different from ♀ Trinidad Euphonia. Above dark olive, below olive yellow, center of abdomen clear yellow.

Se Bolívar [Adj. Brazil, the Guianas.]

The only Venezuelan record is of a bird from Roraima, probably taken at forest edge near the adjacent savannas at about 1200 m.

## PURPLE-THROATED EUPHONIA

*Euphonia chlorotica*
Currunatá Azuquero

4.2″ (10.6 cm.). Forecrown and underparts bright yellow; hindcrown, nape, throat, sides of neck glossy purple black, mantle steel blue. Wings and tail blue black; basal half of remiges white; 2 outermost tail feathers with a large white subterminal oval patch on inner web; sometimes a small patch on 3rd outer feather. ♀: much like ♀ Trinidad Euphonia, differing principally by much larger size and grayish hindcrown and nape. The central underparts are somewhat variable, in some specimens strongly yellowish instead of grayish white.

Tropical zone. S Táchira; w Apure; n Amazonas; nw Bolívar e to the lower Río Caura and in the se corner (*cyanophora*). [E Colombia, the Guianas to n Bolivia, Paraguay, and n Argentina.]

Rain forest, second growth, forest edge, plantations, bushes, shrubbery to 300 m. n of the Orinoco, 100–900 m. s of it. Feeds on mistletoe berries.

## THICK-BILLED EUPHONIA

*Euphonia laniirostris*
CURRUÑATÁ PIQUIGORDO

Pl. 36
4.7" (12 cm.). This and the next species are the only 2 dark-backed euphonias in Venezuela with uniform yellow underparts (no violaceous throat patch). Forecrown and entire underparts bright yellow. Hindcrown, back, sides of head and neck, wings and tail glossy steel blue, 2 outermost tail feathers with a large white patch on inner web. Bill rather thicker than in other species. ♀: above olive green, below yellow with an olive tinge, center of belly bright, clear yellow. Wings and tail dusky, edged olive.

Tropical and subtropical zones. The Sierra de Perijá, Zulia; Táchira and w Apure through Barinas and Portuguesa to the n serranías, thence e to Sucre (*crassirostris*). [Costa Rica to w Peru, n Bolivia and Amazonian Brazil.]

Rain and cloud forests, low second growth, open woodland, deciduous forest, to 1900 m. Coffee plantations, forest edge, savannas, suburban areas, pastures. In pairs or small groups, forages actively from middle to upper heights. Feeds on fruits and mistletoe berries. Call: a pleasant high musical whistle, "fin, fin."

## VIOLACEOUS EUPHONIA

*Euphonia violacea*
CURRUÑATÁ CAPA NEGRA

Pl. 36
4.2" (10.7 cm.). Much like the Thick-billed Euphonia, differing by darker yellow underparts, yellow of head restricted to extreme forecrown, reaching back only to front of eye instead of well behind it, back purplish black rather than steel blue, purple at sides of neck encroaching on sides of throat. ♀: differs by much darker, more olivaceous underparts, belly not clear yellow.

Tropical zone. N Amazonas; generally in Bolívar extending n through the delta of the Orinoco to e Sucre (*violacea*). [The Guianas, e and central Amazonian, and e Brazil, Paraguay, ne Argentina. Trinidad, Tobago.]

Rain forest, high second growth, mangroves, open terrain with scattered trees, to 1100 m. Clearings, savannas, suburban areas, plantations. Alone or in small groups forages in the foliage from low levels to treetops. Feeds on fruits and mistletoe berries. Call: high, melodious, varied, whistled song.

## RUFOUS-BELLIED EUPHONIA

*Euphonia rufiventris*
FRUTERITO VIENTRE RUFO

Pl. 36
4.5" (11.5 cm.). Head, neck, upper breast, back, wings and tail glossy steel blue; lower breast, belly and under tail coverts tawny rufous, small patch at sides of breast yellow. ♀: above olive, grayish on nape. Chin, sides of body and interrupted pectoral band olive yellow; central underparts gray, under tail coverts tawny rufous.

Tropical zone. Amazonas; nw Bolívar e across the Río Paragua to the Río Cuyuni and the Gran Sabana. [Se Colombia to nw Brazil and Bolivia.]

Rain forest, to 1100 m. Clearings, plantations. Forages in middle to upper heights among parasitic plants and epiphytes.

## GOLDEN-SIDED EUPHONIA

*Euphonia cayennensis*
FRUTERITO CAYENERO

Pl. 36
4.5" (11.5 cm.). Glossy purplish black; pectoral tufts golden yellow, tipped ru-

fous. ♀: above dark yellowish olive; chin, sides of body light yellowish olive; central underparts including under tail coverts gray.
Tropical zone. Cerro Auyan-tepui, se Bolívar. [The Guianas, ne Brazil.]
Rain forest, forest edge, 450–1100 m. Forages in the treetops in small groups.

## GOLDEN-BELLIED EUPHONIA
*Euphonia chrysopasta*
FRUTERITO VIENTRE DORADO

Pl. 36
4.8″ (12 cm.). Above olive with a green gloss on back; nape and hindcrown gray; lores and chin white. Below yellow with obsolete olive bars across throat and breast, sides of belly yellowish olive, center of belly and under tail coverts yellow. Under wing coverts and axillars white. Wings and tail blackish, feathers edged olive. ♀: above like ♂, lores and chin white. Underparts pale gray, flanks and under tail coverts olive yellow.
Tropical zone. Amazonas generally; Bolívar from the lower and middle Caura across the Río Paragua to the Gran Sabana (*nitida*). [Colombia, Surinam to n Bolivia and Amazonian Brazil.]
Rain forest, to 900 m. Second growth, shrubbery in open woodland, plantations.

## PLUMBEOUS EUPHONIA
*Euphonia plumbea*
FRUTERITO PLOMIZO

Pl. 36
3.5″ (9 cm.). Upperparts, throat and sides of head glossy dark blue gray. Below orange yellow. Wings and tail blackish, feathers edged gray. ♀: crown, nape and extreme upper back dark gray, rest of back olive. Throat and sides of head pale gray, rest of underparts olive yellow brightening to yellow on center of belly and under tail coverts. Wings and tail blackish, edged olive.
Tropical zone. Amazonas s of the Río Ventuari and across s Bolívar to the tepuis of the Gran Sabana. [Guyana, Surinam; n Brazil.]
Rain forest, open vegetation, shrubs in savannas, 100–1000 m.

## GOLDEN-CROWNED TANAGER
*Iridosornis rufivertex*
FRUTERO CABECIDORADO

Pl. 38
7″ (18 cm.). Feathers of center of crown silky, golden yellow with an orange tinge. Forehead, throat, neck, sides of head and broad collar around upper mantle and breast deep black; mantle shining dark blue; lower back, lower breast and belly dark blue; under tail coverts rufous chestnut. Lesser and median wing coverts shining cobalt blue, wings and tail blackish, feathers edged greenish blue. ♀: like ♂ but slightly duller.
Temperate zone. Sw Táchira on Páramo de Tamá (*rufivertex*). [The Andes of Colombia and Ecuador.]
Dwarf forest, open woodland, low trees and shrubs, páramos, 2800–3000 m.

## SCARLET-BELLIED MOUNTAIN-TANAGER
*Anisognathus igniventris*
CACHAQUITO VIENTRE ROJO

7.5″ (19 cm.). Velvety black. Ear coverts, lower breast and belly flame orange. Wing coverts, rump and upper tail coverts shining light blue.
Temperate zone. Sw Táchira on Páramo de Tamá (*lunulatus*). [The Andes from Colombia to Bolivia.]
Dwarf forest, open woodland and páramos, 2700–3000 m. Forages in thickets.

## LACHRYMOSE MOUNTAIN-TANAGER
*Anisognathus lacrymosus*
CACHAQUITO VIENTRE DORADO
Pl. 38

7.2″ (18.2 cm.). Upperparts dark dull blue, blacker on top and sides of head; spot below eye and behind ear coverts yellow (or forecrown, lores and cheeks and sides of neck dull olive yellow, back dull, dusty, grayish blue, a); rump, upper tail coverts and lesser and median wing coverts glossy purplish blue. Underparts tawny yellow. Wings and tail black, edged blue.
Subtropical to temperate zone. The Sierra de Perijá, Zulia (*pallididorsalis*, a). Sw Táchira on the Páramo de Tamá (*tamae*). The rest of Táchira n through

Mérida to Trujillo (*melanops*). [Colombia to w and central Peru.]
Cloud and dwarf forests, 1800–3200 m. A woodland bird, forages in pairs or small bands in the treetops, seldom near the ground. Call: weak, chirping note.

## BLUE-WINGED MOUNTAIN-TANAGER

*Anisognathus flavinucha*
CACHAQUITO PRIMAVERA

Pl. 38
7" (18 cm.). Forecrown, sides of head and nuchal collar black, center of crown and nape bright yellow. Back moss green (or black, greenish black on rump and upper tail coverts, a; or whole back greenish black, b). Underparts entirely bright golden yellow. Lesser and median wing coverts shining violet blue. Wings and tail black, the feathers edged vivid blue.
Upper tropical and subtropical zones. Sw Táchira along the Río Chiquito (*victorini*). The coastal Cordillera from Yaracuy to Miranda (*venezuelanus*, a). The interior Cordillera in Miranda on Cerro Golfo Triste (*virididorsalis*, b). [Colombia to n Bolivia.]
Rain and cloud forests, 900–2100 m. Usually inside the forest, forages in the foliage of the upper branches in groups of up to 25. Joins other forest species.
Note: Called *Compsocoma* in Lista Av. Venez.

## HOODED MOUNTAIN-TANAGER

*Buthraupis montana*
CACHAQUITO GIGANTE

Pl. 38
8.5" (22 cm.). Head, neck and throat and upper breast black, rest of underparts bright yellow. Upperparts, including wing coverts, glistening purplish blue. Wings and tail black, the feathers edged blue.
Subtropical and temperate zones. Nw Zulia in the Sierra de Perijá; sw Táchira (*gigas*). [Colombia to n Bolivia.]
Cloud and dwarf forests, 1800–3000 m. One of the largest tanagers. Occasionally in scattered trees but usually in dense forest.

## BLACK-CHESTED MOUNTAIN-TANAGER

*Buthraupis eximia*
CACHAQUITO RABADILLA AZUL

Pl. 38
9" (23 cm.). Crown, nape, lower back and rump blue, mantle moss green. Sides of head, throat and breast black, rest of underparts bright yellow. Wings and tail black; lesser wing coverts blue, inner remiges margined green.
Temperate zone. Sw Táchira on Páramo de Tamá. (*eximia*). [The Andes of Colombia and Ecuador.]
Low open forest, 3000 m. One of the largest tanagers.

## BUFF-BREASTED MOUNTAIN-TANAGER

*Dubusia taeniata*
CACHAQUITO MONTAÑERO

Pl. 38
8" (20 cm.). Head, neck and throat black, feathers of forehead and sides of crown tipped milky blue, continued backward to sides of neck forming a long eyebrow. Back dark blue. Band across breast and under tail coverts buff, rest of underparts bright yellow. Lesser and median wing coverts broadly tipped milky blue, greater coverts edge dark blue. Remiges and rectrices black, inner remiges edged dark blue.
Subtropical and temperate zones. Sierra de Perijá, Zulia; the Andes of Táchira, Mérida and central Trujillo (*taeniata*). [Colombia to w Ecuador and central Peru.]
Cloud and dwarf forests, clearings, low, open woodland, 2000–3000 m.

## BLUE-GRAY TANAGER

*Thraupis episcopus*
AZULEJO DE JARDÍN

Pl. 37
6.5" (16.5 cm.). Pale blue gray, darker and bluer on back. Lesser wing coverts violet blue, (or lesser and median wing coverts violet blue, a; or lesser and median wing coverts white, greater coverts blue edged white, b). Remiges black broadly edged blue; rectrices dull blue (or violet blue, a, b). ♀: duller.
Tropical and subtropical zones. N of the Orinoco, except in e Monagas and the

lowlands of e Sucre (*cana*). The low-lands in e Sucre, e Monagas and Delta Amacuro; Bolívar except on the upper Río Caura; extreme nw Amazonas (*nesophila*, a). Sw Bolívar along the upper Río Caura; Amazonas s of the Río Ventuari (*mediana*, b). [Mexico to w Peru, n Bolivia and Amazonian Brazil. Trinidad, Tobago.] Rain and cloud forest edge, gallery forest, second growth, to 2200 m. n of the Orinoco, to 1700 m. s of it. Open woodland, plantations, clearings, isolated trees in savannas, city parks. Alone or in small groups forages usually from low heights to treetops. Often associated with Palm Tanager. Call: a series of high, shrill squeaks.
Note: Called *T. virens* in Lista Av. Venez. and Sp. Bds. S Amer.

## GLAUCOUS TANAGER
*Thraupis glaucocolpa*
AZULEJO VERDEVICHE

Pl. 37
6.5" (16.5 cm.). Very like Blue-gray Tanager but back grayer with top of head and nape not paler than back; lesser wing coverts dull blue, primary coverts dark blue forming a spot on wing. Throat gray, breast and sides of body shining bluish green (contrasting with rest of underparts only in certain lights); center of belly whitish, under tail coverts white. Remiges black edged bright, light greenish blue; tail dark bluish gray. ♀: similar but duller.
Tropical zone. The Caribbean littoral from Zulia to Sucre, including Margarita I., and inland to n Zulia, n Lara, s Miranda and the llanos of central Guárico. [Ne Colombia.]
Tall trees and arid scrub, deciduous woods and clearings; coconut groves, pastures, to 800 m., mostly at low altitudes except in Margarita I. and the Paraguaná Pen. Forages for fruit, usually near the treetops, in pairs or in small groups.
Note: Here regarded as a species distinct from the geographically far removed *T. sayaca*.

## PALM TANAGER
*Thraupis palmarum*
AZULEJO DE PALMERAS

Pl. 37
7" (18 cm.). Mainly shiny olive green,

crown greener, back darker brownish olive, ♂ particularly sometimes has a violet (or bluish, a) wash on chest. Wing coverts and bases of remiges light grayish olive, rest of remiges and rectrices brownish black, edges of remiges grayish olive (or without grayish olive edges, a).
Tropical zone. Throughout except the L. Maracaibo region. Margarita and Patos Is. (*melanoptera*). The Maracaibo region in Zulia, n Táchira and n Mérida (*atripennis*, a). [Nicaragua to Bolivia, Paraguay and se Brazil. Trinidad.]
Many kinds of habitats including forests, xerophytic woodland, palms and city parks, to 1450 m. Alone or in small groups, often in mixed bands, actively forages for fruits and insects from mostly middle heights to near the treetops. Often associated with the Blue-gray Tanager. Call: many high, shrill squeaks.

## BLUE-CAPPED TANAGER
*Thraupis cyanocephala*
AZULEJO MONTAÑERO

Pl. 37
7" (18 cm.). Top of head, nape and sides of head shining cornflower blue, lores black (or lores and sides of head black, malar streak whitish, a). Back, wings and tail yellowish olive. Underparts bluish gray to grayish violet blue (or shining blue like head, b). Thighs and under tail coverts yellow (or thighs and under tail coverts olive, a).
Upper tropical and subtropical zones. The Sierra de Perijá, Zulia, the Andes of Táchira, Mérida and Trujillo (*auricrissa*). Páramo de las Rosas, Lara (*hypophaea*). The coastal Cordillera in Aragua and Miranda (*olivicyanea*, b). The coastal Cordillera in w Sucre and Monagas (*subcinerea*, a). The Paria Pen., Sucre (*busingi*). [Colombia, w Ecuador to nw Bolivia, Trinidad.]
Rain and cloud forests, high second growth, 800–2800 m. Forest edge, clearings, coffee plantations. Forages from medium heights to treetops, in pairs or small groups. Joins other species.

## SILVER-BEAKED TANAGER
*Ramphocelus carbo*
SANGRE DE TORO APAGADO

Pl. 37
7" (18 cm.). Bill black with a conspicuous

silvery white base to lower mandible. Above velvety black with a crimson wash on crown (or uniform dark maroon, a). Throat and breast dark crimson gradually turning to velvety black on belly and under tail coverts (or much brighter, crimson on throat and upper breast gradually darkening on belly and under tail coverts, a). Wings and tail black. ♀: above dark maroon brown brightening on rump and upper tail coverts (or much brighter above, dull maroon, brightening to maroon red on rump and upper tail coverts, a). Below dark maroon brown (or light maroon red, a, b).

Tropical and subtropical zones. Falcón to Miranda s through Cojedes and Portuguesa to Barinas, s Táchira and w Apure (*venezuelensis,* a, b). Ne Anzoátegui to Sucre, Monagas and Delta Amacuro (*capitalis*). Se Sucre at Guanoco (*magnirostris,* b). Generally in Amazonas and Bolívar (*carbo*). [Colombia and the Guianas to Bolivia, Paraguay and se Brazil. Trinidad.]

Open rain and cloud forests, second growth, deciduous forest, to 1900 m. n of the Orinoco, to 1250 m. s of it. Scrub, cultivated areas, thickets, suburban areas. Often near water. Seldom inside forest. Alone or in small groups forages noisily and actively for fruits and insects from near the ground to medium heights. Not shy. Gregarious. Responds to a squeak.

## CRIMSON-BACKED TANAGER
*Ramphocelus dimidiatus*
SANGRE DE TORO ENCENDIDO

Pl. 37

7″ (18 cm.). Both sexes are separable from the Silver-beaked Tanager by their highly contrasting rumps. Head, mantle, throat and breast deep crimson. Rump, upper tail coverts and sides of body bright crimson. Center of belly, wings and tail black. Base of mandible white. ♀: head and throat dusky brown, mantle dull crimson, rump, upper tail coverts and underparts dull red. Wings and tail blackish brown.

Tropical zone. Nw Zulia and the L. Maracaibo region in central Zulia, n Mérida and n Táchira (*dimidiatus*). [Panama, Colombia.]

Open rain forest, low bushy growth, forest edge, to 1300 m. Scrub, thickets, clear-

ings, cultivated areas. Alone or in pairs, active, forages noisily from the lower branches to treetops for fruits and insects.

## HEPATIC TANAGER
*Piranga flava*
CARDENAL AVISPERO

Pl. 37

7″ (18 cm.). Upperparts rosy red (or brownish red, a). Lores whitish, *cheeks dark rosy red* (or brownish red, a). Below light orange red (or dark crimson red, throat paler, a). Wings dark brown edged red; tail reddish brown edged red. Sometimes in splotched red and olive transition plumage. *Bill blackish.* ♀: above yellowish olive; cheeks gray. Below yellow, clouded with olive on breast and sides. Bill blackish.

Upper tropical and subtropical zones. The mountains n of the Orinoco from Zulia, Falcón and Lara to the Paria Pen., Sucre (*faceta*). The tepuis of Amazonas and Bolívar (*haemalea,* a). [Sw US to the Guianas, Brazil, w Peru and Argentina.]

Open rain and cloud forests, second growth, 800–2000 m. n of the Orinoco, to 1800 m. s of it. Forest edge, scrub, orchards, suburban areas. Usually in pairs or small groups, actively forages for fruits and insects fairly high in trees. Dark cheeks and black bill help to differentiate it from Summer Tanager.

## SUMMER TANAGER
*Piranga rubra*
CARDENAL MIGRATORIO

6.5″ (16.5 cm.). Rosy red, darker above. Cheeks not darker than underparts. *Bill pale yellowish brown.* ♀: above yellowish olive; eye ring yellow; below yellow. *Bill pale yellowish brown.* Winter ♂ resembles ♀ but may be splotched with rosy red. In the hand, the outermost primary is equal to the next 2 instead of considerably shorter as with Hepatic Tanager.

Winter resident, Sept.–May. Tropical to temperate zone, throughout (*rubra*). [Breeds in US and Mexico. Winters to w Ecuador, Guyana, Bolivia and Chile. Trinidad.]

Great altitudinal range and correspondingly varied habitats, including mangroves and páramos to 3000 m. Second growth, low open forest, coffee plantations, clearings, forest edge. Solitary, forages from low to fairly high.

## SCARLET TANAGER
*Piranga olivacea*
CARDENAL MIGRATORIO ALINEGRO

6.2" (15.7 cm.). Scarlet; wings and tail black. ♀: above olive; below yellow. Wings and tail dark brown, wing coverts and remiges and rectrices edged olive. Distinguishable from Hepatic and Summer Tanagers by smaller size, darker wings, and darker, less yellowish back. Winter ♂ differs from ♀ by *black wings* and *tail*. In transition plumages splotched with scarlet.
Casual winter visitor. Recorded only from Los Roques, Oct. [Breeds in N Amer. Winters to Colombia and Bolivia. Casual in Aruba and Curaçao.]
Taken in low mangroves.
Note: A new record since the publication of Lista Av. Venez.

## WHITE-WINGED TANAGER
*Piranga leucoptera*
CARDENAL GUAMERO

Pl. 37
5.7" (14.5 cm.). Scarlet; lores, wings and tail black, *double wing bar white.* ♀: upperparts olive yellow, yellower on crown and rump. Underparts yellow, tinged orange on breast. Wings and tail brown, *double wing bar white.*
Upper tropical and subtropical zones. The n serranías from Zulia and Táchira to the Paria Pen., Sucre and n Monagas; Bolívar on Cerro Tabaro, lower Río Caura and the tepuis of the Gran Sabana (*venezuelae*). [Mexico to w Panama. Colombia to w Ecuador, nw Bolivia and nw Brazil.]
Rain and cloud forests, second growth, 650–2100 m. n of the Orinoco, 1000–1800 m. s of it. Forest edge, scrub, cultivated areas. In pairs or small groups, forages from low levels to treetops. Joins bands of other species.

## BLUE-BACKED TANAGER
*Cyanicterus cyanicterus*
FRUTERO LOMIAZUL

Pl. 37
7" (18 cm.). Head, neck, upper breast, back, wings and tail shining cobalt blue; lower breast and rest of underparts bright yellow. Thighs black. ♀: lores and sides of head buffy yellow. Crown, back, wings and tail greenish blue; underparts yellow.
Tropical zone. E Bolívar along the Río Yuruán, an affluent of the upper Cuyuni. [The Guianas, n Brazil.]
Rain forest in the lowlands at about 100 m. Treetops; joins mixed forest flocks.
Note: An addition to the Venezuelan avifauna since publication of Lista Av. Venez.

## RED-CROWNED ANT-TANAGER
*Habia rubica*
CARDENAL HORMIGUERO

Pl. 37
6.7" (17 cm.). Dull pinkish red above, sides of crown dusky (or hardly different from back, a), broad crown stripe pinkish scarlet. Throat and breast scarlet (or bright pinkish red, a, b), abdomen pinkish red (or brownish gray, a), thighs and sides of body brownish gray. Wings brown, remiges edged pinkish red, tail pinkish. ♀: olive brown above, crown feathers basally yellowish. Throat and center of underparts light buff, sides of body olivaceous, under tail coverts buff (or bright orange brown, b).
Tropical zone. The Sierra de Perijá, Zulia (*perijana*). Táchira; the Andes of Mérida and w Lara (*coccinea*). The coastal Cordillera in Anzoátegui and Sucre (*crissalis*, a). E Bolívar on the Río Yuruán (*mesopotamia*, b). [Mexico to n Bolivia, nw Argentina, Paraguay, and se Brazil. Trinidad.]
Rain forest, high second growth, 350–1400 m. n of the Orinoco, 100 m. s of it. Undergrowth, thickets, swampy woods. In pairs or small groups forages noisily and conspicuously in the underbrush and low branches. Joins other forest species.
Note: *H. r. crissalis* replaces *H. rubica rubra* of Lista Av. Venez.

## FULVOUS SHRIKE-TANAGER
*Lanio fulvus*
FRUTERO DENTADO

Pl. 37
6.7″ (17 cm.). Head, wings and tail black. Mantle dull yellow gradually shading to rufous brown on upper tail coverts. Breast patch rufous brown, sides of breast and lower breast dull yellow shading to light rufous brown on under tail coverts. ♀: upperparts olive citrine darkest on crown, shading to reddish brown on lower back and upper tail coverts. Lores and throat pale brownish gray; breast yellowish olive shading to orange buff on belly and under tail coverts. Wings dusky olive; tail dull brown.
Tropical zone. S Táchira; central and s Amazonas; Bolívar from the upper Caura to the upper Río Cuyuni and the Gran Sabana (*fulvus*). [The Guianas, e Colombia to ne Peru and n Amazonian Brazil.]
Rain forest, 350–950 m. n of the Orinoco, 150–1300 m. s of it. Inside forests, forages in the treetops. Joins mixed bands of birds.

[CHARACTERISTIC OF *Tachyphonus* (♂) is black body plumage and often orange or red crest or crown stripe.]

## WHITE-LINED TANAGER
*Tachyphonus rufus*
CHOCOLATERO

Pl. 37
7″ (18 cm.). Shiny blue black; lesser upper wing coverts and under wing coverts snowy white. Lower mandible blue gray. ♀: upperparts, wings and tail rufous brown; orange rufous below.
Tropical zone. Widespread n of the Orinoco, s to n Amazonas, n Bolívar and Delta Amacuro; Margarita I. [Costa Rica to nw Ecuador, se Peru, Paraguay, e and s central Brazil and ne Argentina. Trinidad, Tobago.]
Rain forest, second growth, open woods, scrub, deciduous forest, to 1600 m. n of the Orinoco, to 800 m. s of it. Open fields, suburban areas, plantations. In pairs, actively forages for fruits and insects, usually at low levels. Follows army ants.

## FLAME-CRESTED TANAGER
*Tachyphonus cristatus*
FRUTERO CRESTA ROJIZA

Pl. 37
6.5″ (16.5 cm.). Black; forehead, lateral margins of broad crest buffy yellow, crest orange yellow (or grenadine red, a); rump buff. Narrow throat patch cinnamon buff. The lesser upper wing coverts and under wing coverts white. ♀: upperparts, wings and tail brownish olive (or with forehead, sides of crown and head gray, center of crown rufescent, back dark rufous brown, a). Throat buffy, rest of underparts dull olive ochraceous, becoming ochraceous on under tail coverts.
Tropical zone. Amazonas generally; Bolívar from the upper and lower Río Caura to the upper Río Paragua and Cerro Paurai-tepui in the se (*orinocensis*, a). E Bolívar from Nuria s to the n Gran Sabana (*intercedens*). [E of the Andes to ne Peru; Amazonian and se Brazil and n Bolivia.]
Rain forest, second growth, scrub, open woodland, 100–1400 m. Alone or in pairs, actively forages from middle heights to treetops. Joins mixed flocks in fruiting trees.

## FULVOUS-CRESTED TANAGER
*Tachyphonus surinamus*
FRUTERO CRESTILEONADO

Pl. 37
6.5″ (16.5 cm.) [or 6″ (15 cm.), a]. Glossy blue black; crown patch and rump golden buff; lesser upper wing coverts, under wing coverts and pectoral tufts white; flanks rufous buff. ♀: crown, nape and sides of head dull gray; back wings and tail olive. Below dull, pale grayish, olivaceous on flanks, buffy on under tail coverts (or throat and upper breast light rufescent buff, rest of underparts ochraceous, tinged olive at sides, a).
Tropical zone. N Amazonas s to Cerros Parú and Duida; Bolívar from the Río Cuchivero and the upper Río Caura to the Río Cuyuni and the Gran Sabana; se Sucre and se Monagas s to Delta Amacuro (*surinamus*). S Amazonas from the Yavita-Pimichín Trail s (*brevipes*, a). [The Guianas, e Colombia to e Peru and Amazonian Brazil.]
Rain forest, second growth, to 1400 m.

Open woods, cultivated areas, often near water. Actively forages for fruits and insects near the treetops. Joins mixed flocks in fruiting trees.

## RED-SHOULDERED TANAGER
*Tachyphonus phoenicius*
FRUTERO HOMBROS ROJOS

Pl. 37
6.2″ (15.7 cm.). Glossy black; point of shoulder red; innermost lesser wing coverts and under wing coverts white. ♀: top and sides of head dark brownish gray; the feathers inconspicuously edged pale gray, ocular region blackish. Back, wings and tail dark brownish gray; underparts dull whitish, washed with gray on breast and sides, sides of throat whiter with an ill-marked dusky malar streak. Axillars and under wing coverts white.
Tropical and subtropical zone. Amazonas generally; Bolívar from the upper Río Cuchivero to the Río Paragua and the n Gran Sabana. [The Guianas, e Colombia to Peru and n and central Amazonian Brazil.]
Open rain forest, low second growth, scrub, 100–2000 m. Open terrain with scattered shrubs and low trees. Usually in pairs.

## WHITE-SHOULDERED TANAGER
*Tachyphonus luctuosus*
FRUTERO NEGRO

Pl. 37
5.2″ (13 cm.). Blue black, shoulders extensively white. ♀: crown, nape and sides of head dull gray; back, wings and tail olive citrine. Throat whitish, rest of underparts bright yellow.
Tropical zone. Nw and e Zulia, nw Mérida, nw Táchira (*panamensis*). S Táchira; w Barinas; central Amazonas; Bolívar along the Ríos Cuchivero, Caura and Paragua to the Río Cuyuni and the Sierra de Imataca; n Monagas; s Sucre; Delta Amacuro (*luctuosus*). Extreme n and e Sucre (*flaviventris*). [Honduras to w Ecuador, n Bolivia and Amazonian Brazil. Surinam. Trinidad.]
Rain forest, open woodland, deciduous forest, second growth, scrub, clearings to 900 m. n of the Orinoco, to 1100 m. s of it. In pairs or small groups, actively and noisily forages for fruits and insects

from low to fairly high levels. Joins mixed flocks. Harsh calls.

## RUFOUS-CRESTED TANAGER
*Creurgops verticalis*
FRUTERO CRESTIRUFO

Pl. 36
6.2″ (15.7 cm.). Upperparts, wings and tail dull blue gray, broad coronal streak orange rufous, bordered laterally by blackish. Entire underparts orange rufous. ♀: similar but with plain crown.
Subtropical zone. Sw Táchira along the Río Chiquito. [Colombia to central Peru.]
Cloud forest, 1800 m.

## GRAY-HEADED TANAGER
*Eucometis penicillata*
BACHAQUERO

Pl. 37
7″ (18 cm.). Top and sides of head gray, throat pale gray. Back, wings and tail olive citrine. Underparts bright yellow (with an ochraceous tinge on upper breast, a).
Tropical zone. The Sierra de Perijá, Zulia; Táchira and w Apure to Mérida and w Barinas (*cristata*, a). From Falcón e to Miranda (*affinis*). N Amazonas, along the Orinoco near the mouth of the Río Vichada (*penicillata*). [Mexico to Colombia, n Bolivia, Paraguay and Amazonian Brazil.]
Rain forest, second growth, swampy woodland, to 1200 m. n of the Orinoco, at 100 m. s of it. In pairs or small groups, forages for insects and fruit, often near the ground. Not shy. Follows ant swarms.

## OLIVE-BACKED TANAGER
*Mitrospingus oleagineus*
FRUTERO ACEITUNO

Pl. 37
7.5″ (19 cm.). Forehead, lores, sides of head dark gray, throat somewhat lighter gray. Crown and upperparts yellowish olive green, underparts olive yellow (breast and sides of body darker and more olive, a). Wings and tail dark brownish gray.
Upper tropical and subtropical zones. Bolívar in the Sierra de Lema and Cerros Chimantá-tepui, Sororopán-tepui,

Ptari-tepui and Aprada-tepui (*obscuripectus,* a). The vicinity of Cerro Roraima (*oleagineus*). [Guyana, adjacent Brazil.]
Endemic to Pantepui. Rain and cloud forests on the slopes of the tepuis, 900–1800 m. Often in bands, forages through the forest at mid-level.

## ROSE-BREASTED THRUSH-TANAGER
*Rhodinocichla rosea*
FRUTERO PARAULATA

Pl. 37
8″ (20 cm.). Above dark gray, somewhat tinged olive on crown. Sides of head black; supraloral area extending backward over eye rose red, changing to white behind eye to form a long eyebrow (or with eyebrow only barely indicated, a). Throat, breast, center of belly and under tail coverts bright, rosy, carmine red, sides of belly brownish gray. Wings and tail dusky gray. ♀: differs from ♂ by having the red portions of plumage replaced by ochraceous orange.
Upper tropical zone. The Sierra de Perijá, Zulia (*beebei,* a). The Sierra de San Luis, Falcón; s Lara; the coastal and interior Cordilleras from Yaracuy to the Distr. Federal and Miranda (*rosea*). [W Mexico. Sw Costa Rica to ne Colombia.]
Rain forest, scrub, dense thickets, clearings, 450–1450 m. Usually in pairs, forages for insects on the ground and dense undergrowth. Shy, inconspicuous. Call: melodious.
It is possible that the White-rumped Tanager (*Cypsnagra hirundinacea*) reaches se Venezuela for it has been recorded recently from Surinam.

## HOODED TANAGER
*Nemosia pileata*
FRUTERO DE CORONITA

Pl. 36
5″ (13 cm.). Top and sides of head, sides of neck and breast black. Back, wings and tail all blue gray. Lores and entire underparts white. Iris yellow, bill black, legs yellow. ♀: above blue gray, lores white. Throat and breast pale pinkish buff, rest of underparts white. Iris, lower mandible and legs yellow.
Tropical zone. Zulia in the Maracaibo

region; w Lara, Carabobo; the Distr. Federal; the llanos of e Apure, Guárico, Anzoátegui and w Delta Amacuro; ne Bolívar (*hypoleuca*). [Generally distributed to n Bolivia, Paraguay, s Brazil and ne Argentina.]
Open rain forest, deciduous forest edge, light second growth, gallery forest, near water, to 600 m. n of the Orinoco, to 500 m. s of it. Alluvial areas, plantations. Alone or in pairs, actively forages for insects from undergrowth to treetops, especially on the outer branches and blossoms. Shy. Call: high, sharp, loud "chip."

## GUIRA TANAGER
*Hemithraupis guira*
PINTASILGO BUCHINEGRO

Pl. 36
5″ (13 cm.). Lores, sides of head and neck, ear coverts and throat brownish black, outlined with bright yellow; upper back olive citrine, lower back orange rufous becoming yellow on lower rump. Breast orange ochraceous, center of belly and under tail coverts pale yellow, sides of body olive gray. Wings dusky, coverts and inner remiges like back; tail dark olive. ♀: olive citrine above, brighter and yellower on upper tail coverts. Throat, breast and center of abdomen and under tail coverts yellow, sides of body light gray. Bill yellow, ridge black, legs leaden blue.
Tropical zone. Táchira, Falcón, Cojedes and Barinas e along the n Cordilleras and the llanos to Sucre and Monagas; e Bolívar from the lower Río Paragua to the Altiplanicie de Nuria and the Río Cuyuni (*nigrigula*). S Bolívar from Cerro Ptari-tepui to Roraima and the Brazilian border (*roraimae*). [S Amer. generally to w Ecuador and n Argentina.]
Open rain forest, gallery forest, second growth, suburban areas, scrub, thorny bushes, to 1450 m. Gregarious, in pairs, sometimes in groups of several pairs up to 25, forages for insects from low bushes to treetops. Joins mixed flocks.

## YELLOW-BACKED TANAGER
*Hemithraupis flavicollis*
PINTASILGO BUCHIDORADO

Pl. 36
5″ (13 cm.) [or 4.5″ (11.5 cm.), a]. Top and sides of head, hindneck, mantle,

upper tail coverts, wings and tail dull black. Lower back, rump, throat, sides of neck and under tail coverts bright yellow, rest of underparts dingy white (with a number of blackish bars on upper breast, a). ♀: above olive, below yellow, sides of body olivaceous. Wings dusky, coverts and remiges edged yellowish olive; tail dusky olive. Lower mandible flesh color, legs leaden blue. Best distinguished from Guira Tanager by darker back, yellower underparts, and conspicuous yellowish edges to wing coverts.

Tropical zone to 950 m. Generally s of the Orinoco in Bolívar (except the Río Cuyuni region) and in Amazonas (aurigularis). The Río Cuyuni (hellmayri, a). [Panama, Colombia and generally e of the Andes to n Bolivia, Amazonian and se Brazil.]

Open rain forest, second growth, forest edge, scrub, gallery forest, clearings. Actively forages in the treetops for berries and insects.

## FULVOUS-HEADED TANAGER

*Thlypopsis fulviceps*
FRUTERO CABECILEONADO

Pl. 36

5″ (13 cm.). Top and sides of head chestnut, throat rufous chestnut. Back, wings and tail dark olivaceous gray (or dark gray, a). Breast and sides of body gray, paler than back, center of abdomen and under tail coverts white (or buffy, a). ♀: similar to ♂ but throat whitish.

Upper tropical and subtropical zones. Sierra de Perijá, Zulia (obscuriceps, a). Andes of Mérida (meridensis). N central and ne Cordilleras from Carabobo and n Guárico to Sucre and Monagas (fulviceps). [Ne Colombia.]

Rain and cloud forests, second growth, 800–1900 m. Scrub, open terrain, suburban areas. Thickets, bamboo tangles, lianas. In pairs or small groups forages from undergrowth to medium heights.

## ORANGE-HEADED TANAGER

*Thlypopsis sordida*
FRUTERO DE SOMBRERO

5″ (13 cm.). Top and sides of head cinnamon rufous; ocular region and throat yellow. Breast light buffy gray, center of belly and under tail coverts white,

sides of body light grayish. Back gray with an olive tinge. Wings dusky, the feathers edged gray; tail like back.

Tropical zone. Along the Orinoco in Bolívar and at Soledad, se Anzoátegui (orinocensis). [Se Colombia to n Bolivia.]

Savannas and similar open terrain with scattered bushy vegetation, second growth, plantations to 100 m. Forages in the undergrowth.

## BLACK-CAPPED HEMISPINGUS

*Hemispingus atropileus*
HEMISPINGUS GORRO NEGRO

Pl. 36

6.5″ (16.5 cm.). Crown and sides of head black, long eyebrow from nostril buffy. Back, wings and tail dark olive, underparts lighter, buffy olive green, buffiest on throat and breast, yellowish olive in center of abdomen.

Subtropical and temperate zones. Sw Táchira on the Páramo de Tamá and Río Chiquito (atropileus). [Colombia to nw Ecuador and n Bolivia.]

Cloud and dwarf forests, 2300–3000 m. Forest edge, open woodland, páramos with scattered bushes, clearings.

## GRAY-CAPPED HEMISPINGUS

*Hemispingus reyi*
HEMISPINGUS REY

Pl. 36

6″ (15 cm.). Crown gray; back, wings and tail olive green. Below dull yellow, sides and under tail coverts olive, lighter than back. Upper mandible black, lower mandible dark olive; legs dark flesh color.

Subtropical to temperate zone. The Andes from w Táchira and Mérida to central Trujillo.

Habitat similar to Black-capped Hemispingus, 1900–3200 m.

## SUPERCILIARIED HEMISPINGUS

*Hemispingus superciliaris*
HEMISPINGUS CEJAS AMARILLAS

Pl. 36

5.3″ (13.5 cm.). Upperparts, wings and tail olive green, eyebrow yellow, sides of head blackish. Below yellow tinged olive at sides of breast and belly.

Subtropical and temperate zones. The Andes of Táchira, Mérida and Trujillo (*chrysophrys*). [Colombia to w Ecuador and n Bolivia.]
Habitat similar to that of the Black-capped Hemispingus, 1900–3200 m. Forages very actively in dense vegetation.

## OLEAGINOUS HEMISPINGUS

*Hemispingus frontalis*
HEMISPINGUS OLEAGINOSO

Pl. 36
6″ (15 cm.). Upperparts yellowish olive to olive, eyebrow greenish yellow (or ochraceous orange, a; or buffy white, b). Throat and breast greenish yellow, darker and tinged ochraceous on lower breast and belly, sides more olivaceous (or underparts ochraceous, a; or underparts dull buffy ochraceous, b).
Subtropical zone. The Sierra de Perijá, Zulia (*flavidorsalis*). The Andes of Lara, Trujillo, Mérida and Táchira (*ignobilis, a*). The coastal Cordillera from Aragua to Miranda (*hanieli, b*). In Sucre and Monagas (*iteratus, a*). [Colombia to e and central Peru.]
Cloud forest, 1600–2900 m. Low open forest at the higher altitudes. Alone or in pairs, forages in the underbrush to mid-level of trees.

## BLACK-EARED HEMISPINGUS

*Hemispingus melanotis*
HEMISPINGUS OREJINEGRO

Pl. 36
5.7″ (14.5 cm.). Upperparts gray, brownish gray on rump and upper tail coverts; sides of head black, often with lower eyelid white and occasionally with a white supraloral streak and short eyebrow. Throat, breast and under tail coverts cinnamon, center of abdomen white; sides of body brownish. Wings dusky, feathers edged pale brownish olive; tail grayish brown.
Subtropical zone. Sw Táchira along the Río Chiquito (*melanotis*). [Colombia to w Ecuador and n Bolivia.]
Cloud forest, 1800 m. Clearings, coffee plantations. Feeds on insects.

## SLATY-BACKED HEMISPINGUS

*Hemispingus goeringi*
HEMISPINGUS LOMIPIZARRA

Pl. 36
5.7″ (14.5 cm.). Not unlike Black-eared Hemispingus but much more intensely colored. Crown, nape, sides of neck and head black, long eyebrow and narrow moustacial streak white. Back, wings and tail slaty gray. Entire underparts orange rufous.
Subtropical to temperate zone. Mérida on Páramos La Negra, Escorial and Aricagua; n Táchira on Páramo Zumbador.
Cloud and dwarf forests, 2600–3200 m. Boundary of the upper wooded region of the páramos with scattered trees.

## BLACK-HEADED HEMISPINGUS

*Hemispingus verticalis*
HEMISPINGUS CABECINEGRO

Pl. 36
5.5″ (14 cm.). Head and throat black, broad coronal streak buffy gray. Back, wings and tail dark gray. Below gray, paler than back, center of abdomen white. Imm.: like ad. but throat white.
Temperate zone. Páramo de Tamá, sw Táchira. [Colombia, Ecuador.]
Boundary of dwarf forests with páramos, 3000 m. Open terrain with bushes and scattered trees.

## GRAY-HOODED HEMISPINGUS

*Cnemoscopus rubrirostris*
CNEMOSCOPUS PICO ROJO

Pl. 36
6.5″ (16.5 cm.). Head, extreme upper back, throat and breast gray, palest on throat and breast. Back olive green, lower breast and belly bright yellow, tinged olive at sides of body. Wings dusky, wing coverts and edges of inner remiges olive, primaries edged whitish; tail olive. Bill dark brown.
Subtropical and temperate zones. Páramo de Tamá and Río Chiquito, sw Táchira (*rubrirostris*). [Colombia to central Peru.]
Habitat as in the Black-headed Hemispingus; 2300–3000 m.

## COMMON BUSH-TANAGER
*Chlorospingus ophthalmicus*
CHLOROSPINGUS OJIBLANCO

Pl. 36
5.7″ (14.5 cm.). Crown and sides of head dusky brown to dusky olive, eye ring white. Back, wings and tail olive green. Throat white to buffy spotted with black; breast band greenish yellow shaded with ochraceous; belly grayish white, sides olive green; under tail coverts greenish yellow. Iris white.
Upper tropical and subtropical zones. Sierra de Perijá, Zulia (*ponsi*). Sierra de San Luis, Falcón; Sierra de Aroa, Yaracuy (*falconensis*). W Lara, Trujillo, extreme e Mérida and Carabobo and Miranda (*jacqueti*). Central Lara, w Mérida to s Táchira (*venezuelensis*). [Mexico to nw Argentina.]
Rain, cloud and dwarf forests, 900–3000 m. Inside forest in low dense second growth, clearings. In small bands actively forages for insects and fruits, usually in lower underbrush and thickets but also to the treetops. Joins forest flocks.

## ASHY-THROATED BUSH-TANAGER
*Chlorospingus canigularis*
CHLOROSPINGUS GARGANTIGRÍS

Pl. 36
5.5″ (14 cm.). Top and sides of head dark gray, sometimes indication of white eye ring; throat, lower breast and belly pale gray; broad pectoral band and under tail coverts lemon yellow, sides of body olive. Back and inner remiges olive green; outer remiges and tail dusky brown, edged olive.
Upper tropical and subtropical zones. Cerro El Teteo and Río Chiquito, s Táchira (*canigularis*). [Costa Rica to sw Ecuador and n Peru.]
Rain and cloud forests, second growth, 1250–2000 m., clearings. In pairs or small groups, actively forages from mid-level to treetops.

## WHITE-CAPPED TANAGER
*Sericossypha albocristata*
CUARESMERO

Pl. 38
10″ (25 cm.). Crown and lores snowy white. Throat and upper breast crimson, overlaid with purplish. Body plumage velvety black. Wings and tail glossy blue black. ♀: similar but throat and upper breast dusky purplish.
Subtropical to temperate zone. Páramo de Tamá and Río Chiquito, s Táchira. [Colombia to central Peru.]
Open cloud and dwarf forests, second growth, clearings, 1800–3000 m. One of the largest tanagers. Shy, forages restlessly in small flocks. Called *Pájaro pollo* in Colombia because its call sounds like that of a small chicken.

## MAGPIE TANAGER
*Cissopis leveriana*
MORICHE BLANCO

Pl. 38
11″ (28 cm.). Black and white, with a long tail. Whole head, mantle, throat and breast shiny blue black, the feathers pointed and encroaching raggedly on white of back, and raggedly to a point on white of underparts. Wings and tail black, inner remiges broadly edged white; tail much graduated, the feathers broadly tipped white. Iris yellow.
Tropical and subtropical zones. The Andes of Mérida, Barinas and Táchira, w Apure; Amazonas; Bolívar on the lower Ríos Caura and Paragua and in the se corner (*leveriana*). [Colombia, the Guianas to n Bolivia, Paraguay and Amazonian and se Brazil.]
Rain and cloud forests, second growth, scrub, to 2000 m. n of the Orinoco, 100–950 m. s of it. Clearings, scattered trees, suburban and cultivated areas, near rivers. In pairs or small groups, forages in the middle heights. Call: soft, high whistles.

## BLACK-FACED TANAGER
*Schistochlamys melanopis*
SCHISTSOCHLAMYS CARA NEGRA

Pl. 37
6.5″ (16.5 cm.). Blue gray, paler below, center of belly whitish. Forecrown lores, sides of head and neck, throat and upper breast black. Bill thick, short, curved, blue gray, tip black. Imm.: olive green above, paler olive below, center of belly pale yellow, under tail coverts pale olive with pale yellow tips. Tail much rounded

brownish gray, edged olive. Bill as in ad.

Tropical and lower subtropical zones to 1800 m. Throughout (*aterrima*). [The Guianas, Colombia. E Peru, n Bolivia, Brazil except the west.]

Open woodland, second growth, savannas with scattered bushes, scrub, low open vegetation, cultivated areas. Alone or in pairs forages at low levels for fruits and seeds.

## PLUSH-CAPPED FINCH: Catamblyrhynchidae

CABECIPELUDO

The exact systematic position of this pretty little bird is yet to be determined. Some ornithologists place it with the tanagers, others with the finches; here it is kept as a separate family between the two. The name of the Plush-capped Finch derives from the stiff, erect, plushlike yellow feathers of its forecrown. Its habits are little known. Specimens recently collected in Colombia were found to have eaten small beetles.

**PLUSH-CAPPED FINCH**
*Catamblyrhynchus diadema*
CABECIPELUDO

Pl. 36

5.5" (14 cm.). Forecrown yellow, feathers stiff and plushlike, hindcrown and nape black. Back, wings and tail dark gray. Underparts chestnut. Bill short, thick, stubby, black. Imm.: above uniform grayish olive; below paler washed rufescent, especially on belly.

Subtropical zone. The Sierra de Perijá, Zulia, and the Andes from n Trujillo to ne Táchira (*diadema*). The coastal Cordillera in Aragua and the Distr. Federal (*federalis*). [The mountains of Colombia s in the Andes to w Peru and nw Argentina.]

Cloud forests, 1800–2900 m. Forest edge, clearings, bushes in open areas, bamboo thickets. Alone or in pairs forages for insects in the low vegetation and on the ground. Joins other species.

## CARDINALS, SALTATORS, AMERICAN SPARROWS, SIERRA FINCHES, ETC.: Fringillidae

SEMILLEROS, CANARIOS, CARDENALES

Finches, in the traditional sense, form a very large assemblage of, for the most part, small birds with bills adapted to eating seeds. Most live in rather open country and quite a number are inhabitants of shrubbery and live near the ground. They are found in all types of country from forests, deserts and scrub to snow line. Some species are highly prized as song birds, but many of the South American representatives in the family are sadly lacking in vocal accomplishments. Many species are gregarious except in the mating season, and most are very wary and difficult to approach.

It has been proposed to split this large family in 2: the Fringillidae, represented in the Americas by the siskins (*Carduelis*), and the Emberizidae, containing the rest of the American finches and including the tanagers. The Emberizidae would be split into 4 subfamilies: Emberizinae (buntngs and American sparrows), Catamblyrhynchinae (Plush-capped finch), Cardinalinae (cardinals, grosbeaks, saltators etc.), and Thraupinae (tanagers). As yet there is a certain amount of disagreement about the allocation of certain genera and for this reason the traditional family, Fringillidae, is here maintained. The order followed, however, is much like that proposed by Paynter and Storer in Bds. Wld., *13*, 1970.

## INDIGO BUNTING
*Passerina cyanea*
AZULILLO

5″ (13 cm.). Bright blue, purplish blue on head and breast. Wings and tail black, the feathers edged blue. Bill more or less conical, not particularly thick. ♀: sparrowlike. Above brown, somewhat streaked dusky, below whitish, streaked dusky on breast.
Casual winter visitor. Recorded in December from La Sabana, Sierra de Perijá, Zulia. [Breeds in N Amer. Winters from Mexico to Panama, casually to Colombia. Cuba; Jamaica.]
Forest edge, near grassy savannas, 1000 m.

## BLUE-BLACK GROSBEAK
*Cyanocompsa cyanoides*
PICOGORDO AZUL

Pl. 39
6″ (15 cm.). Dark, slaty blue, blackish on cheeks and throat, shoulders slightly brighter than rest of plumage (or lighter blue; forehead, eyebrow, spot at base of mandible and shoulders pale glossy blue, a). Wings and tail black, edged blue. Bill much thickened, deep at base. ♀: uniform dark reddish brown.
Tropical zone. Nw Zulia, Táchira, w Apure, Barinas and Mérida to the Distr. Federal and Miranda (*cyanoides*). Sucre and Delta Amacuro; generally s of the Orinoco in Bolívar and Amazonas (*rothschildi*, a). [Mexico to w Ecuador, Amazonian Brazil and n Bolivia. Trinidad.]
Rain forest, second growth, plantations, deciduous forest, savannas, near water, to 1400 m. n of the Orinoco, to 1000 m. s of it. Low tangled undergrowth and thickets, forest edge, open woodland. Alone or in pairs, actively forages for berries, fruits and seeds from low dense vegetation to medium heights. Shy. Call: melodious, metallic, whistled chirp.
Note: By some placed in the genus *Passerina*.

## ULTRAMARINE GROSBEAK
*Cyanocompsa cyanea*
PICOGORDO GUARO

Pl. 39
5.5″ (14 cm.). Very like Blue-backed Grosbeak, from which it differs principally by having the rump bright, shiny

blue like eyebrows and shoulders. Bill thick, swollen. ♀: much paler than the Blue-backed Grosbeak; above reddish brown, redder on rump, below light buffy brown.
Tropical and lower subtropical zones. The n Cordilleras from Falcón and s Lara to Sucre and s over the llanos of n Guárico and Monagas (*minor*). [W Colombia. E Brazil and Mato Grosso, n and central Argentina, Paraguay and e Bolivia.]
Open rain and deciduous forest, second growth, 250–1600 m. Scrub, woodland edge, bushes. Alone or in pairs, forages near the ground in undergrowth and thickets and to medium heights.
Note: By some placed in the genus *Passerina*.

## BUFF-THROATED SALTATOR
*Saltator maximus*
PICURERO

Pl. 39
8″ (20 cm.). Upperparts bright olive green. Short eyebrow from nostril white; sides of head, neck and body gray. Chin white, lower throat cinnamon buff, conspicuous moustacial streaks black. Breast gray, tinged buff, center of belly buffy white, under tail coverts cinnamon buff. ♀: similar to ♂ but buff of throat and under tail coverts much paler.
Tropical and subtropical zones. Sierra de Perijá, Zulia to Falcón and Yaracuy and Miranda, s through w Barinas, Mérida and Táchira to w Apure; s of the Orinoco generally in Amazonas, Bolívar and s Delta Amacuro at the mouth of Río Amacuro (*maximus*). [Mid. Amer. to w Ecuador, n Bolivia, Paraguay and s and e Brazil.]
Rain forest, second growth, scrub, to 1650 m. n of the Orinoco, to 1400 m. s of it. Forest edge, thickets, clearings, swampy areas, suburban areas. In pairs or small groups forages for insects, fruits, blossoms, from near the ground to medium heights. Follows ant swarms. Song: rich, varied, and melodious.

## GRAYISH SALTATOR
*Saltator coerulescens*
LECHOSERO AJICERO

Pl. 39
8″ (20 cm.). Upperparts, wings and tail gray (or olive gray, a), short, narrow

eyebrow white. Throat white bordered laterally by wide, black moustacial streaks; breast and sides gray (or olive gray, a) becoming pale buff on belly and under tail coverts.

Tropical zone. Widespread n of the Ríos Orinoco and Meta; s of the Orinoco in nw Amazonas and in n central Bolívar on the lower Río Paragua and e along the Orinoco to Delta Amacuro (*brewsteri*). Se Bolívar on Cerro Roraima (*olivascens*, a). [N Colombia, and e of the Andes to n Argentina and Uruguay. Trinidad.]

Rain forest, second growth, forest edge, to 600 m., rarely to 850 m. n of the Orinoco; to 300 m. s of it. Open, bushy terrain. Clear whistled song.

## ORINOCAN SALTATOR

*Saltator orenocensis*
LECHOSERO PECHIBLANCO

Pl. 39

7″ (18 cm.). Upperparts gray, tail black. A broad, long conspicuous white eyebrow; sides of head and neck black, a white spot at base of mandible. Throat white, rest of underparts buffy white, most markedly on sides and under tail coverts.

Tropical zone. N Zulia, coastal Falcón and w Lara (*rufescens*). From Cojedes s to Apure, thence e through Guárico and Anzoátegui to Sucre, Monagas and Delta Amacuro (*orenocensis*). [Ne Colombia.]

Xerophytic areas, gallery forest, second growth, deciduous forest, to 600 m. n of the Orinoco, to 100 m. s of it. Scattered trees, woodland edge, thorny scrub, cultivated areas. Forages quietly for fruits and blossoms.

## STREAKED SALTATOR

*Saltator albicollis*
LECHOSERO PECHIRRAYADO

Pl. 39

8″ (20 cm.). Upperparts and wings olive green; rump, upper tail coverts and tail gray, eyebrow white, very narrow. Sides of head and sides of throat gray, center of throat white. Below white, heavily streaked with gray on breast and sides of belly. Bill black, tipped yellow.

Tropical and subtropical zones. Zulia s of L. Maracaibo to s Táchira, n through Mérida, and w Barinas to Portuguesa and s Lara, and from Falcón to n Guárico, Sucre and Monagas; Patos I. (*perstriatus*). [Costa Rica to w and ne Peru.]

Open forest, woodland edge, deciduous forest, xerophytic areas, dense dry scrub, open second growth, clearings, cultivated areas, to 2000 m. In pairs or small groups, forages from middle heights to treetops. Shy. Feeds on fruits, seeds, blossoms. Varied, melodious, whistled song.

## RED-AND-BLACK GROSBEAK

*Periporphyrus erythromelas*
PICOGORDO ROJINEGRO

Pl. 39

7.7″ (19.5 cm.). Head, neck, throat and upper breast black; back, wings and tail wine red; underparts and band bordering black on nape and sides of neck bright rosy red. Bill thick, black. ♀: head black as in ♂; back, wings and tail dull olive green; underparts olive yellow, pure yellow in center of belly.

Tropical zone. The Cerro Roraima region, se Bolívar. [The Guianas; ne Brazil.]

Rain forest, second growth, to 1000 m. Alone or in pairs, forages for berries and seeds at medium heights. Penetrating pleasant whistle.

## SLATE-COLORED GROSBEAK

*Pitylus grossus*
PICOGORDO GARGANTIBLANCO

Pl. 39

8″ (20 cm.). Dark gray, forehead, upper breast and sides of neck black; throat white. *Bill thick, crimson.* ♀: like male but without black, these parts being gray like rest of plumage. *Bill crimson.*

Tropical zone. Generally s of the Orinoco in Amazonas and Bolívar (*grossus*). [Nicaragua to w Ecuador, n Bolivia and Amazonian Brazil.]

Rain forests, second growth, to 1300 m. Clearings, low trees, scrub, undergrowth. Alone, in pairs, or small groups forages for insects, usually higher in the forest, lower in the open. Call: varied sequence of pleasant, soft whistles.

## YELLOW-GREEN GROSBEAK
*Caryothraustes canadensis*
PICOGORDO VERDE

Pl. 39
6.5" (16.5 cm.). Olive yellow with a black face. Lores, ocular region and throat black; crown and nape light yellowish olive becoming slightly darker on body, wings and tail. Underparts light olive yellow. ♀: similar to ♂ but crown and nape not yellower than back.
Tropical zone. Generally s of the Orinoco in Amazonas and Bolívar (*canadensis*). [The Guianas, se Colombia, Amazonian and e Brazil.]
Rain forests, second growth, to 1000 m. Clearings, suburban and cultivated areas, shrubs. In pairs or small noisy bands forages for insects and vegetable matter from medium heights to treetops. Joins forest flocks on fruiting trees.

## VERMILION CARDINAL
*Cardinalis phoenicius*
CARDENAL CORIANO

Pl. 39
7.5" (19 cm.). Bright rosy vermilion including long crest, darker on mantle, wings and tail. Chin black. Bill pale bluish flesh. ♀: crest vermilion; sides of head, back and wings light grayish brown; tail rosy red. Chin black, underparts cinnamon buff.
Tropical zone. The arid Caribbean littoral from the Goajira Pen., Zulia, to Carúpano, Sucre; Margarita I. [The e base of the Santa Marta Mts. and the Goajira Pen., Colombia.]
Xerophytic areas, thorny scrub, cactus thickets, to 150 m., usually in pairs.
Note: Called *Richmondena phoenicea* in Lista Av. Venez.

## ROSE-BREASTED GROSBEAK
*Pheucticus ludovicianus*
PICOGORDO DEGOLLADO

Pl. 39
7" (18 cm.). Head, neck, mantle, throat black, upper breast rosy red, encroaching in a point over white underparts. Lower back and rump white. Wings black, median wing coverts and basal part of remiges white. Tail black, outer 3 pairs of feathers with a large white patch on distal part of inner web. Axillars and under wing coverts rose red. ♀: crown blackish brown with a white coronal stripe, eyebrow white. Back reddish brown streaked black; below buffy, streaked heavily with blackish brown. Wings and tail dark brown, wing coverts and inner remiges tipped white. Axillars and under wing coverts yellowish buff to orange buff. ♂ imm. resembles ♀ but has rose-colored axillars and under wing coverts. Winter ♂ ad. rather like ♀ but throat and upper breast dull rose, axillars and under wing coverts rose red.
Tropical and subtropical zones. Winter resident, Oct.–Apr. Nw Venezuela e to Yaracuy and Aragua; Amazonas near Cerro Duida. [Breeds in N Amer. Winters from the Gulf States to e Ecuador and central Peru.]
Open rain and cloud forests, second growth, 600–2000 m., rarely below 1000 m. Cultivated lands, brush. Near streams. Forages for fruits and insects from medium heights to treetops.

## BLACK-BACKED GROSBEAK
*Pheucticus aureoventris*
PICOGORDO PECHINEGRO

Pl. 39
8" (20 cm.). Head, throat, breast, back, wings and tail mainly black, lower breast and belly bright yellow. Shoulders yellow, median and greater wing coverts and base of remiges white; rump yellow; outer 4 pairs of tail feathers broadly tipped white. ♀: above blackish, feathers of crown basally yellow, those of back narrowly edged yellowish buff. Wings and tail dark brown; wing coverts tipped white forming 2 bars; outermost tail feather with a large white tip, next with only a little white. Below yellow spotted black on throat and breast.
Subtropical zone. The Andes of central Mérida (*meridensis*). [Colombia to n Argentina.]
Cloud forest, 2500 m. Forages in pairs or small groups, often in corn fields and orchards.

## YELLOW GROSBEAK
*Pheucticus chrysopeplus*
PICOGORDO AMARILLO

Pl. 39
8" (20 cm.). Head and underparts bright yellow, under tail coverts white. Mantle

black, streaked yellow, lower back and rump yellow, bases of the feathers black showing through, center upper tail coverts black, lateral ones broadly tipped white. Wings black, median and greater coverts and tips to inner remiges yellowish white, base of primaries white, distal part of outer primaries narrowly edged white. ♀: upperparts streaked blackish and yellow, eyebrow and sides of head yellowish white, underparts yellow, under tail coverts white. Wings brown, marked as in ♂; tail brown, narrowly tipped white.

Upper tropical and subtropical zones. The Sierra de Perijá, Zulia; e Lara n to Aragua and e along the coastal Cordilleras to Sucre and Monagas (*laubmanni*). [W Mexico, Mid. Amer. to the Andes of s Peru.]

Rain and cloud forest, but seldom inside it, 950–2000 m. Usually forest edge, low open second growth, cultivated areas. Alone or in pairs, forages from low to upper heights. Song: pleasant, melodious, thrushlike.

## DICKCISSEL
*Spiza americana*
ARROCERO AMERICANO

Pl. 40
6.5″ (16.5 cm.). Crown, nape and sides of head gray, supraloral spot, spot at base of mandible and eyebrow yellow, the latter becoming white posteriorly. Mantle streaked sandy and black, lower back and rump plain grayish brown; shoulders and outer web of wing coverts chestnut, wings and tail dark brown, the feathers edged grayish. Chin and sides of neck white; throat black, black continuing in a point over breast, sides of breast yellow, rest of underparts whitish. ♀: above much like ♂ but browner, eyebrow yellow, wings and tail as in ♂. Below whitish, tinged yellowish on breast, with a few narrow shaft streaks.

Tropical zone. Winter visitor, Nov.–June. N of the Orinoco generally; n Amazonas; n Bolívar. [Breeds in N Amer. Winters from Mexico to Colombia, the Guianas and n Brazil. Aruba. Trinidad.]

Forest clearings, forest edge, llanos, open country, rice fields, and other cultivated areas, to 600 m. n of the Orinoco, at about 100 m. s of it. In small groups and in very large flocks feeds on rice and other seeds on its arrival in Venezuela, eventually dispersing or proceeding further s. In Rancho Grande, Aragua, in Oct., more than 1000 have been seen crossing the divide in 1 hr.

## RED-CAPPED CARDINAL
*Paroaria gularis*
CARDENAL BANDERA ALEMANA

Pl. 39
7″ (18 cm.). Head and upper throat crimson, lower throat black (or crown and nape crimson, sides of head black, throat entirely crimson, a). Back, wings and tail glossy black. Underparts white, the black or crimson of the lower throat encroaching in a point on the breast.

Tropical zone. From Apure and Barinas across the central and e llanos to Anzoátegui and Delta Amacuro; n Bolívar on the lower Río Caura and the Río Cuyuni (*nigrogenis*, a). Amazonas s of the Río Ventuari; s Bolívar along the upper Río Paragua (*gularis*). [The Guianas, e Colombia; n Bolivia; Amazonian Brazil. Trinidad.]

Open forest, gallery forest, second growth, marshy scrub, near water, to 300 m. In pairs or small groups, llanos and cultivated areas.

Note: Called *Coccopsis gularis* in Lista Av. Venez.

## PILEATED FINCH
*Coryphospingus pileatus*
GRANERO CABECITA DE FÓSFORO

Pl. 40
5″ (14 cm.). Crown stripe silky scarlet, sides of crown and forehead black, sides of head gray. Throat and center of belly and under tail coverts white; breast and sides of body pale gray. Back gray. Wings brown, feathers edged gray; tail black. ♀: upperparts wings and tail brownish gray, browner on crown, lores whitish. Throat, belly and under tail coverts white, breast gray, pale-streaked.

Tropical zone. From n Zulia, Falcón and n Lara e to Sucre and across the llanos of Portuguesa, Cojedes, Guárico and Anzoátegui to n Bolívar; Margarita I. (*brevicaudus*). [Ne Colombia. E Brazil from Ceará to Rio de Janeiro.]

Deciduous open woodland, gallery forest, arid second growth, to 750 m. n of the Orinoco, to 100 m. s of it. Thorny, dry scrub, clearings, isolated small trees, xerophytic areas. In pairs or small groups, forages in the thickets and on the ground.

## STRIPE-HEADED BRUSH-FINCH
*Atlapetes torquatus*
CORBATICO

Pl. 39

7" (18 cm.). Crown, nape and sides of head black, crown stripe gray, long eyebrow gray (or eyebrow white, a). Back and wings olive, tail blackish to dusky brown. Below white, pectoral band black; sides of breast gray, flanks and under tail coverts olive gray to olive brown.

Upper tropical to lower subtropical zone. Sierra de Perijá, Zulia (*perijanus*). Táchira, Mérida and w Lara (*larensis*). The coastal Cordillera from Aragua to Miranda and the interior Cordillera in Miranda (*phaeopleurus,* a). The coastal Cordillera in Anzoátegui, Sucre and in n Monagas (*phygas,* a). [Ne and w Colombia to w Peru and nw Argentina.]

Rain and cloud forest, second growth, 900–1800 m. Forest edge, thickets. In pairs or in small groups, shy and inconspicuous, forages in the tangled undergrowth, and in the leaf litter on the ground.

## CHESTNUT-CAPPED BRUSH-FINCH
*Atlapetes brunneinucha*
ATLAPETES GARGANTILLO

Pl. 39

7" (18 cm.). Forehead black, with 3 white spots; crown and nape chestnut, bordered laterally with buff. Back dark olive, wings and tail dusky olive. Sides of head and neck and pectoral band black (or without pectoral band, a). Below white, sides of breast gray; flanks, crissum and under tail coverts dark olive.

Upper tropical to temperate zone. The Sierra de Perijá, Zulia; the Andes of Táchira, Mérida and Trujillo to s Lara; the coastal Cordillera from Carabobo to Miranda (*frontalis*). Sierra de San Luis, Falcón; Sierra de Aroa, Yaracuy (*allinornatus,* a). [Mexico to w Ecuador and e Peru.]

Rain and cloud forests, second growth, 1000–3100 m. Plantations, clearings,

forest edge, thickets. Habits similar to Striped-headed Brush-Finch.

Note: *A. b. xanthogenys* is not regarded as separable from *A. b. frontalis.*

## TEPUI BRUSH-FINCH
*Atlapetes personatus*
ATLAPETES MONTAÑERO

Pl. 39

6.7" (17 cm.). Top and sides of head and the chin chestnut (or chin and throat chestnut, a; or chin, throat and breast chestnut, b); rest of underparts yellow, dark olivaceous gray on sides and under tail coverts. Back dark gray to black; wings and tail dusky.

Upper tropical and subtropical zones. Amazonas; on Cerros Yaví, Camani, Guanay and Paraque (*paraquensis,* a). On Cerro Parú (*parui,* b); on Cerro de la Neblina (*jugularis,* b). On Cerro Duida, Amazonas and Cerro Guaiquinima, Bolívar (*duidae,* b). Bolívar on Cerro Auyan-tepui (*collaris*), on Cerros Ptari-tepui, Aprada-tepui, Chimantá-tepui, Acopán-tepui and Roraima (*personatus*). [Cerro de la Neblina, Brazil.]

Endemic to Pantepui, 1000–2500 m. Cloud forests, low open woodland, clearings, forages in the lower parts of shrubs and bushes alone or in pairs.

## OCHRE-BREASTED BRUSH-FINCH
*Atlapetes semirufus*
ATLAPETES AJICERO

Pl. 39

6.5" (16.5 cm.). Head, throat and breast cinnamon rufous to orange rufous (with white chin and center of throat, a). Back, wings and tail olive green (or dark greenish gray, b). Center of belly yellow, sides of body olive.

Upper tropical and subtropical zones. N Táchira at Seboruco (*albigula,* a). S Táchira and Trujillo (*zimmeri,* b). The Sierra de San Luis, Falcón; Lara; n Trujillo (*benedetti*). The mountains from Yaracuy through Carabobo and n Guárico to Sucre and Monagas (*denisei*). [E Colombia.]

Habits much as Stripe-headed Brush-Finch; 600–2700 m.

## SLATY BRUSH-FINCH
*Atlapetes schistaceus*
ATLAPETES SOMBRERO DE PELO

Pl. 39
6.5″ (16.5 cm.). Crown and nape chestnut; sides of head black, moustacial streak white edged black below, supra loral spot white (or without white spot, a). Lower parts gray, paler on throat. Back, wings and tail dark gray to black.
Subtropical to páramo zone. Sierra de Perijá, Zulia (*fumidus*). The Andes of ne Táchira, Mérida and Trujillo (*castaneifrons*). Sw Táchira (*tamae*, a). [Colombia to se Peru.]
Forest edge, cloud and dwarf forests, páramos, 2000–3800 m. Forages in undergrowth and in low bushes and shrubs in open damp terrain.

## MOUSTACHED BRUSH-FINCH
*Atlapetes albofrenatus*
ATLAPETES DE FRENO BLANCO

Pl. 39
6″ (16.5 cm.). Crown and nape cinnamon rufous, sides of head black, moustacial streak white. Below yellow, sides and under tail coverts olivaceous. Back, wings and tail olive.
Subtropical zone. E Táchira to central Mérida (*meridae*). [Ne Colombia.]
Cloud forest, 2100–2500 m.

## RUFOUS-NAPED BRUSH-FINCH
*Atlapetes rufinucha*
ATLAPETES FRENTINEGRO

6.5″ (16.5 cm.). Forehead and sides of head black. Crown and nape light cinnamon rufous, sides of head, malar streak and chin black, underparts yellow. Back, wings and tail dark gray with an olivaceous wash on upper back.
Upper tropical and subtropical zones. The Sierra de Perijá, Zulia (*phelpsi*). [Colombia to nw Peru and n Bolivia.]
Cloud forest, forest edge, second growth, 1100–2200 m. Forages in the lower parts of bushes and shrubs.
Note: *A. r. phelpsi* replaces *nigrifrons* of Lista Av. Venez.

## PALE-NAPED BRUSH-FINCH
*Atlapetes pallidinucha*
ATLAPETES NUCA PÁLIDA

Pl. 39
7″ (18 cm.). Forecrown cinnamon, hindcrown and center of nape dull buffy white, sides of head, nape and neck black. Back dark gray, wings and tail blackish. Below dull yellow, ill-marked moustacial streak dusky, sides and under tail coverts dull grayish olive.
Temperate zone. Páramo de Tamá, sw Táchira (*pallidinucha*). [Colombia, e and w Ecuador.]
Dwarf forest, humid forest edge, 2450–3300 m. Second growth, clearings, shrubs, bushes.

## BLACK-STRIPED SPARROW
*Arremonops conirostris*
CURTÍO

Pl. 39
6.5″ (16 cm.). Top and sides of head gray, stripes at sides of crown and through eye black; back, wings and tail olive green (or brownish olive; a). Below mostly white, shaded gray on breast and sides (or dark gray on breast and sides, a). Bend of wing yellow.
Tropical zone. Sierra de Perijá, Zulia; n Táchira; n Mérida (*umbrinus*, a). The n mountains from Falcón and w Lara to Sucre; the e slope of the Andes in Barinas e across the llanos from extreme s Táchira and w Apure to Monagas; n Bolívar from Caicara and the Río Cuchivero to the lower Río Paragua (*conirostris*). [Honduras to Colombia. N Brazil in Roraima.]
Rain forests, second growth, xerophytic areas, llanos, to 1300 m. n of the Orinoco, to 300 m. s of it. Clearings, scrub, open fields with scattered trees. In pairs or family groups, actively forages low in thick underbrush and on the ground. Call: a series of accelerated clear notes.

## TOCUYO SPARROW
*Arremonops tocuyensis*
CURTÍO DEL TOCUYO

Pl. 39
5″ (13 cm.). Very like Black-striped Sparrow but much smaller; eyebrow whitish instead of gray; back paler and grayish olive.

Tropical zone to 1100 m. The Goajira Pen., Zulia, e to the Paraguaná Pen. and e Falcón; se Lara. [Adj. Colombia.] Xerophytic areas, low open deciduous woodland, brambles, bushes.

## GOLDEN-WINGED SPARROW
*Arremon schlegeli*
MAIZCUBA

Pl. 39
6″ (15 cm.). Top and sides of head, chin, sides of neck and breast black. Upper mantle gray, rest of back olive. Shoulders yellow, wings and tail dark gray. Throat and underparts white, flanks gray. Bill orange yellow. ♀: similar to ♂ but white of underparts slightly tinged buff, flanks brownish gray. Bill pale lemon yellow.
Upper tropical zone. The Sierra de Perijá, Zulia; s Carabobo; Aragua and the Distr. Federal (*schlegeli*). [Ne Colombia.]
Deciduous forest, forest edge, semi-arid woodland, scrub, thickets, 450–1400 m. Alone or in pairs hops in the bushes and on the ground. Forages to medium heights.

## PECTORAL SPARROW
*Arremon taciturnus*
TICO-TICO

Pl. 39
5.7″ (14.5 cm.). Generally like the Golden-winged Sparrow but at once distinguishable by the striped head. Top and sides of head and chin black, central coronal streak gray, long eyebrow white. Sides of neck and breast black (with a black band across breast, a). Throat and rest of underparts white. Nuchal collar gray, back bright olive green. Wings grayish brown to olive brown, shoulders extensively bright yellow. Tail grayish olive. Maxilla black, mandible yellow (or bill all black, a). ♀: differs from ♂ by having the central coronal streak buffy gray, the underparts pinkish buff (with an ill-marked grayish pectoral band, a). Bill as in respective ♂.
Tropical and lower subtropical zones. Táchira and Apure n through Barinas to ne Portuguesa (*axillaris*). Generally in Amazonas and Bolívar (*taciturnus,* a). [E Colombia, the Guianas, Amazonian and ne Brazil. Se Peru, n Bolivia, Argentina.]

Rain and cloud forests, second growth, to 1000 m. n of the Orinoco, to 1500 m. on the slopes of the tepuis. Actively and inconspicuously, alone or in pairs, forages in the thick undergrowth and from the ground to middle heights of trees. Feeds on insects, fruits and seeds. Call: the only note seems to be a shrill "pssss."

## SOOTY GRASSQUIT
*Tiaris fuliginosa*
TORDILLO AHUMADO

Pl. 40
4.5″ (11.5 cm.). Sooty black with a slight olive wash above; crown, sides of head, throat and breast brownish black, sooty gray on belly and sides. ♀: upperparts, wings and tail olivaceous brown; below grayish brown, whitish in center of abdomen.
Upper tropical and subtropical zones. Sierra de Perijá, Zulia (*zuliae*). Sierra de Carabobo, Carabobo; Distr. Federal (Galipán); e Sucre; Cerro Roraima, se Bolívar (*fumosa*). [Guyana. Upper Magdalena and Patía valleys, Colombia. E Brazil from Pernambuco to São Paulo and Mato Grosso. Trinidad.]
Rain and cloud forests, second growth, deciduous forest, 800–1700 m. Open fields, scrub, rice and corn fields. Forages in pairs or small groups in shrubbery. Feeds on grass and weed seeds.

## BLACK-FACED GRASSQUIT
*Tiaris bicolor*
TORDILLO COMÚN

Pl. 40
4″ (10 cm.). Much like Sooty Grassquit but smaller, back paler and more olive, underparts blacker. ♀: much like ♀ Sooty but smaller.
Tropical zone. The Caribbean coast from the Goajira Pen., Zulia, to Sucre; Mérida; w Lara; the llanos of Portuguesa; Margarita, Coche and Cubagua Is. (*omissa*). La Blanquilla and Los Hermanos Is. (*johnstonei*). La Tortuga I. (*tortugensis*). [Ne and central Colombia. Islands of the Caribbean. Trinidad, Tobago.]
Xerophytic areas, open grassy terrain, rice fields, low thorny scrub, low second growth, trees and scrub near the sea coast, suburban areas, mostly at sea level but to 850 m. in the interior. Restless,

shy, gregarious, in pairs or small flocks forages for seeds and occasionally fruits on or near the ground.

## YELLOW-FACED GRASSQUIT
*Tiaris olivacea*
TORDILLO YERBERO

Pl. 40

4" (10 cm.). Forecrown black, eyebrow and upper throat yellow. Back, lower belly, wings and tail dull grayish olive. Sides of head and neck, lower throat, breast and upper belly black. ♀: nondescript, dull grayish brown, center of belly whitish.
Tropical and subtropical zones. W Táchira to sw Mérida (*pusilla*). [Mid. Amer. to w Colombia. Greater Antilles. Cayman Is.]
Rain and cloud forest edge, semi-open grassy fields with scattered trees and bushes, cultivated and suburban areas, 500–2300 m. Usually alone, forages in low trees shrubbery and for small seeds on the ground.

## PARAMO SEEDEATER
*Catamenia homochroa*
SEMILLERO PARAMERO

Pl. 40

5.5" (14 cm.). Uniform gray (or tinged brown below, a); under tail coverts chestnut. Bill yellow. ♀: above earthy brown, streaked dusky, wings and tail dusky brown. Throat, breast and sides of head ashy brown; belly browner, obscurely streaked dusky; under tail coverts chestnut. Bill yellow.
Subtropical and páramo zones. Sierra de Perijá, Zulia; Mérida on Páramos San Antonio and Nevados (*homochroa*). The cerros of Amazonas from Camani to la Neblina; the tepuis of Bolívar (*duncani*, a). [Immediately adj. Brazil. Colombia to Bolivia.]
Open terrain and scattered low trees and shrubs, 2600–3500 m. n of the Orinoco; 1600–2450 m. on the tepuis. Only found on the open summits, usually in thick cover.

## PLAIN-COLORED SEEDEATER
*Catamenia inornata*
SEMILLERO DESAIRADO

Pl. 40

5.5" (14 cm.). Much like Páramo Seedeater but back streaked black; below

paler gray. Bill brownish flesh. ♀: generally paler than Páramo with underparts much lighter and grayer, without streaks.
Temperate and páramo zones. Páramos de Mucuchíes and San Antonio, Mérida (*mucuchiesi*). Páramo de Tamá, sw Táchira (*minor*). [Central Andes, Colombia to n Bolivia.]
Dwarf forest, páramos, 3250–4200 m. Forages on the ground and in shrubs. Call: pleasant whistle.

## WHITE-NAPED SEED-EATER
*Dolospingus fringilloides*
SEMILLERO NUCA BLANCA

Pl. 40

5" (13 cm.). Head, throat, upperparts, blue black, a white spot on nape and rump, shoulders and wing speculum white. Lower throat, line behind ear coverts and rest of underparts white. Wings and tail brownish black. Bill horn color, thick at base, conical, sharply pointed. ♀: cinnamon brown; throat, center of breast and abdomen white, tinged rufescent. Looks like a *Sporophila* but bill differently shaped.
Tropical zone. Amazonas in the region of Cerros Yapacana and Duida. [N Brazil along the upper Rio Negro.]
Rain forest, 200 m.; forest edge in savannas.

## LESSER SEED-FINCH
*Oryzoborus angolensis*
SEMILLERO VIENTRICASTAÑO

Pl. 40

5" (13 cm.). Head, upperparts, throat, breast, wings and tail, under tail coverts black; belly chestnut. Under wing coverts white. Bill thick, black. ♀: upper parts and wings brown, tail dark brown. Throat and breast reddish brown, shading into cinnamon brown of belly. Under wing coverts white.
Tropical zone throughout (*torridus*). [Mid. Amer. to w Ecuador, Argentina and se Brazil.]
Forest edge, open vegetation near forest, second growth, gallery forest, to 1200 m. n of the Orinoco, to 1400 m. on the slopes of the tepuis. Low open woodland, clearings with low bushes and shrubs. Alone or in pairs, forages at medium heights. Feeds on vegetable

matter. Call: loud, clear, varied, pleasant.

## LARGE-BILLED SEED-FINCH
*Oryzoborus crassirostris*
SEMILLERO PICÓN

Pl. 40
5.5" (14 cm.). Black; wing speculum and under wing coverts white. Bill very thick, pale leaden blue to bluish white, smooth and shiny. ♀: brown above, buffy brown below, under wing coverts white. Sometimes some white at extreme base of tail (not visible in the field).
Tropical zone. Zulia s of L. Maracaibo; central Táchira; central Mérida; e Trujillo; Carabobo; Aragua; Amazonas; nw Bolívar from Caicara e to Delta Amacuro. [The Guianas, n Colombia. Ne Peru, Brazil n of the Amazon. Trinidad.]
Rain forest, second growth, clearings, cultivated areas, savannas with scattered tangled vegetation, to 500 m. n of the Orinoco, to 200 m. s of it. Near marshes. Alone or in pairs forages for grains and seeds in low bushes and thickets. Call: pleasant, bubbling whistles.

## GREATER LARGE-BILLED SEED FINCH
*Oryzoborus maximiliani*
SEMILLERO PICÓN GRANDE

6" (15 cm.). Indistinguishable in the field from Large-billed Seed-Finch. Differs by longer tail and larger, more massive bill, which is bonelike in texture, not smooth and shiny. ♀: differs from ♀ Large-billed Seed-Finch by size and bill texture.
Tropical zone. Nw Bolívar from the lower Río Caura e to Delta Amacuro (*magnirostris*). [Nicaragua to w Panama. Sw and se Colombia. Guyana. French Guiana. Central and e Brazil. Ne Peru. N Bolivia.]
At or very near sea level. Habits similar to Large-billed Seed-Finch.
Note: *O. m. magnirostris* is listed as a race of *crassirostris* in Lista Av. Venez.

[SEEDEATERS FORM A GROUP OF very small birds with rather thick, grosbeak-like bills, usually inhabiting shrubby areas, savanna, forest edge and sometimes swampy land. Males are easily distinguishable; females are very hard to tell apart, but as seedeaters are gregarious and females accompany the males, the difficulty in identification is often overcome. All have more or less similar songs.]

## SLATE-COLORED SEEDEATER
*Sporophila schistacea*
ESPIGUERO APIZARRADO

Pl. 40
4.5" (11.5 cm.). Slaty gray, patch at sides of neck, center of breast and belly and wing speculum white. Bill yellowish flesh color; nails pale-colored. Upper mandible noticeably shallow. ♀: upperparts, wings and tail olive brown. Throat, upper breast and sides of body, pale olive brown, rest of underparts white. Bill dusky, nails pale, instead of black as in Gray Seedeater.
Tropical zone. N Mérida (Sta. Elena); nw and se Bolívar, Delta Amacuro (*longipennis*). [Sw Mexico. Sw Costa Rica; Panama; e and w Colombia, the Guianas; n Brazil. N Bolivia.]
Rain forest and forest edge, second growth, open woodland, open country at, or very near, sea level n of the Orinoco, 300–1000 m. s of it. Cultivated areas, clearings. In pairs or small bands forages for seeds low in the thick tangled undergrowth. Pleasant, long, varied, warbling song.

## GRAY SEEDEATER
*Sporophila intermedia*
ESPIGUERO PICO DE PLATA

Pl. 40
4.5" (11.5 cm.). Very like Slate-colored Seedeater but paler gray. Upper mandible not noticeably shallow, reddish flesh color, nails black. ♀: like ♀ Slate-colored Seedeater but paler and more reddish above; sides of head and neck, throat and breast cinnamon buff. Center of belly whitish. Nails black, instead of pale as in Slate-colored Seedeater.
Tropical zone. Generally s to Apure, n Amazonas, n Bolívar and Delta Amacuro (*intermedia*). [Guyana, Colombia. Trinidad.]
Forest edge, second growth, gallery forest, xerophytic areas, deciduous forest, to 1200 m. n of the Orinoco, to 300 m. s of it. Rice fields and other cultivated

areas, savannas, pastures. Alone or in pairs, seldom in bands, forages for seeds in the lower vegetation.

## PLUMBEOUS SEEDEATER
*Sporophila plumbea*
ESPIGUERO PLOMIZO

Pl. 40
4.2″ (10.6 cm.). Gray above. Wings and tail brownish black, the feathers edged gray; wing speculum white. Chin and moustacial streaks white, throat, breast and sides pale gray, belly white. Bill black. ♀: olivaceous brown above, wings and tail dark brown; below pale buffy brown, buffy white in center of abdomen. Bill horn brown.
Tropical zone. Sierra de Perijá, Zulia; se Carabobo (El Trompillo); Apure along the Río Meta; generally s of the Orinoco in Amazonas and Bolívar (*whiteleyana*). [Ne Colombia; the Guianas; e and s Brazil; Bolivia, Paraguay, ne Argentina.]
Grassy savannas and open fields, to 1100 m. n of the Orinoco, to 1400 m. on the slopes of the tepuis. Gallery forest, llanos, usually in pairs, forages for seeds in the long grass.

## VARIABLE SEEDEATER
*Sporophila americana*
ESPIGUERO VARIABLE

4.5″ (11.5 cm.). Mainly black above, white below. Top and sides of head, back, wings and tail black; rump gray; double wing bar and wing speculum white. Throat, line to behind ear coverts, center of breast and belly white, sides of breast black, sides of body pale gray. ♀: upperparts, wings and tail olivaceous brown; underparts buffy brown, buffier on belly.
Tropical zone. N Sucre (Tunapui); se Monagas (Caño Corozal); n and e Delta Amacuro (*americana*). [Mid. Amer. to w Peru, the Guianas and Amazonian Brazil; Chacachacare I.; Tobago.]
Forest edge and open second growth near mangrove swamps at sea level. Alone or in small groups forages for small seeds at medium heights. Call: like Slate-colored Seedeater.

## LINED SEEDEATER
*Sporophila lineola*
ESPIGUERO BIGOTUDO

Pl. 40
4.2″ (10.7 cm.). Mostly black above, white below. Broad white coronal stripe (rarely absent, occasionally only indicated by a few white spots); band across rump and conspicuous wing speculum white. Throat and sides of neck black, throat bordered by broad, white moustacial streaks, rest of underparts white. ♀: above olive brown; throat and breast buff rather sharply demarcated from white belly.
Tropical zone. Generally distributed n of the Ríos Meta and Orinoco; Delta Amacuro; s of the Orinoco in Amazonas and n Bolívar (*lineola*). [Colombia and the Guianas to n Argentina. Trinidad, Tobago.]
Open woodland, second growth, to 900 m. n of the Orinoco, to 500 m. s of it. Mangroves, gallery forest, savannas with scattered trees and scrub, xerophytic areas, deciduous forest edge. Usually in pairs, forages for seeds in low trees, bushes and grassy fields.
Note: The bird recorded in Lista Av. Venez. as *S. bouvronides* is today regarded as a race of *S. lineola,* confined to Trinidad and Tobago, where the white crown stripe is absent, sometimes only indicated by a few white dots.

## BLACK-AND-WHITE SEEDEATER
*Sporophila luctuosa*
ESPIGUERO NEGRIBLANCO

Pl. 40
4.5″ (11.5 cm.). Upperparts, throat, breast, sides of body, wings and tail lustrous black; base of primaries white on both webs forming a conspicuous wing speculum; belly white. Bill leaden blue. ♀: olive brown above, buffy below.
Usually subtropical, occasionally upper tropical and temperate zones. The Andes of Lara, Mérida and Trujillo; w Apure. [Colombia to w Peru and n Bolivia.]
Cloud and dwarf forest, second growth, usually 900–3100 m. although uncommon at the two extremes; recorded once at 240 m. at La Victoria, Apure. Clearings, wheat fields, suburban areas, grasslands, low brambles. In pairs or small flocks, forages for grass and other seeds.

## YELLOW-BELLIED SEEDEATER
*Sporophila nigricollis*
Espiguero Vientriamarillo

Pl. 40

4.5″ (11.5 cm.). Crown, lores, sides of head, throat and upper breast black; back olive; lower breast and belly pale yellow, sometimes almost white. Wings and tail brown, sometimes wing coverts with pale tips and occasionally a small white speculum present. ♀: like ♀ Black-and-white Seedeater.

Tropical and subtropical zones. N and s of the Ríos Meta and Orinoco (not recorded in s Amazonas); Patos I. (*nigricollis*). [Costa Rica to w Peru, Bolivia and Argentina. Surinam. Trinidad, Tobago.]

Open vegetation, rice, corn and wheat fields. Rain and cloud forest edge, second growth, clearings, grasslands, to 2500 m. n of the Orinoco, to 1400 m. s of it. Deciduous woodland, gallery forest, savannas, xerophytic areas. In pairs or small groups, forages for seeds in the foliage at middle heights, in low open scrub and in grasses.

## DULL-COLORED SEEDEATER
*Sporophila obscura*
Espiguero Pardo

Pl. 40

4.5″ (11.5 cm.). Sexes similar. More or less uniform dull reddish brown, somewhat paler below, especially on center of belly. Upper mandible dusky horn color, lower mandible yellowish flesh color. The bill is straighter, and less thick than in other species. ♀: mandible yellowish flesh only at base. This species somewhat resembles a *Tiaris*.

Upper tropical and subtropical zones. The mountains of Táchira, Mérida and Miranda (*haplochroma*). [Colombia to sw Peru, Bolivia and nw Argentina.]

Forest edge, cultivated areas, clearings, open vegetation, scrub, 900–1300 m. Forages in pairs or small groups from quite low to medium heights.

## RUDDY-BREASTED SEEDEATER
*Sporophila minuta*
Espiguero Canelillo

Pl. 40

4″ (10 cm.). Above brownish gray with an olive cast, rump and entire underparts

rufous chestnut. Wings and tail blackish, wing coverts and inner remiges pale-edged, wing speculum white. ♀: dull reddish brown above, buffy below. Wings and tail dusky brown, wing coverts and inner remiges conspicuously pale-tipped. ♂: breed while still in imm. plumage, similar to that of ♀, except for a white wing speculum.

Tropical and lower subtropical zones. Generally distributed n of the Ríos Meta and Orinoco; Amazonas s to the Río Ventuari; nw and e Bolívar; Los Frailes Is. (*minuta*). [Mid. Amer. to Colombia and the Guianas, n and se Brazil and nw Ecuador. Trinidad, Tobago.]

Rain and cloud forest edge, gallery forest, grassy, swampy areas, clearings, open terrain, to 1600 m. In pairs or groups up to 30, actively forages for grass and weed seeds near the ground.

## CHESTNUT-BELLIED SEEDEATER
*Sporophila castaneiventris*
Espiguero Vientricastaño

Pl. 40

4″ (10 cm.). Mainly blue gray, center of underparts from throat to under tail coverts chestnut. Wings and tail black, the feathers edged gray. ♀: olive brown above; buffy below.

Tropical zone. Sw Amazonas along the Río Negro. [The Guianas, Colombia to n Bolivia.]

Rain forest edge, clearings, low second growth. Open terrain, 100–200 m. Usually in pairs in bushes and fields with low scattered vegetation.

## BLUE-BLACK GRASSQUIT
*Volatinia jacarina*
Semillero Chirrí

4″ (10 cm.). Shining blue black, primaries brownish black. ♀: above dark olive brown, the feathers with a few dark centers, below buffy brown, streaked dusky on breast. Wings and tail blackish brown. Young ♂ resemble ♀ but are blacker.

Tropical, casually subtropical zone. Throughout including Margarita I. (*splendens*). [S Amer. generally to n Chile and central Argentina. Trinidad and Tobago.]

Open terrain, scrub, savannas, second

growth, to 2000 m. Rice and corn fields, xerophytic areas, grasslands. In pairs or in small groups, feeds on grass and weed seeds. Repeatedly jumps vertically about a foot and comes down on the same perch, emitting a sharp see-slik.

## GRASSLAND YELLOW-FINCH

*Sicalis luteola*
CANARIO CHIRIGÜE

Pl. 40
4.7″ (12 cm.). Crown olive, narrowly streaked dusky, lores and narrow eyebrow olive yellow. Mantle olive heavily streaked black, rump plain olive, upper tail coverts olive yellow. Below bright yellow, somewhat clouded with olive at sides. Wings and tail brown, the feathers edged light grayish brown. ♀: like ♂ but duller.
Tropical zone. Ne Falcón; Monagas (Río Uracoa, Caño Corozal); nw (Caicara, Altagracia) and se (Roraima) Bolívar (*luteola*). Andes of Mérida (Páramo de Conejos) (*bogotensis*). [Spottily distributed in open country to Aysén, Chile and Río Negro, Argentina. Mid. Amer.] Open grassy fields, xerophytic areas, mangroves, savannas, wheat fields, to near 2000 m. in the n and at about 1200 m. in the Roraima savannas. In pairs or bands forages near ground.

## SAFFRON FINCH

*Sicalis flaveola*
CANARIO DE TEJADO

Pl. 40
5.5″ (14 cm.). Forecrown orange yellow, back olive yellow, faintly streaked dusky. Below bright yellow, somewhat clouded olive on sides of breast. Wings and tail dusky brown, the feathers edged olive. ♂ imm.: above brown, the feathers with a dark central streak and edged olive; rump uniform olive yellow. Below grayish white; broad band across breast, thighs and under tail coverts olive yellow. ♀: sparrowlike. Above brown, streaked dusky; below dirty white, finely streaked dark brown; remiges edged olive yellow.
Tropical, casually subtropical zone. From Zulia to Sucre s through Portuguesa, Apure and Guárico to n Bolívar, e to Ciudad Bolívar (*flaveola*). [Locally throughout, except in Chile, to central

Argentina. Trinidad. Introduced in Panama and Jamaica.]
Llanos, gallery forest, open woodland, second growth, savannas, xerophytic areas, urban and suburban places, scattered trees, to 1850 m. In pairs or small flocks up to 15, forages on and near the ground for grass and weed seeds. Sings from perches near the treetops. Very tame.

## ORANGE-FRONTED YELLOW-FINCH

*Sicalis columbiana*
CANARIO DE SABANA

Pl. 40
4.5″ (11.5 cm.). Forecrown burnt orange, back plain olive yellow; underparts bright yellow, slightly duller on throat and breast than on belly. Wings and tail dusky brown, the feathers edged olive yellow. ♀: sparrowlike. Upperparts light grayish brown, very slightly streaked, underparts dirty white, with an ill-marked grayer pectoral band. Remiges edged yellowish olive.
Tropical zone. Apure; s Guárico; s Monagas; central Delta Amacuro; nw Bolívar e to Ciudad Bolívar; n Amazonas s to the Río Ventuari (*columbianus*). [E Colombia (Maipures); e Peru; Amazonian and e Brazil. Trinidad.]
Second growth, gallery forest, llanos, open fields with scattered bushes, savannas, cultivated areas, to 200 m. n of the Orinoco, to 300 m. s of it. In pairs or small flocks, forages for seeds near the ground.

## STRIPE-TAILED YELLOW-FINCH

*Sicalis citrina*
CANARITO

Pl. 40
4.5″ (11.5 cm.). Forecrown dull citrine, back dull olive brown, streaked dusky, rump and upper tail coverts olive. Below yellow, clouded olive on breast. Wings and tail dusky brown, wing coverts and outer remiges edged olive, inner remiges edged whitish. Tail blackish, outermost pair of feathers with a large, terminal white patch on inner web. ♀: sparrowlike. Above brown, streaked dusky, rump and upper tail coverts tinged olive. Throat, breast and sides of

body buff, streaked dusky; center of belly and under tail coverts yellow.
Tropical and subtropical zones. The Sierra de Perijá, Zulia, and the coastal Cordillera in Carabobo, Distr. Federal and Miranda; central Amazonas at the base of Cerro Duida; s Bolívar from the lower Río Paragua to the Gran Sabana (*browni*). [Guyana; Surinam; n and central Colombia, n Brazil and in the e from s Pará to Paraná and Mato Grosso. Central Peru; possibly nw Argentina.]
Low open forest, clearings, savannas, grassy slopes, to 1900 m. Does not enter the forest. Shy, Alone or in pairs forages for seeds in the grass and shrubs on and near the ground. Call: low chirping note.

## SLATY FINCH
*Haplospiza rustica*
HAPLOSPIZA APIZARRADO

Pl. 40
5" (13 cm.). Uniform slaty gray. Wings and tail black, the feathers edged slaty gray. Bill conical and sharply pointed. ♀: dark olive brown above. Upper throat whitish, lower throat whitish obscurely streaked dusky, breast and sides olive brown, paler than back and streaked dusky, center of abdomen whitish. Wings and tail like back.
Subtropical zone. Sierra de Perijá, Zulia; Distr. Federal (*rustica*). Summit of Cerro Chimantá-tepui, Bolívar (*arcana*). [S Mexico to w Panama. Andes of Colombia to n Bolivia.]
Low open forest and thick second growth, small trees in open terrain, overgrown clearings, 1850–2600 m. Alone or in pairs, but sometimes in open groups of 10 or more, forages in low bushes and shrubs.
Note: Called *Spodiornis rusticus* in Lista Av. Venez.

## PLUMBEOUS SIERRA-FINCH
*Phrygilus unicolor*
FRINGILO APLOMADO

Pl. 40
5.7" (14.5 cm.). Larger and much paler than Slaty Finch. Uniform blue gray, palest below. Wings and tail black, edged blue gray. Bill conical, sharply pointed, much thicker than in Slaty

Finch. ♀: above brown, below whitish, heavily and conspicuously streaked with black above and below; rump uniform gray.
Temperate and páramo zones. The Andes of Trujillo and Mérida (*montosus*). Páramo de Tamá, sw Táchira (*geospizopsis*). [The mountains of Colombia s through the Andes to Tierra del Fuego.]
Dwarf forest edge, páramos, 300–4500 m. Open terrain with shrubs, bushes and frailejones (*Espeletia*). Very shy, secretive. Solitary or in pairs, often in small loose flocks. Runs on the ground; forages also in tufts of grass and other low vegetation. Frequently along the snow line.

## WEDGE-TAILED GRASS-FINCH
*Emberizoides herbicola*
SABANERO COLUDO

Pl. 40
7.5" (19 cm.) [or 8.5" (21 cm.) a]. Above brown or grayish brown, heavily streaked with black (or black above, the feathers margined with brown, a). Eye ring white. Throat and center of abdomen whitish, breast and sides light brown (or below much whiter, a, b). Wings dusky brown, wing coverts and edges of remiges olive, bend of wing yellow. Tail pale brown, central feathers black centrally (or tail blackish, the feathers narrowly margined with grayish brown, a). Imm.: tinged yellow below.
Tropical and subtropical zones. Generally except for areas occupied by the next 2 races (*sphenurus*). The base of the Andes in w Portuguesa and Mérida; Apure; w central Guárico (Calabozo) (*apurensis*, b). Cerro Duida, Amazonas, 1300–2000 m. (*duidae*, a). [The Guianas and Colombia to s Brazil, Paraguay, e Bolivia, ne Argentina.]
Savannas, llanos, open grassy fields to 1600 m. Secretive, forages on the ground and in tufts of grass.

## YELLOW-BROWED SPARROW
*Ammodramus aurifrons*
SABANERITO FRENTIAMARILLO

Pl. 40
5.2" (13 cm.). Lores, short eyebrow, ocular and malar region yellow. Crown, nape and mantle grayish brown streaked

blackish; below white with a grayish tinge. Bend of wing bright yellow, wings dusky brown. The lesser upper wing coverts edged dull olive, greater ones edged buffy gray, inner remiges edged dull rufescent brown. Tail dusky brown the feathers edged paler.

Tropical zone. From the base of the Andes in Táchira and Barinas to the llanos of Apure; s Anzoátegui; Delta Amacuro (*apurensis*). Sw Amazonas (*tenebrosus*). [E Colombia to w Bolivia and Amazonian Brazil.]

Llanos, savannas, open fields with low scattered vegetation to 300 m. n of the Orinoco, to 200 m. s of it. Gallery and deciduous forest edge, second growth, pastures, cultivated areas; near water. Alone and in pairs forages on or near the ground for insects and seeds.

Note: This and the next species were placed in the genus *Myospiza* in Lista Av. Venez. and Sp. Bds. S Amer.

## GRASSLAND SPARROW

*Ammodramus humeralis*
SABANERITO DE PAJONALES

Pl. 40

5″ (13 cm.). Very similar to Yellow-browed Sparrow, differing by having only the lores yellow, the black streaks of the upperparts edged with chestnut, and the inner remiges edged chestnut. Below dirty white, the breast buffy gray in contrast.

Tropical and subtropical zones. The Goajira Pen., Zulia (*pallidulus*). S of the Andes in Barinas and Portuguesa (*columbianus*). Elsewhere locally (*humeralis*). [The Guianas and Colombia to Bolivia, Uruguay to s Argentina.]

Savannas, grass-covered, bushy open terrain, gallery forest and deciduous forest edge, xerophytic areas, to 1300 m. n of the Orinoco, to 1750 m. s of it. Runs furtively on the ground between the grass tufts; when almost stepped on flies and immediately disappears again in the grass. Tame, perches on protruding rocks, sticks and shrubs. A local name is *Ratonera*. Call: weak trill.

## RUFOUS-COLLARED SPARROW

*Zonotrichia capensis*
CORREPORSUELO

Pl. 39

6″ (15 cm.). The adult differs from any other Venezuelan sparrowlike bird by having a rufous collar around the hindneck. Top and sides of head gray with 2 broad, black coronal stripes; collar around hindneck and sides of breast rufous, mantle reddish brown streaked black, rump and upper tail coverts grayish brown to gray. Throat and central underparts white, a black patch at each side of lower throat, sides of body grayish brown. Wings and tail dusky brown, median and greater wing coverts tipped white forming 2 bars, inner remiges edged chestnut. Imm.: crown brown streaked like back; no rufous nuchal collar; below white finely streaked black on breast and sides.

Tropical, subtropical and páramo zones. Sierra de Perijá, Zulia, s Lara to s Táchira (*costaricensis*). The coastal Cordillera from Yaracuy to Miranda and in Sucre and Monagas; n Bolívar at Caicara (*venezuelae*). The tepuis of the Gran Sabana (except the summit of Roraima) and on Cerro Guaiquinima, Bolívar; on the nw lowlands and on the cerros and serranías of Amazonas, except Cerro de la Neblina. (*roraimae*). The summit of Cerro Roraima (*macconnelli*). Cerro de la Neblina (*inaccessibilis*). [S Mexico to Tierra del Fuego, Curaçao, Aruba. Dominican Republic.]

Open terrain with scattered bushes, rain, cloud and dwarf forest edge, páramos, 800–4000 m. n of the Orinoco, 120–2550 m. s of it. The lowest localities s of the Orinoco are 100 m. near Caicara, nw Bolívar, 120 m. on Caño Capuana, near the mouth of the Río Vichada, Amazonas, and 500 m. near the Gran Sabana, Bolívar. Low open woodland, suburban areas, gardens. In pairs or small groups, forages for seeds and insects, from the ground to tops of low trees. Pleasant, sweet, soft trill. Call: piping sound, transcribed as "it is sweet, cheer here."

[SISKINS ARE SMALL, black and yellow or olive and yellow birds (except for Red Siskin), with short, conical, sharply pointed bills. They are often found in small, restless, swift-flying flocks. They are wary and if disturbed usually fly a good distance away displaying a yellow pattern in wings and tail.]

## ANDEAN SISKIN
*Carduelis spinescens*
JILGUERO TRIGUERITO

Pl. 40
4.7″ (12 cm.). Cap black, back dark, dull olive, upper tail coverts olive yellow. Throat and breast olive yellow, gradually brightening on belly and becoming bright yellow on under tail coverts. Wings black, bases of remiges bright yellow forming a conspicuous patch. Tail black, the feathers bright yellow basally. ♀: differs from ♂ by lacking the black cap; underparts dull grayish, sides of body dull olive yellow, under tail coverts yellowish white. Wings and tail as in ♂.
Subtropical to páramo zone. The Andes of Trujillo, Mérida and Táchira; ne Aragua at Colonia Tovar (*spinescens*). [Colombia.]
Low open cloud forest and dwarf forest, páramos, 2700–4100 m. Forest edge, open terrain with scattered bushes and shrubs, wheat fields. In pairs or small flocks forages close to the ground.
Note: Called *Spinus* in Lista Av. Venez. and Sp. Bds. S. Amer., as were all the species here listed under *Carduelis*.

## YELLOW-FACED SISKIN
*Carduelis yarrellii*
JILGUERO CARA AMARILLA

4″ (10 cm.). Cap black, sides of head and neck and entire underparts bright yellow; mantle dull olive yellow, rump and upper tail coverts bright yellow. Wings black, wing coverts edged olive yellow, remiges basally bright yellow, forming a large patch, inner remiges broadly edged white apically. Tail black, basal third bright yellow. ♀: above dull olive gray, rump bright olive yellow. Below grayish, olivaceous on breast and sides. Wings and tail as in ♂.
Tropical zone. Hda. El Trompillo, se Carabobo. [E Brazil from Ceará to Bahia.]
Open terrain, cultivated areas, 400 m.

## RED SISKIN
*Carduelis cucullata*
CARDENALITO

Pl. 40
4″ (10 cm.). Entire head black, collar around hindneck, rump and most of underparts vermilion, back dark vermilion; center of belly white. Wings black, remiges basally light vermilion, inner remiges edged white distally. Tail black, light vermilion basally. ♀: crown and upper back mouse brown tinged vermilion. Lower back, rump and upper tail coverts vermilion; neck and breast orange red, rest of underparts dirty white. Wings and tail marked as in ♂ but light orange red instead of light vermilion.
Upper tropical zone. The n Cordillera region (no exact localities are given as the bird is much persecuted by bird catchers because of its popularity as a cage bird). [Ne Colombia s of Cúcuta. Trinidad.]
Open grassy terrain with shrubs and bushes. Arid areas, 300–400 m.

## HOODED SISKIN
*Carduelis magellanica*
JILGUERO DE RORAIMA

Pl. 40
5″ (13 cm.). Whole head black. Back olive yellow, brighter and yellower on hindneck and upper tail coverts. Below bright yellow. Wings and tail black. Base of remiges and tail bright yellow. Inner remiges tipped white distally. ♀: differs from ♂ by having no black on head; crown grayish, throat dull yellowish, rest of plumage like ♂ but duller.
Upper tropical zone. Apure on the Río Meta. Bolívar in the Gran Sabana (*longirostris*). [Guyana. Colombia and sw Ecuador to n Chile and s Argentina.]
Open terrain with scattered low trees and bushes, savannas, llanos, 100–1300 m. Gallery forest edge, plantations. Song: a melodious warble.

## YELLOW-BELLIED SISKIN
*Carduelis xanthogastra*
JILGUERO VIENTRIAMARILLO

Pl. 40
4.6″ (11.7 cm.). Black; lower breast, belly and under tail coverts bright yellow. Remiges and tail basally bright yellow. ♀: upperparts dusky olive, throat and breast and sides of body dull olive, paler than back, center of breast, belly and under tail coverts bright yellow. Wings and tail as in ♂.
Upper tropical and subtropical zones. The

n mountains from the Sierra de Perijá, Zulia, Mérida, and Táchira through Yaracuy to the Paria Pen., Sucre (*xanthogastra*). [Colombia to sw Ecuador. N Bolivia. Costa Rica to w Panama.]
Forest edge, plantations, pastures, clearings, 800–2000 m. In pairs, or in flocks up to 30, forages in open terrain close to the ground, in trees from middle heights to treetops.

## DARK-BACKED GOLDFINCH

*Carduelis psaltria*
CAPA NEGRA (♂)
CHIRULÍ (♀)

Pl. 40
4.5″ (11.5 cm.). Glossy blue black above including sides of head; bright yellow below. Bases of remiges white, forming a wing speculum, tips of inner remiges and bases of outer tail feathers white. ♀: light olive above, light yellow below. Wings brownish, median and greater coverts edged whitish forming 2 bars, inner remiges broadly edged white. Tail dark brown, the feathers narrowly edged whitish.
Tropical and subtropical zones. The n Cordilleras from Táchira and Falcón to e Sucre extending s through Barinas. Cojedes, Guárico and Anzoátegui to nw Bolívar at Caicara and Altagracia (*columbiana*). [W US, Mid. Amer. s to nw Peru.]
Open brushy country with scattered trees, xerophytic areas, edge of deciduous woodland, second growth, and gallery forest edge, pastures, suburban areas, gardens from sea level to 2500 m. n of the Orinoco, 100 m. s of it. Restless, shy; in pairs or flocks up to 50, forages from near the ground to treetops.

## ADDENDUM TO PAGE 193

## PERIJA THISTLETAIL

*Schizoeaca perijana*
PISCUIZ DE PERIJÁ

8.4″ (21 cm.). Above olive brown. Superciliaries grayish. Chin spot tawny. Underparts grayish brown. Tail cinnamon brown.
Temperate zone, Sierra de Perijá, Zulia. [Sierra de Perija. Colombia.]

# THE BIRDS OF ISLA DE AVES

An outlying possession of Venezuela is the Isla de Aves (15°42′N–83°40′W) a sandbar less than 500 m. long, 40 to 120 m. wide and 3 m. high lying about 270 km. (180 miles) west of the north tip of Dominica and slightly less than 640 km. (400 miles) north of the Caribbean coast of Venezuela. It is not to be confused with Islas Las Aves, composed of two main islands, Aves de Sotavento and Aves de Barlovento lying between Bonaire and Los Roques, about 80 miles (130 km.) northeast to the coast of Falcón.

Rarely visited except by turtle fishermen, only sea birds nest on Isla de Aves; however, migrants find it a convenient resting place.

The Herring Gull, which has been found there, has not yet been found in Venezuela proper although it has been recorded once in winter from Trinidad and has probably been sighted on Los Roques.

The following 7 species are presently known from Isla de Aves (specimens in the Phelps Collection). A certain number of sight records from the island are not listed.

MAGNIFICENT FRIGATEBIRD
*Fregata magnificens*
TIJERETA DE MAR

RUDDY TURNSTONE
*Arenaria interpres morinella*
PLAYERO TURCO

SANDERLING
*Calidris alba*
PLAYERO ARENERO

HERRING GULL
*Larus argentatus smithsonianus*
GAVIOTA ARENQUERA

LAUGHING GULL
*Larus atricilla*
GUANAGUANARE

SOOTY TERN
*Sterna fuscata*
GAVIOTA DE VERAS

BROWN NODDY
*Anous stolidus*
TIÑOSA

# APPENDIX: SUBSPECIES ILLUSTRATED

## PLATE I

1. *P. haliaetus carolinensis*
2. *C. atratus brasiliensis*
3. *S. papa*
4. *C. aura ruficollis*
5. *C. burrovianus*
6. *C. melambrotus*
7. *M. chimachima cordatus*
8. *P. plancus cheriway*
9. *D. ater*
10. *D. a. americanus*

## PLATE II

1. *B. albonotatus*
2. *B. b. brachyurus*
3. *B. albigula*
4. *B. leucorrhous*
5. *B. n. nitidus*
6. *B. p. platypterus*
7. *B. m. magnirostris*
8. *C. u. uncinatus*
9. *H. b. bidentatus*
10. *A. striatus ventralis*

## PLATE III

1. *G. c. caerulescens*
2. *C. u. uncinatus*
3. *B. albonotatus*
4. *L. schistacea*
5. *H. hamatus*
6. *R. s. sociabilis*
7. *L. cayanensis*
8. *P. u. unicinctus*
9. *C. buffoni*

## PLATE IV

1. *G. melanoleucus australis*
2. *B. albicaudatus colonus*
3. *H. meridionalis*
4. *B. n. nigricollis*
5. *B. a. anthracinus*
6. *B. u. urubitinga*
7. *H. s. solitarius*

## PLATE V

1. *L. a. albicollis*
2. *L. melanops*
3. *C. u. uncinatus*
4. *L. cayanensis*
5. *S. melanoleucus*
6. *S. o. ornatus*

## PLATE VI

1. *M. s. semitorquatus*
2. *S. o. ornatus*
3. *S. tyrannus serus*
4. *O. isidori*
5. *M. guianensis*
6. *H. harpyja*

## PLATE VII

1. *G. melanoleucus australis*
2. *O. isidori*
3. *E. forficatus yetapa*
4. *I. plumbea*
5. *E. leucurus*
6. *G. swainsonii leonae*
7. *F. peregrinus anatum*
8. *F. f. femoralis*
9. *F. r. rufigularis*
10. *F. c. columbarius*
11. *F. sparverius isabellinus*

## PLATE VIII

1. *A. aburri*
2. *P. pipile cumanensis*
3. *P. p. pauxi*
4. *M. tomentosa*
5. *N. urumutum*
6. *C. daubentoni*
7. *C. alector erythrognatha*
8. *S. cunicularia brachyptera*
9. *G. brasilianum medianum*
10. *G. jardinii*
11. *A. h. harrisii*
12. *O. guatemalae vermiculatus*
13. *O. choliba crucigerus*
14. *O. w. watsonii*
15. *O. albogularis meridensis*

## PLATE IX

1. *N. g. griseus*
2. *N. aethereus longicauda*
3. *N. grandis*
4. *T. alba hellmayri*
5. *P. p. perspicillata*
6. *C. v. virgata*
7. *C. a. albitarsus*
8. *C. nigrolineata*
9. *C. h. huhula*
10. *L. c. cristata*
11. *R. c. clamator*
12. *A. flammeus pallidicaudus*

13. *A. stygius robustus*
14. *B. virginianus nacurutu*

## PLATE X

1. *C. a. acutipennis*
2. *H. c. climacocerca*
3. *N. a. albicollis*
4. *C. c. cayennensis*
5. *C. longirostris ruficervix*
6. *C. parvulus heterurus*
7. *C. maculicaudus*
8. *C. n. nigrescens*
9. *C. rufus minimus*
10. *U. l. lyra*

## PLATE XI

1. *P. nacunda minor*
2. *C. rupestris*
3. *C. a. acutipennis*
4. *C. pusillus septentrionalis*
5. *N. leucopyga pallida*
6. *L. s. semitorquatus*
7. *P. c. chalybea*
8. *P. t. tapera*
9. *S. ruficollis aequalis*
10. *A. fucata*
11. *R. r. riparia*
12. *N. tibialis griseiventris*
13. *N. murina meridensis*
14. *N. c. cyanoleuca*
15. *T. albiventer*
16. *A. fasciata*
17. *A. melanoleuca*
18. *H. rustica erythrogaster*

## PLATE XII

1. *S. zonaris albicincta*
2. *C. phelpsi*
3. *C. r. rutilus*
4. *C. cryptus*
5. *C. cherriei*
6. *C. spinicauda latirostris*
7. *C. cinereiventris lawrencei*
8. *C. vauxi aphanes*
9. *C. c. chapmani*
10. *C. a. andrei*
11. *C. b. brachyura*
12. *A. montivagus*
13. *P. c. cayennensis*
14. *R. s. squamata*
15. *M. furcata*

## PLATE XIII

1. *C. colonus poecilonota*
2. *S. nigricans angustirostris*

3. *C. fumigatus ardosiacus*
4. *C. borealis*
5. *A. leucocephala*
6. *M. tyrannus monachus*
7. *F. p. pica*
8. *K. o. orenocensis*
9. *P. poecilocercus*
10. *P. d. decumanus*
11. *C. u. uropygialis*
12. *C. c. cela*
13. *C. l. leucoramphus*
14. *C. holosericeus australis*
15. *C. solitarius*
16. *M. imthurni*
17. *L. tanagrinus guianensis*
18. *Q. l. lugubris*
19. *M. bonariensis venezuelensis*
20. *S. o. oryzivora*

## PLATE 1

1. *N. b. bonapartei*
2. *T. tao septentrionalis*
3. *T. m. major*
4. *C. obsoletus cerviniventris*
5. *C. soui andrei*
6. *C. undulatus manapiare*
7. *C. e. erythropus*
8. *C. v. variegatus*
9. *C. cristatus sonnini*
10. *O. columbianus*
11. *O. g. gujanensis*
12. *O. r. ruficauda*
13. *P. a. argyrotis*
14. *P. m. montagnii*
15. *P. jacquacu grantii*

## PLATE 2

1. *N. violacea cayennensis*
2. *N. nycticorax hoactli*
3. *C. c. cochlearius*
4. *P. pileatus*
5. *T. l. lineatum*
6. *T. fasciatum salmoni*
7. *B. pinnatus*
8. *I. involucris*
9. *B. s. striatus*
10. *Z. undulatus*
11. *D. rufescens colorata*
12. *F. caerulea caerulescens*
13. *S. sibilatrix fostersmithi*
14. *H. tricolor ruficollis*
15. *A. agami*

## PLATE 3

1. *A. g. guarauna*
2. *P. f. falcinellus*

3. *E. ruber*
4. *T. c. caudatus*
5. *M. cayennensis*
6. *P. infuscatus berlepschi*
7. *C. oxycerca*
8. *N. jubata*
9. *O. dominica*
10. *A. brasiliensis*
11. *A. d. discors*
12. *A. flavirostris altipetens*
13. *A. b. bahamensis*
14. *M. armata colombiana*
15. *D. autumnalis discolor*
16. *D. viduata*
17. *D. bicolor*

PLATE 4

1. *M. chimachima cordatus*
2. *I. plumbea*
3. *C. aura ruficollis*
4. *C. burrovianus*
5. *C. melambrotus*
6. *H. c. cachinnans*
7. *B. n. nitidus*
8. *L. schistacea*
9. *G. c. caerulescens*
10. *M. s. semitorquatus*
11. *R. s. sociabilis*
12. *H. hamatus*
13. *C. u. uncinatus*
14. *B. aequinoctialis*
15. *P. u. unicinctus*
16. *H. meridionalis*
17. *B. n. nigricollis*

PLATE 5

1. *F. r. rufigularis*
2. *F. deiroleucus*
3. *F. f. femoralis*
4. *F. sparverius isabellinus*
5. *G. swainsonii leonae*
6. *B. n. nitidus*
7. *B. m. magnirostris*
8. *B. p. platypterus*
9. *H. b. bidentatus*
10. *A. b. bicolor*
11. *A. striatus ventralis*
12. *A. poliogaster*
13. *A. s. superciliosus*
14. *M. s. semitorquatus*
15. *M. mirandollei*
16. *M. gilvicollis*
17. *M. ruficollis zonothorax*

PLATE 6

1. *H. cayanus*
2. *V. chilensis cayennensis*

3. *R. m. maculatus*
4. *R. wetmorei*
5. *A. c. cajanea*
6. *A. axillaris*
7. *P. carolina*
8. *P. albicollis typhoeca*
9. *P. f. flaviventer*
10. *M. s. schomburgkii*
11. *N. erythrops olivascens*
12. *L. exilis*
13. *L. levraudi*
14. *L. v. viridis*
15. *P. martinica*
16. *P. flavirostris*
17. *E. h. helias*
18. *H. fulica*
19. *J. jacana intermedia*

PLATE 7

1. *C. corensis*
2. *C. cayennensis pallidicrissa*
3. *C. speciosa*
4. *C. subvinacea purpureotincta*
5. *C. fasciata albilinea*
6. *S. squammata ridgwayi*
7. *C. passerina albivitta*
8. *C. m. minuta*
9. *C. talpacoti rufipennis*
10. *C. pretiosa*
11. *C. m. mondetoura*
12. *Z. auriculata stenura*
13. *L. v. verreauxi*
14. *L. rufaxilla dubusi*
15. *G. m. montana*
16. *G. violacea albiventer*
17. *G. l. linearis*

PLATE 8

1. *A. ararauna*
2. *A. chloroptera*
3. *A. macao*
4. *A. m. militaris*
5. *A. s. severa*
6. *A. manilata*
7. *A. n. nobilis*
8. *P. chalcopterus*
9. *P. s. sordidus*
10. *P. seniloides*
11. *P. m. menstruus*
12. *P. fuscus*
13. *D. a. accipitrinus*
14. *A. a. amazonica*
15. *A. o. ochrocephala*
16. *A. b. barbadensis*
17. *A. f. farinosa*
18. *A. mercenaria canipalliata*
19. *A. festiva bodini*

## PLATE 9

1. *A. pertinax venezuelae*
2. *A. s. solstitialis*
3. *A. acuticaudata haemorrhous*
4. *A. l. leucophthalmus*
5. *A. wagleri transilis*
6. *P. h. hoematotis*
7. *P. leucotis auricularis*
8. *P. p. picta*
9. *P. e. egregia*
10. *P. rhodocephala*
11. *F. passerinus viridissimus*
12. *N. panychlora*
13. *B. lineola tigrinus*
14. *B. jugularis exsul*
15. *B. c. chrysopterus*
16. *T. p. purpurata*
17. *T. batavica*
18. *T. d. dilectissima*
19. *H. amazonina theresae*
20. *P. pyrilia*
21. *P. caica*
22. *P. barrabandi*
23. *P. m. melanocephala*

## PLATE 10

1. *C. a. americanus*
2. *C. melacoryphus*
3. *C. lansbergi*
4. *C. pumilus*
5. *T. n. naevia*
6. *D. p. pavoninus*
7. *D. p. phasianellus*
8. *P. m. minuta*
9. *P. cayana mehleri*
10. *P. m. melanogaster*
11. *N. rufipennis*
12. *C. viridicyana meridana*
13. *C. a. affinis*
14. *C. yncas guatimalensis*
15. *C. v. violaceus*
16. *C. cayanus*

## PLATE 11

1. *H. mavors*
2. *H. spencei*
3. *M. tyrianthina oreopola*
4. *C. heteropogon*
5. *R. microrhynchum andicolum*
6. *E. cupreoventris*
7. *E. v. vestitus*
8. *H. l. leadbeateri*
9. *H. xanthogonys*
10. *D. johannae guianensis*
11. *D. l. ludoviciae*
12. *C. delphinae*

13. *C. thalassinus cyanotus*
14. *C. c. coruscans*
15. *A. nigricollis*
16. *A. prevostii viridicordatus*
17. *H. l. longirostris*
18. *L. lafresnayi greenewalti*
19. *C. falcatus*
20. *C. l. largipennis*
21. *C. ensipennis*
22. *C. hyperythrus*
23. *S. cyanopectus*
24. *B. f. flavescens*
25. *C. torquata conradii*
26. *C. c. coeligena*
27. *C. bonapartei eos*
28. *C. helianthea tamai*

## PLATE 12

1. *L. stictolopha*
2. *L. ornata*
3. *L. p. pavonina*
4. *L. chalybea verreauxi*
5. *P. langsdorffi melanosternon*
6. *D. longicauda*
7. *C. amethystina*
8. *C. jourdanii andinus*
9. *A. heliodor meridae*
10. *C. mellisugus caribaeus*
11. *C. s. stenura*
12. *A. c. chionopectus*
13. *A. versicolor hollandi*
14. *A. fimbriata elegantissima*
15. *C. n. notatus*
16. *L. goudoti phaeochroa*
17. *S. g. geoffroyi*
18. *A. melanogenys aeneosticta*
19. *A. t. tzacatl*
20. *A. v. viridigaster*
21. *A. tobaci caudata*
22. *A. saucerottei braccata*
23. *T. furcata fissilis*
24. *C. o. oenone*
25. *H. sapphirina*
26. *H. cyanus viridiventris*
27. *L. f. fallax*
28. *C. mosquitus*
29. *K. g. guimeti*
30. *P. theresiae leucorrhous*
31. *P. g. guainumbi*
32. *P. milleri*
33. *C. buffonii aeneicauda*
34. *F. m. mellivora*

## PLATE 13

1. *F. m. mellivora*
2. *P. aurescens*
3. *T. p. pella*

4. *O. underwoodii discifer*
5. *O. guerinii lindenii*
6. *A. recurvirostris*
7. *H. macrocerca*
8. *L. nuna gouldii*
9. *E. e. ensifera*
10. *H. a. aurita*
11. *A. kingi margarethae*

PLATE 14

1. *P. a. anthophilus*
2. *P. g. guy*
3. *P. hispidus*
4. *P. a. augusti*
5. *P. s. superciliosus*
6. *P. bourcieri whitelyi*
7. *P. squalidus rupurumii*
8. *P. longuemareus ignobilis*
9. *P. g. griseogularis*
10. *P. ruber episcopus*
11. *G. h. hirsuta*
12. *T. l. leucurus*
13. *T. ruckeri venezuelensis*
14. *P. auriceps hargitti*
15. *P. antisianus*
16. *T. v. viridis*
17. *T. v. violaceus*
18. *T. m. melanurus*
19. *T. p. personatus*
20. *T. collaris exoptatus*
21. *T. r. rufus*

PLATE 15

1. *C. t. tenebrosa*
2. *N. macrorhynchus hyperrhynchus*
3. *N. ordii*
4. *N. t. tectus*
5. *H. ruficollis bicinctus*
6. *M. mystacalis*
7. *M. fusca venezuelae*
8. *N. rubecula duidae*
9. *B. t. tamatia*
10. *B. m. macrodactylus*
11. *B. c. capensis*
12. *B. goeringi*
13. *B. l. lugubris*
14. *G. l. leucogastra*
15. *G. galbula*
16. *G. r. ruficauda*
17. *G. a. albirostris*
18. *G. d. dea*
19. *J. aurea ridgwayi*
20. *C. a. amazona*
21. *C. a. americana*
22. *C. a. aenea*
23. *C. inda*

PLATE 16

1. *E. b. bourcierii*
2. *C. niger aurantiicinctus*
2a. *C. niger niger*
3. *A. calorhynchus*
4. *A. prasinus albivitta*
5. *A. h. haematopygus*
6. *P. torquatus nuchalis*
7. *P. pluricinctus*
8. *P. aracari roraimae*
9. *P. v. viridis*
10. *P. f. flavirostris*
11. *S. culik*
12. *S. nattereri*
13. *A. n. nigrirostris*
14. *R. a. ambiguus*
15. *R. vitellinus*
16. *R. citreolaemus*
17. *R. culminatus*
18. *R. cuvieri*
19. *R. t. tucanus*

PLATE 17

1. *C. elegans deltanus*
2. *C. g. grammicus*
3. *C. u. undatus*
4. *C. t. torquatus*
5. *C. f. flavus*
6. *C. punctigula punctipectus*
7. *P. rubiginosus meridensis*
8. *P. chrysochloros capistratus*
8a. *P. chrysochloros xanthochlorus*
9. *P. f. flavigula*
10. *P. rivolii meridae*
11. *V. dignus abdominalis*
12. *V. f. fumigatus*
13. *V. kirkii continentalis*
14. *V. passerinus modestus*
15. *V. c. cassini*
16. *M. r. rubricapillus*
17. *M. cruentatus extensus*
18. *D. l. lineatus*
19. *C. m. melanoleucos*
20. *C. p. pollens*
21. *C. r. rubricollis*

PLATE 18

1. *P. c. cinnamomeus*
2. *P. olivaceus tachirensis*
3. *P. squamulatus rohli*
4. *P. spilogaster orinocensis*
5. *P. exilis undulatus*
6. *S. griseicapillus griseus*
7. *G. s. spirurus*
8. *D. longicauda connectens*
9. *D. fuliginosa phaeochroa*

10. *D. merula bartletti*
11. *D. homochroa meridionalis*
12. *L. souleyetii littoralis*
13. *L. affinis lacrymiger*
14. *X. triangularis hylodromus*
15. *X. guttatus polystictus*
16. *X. pardalotus caurensis*
17. *X. obsoletus notatus*
18. *X. picus phalara*
19. *D. c. certhia*
20. *D. picumnus seilerni*
21. *X. promeropirhynchus procerus*
22. *H. p. perrotii*
23. *N. l. longirostris*
24. *C. trochilirostris venezuelensis*
25. *C. procurvoides sanus*

PLATE 19

1. *C. fuscus heterurus*
2. *A. wyatti mucuchiesi*
3. *S. coryi*
4. *L. andicola certhia*
5. *P. candei venezuelensis*
6. *S. gularis cinereiventris*
7. *S. unirufa castanea*
8. *S. cinnamomea bolivari*
9. *S. albescens trinitatis*
10. *S. moesta macconnelli*
11. *S. g. gujanensis*
12. *S. rutilans dissors*
13. *P. rufifrons inornatus*
14. *C. cinnamomea orenocensis*
15. *C. s. subcristata*
16. *C. vulpina alopecias*
17. *C. demissa*
18. *C. gutturata hyposticta*
19. *T. cherriei*
20. *X. minutus ruficaudatus*
21. *X. t. tenuirostris*
22. *X. m. milleri*
23. *M. squamigera perlatus*
24. *P. guttuligera venezuelana*
25. *P. brunnescens rostratus*
26. *P. a. adusta*

PLATE 20

1. *P. boissonneautii striaticeps*
2. *T. virgaticeps klagesi*
3. *T. h. holostictus*
4. *T. f. flammulatus*
5. *F. leucopus longirostris*
6. *S. subalaris olivacea*
7. *A. striaticollis venezuelana*
8. *P. rufus columbianus*
9. *P. pyrrhodes*
10. *P. r. ruficaudatus*

11. *P. e. erythropterus*
12. *A. rufipileatus consobrinus*
13. *A. ochrolaemus turdinus*
14. *A. infuscatus badius*
15. *A. r. roraimae*
16. *H. s. subulatus*
17. *S. a. albigularis*
18. *S. mexicanus andinus*
19. *S. caudacutus insignis*
20. *L. nematura chimantae*
21. *B. rikeri*

PLATE 21

1. *F. viridis*
2. *T. major semifasciata*
3. *C. lineatus intermedius*
4. *T. doliatus fraterculus*
5. *S. canadensis intermedius*
6. *S. melanonotus*
7. *H. rufimarginatus frater*
8. *H. stictocephalus*
9. *H. dorsimaculatus*
10. *H. roraimae*
11. *T. s. spodioptila*
12. *M. b. brachyura*
13. *M. s. surinamensis*
14. *M. guttata*
15. *M. gutturalis*
16. *M. haematonota pyrrhonota*
17. *M. schisticolor sanctaemartae*
18. *M. a. axillaris*
19. *M. menetriesii cinereiventris*
20. *M. behni inornata*
21. *F. grisea intermedia*
21a. *F. grisea rufiventris*
22. *D. mentalis cumbreanus*
23. *T. anabatinus gularis*
24. *D. caudata klagesi*
25. *H. cantator flavescens*

PLATE 22

1. *M. margaritatus*
2. *T. p. punctatus*
3. *T. amazonicus cinereiceps*
4. *T. i. insignis*
5. *T. m. murinus*
6. *T. aethiops polionotus*
7. *T. nigrocinereus cinereoniger*
8. *P. stellaris occipitalis*
9. *P. l. leucostigma*
10. *P. rufifrons minor*
11. *C. nigricans*
12. *C. t. tyrannina*
13. *H. p. poecilonota*
14. *H. m. melanopogon*
15. *T. plumbeus tucuyensis*
16. *T. caesius glaucus*

17. *T. ardesiacus obidensis*
18. *S. n. naevia*
18a. *S. naevia argentata*
19. *M. a. atrothorax*
20. *M. pelzelni*
21. *M. l. longipes*
22. *M. laemosticta venezuelae*
23. *M. i. immaculata*

PLATE 23

1. *A. o. orthonyx*
2. *C. alixi*
3. *C. campanisona venezuelana*
4. *C. ruficauda chionogaster*
5. *G. h. haplonota*
6. *G. guatimalensis regulus*
7. *G. r. rufula*
8. *G. g. griseonucha*
9. *G. ruficapilla avilae*
10. *G. e. excelsa*
11. *H. m. macularius*
12. *M. c. campanisona*
13. *G. f. ferrugineipectus*
14. *G. n. nana*
15. *G. cucullata venezuelana*
16. *G. loricata*
17. *F. analis saturatus*
18. *F. rufipectus lasallei*
19. *F. c. colma*
20. *P. e. erythroptera*
21. *M. t. torquata*

PLATE 24

1. *M. leucophrys angustirostris*
2. *M. myotherinus elegans*
3. *G. rufigula pallida*
4. *H. n. naevia*
5. *H. p. punctulata*
6. *D. cincta*
7. *P. a. albifrons*
8. *C. lanceolata*
9. *T. filicauda*
10. *M. manacus interior*
11. *M. c. chrysopterus*
12. *P. p. pipra*
13. *P. e. erythrocephala*
14. *P. a. aureola*
15. *P. cornuta*
16. *P. serena suavissima*
17. *P. coronata carbonata*
18. *C. gutturalis*
19. *X. atronitens*
20. *C. u. uniformis*
21. *M. regulus zulianus*
22. *M. pyrocephalus pallidiceps*
23. *T. stolzmanni*
24. *T. virescens*

25. *N. c. cinnamomea*
26. *N. chrysocephalum*
27. *P. chloris chlorion*
28. *S. turdinus olivaceus*
29. *S. major duidae*
30. *H. flavivertex*

PLATE 25

1. *M. m. momota*
2. *C. ornatus*
3. *Q. purpurata*
4. *M. atra*
5. *R. rupicola*
6. *P. tricolor*
7. *P. carnifex*
8. *P. scutatus orenocensis*
9. *S. caripensis*

PLATE 26

1. *X. punicea*
2. *C. cotinga*
3. *C. cayana*
4. *A. rubrocristatus*
5. *L. hypopyrrha*
6. *R. simplex frederici*
7. *L. v. vociferans*
8. *L. streptophorus*
9. *L. elegans venezuelensis*
10. *A. tschudii*
11. *P. averano carnobarba*
12. *P. riefferii melanolaema*
13. *P. arcuata*
14. *P. f. formosa*
15. *P. aureopectus festiva*
16. *P. whitelyi kathleenae*
17. *O. cristatus phelpsi*

PLATE 27

1. *T. semifasciata columbiana*
2. *T. c. cayana*
3. *T. inquisitor erythrogenys*
4. *P. polychopterus tristis*
5. *P. a. albogriseus*
6. *P. marginatus nanus*
7. *P. rufus*
8. *P. cinnamomeus magdalenae*
9. *P. castaneus intermedius*
10. *P. v. versicolor*
11. *P. viridis griseigularis*
12. *X. albinucha minor*
13. *P. minor*
14. *A. s. spadiceus*
15. *A. citriniventris*
16. *A. cinnamomeus*
17. *I. isabellae*
18. *C. torquata anthoides*

PLATE 28

1. *M. rixosa flavigularis*
2. *M. fumigatus lugubris*
3. *M. s. striaticollis*
4. *H. f. ferruginea*
5. *S. icterophrys*
6. *T. d. dominicensis*
7. *T. m. melancholicus*
8. *T. albogularis*
9. *T. sulphurea*
10. *T. luteiventris septentrionalis*
11. *C. cinchoneti icterophrys*
12. *C. p. parva*
13. *M. similis columbianus*
14. *M. granadensis obscurior*
15. *M. inornatus*
16. *M. cayanensis rufipennis*
17. *M. maculatus difficilis*
18. *M. chrysocephalus cinerascens*
19. *M. p. pitangua*
20. *P. sulphuratus trinitatis*
21. *P. l. lictor*
22. *L. l. leucophaius*
23. *E. varius rufinus*
24. *E. a. aurantioatrocristatus*
25. *S. sibilator albocinereus*
26. *M. t. tyrannulus*
27. *M. venezuelensis*
28. *M. tuberculifer pallidus*

PLATE 29

1. *P. cinnamomea vieillotioides*
2. *O. fumicolor superciliosa*
3. *O. rufipectoralis rubicundulus*
4. *O. diadema meridana*
5. *O. cinnamomeiventris nigrita*
6. *P. rubinus saturatus*
7. *O. littoralis*
8. *M. v. villosus*
9. *M. b. barbatus*
10. *U. agilis*
11. *K. poecilurus venezuelanus*
12. *C. cinereus bogotensis*
13. *E. euleri lawrencei*
14. *C. fuscatus cabanisi*
15. *M. flavicans venezuelanus*
16. *M. roraimae*
17. *M. f. fasciatus*
18. *T. sulphurescens exortivus*
19. *T. p. poliocephalus*
20. *T. flaviventris collingwoodi*
21. *R. olivaceus flavus*
22. *R. megacephala pectoralis*
23. *R. ruficauda*
24. *S. modestus glaber*
25. *M. viridicata restricta*
26. *M. gaimardii bogotensis*

27. *M. caniceps cinerea*
28. *O. c. coronatus*
29. *E. f. flavogaster*
30. *E. parvirostris*
31. *E. ruficeps*
32. *E. pallatangae olivina*
33. *E. d. dayi*
34. *E. strepera*

PLATE 30

1. *T. a. andrei*
2. *P. platyrhynchos griseiceps*
3. *P. coronatus gumia*
4. *P. mystaceus insularis*
5. *P. flavigularis vividus*
6. *P. r. ruficeps*
7. *T. russatum*
8. *T. c. cinereum*
9. *T. nigriceps*
10. *T. chrysocrotaphum pictum*
11. *T. m. maculatum*
12. *T. sylvia griseolum*
13. *I. granadense andinum*
14. *I. margaritaceiventris impiger*
15. *A. pilaris venezuelensis*
16. *C. galeatus*
17. *L. pileatus santaeluciae*
18. *M. ecaudatus miserabilis*
19. *P. pectoralis brevipennis*
20. *E. meloryphus paulus*
21. *P. murina incomta*
22. *C. obsoletum venezuelae*
23. *I. tenuirostris*
24. *I. subflava intermedia*
25. *S. c. cinerea*
26. *M. stictopterus albocaudatus*
27. *M. leucophrys pallditergum*
28. *O. semiflavum dilutum*
29. *O. inerme*
30. *C. flaveola cerula*
31. *T. viridiflavus chrysops*
32. *T. vilissimus petersi*
33. *T. nigrocapillus aureus*
34. *T. g. gracilipes*
35. *T. e. elatus*
36. *P. griseiceps cristatus*
37. *X. virescens urichi*
38. *P. flaviventris*
39. *P. venezuelanus*
40. *P. ophthalmicus purus*
41. *P. chapmani duidae*
42. *P. nigrifrons*
43. *M. olivaceus venezuelensis*
44. *P. oleaginea chloronota*
45. *L. rufipectus venezuelanus*
46. *L. superciliaris venezuelensis*
47. *L. amaurocephalus obscuritergum*
48. *T. erythrurus venezuelensis*

## PLATE 31

1. *S. unicolor latrans*
2. *S. femoralis nigricans*
3. *S. latebricola meridanus*
4. *C. u. unirufa*
5. *C. griseus minor*
6. *C. n. nuchalis*
7. *T. r. rutilus*
8. *T. genibarbis consobrinus*
9. *T. coraya caurensis*
10. *T. rufalbus cumanensis*
11. *T. leucotis venezuelanus*
12. *H. leucophrys venezuelensis*
13. *H. l. leucosticta*
14. *T. solstitialis solitarius*
15. *T. aedon albicans*
16. *T. rufulus fulvigularis*
17. *C. platensis alticola*
18. *C. meridae*
19. *C. arada urbanoi*
20. *M. marginatus squamulatus*
20a. *M. m. marginatus*
21. *M. ustulatus duidae*
22. *M. bambla caurensis*
23. *M. c. collaris*
24. *R. melanurus trinitatis*
25. *P. plumbea innotata*
26. *P. guianensis facilis*

## PLATE 32

1. *C. leucocephalus leuconotus*
2. *M. gilvus melanopterus*
3. *D. a. atricapillus*
4. *C. m. minimus*
5. *C. a. aurantiirostris*
6. *C. f. fuscater*
7. *C. dryas maculatus*
8. *M. ralloides venezuelensis*
9. *M. leucogenys gularis*
10. *P. flavipes venezuelensis*
11. *P. leucops*
12. *T. fuscater gigas*
13. *T. serranus atrosericeus*
14. *T. fulviventris*
15. *T. o. olivater*
16. *T. n. nudigenis*
17. *T. albicollis minusculus*
18. *T. ignobilis murinus*
19. *T. leucomelas albiventer*
20. *T. f. fumigatus*

## PLATE 33

1. *C. gujanensis parvus*
2. *S. l. leucotis*
3. *S. pulchellus eximius*
4. *V. olivaceus vividior*

5. *V. gilvus mirandae*
6. *H. ochraceiceps ferrugineifrons*
7. *H. b. brunneiceps*
8. *H. m. muscicapinus*
9. *H. semicinereus viridiceps*
10. *H. thoracicus griseiventris*
11. *H. sclateri*
12. *H. semibrunneus*
13. *H. aurantiifrons saturatus*
14. *H. flavipes acuticauda*
15. *M. varia*
16. *V. peregrina*
17. *D. striata*
18. *D. fusca*
19. *D. petechia rufopileata*
19a. *D. petechia paraguanae*
20. *P. pitiayumi elegans*
21. *B. griseiceps*
22. *B. coronatus regulus*
23. *B. cinereicollis pallidulus*
24. *B. rufifrons mesochrysus*
25. *B. nigrocristatus*
26. *B. flaveolus*
27. *B. tristriatus bessereri*
28. *B. culicivorus segrex*
29. *B. bivittatus roraimae*
30. *G. a. aequinoctialis*
31. *S. noveboracensis notabilis*
32. *P. rivularis mesoleuca*
33. *G. p. pelzelni*

## PLATE 34

1. *M. o. ornatus*
2. *M. albifrons*
3. *M. miniatus pallidiventris*
4. *M. brunniceps castaneocapillus*
5. *M. albifacies*
6. *S. ruticilla*
7. *C. s. spiza*
8. *C. c. cyaneus*
9. *C. c. caeruleus*
10. *C. n. nitidus*
11. *D. c. cayana*
12. *D. l. lineata*
13. *D. albiventris*
14. *D. flaviventer*
15. *C. flaveola luteola*
15a. *C. flaveola laurae*
16. *C. b. bicolor*
17. *C. speciosum amazonum*
18. *C. l. leucogenys*
19. *C. a. albifrons*
20. *C. sitticolor intermedium*
21. *D. sittoides dorbignyi*
22. *D. a. albilatera*
23. *D. m. major*
24. *D. carbonaria gloriosa*
25. *D. lafresnayii*

26. *D. h. humeralis*
27. *D. caerulescens saturata*
28. *D. c. cyanea*

## PLATE 35

1. *C. pyrrhophrys*
2. *C. cyanea longipennis*
3. *T. viridis occidentalis*
4. *T. a. arthus*
5. *T. p. parzudakii*
6. *T. xanthocephala venusta*
7. *T. v. vassorii*
8. *T. rufigenis*
9. *T. heinei*
10. *T. nigroviridis cyanescens*
11. *T. cyanicollis hannahiae*
12. *T. c. cayana*
13. *T. c. cyanoptera*
14. *T. g. gyrola*
15. *T. mexicana media*
16. *T. guttata chrysophrys*
17. *T. p. punctata*
18. *T. schrankii venezuelana*
19. *T. nigrocincta*
20. *T. x. xanthogastra*
21. *T. varia*
22. *T. chilensis coelicolor*
23. *T. velia iridina*

## PLATE 36

1. *E. laniirostris crassirostris*
2. *E. v. violacea*
3. *E. xanthogaster exsul*
4. *E. trinitatis*
5. *E. m. minuta*
6. *E. musica intermedia*
7. *E. cayennensis*
8. *E. rufiventris*
9. *E. plumbea*
10. *E. chrysopasta nitida*
11. *H. guira nigrigula*
12. *H. flavicollis aurigularis*
13. *N. pileata hypoleuca*
14. *T. f. fulviceps*
15. *C. ophthalmicus jacqueti*
16. *C. c. canigularis*
17. *C. r. rubrirostris*
18. *H. reyi*
19. *H. superciliaris chrysophrys*
20. *H. frontalis hanieli*
21. *H. a. atropileus*
22. *H. m. melanotis*
23. *H. goeringi*
24. *H. verticalis*
25. *P. melanonota venezuelensis*
26. *C. verticalis*
27. *C. diadema federalis*

## PLATE 37

1. *T. episcopus cana*
2. *T. glaucocolpa*
3. *T. palmarum melanoptera*
4. *T. cyanocephala auricrissa*
4a. *T. cyanocephala olivicyanea*
5. *P. flava faceta*
6. *P. leucoptera venezuelae*
7. *S. melanopis aterrima*
8. *H. rubrica crissalis*
9. *R. carbo venezuelensis*
10. *R. d. dimidiatus*
11. *R. r. rosea*
12. *T. rufus*
13. *T. phoenicius*
14. *T. l. luctuosus*
15. *T. s. surinamus*
16. *T. cristatus intercedens*
17. *E. penicillata cristata*
18. *M. o. oleagineus*
19. *L. f. fulvus*
20. *C. cyanicterus*

## PLATE 38

1. *D. t. taeniata*
2. *A. lacrymosus melanops*
3. *A. flavinucha venezuelana*
4. *I. r. rufivertex*
5. *B. e. eximia*
6. *B. montana gigas*
7. *C. l. leveriana*
8. *S. albocristata*
9. *P. angustifrons oleagineus*
10. *P. viridis*
11. *G. y. yuracares*
12. *G. mexicanus*
13. *I. i. icterus*
14. *I. g. galbula*
15. *I. n. nigrogularis*
16. *I. chrysater giraudii*
17. *I. mesomelas carrikeri*
18. *I. auricapillus*
19. *I. chrysocephalus*
20. *A. i. icterocephalus*
21. *L. m. militaris*
22. *S. magna meridionalis*

## PLATE 39

1. *P. gularis nigrogenis*
2. *C. phoenicius*
3. *P. g. grossus*
4. *P. erythromelas*
5. *P. ludovicianus*
6. *P. chrysopeplus laubmanni*
7. *P. aureoventris meridensis*
8. *C. c. canadensis*

9. *S. albicollis perstriatus*
10. *S. coerulescens brewsteri*
11. *S. m. maximus*
12. *S. o. orenocensis*
13. *Z. capensis venezuelae*
14. *A. c. conirostris*
15. *A. tocuyensis*
16. *A. taciturnus axillaris*
16a. *A. t. taciturnus*
17. *A. s. schlegeli*
18. *A. p. pallidinucha*
19. *A. albofrenatus meridae*
20. *A. schistaceus castaneifrons*
21. *A. brunneinucha frontalis*
22. *A. torquatus larensis*
23. *A. semirufus denisei*
24. *A. p. personatus*
24a. *A. personatus duidae*
25. *C. c. cyanoides*
26. *C. cyanea minor*

PLATE 40

1. *O. (c.) crassirostris*
2. *O. angolensis torridus*
3. *V. jacarina splendens*
4. *T. olivacea pusilla*
5. *T. bicolor omissa*
6. *T. fuliginosa fumosa*

7. *D. fringilloides*
8. *S. l. lineola*
9. *S. luctuosa*
10. *S. n. nigricollis*
11. *S. m. minuta*
12. *S. i. intermedia*
13. *S. schistacea longipennis*
14. *S. plumbea whiteleyana*
15. *S. obscura haplochroma*
16. *S. castaneiventris*
17. *C. h. homochroa*
18. *C. inornata minor*
19. *P. unicolor montosus*
20. *H. r. rustica*
21. *C. pileatus brevicaudus*
22. *E. herbicola sphenurus*
23. *A. h. humeralis*
24. *A. aurifrons apurensis*
25. *S. americana*
26. *S. f. flaveola*
27. *S. c. columbiana*
28. *S. citrina browni*
29. *S. l. luteola*
30. *C. psaltria colombiana*
31. *C. x. xanthogastra*
32. *C. s. spinescens*
33. *C. magellanica longirostris*
34. *C. cucullata*

# BIBLIOGRAPHY

The following bibliography lists mainly books containing color illustrations of birds and books covering contiguous regions that would be helpful in the study of Venezuelan birds.

1961. ALLEN, ROBERT PORTER, Birds of the Caribbean, The Viking Press, New York.

1909. BEEBE, C. WILLIAM, An Ornithological Reconnaissance of Northern Venezuela. Zoologica, *1:* 67–114, New York.

1971. BOND, JAMES, Birds of the West Indies, 256 pp., col. pls. Collins, London.

1968. BROWN, LESLIE, and DEAN AMADON, Eagles, Hawks and Falcons of the World. 2 vols., col. pls. McGraw-Hill, New York.

1916. CHERRIE, GEORGE K., A Contribution to the Ornithology of the Orinoco Region. Mus. Brookl. Inst. Sci. Bull., *2,* No. 6: 133–374.

1972. DAVIS, L. IRBY, A Field Guide to the Birds of Mexico and Central America, col. pls., Univ. of Texas Press, Austin.

1973. DELACOUR, JEAN and DEAN AMADON, Curassows and Related Birds, col. pls. American Mus. Nat. Hist., New York.

1973. FFRENCH, RICHARD P., A Guide to the Birds of Trinidad and Tobago, col. pls. Livingston, Wynnewood, Pa.

1974. HAFFER, JURGEN, Avian Speciation in Tropical South America, 390 pp. Publ. Nuttall Orn. Cl., no. 14.

1968. HAVERSCHMIDT, F., Birds of Surinam. 445 pp. col. pls., Oliver and Boyd Ltd., Edinburgh and London.

1967. MAYR, ERNST, and WILLIAM H. PHELPS. JR., The Origin of the Bird Fauna of the South Venezuelan Highlands. Amer. Mus. Nat. Hist. Bull., *136:* 269–328.

1964. MEYER DE SCHAUENSEE, RODOLPHE, The Birds of Colombia, col. pls., Acad. Nat. Sci. Phila., Livingston, Wynnewood, Pa.

1966. ———, The Species of Birds of South America, Ibid.

1970. ———, A Guide to the Birds of South America, col. pls., Ibid.

1947. PETERSON, ROGER TORY, A Field Guide to the Birds, col. pls., Houghton Mifflin Co., Boston.

1974. ——— and EDWARD L. CHALIF, A Field Guide to Mexican Birds, col. pls., Houghton Mifflin Co., Boston.

1954. PHELPS, KATHLEEN, D., Aves Venezolanas. Cien de las mas conocidas, col. pls., Creole Petroleum Corp., Caracas. English Edition, 1963, Editorial Lectura, 107 pp., col. pls.

1950.  PHELPS, WILLIAM H., and WILLIAM H. PHELPS, JR., Lista de las Aves de Venezuela y su Distribución, Passeriformes. Bol. Soc. Venez. Cien. Nat. *12*, no. 75: 427 pp.

1958.  ———, Lista de las Aves de Venezuela y su Distribución. Vol. 2, pt. 1, No Passeriformes. Ibid., *19*, no. 90: 317 pp.

1963.  ———, Lista de las Aves de Venezuela y su Distribución, second edition, Vol. 1, pt. 2, Passeriformes. Ibid., *24*, nos. 104, 105: 479 pp.

1976.  RIDGLEY, ROBERT S., A Guide to the Birds of Panama, Princeton University Press, Princeton, New Jersey.

1966.  ROBBINS, CHANDLER S., BERTEL BRUUN and HERBERT S. ZIM, A Guide to Field Identification. Birds of North America, Golden Press, col. pls. New York.

1966.  SNYDER, DOROTHY E., The Birds of Guyana, Peabody Museum, Salem, Mass.

1970.  VARESCHI, VOLKMAR, Flora de los Páramos de Venezuela. Universidad de Los Andes, Mérida.

1955.  VOOUS, J. K., De Vogels van de Nederlandse Antillen, col. pls., Natuurvet. Wek. Ned. Ant., Curaçao.

1939.  WETMORE, ALEXANDER, Observations on the Birds of Northern Venezuela. Proc. U.S. Nat. Mus., *87:* 173–260.

———, Lista Parcial de los Pájaros del Parque Nacional de Venezuela. Bol. Soc. Ven. Cien. Nat., No. 40: 269–298.

# INDEX TO ENGLISH NAMES

# INDEX TO SPANISH NAMES

# INDEX TO GENERA AND SPECIES

LIBRARY OF CONGRESS CATALOGING IN PUBLICATION DATA

de Schauensee, Rodolphe Meyer, 1901-
  A guide to the birds of Venezuela.

  Bibliography: p.
  Includes index.
  1.  Birds—Venezuela.    I.  Phelps, William Henry,
joint author.    II.  Title.
QL689.V4D47      598.2'987      77-4033
ISBN 0-691-08188-3
ISBN 0-691-08205-7 pbk.